UNNATURALLY FRENCH

UNNATURALLY FRENCH

FOREIGN
CITIZENS
IN THE
OLD REGIME
AND AFTER

PETER SAHLINS

Cornell University Press
Ithaca & London

First published 2004 by Cornell University Press
First printing, Cornell Paperbacks, 2004
Printed in the United States of America

Library of Congress Cataloging-in-Publication Data
Sahlins, Peter.
   Unnaturally French : foreign citizens in the Old Regime and after /
Peter Sahlins.
      p. cm.
   Includes bibliographical references and index.
   ISBN 0-8014-4142-0 (alk. paper) — ISBN 0-8014-8839-7 (pbk. : alk.
paper)
   1. Citizenship—France—History. 2. Naturalization—France—History.
3. Immigrants—Government policy—France—History. 4.
Aliens—France—History. I. Title.
JN2919 .S24 2004
323.6'23'09440903—dc22   2003020422

Cornell University Press strives to use environmentally responsible suppliers and materials to the fullest extent possible in the publishing of its books. Such materials include
vegetable-based, low-VOC inks and acid-free papers that are recycled, totally chlorine-
free, or partly composed of nonwood fibers. Books that bear the logo of the FSC (Forest
Stewardship Council) use paper taken from forests that have been inspected and certified as meeting the highest standards for environmental and social responsibility. For
further information, visit our website at www.cornellpress.cornell.edu.

Cloth printing   10 9 8 7 6 5 4 3 2 1
Paperback printing   10 9 8 7 6 5 4 3 2 1

CONTENTS

doctrine, as a window onto French immigration and as part of an untold history of nationality law in France of the Old Regime, and in the decades that marked the transition to the New Regime of citizenship, immigration, and nationality.

Most historians believe that such contemporary phenomena had little relevance before the nineteenth century. After all, the numbers of foreigners and naturalized foreigners paled in comparison with the later waves of industrial migration that fed the far more numerous naturalizations of foreigners in France and Europe beginning in the 1880s. And it might seem odd to even think of these Old Regime foreigners as "immigrants," insofar as the "nation-state" in which they settled and to which they became assimilated was fundamentally different from the one today. In the seventeenth and eighteenth centuries, foreigners easily established themselves in the kingdom: in the absence of border controls, passports, and visas, the absolute monarchy had few political tools to mark boundaries and identify foreigners, and little desire to do either. Officially, until the French Revolution, there was no "nation" to which foreigners were expected to assimilate. The kingdom of France knew no statutory definitions of "citizens" and never enumerated their political and civil rights. French "nationality" did not exist: the word only dates from the early nineteenth century. And before the appearance of the nation as a political category in the eighteenth century and, of course, as a sovereign community of citizens during the French Revolution, the different legal privileges of the king's subjects trumped any general definition of French citizenship.

Or so the story goes. Yet foreigners became citizens. Their naturalization—as an administrative and legal procedure—is a key site to investigate the law and politics of citizenship before 1789. The history of naturalization during the French Revolution and under the Napoleonic Empire provides a unique perspective on the changing policies and practices of citizenship and nationality. And naturalization, as part of a social history of immigration in the Old Regime, may indeed be statistically insignificant, but it provides an unusual opportunity to study premodern patterns of foreign settlement in France.

Unnaturally French is a history of the theory, procedures, and multiple meanings of naturalization told in several stages and from several methodological (if not disciplinary) perspectives. As social history, it documents the patterns of geographic origin and identity of foreigner citizens in space and time and reflects on the political and legal conditions that shaped social patterns. As political history, it considers the development of French policy made in the royal councils and in the different administrative sectors of the king's government, including the ministry of foreign affairs; the offices of the royal chancellery, among the controllers-general and directors-general of finance and their staffs; within the local and national treasury bureaux; and often with the assistance of financiers and tax-farmers. The resulting "policy" towards foreigners, immigration, citizenship, and nationality is traced from the sixteenth to the early nineteenth centuries.

TABLES

PREFACE

From the late sixteenth century until the outbreak of the French Revolution in 1789, an average of about fifty immigrants a year, foreigners long established in the kingdom, undertook the costly but ultimately successful quest to be naturalized. Granted letters of naturalization (*lettres de naturalité*) by the French crown, they became French citizens. Yet they remained, in the language of the time, "naturalized foreigners," and they were never fully assimilated into the legal category of French citizens. Foreign citizens were subject to periodic taxes, state proscriptions, property confiscations, lawsuits over inherited property, and other discriminatory measures of state and society, in times of peace and war. Their condition was admittedly far better than the much larger group of unnaturalized foreigners in the kingdom, the tens of thousands of aliens (*aubains*) settled in France but who were unable to inherit or bequeath property, to hold office or religious benefice, and who suffered a range of other civil incapacities. Foreigners and naturalized foreigners occupied distinct statuses in the legal worlds of the Old Regime, but both stood opposed to French "naturals" (for the period did not know the modern vocabulary of "nationality"): those born in the kingdom or descended from French parents born abroad and settled in France. Natural Frenchmen and women (*Français naturels*), of all statuses and conditions, enjoyed as a birthright a common set of "rights, duties, privileges, franchises, and immunities" in the kingdom (according to the text of the naturalization grant). Foreign citizens were those foreigners who became "unnaturally French": their naturalization was a complex legal fiction that gave them, in principle though hardly in practice, the status of "natural Frenchmen" but did not purport to change their nature as aliens.

This book is about the incidence and meaning of naturalization, both from the perspective of foreigners who sought its benefits, and from that of the state that used the practice of naturalization to raise revenue, articulate sovereignty, and define citizenship. It explores naturalization as social practice and as legal

As legal history, the book considers the French lawyers who made nationality law, who constructed, in contestation and collusion with the state, an absolutist model of French citizenship that came to fruition in the seventeenth century. This absolute citizen, defined by the legal distinctions between foreigners and Frenchmen and women, perdured until the 1750s. In its final section, this book considers the unmaking of this absolute citizen and the dramatic mutations of citizenships after midcentury. It then considers this continuing citizenship revolution from 1789 to 1819—during the French Revolution, under Napoleon, and in the early years of the Bourbon monarchy—within the historical movement from the Old to the New Regime.

Research for this book began in 1991 as an attempt to fill a significant gap in the history of immigration to France in the period from the late sixteenth to the early nineteenth centuries—one historian's reaction to the French political debates of the 1990s that often effaced the early history of immigration, nationality, and citizenship. The book was never conceived as a history of the social assimilation or acculturation of foreigners into Frenchmen and Frenchwomen, their "integration" (to invoke the contemporary French concern) in France. Paying attention to the dangers of present-day vocabulary, such local histories of the Old Regime could be written, but they would require sustained and detailed research in a variety of local sources that I have chosen not to consider: parish registers, notarial records, municipal archives, private papers, and others. Some excellent work has been done at the level of capital cities and towns of early modern Europe—the necessary scale at which a history of integration must be framed—and parallel inquiries have been undertaken for Spain, where legal assimilation took shape as a social process at the level of local communities.[1] My initial approach and research strategy, instead, was to use the only sources available at the level of the French kingdom—the legal and administrative traces of naturalization found within the complex bureaucracy of the absolute monarchy. I wanted to describe and interpret the collective profiles (geographic, professional, and temporal) and to reconstruct the motives of a small but revealing group of foreigners who became French citizens.

While searching for materials in the French national archives, I stumbled on the extant rolls of the Naturalization Tax of 1697—the forcible, collective naturalization of foreigners and descendants of foreigners, along with bastards, who had settled in the kingdom during the seventeenth century.[2] I was not alone, nor even the first, in recognizing the importance of this data; my French colleague Jean-François Dubost had used the tax rolls in his study of Italians in France during the sixteenth century, and many genealogists and family historians had extracted the identities of specific groups from these records.[3] Dubost and I decided to join forces in an exhaustive study of the tax, and after nearly a decade of collaboration we coauthored a book with a regrettable title that systematically studied the Naturalization Tax of 1697: *Et si on faisait payer les étrangers? Louis XIV, les immigrés et quelques autres* (And what if foreigners were to pay? Louis XIV, immigrants, and a few others) (Paris, 1999). I patiently coded and statistically exploited the tax rolls to reveal the identities of a certain "foreign France," documented in forty-one maps, figures, and tables that describe the origins, settlement patterns, and taxed wealth of the thousands of immigrants and other "foreigners" settled in the kingdom during the seventeenth century. Dubost plowed through the records of the royal council to understand the political projects of a royal immigration policy and the fiscal practices of an "extraordinary affair" of taxation in the seventeenth century. Our conclusions converged: the Naturalization Tax was a fiscal failure but a revelation about foreigners and nationality under Louis XIV.[4]

More than eight thousand "foreigners" were unlucky enough to be captured on the tax-rolls of 1697–1707. My own compilation of individual naturalizations in the period when records were best kept yielded some six thousand instances between 1660 and 1790 (see appendix 1). Using these two data sets, I set out to write a social history of foreign migration to the kingdom of France. But as I gathered and analyzed the data, it became apparent that a social history of foreign citizens—a small and relatively privileged group of immigrants—must become more than a history of immigration. It must also lay claim to being a legal and political history of the French state, of the law and politics of citizenship and nationality. *Unnaturally French* was rewritten such that a legal history of French citizenship and nationality in the Old Regime (part one) and their transformations after the mid-eighteenth century (part three) incorporate a statistical and descriptive account of the thousands of foreigners who became French citizens (part two). The letter of naturalization—the text itself, the petitioners who requested it, the administrative procedure of its acquisition, its legal significance—became the focus of this book. Instead of proceeding exclusively from the legal and political *theory* of naturalization, this book is grounded in the study of naturalization *practices* at the intersection of state policy and the desires of foreigners themselves.[5]

This book is also about citizenship, although it is not principally about the genealogical origins of modern citizenship as political participation and civic identity, with all its ideological inclusions and practical exclusions. After the 1750s, and especially after 1789, such a notion of the citizen came to the fore, and many historical monographs about citizenship and nationality during the French Revolution and after have appeared.[6] My examination of this political dimension of citizenship takes place within a much broader history and conceptualization of the category. From the perspective of legal history, I focus on the citizen defined primarily in opposition to the foreigner, and on the juridical and bureaucratic passage from foreigner to citizen in the execution of the protocol and procedure of naturalization. In fact, this book is about two kinds of passages, both incomplete: that of foreigners into citizens, and that of the category of citizenship as it moved between law and politics, between the legal practices and political projects of the Old Regime, the French Revolution, the Napoleonic Empire, and after.

This history of naturalization—of citizenship, nationality law, and immigration—ends in 1819, a precise date with a peculiar significance. In 1819, the French government abolished a uniquely French institution, the *droit d'aubaine*. The droit d'aubaine was a royal right of escheat inherited from the feudal world that allowed the king to confiscate the property of aliens, foreigners who died in the kingdom without native heirs, as well as of French citizens who died having established themselves outside the kingdom. A minor feudal right, the droit d'aubaine became the key legal mechanism for distinguishing foreigners and citizens, and the motive force behind thousands of individual naturalizations from 1660 to 1789. After 1789, the droit d'aubaine, like naturalization itself, suffered numerous permutations and reforms until its final abolition during the Restoration. The definitions and uses of the droit d'aubaine by statesmen, lawyers, and foreigners are considered here from the sixteenth to the early nineteenth centuries. A sustained and focused account of this neglected institution brings together, in all their dissonance and convergence, the social, political, and legal histories of citizenship and nationality in France from the Old Regime to the New.

Parts of chapter 4 appeared as "La Nationalité avant la lettre: Les Pratiques de naturalisation en France sous l'Ancien Régime," *Annales HSS* (September–October 2000), no. 5: 1081–108, and are reprinted here with permission of the publisher. Research for this work was generously funded by the National Endowment for the Humanities, the Guggenheim Foundation, the Office of the President of the University of California, and the Department of History at the University of California, Berkeley.

The organizers and participants of a number of academic seminars provided the occasion to rethink the history of French citizenship. I thank those who contributed over the years, in sometimes unintentional ways, at the University of Paris I; the Ecole Normale Supérieure; and the Ecole des Hautes Etudes en Sciences Sociales; the Institut d'Etudes Politiques in Paris; the Central University of Barcelona; the Instituto de Desarrollo Económico y Social (IDES) in Buenos Aires; the Chinese University of Hong Kong (in association with the National Humanities Institute, North Carolina); the University of Maastricht; the European University Institute in Florence; the University of Chicago; New York University; Stanford University; the University of California at Davis; the UCLA Center for Seventeenth- and Eighteenth-Century Studies and the William Andrews Clark Memorial Library; the history and French departments and the Early Modern Studies Group at the University of California, Berkeley.

I am indebted to the many archivists in France who patiently responded to my queries about naturalizations, including Hélène Avisseau, Xavier du Bois-rouvray, Thérèse Burel, Madeleine Chabrolin, Marie-Christiane de la Conte, Jean Courtieu, Jacques Staes, and Françoise Vignier. My greatest archival debts are to Yves Ozanam, librarian of the Paris Bar Association, and Didier Fourny, librarian of the Paris Court of Appeals, who provided me with unlimited access to two of the most important jurisprudential sources for this book.

Inestimable assistance was provided by Deborah Hammon, James Livesey, Lynn Sharp, and Charlotte Eyerman who helped recode the data once I had collected it. David Engerman patiently introduced a novice to the manipulation of statistical databases (notably SPSS); I am most grateful for his efforts. Thanks to my students and research assistants who, over the years, tracked down loose references and gave valuable feedback: Sara Beam, Will Bishop, Carl Freire, Rolando Montecalvo, Marcy Norton, Ethan Rundell, Noah Shusterman, Pierre Terjanian, and, especially, Matthew Gerber. John Ackerman, Karen Hwa, and Cornell University Press magically turned it all into a book, with maps and figures.

More than a decade's worth of intellectual debts would take up far too much space. I have appreciated the input of many colleagues and friends over the years, including Andrew Barshay, Beth Berry, Tom Brady, Natalie Zemon Davis, David Eaton, David Eddy, Robin Einhorn, Michel Feher, Meg Galucci, Xavier Gil Pujol, Jon Gjerde, Daniel Gordon, Josh Greenbaum, Carla Hesse, Lynn Hunt, Geoff Koziol, Pierre Etienne Manuellan, Tom Laqueur, the late Bernard Le Petit, Forest Reinhardt, Jacques Revel, and Randy Starn. In their own ways, my affinal and consanguinal kin have provided unfailing support: deepest thanks to the extended Naddaff family, Elaine and the Seigmans, Julie, and, especially, my parents, Barbara and Marshall Sahlins.

Jean-François Dubost taught me much about the secrets of the French monarchy. Jim Amelang, David Bell, Michael Kwass, and Patrick Weil were terrific readers and friends whose careful and critical comments improved the manuscript and saved me from many egregious errors, but not all. I am most indebted to Ramona Naddaff, of course, whose keen intelligence, editorial sense, and everyday wisdom are only the most evident of her contributions to the final product. This book is dedicated to her, and to our son, Maxwell Naddaff Sahlins, who taught me that history, above all, is telling a good story about what really happened.

UNNATURALLY FRENCH

INTRODUCTION
Citizenship, Immigration, and Nationality
Avant La Lettre

W hat did it mean to become a French citizen in the early modern period? The question might seem historically anomalous. In the world of contemporary nation-states, citizens are variously defined in reference to law, to rights, and to identity. Legally, they are "nationals" to whom are due the rights and benefits of membership in the nation-state. Politically, they are democratic participants in the business of governing, exercising political rights of representation. Socially and culturally, citizens are members of a national community, an "imagined community" constructed from official cultural frames of social belonging within a national state.[1] Identity politics in the early twenty-first century questions whether cultural differences can be accepted within the inherited universal and civic identities of the nation in France. But before the Revolution of 1789, the question could not be asked, and none of these modern aspects of citizenship were relevant.

"Absolutist" France was a monarchy organized hierarchically and legally in privileged estates, corporations, and communities, where individuals shared no common status except as subjects of the king.[2] Old Regime law, especially civil law, was an incoherent composition of customary law, royal decrees, Roman (written) law, and case law of the different *parlements* and sovereign courts of the kingdom. Sovereignty, of course, was located exclusively in the person of the king, but territory was fragmented and administrative and political boundaries were porous (map 1). Neither ethnicity, nor language, nor national identity provided the institutional basis or ideological justification for membership in the polity. The conventional view would have it that only the French Revolution of 1789, "by sweeping away the tangled skein of privilege—regional liberties and immunities, corporate monopolies, fiscal exemptions, vestigial seigneurial rights, and so on . . . created a class of persons enjoying common rights, bound by common obligations, formally equal before the law. It substituted a common law for privilege (etymologically, private law), *citoyens* for *privilégiés*."[3]

Map 1. France 1648–1766

The received wisdom about the Old Regime, the French Revolution, and the invention of modern citizenship can scarcely be contested.

Of course, the ideological origins of this modern citizenship have been traced back to the eighteenth century, among the Enlightened philosophes and ministerial reformers, and ultimately to a stream of resurgent civic republicanism of the eighteenth century. Such currents fed the revolutionary upheaval—or became dominant once the French Revolution occurred, as was the case of the life and work of Jean-Jacques Rousseau. Rousseau's citizen, grounded in classical and contemporary values, claimed a rupture with the past. In a famous footnote to his 1762 *Social Contract* (1:6), Rousseau dismissed the language of citizenship in early modern French political culture, saying that among the French "the name citizen expresses a virtue and not a right." Rousseau chose to identify "citizens" as "associates" who collectively made up the "people." As a community of equals, citizens participate in the sovereign authority that they authorize themselves through the "social contract." Rousseau thus posited an abstract, universal conception of the citizen as the author of sovereignty that reversed contemporary usage and the absolute citizen. As is well known, Rousseau overturned the "citizen-subject" of absolutism even if he never broke completely with the "ancient" citizenship of his native city of Geneva.[4]

In the received wisdom, Rousseau, the Enlightenment, and the French Revolution mark, in global terms, the passage from "ancient" to "modern" citizenship.[5] Ancient or "first citizenship" was a status of persons with proprietary and commercial interests in the Greek *polis* and the Latin *civitas:* it was a status that selectively benefited a relatively small minority of the (adult, male, wealthy) population. The classical examples of Greece (following the rediscovery of Aristotle in the twelfth century) and Rome (notably the sixth-century *Corpus juris civilis* and the *Institutes* of Justinian) provided the model. The thirteenth- and fourteenth-century city-states of the Italian Peninsula (notably Florence, Siena, and Venice) produced the most proximate and elaborate examples of an "ancient" citizenship as a set of political and economic rights and privileges.[6] Late medieval and Renaissance citizenship was fundamentally exclusive: only some wealthy, male members of the elite could enjoy the fiscal and commercial privileges of citizens alongside the right to exercise public office, while the vast majority of the polity's inhabitants and residents (including foreigners and women) did not. More important, as the concept and practice of citizenship spread in the late fifteenth and sixteenth centuries from the Italian city-states to the "New Monarchies" of Europe—France, Spain, and England—citizens lost all claims to the exercise of political rights, and became, in this traditional view, no more than subjects of increasingly absolute monarchies—although some subjects were obviously more privileged than others. Although Hobbes and Locke (and others) in England came to reconceptualize citizens as equals and the basis of a new form of political legitimacy, in France only the Revolution of 1789 was to turn the "subjects" into "citizens."[7]

Citizenship, Immigration, and Nationality Avant La Lettre (3)

"First citizenship," although freed from feudal and religious hierarchies, was nonetheless fundamentally marked by social hierarchy and exclusivity. In practice it amounted to a bundle of privileges and prerogatives held by local and national ruling elites, who more or less—as time went on—participated in the business of governing. In France, the new citizenship, that of Rousseau (who theorized the transition) and the French Revolution (where the practice was first realized), was more inclusive and democratic, at least in principle. It was founded simultaneously on subjectivist and universalist principles, and it required the formal equality of its members, who collectively represented themselves as the source of national sovereignty and state legitimacy.

This story of the citizen's evolution recapitulates the birth of the modern world: in western Europe, it marks the emergence of the nation-state and the concomitant reconfiguration of the social order. The older models of sociologists and others position the appearance of citizenship in the movement from status to contract (to follow Sir Henry Maine), from hierarchy to equality, and from ascription to achievement. To T. H. Marshall, writing in the late 1940s, the developmental pattern was set by England. From "civil" citizenship in the eighteenth century, founded on the concept of civil rights, the category broadened to a "political" citizenship of democratic participation in the nineteenth century; finally, the twentieth century witnessed the emergence of "social" citizenship, founded on entitlements from welfare states, which functioned to legitimize class divisions. In recent years, the "English model" has been revived and contested, but the tripartite scheme appears largely irresistible.[8]

For historians, such models flatten (if they do not eliminate) the history itself of citizenship in the early modern era, especially in Old Regime France. More significant, metatheories about the birth of modern citizenship tend to focus exclusively on the language of rights and the principles of social belonging at the expense of legal citizenship and nationality law. Conversely, legal historians of citizenship often fail to take the social and political dimensions of citizenship seriously. Historians, sociologists, and political theorists of French citizenship assume that the legal notion of citizenship—as nationality—had no meaning in the premodern world. Yet in bypassing the history of legal citizenship after the sixteenth century, the nationality *avant la lettre* examined in this book, historians and others have not taken seriously the one arena where the theory and practice of citizenship was supremely important in early modern France—in the legal passage, both in theory and in practice, of foreigners into citizens.

The Droit d'Aubaine: The Making of Absolute Citizenship in France

In opposition to the identity of the citizen in the modern world, early modern law did not define citizens as rights-bearing subjects. Like many other identities, that of the citizen emerged from the typically early modern reasoning of contrariness (*a contrario*), in opposition and contradistinction to the foreigner's political and civil incapacities or disabilities, to what might be called the "anti-privileges" of foreigners. "Identity and that which marks it define themselves by the residue of differences," wrote Michel Foucault.[9] The general point, originally made about the development of the human sciences at the end of the "classical period" in the eighteenth century, has been incorporated in a wide range of identity studies. Students of citizenship, however, have rarely taken it seriously, especially as an observation about the Old Regime.

Citizens of the kingdom were all those *not* subjected to the disabilities, incapacities, and liabilities of being an alien resident in France. Their identity was determined tacitly, in a singularly unmarked fashion, principally by what they were capable of doing as legal subjects. Citizens appeared less as bearers of rights and never as bearers of political rights; they were not equal before the law, nor were they identified by a shared set of cultural, linguistic, or ethnic identities—the classical characteristics of modern citizenship. They were not defined by statute, or by constitutional law, but contentiously, in the courtroom and the resulting jurisprudence of aliens, citizens, and naturalized foreigners in the Old Regime.

Aliens suffered a number of restrictions and liabilities: they could not hold public office or possess clerical benefices and were subject to special taxes alongside other commercial and economic restrictions. But the most important of the disabilities with which foreigners in France were burdened was the *droit d'aubaine*, a royal right of escheat. At its origins, confiscated from feudal lords in the thirteenth and fourteenth centuries, the droit d'aubaine was the king's right (in practice, that of his financial officers and later tax-farmers) to seize the estates and property of aliens who died in the kingdom unless they had native heirs or had been exempted individually or collectively. The foundations of early modern citizenship thus turned inversely on the capacity to inherit or devolve property in the kingdom, just as modern citizenship, in its transition toward universal male suffrage, rested on the political capacities incurred in property ownership.

The crown and its lawyers originally understood the droit d'aubaine as the king's right to the properties of unexempted aliens, but as of the late medieval period, foreigners in France accumulated other civil incapacities and disabilities: they were barred from political offices and religious benefices, they were subject to special judicial constraints and occasional taxes, they were excluded from some professions and economic activities. These too became part of the "droit d'aubaine" in the kingdom, at least according to the lawyers and apologists of the absolutist state during the late sixteenth and seventeenth centuries. The construction of this amplified droit d'aubaine in the sixteenth and seventeenth century, symbolized in the Naturalization Tax of 1697, provides an unusual and revelatory perspective on the stages in the making of absolutist citizenship. At the same time, the contestations and abolitions of the droit d'aubaine beginning in the mid-eighteenth century, and continuing until its final abolition in 1819, are a key element in the unmaking of French absolutism, in the transition toward a new, postabsolutist regime of citizenship and nationality.[10]

However much it implicates a more general passage into modernity, though, the story is a peculiarly French one. A closer examination of the droit d'aubaine reveals how France's "feudal" inheritance became not only an obstacle but a vehicle through which France entered the modern world. Most medieval European states and polities—indeed, most polities from the pre-Classical to the modern, in Europe and the world—restricted the ability of foreigners to own, devolve, or inherit property; imposed special taxes, duties, and restrictions on their economic practices; and legally excluded them from holding political offices or religious benefices. But no "national" patterns of civil disabilities in the early modern period reeked as much of the feudal world as did those of France, not even those of England, where practices derived from feudal lordship remained a determining element in the notion of "natural allegiance" that formed the basis of English nationality law.[11] In sixteenth- and seventeenth-century France, inheritance restrictions and seigneurial prerogatives that had initially been practiced in the customary and feudal law of northern and eastern France found a renewed and revitalized existence when deployed in the state-building projects of the absolutist monarchy. The droit d'aubaine, in an expansive and political definition of the practice, became the centerpiece of French nationality law. This was the case in practice, in the bureaucracy of naturalization. But it was also the case in politics, where the crown appropriated the droit d'aubaine to tax the alien population of the kingdom, and thus to mark the divisions of citizens and foreigners.

The crown's development of an absolute citizen, and its policies toward foreigners more generally, implicated two contradictory approaches, exemplary of the more general contradictions of French absolutism. On the one hand, the royal state in France invested symbolically in the droit d'aubaine as a mark of absolute sovereignty and a practice of "fundamental law." In the seventeenth and early eighteenth centuries, the monarchy sought to impose this uniform law in the kingdom, including in regions of Roman law and cities where it had not been previously practiced. Such a policy, if this is not too strong a word, dovetails with a model of absolutism found in historical writing since Alexis de Tocqueville, where the crown made every effort to impose uniformity and to level all differences, a project completed only during the French Revolution itself.[12] On the other hand, the monarchy consistently issued privileges as part of its strengthening of royal authority and its continuous need for credit and revenue. Historians since Georges Pagès and his student Roland Mousnier have long noted the inherent contradictions of French absolutism: "full royal authority" contained and was limited by the very privileges and franchises that it conferred.[13] In the specific case of foreigners, this meant simultaneously the extension of the droit d'aubaine to the kingdom and the privileged exemption of individuals, as well as "national" and professional groups, from its levy. Through naturalizations, diplomatic conventions, and collective exemptions, exceptions to the status of aliens were also part of the rule of law.

Given these contradictory tendencies, as the absolutist model crystallized and as naturalization was routinized under Louis XIV, citizenship was hardly a stable and unchanging set of presumptions and practices. Yet the French absolutist model of the citizen from the late sixteenth through the early eighteenth centuries appears in relief when compared to other European experiences, for it took its final shape at a moment when—from England to Hungary and Poland—the civil incapacities of foreigners, especially concerning the right to hold and transmit property, had already waned. Beginning in the late medieval period, inheritance restrictions placed on aliens had diminished, and with the development of international law starting in the sixteenth century, and especially in the period from the publication of Hugo Grotius's *On the War of Law and Peace* (1625) to Emmerich de Vattel's *The Law of Nations* (1758), such restrictions were universally denounced as obsolete remnants of a "feudal" past.[14] In England and the Netherlands, and even in Spain, restrictions on the civil capacities of foreigners to act as legal subjects tended to wane as commercial societies and cultures replaced agrarian and aristocratic ones.

In northern Europe—including Prussia—the question was intimately linked to the juridical incorporation of hundreds of thousands of religious refugees, the French Huguenots, officially banished from the realm when Louis XIV revoked the Edict of Nantes in 1685.[15] While France remained officially a Catholic kingdom, in Holland and Protestant Germany even Jews came to enjoy civil capacities as legal subjects, to become citizens.[16] Beyond the religious question, the public and spirited debate over general bills of naturalization divided Whigs and Tories in England from the 1660s to the 1760s. The 1709 General Naturalization Act and the subsequent proimmigration experiment with the Palatine migration (admittedly unsuccessful) were enacted at the very moment when the model of the absolute citizen in France was perfected.[17] By the time political debates on general naturalization acts had ended, as part of a broader debate over populationism in England during the 1760s, the French monarchy was only beginning to question the droit d'aubaine, and to abolish it in the interest of commerce and communication.

In relation to this uniquely French practice, the crown developed an elaborate mechanism of manufacturing citizens: the letter of naturalization. Its bureaucratic protocol first crystallized in the 1570s, at the moment the royal model of the citizen took legal shape. But the final Old Regime form of naturalization, as fully routinized and stabilized administrative practice, only occurred in the early reign of Louis XIV, a century later, at a moment of the passage from a "judicial" to an "administrative" monarchy.[18]

To escape the levy of the *droit d'aubaine*, and the voracity of the fisc, thousands of foreigners sought individual naturalizations from the crown. To possess religious benefices and political offices, thousands more became citizens in the period from Louis XIV to the French Revolution. The prospect or experience of litigating estates among "foreign" and "native" heirs moved scores of others (and their lawyers) to argue the nature of citizenship in the period from Louis XIV to the French Revolution. The social history of these foreign citizens, and the legal and political histories that frame it, are a window and a reflection of broader patterns of immigration in Old Regime France.

Immigration, Taxation, and Naturalization in the Old Regime

Modern historians have generally neglected the topic of immigration to early modern France.[19] Informed by deep-seated cultural myths about the autochthony of the French population, French historical writing has traditionally treated migration history far more as a "realm of forgetting" than a "realm of memory."[20] This began to change in the 1990s, within a renewed scholarly attention to immigration and movement more generally in early modern France. We have come to learn much about the social and cultural history of foreigners in the Old Regime: about literary figures of the foreigner from the Renaissance to Enlightenment culture; about foreign Freemasons in eighteenth century Paris; about foreigners in the service of the army, the church, and the state; about the roles of immigrants in the economy of the Old Regime; and about the tens of thousands of foreigners a year—tourists, merchants, artisans, pilgrims, aristocrats, philosophers—who passed through Paris, or about the far fewer who settled in Provence.[21] Thanks to older and more recent studies, we have developed social portraits of specific foreign populations and economic groups in the kingdom: Irish traders and clergy in Bordeaux, Dutch merchants in Normandy, Prussian cabinet-makers in Paris, Savoyards in Lyon and throughout the kingdom, Flemish and German artisans in Metz, Italian courtiers in Paris, and so forth.[22] But there have been no attempts to describe synthetically, much less to measure statistically, the foreign population of France. Focusing on the only group of immigrants that can be counted, and whose identities are revealing of the broader patterns of foreign France, this book studies foreigners who became French citizens under the Old Regime.

In fact, there were two distinct groups of foreign citizens: the individual foreigners who from 1660 to 1790 sought to naturalize themselves and their families, or to have their ancestral status of French citizenship affirmed; and those on whom a naturalization tax was imposed at the high-water mark of the construction of the absolute citizen in 1697.

Admittedly, the archives of both kinds of naturalizations reveal only a small and atypical sample of the much larger population of foreigners who traveled and settled in the kingdom during the seventeenth and eighteenth centuries.[23] In the tax rolls of 1697–1707, less than a tenth of the taxed immigrants and descendants of foreigners were naturalized. Among the more recent arrivals, those still alive in 1697, only one in thirty had already become French citizens.[24] Under Louis XIV, the eight thousand or so "foreigners" taxed were but a small proportion of the foreigners in the kingdom, especially if one counts the French population descended from foreigners, as did the Naturalization Tax. The financiers of the tax uncovered less than two hundred artisans in the city of Paris; that same year, an admittedly exaggerated if revealing witness claimed that the working-class neighborhood of artisans and small shopkeepers of the Parisian faubourg Saint-Antoine housed more than fifteen thousand foreigners.[25] However many there were, the number of naturalized foreigners among them must have been an incidental part of the total foreign population in the kingdom.

More broadly, these two data sets of some fourteen thousand foreigner citizens, naturalized by choice between 1660 and 1790 and by force in 1697, formed together a statistically irrelevant portion of the foreigners who traveled through France, especially to Paris, and especially during the increasingly cosmopolitan eighteenth century. In the early 1770s, when Paris as the intellectual and cultural capital of Europe became a magnet for foreign travel, the lieutenant general of police controlled, at least on paper, an average of thirty-eight hundred foreign travelers a year who stayed in Paris. They temporarily resided among its population of nearly half a million souls, themselves in the majority immigrants from the provinces.[26] In those same years, an average of only five established foreigners—a tenth of a percent of the mobile and unsettled foreign population—became citizens.[27] Such stark proportions remind us of just how small the group of foreign citizens was as a proportion of the total "foreign" population.

Foreign citizens were, no doubt, a privileged group of immigrants, although not literally in the Old Regime sense, since only a small proportion were nobles. But these were men and women generally long-established and assimilated into their local communities who constituted if not an elite, than at least a selection of generally successful immigrants to the kingdom who sought to hold offices, benefices, and to pass on their inheritance to families and children. If privileged, they were also synechdotal: the geographic origins of foreign citizens were largely comparable to those of immigration flows more generally, even if the socioprofessional profiles differed among the two kinds of foreigners.

The social, professional, and "national" identities of foreign citizens can be known, alongside other consistent markers of civil status, precisely because of the French state's monopoly of naturalization procedures. Unlike Spain and Spanish America during the Old Regime, the passage from outsider to insider necessarily entailed the state's intervention.[28] In France, only the king and his royal administration, and not local municipalities or seigneurs, conferred the privilege and title of a citizen or "natural Frenchman." Inevitably, then, a social history of foreign citizens in the kingdom considers them through the prism of the state. Individually and collectively, naturalized foreigners were caught up, actively (as citizens, to paraphrase Rousseau) and passively (as subjects) in the projects of state-building. Foreign citizens were agents and victims of the construction, and the eventual dismantling, of the absolute citizen.

Thus legal and political histories necessarily frame the social history of naturalized foreigners from 1660 to 1790. The jurisprudence and case law surrounding each particular group of foreigners shaped the social, geographic, and professional patterns and profiles of naturalization. For despite the monarchy's unintentional construction of a universal category of "foreigner" in the collective naturalization and tax of 1697, the privileges and statuses of different "national" groups varied considerably, and they were harshly contested within the jurisprudence of the sovereign courts. The social history of naturalization, in this sense, needs to take the law seriously, to explore how legal frameworks determined—or at times, did not—the practices of naturalization. At the same time, the legal framework was subject to abrupt political mutation, not only by the continual if episodic wars and international treaties of the Old Regime, but also by the decisions of kings and councils that dramatically intervened to modify politically these laws and privileges of distinct "national" groups, and others. The Naturalization Tax of 1697 was unique, but it showed how politics redefined the law, as well as the practices, of citizenship in France.

Legal and political histories alone cannot sufficiently account for the distinct profiles and different rates at which specific "professional" and "national" groups of foreigners became citizens. There were professionally specific patterns (of clergy, merchants, and artisans); there were nationally specific patterns (of German and Austrian clerics in the Alsace or Flanders, of Genoese sailors and merchants in Provence, of Dutch merchants in Rouen, of Savoyard clerics in Dauphiné). There were geographically specific patterns. (It will come as no surprise to learn that border regions produced the largest groups of foreign citizens in the Old Regime: the Low Countries [Spanish, then Austrian in 1714] and the bishopric of Liège in the northeast; Lorraine and the Rhineland principalities in the east; the duchy of Savoy [after 1718, the kingdom of Piedmont-Savoy, including the counties of Savoy and Nice in the south]).

There were temporally specific patterns to naturalization as well. Between 1660 and 1790, naturalizations fall into three distinct periods. First, coinciding roughly with the reign of Louis XIV (1660–1709), individual naturalizations declined, especially during the wars and economic downturn of the 1690s. Second, from near the end of the reign of Louis XIV until the middle of the Seven Years War (1710–1759), a period of relative economic prosperity witnessed the dramatic increase in numbers of naturalizations. Finally, within the crisis of the Old Regime

(1760–1790), individual naturalizations declined precipitously, anticipating slightly but confirming the citizenship revolution of the eighteenth century.

The Citizenship Revolution in France: Before 1789

The citizenship revolution began in the 1750s, continued across the revolutionary decades and during the French Empire (1804–1814), and was marked by the final abolition of the droit d'aubaine in 1819. In some sense, this transformation remained incomplete: a strong argument could be made that the citizenship revolution only came to fruition in the 1880s, with the consolidation of French nationality law and the political institutions of the nation-state during the French Third Republic.[29] But in the initial passage from the Old Regime to the New, the fate of the droit d'aubaine defined the citizenship revolution, just as the French Revolution, followed by the Napoleonic reforms and those of the Bourbon monarchy, marked the decline and final abolition of the droit d'aubaine. Rather than a simple passage from subject to citizen, the citizenship revolution can best be traced as the dialectical movement of the droit d'aubaine—and the category of citizen itself—between the realms of law and politics.

In early modern France, the citizen moved between a political being and a legal subject.[30] In the sixteenth century, during the endemic religious and social unrest of the Religious Wars, the citizen appeared above all as a political being, a member of a limited social category that excluded women, the poor, and many others. In the key decade of the 1570s, however, the monarchy drew on the jurists and jurisprudence to create a model of the absolute citizen, founded on the droit d'aubaine. Citizenship became an enlarged, socially inclusive membership category, a juridical condition pertaining to men and women, peasants and nobles, children and adults, servants and masters—and accessible to foreigners by naturalization. This movement of the citizen from politics to law crystallized in the late seventeenth century, as did the protocol and procedure of naturalization. On the one hand, divested of political content and routinized as administrative law, naturalization became a legal and bureaucratic procedure of manufacturing citizens. Naturalization and citizenship, in the routinized practices of the absolute monarchy, remained the province of law, not politics. On the other hand, naturalization became a tool of state building, although ultimately an unsuccessful one: the forced naturalization of 1697 marked the political appropriation of a legal practice.

Between the 1697 Naturalization Tax and the 1750s, the droit d'aubaine and naturalization returned to their status as legal and administrative procedure, but in the middle decades of the eighteenth century, especially in the period coinciding with the Seven Years War (1756–63), a profound and largely undocumented revolution took shape. Citizenship shifted its locus again, this time from the domain of law to the domain of politics. A postabsolute citizen began to take shape in the 1750s and 1760s in a citizenship revolution that continued and deepened through the French Revolution itself (1789–99), under the Napoleonic Empire (1804–14), and into the nineteenth century. The citizenship revolution was eventually to produce the modern distinction between political citizenship and legal nationality, and to establish the modern significance of naturalization.

The citizenship revolution before 1789 was defined by two seemingly incongruous processes whose near simultaneous appearance before and after the Seven Years War suggests their interrelatedness, and also their common origin. First, the citizen emerged as a central rhetorical figure and key concept in the new political culture of the late eighteenth century, at a moment of the transformation and decline of absolute monarchy. This political reinvention of the citizen coincided with the second aspect of the citizenship revolution of mid-century: the French monarchy's systematic abolition of the droit d'aubaine, a policy that effaced the principal legal distinction between foreigners and citizens, and thus overturned the model of the French absolute citizen.

The citizenship revolution that ruptured with earlier expressions of absolutism coincided with a broader mutation of French political culture in the 1750s, the subject of extensive scholarship for at least two generations.[31] In the context of an exploding number of printed pamphlets and books circulated among an increasingly wide readership that both supported and opposed the Enlightenment, the "public sphere" was born, the ideas of "publicity" and "public opinion" became legitimating principles of politics, and "public law" was reborn.[32] In this broader arena, beyond the practice of the law and more widely diffused than the radical challenges to the principles of absolutism, the citizen became a key word of eighteenth-century political culture.

Beginning with the debates of the 1750s between the parlement, opposed to new "universal" taxes and the continued imposition of religious conformity, the language of the citizen passed from the narrow discourse of legal specialists to broader arenas of political debate where it intersected with a growing political language of "rights."[33] In these debates, and in the politics of the monarchy itself, especially in the face of France's humiliation during the Seven Year's War and the fragmentation engendered in the strife over taxation and religious policy, the "citizen" was increasingly linked to the "nation" within a recognizably modern ideological program of nationalism.[34] Within and alongside the nation, the citizen became a key word of the second half of the eighteenth century (as did "fatherland," "society," "utility," and "happiness"). The "citizen" appeared in the discourse of the Enlightenment, but also among its enemies; in the discourse of controllers-general and foreign ministers, but also in the writings of opponents of royal despotism, republican and other. The status of the "citizen" was central to the struggles for religious toleration, and the language was used by those seeking to preserve confessional unity. And the language of citizenship appeared in the confrontations between sovereign courts and royal authority, mostly concerning the increase in direct taxation. The multiple and varied significations and political uses of the word forced the "citizen" to shed its inclusive, juridical frame, and to become a central term of political debate in the second half of the eighteenth century. The story of how this happened still awaits its full-fledged historical treatment which this book, despite the attention that I give to the political citizen in chapter 7, does not provide.[35]

More important is the coincidence of this invention of the political citizen with the dismantling of legal citizenship in France. In this second dimension of the citizenship revolution, a far less public and more silent process, the absolute citizen, quite simply, disappeared.

Beginning in 1766, the French foreign office and the finance ministries, partially inspired by the contemporaneous philosophical critique of the droit d'aubaine, began to systematically dismantle the droit d'aubaine. The foreign office, under the influence of Enlightened reformers and a series of controllers-general and directors general of finance from Séchelles to Turgot to Necker to Calonne, abolished the droit d'aubaine in the interest of populationism, and especially of "commerce" and "communication." Such an abrupt shift in French foreign policy has been heavily occluded by the more visible "diplomatic revolution" of the mid-eighteenth century (reversing the traditional French and Austrian enmity) as well as the philosophically informed "new diplomacy" of the late eighteenth century, to which the French monarchy's shift of attitudes in relation to the droit d'aubaine were related.[36] The policy reorientations helped to frame the monarchy's full-scale assault on the principal juridical distinction between French citizens and foreigners, the droit d'aubaine, although the result was full of unintended consequences. Having invested symbolically in the droit d'aubaine as a mark of absolute sovereignty and the heart of French nationality law since the late sixteenth century, the monarchy inevitably undercut its own authority when it began to dismantle the droit d'aubaine, and produced the conditions for the rise of the postabsolute citizen.

In a series of some sixty-six international treaties and collective grants signed between the early 1766 and 1782, the French state abolished or exempted (albeit in a conditional and reciprocal manner) nearly every foreigner in France from the droit d'aubaine, and thus (at first unintentionally, but later explicitly) put into question the legal definition of aliens and citizens. The piecemeal but consistent elimination of the most important juridical marker of difference was a far more silent and largely unnoticed policy of the French state. It took place out of the "public sphere," even as it was negotiated extensively as a matter of international diplomacy under Louis XV and Louis XVI. Historians of the Old Regime, including specialists of French foreign policy and biographers of the key state ministers, have systematically ignored these treaties.[37] And so did contemporary publics: the dismantling of the droit d'aubaine, the abandonment of the absolute citizen that had crystallized under Louis XIV, was largely invisible, and went virtually unnoticed. Memorialists and chroniclers of the period gave scant attention to the treaties and grants negotiated and conferred between the end of the Seven Years War and the outbreak of the Revolution. Occasionally they published word of a negotiation, the signing and ratification of an international convention, or the registration of treaties and grants made to specific "national" groups of foreigners by the sovereign courts. But publicists, pamphleteers, and memorialists left no traces of any public discussion, much less a debate, over these conventions and grants.[38] Nor were they part of a "public" record in the subsequent memoirs of ambassadors, either foreign or French, or even in the formal diplomatic instructions to French ambassadors from the foreign office. The dismantling of the droit d'aubaine, if not exactly a "royal secret" (as Louis XV's personal foreign policy has been called), was nonetheless largely invisible.[39] If the first instantiation of the citizenship revolution was unrelentlessly public, the second fell into the domain of the "private"—that is, not only of the publicly unspoken, but also the realm of private, civil law.

Both dimensions of the citizenship revolution before 1789 coincided with Louis XV and his ministers' mid-century structural reforms of the monarchy that began the final phase of absolutism. As historians since Alexis de Tocqueville have long noted, the reform projects to impose "universal" taxes abandoned the monarchy's earlier efforts to shore up the privileges (and tax exemptions) of officeholders, nobles, provinces, and other corps and communities of the realm. Everything happened as if, under the impact of fiscal crisis that resulted in part from the Seven Year's War, the Crown resolved the dualism of Louis XIV's political rule in favor of the homogenizing, totalizing qualities of absolute sovereignty. Abandoning the corporatist vision of the social order, ministerial reforms under Louis XV and Louis XVI turned the idea of "privilege" into a common law founded on general interests. Historians have variously described this "bureaucratic revolution" of an "enlightened monarchy," the struggle between a modernizing state (accused of "ministerial despotism") against the privileged groups of the realm, but they have only seen within it the first instantiation of the citizenship revolution, the birth of the political citizen.[40]

The two dimensions of the citizenship revolution—the discursive and political appropriation of the citizen, and the abolition of the droit d'aubaine—took place nearly simultaneously but in different contexts and with contradictory implications. The first constituted the ideological origins of revolutionary citizenship; the second launched debates in the courtroom, among lawyers arguing the cases of foreigners and citizens, that raised without consistently resolving the meaning of French nationality. Before 1789, the identity of the postabsolute citizen was still incomplete.

The Citizenship Revolution from the French Revolution to the Final Abolition of the Droit d'Aubaine

The revolutionary experiments concerning the droit d'aubaine and naturalization, the Napoleonic Empire's reforms, and those of the restored Bourbon monarchy that reconstituted and ultimately abolished the droit d'aubaine between 1789 and 1819, represent a second phase of the citizenship revolution. The twisted history of the droit d'aubaine in these years is the story of its oscillation between the poles of law and politics, between the courtroom and the public sphere, and from the Old Regime to the New. The legal and political frameworks governing the droit d'aubaine, and the practice of nationality and citizenship more generally, changed frequently and abruptly. The reconstruction of these histories—at once social, political, and legal—can illuminate the meaning of revolutionary citizenship and nationality.

The early French revolutionaries drew on the efforts of the late Old Regime monarchy to break with its classical absolutist past, although they went further, as we shall see, in abolishing the droit d'aubaine outright in 1790 and 1791 on the basis of universalist, cosmopolitan, and Enlightened rhetoric. The droit d'aubaine was swept off the historical stage as dust from the feudal world. At the same time, the early revolutionaries turned naturalization into an automatic and statutory process, and individual naturalizations came to an end—except for the philosophical and political naturalizations of the radical Convention in 1792. But slightly more than a decade after the French revolutionaries had abolished the droit d'aubaine, Napoleon reinstituted a redefined version of the droit d'aubaine on a reciprocal basis in the first article of the Civil Code concerning the status of persons (1803), and in the same year reintroduced the practices of sovereign and discretionary naturalization. More important, the Civil Code crystallized a distinction between civil and political rights in France that made naturalization far less attractive and popular than it had been under the Old Regime, except for particular groups of soldiers, government employees, and others. In 1814, both the droit d'aubaine and naturalization were reaffirmed, albeit with modifications. The French constitutional assemblies of the Restoration only debated and narrowly approved the final abolition of the droit d'aubaine (as a central element in French immigration policies) in 1819, after a half century of high political drama in which it had played a not insignificant role.

For historians of the nineteenth century, 1819 is a date without significance in the development of modern French nationality law and citizenship. But seen from the Old Regime, it is deeply symbolic of the broader citizenship revolution that spanned the turbulent years from the 1750s through the revolutionary decade, the Napoleonic Empire, and the Bourbon Restoration.

The absolute citizen, constructed during the sixteenth and seventeenth centuries, had rested on a principal legal marker of difference between the citizen and the foreigner. This legal boundary, written into the droit d'aubaine, was fictionally effaced in the letter of naturalization and politically dismantled during the first phase of the citizenship revolution of the late eighteenth century. The French Revolution, of course, amplified the political liberation of the citizen from the language of the law, but it also went much further: the revolutionaries broke explicitly with the Old Regime practices of the droit d'aubaine, even its serial and reciprocal abolitions, as well as the authority of the government to grant discretionary naturalization. Yet under Napoleon, both the droit d'aubaine and naturalization were reinstituted—although a more accurate account will describe their reinvention—and the droit d'aubaine was only dismantled, after much debate, in 1819.

The legal, social, and political histories of the droit d'aubaine after the 1750s, like its uses and abuses in the construction of monarchical absolutism during the sixteenth and seventeenth centuries, come together as histories of nationality law, citizenship, immigration, international relations, and state building in France. These, in turn, propose a single story about the emergence of modern nationality (as legal membership) and citizenship (as political rights, and eventually as social belonging). The French Revolution occupies a less central place in this story than in standard accounts, which are too often premised on a misleading distinction between "traditional" and "modern" citizenship, and which fail to distinguish between the discourses and practices of the citizen in law and in politics. This book attempts to correct the received wisdom about the transition from early to modern citizenship in France through the largely untold stories of how foreigners became French citizens between the late sixteenth and the early nineteenth centuries.

PART ONE

FOREIGNERS & CITIZENS IN EARLY MODERN FRANCE

THE MAKING OF THE ABSOLUTE CITIZEN

The absolute citizen was, above all, a creation of the law and the lawyers of early modern France. No one denounced this more forcefully than Jean-Jacques Rousseau. In a famous footnote to his *Social Contract* (1762), Rousseau impatiently dismissed all previous definitions of the citizen offered by legal commentators, dictionary authors, and other French writers who "did not know what [the word] means." In particular, he singled out the sixteenth-century humanist and jurisconsult Jean Bodin (1529–96), noting that "when Bodin wanted to speak of our citizens and burgesses [*bourgeois*], he made the gross error of mistaking the one for the other."[1]

The criticism of Jean Bodin is deeply unfair. It reveals more about the prejudices of the self-proclaimed "citizen of Geneva"—and of the citizenship revolution in the eighteenth century—than about Rousseau as a close reader of texts. In fact, Jean Bodin devoted great attention in his 1576 treatise, *Les Six livres de la République*—book 6, chapter 1 (ironically the same citation as Rousseau's)—to the distinction between a "bourgeois" in a town or city and the "citizen" of the kingdom. For Bodin, the former was not a "true" but rather a merely "honorary" citizen—a distinction that Rousseau would overturn with a vengeance. What mattered most, for Bodin, was the legal definition of citizen in the kingdom as a whole.[2]

Bodin's treatise is known by historians and political theorists of early modern France for offering, most famously, a durable justification of indivisible sovereignty, "absolute and perpetual power." Written in the midst of the religious and civil wars, and published following the disastrous events of the crown's implicit participation in the massacres of Protestants on Saint Bartholomew's Day in 1572, Bodin reacted by putting the problem of social "order" at the center of his political reflections, and advocated a strong monarchy as the necessary solution. Traditionally, unwittingly following Rousseau, commentators have debated the extent of Bodin's "absolutism," but have rarely examined the place of the "citizen" in Bodin's thinking or have dismissed its importance as a mere

synonym of the "subject."[3] But the equivalence is misleading, for it fails to illuminate the legal, as opposed to the merely political, dimensions of absolute citizenship in the period, and the key place of Jean Bodin in the philosophical
elaboration of citizenship and nationality law in early modern France.

Jean Bodin and French Jurisprudence

Jean Bodin worked briefly as a legal practitioner, a barrister who plead cases
at parlement, then as a professor of law (at Toulouse and Paris). Above all, Bodin
was a philosopher and political theorist who, in his treatment of the citizen,
wrote within a tradition of "scholarly law" (*droit savant*) that was several steps
removed from the technical exigencies of litigation and courtroom argument.
His treatise was deeply and critically immersed in the terms of Roman law, and
his text was inflated with a constant recourse to examples drawn from Rome.[4]
But his relation to Roman law was not unmediated, as Bodin followed the Italian jurists, Baldus, Bartolus, and the other *commentatori* on Roman law and the
jurisprudence of the late medieval Italian city-states. Like his contemporary jurists in France, Bodin turned their Latin city (*civitas*), by metaphoric extension,
into the kingdom: "All the realm being one great city," he wrote, "after the
fashion of the Roman Empire."[5] The identification of the civitas with the kingdom entailed important consequences. First, Bodin recognized a population of
millions of people under the sovereignty of a single individual was not like that
of a small city-state. France was a commonwealth "diversified in its laws, its
customs, its religions, its nations." Citizens did not share a common culture or
even common laws—except, of course, for the law of shared obedience to the
king. A Republic was "a lawful government of many households or families and
of what belongs to them in common, with sovereign power," and the magni-
tude of France was also a City, "even though its citizens are divided into many
towns, villages, or provinces. For the town does not make up the City [*la ville ne
fait pas la cité*], as many have written."[6]

This metaphoric reworking of the civitas justified and anticipated the extreme
devalorization of local or municipal citizenship in relation to the citizen of the
French kingdom, and made for a unique political and legal framework of citizenship in early modern Europe. In England, it is conventionally argued, nationality
emerged historically out of municipal law(s), and this at a relatively late date.[7] On
the Italian Peninsula, as throughout the Germanies, municipal citizenship within
cities and hometowns flourished as long as territorial states made no efforts to
constitute "citizenship" at the level of the kingdom or principality—and they did
occasionally, as in Naples under the Bourbons or in Prussia under the Hohen-
zollerns. In Spain and Spanish America, despite the existence of a monarchy with
absolutist pretensions (as in its experiment with the Nueva Planta in 1714), cities,
towns, and villages continued into the eighteenth century to make citizens

(*vecinos*) and to define "nativeness" (*naturaleza*) by drawing boundaries that excluded "bad" immigrants, in the process identifying the rights and privileges of the citizen in the kingdom and its colonies.[8] But the French kings had, since the thirteenth century, presumed the prerogative of identifying "citizens" of the kingdom, within the medieval practices of "letters of royal bourgeoisie," over and above those of a town or city. By 1576, when Bodin published his treatise, local or municipal citizenship (*droit de bourgeoisie*) was clearly disassociated from the conferral of royal or "national" citizenship through grants of naturalization.

In France, municipalities continued to confer the statuses and privileges of local citizenship until the French Revolution, despite the monarchy's fiscal absolutism over its towns. Local privileges of citizenship involved a shifting set of social actors and economic privileges granted by and in the municipality.[9] But towns and cities after the sixteenth century did not claim to confer national citizenship—except of course for those that Bodin did not live to see, the special and contested cases of Strasbourg, Metz, and other towns in the provinces of Alsace, Lorraine, and Flanders during the seventeenth century. Through the eighteenth century, these towns and cities sometimes claimed the right to draw the boundaries of "royal" or "national" citizenship. Most often, they were unable to overturn the normative prerogative established by the absolutist monarchy, the one for which Jean Bodin provided the philosophical and ideological foundations. Citizenship in the kingdom took logical, legal, and political precedence: it became part of "common law" set against the "privileges of bourgeoisie."[10]

Bodin thus defined the municipal citizen in purely "honorary" terms, with his—the gendering of the citizen was explicit—status and rights strictly identified with the municipality where he lived. It was not just a question of scale: the local citizen or "bourgeois" (the word derived from the French town or "bourg") might have a "right to vote or to hold the status of bourgeois by his merits, or by the favor granted to him," but this too was merely an honorary privilege. He was not a "true citizen, since he is not a subject." This was central, since Bodin defined the citizen on three separate occasions in the sixth chapter of book 1 as "the free subject depending on the sovereignty of an Other." He thus rejected the classical and Aristotelean definition of the citizen—as one who "rules and is ruled in turn"—in favor of political subjection. "The fault is greater to say that he is not a citizen who is not part of the magistracy and deliberative assemblies of the estates of the people, as a judge or participant in the affairs of state."[11] In this fundamentally antipolitical and anti-Aristotelean world, the citizen was completely divorced from a public role, and placed at the receiving end of sovereignty.

To be a "free subject" in sixteenth-century France was not to be a public or political actor, because sovereign power was indivisible and located exclusively in the monarchy. Nor was it to be one among equals before the law, the essence of modern citizenship. Bodin of course recognized that "citizens" in the monarchy were unequal in their privileges. France was, he wrote, a "society of orders," what modern historians have called a corporate society, and Bodin thought the inequality of the three estates and their privileges, among others, was "good and valid." Bodin knew that he lived in a legally fractured and fragmented world, where endless distinctions (based on rights and privileges) divided the unitary category of citizens. If one were to define citizens on the basis of their different rights and privileges, Bodin reasoned, one would find "fifty thousand definitions of citizens, according to the infinite diversity of prerogatives that citizens have over each other, and over foreigners." What defined a citizen was not his "rights" or "privileges" but his sense of duty and obedience, exercised in exchange for the protection of the king: "It is thus the gratitude and obedience of the free subject towards his sovereign prince, and the tutelage, justice, and protection of the Prince towards the subject, that makes the citizen . . . the other differences are incidental and accidental."[12]

Such a depoliticization did indeed transform the citizen into a subject. But it also expanded the membership boundaries of citizenship. Citizens (legal, and not just political, subjects) came to include more than just wealthy, elite, and privileged males. Instead of exercising rights and privileges (especially political ones), the citizen became part of a socially inclusive membership category, what sociologists have sometimes called "an instrument and an object of closure."[13] The qualities of a citizen were thus not restricted to (male) heads of households or families; citizens included "women [and] children of families who are free of all kinds of servitudes, and their rights and liberties, and the power to dispose of their goods, are not in any way curtailed domestic authority."[14] The household was not the city: every man, woman, and child may not have held extensive rights, but they were nonetheless legal citizens of France. In a distinct reversal of the late medieval idea of the citizen in Italy and elsewhere, Bodin turned the citizen from a political being into a legal subject.

The intellectual historian J. G. A. Pocock formulated a reverse movement from politics to law in the classical age: the shift from the political being (*zoon politikon*) of the fourth-century B.C.E. Greek philosopher Aristotle to the legal person (*legalis homo*) of the early second-century C.E. Roman jurist Gaius. Aristotle's citizen (*polites*), the citizen of the Athenian city-state, was classically defined as a man who rules and is ruled in turn: he was a privileged member of the Athenian *polis*. Citizenship, here, was a "limited membership category": the exclusive prerogative, if not exactly the privilege, of males, slave owners, and patriarchs. The Roman jurist Gaius's citizen, by contrast, was a legal being, existing and acting in a world of persons, actions, and things regulated by law. As Pocock points out, Gaius's citizen came into being through the possession of things and the practice of the law:

His actions were in the first instance directed at things and at other persons through the medium of things; in the second instance, they were actions he took, or others took in respect of him, at law—acts of authorization, appropriation, conveyance, acts of litigation, prosecution, justification. His relation to things was regulated by law. . . . A "citizen" came to mean someone free to act by law, free to ask [for] and expect the law's protection, a citizen of such and such a legal community.[15]

Of course, this "citizenship" was still a socially limited category, and under the Roman republic, property ownership had been an important, although not determining, qualification. But the Caracalla edict of the early third century CE (the so-called Constitution of Antonin) extended Roman citizenship universally through the legal fiction of Rome as "common fatherland" (*communis patria*) and set its limits not by property or the ability to hold office—to act politically—but on another distinction that Aristotle also knew well: between citizen and slave, the *summa divisio* of classical and especially Roman law.[16]

Fourteen centuries later, in the turmoil of religious and civil warfare that tore apart the social fabric of France, Bodin effectively reversed the movement from the political citizen to the legal subject. He implicitly made the slave into a French citizen: although the slave was hardly a "free subject," the French legal adage was upheld: "There are no slaves in France." And he turned the foreigner into a kind of slave, despite the complementary aphorism, oft-repeated in the Old Regime, that the foreigner in France "lives free and dies a slave" (*Liber vivit; servus moritur*).[17] Better put, Bodin's text gave expression to the renewed emphasis, especially among the jurists of the early modern monarchy, on the legal distinction between citizens and others where such others were not slaves, as in classical times. Writing toward the end of the sixteenth century, and in the context of a widespread xenophobic reaction against Italians, Germans, and Spaniards in France, Bodin—and after him, the king and his council as well as the courtroom lawyers—defined the legal citizen in opposition to the foreigner (*étranger*). If the citizen/foreigner distinction was not actually the *summa divisio* of French civil law, it was nonetheless the central organizing distinction for the boundaries of membership in the polity.

Bodin's presentation of the "citizen" was unusual in the late sixteenth century, and even more remarkable in the context of juridical writing more generally in the Old Regime. No other treatise of politics or law considered the problem of the citizen so generally and abstractly; indeed, not until Rousseau did the citizen figure so centrally in a work of political theory. Lawyers and jurisconsults in France after Bodin tended to treat the "citizen" exclusively in legal terms, and as a practical matter in relation to the jurisprudential status of the "alien." Much of their writing involved a technical and highly elaborated gloss on juridical and administrative practices. Yet it is no coincidence that Bodin penned his work when he did, because he composed his text at just the moment when the juridical model of the absolute citizen took shape in the 1570s.

In the years surrounding the publication of Bodin's treatise, three other jurists published texts that elaborated on the legal definition of the citizen, as well as the legal disabilities of aliens and the meaning of "naturalization" (a word that first appeared in 1566). None were of the quality and sophistication of Bodin's. Jean Bacquet (1520–97) was attorney at the Paris parlement before becoming the royal solicitor (*avocat du roi*) in the Chambre du trésor (the sovereign courts responsible for registration of patent letters and disputes over domanial taxes). In his collected works published the year after Bodin's treatise, he included a seminal *Traité du droit d'aubeine* that exhaustively elaborated a "doctrine" of the royal citizen in French civil law through a discussion of alien disabilities.[18] The following year, Jean Papon (1505–90) published an administrative manual for the use of civil law practitioners that contained an elaboration of the juridical model of the citizen, constructed in contrast to the civil, religious, and political incapacities of foreigners, and an idealized vision of the administrative process of naturalization (*Secrets du troisième et dernier notaire*, 1578). Papon, a hack lawyer, compiled with no particular accuracy the jurisprudence and treatises of earlier sixteenth-century jurists (le Maistre, le Coq, Pape, etc.). He was one of the first best-selling authors of those widely sold legal dictionaries (*dictionnaires d'arrêts*) of dubious value (*Recueil des arrêts notables des cours souveraines de France, ordonnez par titres. . . .* [first edition, 1565]). Finally, René Choppin (1537–1606) published an important treatise on royal authority two years before Bodin, and was closer to him in intellectual stature, although far more attentive to French customary law than to Rome. The Angevin humanist and royal apologist was a great commentator on the customals (the redacted customs of the northern provinces) and his *Traité du domaine de la couronne de France* (Latin edition, 1574; first French edition, 1603) included an important section on the customary law precedents of the king's rights over aliens and the meaning of naturalization.[19]

These works appeared simultaneously, in the space of five years, as an expression of a broad xenophobic wave of French public opinion in the 1560s and 1570s. A period of general economic regression, religious violence, and political turmoil, these decades constituted a low-water mark in the authority of the monarchy. Questions of royal succession divided France into parties organized along social, political, and confessional lines.[20] The foreigner became an important site for thinking about French unity. Printed pamphlets and diatribes against the Italians, Spaniards, and Germans present in France at the beginning of the Religious Wars created a cacophonous discourse against the foreigner. At the Estates General at Orléans (1560) and Blois (1576), the Third Estate, dominated by noble magistrates and barristers, underscored their fear of the foreigner, especially in economic terms.[21] Jurists were among the most vocal in arguing strenuously for increased restrictions on the admission of foreigners and especially on their legal assimilation as Frenchmen and women.

The lawyers and magistrates involved in the religious and civil struggles from 1562 to 1598 were assuming their role as "political men" (*homo politici*), as the barrister François Baudouin claimed about jurisconsults in 1559.[22] Some took an active part in political life, writing pamphlets and libels, and acting in the various Estates General or in the sovereign courts of the kingdom. Most tended to support (with notable exceptions such as René Choppin) the Politique party of religious toleration under the leadership of Henry IV during the later stages of the French Wars of Religion. Reflecting their explicitly political role, they relied extensively on the language of the "citizen." In their writings, the word tended to refer less to the distinction with "foreigners" and more to the public, ethical, and civic spirit of disinterested and political action. France's disorder resulted from the corruption of "good citizens," who should never act out of narrow, sectarian, intolerant motives but only in the service of the public good.[23]

These political claims, along with the lawyers' public roles as citizens, came to an end with the reconstitution of royal authority under Henry IV. Among the jurists, the Age of Eloquence passed away in the early seventeenth century, as the prestige of the Palais declined, and juridical discourse about the citizen returned to the more technical, legal language that had developed in and around the practice of civil law. Within the language and practice of jurists in the course of the early seventeenth century, the citizen moved from politics to the law. Defining citizens became a matter of "private," not "public," concern, the domain of the law and administrative courts, not public declarations of royal authority or public opposition to the crown. Like public law itself, citizenship was submerged in the workings of the administrative monarchy. In 1692, Gabriel Argou could write revealingly about how "private citizens concern themselves little in France with what relates to public law, knowledge of it being for them more of a curiosity than useful."[24]

Despite having provided the philosophical justification of this movement, Jean Bodin was *not* the principal influence on subsequent treatises on royal rights and the jurisprudence of case law about foreigners under the Old Regime. For one, he did not share the xenophobic sentiments of his practicing colleagues who sought to restrict legal citizenship as much as possible. More generally, his text stood apart from the more technical exigencies of legal practices on which French law rested, and must be distinguished from the work of legal technicians and practitioners that was dominant after the sixteenth century.

With Bacquet and Bodin, subsequent jurists insisted on the legal, rather than political, identity of citizens, defined jurisprudentially in contrast and opposition to foreigners. In this regard, jurisprudence and legal doctrine provided essential materials for the political construction of absolute monarchy from the late sixteenth to the late seventeenth centuries. In this first moment of French absolutism, from the reigns of Henry II to Louis XIV, the absolute citizen took shape in the collusion (and sometimes conflict) between jurisprudential practice and royal policy toward aliens and toward their naturalization as French citizens.

To understand the collusion, but also the slippage, between the juridical and the royal citizen in early modern France, it is important to identify the several kinds of jurists who created the legal theory and practice of French citizenship, as well as the basis of French public law in the sixteenth and seventeenth centuries. As summarized by the royal humanist Etienne Pasquier in the 1560s, "The Common Law of France rests on four points: from royal ordinances; the different customs of the provinces; the general decisions of the sovereign courts; and in certain moral ways that, by a long and ancient usage, we possess in faith and hommage to Rome."[25] Roman law occupied an ambivalent status within late medieval and early modern France. The French kings borrowed from Rome, by way of the Italian Commentators, key formulas of legislative power, yet they formally rejected the corpus of Roman law as the basis of French law. Such was the ideology of the jurists as well: Jean Bacquet, to cite but one example, wrote that "this Kingdom is in no way subjected to Roman laws and Imperial Constitutions," eliding the complex relations between French and Roman law in the sixteenth century.[26] For the "faith and hommage" to Rome translated into an insistence on the value of Roman law, especially the *corpus juris civilis* and Justinian's *Institutes*, as "written reason" to fill the gaps where other sources of law failed to cohere, and as the clearest expression of natural law.[27] The principal sources of French law, as Pasquier listed them, were in the thousands of royal ordinances and edicts, in the redacted customals of the northern provinces, and in the case law emanating from the sovereign courts, and especially the Paris parlement. Given the declining influence of scholarly law "with its infinite digressions on Roman law," it was left to the jurists to sort these out and to establish "doctrine."[28]

The first group directly engaged in this project were the dozens of collectors and compilers of court decisions (*arrêts*) known in the Old Regime as *arrestographes* or *arrêtistes*. Their reputation, as Christiane Chêne has pointed out, was ambivalent at best. At the end of the seventeenth century, the Parisian barrister Berroyer wrote that "there are two directly opposed opinions concerning the use made of legal decisions: the one is that they form a part of our French law; the other is that even the most precise of these compilations contains something dangerous." It was the latter opinion that initially dominated, and barristers and attorneys, including those who produced ever more compilations of decrees, denounced their imprecise, haphazard qualities.[29] Apprenticeship in the law was a long and tortured process: "Thirty years of study barely suffices to train a jurist," wrote a weary eighteenth-century lawyer, François Chavry de Boissy. Although *procureurs* (attorneys or solicitors) could practice after seven years' apprenticeship as clerks, *avocats* (barristers) required university training (the *licence*) and more apprenticeship before being able to plead their cases before magistrates.[30] Given the widespread demand among practitioners, the compilation of court decisions as virtual "manuals" of jurisprudence was indeed "a temptation of beginners." These collections of decrees, however imperfect and despite their "doubtful science," were widely consumed during the necessarily long training period of becoming a practicing lawyer, and in the practice of civil law itself.[31]

The sixteenth- and seventeenth-century arrestographes, whose works were reprinted until the French Revolution, tended to treat separately the decisions of the different parlements and sovereign courts of the kingdom. The Paris parlement, with half of the kingdom's population in its jurisdiction, was the object of specific compilations (Bardet, Loüet, or Soëfve), but so were other smaller regions of customary law such as Brittany (Frain, Hévin). The southern regions of written Roman law (*droit écrit*) were also heavily represented: Provence (Boniface), Grenoble (Basset, Pape), or Toulouse (Albert, Catellan, Maynard, La Roche-Flavin).[32] These regional compilations formed the basis of eighteenth-century "national" dictionaries and collections by lawyers who sought to constitute a civil jurisprudence at the level of the kingdom, one that included the law governing "foreigners" and "citizens." Among these compilers who shed their negative reputation as they developed the modern notion of the repertoire were Jean-Bapiste Denisart (1712–65), solicitor at the Châtelet court in Paris, and his posthumous editors. The ninth edition of his *Collection de décisions nouvelles et de notions relatives à la jurisprudence actuelle*, organized alphabetically, was published as a semiofficial enterprise after his death in an attempt to create a comprehensive jurisprudence of the kingdom.[33] The Parisian barrister Joseph Guyot (1728–1816) also produced a repertoire of considerable if unwieldy size, in collaboration with his colleague Boucher d'Argis, that went through four editions before 1783. Pierre-Antoine Merlin in 1784 then reworked the dictionary as a seventeen-volume "supplement" that was republished several more times during the turbulent revolutionary decades.[34]

The arrestographes, then, were a key group in the production of "French law," and in this instance the doctrines governing the status of foreigners and the identity of citizens. A second group of jurists involved in the project of founding "French law," and within it the droit d'aubaine, were specialists both inside and outside the academy. University chairholders in French law, established in Paris and elsewhere in 1679 (including the Roman-law provinces of the kingdom) compiled specialized treatises on the civil capacities of persons.[35] None was more famous, nor more influential, than Robert Joseph Pothier (1699–1772), whose treatises on inheritance law, adopting the categories of Justinian, influenced directly the authors of the Civil Code. Lesser academics also made their impact, in particular by re-editing and commenting on the classic treatises of Bacquet and Lefebvre de la Planche. Claude Joseph de Ferrière (1666–1747), son of the dean of the Paris law school and himself a chairholder of French law at Paris, re-edited with commentary the 1744 edition of Bacquet's works, including his *Traité du droit d'aubeine*, Paul Charles Lorry (1719–66) was a Romanist law professor at Paris who edited the treatises of Lefebvre de la Planche. In their hands, the droit d'aubaine became an essential part of French law.

Not all jurists who helped in this project were at the universities; other barristers benefited from more informal patronage and worked from outside the heavily Romanized traditions of scholarly law. The astounding success of the works of Gabriel Argou (1640–1703), a great specialist of feudal law, testify both to the various demand among lawyers for such synthetic works, and to the patronage of the crown. Argou's *Institutions du droit français*, initially published in 1692 at the instigation of the abbé Fleury, was reprinted eleven times in the next century, the last time by Boucher d'Argis in 1787, and represented, according to Chancellor d'Aguesseau, the best introduction to French law, "more than any other one that can be useful to beginners."[36]

The third and last group of legal practitioners who participated in the construction of a "French" jurisprudence of foreigners and citizens were the royal solicitors and attorneys-general who engaged in litigation before the courts concerning foreigners and authored protocols and treatises. Jean Bacquet, royal solicitor (*avocat du roi*) at the Paris Chambre des comptes, was to become the most oft-cited expert on the subject of the citizen and the alien. Subsequent jurists in the seventeenth and eighteenth centuries quoted and annotated his text with far greater frequency than that of Jean Bodin, whose work remained far removed from the exigencies of courtroom practice. Bacquet's treatise became the definitive text on alien law, at least until the posthumous publication of Jean Jacques Auguste Lefebvre de la Planche's (1668–1738) *Traité du droit d'aubaine*. The author had been an attorney at the Paris parlement, then royal solicitor of the Chambre du domaine, and archivist of the council of finances (among other commissions) until his retirement in 1732; his works were published in 1765, edited by Lorry.[37] Finally, Henri-François d'Aguesseau (1668–1751) contributed extensively to the jurisprudence of citizenship, and to the making of French civil law more generally. Descended from a distinguished family of Bordeaux magistrates, members of the robe nobility, d'Aguesseau plead cases as royal solicitor-general (*avocat général du roi*) of the Paris parlement in the 1690s before embarking on his career as chancellor under the regency of Cardinal de Fleury in 1717. Exiled in 1727, he returned to the office in 1737 and then attempted to codify the practices of French civil law.[38]

The compilers of court decisions, university law professors, and royal attorneys and barristers all contributed to the model of the absolute citizen within their broader construction of French law in the early modern period. Yet they did so in an unfamiliar and distinctly premodern vocabulary.

For educated Frenchmen and women under the absolute monarchy, the term *citoyen* was usually reserved for discussions of the members of ancient republics such as Athens and Rome. Jacques-Benigne Bossuet, for example, the theological apologist of Louis XIV's absolutism, used the term extensively to decry the "excessive love of liberty" in these defunct polities.[39] The legal vocabulary of the Old Regime jurists was, by contrast, specialized, even esoteric. In their jurisprudential commentaries on court decisions involving litigation over the inheritance rights of aliens, and their descriptions of the procedure of naturalization, the lawyers tended to shy away from the lexicon of scholarly law and its theoretically clean opposition, used by Jean Bodin and adapted from Roman law, between "foreigners" and "citizens." Just as legal practitioners distanced themselves from the university traditions, and from Latin as the language of law—after the sixteenth century, they wrote almost exclusively in the vernacular, befitting the pragmatic and utilitarian vision of their works—so too did they distance themselves from Roman precedents and the vocabulary of the civitas. Although some French jurists continued to use the term *citoyen*, especially the learned jurisconsults steeped in Roman law, most legal practitioners—in keeping with their declining role as political theorists—resorted to a different set of terms altogether in their jurisprudential discussion of "nationality."

The word "nationality" (*nationalité*) itself was a postrevolutionary invention. Its first literary usage appears to have been in Germaine de Staël's 1807 novel *Corinne and Italy*, where it referred to a "spiritual force" of belonging. The German connection was to deepen in the course of the nineteenth century, making nationality into a subjective, sentimental attachment. At the same time, as a term of legal membership in the state, the word was used, along with the noun "nationals" (*nationaux*), in administrative documents of the Napoleonic Empire, and *nationalité*, in its juridical sense of state membership, entered common legal usage in the 1840s. Yet it was only in 1874 that it appeared in the title of a governmental or constitutional act.[40] Until then, lawyers and politicians of the early nineteenth century debated the criteria for the "quality of [a] French[man]" (*qualité de Français*) as a mode of recognizing or attributing general membership in the state.

As a category of sentimental belonging and cultural identity, nationality may indeed be a nineteenth-century invention; as a legal category of citizenship, though, the concept and practice existed long before the word. In the early modern period, lawyers produced the idea of the French citizen as a "national," in contrast and opposition to the foreigner, and argued about the applicability of definitions in hundreds of cases of contested inheritances and seizures by the droit d'aubaine. They relied little on the term *citoyen*, deploying a lexicon of more technical words, "terms of chancellery and court," as the *Encyclopédie* was to note in 1752: thus *naturalité* ("nativeness"), *regnicole* ("native resident"), *sujet* ("subject"), *Français naturel* ("natural Frenchmen and women"), and *naturels Français* ("French 'naturals' "). Concerning the latter two, everything happened as if the Latin cognates of the "nation" (*natio*) were taken seriously: the "nation" was constituted by a community that shared the condition of being born (*nasci*) and, thus, was of the same nature (*natura*). Beginning in the thirteenth century, the native subject was called a "natural" (*naturel*, from the Latin *naturalis*), identified by his birth in the kingdom; shortly thereafter, in 1270, the term "nation" (*nation*) made its first appearance in the French vernacular. Although the nation, as a political construction, developed only in the course of the eighteenth century (as David Bell has so persuasively argued), by the end of the Middle Ages, at least semantically, "the French were united . . . by ties that, secreted by nature, could not be broken."[41]

If, in the technical language of the law, early modern jurists consistently avoided mention or discussion of the "nation," they nonetheless worked out extensively the theory and practice of French nationality avant la lettre using the synonyms of French nativeness, *citoyen*, *regnicole*, and *naturel français*. The definition of French nationality turned on the idea of the "alien" (*aubain*). Most jurists and publicists of the Old Regime, following Bacquet, derived the term *aubain* from *alibi natus*, born elsewhere. Happy etymology, even if false: the word most certainly derives from *ali ban*, those belonging to another seigneurial jurisdiction.[42] Already in the fourteenth century, aliens were defined by their place of birth, not their allegiance; by the sixteenth century, birth was a commonplace marker of foreignness. In his definitive treatise, Bacquet wrote: "We hold in France that any man who is not born in the Kingdom, Countries, Lands, or seigneuries under the obedience of the king of France is called *Aubein*, or Foreigner: whether he resides continually in the kingdom, or whether he is a simple traveller or passing through." In fact, Bacquet's apparently simple negative definition was complicated by two sixteenth-century concerns. On the one hand, Bacquet still acknowledged the medieval distinctions of "aliens" from proximate lands (*aubains*) and those from distant ones (*épaves*), following the extracts that he reproduced from the registers of the Paris Chambre des comptes. And this despite the generalization of the principle of birth outside the kingdom since the first half of the fourteenth century. More importantly, he formally delimited three kinds of aliens: "true aliens" (where the identity of "foreigner" and "alien" was complete); exempted aliens (where the statute of persons and of their goods was distinguished: they were exempted from the droit d'aubaine); and lastly, "reputed aliens," those born in lands previously under the control of the French crown.[43]

After Bacquet, the multiplicity of the alien decreased in importance. Although early seventeenth-century financial officers and their apologists, such as François de Maisons, could still invoke them, the tendency under absolutism was precisely to collapse these different categories of aliens into a single one—and to define, tacitly, the singular category of the citizen. Thus by the 1730s, Lefebvre de la Planche's royalist revision of Bacquet no longer reproduced the sixteenth-century distinctions, and among the jurists more generally, "alien" and "foreigner" became synonymous.[44]

The eighteenth-century jurists—among them Robert Joseph Pothier, whose work on civil law was to inform the text of the Civil Code, Joseph Guyot, and Pierre-Antoine Merlin—all repeated the negative definition of Bacquet. For the jurists, "foreigner" and "citizen" were mirror images, understood *a contrario*. Such reasoning was perhaps best expressed by Chancellor d'Aguesseau, who, in 1694, as solicitor-general pleading before the Paris parlement, wrote an important opinion about a highly complex inheritance dispute involving the descendants of a Frenchman born abroad: "Native resident is opposed to alien; and as contrary things should be defined mutually and respectively, by defining the term alien, we will know the extent of that of native resident [*regnicole*]."[45] If the jurists defined an alien as a person not born in France, a native resident was defined inversely as a native and resident subject of the French crown, despite the strict interpretation of its etymology as "inhabitant of the kingdom."[46] Again, d'Aguesseau, paraphrasing the late sixteenth-century jurist Antoine de Loysel, put it succinctly: "To be a *regnicole*, one has to exclude these two conditions: birth and residence outside the kingdom." In other words, a native subject and legal citizen was a person who was not an alien in the kingdom, any person not subjected to the civil and political disabilities of the law, the "anti-privileges" of the aubain.

The "Anti-Privileges" of the Alien

Aliens in the kingdom, or simply "foreigners" in the language of Jean Bodin, suffered from a number of legal incapacities or disabilities (*incapacités*), a notion widely used in the common law traditions of the early modern period that derived ultimately from Roman law.[47] Incapacity was the inability of a person to give or receive things, which early modern jurists glossed as the "vice" (*vice*) or "stain" (*tache*) or "blot" (*macule*) of a person, a legal and moral quality determined principally by nature and birth.[48] The greatest incapacity of the foreigner, according to Jean Bodin, was the inability to legally draw up a will or to deed property *ab intestat*, without a will. That incapacity was explicitly and indelibly linked to the lord's (or king's) right to seize the alien's property at his or her death: "The most notable privilege that the citizen has over the foreigners is that of being able to make a will and dispose of his goods according to custom, or to leave his own kin [*parents*] as heirs: the foreigner has neither the one nor the other, and his goods are acquired by the seigneur of the place where he died."[49]

Bodin called this incapacity the "droit d'aubaine," and he saw nothing unique about it. Countering the complaints of Italians in the kingdom (a wealthy and highly visible group of foreigners that was the subject of a xenophobic backlash in the 1570s, and was no doubt targeted by the royal treasurers), Bodin argued that the droit d'aubaine was neither a distinctively French nor a relatively new law. In a whirlwind survey of European practices, he referred fleetingly to other polities where the droit d'aubaine was levied, including Naples, Sicily, "and the entire Empire of the East." Nor was Bodin alone in defensively arguing about the universality of the droit d'aubaine. René Choppin, his contemporary, added England, Spain, and Hungary to places where the droit d'aubaine was practiced, and Jean Bacquet repeated the list and added Scotland as well as "the entire Empire of the West."[50]

Yet in the writings of these and other jurists, as in modern histories of the droit d'aubaine, it is not clear of what this common, universal institution consisted. Indeed, brief mentions of other European examples of the "droit d'aubaine" (glossed as *ius albiganii* in the Latin of the early modern jurists) masked a variety of legal restrictions on foreigners' ability to hold, devolve, or inherit property; royal prerogatives to the property of dead foreigners; and inabilities of foreigners to hold offices and benefices. For rhetorical and political purposes, Bodin and other early modern jurists collapsed these into a singular "droit d'aubaine," and turned the French experience into a common European one—most often with Roman origins. At the same time, they provided the absolute monarchy in France with the legal materials out of which it constructed a royal model of the citizen. Yet a closer look at some other European practices, and at the French juridical elaboration of the institution itself, reveals the singularity of the French droit d'aubaine, its fragmentary origins in the late medieval period, and its uses (and abuses) as a tool of absolutist state building in the sixteenth and seventeenth centuries.

In late medieval Italy, the most proximate example to ancient Rome, the heirs of dead foreigners did not suffer the confiscation of their properties, and the "droit d'aubaine" as such was unknown.[51] In early modern England, there were many legal distinctions between subjects and aliens, and the crown's frequent restrictions on "foreigners" often targeted the merchant classes more than aliens. Although municipalities regulated access to local citizenship and its privileges, the crown passed general edicts against foreigners, "alien friends" and "alien enemies" alike. Foreign merchants and others were free to ply their trades, but they could not employ fellow aliens (a restriction that fell into disuse in the sixteenth century); they could not own real property in the kingdom, and thus could not inherit or bequeath immovables; they were proscribed from certain kinds of legal actions, including guardianship; they had no capacity to exercise political rights. The foreigner could remove some of these disabilities by a public grant of "letters patent of denization" from the crown that created the category (for which there was no French parallel until 1803) of "alien resident." Or, if they sought to acquire immovables or gentry status, foreigners needed a much more expensive, private act of naturalization, issued by Parliament. But even without an alien's denization or naturalization, the crown almost never claimed the prerogative as such of seizing the property of a foreigner who died in the kingdom without native heirs.[52]

In early modern Spain, foreigners could not engage in trade with the Indies or hold secular or religious offices or benefices. Yet here also the crown did not claim the right to seize the property of foreigners who died in the kingdom against the claims of their kin.[53] In 1169, Alexander III had abolished all inheritance restrictions on foreigners in the Papal States, but the pope had never confiscated the estates of dead foreigners. In the Holy Roman Empire, access to "citizenship" was regulated on the municipal level and that of the principality; foreigners could acquire the ability to hold office and economic privileges, but they do not seem to have been restricted in their ability to inherit. Emperor Frederick II had explicitly abolished a princely claim to the properties of dead foreigners by the *Omnes peregrini* in 1220, even if the law was not immediately put into practice; and although property leaving a jurisdiction (commercial transactions as well as inheritance) was often taxed, the dues of 5 or 10 percent (glossed as the *Abzug*) befell native residents and foreigners alike.[54]

Judgments about the "universality" of the droit d'aubaine, whether in the sixteenth century or among contemporary historians, conflate several rather different things. They equate the droit d'aubaine with a lord's right of escheat (*déshérence*, of an alien or anyone who died without known heirs) or his right to abandoned or unclaimed objects (*biens vacans* or *épaves*); or they equate the droit d'aubaine with the specific prohibition that foreigners could not bequeath or inherit property; or they enlarge its scope to include a variety of other civil, religious, and political incapacities that surrounded the foreigner. As such, the early modern juridical commentary on the droit d'aubaine anticipated, just as it provided the ideological materials for, the royal project of constructing a legal, absolutist citizenship.

It is thus no surprise, then, that even the great comparativist Jean Bodin, much less his fellow jurists, cast only a fleeting glance across the European landscape in search of parallel measures to that of the ability of the French monarch; and it is no surprise that, failing to elaborate any in detail, they turned more systematically to Greece and especially to Rome for precedents, if not the origins of, contemporary French practices. Jean Papon, in his 1568 treatise, wrote that the Roman *Lex faldicia [de legatis]*, which forbade foreigners to draw up wills, "is exactly observed in France." René Choppin and especially Jean Bacquet, writing in the 1570s, both identified the *aubain* with the Roman *peregrinus* (foreigner, alien) and his civil law disabilities, including the inability to will property.[55] As late as the 1690s, the jurisconsult Jean Domat still traced the origins of the droit d'aubaine to Rome, despite his effort to constitute French law on a natural and rational basis. For legal commentators on the droit d'aubaine until the middle of the eighteenth century, especially those of scholarly law, Roman law provided the origins and justification of the droit d'aubaine.[56]

As the eighteenth century was to finally discover, the origins of the droit d'aubaine in its strictest sense came not from Rome but from the late medieval practices of the nascent French state in its struggles against seigneurial authority.

Modern historians, in particular Bernard d'Alteroche, have exhaustively treated this story of thirteenth- and fourteenth-century state building: the crown's appropriation, at the level of the kingdom, of a variable and widely diversified set of seigneurial rights within the regions of fragmented and decentered customary law at the height of the feudal regime.[57] The droit d'aubaine, as it became part of royal law in the late medieval period, derived from Germanic practices in a small area of customary law in northwestern Europe that, already in the ninth century, empowered seigneurs to control the possessions of "aliens" who died in their seigneuries. The definition and condition of alien was far from settled and unitary, however, even in the fourteenth century. In the southern, Roman-law provinces, "aliens" suffered relatively few disabilities; in Champagne and Vendomois, in the north, the aubain approached the status of a serf. Throughout the customary law regions of the north and east, the alien was often taxed for marriages outside the seigneurie in the *droit de formariage*, and alien household heads (*chefs*) paid annually a due known as the *droit de chevage*.[58] In the most onerous conditions of customary law, the alien could not inherit, and the status of his or her property was akin to the property of serfs and others that befell by "dead hand" (*mainmorte*) the lord. In general, the condition of the alien converged with the other "anti-subjects" of feudal law, including serfs and bastards: seigneurs retained similar kinds of rights over the property of each, ranging from inheritance rights over goods without heirs to specific prerogatives to acquire the property of an alien who, denied the right to bequeath property, died within a seigneurial domain. These "anti-subjects" shared certain incapacities, the "vices" that made them incapable of acting in civil law, and their lords acquired property rights over their goods and persons.

The French monarchy's first steps in securing the droit d'aubaine from the lords were tentative, but by the early thirteenth century, in conjunction with a new elaboration of the king's political authority and its extension to the kingdom (symbolically identified as the *patria*), the crown consistently claimed rights over the properties of "aliens" in the royal domain, and thus asserted its prerogatives over seigneurs. The infamous *Institutions* of Louis X in circa 1270, extending a customary practice from the Paris region, proclaimed:

> If any *aubain* or bastard dies, without heirs or descendants, the king is his heir, or the lord whose man he is, if he dies a chattel serf. But a bastard or *aubain* cannot take any lord but the king in the territories directly obedient to him, nor let it be established in other seigneuries which are the jurisdiction of his justice, according to the usage of the Orléanais and Sologne customs.[59]

This usurpation of a seigneurial privilege became by the fourteenth century a double movement: toward a definition of the droit d'aubaine as the king's claim to the property of a dead alien, and toward an expansion of the droit d'aubaine, beyond the royal domain, to all foreigners in the kingdom. The process was exceedingly long, complex, and uneven, but such state building was a crucial, although underexplored, aspect of the medieval making of the French "nation." Historians and literary critics have explored the French nation through its symbolic productions, its myths, royal rituals, and related ideological and historical claims that reinforced the sacrality and the cultural and political centrality of the French monarchy.[60] But they have never considered the implications of these symbolic constructions in relation to the simultaneous appearance of the process of confiscating the droit d'aubaine from the lords as a marker of "national" differences between "aliens" and "naturals."[61] Of course, the nation was not directly linked to the droit d'aubaine: at stake was exclusively a royal prerogative of confiscating the goods of aliens in the French kingdom that took shape toward the end of the fourteenth century.[62]

The monarchy's "invention" and acquisition of the droit d'aubaine was assured by the time Bodin penned the *Six Books of the Republic*, even if the victory was not yet complete. Most of the customary law redacted in the sixteenth century attributed the droit d'aubaine to the crown.[63] Barristers and attorneys of the period had already identified the droit d'aubaine, in Bacquet's words, as "sovereign, regal, honorific," and belonging exclusively to the king as "one of the jewels of his crown." Antoine de Loysel, also writing in the 1570s, claimed unconditionally that it was "royal, sovereign, annexed to the crown, not separable, not to be given or ceded to any seigneur in the realm": Should the king give the prerogative of dispensing justice to a lord, he still reserved for the crown the droit d'aubaine, as with other "royal matters." It was but a small step to define the droit d'aubaine as a "fundamental law" of the kingdom: Pierre Dupuy, in his *Traité des droits du roi* (1656), intimated as much, and Lefebvre de la Planche, the king's solicitor (*avocat au roi*) at the Paris Chambre du domaine in the early eighteenth century, was even more explicit. For Lefebvre, as for his eighteenth-century contemporaries, the droit d'aubaine had quite simply become "a domanial right inherent in sovereignty, so ancient that its origin is not known, no more than the other fundamental laws of the monarchy." Yet even at this late date, the monarchy was forced into litigation initiated by high noblemen, including the marquis de Belle-Isle in 1719, the duc de Bouillon and the duc d'Uzès in 1721, and no less than the duc d'Aiguillon in 1756. These nobles and others contested the monarchy's claims to the property of foreigners as part of the rights and jurisdictions on domanial lands ceded by the crown, and on the basis of their seigneurial rights of escheat—although their claims were never successful.[64] It is significant that in 1790, the politicians who dismantled the "feudal system" during the French Revolution felt compelled to abolish the droit d'aubaine, not only as "public law" but also alongside other seigneurial privileges.[65]

Strictly defined, the droit d'aubaine was the king's right of escheat to the property of an unexempted foreigner, and thus the incapacity of the foreigner to make a will. Yet beyond the inability to bequeath property, either by a testamentary act or ab intestat, aliens in France accumulated a variety of civil, religious, economic, and political disabilities in the sixteenth and seventeenth centuries. The inability to inherit property, the inability to hold offices or ecclesiastical benefices, the requirement to post bond before trial (the famous *cautio judicatum solvi*), the subjection to bodily restraint, and the imposition of special taxes and charges that citizens did not pay: such were the principal ones. Historians have sometimes distinguished these disabilities from a "droit d'aubaine" *strictu sensu*, but they have not fully considered how jurists and apologists for the French monarchy invented an expanded absolutist "droit d'aubaine" defined as a collection of inheritance restrictions and family disabilities alongside a host of others.

According to the French jurists, foreigners "lived free": with respect to their property, wrote Gabriel Argou in the early eighteenth century, they were considered

> capable of drawing up all contracts among the living; they can acquire and possess immovables; they can sell them, contract marriage in France with French women and with other foreigners; they can make and accept gifts among the living, even mutual donations, whether of property or of usufruct; they can borrow, and in all these and similar contracts, they are treated in the same way as true French.[66]

Yet civil, political, and economic incapacities and "anti-privileges" attributed to aliens began to accumulate in the later Middle Ages, and especially during the sixteenth century, belying the legal aphorism that only the foreigner "dies a slave." Thus the tension between the civil rights of foreigners while alive, and their inheritance disabilities on death, as expressed in the "nice quatrain," cited by the jurist Loysel, of the minor sixteenth-century poet Pibrat: "To the foreigner, be humane and kind / if he complains, bow to his reason / But to give him the goods of the house / Is an act, toward your own, of treason."[67]

The growth of economic and political incapacities during the sixteenth century was at times the result of the crown's own ordinances, as we shall see. But most of these and the civil incapacities as well resulted from the jurisprudential decisions of the sovereign courts and their regulatory ordinances, notably that of Paris. In fact, the Paris parlement's xenophobia during this period, and especially in the sixteenth century, translated the diffuse antiforeigner sentiment of the French Wars of Religion into a specific set of juridical incapacities.

The legal and political construction of an amplified droit d'aubaine—which the jurists then likened to other European practices—thus extended far beyond the capacity of a foreigner to make a will ("active succession") in the French kingdom. According to Jean Bacquet, an alien was not only prohibited from making a will, even to "charitable works,"[68] but from all modes of passing on property through succession (except freely contracted donations, including marriage contracts, made when the foreigner was alive). The droit d'aubaine was also extended to include the right of inheriting property ("passive" succession) within Bacquet's argument. The kin of a foreigner born outside of France could not inherit from the (unexempted) alien any goods bequeathed to him within the kingdom, unless he or she had first taken letters of naturalization. Such a proscription of "passive" succession, of being unable to inherit property in the kingdom, was attenuated slightly by the juridical recognition of the capacity of those children born in the kingdom of a legitimate marriage to inherit, a principle which became "one of the rules of French law" by the eighteenth century.[69] Nonetheless, passive successoral incapacity was evidence of the more comprehensive and totalizing inheritance restrictions on aliens that were already coming into practice during the late fifteenth century.[70] Foreigners could not inherit property from other foreigners, from French citizens, or from their own ascendants. The sixteenth-century lawyers developed a consensus that the king's right to seize the property of a dead foreigner was linked to the civil nonidentity of aliens: as both Antoine de Loysel and Pierre Jacques Brillon put it, more than a century apart, the foreigner had "no family."[71]

Neither could foreigners then have "fictive" families, that is, function legally in such a way as to presume their existence as (French) parents or children. As property owners, foreigners could not exercise the *retrait lignager*, the sale of property that could eventually be recuperated within a lineage after several generations. They could not establish or be charged with trusts (*substitutions*), they could not act as tutors to minors, and so forth. The equation of foreigners and bastards without known or legitimate family was far from coincidental. Thus, a fourteenth-century definition of the aubain recorded from the registers of the Chambre des comptes by Bacquet in the 1570s defined aliens as those people who ignored their own birthplace, their own parents, or were unbaptized. Such a persistent linkage between aliens and bastards persisted in the fact that the king collected the droit d'aubaine from both groups, both individual foreigners and in the "foreign" population forcibly naturalized and taxed in 1697.[72]

Already in the sixteenth century, then, foreigners were incapable of acting in all matters of succession—not despite but because the king enjoyed the right (over and above local seigneurs) to their property. The inability to bequeath or inherit property, or to act in any capacity in family law governing the cross-generational transmission of property, however, was just the beginning of the crown's and the lawyers' efforts to enlarge the scope of the civil disabilities of foreigners. Beyond family law, alien foreigners came to suffer a host of other restrictions in the early modern period. Following a regulatory ordinance of the Paris parlement in 1552, the foreigner had to furnish a bond in order to plea a case in court (whether suing or defending himself), the infamous *cautio judicatum solvi*. The crown extended this obligation to provinces, such as Languedoc and Provence, that were until the late seventeenth century largely exempt from the strict definition of the droit d'aubaine.[73] The status of aliens was similar to French natives as it concerned penal bodily restraint (*contrainte par corps*), but the royal ordinance of 1667 that abolished this "absurd and barbarous principle" in France continued to apply to aliens, at least according to the jurisprudence of the late seventeenth century. By a parliamentary decision of 16 April 1737, foreigners could not even "make use of charitable funds to get out of prison."[74]

Economic restrictions also accumulated in the late medieval and early modern period. Already in 1358, the crown forbade foreigners the exercise of the professions of "bankers" of all kinds (agents, brokers, money changers, etc.) because they were suspected of regularly "transporting gold and silver outside the kingdom." Francis I reiterated the edict in 1534 and after, increasingly informed by early mercantilist precepts about the need to preserve the crown's control over bullion. But it was the Estates General at Orléans in 1560 that took the lead, as the Third Estate decried the transport of capital outside the kingdom by foreign merchants and bankers. After further complaints in the next Estates General, the Blois ordinances of 1579 permitted foreigners to serve as bankers only after having furnished a 150,000 livre bond, renewable every five years. A 1565 decision of the Paris parlement denied the foreigner the capacity to declare bankruptcy in France: as Jean Bacquet put it in a gruesome metaphor, "otherwise the foreigner would be able to suck out the blood and marrow of the French to his own advantage, then pay them off in scraps of paper."[75] In its edict on commerce in 1673, the culminating moment, under Colbert, of the mercantilist program, Louis XIV reiterated the prohibition, and the sovereign courts of the northern and eastern provinces of the kingdom, until the end of the Old Regime, were to invoke that same edict. At the same time, the monarchy ceded to the xenophobic claims of the urban professions. As of 1543, the crown officially forbade foreigners from joining the guilds, responding to pressure from the corporation merchant haberdashers in Paris; and in the 1630s, it was the quill-makers' guild of Paris that required its members to be naturalized.[76]

In conditions of fiscal distress, the monarchy naturally tried to extract the wealth of foreigners in the kingdom. Francis I and Henry II were frequently forced to turn to the Italians for loans, and in 1578 Henry III taxed foreign bankers, whether or not they had been naturalized. In 1587, a royal edict required all foreign merchants and courtiers to pay for letters of naturalization, even if they already had them. Under Louis XIII and Louis XIV, the crown taxed foreigners on several occasions. (If the tax of 1639 was quite expansive in principal, those of 1646 and 1657 specifically targeted wealthy foreigners and merchants). Then, in 1697, at the end of the century's costliest war, Louis XIV imposed an "extraordinary tax" on the entire foreign population of the kingdom, including the descendants and heirs of immigrants who had arrived after 1600, along with the bastards in the realm. In 1709, having experienced the dramatic defeat of this initiative, the monarchy abandoned the idea of a tax and imposed instead what amounted to a forced loan on the richest foreigners, requiring them to purchase 5 percent bonds.[77]

It is by no means clear that all such restrictions, incapacities, and taxes were assimilated under the droit d'aubaine; many, such as the necessity of posting bond, were not. But as the judges and lawyers of the sovereign courts placed new disabilities on aliens, especially in the domains of civil law and beyond, the definition of the droit d'aubaine expanded concomitantly, at least in the rhetorical strategies of the jurists and royal publicists. The accumulation of restrictions on aliens with regard to religious benefices and political offices, far beyond the realm of civil and family law, were increasingly linked to a revitalized—an absolutist—definition of the droit d'aubaine during the sixteenth and seventeenth centuries.

As late as the fourteenth century, several royal ordinances had actually conferred high-ranking royal offices on foreigners, preferring them to natives. According to the sixteenth-century jurist Papon, this was because foreigners were "sequestered from all familiarities, favors, hatreds, and other specific affectations" and thus able to render justice neutrally. Papon's opinion was to be echoed and philosophically amplified, ironically, in Rousseau's idea of the legislator within a new republican citizenship of the eighteenth century. A foreigner alone was capable of manifesting the General Will, without sectarian conflicts of interests.[78]

Within the construction of the absolute citizen, customary prohibitions, royal ordinances, and parliamentary regulatory decisions accumulated to prohibited foreigners from holding office. The first prohibition of holding financial offices in 1323 was evidence of the crown's concern to limit the influence of Italian accountants (*receveurs*) in its finances, a prohibition reiterated in 1348 ("That no Italian or other foreigner be charged with collecting taxes for the king") and in the next decade extended to money changers. Royal ordinances extended the prohibitions on office holding to judiciary positions in 1493 for the Paris parlement, and in 1616 to the totality of public offices in the kingdom, including lawyers, royal secretaries, and officeholders in the fiscal and sovereign courts of the kingdom.[79] "The foreigner's faithfulness is suspect, as long as it hasn't been certified" by naturalization, according to the jurist Bourjon. It was possible, according to the jurisconsult Le Bret in 1689, that office could be given to foreigners "when it becomes a question of recognizing the virtue and services of some great person"—as the well-known examples of Charles de Gonzague, Cardinal Mazarin, John Law, the duke of Berwick, Jacques Necker and others suggest. And Bourjon noted that "the king often accords permissions (*brevets*) to foreigners to hold offices or benefices in France; but these permissions, although dated and enounced in their provisions of office, do not stop the king from acquiring by the droit d'aubaine their goods when they die." But the early modern jurists agreed unanimously with Bacquet, who argued that that foreigners were in principle excluded from office, and that the possession of offices never naturalized their holders.[80]

The jurisprudence on ecclesiastical benefices was similar. A royal edict of 1431 prohibited foreigners from holding them, the first such surviving prohibition. The edict expressed a nascent set of Gallican principles, the defense of the French church against Ultramontane influences, which were to take formal shape six years later in the Pragmatic Sanction of Bourges (1437). Against the backdrop of growing Italian and English influence in the high clergy, the 1431 edict specifically targeted archbishops, bishops, and cathedral canons. But the prohibition became a central "liberty of the Gallican Church," as the barrister Pierre Pithou explained: "No one, of whatever status, can hold any benefice, either directly or indirectly in this kingdom, if he is not a native, or if he isn't naturalized." The proscription applied to foreigners who were nonetheless exempted by collective privilege or treaty from the droit d'aubaine. Repeated several times in the sixteenth century, the decrees suggested indirectly the scale of the practice: royal edicts of 1493, 1522, 1535, and 1560 reiterated the injunctions. The Blois ordinances of 1579 extended this disability to naturalized foreigners, and for consistorial benefices as well as church wardenship). These ordinances, glossed Antonine de Loysel, "were decreed to assure that the practices of foreigners not bring any diversity or difference to the customs and laws of the kingdom, and that our ancient discipline not be corrupted by a foreigner."[81] Papon, his contemporary, pointed specifically to the linguistic problem: foreigners were prohibited from preaching because of the "diversity of languages of the shepherds and their flocks that forbids mutual comprehension." But other sixteenth-century lawyers saw that this "incapacity is more political than ecclesiastical," as the Parisian barrister Boutaric commented, also in the 1570s.[82] Although occasionally contested in court, this prohibition became part of "French law" in the seventeenth and eighteenth centuries, and in 1681 Louis XIV reiterated the prohibition against foreigners, including naturalized ones, holding benefices in the so-called annexed provinces.[83]

As the inheritance disabilities, economic restrictions, and reiterated prohibitions against foreigners holding religious benefices and political offices increased dramatically, the jurist's definition of the droit d'aubaine expanded concomitantly. Rhetorically and in practice, an enlarged droit d'aubaine was already visible in the treatises and commentaries of the late 1560s and 1570s: the jurists who universalized the droit d'aubaine simultaneously amplified its extension. In 1607, Jérôme L'Huillier, the king's attorney (procureur du roi) at the Paris Chambre des comptes from 1596 to 1619, argued against the claims of a Genoese for exemption from the droit d'aubaine: his definition of the term was that it "consists principally in forbidding the foreigner from holding office or benefice in France, from inheriting or fathering a succession, or from disposing in any way of his causes at his death."[84] Note that he began, as did other contemporaries, with the question of offices and benefices. Such an amalgamation of distinct incapacities was to establish the robust, muscular version of the royal droit d'aubaine during the seventeenth century.

The forced collective naturalization by Louis XIV at the end of the War of the Augsburg League—the Naturalization Tax decreed by the royal ordinance of 22 July 1697—crowned the process by which the monarchy appropriated the droit d'aubaine, turning law into fiscal and political expediency. The "extraordinary tax" was one of several desperate efforts of the crown in a moment of severe fiscal constraint brought about by the long wars of Louis XIV.[85] The tax revitalized and further expanded the droit d'aubaine that the lawyers had constructed during the sixteenth and seventeenth centuries, a process that transformed a feudal right into a major political stake for the absolute monarchy. In this context, the French monarchy was truly the highest form of (fiscal) feudalism, since it politically reactivated certain prerogatives of seigneurial lordship, and added to these the accumulated civil, economic, religious, and political disabilities of foreigners. This political "confiscation" of an amplified, absolutist droit d'aubaine was made evident in the text of the declaration itself. The law revoked all previous individual and collective naturalizations and imposed a tax, which stood in lieu of naturalization, on foreigners and descendants of immigrants who had settled in the kingdom since 1600. The crown legitimated this forced collective naturalization by invoking the long obsolete practice of a special tax on foreigners (*droit de chevage* and *formariage*); but it also justified the project, in the first instance, with a final, "absolutist" version of the droit d'aubaine.[86] The droit d'aubaine was a fundamental right, according to the July edict, that included the foreigner's inability at his death to pass on property in the kingdom and to exercise neither "offices, charges, dignities, commissions nor employment, nor contract to collect taxes, nor practice banking, money exchange, brokerage, or other professions." A pamphlet justifying the tax, written at the instigation of the royal council against the complaints of the Dutch, English, and Spanish ambassadors gathered to negotiate the Ryswick Treaty, gave an even more comprehensive definition of the droit d'aubaine, one far beyond that of even the most royalist jurists of the seventeenth century. Moreover, in defining the droit d'aubaine, the pamphlet began with its public or political aspects:

> It consists specifically of excluding foreigners from all charges, offices, and public commissions, of all rights of local citizenship in the towns [*droit de bourgeoisie*] and association in the different artisanal and professional communities, and of removing the freedom to dispose of their goods by last will and testament, which goods become the possession of the Sovereign, to the exclusion of their heirs and kin, even if natives of the country.[87]

Using a politically expanded and juridically grounded notion of the droit d'aubaine, the monarchy turned the droit d'aubaine into what it believed might be a major potential source of revenue to the crown. In practice, by contracting the 1697 Naturalization Tax to the financier (*traitant*) Nicolas Damour, who then sold the contract to others, the crown barely received any income from the experiment.[88]

Not that the droit d'aubaine itself, as levied in particular instances against purported aliens, had ever yielded much revenue for the French crown. Until 1669, the responsibility for collecting the droit d'aubaine lay with the treasurers-general; but when Louis XIV instituted the regime of tax-farming of "domanial products" (including fixed revenues of the crown and a variety of "feudal" dues owed to the king), the contracting tax-farmer retained a significant proportion of the dues. In 1692, the barrister Argou wrote that "the domanial tax-farmers have, in virtue of their contract, all the properties in escheat that do not exceed the value of 2,000 livres, as well as a third of those that are greater, such that the portion due to the tax-farmers amounts to at least 2,000 livres." The edict of 1693, under conditions of extreme fiscal duress, reorganized the royal treasury, affirmed the practice and organization of royal tax-farming, and guaranteed income from domanial rights to the tax-farmers themselves.[89] Beyond the sums collected by the tax-farmers, whose incentives were thus doubly built in to their contracts, the remainder of the estate befell a beneficiary of the king, most often a recipient of royal largesse at court. The political recycling of alien properties became part of the absolute monarchy's construction of clientage and patronage, just as it reaffirmed its "feudal" character.[90] In other cases, the recipients of the monarch's gift of property were the widows, mothers, and other foreign kin who had been deemed legally incapable of inheriting in the first place, affirming the crown's sovereign authority to take exception from the letter of the law.

More important, at least to those purported "foreign" heirs who continued to claim the estates of their kin, the fisc took possession of these estates without waiting for a court sentence adjudicating the property, beyond the initial inquiry that established the alien status of the deceased by the courts of the treasurers-general. Even if some jurists argued that it was the foreigner's burden, or that of his descendants, to disprove his alien status, most of the jurisprudence recognized that the presumption of proving alterity was that of the fisc. But since confiscations of estates by the tax-farmers were preemptory, and took place before litigation was resolved, a constant stream of appeals to the Chambre du trésor at Paris, and then to the Paris parlement, continued unabated. Such a "system" encouraged both vast delays and endless litigation; and it gave free rein to the tax-farmers, whose avarice in collecting the droit d'aubaine was matched only by their expediency in seizing the properties of dead foreigners (or those supposed to be foreigners) throughout the period from Louis XIV to the French Revolution.[91]

The French monarchy's collection of the droit d'aubaine and its accumulation and assimilation of the family and civil incapacities of foreigners during the early modern period represents a distinct "counterexperience" (to borrow the phrase of Pierre Vilar, who was referring to Spain in the nineteenth century) in the broader processes of Europe's modernization. By the seventeenth century, most European states were abandoning—or at least, debating the abandonment—of civil law restrictions on property ownership and especially on the transmission of property across generations. In part, elsewhere in western Europe by the seventeenth century seigneurial authority was in decline, and with it passed away a lord's right of inheriting all unclaimed property. More ideologically, within the growth of doctrine in international law during the seventeenth century (the *ius gentium* or "law of nations" founded on natural law theory), authors from Hugo Grotius (1583–1645) to Samuel Pufendorf (1632–94) tended to downplay the civil law restrictions on property. Although the restrictions on and legal incapacities of foreigners that had been so widespread in kingdoms and principalities of the later Middle Ages were rarely abolished outright, many (including those in England) fell into disuse. Modernity, constituted as the decline of such feudal rights as the droit d'aubaine, justified by the natural law theorists of the seventeenth century, was clearly in this instance founded on the unfettered transmission of property across the generations.

Already in *The Law of War and Peace*, first published in 1625, the Dutch diplomat and jurist Grotius noted:

> The fact that the right to make a will is not everywhere granted to foreigners is not due to a universal principle of law, but to a special statute of a particular state; and unless I am mistaken, the restriction goes back to a time when foreigners were considered almost as enemies. In consequence, among the more civilized nations, this restriction has deservedly fallen into disuse.[92]

As a Dutch refugee in France who had sought a letter of safe conduct from the French king in 1623, Grotius himself would have been exempted from the droit d'aubaine in France, for Louis XIII had welcomed Dutch refugees as his "natural subjects."[93] More important, perhaps, Grotius was writing in a rare moment of peace in the French kingdom during an otherwise extraordinarily bellicose century. Elsewhere in Europe, warfare did not stop states from abandoning, or at least debating the utility, of the civil law incapacities of foreigners that were often deemed by French jurists to constitute examples of a near-universal "droit d'aubaine." In England, a general debate on collective naturalization took place from the 1660s through the Naturalization Bill of 1753—at exactly the same moment that the French monarchy reinforced its commitment to the incapacities of foreigners through its consolidation of the droit d'aubaine. In Spain, the establishment of a new public law under the Bourbon dynasty unified "Spanish" citizenship, even if local authority to restrict foreigners from holding offices or benefices, or trading and settling in the empire, was not attenuated in the eighteenth century. In France, by contrast, ancient feudal practices (including the droit d'aubaine) were reactivated and expanded in a process occasioned by the fiscal needs of a bellicose absolute monarchy, and ideologically prepared by the juridical accumulation of civil incapacities.

The financial needs and authoritarian pretensions of an expansionist state in France, during the long wars of the seventeenth century, used the arguments of the jurists in reinvigorating the droit d'aubaine and amplifying its practice. The droit d'aubaine was applied, in principal, to the entire kingdom; it was levied on all "national" groups in France; and it was redefined to include a wide range of civil and political incapacities distinct from the ability to inherit or bequeath property.

Under such conditions, it became clear that the sixteenth-century search for the origins of the droit d'aubaine, especially in Roman law, could perhaps "pleasantly amuse commentators," wrote d'Aguesseau, then royal attorney at the Paris parlement, but it distracted the courts from expediting their business.[94] Instead, the lawyers turned to more instrumental explanations of the droit d'aubaine, outlining three functions it played, all of them inevitably of value to the crown itself.

First, following Bacquet, the lawyers noted that the droit d'aubaine existed simply in order "to have knowledge of he who is born in the kingdom, and he who is not, but has come to live here, and to mark the difference between them." Jérôme L'Huillier, the king's attorney at the Paris Chambre des comptes in the early seventeenth century, elaborated on this function of the droit d'aubaine:

> Civil reason, following which the laws and political regulations were made, does not permit a foreigner to be of the same condition as a citizen and natural subject. That is why, in all well-administered states, they are always placed apart and separated, and principally in France, where the droit d'aubaine practiced against foreigners is so real and ancient that we ignore its origins.

Such a functionalist—and antihistorical—reading of the droit d'aubaine, taken up by the barrister Gabriel Bouchel in 1671, subsequently informed the political and fiscal policy of Louis XIV and justified the levy of the Naturalization Tax in 1697.[95] Some lawyers sought to infuse this distinction with a difference, justifying the separation of foreigners precisely because of their "different mores and maxims," which, mixed with those of the French, "produces a poisonous corruption, and which gives birth to much trouble, and sometimes the desolation of the country that had so favorably welcomed them."[96] But the crown itself never justified its use of the droit d'aubaine based on cultural difference or "corruption," only on the abstract principle of marking difference.

Except, perhaps, in the context of mercantilist doctrine. For the second function played by the droit d'aubaine was cast in fiscal and political terms, and dovetailed neatly with the reigning economic policy of the absolutist monarchy. Already in the late sixteenth century, the barrister Antoine de Loysel insisted that the principal function of the droit d'aubaine was to exclude the foreigner from all inheritances and thus "to prohibit goods in the kingdom from moving to foreign countries." This fiscal and mercantilist rationale was to be increasingly heard in the late sixteenth and early seventeenth centuries, as the "doctrine" took shape alongside the royal model of French citizenship.[97] In fact, mercantilist arguments were hardly doctrinal, and appeared first in practice before they did in theory. The early seventeenth-century *Traicté de l'oeconomie politique* (1615) by Antoine de Montchrétien (1575?–1621) contained all the ambivalence of mercantilist policy, as did Bernard de Laffemas's reports to Henry IV: a xenophobic ideology that sought to exclude foreigners from commerce and trade sat uncomfortably with the "rationality" of recruiting foreign artisans in the service of "national industry."[98]

Finally, the political and economic rationales for the droit d'aubaine coexisted with a third perception of its functional value: introduced into France by reason of reciprocity, the droit d'aubaine was practiced to assure the reciprocal interests of France when "neighboring princes and lords collect the droit d'aubaine on their lands from those who come from the kingdom of France," according to Jean Bacquet.[99] The principle of reciprocity, which was to become so key to the abolition and reinstitution of the droit d'aubaine during the late eighteenth century, was already present in the monarchist rationale for the droit d'aubaine's existence.

Some jurists argued all three reasons, others invoked only one, but all concurred that the droit d'aubaine was, in theory, an unquestionable mark of sovereignty. In practice, the question was full of contradictions.

The Droit d'Aubaine within the Political Contradictions of Absolutism

If the monarchy's fiscal stake in collecting the droit d'aubaine was slight, and its desperate attempts to use a collective imposition of the droit d'aubaine on all foreigners in the kingdom was a total failure, the crown's political interests in the droit d'aubaine were nonetheless significant. As plaintiffs and defendants engaged in civil litigation involving collateral relatives of dead foreigners, tax-farmers, and the beneficiaries of royal largesse, the droit d'aubaine increasingly became viewed as not merely a fiscal matter but an issue about the extension of royal authority—and of sovereignty—itself. More generally, the reactivation and reconfiguration of the droit d'aubaine took shape within an absolutist dynamic that sought to impose uniform laws on the kingdom, and on all persons therein, including the law of the droit d'aubaine. This was not an easily achievable project, because a large part of the kingdom, especially the southern provinces that followed principally Roman civil law, were traditionally exempted from the droit d'aubaine on the basis of local and regional customs and privileges. Because the droit d'aubaine was so intimately linked by the lawyers to sovereignty, from a strictly absolutist viewpoint it could not be fragmented as long as sovereignty remained indivisible (as Jean Bodin had so persuasively argued about the nature of sovereignty itself). The very absolutist royal attorney Lefebvre de la Planche wrote in the 1730s that nothing "should diminish a royal right which is exercised in the entire extent of the kingdom and which cannot be restricted by [the] usages, customs, and particular laws of any one of its provinces."[100]

The extension of the droit d'aubaine to the southern provinces of Provence and Languedoc and to the eastern province of Metz (all provinces of Roman law that had either been exempted or never recognized the droit d'aubaine) illuminates the absolutist dynamic at work, especially in conjunction with the imposition of the 1697 tax. That dynamic, as historians of the French state have long noted, involved the crown's imposition of "universal" laws and taxes that ran roughshod over specific regional and local privileges. For over half a century after the French crown inherited the county of Provence in 1481, for example, the monarchy did not collect the droit d'aubaine; having promised to uphold all the privileges of the province, it dared not touch the exemption. But in 1539, in a first surge of absolutist pretensions, Francis I ordered the imposition of the droit d'aubaine in the province, thus beginning a lengthy struggle that, by the eighteenth century (and despite the opposition of the lawyers from the parlement of Aix), resulted in the regular collection of the droit d'aubaine—albeit at a significantly lower incidence than in the parliamentary jurisdictions of customary law, including Paris.[101]

In neighboring Languedoc, which the crown had also exempted from the droit d'aubaine in 1475—a privilege confirmed in 1483 by Charles VIII at the Estates General of Tours—the struggle was more drawn out, and ultimately even less successful.[102] In the late sixteenth and early seventeenth centuries, the royal solicitors-general of the Toulouse parlement successfully authorized a partial collection of the droit d'aubaine, despite the claims of the lawyers (Cambolas, Maynard, La Roche-Flavin) who compiled the case law of Languedoc in the seventeenth and eighteenth century.[103] A developing jurisprudence gave the French king the legal right to collect the droit d'aubaine, and a small but consistent number of foreigners sought letters of naturalization that were registered at the Chambre des comptes in Montpellier. But it was the 1697 tax itself that sounded the death knell for the privilege of exemption in the eighteenth century: after 1700, and throughout the eighteenth century, Languedoc's exemption from the droit d'aubaine "does not appear to be consistently recognized," as Lefebvre de la Planche put it. The case was understated, although again, the number of naturalizations from the entire province of Languedoc (the jurisdiction of the Montpellier Chambre des comte) was significantly less, in both absolute and proportional terms, than those in other regions.[104]

By the 1730s, there were still islands of resistance to the application of the droit d'aubaine, including the port cities of Bordeaux, Marseille, and Dunkerque, where settled foreigners were exempted by specific privileges of the crown. The difficult case of the Three Bishoprics of Metz, Toulon, and Verdun continued to pose problems more than two centuries after Henry II had taken Metz and claimed possession of the eastern borderlands in 1552. The town and jurisdiction of Metz had long claimed an exemption from the droit d'aubaine on two grounds: local customs, which reciprocally exempted foreigners from Lorraine living in the Three Bishoprics and French subjects living in the duchy of Lorraine; and the third article of the Metz redacted custom of the sixteenth century, which offered an automatic naturalization based on minimal conditions of residence and marriage. The "naturalization" in question, which permitted the foreigner to acquire the status of a "bourgeois of Metz," could be had with alarming facility (from the crown's point of view): according to the customal, any foreigner marrying a native of Metz received the status of bourgeois. Until the last decades of the seventeenth century, the jurisprudence tended to uphold the exemption of foreigners who became bourgeois of Metz from the droit d'aubaine—and thus gave municipal statutes the power to confer the principal marker of national difference. But around the time of the Naturalization Tax, things began to change.[105]

The problem was inextricably tied to the character of Metz as a frontier province. By the late seventeenth century, the Three Bishoprics were neither considered a "conquered province" nor were they on the front line of battle with the Holy Roman Empire and its constituent principalities. But if the military frontier had been pushed east, the district (*generalité*) of Metz was still not a province like the others. As the intendant Turgot responded to the instructions of Beauvillier for the duke of Burgundy in 1697,

> That it is not a contiguous province and district that came to France at one time, with its own ordering principles and uniform government; it is only a series of places and pieces, detached to different degrees from the various dominions of Spain or of Lorraine, which bring and maintain their usages, and which were unified to form this portion of the frontier.

In this province bordering not only Spanish Flanders and Lorraine but also the county of Luxembourg, the electorate of Trier, and the Palatinate, the result was an administrative imbroglio that rested on a tacit recognition that the droit d'aubaine simply could not be levied. Local juridical customs and traditions were such that the inhabitants "must give to themselves and each other all the shared advantages of transferring [themselves] from one country to another, of inheriting, [and of] engaging in commerce at all times, without which such districts, so intertwined, could not subsist [especially] if one sought to govern them absolutely as if they were delimited and different states."[106]

Moreover, Metz had survived the disastrous population losses of 1630–50 during the Thirty Years War only through persistent immigration, and the need to exempt new and settled immigrants from the droit d'aubaine was upheld by the parlement of Metz on 9 April 1689.[107] But in 1700, at the moment when the royal council heard claims of exemptions to the 1697 tax, it refused to authorize any municipal citizenship (*droit de bourgeoisie*) to confer a privilege or exemption equivalent to the naturalization of foreigners as royal subjects. After all, the French monarchy had spent the better part of three centuries wrestling away the right to naturalize at the level of the kingdom from lords, towns, and provinces. The application of the 1697 tax provided a remarkable opportunity for the crown: in particular, it was the appropriate moment to respond to the encroachments— actual, possible, or merely fantastical—of the duc de Lorraine on the possessions of the French king. Thus the royal council engineered the triumph of the royal right of the droit d'aubaine over local privileges in Metz, and forbade any exemptions, both within and after the imposition of the 1697 tax.[108]

The application of this muscular version of the droit d'aubaine was felt as a political necessity to mark the sovereignty of the king over Metz, especially because the Treaty of Ryswick and the abandonment of the "reunions" signified the restitution in 1697 of the duc de Lorraine to his estates, which had been occupied by the French since 1670. The Naturalization Tax helped the king claim a stake and sovereignty in a territorially disaggregated and politically contested province. In May 1701 a royal declaration clarified the rights of the king to collect the droit d'aubaine among all foreigners in the Three Bishoprics. By the early eighteenth century, as Brillon was to note, "the city of Metz no longer enjoys its privilege previously accorded by the emperors to naturalize foreigners who came to settle," even though individuals sought unsuccessfully to challenge the crown's right in the local courts until the 1760s.[109]

Despite the modest success of the crown in imposing the droit d'aubaine in the Roman-law provinces of Provence and Languedoc, and in the jurisdictions of Metz that held on to their customs of municipal citizenship, the king's right to seize the property of a foreigner who died without native heirs (or previous exemption) was, by the late seventeenth century, hardly universally applied throughout the kingdom. True, the issue of whether the droit d'aubaine was to be applied to France's growing colonies, especially in North America and the Caribbean, had been settled by a series of administrative circulars during 1717 and 1718. Foreigners were to be subjected to the droit d'aubaine, and slaves held by foreigners who died in the colonies were to be considered "movables" subject to the droit d'aubaine.[110] But in the "metropole," as the Provençal lawyer Boniface was to note in the last decade of Louis XIV's long reign, "the law of aubaine, which is a law of the kingdom, is not a general one, either for all the provinces of France, nor for all states [of origin] of foreigners, as it is tempered and suffers from a great number of exemptions."[111] Put another way, the foreigner did not have the same legal status throughout the kingdom: if, on the one hand, the monarchy sought to impose a unified and expanded droit d'aubaine throughout the kingdom, on the other hand, Louis XIV continued the long tradition of using exemptions from the droit d'aubaine in its monarchical politics of immigration and state building.

Indeed, throughout the early modern period, jurists from Bacquet to Lefebvre de la Planche, Denisart, Guyot, and Merlin successively rehearsed these exemptions, commenting extensively on the particular jurisprudence surrounding each, and generally organizing them into three categories: those foreigners exempted on the basis of their "national" origins, their place of residence in the kingdom, or their professional status.[112]

National groups that found themselves exempted, most often by international treaties, grew proportionately during the Old Regime. In his 1763 *Dictionnaire raisonné des domaines et droits domaniaux,* just before the movement to systematically abolish the droit d'aubaine, Bosquet listed a range of exemptions enjoyed by the Avignonnais, the English, the Hanseatic towns, the Flemish, the Genevans, the Dutch, the Lorrains, the Portuguese, the Savoyards, the Swedes, and the Swiss established in the kingdom, although he did not mention earlier exemptions that had been enjoyed by the Scots or the Venetians or the Milanese and others.[113]

Several of these "national" groups received exemptions because they were from territories over which the French king maintained some kind of claim: hence, according to the jurisprudence until the late seventeenth century, the Flemish or Milanese or, before the king's acquisition of the county in 1678, Burgundians of the empire (the Franche-Comté) were reputed to be "natural Frenchmen" even if they were encouraged to seek letters of declaration of naturalization. These and other "national" groups also received exemptions from the droit d'aubaine as a result of international peace and commercial treaties, or as a result of particular accords between the French crown and its allies. Until the mid-eighteenth century, exemptions from the droit d'aubaine appeared regularly in international peace treaties and treaties of commerce, only to disappear in practice as quickly as warfare was resumed. Thus the rapidly changing status of the inhabitants of the Dutch Low Countries, who were repeatedly exempted from the droit d'aubaine by a succession of treaties including those of 1526, 1529, 1544, 1598, 1648, 1668, 1678, 1697, 1713, and 1748! The meaning of such exemptions, of course, remained contested among direct and collateral heirs, and among the tax-farmers and beneficiaries of royal donations of the droit d'aubaine, in a vast jurisprudence that filled the dockets of the Paris and regional parlements. This was the case even among the inhabitants of Avignon and the Comtat Venaissin, for example, those isolated enclaves of papal jurisdiction within Provence. Even though the Avignonnais were consistently granted exemptions from the droit d'aubaine and the full recognition by the royal council and its lawyers that the inhabitants would be treated, in terms of their successoral capacity, as French-born natives, litigation over the estates of purported foreigners persisted until the incorporation of the papal territories during the French Revolution.[114]

In addition to these "national" exemptions, the crown offered "professional" ones as it recruited specialized labor and offered immigrants willing to settle in the kingdom exemption from the droit d'aubaine. Such was part of the mercantilist, and especially Colbert's, goal of using the special talents of foreigners in the service of the kingdom, and this despite the more general economic protectionism associated with the practice of seventeenth-century mercantilism.[115] Dutch swamp-drainers and Flemish tapestry workers throughout the seventeenth century, and under Louis XIV, foreigners working in the Gobelins manufactories (1667) or those in Beauvais (1722), sailors and other mariners (1687), Venetian glassmakers (1665), soldiers employed in the French armies (1715), and others all received exemptions (ranging from ten years to perpetuity, and sometimes conditionally) from the droit d'aubaine. Such exemptions, equally a part of mercantilism, continued until the end of the Old Regime, with English working in the mines of lower Brittany in 1755 and sailors and foreigners working to clear land in a district of Bordeaux each receiving exemptions in 1762, for example. So too were students exempted (although their status was often debated), as well as ambassadors and those who served in foreign diplomatic corps.[116]

Parallel to the exemptions of "national" and "professional" groups were collective privileges given to towns and cities of the kingdom in order to recruit settlers, especially merchants. Such exemptions from the droit d'aubaine had medieval precedents, but they appeared more consistently within early modern royal policies that sought to repopulate the coastal and frontier cities by attracting immigrants. Bordeaux (1474), Metz (1552), Lyon (from 1569 to 1615), and Calais (1567) all acquired their exemptions (or retained their privileges) in the sixteenth century, while Dunkerque (1662), Marseille (1669), and Sarrelouis (1682) received exemptions from Louis XIV's royal council.[117] Despite the monarchical efforts to extend the droit d'aubaine to the entire kingdom, Louis XIV and his predecessors tolerated and even reactivated or invested new cities with the privilege of exempting immigrants from the droit d'aubaine. In a policy that ran directly counter to the crown's attempt to diminish the prerogatives of local and municipal citizenship, the seventeenth-century monarchy used the grant of municipal citizenship to exempt established foreigners from the droit d'aubaine. In most cases, a foreigner's acquisition of such a droit de bourgeoisie was contingent on various degrees of evidence about social assimilation, as the monarchy sought to ensure that wealthy and established foreigners, permanently settled in the kingdom, would be the beneficiaries of such collective exemptions. In these cases, the attempts to encourage immigration and increase the commercial wealth of the kingdom actually displaced the juridical and political construction of absolutist homogeneity, even as the rhetoric of royal privilege invoked the example of Rome and international law.[118]

In much the same spirit that exempted frontier cities and maritime ports from the droit d'aubaine, royal and diplomatic exemptions of frontier provinces left the kingdom far from unified in the application and collection of the droit d'aubaine. The peripheral exemptions from the droit d'aubaine expose the limitations—or, perhaps better, the contradictions—of the practice of absolutism in France. French jurisprudence concurred with an emerging body of international law that conferred on inhabitants of "conquered provinces" the reputation of "French natives," and the new subjects of absolutism were thus not required to take individual letters of naturalization, even when they settled in other provinces of the kingdom. It is true that some barristers dissented, and an extensive jurisprudence developed about the annexation of territory in the late seventeenth and eighteenth centuries, especially concerning the nature of "permanent" territorial acquisition. (Some lawyers, such as Bosquet and Guyot, argued that inhabitants of the conquered provinces should be required to seek individual naturalizations, but such an opinion was in the minority.) Meanwhile, lawyers from these conquered territories often went to great lengths to demonstrate that, as the jurisconsults of Ypres explained to Louis XIV in 1690, "the droit d'aubaine was not collected" in Flanders (or Liège, Artois, the Franche-Comté . . .).[119]

By both international treaties and specific judicial decisions of the parlements and the royal council, the crown recognized the special status of frontier provinces, and tended to reciprocally exempt foreigners from neighboring states who had settled in these provinces. Before its definitive acquisition by the crown in 1678, the Francs-Comtois were exempted from the droit d'aubaine in the province of Burgundy, and reciprocally, Burgundians were exempted in the Franche-Comté (although a complicated jurisprudence tried to settle the question of what happened during the period of conquest itself). The Treaty of the Pyrenees in 1659 established a reciprocal exemption between the Catalans of the Aragonese crown and the inhabitants of Roussillon and the borderlands of Cerdanya. Savoyards were exempted from the droit d'aubaine in the Dauphiné, and could even hold benefices there, according to the jurisprudence of the Grenoble parlement. And in the eighteenth century, the Paris parlement, ruling on a disputed inheritance concerning an inhabitant of Mons in the district of Hainault, declared that the droit d'aubaine was not applicable in the frontier provinces of the northeast.[120]

Beyond these "national," "professional," and "geographic" exemptions, there was the special question of the Jews in France and their relation to the droit d'aubaine. According to the jurists, until the middle of the eighteenth century, the Jews were not considered "aliens," since they were not subjected to the droit d'aubaine.[121] Nor, of course, were they considered "citizens" or "natural Frenchmen," since by the letter of the law, reiterated by Marie de Medici in 1615, they had long been expelled from French territory. In fact, earlier legislation in the fourteenth century had removed them from the "core territory of French rule," but by the end of the Old Regime three distinct groups existed on the peripheries of the kingdom: the Sephardim within the généralité Bordeaux (and in particular, the Bayonne suburb of Saint-Esprit), some three thousand strong and wealthy at the end of the Old Regime. They were not unlike the merchant Jewish families of the Papal States in Provence, many of whom migrated to Bordeaux in the eighteenth century. Both groups were far smaller but more privileged than the Ashkenazim communities of the east (the thirty thousand Jews in Lorraine, Metz, and Alsace).[122]

Despite juridical attempts to collapse the different legal statuses of these groups into a singular category of "Jews," the various communities all had distinct "national" statuses. The "Portuguese merchants" had acquired a status that approximated, with respect to inheritance law, the status of French native residents. In August 1550 Henry II had issued a collective naturalization to some twenty-six merchant families giving them the right to establish themselves, and to acquire and to inherit properties, with the same privileges as the "natural subjects of the king." Their descendants laid claim to this privilege of the "New Christians" of Bordeaux, and they received a confirmation of their ancestor's grant in 1574 and 1656, at the beginning of each reign of a new monarch.[123] In 1722, when Louis XV came of age, he ordered the seizure and inventory of all properties of the "Portuguese" Jews, who bought back their privilege with a "royal advent" gift of one hundred thousand pounds (a tax also imposed on all naturalized foreigners in 1723, but not consistently collected). Yet even in 1723, as in each previous renewal, the privilege restricted their rights and their residence to the jurisdiction of the Bordeaux parlement.[124] In the context of the increased migration of the Portuguese Jewish (and Avignonnais) families to Paris during the eighteenth century, and in the broader historical context of the citizenship revolution after the 1750s that abolished the fiscal category of aliens, a few Jewish families succeeding in acquiring letters of naturalization after the 1750s.[125] As for the Jews of Metz and Alsace, they were far less assimilated juridically than the Portuguese of Bordeaux, although their privileges were confirmed by Louis XIV when he arrived in Metz in 1657 and in Strasbourg in 1682. Still, neither subjects nor aliens, the Jews were qualified as a "singular case" by Turgot as late as the 1770s. He emphasized the usefulness of this status to the crown (they were better businessmen than their gentile counterparts) and invoked a "reason of state" (*raison d'état*) in maintaining their ambiguous status.[126]

→→

The ambivalent attitudes of the monarchy toward the Jews, especially in the reign of Louis XIV, were in this instance similar to the contradictions of monarchical policy more generally toward foreigners. The absolutist reaffirmation of the droit d'aubaine on foreign (and, indeed, French-born) subjects in the late seventeenth century ran roughshod, especially in the Naturalization Tax of 1697, over the previous (and contemporaneous) royal privileges and exemptions of foreigners. More, the revitalization of the droit d'aubaine ran counter to the traditional politics of welcoming (and seducing) immigrants, especially those with valuable labor skills. Ideologically speaking, the political confiscation and amplification of the droit d'aubaine ran counter to the more generalized monarchical propaganda that France was a kingdom of "liberty" that welcomed religious and political refugees.[127] How to account for what was at best ambivalence, and at worst a frightening contradiction, at the heart of the monarchy's policies toward immigrants?

The two-faced policies of the crown were not simply the result of royal vacillation.[128] For one, the crown's contradictory policies toward the droit d'aubaine can be explained by pointing to the distinct groups within the personnel of the administrative monarchy that had different interests in the droit d'aubaine and in the presence of foreigners more generally. Indeed, the apparent ambivalence toward the droit d'aubaine reveals an essential tension between not only two groups but also two "ideologies," for want of a better word. On one side were the financiers and the tax-farmers, supported in large part by the jurists, with whom they were sociologically linked. For these partisans of royal rights, the interest in the droit d'aubaine as an inheritance incapacity was obvious, as was the interest in the politically redefined droit d'aubaine in the Naturalization Tax of 1697, which extended over the entire kingdom.[129] Such "interests" were grounded in a concern to enforce the crown's domanial rights over the entire kingdom, and as a result ignored the vast wealth and income generated in the movement of foreigners into the kingdom. Not that the tax-farmers and financiers were motivated solely by their personal interests in the collection of the droit d'aubaine; rather, their positions reflected the ideology of an "immobile France," of a state grounded on the extraction of wealth and taxes from the land.[130]

On the other side, the administrative elite of the kingdom was seduced by the solicitations and interests of the "France of movement"—the vital service and commercial sectors of trade and finance, in which foreigners, especially Protestants, played significant roles. The intendants and government personnel were more frequently partisans of a politics of attracting foreigners and exempting them from the droit d'aubaine.[131] Their ideals were reflected in the clauses of international treaties in the seventeenth century, and nearly surfaced during the widespread opposition to the monarchy at court in the 1690s. The classical mercantilist doctrine as elaborated by Montchrétien and others, made into consistent policy by Colbert in the 1660s, was ambivalent in its attitudes toward foreigners, on the one hand restricting their access to national commerce, and on the other offering privileges to skilled artisans and manufacturers in the service of the crown. But generally speaking, it was the xenophobia of Montchrétien that prevailed, and the French monarchy adopted a highly restrictionist policy toward immigration under Louis XIV.

In the 1690s, during the desperate years of the War of the Augsburg League and its aftermath, the king was faced with a choice.

At that moment, Fénelon, tutor of the royal princes and central figure of the "Burgundy Circle," challenged the traditional mercantilist doctrine found among the highest-ranking (although frequently dismissed) ministers at court. His *Aventures de Télémaque*, an allegorical critique of Louis XIV (and of the absolutist reconfiguration of the droit d'aubaine), represented a stream of liberal thought and reform that flowed underneath the restrictionist mercantilist mountain of absolutism. Young Télémaque, before he became king, traveled throughout the ancient world with an insatiable curiosity. Marveling at the prosperity of the Phoenicians (behind whom the late seventeenth-century reader would have no trouble identifying the Dutch), Télémaque asked how he could make his own kingdom flourish. The response, given by the captain of a Phoenician boat, was an unequivocal endorsement of an "open door" policy of immigration:

> Do as we do here: receive foreigners in your ports well and with ease; give them a sense of security, ease, and complete freedom. . . . Above all, do not undertake anything that is an obstacle to commerce. A prince should not get involved, for fear of disturbing it, and should leave all profits to those who have made efforts, or else he will discourage them; the prince will gain enough by the great wealth that enters his States. . . . Only profit and ease will draw foreigners toward you: and if you make commerce more difficult and less useful, they will imperceptibly leave and never come back, for other peoples, profiting from your imprudent judgment, will draw them away, and accustom them to get along without you.[132]

But in 1697 Louis XIV abruptly turned his back on "commerce" and the free movement of people and goods into and out of the kingdom. Instead of supporting a "France of movement" fed by the flows of wealthy and enterprising foreigners to the realm, he chose to amplify that "ancient" custom of the feudal world, the droit d'aubaine, and used it to collectively and forcibly tax the foreign population of the kingdom.

In 1697, at the end of the disastrous War of the Augsburg League, and in the midst of demographic collapse and economic stagnation, the monarchy decided between these two "camps," these two "ideologies." Ultimately, Louis XIV compromised the long-term interests of the kingdom, gambling that the immediate fiscal imperatives were more important. The wager was lost, since the Naturalization Tax of 1697 failed to produce any significant revenue to the crown, and led to the questioning (if not yet public critique) of the absolute citizen.

Beyond the question of competing personnel and ideologies, the ambivalent policies of the crown toward the droit d'aubaine represent an essential contradiction of French absolutism, and find their parallels in the monarchy's attitude toward venal officeholding, ennoblement, and taxation more generally. On the one hand, the crown sought to reinforce privilege so as to raise money, by selling patents of nobility and offices that multiplied the legal and fiscal distinctions among its subjects. On the other hand, at various moments within the construction of absolutism, but especially beginning with Louis XIV, the crown sought to abolish such privileges in order to strengthen royal authority. Nearly the entire twentieth-century historiography of French absolutism, from Georges Pagès to Roland Mousnier, David Bien, Gail Bossenga, and Michael Kwass, has elucidated this fundamental contradiction and named its motive: the endless pursuit of revenue.[133] Although the history of the droit d'aubaine does partake of this more general contradiction of early modern French absolutism, it must also be explained differently—especially because the droit d'aubaine, in its individual occurrence or its collective imposition in 1697, was singularly ill-designed to increase royal revenue.

The ambivalent, if not fundamentally contradictory, policies of the crown toward the droit d'aubaine, and toward immigration and citizenship more generally, must be found in the ambiguous status of the royal prerogative itself. The multiple and contradictory uses of the droit d'aubaine stemmed from the fact that the legal frameworks of the Old Regime did not always make a clear distinction between "private" and "public" law, even if the droit d'aubaine— and hence the identity of the citizen in early modern France—stood at the intersection of both. In "public law," the droit d'aubaine had a double significance that reiterates the general contradictions of French absolutism. On the one hand, it supported the absolutist project to extend royal authority to the kingdom as whole, including its southern Roman-law provinces and previously exempted municipalities. On the other hand, exemptions from the droit d'aubaine belonged increasingly to the growing sphere of international public law, the object of negotiations in the peace treaties of the early modern period. Yet in everyday practice, the status of "aliens" was firmly located in "private" or civil law, within the vast contestations over succession and inheritance, through which was elaborated a "doctrine" about the juridical incapacities of foreigners and the meaning of citizenship.[134] The "public" dimensions of the droit d'aubaine alternately amplified its definition (as part of the absolutist claims of the crown) and reduced its extension (through the numerous exemptions). But the legal contestations over the droit d'aubaine that made up the *practice* of citizenship were grounded in the sphere of (private) civil law, and in the hands of the magistrates, barristers, and attorneys. In the Old Regime, these jurists became the border guards of French citizenship in everyday life.[135]

Defining Natural Frenchmen and Women

In the 1697 Naturalization Tax, the monarchy deployed an expanded version of the droit d'aubaine to justify, initially at least, the taxation of all foreigners and their descendants or heirs that had settled in the kingdom after 1600. "Foreigners," in this amplified understanding of the term spelled out in the ordinance of July 1697, included native Frenchmen and women whose ancestors had immigrated to France after 1600—as many as three generations earlier—and who had bequeathed their estates in the kingdom to native heirs. In this instance, the crown turned its back on the jurisprudential definition of the foreigner. The state appropriated the law for political purposes, but neither prior nor subsequent jurisprudence offered any justification for the 1697 tax and the denial of the quality of French citizens to individuals born in the kingdom of foreign parents. Indeed, the jurisprudence of the early modern period more generally, despite the persistent xenophobia of the lawyers, tended to shrink the category of "aliens" and offered from the sixteenth to the eighteenth centuries an increasingly expansive definition of who could be considered a "natural Frenchman." This cumulative extension of the citizen in the period from the sixteenth century to the French Revolution, a growing liberality in the attribution of French nationality in the jurisprudence of case law, reflected and was reflected in the increasingly automatic procedure of naturalization itself (see chapter 2). It resulted essentially from the juridical modalities by which nationality was determined, and was occasioned by the social fact of French emigration in the sixteenth and seventeenth centuries, and especially the Huguenot diaspora before and after 1685.

The paradox of largely xenophobic lawyers developing ever more liberal and inclusive interpretations of who was a French citizen resulted from the specific mode in which the "doctrine" of citizenship came to be elaborated. Litigants and collateral heirs fought among themselves over the property of reputed aliens, including foreign-born offspring of French natives, while those reputed to be foreigners brought court challenges against the tax-farmers, royal treasury officials, and noble and courtly recipients of the king's donations of property from the droit d'aubaine. Within a wide variety of lawsuits over disputed claims to inheritances, offices, and benefices, the lawyers produced "doctrine" about the "rights and privileges" of French citizenship.

"Doctrine" remains within quotation marks as a misnomer, insofar as the elaboration of a set of more general legal principles emerged as glosses of specific arguments in specific cases argued before the courts. Each of these cases might contain numerous questions of civil law: in the infamous case concerning the duke of Mantua's succession in 1651, the Parisian barrister Soëfve argued nine separate points relating to the privileges of sovereign princes, the nature of residence, domicile, and inheritance capacity, and the value of letters of naturalization, their registration, and their retroactive effect.[136] The courts ruled not on the conditions of nationality per se but on the capacity of specific individuals to inherit property; in the hands of the barristers and the arrestographes, the particular value of their particular circumstances were elevated to a more abstract set of conditions (relating to origins, the nature of exemptions, the value of letters of naturalization, the definition of residence, and so forth). Inevitably, at the heart of these particular circumstances—and of the determination of nationality law—was the question of the capacity of the claimant to inherit property. As the legal historian Vanel saw it,

> One did not seek to specify the quality of an individual except at the moment when this determination became necessary to solve a practical problem. . . . Juridical rules primarily evolved through questions of inheritance, as a purely private set of interests. The theory of citizenship needed to be specified solely because the inheritance of an estate raised questions about the nature of citizenship. . . . Otherwise put, an individual did not inherit because he was French; he was French because it was logical that he inherit. It was thus normal that the rules of citizenship were modified solely as a function of new cases presented before the parlements.[137]

Unlike naturalization law after the French Revolution, which proceeded from the declared interests of the state or the nation, the doctrines of the Old Regime appear as the unintentional by-product of individual claims of reputed foreigners and would-be citizens within case law.

To understand these rules attributing French citizenship before the French Revolution, Vanel, like other legal historians, made use of the Latin terms invented by later nineteenth-century jurists, the principles of *ius soli* (law of soil, birth on French territory) and *ius sanguinis* (law of blood, birth of French parents) as modes of attributing French nationality. These terms have since passed into contemporary public and republican debate about the attribution of citizenship. Vanel recognized the "arbitrary and rigid" nature of the strict opposition that had no significance to lawyers and judges of the early modern period, yet she insisted on using it.[138] Indeed, early modern juridical discourse rarely used these Latin terms, no matter how strong the attachment of some jurists to Roman law.[139] For, unlike Bodin or Rousseau, the lawyers and judges of the period were singularly uninterested in developing a general set of principles about the attribution of French nationality, much less in an elucidation of the "rights and privileges" of French citizenship. Rather, they were concerned with the question of successoral capacity—which in fact they generalized, consistently but most often implicitly, into three categories or criteria: birth in the kingdom, birth of French parents, and permanent residence under royal jurisdiction.[140] Thus when modern historians of French nationality argue (contra Vanel, as is often the case) that ius soli was originally a feudal practice that persisted as the dominant mode of attributing French citizenship until the Civil Code (1803), their language caricatures practices of both the medieval and early modern periods.[141] Although not altogether wrong, the terms tend to limit our understanding of the early history of French nationality law—of nationality avant la lettre.

In historical retrospective, the best evidence of a "traditional" French "law of soil"—the attribution of nationality on the basis of birth—can be found reversely stated in Bacquet's 1577 definition of the alien (repeated throughout the early modern period) as someone *not* born in the "kingdom, countries, lands, and seigneuries" under the sovereignty of the French king. At the same time, and already in the early sixteenth century, the Paris parlement upheld several claims of children born in France of un-naturalized foreign parents to inherit estates—the so-called softening of the droit d'aubaine. Louis Charondas Le Caron, an early and often sloppy arrestographe, reported a 23 February 1515 decision of the Paris parlement that he generalized as the following claim: "Children born in France of a foreigner and residing in the kingdom, even if their father was not naturalized, are reputed to be French, and inherit from their father or mother by their birthright, something that few legal practitioners have understood." His contemporary, Jean Papon, cited four other decisions of the Paris parlement to that effect, and the magistrate Jean de Cambolas, president of the Toulouse parlement, reaffirmed the "principle" in 1602 (implicitly recognizing, in the process, that the droit d'aubaine might be applied in Languedoc). As Lefebvre-Teillard has noted, the early decisions were not very well cited, and often impossible to verify.[142] But by the seventeenth century, jurists consistently attributed the ability to inherit to children born in the kingdom of foreign parents, a tendency that can be considered, in retrospect, an oblique assertion of a general "law of soil."

Why, then, did some sixteenth-century jurists, contra Jean Bodin, insist not only on birth within the kingdom but also on the centrality of maternal descent? Jean Papon, among them, believed that in addition to being born in the kingdom, the claimant needed to have been born of a French mother, "of a wife taken in the kingdom and not a foreigner, and also that they be residents of the kingdom, for one without the other does not suffice." Bodin himself had remarked, in his definition of what he called the "natural citizen," that "before, to be a citizen, it was necessary to have [both] father and mother who were citizens," although such was no longer the case.[143] But the belief that in "past times" one had to have been born of French parents (or especially mothers) before being able to inherit was itself an ideological construction corresponding to the belief common among sixteenth-century jurists (as voiced in the complaints of the Estates General in 1588) that citizenship was too widely available, and naturalization was too easily accomplished. It was also evidence of the jurists' efforts to give primacy to the principle of descent in the attribution of citizenship. In truth, neither fifteenth- nor sixteenth-century jurisprudence—nor that of the later period—ever accepted the principle that, to inherit, a man had to be born of a native mother, much less two native parents, but only of a legitimate union (for bastards, of course, also suffered the incapacities of inheritance).[144]

Yet even in this case, the jurists were commenting on the conditions under which an individual could inherit, which was not quite the same thing as arguing about the condition of being French—although that would flow from the decision. They did not seek to establish a general principle of ius soli; they assumed that an important component—but certainly not an exclusive criteria—of being able to inherit was having been born within the kingdom. At the same time, beginning in the late sixteenth century, a series of cases were presented before the sovereign courts that were to expand the boundaries of inheritance capacities, and thus of French citizenship, and to include a growing insistence on the principle of descent, what the nineteenth-century jurists would call the "law of blood" (ius sanguinis).

More than the modalities of attributing inheritance capacity, social factors determined the increasing importance of descent in the attribution of French citizenship between the sixteenth and eighteenth centuries. It is probably an exaggeration to state that France was more of a country of emigration than immigration in the early modern period, but emigration was important (if historically understudied), and it was the claims of descendants of French emigrants who had returned to the kingdom that drove the expansion of the rules attributing citizenship.[145] Such emigrants were principally of two kinds. Although France under the Old Regime never developed a full-fledged and consistent policy of settlement in overseas colonies, the economic interests of individual French merchants increasingly drove them to establish businesses and "residence" beyond the boundaries of the kingdom—and sometimes even to seek naturalization abroad.[146] Their children, born abroad, often returned to France to claim inheritances (and frequently to enter into litigation with collateral heirs). As we shall see, many of them took "letters of declaration of naturalization," such as Aubry in 1715, whose "father had been sent to the island of Tarques in Africa by the Company in Marseille to administer their goods, and there he married the said Angela, daughter of a Genoese, of whom the claimant was the outcome of their marriage." Such letters of declaration, the jurists argued, were not strictly required as long as the descendants settled permanently in the kingdom.[147]

More important and numerous were the children of Huguenot refugees. Between the mid-sixteenth and the mid-eighteenth centuries, concentrated around 1685, when Louis XIV revoked the Edict of Nantes, nearly a quarter of a million French Huguenots left the kingdom, settling in England, Prussia, Holland, Geneva, and Acadia. A large body of legislation came to govern the status of their children born abroad. "De-naturalized" along with their parents as part of the reiterated prohibitions on Protestants leaving the kingdom (declarations of 18 May 1682, 31 May 1684, 7 May 1686, 3 September and 4 February 1699, and the royal ordinance of 18 September 1713), they shared a civil status similar (although far from identical) to the legal category of aliens.[148] In fact, according to the official doctrines of both the monarchy and the jurists, Protestants—and indeed, all emigrants—who permanently settled abroad lost all rights to inheritance and legally became "aliens."[149] According to Bacquet, "The Frenchman who has removed himself and settled outside the kingdom . . . becomes a foreigner in his native land, and cannot in any way inherit in France." A generation later, Antoine de Loysel was even more strict: a citizen who abandoned his sovereign to live elsewhere "has no legitimate heir and can have none." Such a position was reinforced by the famous royal edict of 1669 that forbade French men and women from emigrating and disinherited their children, prohibiting the latter from ever being naturalized. Initially motivated by mercantilist principles of economic protectionism, the edict became inextricably linked to the question of the Protestant diaspora before and after 1685.[150]

Yet in practice, a small number of children of French refugees abroad—a statistically insignificant but legally important element within the Protestant diaspora—returned to France, converted to Catholicism, and armed themselves with letters of declaration of naturalization in disputes over estates. After 1685, the cases and litigation became more frequent. To cite only one, Pierre Ardesoif had fled to England with his father in 1686 at the age of six, but returned to d'Alençon in Normandy in 1703, upon his father's death. Eleven years later, he sought a declaration of naturalization. Litigation involving converted children of the diaspora who received declarations of naturalization clustered in the 1720s and 1730s, as a first generation of Protestant refugees after 1685 died off or at least settled their estates.[151]

Not that these children and their lawyers argued explicitly about their past Protestant identities, or those of their parents: given the normative proscription against Protestants, even before 1685, they were unlikely to do so. Their barristers downplayed, and sometimes even omitted mentioning, their Huguenot ascendance, which was considered irrelevant to the arguments and claims of inheritance based on the principles of descent. The most famous case in the sixteenth century, one that set precedents for the entire Old Regime, was that of Marie Mabile, who was declared a "true and natural Frenchwoman" in 1576 despite being born, raised, and having married in England. Mabile l'Anglese was descended from two Huguenot French parents who had taken refuge in England, and when her English husband died, she had returned to France, taken letters of naturalization, and sued for a share of her maternal grandmother's estate. According to the lawyers, the letter of naturalization had not been absolutely necessary, but was evidence of her desire to permanently establish herself in France. Resident in the kingdom, descendance from French parents: these two conditions were sufficient to allow her to be considered a "natural Frenchman [*sic*]."¹⁵²

Just months before the Mabile ruling, the royal edict of May 1576 recognized as French natives those individuals born abroad of parents who had fled during the Wars of Religion, provided they return to the kingdom. In a moment of religious conciliation, Henry III had identified the children of Protestant refugees as "French naturals" without their need to retain special letters, if they resettled in the kingdom.¹⁵³ This political overture, offered in the context of a momentary peace between Huguenots and Catholics, had no formal juridical precedents. Nor did subsequent royal legislation about the civil status of French Protestants in the kingdom before and after 1685 rest on the findings of French case law. But case law concerning the children and grandchildren of Protestant refugees tended to diffuse the notion that French citizenship, as the capacity to inherit property, could be extended both to emigrants who returned to the kingdom to claim inheritances and to children born of French parents abroad who returned to reside in the kingdom.¹⁵⁴

The principle that citizenship was inherited might even be extended back several generations. In a case heard by the same court in 1694, the existence of one French grandfather was recognized as a sufficient basis to claim such a capacity, provided that the claimant establish his permanent residence in the kingdom. The case involved a Protestant merchant, Adrien de Rocquigny, who left France in 1596 (for religious reasons, no doubt, fleeing the French reconquest of Normandy) and married a French émigrée in England, where they had settled. Their son, Adrien, was born in England two years later and eventually married a Frenchwoman who had also fled the persecution of Protestants in France. Their son, Guillaume de Rocquigny, although born in England in 1632, at the age of two came to live with his father, who had returned to Caen and taken letters of naturalization (that did not in fact name his son as a beneficiary). Guillaume grew up in France, became a banker, and traveled widely in the North Atlantic world. When he died, French fiscal officers seized his estate, but his direct heirs successfully proved, in a case argued by d'Aguesseau himself, that Guillaume was to be considered a "natural Frenchman."¹⁵⁵

The court established Rocquigny's citizenship not only on the basis of his French ancestry but also because he had offered proof of his desire to become French by returning to the kingdom and establishing permanent residence there. The same "condition" of residence can be found throughout early modern French jurisprudence that recognized the capacity of French-born children of foreigners to inherit and the ability of foreign-born children of French parents to inherit if they settled in the kingdom. For d'Aguesseau, arguing the Rocquigny case, the Roman *iuris postliminum*, the "right of return," justified the latter's prerogative.¹⁵⁶

More generally, the barristers did not explicitly draw on Roman law, but they understood the voluntary establishment of residence as a key element, an essential if insufficient condition, for the attribution of Frenchness. For the jurists, often unconsciously following Bartolus and medieval Italian jurisprudence, this "law of domicile" (*ius domicilium*) dovetailed with an oft-cited "spirit of return" (*esprit de retour*) inherited across generations whose proof was found in the simple desire to reside in the kingdom.[157] This spirit of return could be actualized by children or even grandchildren who, although born abroad, established their residence in France—and the spirit of return could be invoked even in cases where parents themselves had abandoned the idea of returning to France, having taken letters of naturalization abroad. In a general principle elaborated by the jurisconsult François Tronchet throughout his three decades of legal practice before the French Revolution, fathers could not deny their offspring the quality of a Frenchman.[158]

Thus the arguments of barristers in defense of their client's claims to inherit, especially after the late sixteenth century, came to insist on the growing importance of bloodlines in families—no surprise, in a society that increasingly emphasized the ideas of lineage and descent, especially among the nobility.[159] Despite the judicial consensus that French civil law was distinct from that of Rome, paternity law that drew on the principles of Justinian experienced a modest revival among civil law jurists of the seventeenth and eighteenth centuries, especially those needing "written reasons" for the ability of children to claim the French identity of their parents.[160] From the barrister Le Maistre in the early seventeenth century to the jurisconsults Pothier and Tronchet in the late eighteenth century, lawyers won almost every case for clients, born abroad of French parents who returned to France to inherit property. This renewed deployment of the Roman law precepts of paternity and descent was already present in the written law provinces of the south, but it penetrated and infiltrated the civil jurisprudence of the northern, customary law regions in the seventeenth and eighteenth centuries. As such it helped to shape a distinctively "French" nationality law that, in certain interpretive cases, even gave primacy to the principle of descent.

Thus, in the course of pleading a case before the Paris parlement in the 1630s, Le Maistre (who would later publish his own compilation and dictionary of case law) argued rhetorically that the principle of filiation was even more determinate than that of birthplace. The case, decided on 26 June 1634, concerned an estate contested between members of the same family: the children born in Savoy of a French native, Jean du Bail, and his French mother, who sought to exclude them from the inheritance based on their status as foreigners. Le Maistre argued, successfully:

Is it not more reasonable that a Frenchman engender Frenchmen everywhere and not that he engender a Spaniard if his wife gives birth in Spain, a Savoyard in Savoy, an Englishman in England? Would it be that a father, who has only one country, have children of different nations? And who can doubt that it be more [important] to be born of a Frenchman than to only be born in France, that the father is more [important] to his son than the place where he came into the world: the father is natural to him; the place itself is foreign. In one case, it is the blood that is French; in the other, it is only the air that is French.[161]

This astonishing rhetorical claim invoking French "blood" was extremely rare in the early modern period, although, arguing the opposite claim, radical republicans in the French Revolution sometimes insisted that breathing the air of liberty was enough to acquire French nationality. (Had these terms become dominant as legal principles, the central opposition in the debates over French nationality during the modern period might have taken shape as the opposition between *ius soli* and *ius aerius!*) More generally, it was rare to find such a stark opposition of "principles" as the basis of jurisprudential reason. When the magistrates of the Paris parlement pronounced in favor of Le Maistre's arguments, they in fact confirmed not a general proposition of the attribution of citizenship but a specific proposition about the capacity to inherit of children who were born outside of the kingdom of a French father. Moreover, although convinced by the lawyer's arguments, they also emphasized the condition that such children inherit "provided that they wish to reside and make their home there at the time of the claim." Only by this residence was the "vice of their origin entirely purged."[162]

Indeed, the principal reason why the modern terminology in Latin guise of "soil" and "blood" remains inadequate to an understanding of early modern French citizenship has to do precisely with the law of residence, a certain *ius domicilium*. The increasing emphasis on residence within the jurisprudence of alien law, in combination with birth and descent, marks the decidedly non-Roman origins of early modern French citizenship. For there was nothing Roman about the claim that residency was essential to the definition or exercise of citizenship. After the social wars, by the decree of the Emperor Caracalla in 212 C.E., Roman citizenship was extended to all the inhabitants of the empire (except *deditices*, subjects of Rome who had surrendered their rights). But this "right of origin," according to Yan Thomas, had been firmly grounded in a notion of genealogical descent. The late medieval interpretation, among the glossators of the thirteenth-century Italian city-states and later in France, began to eliminate this genealogical depth, and came to understand the attribution of citizenship solely on the basis of birth in the city, without concern for paternal ascendance.[163] In the treatises of the 1570s, French jurists made residual ideological claims about the importance of descent in the attribution of French citizenship. But French jurisprudence by the late sixteenth century recognized both birth in the kingdom and genealogical descent from a French native in the attribution of inheritance capacities—provided that the claimant resided permanently in the kingdom. Such an emphasis on what could anachronistically be labeled a "law of residence" dovetailed neatly with "feudal" practices that attributed belonging and identity not on the basis of birth but to those who had voluntarily sworn oaths of fealty and obedience. In the late medieval period, French jurists inherited the Italian jurisprudential reworking of the Roman notion of *origo* and, alongside and within the customary and feudal practice of vassalage, created a notion of citizenship in the kingdom that was to be grounded on birth. But increasingly in the seventeenth and eighteenth centuries, descent became important, as did the necessary (if not in itself sufficient) condition of residence.

The evolution of French nationality law toward a set of rules attributing citizenship that was more inclusive, although increasingly dependent on the condition of residence, was thus occasioned by the growing number of claims, especially by children of the Protestant diaspora, to escape the onerous status of aliens and to inherit family estates in the kingdom. Combined with a renewed attention to Roman paternity law, and in the context of a broader emphasis on lineage and descent in French family law, these claims pushed the barristers to argue that the "quality" of a natural Frenchman or woman could be acquired through filiation and descent (but also residence) as well as birth in the kingdom (but also residence). Jurists and legal practitioners of nationality law, working through the vast litigation over property rights between reputed foreigners and French native-subjects, tended toward increasingly expansive definitions of the identity of French "nationals" or "citizens," and this despite—or rather, as an unintended consequence—of their general xenophobia. By increasingly recognizing the principle of descent, sometimes well beyond existing juridical norms, some lawyers—including the jurisconsult Tronchet, who was to play a central role in the definition of French nationality by descent in the Civil Code of 1803—virtually displaced the definition of French citizens as those born in France in favor of descent from French parents, contingent on their residence in the kingdom.

The juridical model of French citizenship, as it took shape after the late sixteenth century, was thus defined by an increasing porousness of its boundaries. But in their commentaries and judgments about the droit d'aubaine in the sixteenth and seventeenth centuries, the jurists also helped to constitute an ever-sharpening distinction between foreigners and citizens. Such were the opposing tendencies of the absolute citizen in the definition of which the history of the droit d'aubaine played such a disparate and contradictory role.

The French citizen from the late sixteenth through the early eighteenth centuries was first and foremost a legal being, defined in contrast and distinction to the foreigner. The legal fiction of *becoming* French during this period—the theory, protocol, and practice of naturalization—provides additional clues about the meaning of the absolute citizen, at the same time that it reveals further slippage between the juridical and royal models of citizenship in early modern France.

◂← CHAPTER TWO →▸

THE LETTER OF NATURALIZATION
IN THE OLD REGIME

In the sixteenth century, the legal practitioners of civil law and the crown developed rather different ideals about the qualities and prerequisites of foreigners who sought naturalization. On the one hand, the juridical model insisted on a residual, political dimension of citizenship as honor and merit and on the incomplete nature of assimilation enacted through a grant of naturalization. On the other hand, the royal model of citizenship presumed the crown's sovereign authority and correspondingly diminished the political implications of citizenship and naturalization. Despite the opinions of the jurists, the royal model of naturalization was to triumph. It crystallized early in the reign of Louis XIV: between 1660 and 1789, the protocol, procedure, and practice of naturalization embodied this absolutist model.

Of what did this royal model consist? Philosophically and legally, by a grant of naturalization, the king exercised his sovereign authority and removed the foreigner's "vice of origin," turning an alien into the juridical equivalent of a French native.[1] Unlike contemporary practices of naturalization, there were no formal a priori requirements about "integration" or "assimilation"—such as speaking French, practicing French customs, or subjectively identifying with France—other than an expressed desire to "live and die" in the kingdom.[2] The official, royal model of absolutist citizenship did not refer to the modern notion of nationality, either in sharing a common culture or being attached sentimentally to France (other than the implicit ideal of loyalty to the king, assured by the very fact of residence). Nor did the royal model and practice of naturalization necessitate the expression of patriotism. The royal chancellery turned down few, if any, requests from foreigners seeking to be naturalized, except those petitioners who failed to follow the appropriate protocol. Between 1660 and 1790, thousands of men and women, usually long established in the kingdom, received letters and declarations of naturalization. They became legally identical to French natives, especially regarding their capacity to transfer property inheritance across generations. But did they actually become French citizens?

According to Jean Bodin, who provided the philosophical foundations of legal citizenship in early modern France, "natural" and "naturalized" citizens were absolutely equivalent.[3] But most of his contemporary jurists thought differently, and were less certain that the two terms were synonymous. Practicing barristers and other legal technicians, after all, mostly used a different language and wrote consistently not about "naturalized citizens" but about "naturalized foreigners." The administrative apparatus of the crown followed suit in its identification of foreigners who acquired French citizenship. The difference is significant, both philosophically and politically. Among the sixteenth-century jurists, naturalization never bridged the deep xenophobic gap between foreigners and "natural Frenchmen" (and women). Naturalization as administrative practice, moreover, never fully protected the foreigner from all the civil incapacities, especially the liability to special taxes, that accumulated during the early modern period. Naturalized citizens remained foreign citizens. The term "naturalized French" only appeared very late in the Old Regime, revealing the way in which the more public discourse of the "nation" set the stage for naturalization to become a more totalizing process: one could "belong" only to one "nation," and in a world of imagined nation-states, naturalization became more exclusive.[4] So too was the modern invocation of the "rights of the citizen" absent in the Old Regime, although the phrase once or twice appeared within naturalization grants during the 1770s, in the period of the citizenship revolution.[5]

Until then, the official model of royal citizenship operated on a different kind of fiction. Foreigners acquired "letters of naturalization" (*lettres de naturalité*, more literally "letters of nativeness") that "had the effect of returning [foreigners] to the same condition of those born [in the kingdom]," to quote the late seventeenth-century Jansenist jurisconsult Jean Domat. The standardized formula of the letter stated that the foreigner would be treated in all respects "as if he [or she] were born in the kingdom."[6] The absolutist model, then, rested on a central legal fiction . . . that was false.

Fictions of Naturalization

A legal fiction, wrote the medieval Italian jurist Cino of Pistoia (1270–1336), was "the elevation to the ranks of truth of a thing that is certainly contrary to the truth." To Renaissance jurists of learned law, the use of fictions, although dangerously close to cavillation, was an approved intellectual procedure. Inexact and false, legal fictions were necessary (to produce practical results) and limited (done in the name and principle of equity and in the interest of the public good). But legal fictions were of various kinds, some more "truthful" than others, just as they had been in Roman law.[7] In the French royal model of naturalization, the fictional equivalence of "naturalized foreigners" and "citizens" was deeply misleading. The falsifying qualities of naturalization was most disturbing to the sixteenth-century French jurists who were inspired by what can be called, despite tremendous variation in practice, the "Italian model" of becoming a citizen.

Within a vast and highly variable jurisprudence of citizenship practices in the medieval Italian city-states, the assimilation of a foreigner as a citizen was a more truthful legal fiction than it was to become in the early modern French state. In the Italian city-states, foreigners received grants of citizenship based on evidence of their social assimilation and political loyalty, for the "honor" of becoming a citizen of Venice or Siena depended on a foreigner's merits, moral worth, and degree of assimilation into the local community. Foreigners who received grants of "citizenship" (the word "naturalization" was only reintroduced into Italian after its appearance in France in the 1560s) were generally required to demonstrate a lengthy prior residence, the purchase of property or shares in the public debt, or even marriage and establishment of a family in their adopted city. The act presupposed that the foreigner had adopted the values and beliefs, as well as the customs and habits, of a native citizen (whose own origins were increasingly defined by his place of birth, not his ascendance). Above all, citizenship was a restricted political category, since the acquisition of citizenship was universally considered an honor that rewarded active proof of virtue, merit, and evidence of social assimilation.[8]

In this way, citizenship in the Italian city-states was a limited social category defined by gender, wealth, and social status. Citizens were men of independent means, a far smaller portion of the population than ordinary "inhabitants" and "residents," including foreigners. Because citizenship was first and foremost a political act that conferred in practice the rights of political action—of voting and officeholding—it was limited to adult, wealthy heads of household who had long established themselves in the community, in this way following the Roman republican model.[9]

The legal fiction of becoming a "natural citizen" developed by the Italian lawyers and jurisconsults recognized the essential and transformative power of custom and civil law. The jurisprudential presumption was that citizenship was part of civil law, and by the fourteenth century, "created" citizenship—whether by privilege (*per privilegium*) or treaty (*per pactum*)—was increasingly equated with citizenship of origin (*per origo*). According to a *consulta* of Baldus of Ubaldis (d. 1400), "true citizenship stems not from nature but art, for citizenship is something which can be made and is not only born, but created."[10] Such unequivocal proclamations, however tempered in specific jurisprudential claims, were nonetheless significant in their unreserved endorsement of the identity between what Bodin and French scholarly law would call a "natural" and a "naturalized" citizen. Their equivalence lay precisely in their "unnatural" or civil foundation.

The origins of this thinking can be traced from Baldus back to his teacher Bartolus of Sassoferato (d. 1357), for whom "original citizenship" and "created citizenship" amounted to exactly the same thing: they were species of the overall genus of *civilitas*, and were both equally "true" forms of citizenship.[11] But the roots are even deeper. Jules Kirshner has argued that a "steering assumption" of Baldus's conception of citizenship was the idea of "second nature," a civic identity constituted "between nature and culture." The notion of a second nature was ultimately drawn from Aristotle's *Nicomachean Ethics*, and more immediately from Saint Thomas Aquinas and other scholastic commentators of the later Middle Ages. "For it is harder to change nature than a habit, yet it is difficult to change a habit too," wrote Aristotle, "for the very reason that habit is a second nature." Second nature was produced by *habitus*, a notion that the Italian Commentators of Aristotle understood to mean the timeless repetition of actions that formed a person's "natural" disposition.[12]

Of course, such philosophical claims were stated in rather more prosaic and pragmatic circumstances: the Italian Commentators offered their jurisprudential opinions (*consilia*) with respect to specific claims of foreigners to enjoy the economic benefits, commercial privileges, and political rights of citizenship. Thus Baldus developed the argument in an unusual late fourteenth-century opinion about the cloth merchant Titius's claim to Venetian citizenship. His principal argument was not that Venice and Vicenza had a reciprocal treaty that mutually conferred the economic privileges of citizenship, exempting each other's merchants from specific customs duties, but the fact that the *practice* of Venetian citizenship over time had become second nature to his client. Baldus likened Titius to a plant transferred from his natural habitat to an alien field where it took hold because he had resided in Venice for decades having established his roots as a merchant, a father, and a citizen. Titius was, literally, naturalized by his long-term residence in the city, by the endless repetition of activities and thoughts that produced over time feelings of love and loyalty for his adopted city. As a consequence of his de facto naturalization, Titius now sought to make his condition a legal one, to be guaranteed the same rights and privileges as a natural citizen.[13] To Bartolus and the Italian Commentators, this form of naturalization was first and foremost social; it was then recognized (by a variety of kinds of grants, depending on the legal practices of the particular city-states involved). In theory at least, and increasingly during the fourteenth century in practice, no distinction remained between citizens by birth and those conferred the status by law or privilege.

As the jurisconsults of scholarly law and the French crown selectively adopted the principles of the Italian Commentators and the jurisprudence of the late medieval Italian city-states, they introduced important differences, and ultimately diverged in their understandings of naturalization. First, in the hands of sixteenth-century French lawyers as in the policies of the crown, the presumption of the complete and prior assimilation of foreigner into citizen was tempered by a persistent and widespread xenophobic predisposition: even "naturalized citizens" could be restricted in their exercise of civil actions, and they were subjected to special and onerous disabilities. Second, and as a result, the legal fiction that allowed the monarchy to treat foreigners "as if" they were French natives did not mark their complete social or political assimilation. They remained foreign citizens.

It is true that many of the best minds of French jurisprudence, from Bodin to d'Aguesseau, concurred that the status of a naturalized citizen was absolutely equivalent in theory to that of a natural citizen. In practice—especially in the 1570s, and later under Louis XIV—the equivalence between natural-born French and naturalized foreigners was never complete, evidenced by the striking absence of biological metaphors of naturalization in the writing of the jurists.[14] In the late sixteenth century, Bacquet, Papon, and Choppin, who elaborated a model of citizenship in the 1570s founded on the incapacities of foreigners, also expressed considerable resistance to the "fiction" of complete assimilation. Decrying foreign officeholders in the kingdom, Bacquet noted that "in the heart of the foreigner ... there is a suspicion of some hidden poison, dare I say treason." For Jean Papon, even a naturalized foreigner remained tainted, since "the foreigner will never be as faithful as a native, who will always have friendship, love, and care for the health of the fatherland [patrie], and who would rather suffer than betray it; a condition that a foreigner most likely could not attain nor even seek." Papon was convinced that "the prince will never be able to claim nor recognize any foreigners as faithful and dedicated to his service as are his true and native subjects born in the kingdom."[15] And in the crown's own policies, naturalized foreigners still suffered discrimination and were subject to disabilities and special charges, as the Naturalization Tax of 1697 was to prove so painfully.

At the same time, the sixteenth-century jurists asserted in their treaties that foreigners ought to prove their worthiness as well as their social assimilation before becoming naturalized. This aspect of the "Italian model" was shared by the provincial estates in late medieval Languedoc (where Italian jurisprudence penetrated easily, thanks to geographic proximity and a common Roman-law tradition). It was also a tenet of jurisprudential thought among legal commentators writing in the other regions where civil law was grounded on the inheritance and practices of Rome. But the expectation that naturalized foreigners should be assimilated was not simply a regional demand. The Estates General of Tours of 1483 insisted on evidence of social assimilation and merit, and the call to closely assess the moral worth and social integration of foreigners before naturalization echoed throughout the sixteenth century among jurists from customary law regions. The humanist jurisconsult Pierre Rebuffi (1487–1557) had argued that it was the foreigner's responsibility, following the examples of Athens and Rome, to provide evidence of his "virtues" and "merits" before becoming naturalized.[16] In ancient Greece and republican Rome, according to the Renaissance jurists more generally, citizenship was an honor to be conferred only in recognition of exceptional services rendered and of complete social assimilation.

In the 1570s, lawyers and jurisconsults underscored the importance of virtue and social assimilation; they argued that naturalization should only be made on the basis of merit. René Choppin noted how, "anciently" in France, naturalization was conferred "to recognize services" given to the crown, and how France would do well to follow the celebrated republics of Sparta and Athens that severely restricted citizenship. "In the same way, one can infer that the State of France would be much better off if this regulation had held, so as to abolish this too large and excessive affection towards foreigners, called by the Greeks *xenophilia*, which is nothing but the too great and unchained love of foreigners, and the too dangerous permission they are given to commune and associate [with the French] in the middle of France."[17] The problem was one of the inadequate socialization of foreigners, who were naturalized without evidence of social assimilation. Hence the juridical claim, already examined, which purported to attribute French citizenship only to those born in France of French parents or a French mother.[18]

Such were not simply the learned musings of jurisconsults or the xenophobic practices of legal practitioners. At the meeting of the Estates General in Blois in 1576, the Third Estate (dominated by lawyers) proposed a strict set of requirements for naturalization, including a previous ten-year residency, legitimate marriage and children, and possession of at least two hundred livres in property.[19] In truth, such requirements harkened back less to Greece and Rome than to the statuses of the citizen in the medieval Italian city-states. But the Blois ordinances were never incorporated into law, and the crown's more "liberal" and inclusive policies toward naturalization ultimately prevailed.

The official model of naturalization that took shape in the sixteenth and seventeenth centuries—less a theory than a set of implicit assumptions within the practice of naturalization itself—turned its back on the rhetorical and political claims of the jurists. In turning naturalization into an exclusively royal and sovereign privilege, the monarchy downplayed any requisite criteria of merit and social assimilation. Although the royal courts responsible for the verification of the grant of naturalization sometimes enacted a pro forma inquiry into the "life and habits" of a petitioner, the French monarchy turned naturalization into a routinized administrative procedure, an increasingly bureaucratic and even automatic grant.

The contrast with other European monarchies, notably Spain, is striking. The legally distinct territories of the Habsburg Empire on the Iberian Peninsula maintained the prerogative of defining "nativeness" and of naturalizing foreigners through patent letters issued by the regional parliaments in Castille, Aragon, Catalonia, and Navarre. At the same time, the sixteenth century witnessed the development of legislation against foreigners trading in the Americas, and early in the seventeenth-century the crown began to issue concessions of "naturalization to trade in the Indies."[20] But it was only with the reforms of the new Bourbon monarchy in 1715 and the abolition of regional "public laws" that the crown formally abolished "foreignness between kingdoms" and promised not to concede naturalization to foreigners unless approved by the cities and towns with votes in the Cortes. In fact, independent of the naturalizations as formal letters patent, foreigners in eighteenth-century Spain and Spanish America were "naturalized" following customs and social processes regulated at the municipal level. Municipalities often protested the ease with which the crown could proffer grants of naturalization without prior evidence of social assimilation, complaints also voiced by the Estates General in late sixteenth-century France.[21]

In contrast to Spain, the French crown became at an early date the exclusive source of naturalizations. Citizenship was routinely acquired through the royal chancellery without any prior evidence of social assimilation, or even of prior residence (even if the registration procedures of the magistrates in the Chambre des comptes faintly echoed the claims of sixteenth-century jurists). In this way, French practices diverged significantly from Iberian ones in the Old Regime, just as they diverged from the practices of "naturalization" and "denization" in England. Unlike England, France developed no intermediary legal condition between the foreigner and the citizen before the Civil Code of 1803, although postrevolutionary practitioners of naturalization would argue that French "naturalization" resembled English "denization."

It might be argued that the unbridged xenophobic gap between the royal and administrative fiction of naturalization and its idealization by the French jurists had its roots and justification in the early modern recognition that the king's power over nature was limited. The most absolutist of jurists—even those later so critical of the "tyranny" of Louis XIV—implied that the king's power was equivalent to that of nature: thus Chancellor d'Aguesseau, who argued that children born before letters of naturalization were issued to their parents were nonetheless "Frenchmen by birth, since the grace of the Prince has the right to make citizens, as Nature does; and when the stain of their origin is effaced, one can no longer distinguish who is born French and who has become French."[22] But other jurists, especially when treating the condition of nobility, recognized the illusion of the king's power over nature. "The law certainly imitates nature, but it does not have equal power," wrote Cardin Le Bret, placing clear limitations, despite his royalism, on the king's ability to alter blood and race.[23] "Nature is not within the power of the Prince, but rules alone," wrote Jean Papon in his own treatment of ennoblement. The examples he cited included that of Emperor Claudius, who, according to Suetonius, "tried to make a young male child into a female. He had his testicles torn off, then dressed, styled, and dissimulated him in such a way to represent a female. But he could not do enough, and the child always remained a male." Ennoblement, by contrast, worked because the king's transformative authority was joined to "civil transfiguration of commoners . . . [who] with time learn to live virtuously, and thus become valiant, courageous, and give themselves over to doing good and pleasing both the prince and his people. Even without said letters of ennoblement, by their correct lifestyle, they can ennoble themselves sufficiently."

The similarity between ennoblement and naturalization was greater in administrative practice than in juridical theory.[24] For just as a commoner could not become noble simply by adopting the lifestyle and values of nobility, neither could a foreigner resident in France his entire life become French by a purely "civil transfiguration." Neither residence nor evidence of social assimilation alone could ever naturalize the foreigner (unlike in the Italian city-states and in early modern Spain). More importantly, in the French royal practice of naturalization, "civil transfiguration" was never an explicit requisite condition for a foreigner to become a French citizen.

By the reign of the Sun King, the procedure of naturalization had become largely automatic, and it was to become even more routine during the course of the eighteenth century. By then, the jurists had come around, abandoning all requirements for evidence of merit or assimilation. As Lefebvre de la Planche, the king's solicitor at the Paris Chambre des comptes until the 1730s, was to write:

> Some authors claim that the privilege of naturalization should never be accorded except to those who merit this honor by stunning actions. They found their arguments on the practices of Athens, and elsewhere. . . . But this rule is never observed in France: without judgment about merit, letters of naturalization are accorded to all foreigners who come to France with the desire to establish themselves here, provided they practice Catholicism.[25]

As we shall see, the author was wrong to presume that Catholicism was a condition of naturalization, an error corrected by the solicitor Jean-Baptiste Denisart in his widely reprinted collection of judicial decisions. In the 1773 edition of his work, Denisart noted that "foreigners who request these letters are never refused," which certainly seems to have been the rule from Louis XIV to the French Revolution.[26]

The royal model, then, did not consider naturalization to be a meritorious reward, nor did it require social assimilation of the foreigner. Instead, the crown used two master metaphors found in the jurisprudence of the Italian Commentators and elaborated by the French jurisconsults and practitioners of the 1570s: the metaphors of a civil law contract and of adoption. Both of these metaphors presumed the absolute and sovereign authority of the king. In the first instance, the jurists likened naturalization to a kind of "social compact," not—as for Rousseau—among citizens who were equals, but between a foreigner and the king, who most emphatically were not. True, the privilege of naturalization was a completely discretionary "gift" of the king, who, enacting a legal fiction, thereby allowed a foreigner to be treated "as if" he were a natural-born Frenchman. Yet the privilege was without effect—it had no force of law—if the foreigner did not request and accept the grant. Even Bodin, who insisted on the absolutist prerogative of this sovereign grace, turned to civil law in justifying the acquisition of the "rights and privileges" of a citizen: a foreigner had to request to be naturalized, "for as such the gift is worthless if the giver has not presented it, and the recipient has not accepted the offer made to him." Despite his attraction to Rome, Bodin used a remarkably "feudal" language, one common among sixteenth-century jurists. Like him, Jean Bacquet under-scored the "mutual obligation between the prince and subject, just as between the feudal lord and vassal, which can only be contracted by mutual consent."[27] For Bacquet and others, the demand for letters and their subsequent registra-tion and verification in the courts at the instigation of the claimant represented the symbolic performance of a contract by mutual consent.[28] By the seven-teenth century, jurists such as Hyacinthe Boniface (d. 1699), rector of the Paris law school, abandoned the language of feudal lordship and vassalage and spoke more simply of the "reciprocal contract" by which the king allowed a foreigner to enjoy the privileges and rights and protection of a natural subject; and the naturalized foreigner was obliged to conform to the laws of the state.[29] The emergence of this notion of reciprocal contract reflected and informed the civil law definition of citizenship as a legal, as opposed to a political or social, condition.

Second, naturalization appeared to the learned jurisconsults as a form of adoption, and more broadly, a specific articulation of the "family model" of ab-solutist sovereignty. The irony, of course, was that adoption was not considered part of French law. "While adoption," noted the seventeenth-century jurist Denis Le Brun, "has always been commonly practiced in most nations, we no longer practice it in France." In the eighteenth century, barristers such as Boutaric were to decry adoption as "contrary to the laws of nature and of Christianity." Yet in practice, innovative work of social history has shown how adoption survived in Lyon (in part the heritage of Roman civil law in the south) and tacitly but legally in sixteenth- and seventeenth-century Paris.[30] More im-portant, civil law jurisconsults dwelled on the legal problem of adoption in re-lation to Roman law practices and to the jurisprudence of the Italian Commen-tators as they constructed a distinct *mos gallicus*.[31]

In the fourteenth century, Baldus had argued that citizenship by statute en-tailed an "adoption" of "children" by the city ("their mother") and the prince ("their father").[32] French jurists of the early modern period borrowed freely and with abandon the metaphor of adoption in their glosses of naturalization. Indeed, the terms were synonyms: Jean Bacquet called letters of naturalization "letters of adoption, because someone who is adopted, or given to replace a lost child by the kindness of the prince, is considered to belong to the family of adoption." Two centuries later, Lefebvre de la Planche concurred: "The letters which the foreigner needs in this case can only be accorded by the king who, as the father of his peoples [*père de ses peuples*], is alone able, through the quality of sovereignty accorded to him, by a kind of adoption, [to] admit the foreigner to the ranks of his children." Commentators on learned law and legal practitioners alike in sixteenth-century France deepened the metaphoric identity of the prince as father, and thus pushed the metaphor of adoption even further. In the French theory of naturalization, the naturalized foreigner became an "adopted Frenchman."[33] Given official strictures against adoption, it is no surprise that naturalized foreigners were never completely assimilated in Old Regime law, that they remained foreign citizens.

The notion of naturalization as adoption took its force from the "family romance" of absolutism, the metaphoric equivalence of king and father that informed so centrally the political culture of absolutism. Once again, it was Jean Bodin who provided the seminal equivalence: "The well-behaved family is the true image of the Commonwealth, and domestic authority resembles that of the sovereign; thus the good government of the house is the true model of the government of a Commonwealth." Scholars in the last twenty years have made much of the "marriage" of the king and the kingdom in ritual actions (the coronation and *sacre*) and in political discourse, especially in the sixteenth century. At that moment, magistrates of the Paris parlement as well as lawyers including Choppin and Bodin commented extensively on the political metaphor of the royal marriage in which, by the explanatory legal fiction, "the king is the husband of the kingdom."[34] Given this family romance of the Old Regime, it was only logical that French subjects and native inhabitants were considered as children. It is no surprise, then, that beyond the use of the term in scholarly law, adoption was a widely disseminated metaphor in the juridical discourse of naturalization—even if actual adoptions were not officially practiced in the early modern period.

The juridical theory of naturalization, then, derived from the Roman law traditions as found in the jurisprudence of the Italian Commentators; yet the reworking of these traditions in sixteenth- and seventeenth-century France produced some notable changes, both in the writings of the jurists and the practice of the monarchy itself. First, the jurisconsults never accepted the complete assimilation of foreigners as naturals, although they recognized the sole authority of the king in perpetrating the legal fiction that allowed foreigners to be treated "as if" they were native Frenchman. Second, they continued to insist on naturalization as evidence of social assimilation and political merit, a principle not adopted by the official model and practice of naturalization in the Old Regime. Finally, French nationality law in this period drew on the metaphors of civil contract and especially adoption, within the family metaphors of royal sovereignty, in its epistemological and practical justification of naturalization.

Yet the *practice* of naturalization—the letter of the law—differed significantly, since neither contract nor adoption was found within the rhetorical formulas of the grant. Letters patent of naturalization never mentioned adoption, contract, or the notion of *habitus*, nor did they include a statutory set of requirements about social assimilation and integration, or even about the merit and virtue of the foreigner in question. The practice of naturalization in early modern France failed to include any statutory requirements about the foreigner's "civil transfiguration," his assimilation or integration into the life of the community. Instead, both the text and the protocol relied on a simple and largely unjustified legal fiction that by the age of Louis XIV had become a routinized and banal administrative procedure of the absolute monarchy, and a highly regulated bureaucratic practice. Despite its formulaic character, the letter and procedure of naturalization reveal much about the legal and administrative fictions of becoming a French citizen, and also about the disconnection between the letter of the law and the multiple uses of naturalization itself.

The Letter and Practice of the Law: The Conditions of Becoming French

The early modern state's administrative practice of granting letters of "nativeness" or "naturalization" (*lettres de naturalité*) in France developed slowly from the monarchy's first grants of "royal bourgeoisie" in the early thirteenth century. The regal grant of royal bourgeois (*burgesias regni nostri*) appeared in the thirteenth century as a means of affirming and extending royal power against the lords, and was conferred on adult men (and women) who settled in specific towns under the direct dominion of the king.[35] Yet the actual privileges and grants to individual foreigners, especially foreign merchants—what became known as *lettres de bourgeoisie*—evolved slowly in several stages. At first, the crown bestowed ordinary grants and privileges on foreigners, and in the first half of the fourteenth century many of these were still restricted to specific royal towns and cast in negative terms: thus "Lombards" were permitted to exercise freely their trades in specific royal towns (Paris, Rheims, for example), and were, in a kind of reverse legal fiction, not to be treated as foreigners (*non tanquam Lombardus sed ut ceteri burgenses regni Francie*).[36] By the middle of the fourteenth century, however, the crown began issuing individual lettres de bourgeoisie, which from the beginning were occasionally called lettres de naturalité. Significantly, not only were these valid within the entire kingdom but they were also stated as "positive" fictions, in that they exempted their beneficiaries from the civil incapacities and constraints imposed on aliens, especially the droit d'aubaine. Although the denomination of "letters of royal bourgeoisie" persisted among certain sixteenth-century jurists, notably the customary-law specialists such as René Choppin and Antoine Loysel, such royal grants became widely and commonly known as "lettres de naturalité" by the late sixteenth century.[37]

Yet before then, such letters were relatively few in number, unevenly distributed geographically, and restricted socially to a small class of nobles. Half of the collection of 258 letters gathered by Bernard d'Alteroche between 1336 and 1599 were given after 1550.[38] Between the late fourteenth and the late fifteenth centuries, more than half of the letters were granted to nobles, and the largest concentration of grants were to foreigners settled in the customary law regions of eastern France. Moreover, the absence of a single juridical regime governing the incapacities of aliens resulted in an extreme diversity of juridical acts, both in form and in content. Letters of naturalization varied in their formula and vocabulary about residence, successoral capacities, and manifestations of sovereign authority. They included a wide variety of clauses, at once preliminary, dispositive, and executionary, and they did not yet systematically reproduce a consistent formula that allowed their beneficiaries to inherit or devolve property, or to hold benefices or offices in the kingdom.[39]

Already under Francis I (1515–47) and certainly by the second half of the sixteenth century, in the midst of the religious and civil wars that saw widespread xenophobia against increased naturalizations of foreigners in the kingdom (Italians, especially, and Germans), a more stable model of the royal patent lettre de naturalité crystallized. Grants of naturalization were common and easily acquired . . . much to the chagrin of the jurists, as we have seen. In concrete terms, according to Jean-François Dubost's comprehensive assessment, grants of naturalization seem to have peaked in 1565 and 1566, at around 125 per year (more than a third Italians) then stabilized after the 1570s, averaging forty a year until the early reign of Louis XIV.[40] This surge of demand for naturalization unleashed at the beginning of the Religious Wars in France was a response to the xenophobic climate of the time, and resulted in an initial normalization of administrative practices that were finally to crystallize in a more complex bureaucratic form early in the reign of Louis XIV.[41]

Early modern letters of naturalization were a particular instance of patent letters on which the chancellor officially placed the royal seal with green wax on red and green silk, with a double tail, signifying the perpetual effect of the charter. As a "grace" of the king, they were similar in form to other "royal letters in the form of charters" that transformed the status of a person, such as letters of legitimation or of ennoblement. (Such "letters of grace" were sometimes contrasted with "letters of finance" and "letters of justice.") By definition, they were a sovereign and discretionary act of the king, "accorded by favor to whomever he pleases, without being obligated by any sense of justice or equity, such that he can refuse to give those that he deems inappropriate."[42] Issued by the Great Chancellery, however, the vast majority of naturalizations never engaged the king personally. Instead, the key figures involved in drafting the letters and assuring their passage through the complex bureaucracy of the chancellery were the royal secretaries attached to the office of the chancellor (officially known as *notaires et secretaires du Roi, Maison et Couronne de France*).

Foreigners (even those exempted by statute or treaty from the droit d'aubaine) were naturalized through the offices of the royal secretaries responsible for drafting and authenticating all royal acts including the decisions of the sovereign courts. In the Old Regime, these officials were venal officeholders of extraordinary wealth and privilege whose numbers varied but stabilized at three hundred during most of the eighteenth century. Most offices were pure sinecures: nearly one in four royal secretaries never worked at all, although the monarchy preserved the charge since it depended on investments in these ennobling offices as part of its "system" of loans and credits. But those who worked—or rather, whose clerks did the work of producing drafts of patent letters, which were then expedited by the secretary of the royal household—were exclusively empowered to redact letters on the basis of requests made to them by foreigners seeking naturalization.[43]

In the late sixteenth century, the redaction of chartered privileges was already fixed by a long tradition. Royal secretaries had recourse to collections of model texts on the basis of which they established drafts (*minutes*) that were reread and corrected before being expedited. (Of course, lesser officials and clerks in the chancellery, from seal-warmers to bailiffs, oversaw and produced the transcription of the draft onto parchment, received the expedition order and signature, and then had the chancellor impose the royal seal—a process overseen by a group of working royal secretaries known as *grand audienciers*).[44] Beginning in the seventeenth century, and certainly by the reign of Louis XIV, however, the royal secretaries' control of the procedure of naturalization was partially overshadowed by the growing importance of the secretary of state for the royal household. Although generally considered a "frivolous" office of little functional value in the making of royal law, in this one domain the secretary of state took over the authorization or the expedition (*jussio*) of the letter, and himself signed the king's name.[45]

Louis XIV institutionalized the administrative procedure, assuring the monopoly of royal secretaries in presenting requests for naturalization, and allowing only a single clerk, registered at the chancellery, to sign the royal secretary's name (royal ordinance of 1672). Two years later, the monarchy began to archive the registered drafts (*minutes*) of letters submitted by the royal secretaries to the secretary of the royal household (ordinance of 20 May 1674)—the basis of the statistical work in this book.[46] Yet even as this administrative practice stabilized, neither the king nor any of his councillors normally intervened in the process of granting naturalization. Naturalization, following the correct protocol and procedure, gained an automatic quality, and only in special and extenuating circumstance was it subjected to the discretionary opinions of the king or his councillors.

To claim that naturalization gained an automatic quality seems counterintu-itive, because legally speaking the privilege was a discretionary gift of the king. In fact, the increasingly automatic procedure of naturalization was the adminis-trative counterpart of the shift of citizenship from politics to law, the depoliti-cization of French citizenship in early modern France. Especially beginning in the reign of Louis XIV, everything turned on administrative law, on protocol. If that protocol—including the proper registration of the letter—was correctly executed, the crown denied few if any individual petitioners for naturalization, and the provincial tax courts verified them automatically as well. Of course, this kind of "automaticity" differed greatly from that of the French Revolution, when the written laws and constitutions included statutory requirements that, if fulfilled, would automatically confer the quality of French citizenship.[47] In the Old Regime, although the king retained the discretionary authority to nat-uralize, the practice of naturalization was dependent on the correct execution of the letter of the law.

Such a normative routinization of naturalization was not, of course, without exceptions, if only because the process was often opaque to foreigners seeking naturalization. It is not surprising at all, for example, to find foreign residents, especially established and noble ones, reaching high into the networks of clien-tage and protection when requesting naturalization. The archives of the royal secretaries and the ministries of foreign affairs, of war, or other ranking offices contain the traces of such requests, which illustrate at once the obscure nature of the protocol and the appeals by claimants through ministerial networks of clientage and protection—even if, in the end, the normal protocol and proce-dure tended to prevail. In November 1756, for example, a Hungarian military officer, Marczy Cristel, wrote to the comte d'Argenson, then minister of war, requesting naturalization for himself and his wife, Marie Anne Beckerine of Vasheim in the Palatinate. The request was referred to the chancellery and pro-cessed the following January through the ordinary procedures following a for-mal demand by a royal secretary.[48] The case of Venier Candie, an Italian mili-tary officer in the Navarreins regiment who finally received his letter of naturalization in 1738, reveals how connections at court could complicate and delay what had become, by then, a relatively automatic procedure. Venier Can-die had written to War Minister Nicolas D'Anervilliers, humbly supplicating him for letters that would "keep for a niece the few furnishings that he left when he died." Candie was informed that he had to make a request to the chan-cellery: having launched two procedures for securing his letters, Candie had to withdraw one of them. He then wrote back on 24 June 1738 to d'Anervilliers: "Although I have had the advantage of receiving my naturalization directly from His Majesty, this does not stop me, Monsiegneur, from being humbly rec-ognizant of the greatness of your signs of protection which I will keep all my life, profoundly inscribed at the bottom of my heart."[49] Significantly, this rhetorical flourish of fidelity and identification far surpassed the language of the grant itself. Inscribed on his heart were not the sentiments of loyalty to the nation, nor even to the king, but the expression of personal reconnaissance that, although in the end useless, was often voiced by petitioners seeking letters of naturalization.

Even when the protocol became routinized, it was still possible and sometimes necessary for well-connected foreigners to receive a hearing at one of the royal councils—usually the council of dispatches, but occasionally others. But the ordinary procedure, the one that became increasingly the norm over the course of the Old Regime, was that requests for letters had to be made by royal secretaries at the chancellery and expedited by the secretary of state of the royal household. The procedure, affirmed by counterexample in the case of the Roman knight Ghezzi in 1725, was to send requests directly to the Great Chancellery in order to be processed.[50]

There were at least two general exceptions to the procedural rule. For those seeking to be ennobled at the same time as their naturalization, such as the Polish prince Jablonowski in 1771, the letters would necessarily have to go through the council of dispatches: otherwise, wrote Chancellor Maupeou to Foreign Minister d'Aiguillon, if the letters were "pure and simple, I will have them sealed as soon as they are presented to me."[51] The other significant exception involved requests for naturalization with permissions to hold benefices among natives of the Austrian Low Countries, especially in the 1780s. As we shall see, the question involved the principles of international reciprocity, and the foreign ministry sought to assure a changing system of mutual permissions and accords with the provincial government in Brussels that gave the foreign office the formal right to approve or deny grants of naturalization.[52]

Just as the procedures routinized, so too did the text become fixed. In fact, since at least the fifteenth century, the royal secretaries and their clerks relied heavily on model texts, templates that circulated in and around the Great Chancellery; their own texts simply enacted as particular instances the legal principles and fictions stated in the ideal type. The evolution of these model texts reproduces the tendencies toward routinization of procedures, and further underscores the early reign of Louis XIV as the moment when the administrative process and the legal fictions of royal naturalization took their definitive form.

Although the lettre de naturalité is mentioned in an unprinted late-fifteenth-century model text (in the context of permitting a *maître de requêtes* to sign the king's name),[53] the printed model texts and manuals of the sixteenth and early seventeenth centuries show a remarkable neglect of that privilege by name. The earlier printed manuals, such as the anonymous *Grand stile et prothocolle de la Chancellerie de France* (first surviving edition was 1514; republished in 1532 and 1548), did not mention lettres de naturalité at all, but provided a model of a patent letter for becoming a bourgeois du roy.[54] Jean Papon, in his published and widely reprinted treatise of 1578, reproduced several model texts of lettres de naturalité, but it was only at the end of the sixteenth century, in the anonymous *Thrésor du nouveau stile et prothocolle de la chancellerie de France* (1599), that a formulaic lettre de naturalité made its appearance in an administrative manual that circulated in the Great Chancellery. The text went virtually unchanged in L'Escuyer's *Le Nouveau stile de la chancellerie de France* (1622), but received an important elaboration in the hands of a chancellery bailiff du Sault. Writing a generation later, he stiffened the condition of residence in his *Nouveau stile des lettres des chancelleries de France* (Paris, 1666). A decade after that, manuscript versions of sample letters or templates were circulated among royal secretaries and their clerks; assembled by the chancellery in the 1670s, they coincide with the moment that Colbert took charge of regularizing the registration of expeditions from the royal household. By then, the style was fixed, and the only model texts that survive from the eighteenth century ironically reproduced verbatim examples of naturalization from the reign of Louis XV.[55]

It is worth considering in some detail the formulas of the stabilized model letter and practice, for, however great its rigidity and automaticity, the letter of naturalization discloses the guiding legal fictions, not of juridical theory but of monarchical practice. At the same time, the actual practices of claimants occasionally diverged from the letter of the law, constituting a set of administrative fictions that took shape in the collusion between foreigners and the monarchy—especially the fiction of a Catholic France.[56] Finally, the letter of naturalization was the subject of extensive jurisprudential commentary that itself attempted to normalize a set of divergent practices. A close reading of examples of formulas, and commentary thereon, reveals much about the various legal and administrative fictions of naturalization, explored in the remainder of this chapter.

The letter was in three parts: the initial protocol (containing the salutation, the address, and the exposition); the dispositive (where the legal fiction was enacted); and the expedition (the authorization and address of the letter for its registration in the sovereign and fiscal courts).

The formula of being a "letter" was taken literally. The salutation (*salut*) was done in the voice of the king, who addressed a universal audience and greeted the claimant: "Louis by the Grace of God King of France and Navarre to All Those Present and to Come." The address was normally followed immediately by an exposition (*exposé*) that introduced the claimant—or the claimant and his family—as foreigners, and that most frequently but not necessarily identified them as practitioners of the Roman Catholic and Apostolic faith. The exposition was cast as a request in which the supplicant identified himself or herself (generally in a highly abbreviated manner) and explicitly asked for the privileges conferred by letters of naturalization. Thus, a typical opening protocol from a typical Old Regime letter:

> Louis by the Grace of God King of France and Navarre to All Those Present and to Come greets our beloved Bitter Kaum, native of the parish of Vernes, diocese of Munster, a tailor professing the Roman Catholic and Apostolic Faith, has had represented to us that it has been more than twelve years since he established himself and married in the town of Dijon where he desires to fix his residence and finish his days in our kingdom, but that in order to participate in the advantages and privileges that our subjects and native residents enjoy, he needs our letters of naturalization, that he has very humbly requested be accorded to him.[57]

As we shall see, the exposition might be more or even less elaborated: in upward of 90 percent of the sample, there was rarely even this much description of a life's trajectory that contained, implicitly or explicitly, statements of loyalty and national belonging.[58] But the one consistent element in the exposition, according to the jurists, was the identification of the *foreign* origins of the foreigner. The recognition of the claimant's foreign origins had been consistently present in the letter of naturalization since the 1340s.[59] According to Jean Papon, it was very important that the particular "national" origins of the foreigner be identified:

> It is absolutely required that he give an account of where he is from, from which town, such as from Genoa in Italy, from Vic in Spain, or from elsewhere. In this he must not be misleading, which would be very prejudicial to the claimant, for without being misleading, and expressing the truth, he could obtain that which he seeks, that is, the dispensation of nativeness [*dispense de naturalité*]. A false account will always have the presumption of malice. *Because all nations are different*, this one is treated more favorably than another, or at least is less suspect and to be feared less than another, it is necessary to admit to the truth, to be Spanish, Italian, English, Scottish, Polish, Jewish, Turkish, Marrano, or something else, without dissimulating anything, nor claiming one nation as another. For if that were to be done, the claim is false and the claimant incapable of receiving the grace that the Prince had chosen to confer.[60]

In practice, the letters of naturalization rarely insisted on the "national" origins of the petitioner, as they tended to rely on the parish and diocese: thus our friend "Bitter Kaum, native of the parish of Vernes, diocese of Münster."[61] Within perhaps half the expositions, the petitioner described his profession or social status; much more rarely did the claimant list his or her genealogy and filiation, the names of her father and mother, and their places of birth. In cases involving supplicants born abroad of French parents, such a genealogy is expected, and indeed widely found; but among foreigners born abroad without French ancestry, family ties are rarely mentioned. Their absence is further evidence of the alien's juridical lack of family, and the primacy of the geographic location of birth over filiation and descent in the definition of a foreigner. In all cases, the preamble ended with the petitioner exposing his motives and particular circumstances, and humbly requesting to "participate in the advantages and privileges that our subjects and native residents enjoy."[62]

The dispositive section (*dispositif*) of the letter constituted the essence of the privilege and was introduced by a declaration of royal will: "Wishing to favorably treat the aforementioned Bitter Kaum, we have, by our special grace, full power, and royal authority, recognized, deemed, held, and reputed him to be . . . a true and natural subject and native resident." But until the 1660s, and indeed until the end of the Old Regime, the letters varied widely in what followed: some were more elaborated, others more abbreviated. In the 1570s, even as the French juridical ideals of the citizen took shape, the royal model of naturalization permitted, in the texts themselves, a wide variety of styles, including the dispositive sections. Jean Papon's administrative manual reprinted two model texts, and the author noted that there were others. "And others of this kind are drawn up in a variety of styles, as it pleases the [royal] secretaries. I do not know what reason moves them to make some more abbreviated and others more ample."[63] Amplified or not, at a minimum the dispositive contained three clauses: (1) the petitioner was permitted to reside wherever he wanted in the kingdom; (2) he or she was to enjoy all the privileges of a natural-born subject; and (3) he or she could inherit and devolve property freely.

"THAT HE CAN *and it be permissible for him to establish himself and reside in such town or place of our kingdom, countries, lands, and seigneuries of our dominion as he wishes*"

The permission to establish legal residence wherever in the kingdom the beneficiary wanted was a formula that dated from the mid-fourteenth century, and underscored the prerogative of the king to offer a privilege pertaining to the kingdom as a whole, beyond the variety of royal jurisdictions of which it was made up.[64] At the same time, the formula echoed the king's own will, as expressed in the letter, insofar as it permitted residence at the discretion of the beneficiary himself.

Most important, unlike modern practices in France and Europe, naturalization did not require prior residence, although only a very few demands to be naturalized emanated from foreigners established outside the kingdom.[65] Rather, it was the future residence (and eventually, death) in the kingdom that came to be stated as a condition of the letter's validity, beginning with a royal ordinance of Louis XII in 1498, and increasingly so—despite some such exemptions—as the Old Regime evolved.[66]

It is true that Louis XIV offered dispensations, even as the jurists insisted on the clause of residence: almost two-thirds of the forty dispensations in the data sample date from the reign of Louis XIV. The king issued most of these, of course, to princely families and members of the royal household or to high-ranking foreign nobles. Thus Louis XIV's letters of March 1697 to the children of the prince de Carigan, "although resident outside the kingdom, to be able to own all kinds of goods, even offices and benefices, inherit them and dispose of them or transmit them to their legitimate heirs, even though they do not reside in France." A similar clause was added to the letters given in January 1698 to the princes and princesses born or to be born of the grand duke of Tuscany's marriage; to those of July 1702 given to the duke of Savoy; and to those of 1727 issued to the duke of Württemberg, to the prince of Montbéliard in 1713 (who was also dispensed from the practice of Catholicism), and others.[67] Nor was it only the families of foreign princes: abbot Zongo Oudedey de Pezzaro in 1704 and the abbots Louis and Jacques de Qualterio in 1723, all nephews of cardinals, received naturalizations with exemptions of residence. It is true that litigation continued to surround these cases, particularly concerning the inheritability of the exemption. To mention but one example: the twelve-year lawsuit surrounding the estate of Alphonse Henri del Pozzo, marquis de la Cisterne, who was naturalized with a dispensation to reside outside the kingdom, and whose eldest son and sister in 1754 claimed the right to benefit from such an exemption. The solicitor-general of the Paris parlement, Joly de Fleury, argued that such a dispensation was not inheritable (despite the text of the letter), and the marquis's heirs were denied their claims.[68] More important, after the reign of Louis XIV, there were fewer such exemptions, although they were not completely exceptional. Among others, in 1771, Emile Lante de la Rovère, abbot of Grand Selve in Rome and the grandson of an Italian duchess naturalized by Louis XIV, received his own naturalization with permission to hold benefices of up to thirty thousand livres and a dispensation of residence.[69] The king's power to exempt highly connected individuals suggests only that his sovereign power stood above the "common law" of the kingdom, not that the legal norms failed to take the residency requirement seriously.

Another, seemingly minor, exception to the rule permitting the foreigner to reside freely "wherever he wants in the kingdom" masked a major fact of religious difference. Some one hundred cases that appear in the database of this book subtly restricted residence to "towns and places" in the province of Alsace. In certain cases, this was a restriction stated negatively: Dietrich Jacob Ayme in February 1733 "could not settle in any other part of our kingdom but the province of Alsace." In others, it was cast more positively: Jean Georges Bockshammer from Montbéliard received his letter in May 1736 and was permitted to "live in whichever city or place in our kingdom in our province of Alsace which pleases him."[70]

The beneficiaries of these letters of restricted residence were all members of the Protestant faith, either Lutherans or Calvinists, for only in the Protestant districts and principalities that made up "Alsace" (including Colmar) was the practice of the "reformed religion" permissible after the conquests of Louis XIV.[71] Elsewhere in France, between the revocation of the Edict of Nantes in 1685 and the Edict of Toleration in 1787, Roman Catholicism was the only officially recognized faith. Foreign Protestants could, of course, come to France after the revocation of the Edict of Nantes. Indeed, the royal council specifically encouraged them to do so in ordinances of January and June 1686 as it countered rumors that all Protestants were banished from France. The edict was repeated by the royal declaration of 14 May 1724, and throughout the eighteenth century many foreign Protestants did settle in the kingdom.[72] Central to the banking and financial communities, foreign Protestants, living and dead, were tolerated around the Swedish and English embassies in Paris, Marseille, and elsewhere.[73] In many ways, foreign Protestants had a more viable civil status in France than native ones; in any case, and despite the threat that the droit d'aubaine would be collected at their deaths, they appear to have been in a better condition than foreign Protestants who had become French citizens before 1685. The latter were forced to convert, and frequently punished for relapse by having their properties seized at their death. Such was the sorry case of Gerard Pitters, born in Amsterdam, naturalized in April 1673 along with his Dutch wife Margueritte Bernard, after having lived in Nantes for over thirty years. Like the rest of the naturalized Protestants, he was required by the revocation of the Edict of Nantes, to become Catholic or to flee. He stayed but was found to have relapsed, for on his death in 1701 his estate, worth thirty thousand livres, was seized and offered as a royal gift to a faithful Catholic subject of the king.[74]

Foreign Protestants, especially German Lutherans, who naturalized after 1685 sometimes made explicit their religious faith in the expository address of the letter, and were restricted in their residence to Alsace. But some were ritually and textually identified as "Catholics" whose residence was then restricted to Alsace: this was one of several administrative fictions that permitted Protestant foreigners to become citizens.[75] Beginning in the 1750s, royal officials and barristers increasingly recognized these administrative fictions as means to overcome legal prohibitions on the exercise of the so-called Reformed Religion in the kingdom. As the keeper of the seals wrote in 1785, "Letters of naturalization are given to Protestants on the condition that they reside in a province where this religion is tolerated, for example Alsace, where they are obliged to have them registered. And if for their business or other reasons they were obliged to move their residence to another province, they could only do it after obtaining a simple permission of residence in the province of their choice."[76] Yet such simple permissions were rarely necessary, since the royal administration willingly played into the ambiguous legal distinction between "residence" and "domicile." Thus the letter issued to Raymond Archer and his family, Protestants from Geneva, in 1785. Even though they were listed as "currently living in Port-au-Prince, in Saint Domingue," the Archers were given a naturalization that restricted their residence to Alsace. The royal secretary who drafted the letters requested of the chancellery that they be expedited and signed "if nothing opposes them," and apparently nothing did.[77] In this and dozens of other cases, then, it became possible for foreign Protestants to acquire French nationality in the Old Regime long before French Protestants. They did so by taking advantage of the administrative fiction of residence that the monarchy devised in conjunction and collusion with foreign Protestants themselves.

"THAT HE ENJOY *the privileges, franchises, and liberties that our true and original subjects and native residents possess*"

In many ways, this second clause of the dispositive section of the letter of naturalization might seem to lie at the heart of the legal fiction of naturalization. After all, nothing could be more explicit than a general declaration that the foreigner would partake of all the "privileges, franchises, and liberties" enjoyed "as if" (to follow the fictions of the jurists) he or she had been born (and was resident) in the kingdom. Yet the phrase was without substance, precisely because of what Jean Bodin had argued: that to define the "citizen" in terms of his "privileges" would inevitably result in a multiplicity of definitions. The Old Regime monarchy never elaborated the statutory content of what it meant to become a French citizen, nor did jurists ever attempt to lay down what those common privileges and "rights" might be. Only the French National Assembly in 1789 made explicit the "rights of Man and the Citizen"; only the Constitution of 1791 set down, in public law, the conditions of becoming French; and only in 1803 did the French Civil Code define "nationality" (the quality of being a Frenchman or woman) as a status of persons. Instead, under the Old Regime, the logic of naturalization left these privileges of the French citizen defined essentially by what they were not—foreigners with civil incapacities, especially surrounding property inheritance. Thus the third formula of the dispositive section of the letter, which addressed the principal legal disability of the alien.

"THAT HE BE *able to inherit, have, and possess all goods both movable and immovable that he has acquired and could acquire subsequently, or that would be given to him, resigned in his favor, and left to him in whatsoever manner; and of these goods, to enjoy, control, and dispose of by last will and testament, donations among the living, or otherwise, as he is allowed by the law; and after his death, his heirs and others to whom he has given the said goods can inherit from him as long as they be native residents* [regnicoles], *everything as if the claimant had been born in the kingdom.*"[78]

This central legal fiction, the privilege of allowing foreigners to inherit and devolve property, lay at the core of the letter of naturalization. Its evident referent was to the droit d'aubaine, and the remainder of the dispositive section of the letter explicitly underscored the foreigner's exemption from the king's claims to the droit d'aubaine. The claimant was given the letters "without, by means of any laws or regulations, his being given any trouble or impediment, nor that we be able to make a claim [to properties] by the droit d'aubaine or by any other means." The ability to transfer property across generations, identified with the king's relinquishment of the droit d'aubaine, was at the heart of becoming a citizen, and indeed of citizenship itself in the Old Regime, at least before the mid-eighteenth century. Afterward, in the New Regime, property was to become a condition of citizenship, as in the enlightened reform projects of the Physiocrats and ministers, or in the nineteenth-century constitutional regimes of property qualifications. In the New Regime "citizenship" (as political rights) was premised on the ownership of property, while "citizenship" (as nationality) in the Old Regime was organized around the transmission of property and the capacity to inherit.

This principal clause of the dispositive, cast as a legal fiction that allowed foreigners to act with respect to their property "as if" they were born natives, is found without elaboration in the majority of the six thousand individual grants of citizenship collected for this book. Yet more than a third of the naturalizations correspond in addition to another of Jean Papon's model texts of the 1570s, in which naturalization appears as the mechanism "to qualify the foreigner to hold spiritual benefices or temporal offices." In these letters, the dispositive includes a further clause:

> And that [the recipient of the letter] can accept, hold, and possess in our kingdom and lands of our dominion all and each of the benefices that he is given and canonically conferred by good and just title without derogating the said decrees, concordats, privileges, and liberties of the Gallican Church, up to the sum of [e.g., 1,500] livres of annual revenue, all charges deducted; and he can take possession and enjoy these benefices like one of our natural subjects and original Frenchmen [*sujet naturel et Français d'origine*].

The privileges permitting foreigners to hold spiritual or temporal benefices varied substantially, but there were three distinct sets of conditions that could be imposed.[79] One variant made explicit that should any "differences" or lawsuits result from these benefices, they must be resolved before "our judges."[80] Another specified, in cases involving pontifical benefices, the derogation of the Boulogne Concordat, which since 1516 had regulated the relations between the papacy and the French crown. It required that the claimant "within six months bring and place in the hands of our Chancellor of France an Apostolic Brief in which our Holy Father the Pope accords and consents that although the said benefices were opened in Rome [the claimant] be nonetheless given them only by our nomination or the nomination of those in our kingdom that have the right to nominate, under the penalty of forfeiture."[81] A third category included a set of restrictive clauses stipulating that the intendants, administrators, and vicars general of the beneficiary in charge of souls must be French.[82]

In the sixteenth and early seventeenth centuries, such grants to hold ecclesiastical benefices were distinct from letters of naturalization, and until the end of the Old Regime it was still possible for clerics to seek naturalization separately from the explicit permission to hold ecclesiastical benefices (although the former was required in order to devolve the accumulated inheritance of such benefices). But such examples become rarer under Louis XIV, and in the century and a half before the French Revolution, the vast majority of foreign clerics sought naturalization that included the clause of permission to hold benefices.

If Papon's two "model letters" of naturalization accounted for nearly all the six thousand letters sampled between 1660 and 1789, there were nonetheless a number of outliers, evidence of an extreme fragmentation of practices. Occasionally, grants of naturalization would make specific references to the uses to which the letter would be put. For example, Jacques Behr from Liège received letters of naturalization in 1788 that included a request to have recognized and validated the law school degrees he had received at Rheims in 1787, even though he was a foreigner. Louis Berthollet, born in the parish of Talloire near Annecy (Savoy), had been received as a doctor at the medical faculty of the University of Turin in 1770, and his naturalization of February 1778 explicitly recognized the validity of his foreign credentials in France.[83] Other letters (ten in the sample) combined royal legitimation with naturalization, such as those given to Antoine Mathieu, for his son, in 1663. Mathieu, born in Sweden, was a struggling draper who, after settling in Lyon, had an illegitimate son with a Lutheran woman, whom he sought to benefit by naturalizing and legitimating.[84]

There were twenty-six cases involving ennoblement (or the recognition of noble status) and naturalization. An illustrative example of naturalization and ennoblement was that of Jean Ernest Terwell from Westphalia, orphaned at the age of twelve, sent to Holland to learn the sciences, who died at Sedan in 1678, after having left one the first modern cadastres of Champagne.[85] The jurists were ambivalent about foreign noble status: Charles Loyseau (son of the Paris barrister Antoine Loysel), for example, asserted that "foreigners who are certainly noble in their own country . . . will be taken for nobles in France." But he also claimed that noble foreigners could not acquire the privileges of their rank in France by simple naturalization, "for not being citizens of France, much less can they be nobles. . . . and just as legitimation does not include ennoblement, as I said, neither do lettres de naturalité." In fact, since the fourteenth century, the acquisition of nobility was independent of nativeness.[86] The occasional "recognition of nobility" that accompanied naturalization inevitably was approved by one of the royal councils, and had, in addition, to be addressed and registered at the Cour des Aides as well as the fiscal law courts.[87]

Finally, the sample of naturalizations includes a handful of letters that gave to the foreign petitioners the same rights to inherit or devolve property as in the model letter of naturalization, but they were specifically not called letters of naturalization, as the petitioner failed to fulfill one or more of the conditions required by the letter of the law—normally, but not exclusively, the status of being a Catholic. Such letters represent what can only be termed "double fictions": on the one hand, they granted the same rights of acquiring and disposing property through inheritance "as if" their recipients were native Frenchmen or women; on the other hand, they were not called lettres de naturalité but had the same effect, "as if" they were letters. Identical in their formula, the difference was nominative, not substantive. Such doubly fictional letters implicated two groups in particular. First, there were a small number of Protestants who benefited from such letters, such as the English gentleman Samuel Hayes in 1733, whose lawyer—in a petition to the French foreign ministry—cited a number of precedents, Protestant and non-Protestant alike, including the marquise of Pianesse in 1669 and the comte de Hoim in 1727.[88] Second, a handful of Jewish families from Avignon and Bordeaux living in Paris received doubly fictional letters, giving them the same inheritance rights as both naturalized foreigners and native Frenchmen. These were among the numerous instances of administrative fictions whereby non-Catholic foreigners (but not Muslims) could acquire the same civil status as French citizens, at a moment when only the Catholic faith was officially recognized in the kingdom.[89]

More significant, in a statistical and legal sense, was the distinction made by the jurists and other commentators between letters of naturalization and letters of declaration of naturalization (*déclaration de naturalité*).[90] The latter, sealed on yellow wax with a single tail to signify the "transitory" nature of the act, had no retroactive effect. In contrast to letters, declarations of naturalization did not purport to change the nature of the claimant, however fictionally. Following the jurisprudence of the seventeenth and eighteenth centuries, they were limited to recognizing a preexisting state or quality, "to lift an impediment that had suspended its execution," according to the then royal solicitor-general at the Paris parlement, Henri-François d'Aguesseau.[91] The crown had originally issued declarations for natives of territories and districts believed to have been part of its "ancient domain" following the example of those issued by Francis I to Flemings after the Treaty of Cambrai, and continued episodically to do so in the eighteenth century.[92] But by then, the privileged treatment of "near foreigners," natives from the Spanish (and after 1714, the Austrian) Low Countries fell into disfavor. In 1779, the foreign minister insisted that foreigners born in the Austrian Low Countries "are as much foreigners in France as the other subjects [of the empire] and I know of no act that establishes any exceptions in this regard concerning the former."[93] The use of declarations grew substantially in the seventeenth and eighteenth centuries as they became sought by

Frenchmen and women born abroad who returned to the kingdom to reclaim their original identity. Examples include the daughter of a high-ranking French father born outside the kingdom, and Marie Caroline Léocadie des Ursins, born in Liège in 1720 of a French mother whose own father was Maréchal de France, who was instructed to take letters by her "honorary tutor" François duc d'Harcourt, a peer of France.[94]

In practice, however, the Great Chancellery did not always follow established rules and norms: not all petitioners born outside the kingdom of French parents received declarations, nor were declarations alone given to petitioners born of French parents outside of France. Even some native subjects of the French king descended from foreigners received individual naturalizations (not declarations) as was the case in 1776 with Jean Hans Delap, born in Bordeaux of Irish parents. Although the letters of the privilege of naturalization and the vast jurisprudence on the question attributed the "quality of Frenchness" to such individuals, there were many who, like Delap, "fearing to be disturbed with the excuse that he is a son of a foreigner," sought and received naturalization.[95] Perhaps the memory of 1697, when Louis XIV had named as "foreigners" families descended from immigrants who had arrived in the kingdom since 1600, was still alive late in the Old Regime. Certainly, a large number of descendants of foreigners throughout the eighteenth century sought formal declarations of their original nationality, so as to enjoy without disruption the civil law capacities that were due to them with their birth in the kingdom.[96] Aliens—both long-term residents in the kingdom and Frenchmen and women whose French parents had settled abroad—were more likely to seek to be "declared naturalized" than to seek full-blown letters of naturalization because the latter cost twice as much. Whether it was the result of pressure from petitioners and their patrons or the inevitable sloppiness of bureaucratic procedure, the Great Chancellery and the royal secretaries charged with redacting the letter often deviated from the norms in their decisions about who should be fully naturalized, and who might be simply recognized by declaration as fictionally equivalent to a "natural Frenchman."

There were, nonetheless, at least three principal conditions and limitations placed on the naturalized foreigner and the recipient of a declaration of naturalization in the dispositive section of the letter. First, property could be deeded to "children or heirs" only if they were native residents of the kingdom (regnicoles), a caveat that was regularly added to the main section of the dispositive in the 1670s. Second, the dispositive section of the naturalization grant ended with a mobility and residency restriction: the foreigner agreed to "finish his days in France," and—especially in letters after 1666 and at times of warfare— "not to leave the kingdom without the express written permission of the king." The third limitation was that the foreigner "not enter into relations with [s'entremettre avec] other foreigners." A fourth condition, implicitly required by its usual presence in the narrative exposé of the protocol, and according to most historical accounts, was the condition of being a Catholic.

"PROVIDED HIS HEIRS *are native residents*"

The first condition—*proviso quod heredes* (or *heredes impetrantis*) *sint regnicolae* in the Latin still common among the learned lawyers of the sixteenth century—was universally acknowledged by early modern jurists as essential to the fiction of naturalization, even when they disagreed about the definition of a native resident.[97] Jean Papon, Jean Bacquet, and other sixteenth-century jurists acknowledged that the legitimate children born of a man who had "taken a wife in France" and who resided in the kingdom were "reputed to be French." In practice, no such formal marriage requirement of the foreigner petitioning for naturalization ever entered into the jurisprudence (nor did marriage serve to transmit nationality, as it did in the New Regime). But the jurists concurred early in the legal fiction that a child of a foreigner, born in France, was not subject to the droit d'aubaine, and thus was "reputed to be" French.

Just as the jurists invoked an "ancient," "common," and "French" tradition in restricting the capacity to inherit to a native subject, so in practice did chancellery officials seek to ensure that the restriction appeared on all letters and declarations, at least according to a memoir of the 1630s.[98] Both understood that in the case of the offspring born in France of a foreigner who died without legitimate family members to succeed him, the inheritance belonged to the king "by the right over aliens [*à titre d'aubain*]." The rule applied not only to first-generation descendants but to a projected and imagined "lineage" that came to define the aubain. Thus, wrote the barrister Bosquet, elaborating on the remarks of Bacquet a generation earlier, "the droit d'aubaine is levied *in infinitum* toward persons descended from foreigners." His contemporary, the hack legal compiler Papon, commented more expansively that

> the said droit d'aubaine does not stop and end, but endures in the persons of the said children, nephews, offspring, or other descendants, infinitely and without exception. If any of these die without children, or their children without children, the said fisc inherits from them, in all cases, by the droit d'aubaine. There is no difference between these descendants and the [original] father, except that the latter could not draw up a will, and the fisc inherited as a result. But none of this applies to children born in France, who are not foreigners, and who by law can make a will and dispose of their goods, having been born in France . . . [99]

Some jurists—especially from customary-law regions—diverged with this view, but only because they insisted that seigneurs who had privileges of "higher justice" (*seigneurs haut-justiciers*) should inherit when such an individual died in their jurisdictions without heirs (as per their seigneurial privileges of escheat). Such were the arguments of Charles Loyseau and Pierre Basnage, both learned commentators on customary law, the former of Paris, the latter of Normandy. But regardless of who might be the appropriate recipient of the escheat confiscated from the descendants of a foreigner, all jurists agreed that the restriction requiring a foreigner to pass on property to a native subject went on "infinitely."[100]

An unintentional effect of this practice was to constitute a notion of lineage that was attached to the condition of foreignness. In the 1750s, in the spirit of an Enlightened thought that would help dismantle the droit d'aubaine as a remnant of servitude, the attorney Jean-Baptiste Denisart returned to the medieval vocabulary of *aubenage* ("alienness") in declaring that that "alienness is a personal vice. The stain of foreignness is not transmittable."[101] But in fact, the "stain" or "vice" was transmitted across generations, if not exactly as blood or race, then nonetheless within the "natural order" of property succession. The widespread belief that native-born Frenchmen were tainted by their parents or grandparents' origins helps to explain the definition of foreigners that informed the 1697 Naturalization Tax: foreigners were not only immigrants resident in the kingdom but also the descendants of immigrants from as many as two generations earlier. In the eighteenth century, the barristers and magistrates who adjudicated individual questions about the applicability of the droit d'aubaine did not make use of the sweeping definition of the "law of blood" or the general principle of descent, but they did share the conception that "foreignness" was essentially a quality transmitted through families in their inheritance of property.

"To FINISH HIS *days in the kingdom*"

The first part of this laconic formula was in fact of supreme importance to the jurists and to the royal council in the seventeenth and eighteenth centuries, even if its actual meanings (the relation between residence and domicile, for example) were the subject of much jurisprudential debate. Legal historians have sometimes argued that the requirement of residence became less stringent in the course of the early modern period, as witnessed by the large and apparently increasing number of "exemptions" issued by the French chancellery in this period.[102] But the number of exemptions actually peaked under Louis XIV and declined during the eighteenth century. More, their conferral represents a set of exemplary exceptions of an increasingly entrenched and contrary norm: that the foreigner was required to finish his days in the kingdom.

In fact, the residence clause does not appear in any of the model texts of naturalization before Du Sault's 1666 manual. Nor did the sixteenth-century juridical model emphasize the question of future residence until death in the kingdom (although it could be argued that they assumed a permanent residence based on their presumption of the social integration and assimilation of the naturalized foreigner). But by the middle of the seventeenth century, both the juridical and the royal model of naturalization adopted the requirement that the foreigner "finish his days in the kingdom," a phrase that quickly became part of French common law.[103] A century later, the requirement of residence became a necessary condition of naturalization. Lefebvre de la Planche in the 1730s wrote that even if the clause were omitted in the letter itself, the Chambre des comptes, responsible for verifying the letters, inserted it: "The conditions of this adoption are no less constant: there is only one required, which is a faithful commitment to make a continuous residence in the new country that the foreigner has chosen, and where he has been granted the privilege of being received." Bourjon, in his best-selling dictionary of French law, concurred: "The nonresidence of the foreigner destroys the effect of letters of naturalization that he [has] obtained: it is a renunciation of the right that resulted from them; it is the nonexecution of their tacit condition which, as a result, annuls them."[104] Such an apparently incontestable claim was, of course, the subject of an extensive jurisprudence in the sixteenth and early seventeenth centuries. But by the reign of Louis XIV, the interests of the crown and the presumptions of the jurists about residence had already converged in the text of the privilege of naturalization: the permanent residence in the kingdom until the death of the beneficiary of naturalization was a sine qua non of the privilege itself.

Residence mattered in the Old Regime. Not that it hadn't mattered on specific occasions in the later middle ages or the Renaissance. In 1499, Louis XII had annulled the naturalizations of Italians who had not established their residence in France.[105] But it was only under Louis XIV and after that both the royal and juridical models of naturalization took seriously the residency requirement, even as Louis XIV gave out dispensations as royal privilege. Under his successor, in 1718 and again in 1720, faced with a significant increase in naturalizations of Genoese sailors who evidently failed to establish residence, the crown revoked all such grants to nonresident foreigners. In the eighteenth century, the jurists concurred unanimously, following the commentary of Paul Charles, a royal professor of French law at Paris, that exemptions of residency in the letters amounted to further "privileged exemptions" ("*exemptions d'aubaine et de privilège*") and not "rights of naturalization with a dispensation of residence" ("*droits de naturalité avec dispense d'incolat*"). They were exceptions that did not contradict in any way the general rule "that the adoption by a State of a new citizen presumes, on the part of the citizen, a sincere desire to establish himself in the kingdom."[106]

Moreover, the increased importance of residence at the end of the Old Regime was attested by the fact that not all requests for exemption were granted. Thus the case of the very noble (but apparently not well connected) Jean Nepomuc Joseph-François Xavier François de Paul de Nortlitz et de Reinech, comte du Saint-Empire, who made a "request for simple letters of naturalization, without title, privileges, or rank" in 1780. An unsigned letter from the chancellery summarized the case: "He claims that for reasons of health, following the advice of doctors, he wishes to pass part of the year in the southern provinces of the kingdom where he has designs on a small plot of land which, in case of death, he would like to devolve to his children." Chancellor Maupeou and Foreign Minister Vergennes agreed that naturalization, in this case, was not appropriate:

> A simple permission to acquire, possess, and dispose of property in France would be less subject to obstacles [*inconvenients*] than letters of naturalization. Since these letters need to contain the clause of fixing a domicile in the kingdom and since M. le comte de Norlitz does not appear to have this project, it would be necessary that he regularly get specific permissions to leave France, which would result in embarrassment and danger.[107]

In the eighteenth-century jurisprudence about the residency clause, those barristers who argued for its necessity tended to be upheld in the decisions of the courts. Such was the result in a contested inheritance between the Prince of Loewenstein Wertheim, defendant, against the claims of the Sieur de Giovanni and the Prince de Condé in 1764. The latter argued that Loewenstein Wertheim, naturalized in 1751, was domiciled in Lorraine, and that Lorraine was not legally part of the royal domain. But much of the case turned less on the legal status of Lorraine than on the clause in the letter itself, that of "finishing his days in the kingdom." The Prince of Loewenstein's lawyer, maître Gin, argued that the phrase did not require an "actual domicile." Citing the lawyer Argou, and thickening his case with legal precedents (Bignon's successful arguments in the Vanelli case of 1641), he distinguished between "domicile" of intention and of fact. The "promise" in the letter proved, in fact, merely the intention; the interval of Loewenstein's absence from the kingdom was without bearing on that intention, since it constituted a mere domicile of "fact."[108] Loewenstein's lawyer's verbal gymnastics were not convincing, and he lost the case.

Residence, for the jurists, might be considered the palimpsestic trace of social assimilation and integration; for the crown, it was the only stated condition, however unelaborated, that signified the permanent loyalty of the foreign citizen. In fact, nearly all demands for naturalization came from long-established foreigners in the kingdom, who naturally, it might be supposed, would finish their days in the kingdom; and it was only in litigious cases involving claims of natives and purported foreigners, or those who had been naturalized, that the question was raised to the level of jurisprudential consideration. At this level, the jurists and the crown concurred: they both argued the principle that future residence "until death" was a necessary condition that made the letter of naturalization legally valid.

The Loewenstein case further raised the second part of the residency requirement: the clauses at the end of the dispositive section of the letter that forbade its recipient to leave the kingdom without a royal permission that was explicit (and written, as the eighteenth-century formulas and examples of naturalization were to add). To require that a naturalized foreigner receive written permission to leave the kingdom seemed to place him ostensibly in the same category as citizens, who by royal legislation under Louis XIV, and especially in the infamous ordinance of 1669, were theoretically subject to the same requirements. Modern historians, implicitly following the commentary of Lefebvre de la Planche, have pointed to the 1669 ordinance as a significant turning point in the royal policies and laws of the French state, which increasingly sought to restrict mobility and movement. They have also linked the ordinance explicitly to the problem of "fugitive citizens," the families of Protestants who had fled France both before and after the Edict of Nantes. In fact, the preamble of the 1669 ordinance reveals explicitly that the law was not directed toward the Protestant flight, but was conceived with a mercantilist concern to stem the drain of skilled labor from the kingdom, especially those engaged in naval construction.

> During the recent times of disorder, several of our subjects, forgetting what they owe from birth, have gone to foreign countries and worked there in all areas of their expertise, even in shipbuilding [and] maritime transport. . . . We forbid all our subjects to establish themselves definitively without our permission in foreign countries through marriage, the acquisition of lands, the settlement of their families and goods in order to set up a stable establishment without intention of returning, with the penalty of seizing their bodies and goods without the ability to be reestablished or rehabilitated, or their children naturalized, for whatever reason.[109]

The 1669 ordinance rendered those Frenchmen and women who established themselves abroad, without the consent of the king, incapable of inheriting property in France, thus affirming what was already a "traditional" doctrine. But it also made their goods subject to confiscation and refused to allow their heirs to become naturalized.[110] As such, French natives were placed in a considerably more onerous position than that of aliens. As Denisart noted nearly a century later, the Frenchman who went to live abroad did not even possess the privilege of the foreigner, who may have been incapable of inheriting but who could nonetheless freely dispose of his goods in the kingdom during his lifetime.[111]

It is true that the 1669 ordinance, originally conceived as part of the highest form of mercantilism under Colbert, was reinterpreted within the religious controversy surrounding the king's withdrawal in 1685 of the Edict of Nantes.

In the royal ordinance of 1698, such a slippage was made explicit, and its conditions clarified, when Louis XIV permitted the offspring of Protestants who had fled France to return to the kingdom and become legal heirs, provided they produced a certificate of Catholicity. But was 1669 such a turning point? Lefebvre de la Planche, writing in the 1730s, believed that earlier edicts and royal legislation before 1669 had assumed that the "mutual obligations of sovereign and subject" did not cease with the emigration of a French citizen, and he cited Bodin as proof. Other sixteenth-century authors, according to Lefebvre, had also clearly distinguished transitory and ephemeral exit from the kingdom from definitive emigration, as evidenced by marriage, officeholding, or letters of naturalization taken from a foreign prince. Certainly the question was hotly contested, as the crown attempted to regulate the status of the children of the diaspora in the 1720s and 1730s. But by the 1730s, the normative presumption was that French citizens could leave the country, and that their children born abroad could inherit, provided they returned to reside in the kingdom.[112] The edict, however, was frequently invoked as an argument in court cases set in the borderland provinces, especially Alsace, and within litigation between direct and collateral heirs of Protestant refugees.

Residence in the kingdom, then, was a critical component in the royal and juridical models of French citizenship and naturalization. Not that residence alone was ever a sufficient condition of citizenship in France. Unlike Spain in the same period, where residence and the local acquisition of citizenship established "nativeness" in the different parts of the Spanish Empire (defined principally by the ability to hold benefices and offices, but also to trade with the New World colonies), the acquisition of French citizenship depended entirely on the crown's sovereign intervention in the letter of naturalization. Unlike England (despite the claims of Lefebvre de la Planche and others), French law never recognized a "natural allegiance" that persisted despite emigration from the kingdom; allegiance and loyalty were premised and guaranteed on the basis of legal and permanent residence in the kingdom.

"To NOT ENTER *into relations with other foreigners*"

The third condition of the dispositive section within the letter of naturalization seems to have been of a different order than the requirement for residency: its meaning is more ambiguous, and it occasioned no jurisprudential debate. No civil litigation over contested inheritances ever turned on this clause, even in the frontier provinces, nor did the frequent contestations between "foreigners" and native residents over the acquisition and exercise of benefices and offices make reference to it. Obviously, the formula did not target or describe the everyday relations of naturalized foreigners living in the borderlands of the kingdom, in Artois, Metz, Provence, or the Pyrennean districts. Nor did it generally apply to commercial and economic relations that brought foreigners into daily contact with French citizens, especially in the port cities of the kingdom and in Paris. It is true that, within the mercantilist precepts of the crown, French natives were discouraged from employing foreign commercial agents. But such strictures were unenforceable and, if enforced, would run counter to the economic interests of the king and the kingdom. Rather, the clause seems to bear traces of the mercantilist precept that sought to protect the wealth of the kingdom at the expense of foreign states, and an even more ancient and xenophobic fear that capital might be in the hands of other than natural-born French subjects. These were concerns expressed in royal legislation, especially that covering the frontier provinces.[113] But the letter of naturalization failed to invoke the "public" dimension of the prohibitions that were occasionally mandated by the king, and in practice the strictures against "having relations with" foreigners seems to have had a more political connotation. If anything, the phrase makes reference to the "police" of foreigners in the capital under Louis XIV, and especially within the diplomatic and ambassadorial milieus, the subject of the admirable work by Lucien Bély.[114] Once again, the condition does not appear in either the naturalizations or the legal commentary of the sixteenth and early seventeenth centuries, but it was used consistently after the 1660s—and continued well after the abandonment of traditional mercantilist economic policies.

Periodically and occasionally, during the eighteenth century, an additional clause and condition pertaining to the economic rights of naturalized foreigners makes its appearance: "The claimant can enjoy the privileges and advantages of our subjects in commercial relations following the treaties signed with different nations only after having lived in France during six consecutive years, and with the condition of bringing a proper and legal certificate by the magistrates of the places [where he has lived]." This specific condition of the disposition of naturalizations can be found among letters given to the Genoese and other Italians in 1718 and the early 1720s, and to other foreigners sporadically from the late 1730s until the 1770s. Here, the remnants of mercantilism moved into a more general economic protectionism. The target was not so much the flight of capital per se but the all-too-common practice of taking letters strictly to enjoy the privileges of French merchants while not establishing residence in the kingdom. In this sense, the clause simply reinforced the growing requirement of residence as the sine qua non of naturalization during the Old Regime.

"AND PROFESSING THE *Catholic, Apostolic, and Roman faith*"

It should be clear by now that historians who assume the existence of a fourth condition, religious conformity, have not adequately understood the legal fictions by which Protestants and Jews acquired French citizenship.[115] In this, they follow the lead of the apologists of the monarchy, at least its most conservative elements. The king's attorney at the Paris Chambre des comptes,

Lefebvre de la Planche, whose anti-Semitic diatribes backfired in forcing the state to grant individual naturalizations to Jewish families from Bordeaux, Avignon, and Metz, noted how easy it was to acquire letters in France. "Without inquiry into background, letters of naturalization are given to all foreigners who come with the intention of establishing themselves [in France], provided that they be of the Catholic faith."[116] True that the preamble of the definitive model text produced early in the reign of Louis XV included the clause that the petitioner professed as a Catholic, and several examples of naturalization and declarations of naturalization from the eighteenth century even include the condition as a dependent clause at the end of the dispositive section of the letter. Thus the case of a letter to the Englishman Jean Stone of January 1733 to which, in draft form, the clause was added in the dispositive section: "provided nonetheless that he profess the Catholic, Apostolic, and Roman faith."[117] Such a formal condition in the dispositive of the letter can be found even before the revocation of the Edict of Nantes in 1685, when, for example, the Irish merchant Matthieu Porter and his family, fleeing religious persecution as Catholics in England, settled in France and received a letter of naturalization in 1665 that underscored their identity as Catholics in the dispositive clause of the letter.[118]

But the requirement was hardly universally applied. Although such sixteenth-century jurists as Papon, Bacquet, and Choppin commented extensively on the residency and inheritance clauses, none mentioned the requirement of Catholicity. Even Chancellor Michel de l'Hôpital, advocate of the Politique position, explicitly stated in 1561 that "many can be citizens who are not Christians"—although, of course, he did so within a Latin lexicon, and was referring to the political dimensions of citizenship as service to the public good.[119] Only after the Edict of Nantes in 1598 allowed Protestants to publicly practice their religion under conditions specified by the monarchy, and only after the death of its author, Henry IV, in 1610, did the chancellery and royal secretaries begin to add a standard rhetorical clause to the initial protocol and exposé about the petitioner, claiming that he or she "professed the Catholic, Apostolic, and Roman faith." By the 1640s, most letters contained this clause; thus, even before the revocation of the Edict of Nantes in 1685, the presumption and normative practice was to identify Catholicism and citizenship.

But many foreign Protestants, naturalized by the crown, escaped the conditional requirement of being practicing Catholics as stated in the dispositive section of the letter. Sometimes, the clause was simply omitted, and the religion of the claimant went unstated in the exposé: such was the case in letters of naturalization given to John Law in 1716, registered at the Paris parlement; and those given to the maréchal de Berwick in 1703, his wife Anne Berkeley, and his son Jacques Fitz James, in April 1714.[120] These—and there were others—involved high-standing nobles whose services to the monarchy "effaced the stain of heresy." It is true that not all Protestants were so privileged, for in

1756 a German Lutheran named Le Coq was turned down for a letter of naturalization. An official in the ministry of foreign affairs, de Bussy, reiterated the "official" argument that as long as foreigners were not Catholics, they could not obtain letters. Fictions were of no use: "The disguise cannot take place and would serve no purpose; the first thing demanded will be the extract of the baptismal act, and as soon as it is seen to be signed by a Lutheran minister, the declaration of naturalization will be refused, and will only be given with an act of abjuration by a Catholic priest."[121] Yet as we have already seen, the "disguise" often *did* take place by restricting residence to the province of Alsace, as was the case of the Protestant Jean Heylaud in 1757, whose letter of naturalization was signed and sealed despite the fact, explicitly noted, of "a difference of religion."[122] Here might be the one exception to the rule of procedural automaticity: connections among Protestants may well have counted in their ability to secure naturalization before the second half of the eighteenth century.

After the 1760s, however, and in the context of widespread public debate about the citizenship of French Protestants, legal commentators increasingly drew attention to the administrative fiction of Catholicity and argued for the removal of any residual Catholicity clause. Paul Charles Lorry, the editor and glossator of Lefebvre de la Planche, corrected the author's claim that Catholicity was a necessary condition of naturalization:

> In the formulary letter of naturalization, a clause was introduced, "after it has been shown to us that [the petitioner] is of good moral standing, relations, and of the Catholic faith," but, 1. Letters are registered without any inquiry or verification of the facts; and 2. they are accorded without this clause and no one has complained. The prince gives to religion the respect that is owed when he does not permit the public practice [of] a religion other than his own . . . but in fact [others] live happily and quietly in the heart of France: let us thus abandon a fiction which, too contrary to the facts, is a source of the civil order's deformation.[123]

Still, the fiction was never fully abandoned in the Old Regime's practices of naturalization, and sometimes the monarchy resorted to the doubly fictional letter of naturalization, such as the patent letter given to Samuel Hayes, a Protestant gentleman, and his wife, permitting him "to dispose of his goods in France and to reside there." The letter resembled in form that of a grant of naturalization, but there was no Catholicity clause: the phrases granted him "the same rights, faculties, exemptions, advantages, or privileges that our natural or naturalized subjects enjoy" provided—as in the letters of naturalization—that the petitioner commit himself to "finish his days in France." So too did the Protestant military commander maréchal de Saxe in 1746 receive a patent letter with "permission to settle in France, to acquire and possess all kinds of goods, to dispose of them, with dispensation of inquiry [into his background]." And a handful of Jewish families from Bordeaux, Metz, and Avignon also received these doubly fictional "naturalizations" after 1759.[124]

These double fictions—of patent letters that had value "as if" they were naturalizations, which themselves conferred on foreigners the status to be treated "as if" they were natives—were extremely rare in the Old Regime. In other cases of religious differences, royal secretaries and the chancellery relied on other administrative fictions, such as restricted residence, that masked a confessional diversity. And among the corpus of letters used in this book, the vast majority did not involve foreigners other than Catholics, but deployed other legal and administrative fictions that both revealed and obscured the practice of becoming French.

The dispositive section of the naturalization letter ended with the king's renunciation of any taxes or financial gain for the privilege given to a foreigner. In the seventeenth and eighteenth centuries, naturalization was most often, literally, a gift from the king, and the standard formula was that the king "herewith dispenses without justification [*sans que pour raison due*] the requirement to pay to the kings our successors any tax or indemnity; of whatever sum imposed, we give and shall give a right and remission." Such had not always been the case. Letters of bourgeoisie of one or several towns, or of the kingdom, had been granted for free until 1341, and the jurists of the 1570s collectively remembered that the king had previously received a "finance" (tax) paid at the moment of naturalization "to indemnify the sovereigns for their *droits de chevage, formariage, et aubaine.*" (The first two "feudal" rights had not been levied by the crown since the fourteenth century; the last, of course, was increasingly important in the late sixteenth century). Papon noted that the tax had been proportional to the financial wealth of the naturalized foreigner (following an inquiry undertaken by local judicial officials of his or her place of residence), and Bodin dismissed it as a "modest sum," one hundred écus.[125] After 1570, few naturalizations claimed an indemnity in compensation for the aubain lost to the king, a shift deplored by L'Huiller, royal attorney at the Chambre des comptes, in the early seventeenth century:

> This tax paid by those who are legitimated, naturalized, or ennobled is ancient and domanial; but since other, more important ones came about, such as *gabelles, aides, tailles, fermes* and other extraordinary impositions [in fact, the principal sources of indirect and direct revenue for the crown], attention has not been paid for thirty or forty years to such royal and domanial rights. Presently, of about one hundred legitimations, naturalizations, or ennoblements that are issued every year, there are only a dozen where the [king's] remission [of the fee] has not been given.[126]

If naturalization was in principle a gift, the letter itself did not come cheap. In the reign of Louis XIV, the tariff levied by the chancellery for the seals (*droits de sceau*) rose from 74 livres 9 sols for an individual grant in 1674 (two-thirds of which went to the royal secretary's honorarium, and another modest sum was added for the signature) to over 106 livres in 1704, fees that seem to have stabilized in the eighteenth century.[127] But these sums, already important, were to be amply supplemented by the fees involved in the letter's expedition.

Expediting the Letter: The Routinization of Naturalization from Louis XIV to the French Revolution

The efficacy of the letter of naturalization rested on its legal expedition (*jussio*), the final section of the patent letter of naturalization. The expedition began with the words, "This we give and send" (*Si Donnons et Mandons*), and was addressed first to the magistrates of the appropriate Chambre des comptes of the kingdom, the eight sovereign fiscal courts whose jurisdiction covered the domanial rights and dues of the crown.[128] It instructed these judicial and financial officers to verify and to register the letter, ordered them to undertake an inquiry ("having gathered information on the life, mores, goods, and qualities of the recipient"), and authorized them to levy a tax proportional to the apparent wealth of the claimant. After which, the king thus ordered "the cessation present and future of all troubles and obstacles, notwithstanding anything to the contrary, to which we have given remittance." This registration of the letter of naturalization—in fact, its verification (*vérification*)—by the Chambre des comptes was the subject of an elaborate juridical commentary from the sixteenth to the eighteenth centuries that produced a firm consensus.[129]

The jurists placed the responsibility of having the letters verified at the appropriate Chambre des comptes (in principle corresponding to the place of declared residence) squarely on the shoulders of the claimant, who generally had one year in which to do so. Although barristers and solicitors differed on the exact meaning of verification and registration (as a matter of fiscal law? As evidence of the "civil" contract between king and foreigner?), they agreed that such a procedure was key. Chancellor d'Aguesseau noted that "this sole failure of protocol renders the letters useless," as was found in a number of legal cases, from the widow Flandio's claims to inherit from her husband (by the law *unde vir et uxor*) in 1738, to the more famous case of the inheritance of the duc de Mantua, whose successors lost their case in part because of the duke's failure to have his letters registered at the Chambre des comptes—even though he did have them registered at the Paris parlement.[130]

It was on the occasion of the verification and registration of the letter in the Parisian and provincial Chambres des comptes and the offices of the royal treasury that magistrates, jurists, and fiscal officers became, momentarily and in theory, the gatekeepers of access to French citizenship. On paper, the Chambres were usually ordered, within the expeditionary clause, to undertake an "inquiry" into the moral qualities of the foreign petitioner, his "life, mores, goods, and condition." When they did execute this clause, provincial officeholders of the fiscal courts and bureaux implicitly enacted a pale version of the "juridical model": they pointed to a set of conditions involving the prior social assimilation or the meritorious claims of the resident foreigner in question. In practice, however, they did not insist, beyond a ritualized appraisal, on the moral qualities or social identity of the claimant.

These local inquiries, their appearance and variation in time and space, are notoriously difficult to locate, given the wholesale absence of archival records for the Paris Chambre and most of the provincial ones (see appendix 1). But it would appear that local judicial officials rarely took advantage of their mandate to act as the border guards of French citizenship. Judges and their officials generally did not prioritize such inquiries, their offices being preoccupied with more pressing matters no doubt, but also out of an implicit recognition of the political stakes involved. If the Chambres des comptes were to deny naturalization (and there is no evidence that they ever did so successfully), their act would amount to a direct challenge to the discretionary sovereign authority that had conferred the patent letter itself, and thus to the royal model of legal citizenship that placed the law over politics.[131]

In fact, letters of naturalization that included surviving formal inquiries by the provincial Chambre des comptes make up an extremely small proportion of the sample letters of naturalization and declaration, although how small is difficult to say. The surviving traces of inquiries tend to come from outside the jurisdiction of the Paris Chambre des comptes, and many were undertaken in an irregular fashion. For example, in the 1690s the Rouen Chambre produced a spate of surviving inquiries, but its registers before and after that decade contain relatively few traces of inquiries.[132] More generally throughout the kingdom, such inquiries tended to be more frequent early in the reign of Louis XIV, and much rarer during the eighteenth century.

Among those that survive, in Rouen and elsewhere, the formal investigations of the moral worth and degree of social integration and assimilation of the foreigner were turned into highly stylized and pro-forma bureaucratic procedures. In April 1687, Claude Marteau, aged 68 and born in Laôn in Picardie, received letters on behalf of Julia Bonnardy, his wife aged 59, and their six children born in Venice. The Paris Chambre ordered an inquiry, undertaken by the office of the royal solicitor. Claude Marteau was a jeweler by trade, although not a very successful one: his boutique and movable goods, according to witnesses at the inquiry, were worth one thousand livres at most. The witnesses, who included a lawyer at the Paris parlement and two merchants in Laôn, all offered a similar version of Claude's life: son of a royal notary, he left Laôn when young, settled in Venice and married, and returned twenty years ago. They testified that the family "lives most honestly and without reproach, having always lived properly and most loyally in the service of the king," a ritualized description of loyalty and identity founded on the codes and customs of civility.[133] A year earlier, the Paris Chambre inquired into the life and manners of Louis Pompe, an Italian and Spanish teacher born in Naples. The inquiry into his "life, mores, and religion" was a positive if neutral appraisal: he was "attached to the service of the king, and is neither business agent nor merchant of any foreigner."[134] In these and dozens of other cases, the petitioner was inevitably found to be "of good moral standing," and often to own substantial property, as testified by royal judges, municipal councillors, and local dignitaries who presented themselves before the royal attorney at the local Chambre des comptes. Such testimony, in my investigation, only very rarely produced negative judgments; for the most part the inquiries are platitudinous, ritual formulas about the moral character and the fidelity of the foreigner requesting citizenship.

Only in the case of Protestants, and especially in the years immediately before and after the withdrawal of the Edict of Nantes, did the provincial fiscal courts occasionally contest the royal grant of naturalization, thereby standing up to the king's authority in conferring the grant. In February 1671, the Nantes Chambre des comptes refused to register a letter given to Etienne Procter, an English merchant, until he brought back, within three months, "letters expressing the royal will" concerning his religion, which wasn't mentioned in the original grant. The letters that Procter finally obtained in August 1672 ordered that "without concern about the omission of the clause claiming profession of the so-called Reformed Religion, it be ordered to proceed with the pure and simple registration of the said letters." And as late as 1615, the Paris Chambre had returned a letter to the chancellor "on the basis of it being found that he was of the so-called Reformed Religion," although the letters were subsequently registered.[135] Apart from these isolated cases, always resolved in favor of the crown, the local magistrates never explicitly judged foreigners as unworthy of becoming French citizens. They never adopted in practice the principles, elaborated in the 1570s, of the juridical model of citizenship and naturalization.

Every act mentioned within the expedition (the executionary clause) cost the claimant money, and great effort, since the letter of naturalization was not valid until it was executed, and the costs of doing so increased persistently during the course of the eighteenth century. If the letters patent of naturalization were "gifts of the king" who explicitly renounced his financial interest at the end of the dispositive clause in the letters, such a "gift" was nonetheless frequently matched by a "countergift" required of the foreigner at the moment of registration at the Chambre des comptes, a "tax varying according to the wealth of the recipient," according to the formulaic clause of the letter. Already in the 1570s, Bacquet noted that the Chambre taxed "a small sum such as it wished," but by the eighteenth century the Chambre des comptes more often than not exempted the claimant from such a tax as part of a stylized formula.[136] When such a sum was requested, it was on average around twenty livres, although the tax could run as high as fifty or even one hundred livres. More rarely, it was either remitted to the claimants on the basis of their extreme poverty or left to the entire discretion of the foreigner in question.[137] In the seventeenth and eighteenth centuries, the Chambre des comptes fictionally remitted and transformed the tax into a charitable donation. There were many precedents for doing so. In a royal edict of 1574, Henry III, invoking even earlier edicts, directed that donations made in Paris be given toward the "poor children of the Holy Trinity Church." Such forced charity of the foreign citizen might cost between ten and one hundred livres, at the discretion of the Chambre.[138]

The "gift-tax" of the claimant at the Chambre des comptes was then matched by another gift-tax imposed by the Chambre du domaine et du trésor, where until 1693 the foreigner was further required to register his letter. (After that date, the expeditionary clause of the letter was addressed to the "presidents, treasurers and treasurers-general of France, and to all other relevant fiscal and judicial officials," and registered in the newly reorganized Chambre du domaine and the local financial bureaux.) The requirement of registration at the Chambre du domaine—failure to do so would result in the nullification of the letters—resulted from the famous patent letters of Henry III in 1582, who ordered it done for purely bureaucratic reasons—"for our prosecutors and other offices to consult when needed." In so doing, royal authority claimed to protect the beneficiaries of naturalization from the avarice of the treasury officials, and especially the king's prosecutor of the Chambre du domaine. The 1582 ordinance was considered an act of "publication" that would make known, officially, that a particular beneficiary was to be exempted from the droit d'aubaine.[139] But in practice, of course, the need to register at the Chambre du trésor, and after 1693, the Chambre du domaine and the local financial bureaux, became an added burden and cost to the recipient of a naturalization or declaration—even when the fiscal courts, like the Chambre du domaine, commuted payments into charitable donations.

Such a transformation of the "tax" into an act of charity, however formulaic it was to become in practice, was nonetheless a revealing and significant act. Paul Charles Lorry, annotating Lefebvre de la Planche's text in the 1760s, speculated that such charity to the poor was a "contribution to the needs of the society where the naturalized foreigner settled."[140] Symbolically, forced charitable donations were also a trace element of the juridical model, of naturalization as a meritorious reward for contribution to the public good. Such a faint and "thin" administrative fiction stood in stark contrast to the absence of formal conditions requiring that the foreigner demonstrate either his or her social assimilation or virtuous contributions to society.

According to the jurists, the registration of the letters at the local financial bureaux of the royal treasury after 1693 was an essential condition for the validity of the letter. Such was the judgment in the case of the comte de Mortaigne, a Swabian lieutenant general of the king's army, born in the principality of

Hesse in the Rhineland, and naturalized by Louis XIV in 1705. The count registered his letters at the treasury offices, and his son was forced to seek naturalization again in May 1748. According to Lefebvre, the fiscal registration was a necessary formality that had to be accomplished at the request and initiative of the foreigner himself, and could not be done without his consent (that is, post facto by his heirs).[141] The fiscal officers also undertook, in principle, a formal inquiry into the social standing of the foreign claimant. Like the magistrates of the Chambre des comptes, they never denied these claimants naturalization (although their inquiries produced the raw materials of local social histories).[142]

Under Louis XIV, the executionary clause grew longer as further royal institutions were listed as the addressees of the letter. A royal edict of December 1703 required that letters of naturalization be "insinuated" along with all civil acts and transactions in the kingdom at the offices of the treasury officials where the claimant resided. For foreign citizens, this meant an additional expense. In 1722, the tariff was set at one hundred livres per individual beneficiary.[143] Although jurists such as Joseph-Nicolas Guyot had argued that the failure to register the letters at the treasury bureaux rendered them invalid, most lawyers followed Denisart (who cited a decision of the Paris parlement of 1740) in his understanding that the neglect of this formality did not render them legally void.[144] Nor did the "imprudent declaration" of 8 December 1723 and the reestablishment of advent taxes in a formal *lit de justice* of 1 July 1725 become a requirement for naturalized foreigners, despite the arguments of historians Mathorez, Boizet, and others. Many naturalized foreigners were required to pay the tax, but this fiscal expedient on the part of a monarchy perpetually short on revenue was not to be reproduced in the Old Regime.[145]

The Old Regime jurists were divided, however, over the question of whether registration at the sovereign court of parlement was necessary as well. On this point, royal legislation appeared uncompromisingly clear: an ordinance of 14 October 1571 enjoined treasury officials to have no regard for letters registered at the parlement, and that ordinance was followed by another in 1579 that required their exclusive registration at the Chambre des comptes.[146] But in practice, a large number of letters were addressed to and registered by the Paris parlement throughout the Old Regime, especially those of foreign clerics seeking naturalization with permissions to hold benefices. Occasionally, drafts of letters concerning high-ranking clerics came back annotated by an official at the chancellery noting, in the expeditionary clause, that the letter "must be addressed to the Paris parlement," and Denisart argued as well that "it was customary" to do so.[147] Nearly a quarter of the letters studied in this sample were addressed to or registered at the parlements or other sovereign courts, other than the Chambres des comptes, of the kingdom.

Did it matter? In what was a prescient opinion from an otherwise uninspired lawyer arguing a case of contested inheritance before the Paris parlement in 1641, the barrister Bignon contended that registration in the Chambre des comptes could be counted as a mere fiscal matter of the crown. Registration at the Paris parlement, by contrast, was relevant in all civil matters regarding inheritance and the transmission of property across generations. Bignon was arguing in favor of the duc de Mantua's heirs, and he lost his case. His losing claim was that "the efficacy of these letters in cases of succession and other rights belonging to the subjects of the king is only determined and declared in parlement." This argument was to resurface in the eighteenth century, first concerning the inheritance of the English wizard of high finance John Law, who was naturalized in 1716 (but only registered his letters in the Paris parlement) at the moment that he put into place his disastrous "system" of stock options. When Law died in 1734, his collateral heirs disputed the succession; the controller-general intervened in the lawsuit, in the name of the king, and successfully argued that the letters were valid despite the failure to have them registered in the Chambre des comptes.[148]

Late eighteenth-century lawyers, arguing cases of civil litigation involving "foreign" claims, were to refer to Bignon's arguments, in the context of debate over whether the international and reciprocal collective abolitions of the droit d'aubaine in fact enacted the right to foreigners to inherit property from each other or even from French natives (see below, chap. 7). But even before that, foreigners seeking naturalization had to take the questions of registration and protocol into account, especially because the courts pointedly upheld their prerogatives in the matter. Thus, to take but one example, the case of Gayetan Pietre, a merchant born in "Albania," under the jurisdiction of the Papal States, who had lived in Marseille and Aix for many years. There he had five children and bought a considerable number of properties (evidence of his "firm resolve to live and die in the kingdom"). Pietre was naturalized in 1788, but the original letters were addressed "to the parlement and the Cour des comptes of Provence. The parlement registered them," he explained, "but the Cour des comptes refused to register them after the parlement" had done so. As a result, the chancellery was forced to make a duplicate set of letters (no doubt, at the expense of Pietre), which were sealed and sent to the Chambre des comptes at Aix.[149]

The expeditionary section of the letter ended with these injunctive clauses, ordering the registration of the letter; the patent letter was dated (by month for naturalizations, by date and month for declarations), signed in the king's name, and appropriately sealed. The tariffs of the seal were fixed by ordinance, and increased from 74 livres in 1672, to 79 in 1674, to 106 livres per beneficiary in 1704, with a sum half again as much in "honorarium" to the royal secretary.[150] Of course, the king's signature was imitated: notarial manuals from the late sixteenth century state that even a master of requests (*maître de requêtes*) in the chancellery could sign the king's name, but such seems to have been rarely, if ever, the case in the seventeenth and eighteenth century letters of naturalization. Nonetheless, the letter of naturalization, like so many other patent letters, always had the "alleged signature of the king," that "indecent prostitution of which no one is the dupe," according to the cynical duc de Saint-Simon in his memoirs.[151]

Thus the letter of naturalization. It was a costly bureaucratic procedure: including all "taxes" and "gifts" relating to its registration and verification, the letter of naturalization could cost more than six hundred livres by the middle of the eighteenth century, although it might in some instances cost half as much. According to common wisdom at the time, letters of declaration were half the price of naturalizations, but this still might be a substantial sum—at least two years' salary of a skilled artisan in the Parisian building trades or ten seasons of work for a day laborer in the seventeenth century.[152] Of course, the payment of these "taxes" in the execution of the protocol did not include what may have been considerable kickbacks to royal secretaries and others who intervened in the administrative process, not to mention the expenses involved in traveling to the courts and bureaux where the letter had to be verified and registered.

The intervention of the king or his councillors, however, was less important than the bureaucratic procedures routinized—but with room for exceptions—during the Age of Louis XIV. Just as the letter stabilized in form, so too did the procedure regularize and normalize in practice. It is true that hundreds of letters in the period from Louis XIV to the outbreak of the French Revolution were initially denied because of some minor infraction in the strict protocol of the letter's delivery, including the delays for registration which, if exceeded, required that the recipient seek additional "letters of superannuation." There were many more letters that were issued by the Great Chancellery and never registered, which sometimes required the descendants of foreigners to repeat the procedure again.[153] And there are numerous examples of letters issued and reissued because of concerns, voiced by their recipients, that mistakes had been made involving the spelling of their names, dates of birth, or origins.[154] These naturalized foreigners feared for the validity of their letters, and they were no doubt justified: dozens of naturalizations became the object of litigation between naturalized foreigners and native heirs, who were likely to question procedure and protocol in their challenges to a naturalized foreigner's estates. But, to confirm the judgment of Lefebvre de la Planche, and excepting the cases of a few Protestants, no requests for naturalization that followed the protocol of text and procedure seem to have been denied by the monarchy or its royal officials.

If procedure was everything, patriotism was nothing. There was little evidence of "citizenship" in the formulas of the letter and declarations of naturalization, if by citizenship we understand the recognition of service to the public good or meritocratic actions, or even of proof of social assimilation. The juridical model, articulated by lawyers in the 1570s, had completely dissipated by the time the royal model and the practice of naturalization crystallized at the beginning of the reign of Louis XIV. Instead, in the text of the letter and the procedure of its expedition and registration, a set of legal and administrative fictions assured only a future condition: that a foreigner would be treated "as if" he were a native Frenchman or woman, especially concerning his or her right to inherit or devolve property, if he or she promised to reside permanently in the kingdom. To quote once again Lefebvre de la Planche (because he was so central in the affair), "The conditions of this adoption are no less constant: there is only one required, which is a faithful commitment to make a continuous residence in the new country that the foreigner has chosen, and where he has been granted the privilege of being received."[155] Yet if residence was a synecdoche for allegiance and loyalty to the king within the royal model of naturalization, there was more meaning to the procedure than the legal and administrative fictions that have been analyzed in this chapter. From the perspective of many foreigners and descendants of French who sought through the letter of naturalization to claim French citizenship, or to reclaim their native status, a set of vernacular fictions of citizenship made their appearance within the claimant's exposition of his or her case.

CHAPTER THREE

THE USE AND ABUSE OF NATURALIZATION

B y the reign of Louis XIV, the letter of naturalization had become an exclusive and discretionary act of royal authority—and to a great extent, a routinized, bureaucratic affair. The royal model converged with juridical doctrine in the administrative act of naturalization. But these differed, at times substantially, from the vernacular models and practices of citizenship—the foreigners' conceptions of what it meant to become Frenchmen and women, and the reasons why they sought to be naturalized. Formulaic, imprisoned by the protocol of royal privileges, royal grants of naturalization might appear an unlikely place to look for traces of how foreigners, seeking to be naturalized, conceived of French citizenship. Yet the voices of some foreigners can be heard faintly, mediated by layers of clerical and secretarial intervention, in the expository section of the letter. There, the claimant identified the motives and particular circumstances that justified his or her request to "participate in the advantages and privileges enjoyed by our subjects and native residents."

The expository preambles of naturalizations were not all drawn from model texts—even if the model texts circulating in the seventeenth and eighteenth centuries do provide narratives full of stock expressions and formulas. Already by the sixteenth century, according to the legal scholar Michaud, the exposé was "conceived in largely invariable terms, and became for the [royal] secretaries and their clerks a routine affair." In the Old Regime, the preamble was largely the discretionary work of the royal secretary charged with redacting the letter. Such was the assumption of the financier Nicolas Damour, who had contracted to collect the Naturalization Tax of 1697, and who assumed that whatever the secretaries included in these narratives, they could not change "a royal right dependent on the crown." But the variation in the narrative sections of the preambles was structured independently of any single secretarial set of choices.[1] In several hundred of the individual naturalizations consulted for this book, individual foreigners offered more extensive renditions of their life histories. Like the narratives in royal letters of remission or pardon—structurally similar, but generally much longer and more elaborate—the texts contain the life stories of hundreds of individual foreigners seeking to be naturalized.[2] Recast in the voice of the king himself, these narrative and vernacular fictions reflect, or at least refract, the explicit and sometimes unstated motivations and the petitioner's conceptualizations of the meanings of naturalization.

Yet how are these claims to be interpreted: As transparent reflections of true desires, or as the instrumental manipulation of stock phrases from motives of obvious self-interest? Did becoming a citizen in Old Regime France mean claiming some participation in the ideal of public service, meritorious action, and virtue, for which naturalization was a reward—even if the absolutist model of naturalization never required such claims? Do narratives in the preambles of naturalizations and declaration reveal only the strategic value of the grant of nativeness itself, or should the rhetoric of devotion to the public good, when it did make its appearance, be taken seriously? The answers to these questions are to be found within a corpus of some five hundred letters that reveal not so much a unified opinion or doctrinal response as a shared and vernacular set of fictions about becoming French.

A legal fiction, in the Renaissance definition, treats a person or a thing "as if" that person or thing were of another nature, in the interest of both equity and the public good (chapter 2). But the vernacular fictions treated here take on a different meaning. On the one hand, fictions make reference to the acts of lying, dissimulation, and dishonesty: a fiction, in this instance, stands opposed to the truth. On the other hand, following Natalie Davis, vernacular fictions partake of the meanings imparted in the Latin root *fingere*, the shaping, creating, and crafting of a narrative, a story.[3] Vernacular fictions of naturalization both conceal the motives, intentions, and interests of the foreign claimant and provide the materials with which foreigners shaped stories about their lives. That the "materials," in this instance, were often a stock set of narratives is itself revealing, not so much of the individual intentions of naturalized foreigners but of the language in which they expressed their desire to become naturalized.

The vernacular language of citizenship does correlate with the "official" language of the law, the juridical doctrines about descent, belonging, and residence that developed from Bacquet to Lefebvre de la Planche and beyond. Indeed, as we shall see, key notions in the legal vocabulary of citizenship—such as the "spirit of return" that a Frenchman born abroad is assumed to retain, or the notion of "accidental birth" in the kingdom—reappear consistently in the narrative exposés of the letter. In this sense, there is a certain convergence between the language of the jurists and that of the recipients of naturalization, even if it was extremely rare for foreigners and royal secretaries to cite lawyers in their claims to be naturalized.[4]

At the same time, the letter of naturalization contains (at least) two voices: there is, inevitably and evidentially, a slippage between juridical norms (the "theory" of the jurists) and vernacular practices (the narrative claims of foreigners petitioning for citizenship). This slippage both broadened the criteria for admission into the French polity and suggests how a certain idea of nationality—as legal status, sentimental attachment, and even, at moments, of cultural identity—already existed in the claims of foreigners seeking to be naturalized under the Old Regime. Such was not simply a residual trace of the classical or "Italian model" of political citizenship; in many ways, it anticipated a more modern understanding of citizenship as social belonging and identity. In the cases of descendants of expatriate Frenchmen and women, religious refugees and economic adventurers whose sons and daughters returned to the kingdom, there were arguments to be made about "eternal Frenchness" passed through bloodlines and affirmed by moral sentiment.

The striking aspect about these stories is that they were told at all. Despite the desire of certain jurists (and others) in the 1570s, the absolutist model of the citizen was not to be contingent on the moral character of the foreign claimant, his or her social assimilation, or virtuous acts. Literally nothing could be said in the expository preambles that would affect the Great Chancellery's "decision" to grant the privilege, because what mattered most, as we have already seen, was procedure, routine, and the letter's affirmation of future residence until death. Although the foreigner's moral character was occasionally brought to the fore during verification procedures, this, too, was largely incidental in the administrative procedure of naturalization, and rarely, if ever, affected the outcome of a request. The majority of letters followed the routinized, bureaucratic procedures and practices, moving through the "system" more or less quickly and depending, at times, on clientage and patronage networks that helped expedite, but otherwise did not influence, the grant of naturalization. The contents of the foreigners' statements in the preamble of the grant were never taken seriously.

If no foreigner with a procedurally correct petition for naturalization was ever turned down, why bother to tell a life story? Perhaps for the same reason that so many foreigners, already exempted from the droit d'aubaine, sought letters in the first place: in an attempt to assure or guarantee the efficacy of their statutory exemptions. In legal terms, a great many letters (how many can never be determined) were considered *ad majorem cautelam*, sought for the purposes of guarantee against other claimants in inheritance disputes, against the royal fisc, or against competitors for a monastic office.[5] In these cases, letters of naturalization and declaration were an insurance policy for an orderly succession or promotion to office—and many petitioners admitted that "they had been counseled" to take them. Moreover, foreign petitioners, however long they had been resident in the kingdom and knowledgeable about its customs, can hardly have known that it simply did not matter within the royal bureaucracy what their background or values might be. The narrative strategies and choices in these letters respond to a *perceived* set of norms and expectations about what it would take to make a convincing case about Frenchness. That is why, in part, they have a sometimes formulaic quality; at the same time, taken together, the corpus of stories offers a set of folk claims, a vernacular language of citizenship in the Old Regime—stories not about being but about becoming (or even re-becoming) French.[6]

Fictions and Lies: From Public Good to Self-Interest

It is indeed sobering to discover the extent to which the expository section of the letter of naturalization could be challenged juridically within the vast litigation over inheritance, and the extent to which the fictions it told were, in some cases, outright lies. Such deceit is revealed most unusually in an obscure and endlessly complex court case in Alsace during the 1730s and 1740s that was revoked on two occasions to the royal council in Paris. The claimants were Marie-Josephe-Marguerite Gumpp and her brother, Philippe Antoine, in the name of their mother, Marie Marguerite Sommer-vogel. The plaintiffs were Joseph-Clement-Marie Joner and Leopold Wimpf and his "consorts," involving nearly a dozen individuals from Alsace, both direct and collateral heirs, all related as maternal first cousins, paternal second cousins, and maternal and paternal grandchildren to Jean-François Joner, who died in Alsace in September 1731. The case was complicated because the local districts where the properties were found in Alsace had been conquered and finally annexed in 1682, and also because all the families, headed by ambitious officeholders of different kinds, including some high-ranking nobles, had moved between the Holy Roman Empire and France continuously since the mid-seventeenth century.[7] The merits of the different arguments, put forth by determined if not always particularly eloquent or original barristers, turned on the *summa divisio* of whether claimants were native residents or foreigners, and especially whether the "foreign citizens" in question had legitimately received their letters or declarations of natural-ization that enabled them to legally inherit property in the kingdom. Chal-lenging their opponents' letters, both parties revealed the multiple fictions of naturalization.

Briefly put: Marie Marguerite Sommervogel, the maternal first cousin of the dead foreigner in question, received letters of naturalization in October 1732 in order to claim her share of the inheritance. When she learned that such privileges had no retroactive effect, she took recourse to letters of declaration of naturaliza-tion, which were granted on 28 January 1732 and then registered by the sovereign council in Colmar. The expository section of the preamble read as follows:

[She] claims that she was born in about the year 1667 of the marriage of Jean Pierre Sommervogel and Barbe Joner, natives of the province of Alsace; that having married Sr. Gumpp in the village of Kintzingen in Brisgau, a district ceded by Peace Treaty to the [Holy Roman] Empire, she resided with him for several years in the said province of Brisgau, and came, after the death of her husband, to the province of Alsace to restore her privileges and rights of her fatherland [*droits de sa patrie*]. Since the parish registers of most of Alsace were lost in the religious troubles and during the wars, the claimant cannot justify her place of birth by an extract of her baptismal record, and she was therefore counseled to have recourse to our letters of declaration of naturalization that she very humbly requests that we accord her, by means of which she could participate in the rights and advantages that her mother and father had acquired at birth.[8]

In response to objections concerning obvious gaps in these letters, notably the justification of her birth, Sommervogel took additional "letters of amplification" in 1733 that further specified her place of birth and made more explicit the conditions of her husband Gumpp's voyages outside of France.

Her legal adversaries, especially Joseph-Clement-Marie Joner from Munich, claimed that the narratives in Sommervogel's declaration and amplification of naturalization contained a string of unbroken lies: they were full of both commissive errors (*subreptice*) and willful omissions (*obreptice*). Not only did the letters leave out her exact place of birth (against the strictures of the jurist Papon), but their "authors" had lied about the parish archives being burnt. Further, the letter of declaration was misleading about the annexation of Brisgau (not mentioning its cession in 1648, nearly ninety years before the claimant took her letters), where her "several years" really amounted to "at least thirty or forty"; and so forth.[9]

It is worth underscoring that the defendant, Joseph Joner, offered these criticisms only a year after he had returned to France from his native Bavaria and had taken letters of declaration of naturalization to claim the inheritance. Sommervogel's lawyers, in turn, attacked Joner's letters of 1732 as also being full of omissions and deliberate distortions, notably in their failure to state that his father had gone to the imperial court in Vienna where he had been tutor to the emperor's children, and where he had clearly established a permanent residence. Despite these attacks, the magistrates at the sovereign council of Alsace remained convinced by Joner's arguments: by a decision of 8 July 1734, they declared invalid Sommervogel's letter of declaration and upheld Joner in his claim to the succession a year later. At that moment, another collateral claimant to the estate, Dame Wimpf and consorts, paternal second cousins who had remained in Alsace after the conquest, requested the royal council of state to overrule the sovereign council's decisions and to declare both sets of declarations of naturalization to be fraudulent lies. A fascinating if endless discussion of obreptional and subreptional proofs followed: lawyers for all parties saw in the narratives of the expository preambles of these declarations of naturalization not simply empty rhetorical formulas but outright lies that rendered the letters and declarations legally invalid. Although the final decision of the royal council was not located, it appears that Dame Wimpf and consorts emerged victorious in their claims to dismiss both sets of letters of the contending parties, identifying them as foreigners and thus incapable of inheriting in France.

The case is important on several scores. First, it shows how barristers could twist their claims about the "private" capacity of individuals to inherit into public arguments for the "interests of the nation," even if this was surprisingly rare in litigious cases involving foreigners, even in the late eighteenth century.[10] More important, the case reveals the most fundamental meaning of vernacular *fiction* in the letter of naturalization: the exposition of the letter as a series of lies told about one's origins and history in the interest of securing the right to inherit property.[11] This abuse of naturalization—or in this case, of declarations of naturalization—stands at the extreme end of a continuum that stretches between two rhetorical poles: on the one hand, the textual invocation of public interest and the honorary quality of citizenship; on the other hand, the explicit mention of the self-interested utility of naturalization and declarations. Beyond the letter of naturalization as an outright deceit, it is worth taking a closer look at the tropes, both formulaic and original, of this vernacular language of citizenship.

The juridical model of naturalization, put forth by the lawyers in the 1570s, had insisted on the "qualities and merits" of the foreigner who received a letter of naturalization: the grant of nativeness was considered a rare privilege that recognized both his virtue and social assimilation. The royal and absolutist model never adopted such claims within the administrative protocol or the text of the grant, nor even in the verification procedures of the royal Chambres des comptes or the local treasury bureaux. The juridical claims were, on the one hand, nostalgic: the idea of citizenship *per privilegium* harkened back to the medieval Italian city-states and, beyond that, to Rome itself. On the other hand, such claims were revived in different ways within the eighteenth-century language of republicanism and patriotism, within which can be found the birth of "nationalism" itself—the political project of constructing a community of citizens.[12] But neither corresponded to the royal model of naturalization that was to become dominant between the reign of Louis XIV and the French Revolution.

Yet the vernacular versions of the "citizen" who acts in the interest of the public good, and whose status could be acquired only through the expression of disinterested deeds, remained under the Old Regime an enduring trope in the narrative preambles of foreigners seeking letters of naturalization. The persistent vision of naturalization as a special honor conferred on foreigners for their service to the crown—through their arts and industry, commerce or science—can be found in perhaps a quarter of those letters where a narrative existed at all. (Such an ideal was revived and transformed during the French Revolution as a means of recognizing foreign "benefactors of humanity," as we shall see.) Among the more famous examples of the Old Regime, Louis XIV awarded naturalization in 1673 to the Genoese cartographer and geometer Jean Dominique Cassini, already a member of the French Royal Academy, who had been recruited by the crown to complete the first triangulation of French territory. Cassini's privilege explicitly recognized the letters as a reward for service, and only required that the claimant "finish his days in the kingdom."[13] More generally, one of the rare expository sections of the preamble of naturalization restated the royal and mercantilist tradition of recruiting foreign labor and awarding naturalization in return: "The desire we have to contribute to the perfection of the arts and to excite the emulation of our subjects engaged us to take under our protection and fix in our kingdom foreigners who distinguish themselves by their industry."[14] Such a moment of "pro-immigration" in royal policy coincided with naturalization as a reward that recognized social utility, if not virtue and merit.

Although neither virtue, nor evidence of social assimilation, nor criteria of social utility were deemed a conditional requirement for naturalization, a wide range of foreigners (from courtiers to bankers to military officers to merchants) all framed their narratives as exempla of public service, of contributions to the general welfare of the kingdom, if not specifically the good of the king himself. Service to the king at court put the foreigner in a good place to request and receive naturalization. Estienne Padry, "of the Athenian Nation" (as he called himself), was a translator of Oriental languages at Versailles; as he recounted in his letter, he was decorated as a knight in the Orders of Notre Dame de Montcarmel and Saint-Lazare de Jérusalem, and had received a pension for his son in the Jesuit College of Paris. His naturalization followed logically as a reward for his services.[15] Joseph Nicolas Pancrace Royer, born in Piedmont and naturalized in 1751, served as music instructor to the royal children, although he rested his claims on his father's contributions to the construction of the gardens and fountains of Versailles.[16] But service to the king was not restricted to those at court, as long as the petitioner made a claim about the utility of his presence to the French kingdom.

More frequently, petitioners claimed to contribute to the wealth and prosperity of the kingdom or its colonies. François Caron, a Protestant merchant from Brussels, received naturalization letters in July 1665 for himself, his Japanese wife, and five children, explaining how he had been part of the Dutch East Indies Trading Company, investing a "considerable sum of the capital" and traveling to China and Japan, where he spent more than twenty-five years.[17] His service in the interests of a mercantilist France, and a "France of movement" more generally, were rewarded with a grant of naturalization.[18] On other occasions, supplicants referred to their provision of essential economic services to a local public. Jean Baptiste Castiglioni, born in Milan, offered a lengthy exposé of his "happiness in attracting the confidence of the merchants and councillors of Lyon" by being chosen in 1708 "to seek out wheat in Italy after the harvest was ruined"; he then narrated his own climb up the local ladder of power, ending with his nomination as alderman of that city in 1719.[19] The theme of providing grain for a starving population was used widely among foreigners living in different parts of the kingdom: it was as if supplying grain in times of famine was a meritorious act in the public interest, even if the individual might have made much money on the transaction (a fact that went unmentioned in the narratives of the letter). Jean Baptiste Mainetto of Genoa received his letter in July 1743 after having claimed to have shown his zeal on all occasions necessary to the public interest, "and notably the grain shortage of 1729, when by his own credit and hard work, he had more grain brought in than necessary to assist the districts of Grasse, Draguinan, and Saint Paul, so much that the price dropped . . . which won him the esteem and goodwill of his fellow citizens."[20] Municipal citizens, of course. And even Jews, who came to acquire citizenship or its functional equivalent—the doubly fictional grant of naturalization—invoked their role in providing subsistence to their local communities in times of need. Cerf Berr, leader of the Alsatian Jews in Strasbourg appealed to the king and received in 1775 a doubly fictional grant of nativeness ("permission to acquire goods and to dispose of them") after listing in his narrative a large number of his enterprises relating to "military service and the public good," including his assistance during the famine of 1770 and 1771, which gave him "occasions to give proof of the zeal with which he is animated for the good of our service and that of the state."[21]

Just as the protocol of expediting the letter of naturalization ritualized foreigners' contributions to public works, so too did individual foreigners seeking naturalization claim to have made contributions to "charitable works." Elizabeth Joseph Sapin, born in Ghent, was naturalized in July 1789; in her letter, she stated that she had run an orphanage with twelve children, and now sought to enter a convent "to be continuously employed, for the rest of her life, serving poor, sick people" in her parish. Antoine Thibault, a master surgeon who had lived in Paris for over thirty-three years, described how he only "works with honor and integrity for the public contentment and the relief of the poor."[22] In some fourscore cases, arguments involving medical contributions to the kingdom were deemed appropriate, especially when they came from a group of foreigners, like Thibault, who served in the health care professions. Doctors and surgeons, perhaps not unexpectedly, elaborated narratives about curing the sick body of the kingdom, if not the king himself. Joseph Vinache of Naples received letters that served to "mark the satisfaction which his work deserves, work done by order and for the service of Louis XIV, and the discoveries he has made for the curing of illness that had until then appeared incurable."[23] Jean Grecy from Tuscany had served the royal health officers in Portugal, and his desire to come to France, he claimed, was fed by the success of his various remedies and potions. He received letters in 1754 authorizing him to practice in France and was even given the charge to be aware of "abuses perpetuated in our kingdom by people out to fool the public." The medical doctor's naturalization involved a happy conjunction of his personal interest and that of the kingdom: "The advantages he has found in France in the justice which has rewarded his talents has given him the desire to finish his days in the kingdom."[24]

The most expansive claim based on medical expertise in the public service was that of Antoine Tristan Anty d'Isnard, born of French parents from the Auvergne. His father Jacques had been a "medical counsellor" and was "very experienced with pestilent diseases for the healing of which he had a special secret." So armed, he had left the country in November 1661 to go to England to treat plague victims, and had been rewarded by the king of England for his work, both then and again in 1666. Pestilence brought him back to France in 1668, when Louis XIV requested his return "for the interest of our service and the good of our subjects." His son, wife, and four grown children, all born in England and resident in France for twenty-three years, sought in 1692 to be naturalized.[25] The family's claim described the doctor's contribution to the public good in his defense of the realm against epidemic disease, often perceived in the early modern period as having foreign origins. In this case, as in other petitions by medical personnel, foreigners petitioned as the ultimate insiders battling an external "invasion" of the body politic. It was a logical strategy in a period of recurrent xenophobia, both official and popular, during the seventeenth century.

Beyond the provision of foodstuffs and the contribution of medical expertise, the easiest and most common public service to demonstrate was military service. Although the jurists were unanimous that soldiering in the French armies, like officeholding in the kingdom, did not in itself naturalize foreigners, the royal recruitment of foreign mercenaries sometimes offered collective naturalizations and exemptions from the droit d'aubaine as a reward. But many foreign soldiers, already thus naturalized, nonetheless sought to be naturalized individually. In their letters, the idea of public service merged with a claim of personal sacrifice and willful neglect of self-interest. The idea of selfless and virtuous service to the king and crown revived not only a feudal ideal of loyalty (*fidelitas*) to a lord (*pro domino*) but a classical notion of heroic self-sacrifice of life and limb—*pro patria mori* as an extreme example of love and devotion to country.[26] In the expository preambles of the letter, there was no invocation of a religious dimension to this rhetoric: rather, it was cast in genealogically specific terms, often contaminated by the persistent language of feudal loyalty. Thus the tediously long account of an ancient and illustrious noble family that had long served the king for over eight centuries by Jean Baptiste Desmonts, the comte de Walers, himself born in the duchy of Clèves in the Austrian Low Countries.[27] Alphonse Marie Louis Saint Severin d'Aragon, a colonel in the

Italian Royal Regiment and ambassador to Sweden, wrote of the illustrious service record of his family, noting how an uncle was honored by Charles VIII with the title of knight in his orders, and how Francis I had permitted him to live in France and enjoy the privileges enjoyed by "our original subjects and regnicoles."[28] Indeed, prior naturalizations of ancestors reveal at once how the privilege could become a specific family tradition and also how the vernacular fictions of past naturalization could be used to signify the loyalty of the actual claimant. Such was the case of Philippe François Madrid de Montaigle, born in Liège, who in 1775 insisted that his great grandfather, originally from Cologne, had been naturalized (and ennobled) by Louis XIV over a century earlier.[29] But more than descent, military narratives focused on personal sacrifice and, most dramatically, the loss of life in major battles to defend the French kingdom. Or if not life, then at least limb. Robert de Stack, who rose to the rank of infantry colonel in the Irish regiment of Clare from 1728 to 1757, ended his career in a naval battle against the English "where he lost his left arm . . . giving us proofs of his courage and bravery."[30]

The idea and ideal of service and sacrifice—to the king, the kingdom, or the local community—thus had an important place in the supplicant discourse of naturalization. Foreigners narrated stories as if naturalization were a reward for their public actions and personal sacrifices. Citizenship, in this instance, was not just about legal membership, nor was it explicitly about political "rights" or even participation. Rather, the vernacular version of the absolute citizen put forth the "citizen" as a category of social belonging that merged with the ideal of public service and even virtue. It echoed the presumptions of the juridical model of "honorary citizenship" put forth in the sixteenth century, but the political character of the (naturalized) citizen was limited, as a subject of the absolute monarchy, to manifestations of public service to the greater good of community, kingdom, and king. Such narratives, without legal or practical effect on the procedure or acquisition of grants of naturalization in the Old Regime, persisted within a set of rhetorical tropes that foreigners perceived to be part of the language of absolutist citizenship.

The fiction of public service lay at one end of a rhetorical continuum that stretched between the public good, on the one hand, and private self and family interest, on the other. Although some foreigners chose to tell stories of devotion as public, if not truly political, citizens, others opted to state simply and without equivocation the strategic and instrumental logic of their requests to be naturalized. In particular, those who sought offices or ecclesiastical benefices most frequently acknowledged (without other justification) how royal letters would allow them to purchase offices, to inherit them, to be formally accepted by the corps or corporation that regulated that profession, or even to exercise the offices that had already been conferred on them. Such was the case, for example, of Joseph Michel Arnould, born in Hainault, who stated that he wanted to hold the office of royal notary in the village of Nuits in Burgundy, but feared that his foreign birth was an obstacle.[31] Becoming naturalized, in such cases, meant getting "regularized" and protected, by royal privilege, against competing claims of native residents to offices or inheritances. Claude Mathieu, born in Lorraine, was royal solicitor in the Waters and Forest administration in Alsace, having moved there in 1692 after rising through the ranks of lawyers at the Paris parlement from lowly registrar (greffier) to royal solicitor to barrister. In 1725, after more than thirty years of royal service, he was finally naturalized.[32]

Given the strict injunction against foreign ecclesiastics holding religious benefices and offices, including monastic appointments, many foreign clerics who sought to be naturalized were quite explicit about their motivations.[33] Even when they were not prohibited from entering French convents, they might seek to be naturalized when engaged in a divisive contest over posts and benefices within their religious communities. Such was the case of Jean Lallemand in 1713, who received his naturalization only when forced to by the opposition of an abbot of Ferny (Soissons), of the Benedictine order of Saint-Benoît, as he explicitly pointed out.[34] Or, like secular officeholders, many holders of ecclesiastical posts and benefices sought post-facto naturalizations to ensure the possessions of their offices, or to increase the benefices that they already enjoyed as a result of specific permissions by the crown. The comte de Lewestein, for example, received letters of naturalization in December 1688 in order to take possession of the benefices conferred on him, without derogation of his canonate in the metropolitan church of Cologne. He did not, however, register those letters until twenty years later, when he retold of his rise within the ecclesiastical hierarchy, having since become deacon of the Strasbourg Cathedral, and then bishop of Tournai.[35]

There were a wealth of reasons, other than officeholding and the enjoyment of ecclesiastical benefices, that drove foreigners to become citizens, and these were often explicitly mentioned in the grants of naturalization and declaration. Anselme Coste, "called in the language of Piedmont Contaz," petitioned for a declaration in March 1718 at the age of thirty-one. He told the story of having been sent by his parents to earn his living in France, where he became a wood merchant after having worked for several years in the business for a "bon bourgeois who, in addition to setting him up, arranged for a marriage." Coste cited, somewhat unusually, Henry IV's royal declaration that exempted Savoyards in France from the droit d'aubaine, but claimed nonetheless that "for the scruples of the people with whom he works, and to establish himself in France with greater security," he sought to be naturalized.[36] Other petitioners cited pressure from their families, or prospective families: Alexander Prainsendorf was a "poor tailor's assistant" who was forced to abjure his Protestant beliefs and to obtain letters of naturalization in 1715 by the father of his fiancée. And it was simply the "interest of his family" that made Jacques Hooghstoel, a merchant from Bruges, seek to be naturalized in 1712, the same year he was married.[37]

Interest, not public service, stood at the heart of the vernacular discourse of naturalization in the Old Regime: interest in offices, in benefices, but mostly in the capacity to inherit or devolve property, to escape the onerous status of alien that put the beneficiary at a disadvantage against collateral heirs born within the kingdom. Naturalized foreigners were surprisingly explicit in their letters, appealing to the king for the privileged fiction of being treated "as if" they were native or "natural" Frenchmen and women in order to escape the royal officers of the treasury bureaux and the tax-farmers who collected the droit d'aubaine. In 1660, Thomas Platte, born in England, humbly entreated the king to grant him and his wife Jeanne Boudon letters of naturalization. "As foreigners, [they] fear that our [royal] officers could bother them and after their death stake claim to the goods that they might acquire."[38] Indeed, the fear that the tax-farmers would seize the property of a foreigner even though he was already exempted by treaty or collective privilege provided a frequent rationale for the acquisition of letters of naturalization. Even the royal council recognized the need to protect foreigners, especially important ones, from the voraciousness of its own fiscal administration, as revealed by the correspondence between Chancellor Lamoignon, Foreign Minister duc de Choiseul, and the royal solicitor of the Paris parlement, Joly de Fleury, concerning the case of the Swedish king's sister, Princess Anhalt Zerbst of the Holy Roman Empire. In April 1760 the princess sought refuge in France, "sheltered from the violence which the Prussian king undertook on her lands." She fell ill in Paris and, having contracted during her stay a great number of debts, feared that if she were to die, the domanial tax collectors would seize her property, given her quality as a foreigner. The chancellor moved expeditiously and issued letters of naturalization on 22 April 1760. Lamoignon then asked for their prompt registration, for "independently of the dangerous state in which Madame Anhjalt finds herself, and the just treatment due to a princess of her character. . . . His Majesty believes it necessary to take precaution against the interests even of his kingdom, to prevent her inheritance from being consumed in court procedures and attendant useless costs."[39]

If self-interested protection from the tax-farmers and treasury courts was sometimes a stated objective within naturalization narratives, more frequently such motives were masked by the language of the public good—of good citizenship, if not patriotism itself. The slippage can be seen most clearly in the rare and revealing case of Marczy Cristel of Hungary, whose actual petition for naturalization has survived along with the draft presented by the chancellery for expedition by the secretary of the royal household. In November 1756, Cristel wrote Secretary of War comte d'Argenson, asking for his "powerful protection" in acquiring for himself and his wife letters of naturalization. Cristel and his wife, Marie Anne Beckerine from Vasheim in the Palatinate, owned only a house in Molsheim (Alsace), along with "the little he could save from his annual pension of eight hundred livres." Seeking the protection of the king against his own fiscal officers, Cristel wrote: "As they have seen several times in France, a month after their parents' death, children have their goods seized by the fisc, and thus are poor widows and children reduced to utter poverty." D'Argenson did accord his "protection," by which he simply transferred the dossier to a royal secretary at the chancellery, who processed the letter a mere three months later. But the text of the letter of naturalization dated January 1737 made no mention of the petitioners' need to protect himself from the tax-farmers contracted to collect the domanial taxes. Instead, the citizenship grant spoke, in the king's name, only of Cristel's valiant service record in the regiments of Berchiny and Pollereszky.[40]

Naturalization could thus be an instrumental act, obscured by the rhetoric of public service, to protect a resident foreigner from the avarice of the tax-farmers. More generally, foreigners sought to be naturalized and declared native Frenchmen and women out of a calculus of interests that revolved around the question of family and inheritance. Some were quite explicit about using letters of naturalization in actual or future contestations with collateral relatives over their properties. Jean Aillaud, a pharmacy clerk born in Savoy, pointed out in 1735 that although foreigners from the county of Nice did not need such letters, he, fearing nevertheless "that his heirs would find obstacles in the ordinary order of successions," sought to be naturalized.[41] But others were more understated—or even lied about—their proprietary interests, and those of their heirs. Yet even when property was not explicitly mentioned, the vast majority of foreigners' exposés were founded on narrative accounts of belonging and identity in which the family (and lurking behind it, property relations in the family) figured centrally.

The Absolute Citizen: Family, Gender, and the King

The articulation of family and citizenship has a long history in the political theory of the absolutist monarchy, and in the historiography of French state building during the early modern period as well. Recently, historians have focused not simply on the models of family and state that informed political theory and practice in Old Regime France but on the material and ideological engagements of royal officeholders and the king: thus Sarah Hanley's "Family-State Compact," the idea that the strengthening of royal authority depended on, as it affirmed, patrilineal family relationships within the robe nobility.[42] In the case of naturalization, not only did the metaphor of family as state function in legal theory but it also made sense in practice: individuals legally naturalized themselves, their consorts, and their children in attempting to assure the transmission of property along family lines. In the New Regime, especially after the radical Republic, citizenship was to become premised on property ownership; in the Old Regime, it was determined by conditions of property transmission, as bequests or inheritances. But the relation of king, family, and citizenship is even more complex when the vernacular fictions and rhetorical strategies of naturalized foreigners are considered. In their narrative expositions, foreigners represented a variety of family practices in which the king played diverse roles in the narrative, guaranteeing, reconstituting, or replicating the model of the family.

Independent of the ideas of self-interest or service, petitioners' claims in their expositions incorporated notions of birth, lineage, and what can only be called family values to constitute an even more expansive idea of French nationality than that of the jurists. By the eighteenth century, lawyers who successfully argued the cases of descendants of French citizens who had established their residence abroad—whether out of commercial interests, in flight from religious persecution, or even in service of the French king—imposed increasingly liberal standards on who could be considered French, expanding the "rules" of access to French citizenship in the seventeenth and eighteenth centuries. The expository narratives of those "aliens" who sought declarations, and, more rarely, naturalizations tended to expand the criteria of admission to the French polity. At the same time, they—alongside foreigners born abroad of foreign parents— developed a vernacular model of the absolute citizen, one far more likely to attribute a specific cultural, moral, and emotional content to the political ideal of belonging than was found in the legal formulas of naturalization.

In the seventeenth and eighteenth centuries, foreigners seeking citizenship, although rarely citing verse and text, put the legal doctrine to use, added important rhetorical flourishes, and even expanded the normative rules attributing French citizenship. In their petitions, they—through the clerks of royal secretaries responsible for drafting the letters—consistently deployed two legal tropes, the "spirit of return" (*esprit de retour*) and the idea of "accidental birth" (*naissance accidentelle*), which they spun into narrative stories about their families. And in these narratives they underscored the idea of a distinct social, if not ethnocultural, filiation as well as the practice and inheritability of patriotism— of an emotional attachment not only to the French king but to an abstract notion of France and French culture. This construction of an idea of French nationality, not simply as a legal membership category but also as an emotional bond and identity, went beyond purely juridical arguments. Anticipating the more modern notion of "nationality" that took shape in the nineteenth century, foreigners claiming to be French infused the vernacular citizen of absolutism with an essential identity of Frenchness.[43]

The idea of "accidental birth" was widely used for sons or daughters born far outside the kingdom of French parents who had emigrated for economic or religious reasons. Ritte Palyart, born in Portugal of a French father whose own father, Louis, had been naturalized (his letters had apparently perished in 1755 in the Lisbon earthquake and fire), established himself in Rouen in 1767 where, as a merchant, he served as consul general of Portugal in that port city of Normandy. Yet Palyart still claimed that he had "been born accidentally in a foreign country," and received letters of declaration from the chancellery in 1785.[44] Petitioners born just outside the shifting boundaries of the kingdom, north, east, and southeast, whose French parents still maintained their principal residence in the kingdom, made frequent use of the concept. Thus the succinctly stated but moving case of Jean Baptiste Collet, whose family was originally from Cubris in Provence, but whose mother was from the nearby village of Rigaud, across the kingdom's boundaries, in Savoy. His pregnant mother was counseled to return to her village "to take her native air," and there she gave birth "accidentally" on 12 February 1711 to the petitioner, "and died there following her pregnancy." The petitioner was taken back by his father to France, where he was raised and ordained a priest by the bishop of Marseille. In 1753, he sought and received a declaration of naturalization.[45]

But if people moved across boundaries, and gave birth there "accidentally," boundaries also moved across people, turning children of French parents into accidental foreigners. Or so argued a number of petitioners from the border regions, territories conquered and returned under the reign of Louis XIV. In June 1759, Jean Guillaume Wolf, native of the electorate of Trier, sought to be naturalized at the age of sixty-six. Born during the ephemeral French rule of the Rhineland in the 1690s, he noted in his letter how the French had been present between 1703 and 1705, and again shortly before the Utrecht Treaty. Arguing that since "the time of his birth and the time he came to France" coincided with French control over his homeland, "he should be assured the enjoyment of privileges attributed to true and original subjects." He was right, according to the jurisprudence; nonetheless, to guarantee those privileges, he acquired a declaration of naturalization.[46]

From an "accidental" birth outside the kingdom to the "accidental" character of the foreigner there was but one step, easily taken by Jean Glorieux, novice in the Capuchin monastery of Valenciennes, born in Dottighiers in the Low Countries, who requested a declaration of naturalization in 1773. He argued that he was born when his parish formed part of the Lille châtellenie, "but currently, by the rectification of the frontiers of the kingdom, this parish is under the submission of the Empress." Consequently, the petitioner, although born a "subject and native" of France, feared that "because of his accidental quality as a foreigner, [he would have] difficulty making his vows in the convent."[47] In fact, the eighteenth-century jurists increasingly distinguished between "true" foreigners (born abroad of foreign parents) and "false" ones (descendants of French parents born abroad). That distinction was shared by the French foreign ministry, as when, for example, in 1776, the comte de Vergennes elaborated on the distinction between the letters of naturalization (for "true" foreigners) and declarations of naturalization (for "true" Frenchmen and women). A true Frenchman, he wrote, echoing the jurists of the time, "cannot lose during a temporary stay abroad his quality of being French. The birth of his son in a foreign country is a pure accident: hence the distinction between letters of naturalization and declarations."[48] Such a distinction, we have seen, glossed a great diversity of practices, even in the later decades of the eighteenth century.

If some descendants of French parents insisted on their "accidental" birth outside the kingdom, and by extension on the "accidental" character of their foreignness, others developed in their petitions the idea that their parents, while living abroad, had always maintained a "spirit of return" that was remarkably inheritable and reactivated by their own return to the kingdom. Catherine Brun, born in Denmark of a French father and Danish mother, noted that her father had always kept the "spirit of return" and the "natural intention to return to the kingdom."[49] In one of the more elaborate petitions, which reflected the transformations brought on by the beginning of the French Revolution, the declaration of naturalization issued to Jean Ambroise Parin on 2 August 1789 developed both the idea of accidental birth and the spirit of return. Parin's petition stated that his parents were born in France, and established in Besançon; their residence in the states of the Prince Bishop of Basel was only temporary, since of three children, two were born and resident in the kingdom. Thus he claimed that "the birth of the petitioner was only accidental, that his father and mother had maintained the spirit of return which is in the heart of all Frenchmen, and that following their wish and consent the petitioner drew up his request to be reestablished in all the rights of citizenship and of our subjects which his accidental birth in a foreign country could not suspend or alter."[50]

Some petitioners elaborated on the spirit of return to a voluntary, but inheritable, affirmation of loyalty on the part of their parents who themselves could not, for a variety of reasons, complete the project of returning to France. A parent's spirit of return might have gone unrealized because of his untimely or unexpected death; and even the failure to seek naturalization in a foreign country could be used as proof of a desire to return to the kingdom. Antoine Tarin, an apprentice hatmaker born in Munich, claimed that his French mother and father were never naturalized in Bavaria "because their intention had always been to return to our kingdom after the Peace of Ryswick, [which they would have done] if they had not died." Tarin was faced with the fact that collateral relatives of his mother's and father's families opposed his succession on the basis that he was born in a foreign country, as were his wife and three children; his naturalization in 1710 empowered him in this context.[51] And in letters issued in 1750, Thomas Patrick Lee admitted that his grandfather came from Ireland and established himself in Bordeaux in 1658, taking letters of naturalization several years later, as did many Irish merchant families in the eighteenth century. His father, during a business trip to Ireland, married Marie Lambert, who gave birth in 1725 to the petitioner. The father, according to Thomas, had "always preserved the spirit of return," but died unexpectedly, and today the petitioner, born of a French father descended from a naturalized grandfather, sought "to enjoy the advantages and privileges acquired of that paternity" by seeking a declaration of naturalization.[52]

Foreigners seeking citizenship, or descendants of French citizens born abroad who reestablished their residence in the kingdom, thus claimed that they already enjoyed a devotion and attachment to France, a social and sentimental sense of belonging, if not a cultural identity as Frenchmen and women. Devotion and attachment to France were integral to the vernacular discourse of nationality under the absolute monarchy, the foreign claimants' version of the absolute citizen. Many claimed that they were explicitly raised by their families with a "special attachment to France," as was Vincent de Pellas, born in Genoa of French parents. These "sentiments for the fatherland of his fathers in which the petitioner was nourished from his earliest childhood have influenced him to come and fix his residence" in France and to seek naturalization.[53] Sophie Louise Jeanne Françoise Desnoyer, born in Dresden (Saxony), told how she was raised by her mother "in the principles of piety and virtue according to the mores and norms of our kingdom . . . and even though attached to France by the most sacred bonds, having married a Frenchman with whom she had several children," she still feared that her birth in a foreign land would one day create objections. She was naturalized in June 1764.[54] Pierre Mobre, a merchant born in Vienna of French parents, had been raised ever since the family's return to France "with a special attachment which he had always kept for our kingdom; the sentiments with which he was nourished since his childhood would make him stand out today notwithstanding the reputation he had acquired by his business in the place of his birth." He was made the equivalent of a "natural Frenchman" by a grant of June 1722.[55] Such stories were impoverished in their literary elaborations of "Frenchness." But petitioners underscored rhetorically their identity as Frenchmen and women and their sentimental attachment to France, the result of their upbringing by families that had instilled in them such feelings and sentiments. As such, the stories responded to a perceived normative practice that French citizenship was not solely a juridical status but also an emotional bond, and even a cultural identity.

Moreover, foreigners petitioning for naturalization considered how such values and sentiments formed part of their own nature, transmitted from their parents and ancestors to their own children. Here, they unwittingly linked the cognates of the Latin *natio* (nation), *nati* (birth), and *natura* (nature). "Foreigners," both true and false ones, did not make claims about Frenchness in terms of individual rights and natural law. Rather, they cast their arguments in terms of family upbringing, as well might be expected given the purpose of the letter in assuring the continuation of property ownership and the survival of property across generations. Thus Emmanuel Frédéric de Tane, born in the village of Quiers in the Piedmont, claimed to have lived in the Auvergne since his youth where he had been "raised with sentiments of faithfulness and attachment to our Crown to which his maternal ancestors had given expression on numerous occasions, and which he has not ceased to inspire in his children with the intention that he has always had to live and end his days with his family in our kingdom."[56] Petitioners also underscored their natural affinity, attraction, or inclination to France—a bond created through their families that would thus make them "natural" Frenchmen and women. And after the death of his mother and father in 1700, Charles Philippe Forest, born in Venice, sought to be naturalized and to return to his paternal family in Jouy, near Paris. The petitioner claimed that the "sentiments which his father inspired and the French inclination in which he was raised" made such a desire only "natural."[57]

Many other such examples of foreigners born of foreign parents abroad could be cited. But the rhetoric of natural belonging, an identity transmitted through the family, was especially frequent among "aliens" born abroad but descended of French émigrés, who had left for religious or professional reasons. These petitioners sometimes mentioned in passing their upbringing in the French language, or their acquisition of French after their settlement in the kingdom. More frequently, they insisted on their de facto identity as French men and women, the result of their family ties. Their sense of belonging to France was thus a "natural" extension of the attachments inculcated by their families.

In this sense, although it contained elements of what scholars consider to be modern notions of nationality, such an ideal of belonging and identification with France was firmly grounded not in an ideal of patriotism per se but in family ties and loyalty. More important than any myths and symbols of Frenchness was the importance of the symbolic world of belonging created through family ties, the *lieux de mémoire par excellence* of the Old Regime. The result was that personal and family narratives invoke the existence of truly naturalized foreigners, beyond the legal fictions of administrative law and letters. Unlike bureaucrats and barristers, who contributed to the making of French citizenship, the foreigners themselves took naturalization seriously, underscoring the affinity, attraction, or natural inclination for France, created through their families, that made them already "natural" Frenchmen and women. Naturalization, in this vernacular, recognized a de facto social affiliation and even a cultural identity.

The family was thus the primary framework of socialization that made French citizenship in the Old Regime into a category of social belonging.[58] The absolutist model only underscored the necessity of perpetual residence as a condition of acquired nativeness. In fact, the official and vernacular models were not really opposed in the practice of naturalization: in the Old Regime, family and belonging were orchestrated implicitly within the concept of perpetual and future residence. Resident and established foreigners in the Old Regime who sought naturalization were presumed to have acquired the loyalty and even the identity of natural Frenchman through their families. In the New

Regime, by contrast, it was not the family but the state that assured the assimilation of foreigners as citizens.[59]

If family counted for much in the vernacular practice of naturalization under the Old Regime, however, the state was not entirely absent. In their narratives of belonging, foreigners seeking naturalization nonetheless cast the king and the kingdom in central roles. In the celebrated court case of Rocquigny in 1694, Henri-François d'Aguesseau, then royal solicitor-general at the Paris parlement, considered the question put before the court of whether the son of a Frenchman born in a foreign country where his father was established should be considered French when he came to live in France and took letters of naturalization. D'Aguesseau claimed that he needed no letters because "nature gave him once the quality of citizen, which was only temporarily suspended, and can be easily recovered." Such recovery, moreover, was easy because, according to d'Aguesseau, arguing the same case, "the fatherland [patrie], like a good mother, opens her arms to her children, and invites them to return to their duty."[60]

The mixed metaphor of the fatherland as mother was, in fact, the complement of the widespread tropes in legal and political thought that identified the king as "father" and considered naturalized foreigners as "adopted children."[61] The adoption metaphor, as we have seen, was never found within the dispositive and executionary clauses of the patent letter of naturalization, even if it had formed part of the juridical vocabulary of the Old Regime. But the expository preambles of the letter frequently invoked the experiences of abandonment and being an orphan, and pointed to the role of the king as father.

Such stories of being orphaned can be found widely among converted Protestants, Jews, and Muslims, who abandoned (or were abandoned by) their families and became French. Thus the story of David da Costa's conversion from Judaism, as told in his 1743 letter of naturalization. Born of Jewish parents in Livorno (Italy), da Costa explained how at the age of sixteen, after traveling throughout Europe, he came to settle in the town of Rennes with his uncle "to learn the French language." It was at that time, he continued, that he "saw the truth" of the Christian religion and decided to convert. His uncle tried to dissuade him, and when he failed, chased David from the house, "and he thus was deprived of all the help from his family." Notwithstanding his abandonment, David was baptized on 17 May 1728, and took the name "Jean-Jacques Coste, that he saw could be better accommodated to the pronunciation of the French language." Jean-Jacques married five years later, and he began to use his inherited family name, da Costa, even as he had his five children baptized. Now, with confusion over his children's names, and given his own desire to stay in France and perpetuate his original name, David sought a royal grant of naturalization, with provision for his name to be changed back to the name of his ancestors.[62]

In many ways, da Costa's case was singular. His letter of naturalization contained a lengthy exposé of his life story, rare among the usually laconic, formulaic character of the grants. His attention to the French language, highlighted in the exposé, was also distinctive. Most letters of naturalization made no mention of name changes, even if it "was the practice" for non-Catholics to take a new name when they abjured their old religion and were baptized.[63] But if retaking his family name was unique, da Costa's tale of abandonment by his family was not. Nor was the narrative of conversion, which figures centrally in the letters of non-Christians who came to France.

Such was particularly the case among converted Muslims and Jews born in the Ottoman Empire, who for a variety of circumstances found themselves in France seeking citizenship. Louis Albohère, naturalized in August 1754, was from Istanbul (still called Constantinople in the letters of the eighteenth century), and defined himself "of the Jewish nation, brought up in the religion of Mohammed, and professing the Catholic, Apostolic, and Roman faith." He had come to France as the treasurer of the Ottoman emperor, and had converted while in Paris in 1722.[64] Other subjects of the Ottoman emperor had been orphaned and brought to France in less voluntary circumstances. Louis Elisabeth Ally was captured in 1686 in Belgrade by the emperor's troops and lived in the Palatinate until 1689 when he was recaptured by the French and brought to Versailles in the retinue of the duc de Bourbon, who had him baptized in 1690.[65] Several other Muslim children, including Lucie Esmer Fontana, baptized in 1697, had been brought to France by the Sr. de Fériol when he left the post of ambassador of Louis XIV at the Ottoman court. But others left their families and came to France specifically to convert to Catholicism. Thus the solemn story of Jean Marie Alix de Boullomoranges, born in Philadelphia (in the Ottoman Empire) in 1715, and naturalized in 1743 within a year of coming to the kingdom. He had left his family and come to France after having made a vow, while deathly ill, to "leave the errors of Mohammedism." Four months after converting, he sought French citizenship.[66]

Many of the narratives of Protestant, Jewish, and Muslim converts to Catholicism include descriptions of the ways in which they were abandoned, like David da Costa, by their families. Religion and family went together: Jean Lampe's abjuration of "the errors of Calvinism that he had the misfortune of imbibing with milk" in 1779 used an ancient biological trope of French culture.[67] Jean Rhode dit Le Roux, master clothier from Schomberg (Saxony), claimed that he abjured "in his earliest youth the errors of the so-called Reformed Religion in which he had the misfortune of being born" and that he left his family and came to France "to have the liberty of practicing the Catholic faith."[68] Even though he had been born a Muslim in Athens, Jean Baptiste Panallioti was baptized on 30 October 1689 when he arrived in Nîmes. "He was but eight or nine, and luckily he received the faith and formation of our kingdom, such that he has retained nothing of his country, not even the name of his father or mother, of which he has no memory," and certainly none of their religious faith.[69] It is no surprise to find the occasional case involving both naturalization and legitimation among religious refugees and converts. Thus Marie Madelaine Demarseille took her last name from the town where her mother had settled when she immigrated from Greece. Her mother had married and fled to Algeria, leaving her daughter alone to be "brought up and instructed in the Catholic religion and kept at our expense in convents." Thankful for all that she received, she nonetheless "wanted more than anything to enjoy the advantages of [the king's] natural subjects," and sought naturalization and legitimation.[70]

The stories of foreign petitioners born Catholics were less about abandonment than about being orphaned: relating anecdotes about the death of their parents or spouses, the narratives implicitly identify the king as the central male figure who would reconstitute metaphorically a family unit. Within a month of her parents' death, Louise de Moupes de Casseneuve, born in Spain of French parents but long resident in France, engaged a royal secretary to be naturalized by the Great Chancellery. She did so "to assure her estate and her rights, to put herself under shelter from any trouble and difficulties that she might encounter under the pretext of her birth in a foreign country, and to participate in the advantages and privileges that her father had acquired by birth."[71]

Among female petitioners, the king often figured in a more evident manner than among men in the reconstitution of the unity of the family or the household; women were more likely to make their claims at the moment of the death or disappearance of their fathers than of their husbands. As Jean Bacquet pointed out, the foreigner in France lived under the aphorism "*licet liber vivat,* such that he can give his goods, sell them, exchange them, and dispose of them freely while alive," but

> the opposite is practiced in France toward married women who *serve vivunt* [live as slaves] because during their marriage they cannot in any way contract obligations, whether by sale, exchange, or donation, or otherwise . . . but married women can freely dispose of their goods, and by last will and testament they can deed all their movable property . . . without the consent or authority of their husbands.

Thus when a foreign women lost her husband or father, sometimes claiming to inherit *in uxor* his estate, it was only "natural" that she sought to be naturalized.[72]

Some women's claims went further than those of Bacquet and the jurists, as they put further pressure on the legal boundaries of belonging. The lawyers, for example, never considered how a foreign women's marriage to a Frenchman might confer on her the qualities of French citizenship—although it might help prove, in certain cases, that the petitioner had established the intention to reside in the kingdom.[73] Yet female petitioners frequently claimed that the act of marriage implied the transmission of citizenship. Jeanne Coudurier, born in Cluse, Savoy, married an ironworker from Savoy and lived in Marseille for seventeen years. At the age of thirty-three, in 1722, she offered an extensive review of the reasons that she ought already to be considered French: her husband had acquired the "right of nativeness" (*droit de regnicole*) by his twenty-two-year residence, his commercial activities, and his acquisitions; that she, by marriage as well as by royal edicts of 1669 and 1703, should be considered French. But to guarantee her rights to the estate, she petitioned for and received a letter of declaration.[74] Women also used the claim of marriage to a Frenchman as a rationale for being considered French already, as Cécile Conti did in her 1782 naturalization. Born in Aleppo, in the Ottoman Empire, of a Venetian father and a French mother, she had married a French merchant there in 1769, and had subsequently settled "irrevocably" in Marseille. Thus "she could be considered by virtue of her marriage to one of our natural subjects as if she were our true subject and *regnicole*." But to avoid troubles that might result from her foreign birth and marriage in a foreign country, "she had been counseled" to seek letters of naturalization.[75]

If women enlarged the legal criteria of what constituted a citizen in their arguments to be naturalized, they nonetheless insisted on the central role of the king. Their husbands had left them property, no doubt, but also a new aspiration to become French, and at the death of these male kin, women called on the king to fulfill their desire. Catherine Philippine Thiriard, born in Cologne, petitioned in 1759 with her two daughters for a declaration of naturalization. She was the widow of Mathieu Bressole, a Frenchman born in Lyon and chief cook of the duc de Lorraine, then also king of Poland. Bressole had lived for several years in Dresden before developing the idea of returning to France, and just at the point when he sought to leave, he died on 13 April 1757. "Wanting nonetheless to follow the will of her husband," the widow and her two children came to Lyon and petitioned for citizenship.[76]

But husbands could also constrain the desires of their wives or fiancées, and their deaths might provide the occasion for the king to liberate a woman from her condition and to fulfill her wishes through naturalization. Honorée Etienne sought her letters on learning of the death of her fiancé. Born in Lisbon of French parents from whom she had always "felt the inclination for the French nation," Etienne had resided in Paris with her parents on their retirement until her engagement to another French merchant. Her fiancé had "forced her" to establish her residence in Lisbon; she had not yet departed when she learned of his death. "Finding nothing else to engage her to go" and, by contrast, everything to make her stay in Paris "in the bosom of her family," she sought to be naturalized in 1752.[77] In a similar fashion, Marie Aurore, countess of Rutouska, born in Silesian Prussia, petitioned in 1756 for naturalization. She claimed that as a legitimate daughter of the king of Poland, she had always wanted to live and die in France, but the obligation to follow her husband made her suspend that plan, although she sent her son to Lyon to study. She followed her husband to Turin when he was named ambassador to Savoy, and finally to France when he was posted there. Indeed, she was about to join him in Paris when he died, at which point she sought citizenship.[78]

In all these instances, women took care in their narratives to cast the king as a replacement for a central male figure—father, husband, fiancé—while expressing their own will and volition to reside in France. More generally, petitioners for naturalization consistently invoked their voluntary choice in moving to France, or returning to their hometowns or villages, in order to remain there until their deaths. This was, of course, one of the principal criteria for a valid letter: the formula of the letter declared that the charter would only be valid if the petitioner "reside and finish his days in France." Naturalization was an agreement, a "contract," that symbolized the foreigner's willingness to identify with the kingdom and to enter into a relation of fidelity to the king.

In the official model of the absolute citizen, an expression of will was also a central element in the conditions and mechanism of becoming naturalized. French legal historians have sometimes emphasized the element of will as the foundation of allegiance in the jurisprudence of citizenship under the Old Regime. In England, allegiance was "natural" and "perpetual," received at birth, and impossible to shed. By contrast, in France, allegiance was constituted in the acts of will implicit in the establishment of permanent residence.[79] The foreigner's expression of will was not tied to a specific cultural identity, nor was the voluntary and contractual nature of naturalization dependent on prior social assimilation. Yet the vernacular fictions of the petitioners occasionally emphasized cultural identity—sharing French "mores and customs"—as a claim to French citizenship. Such a notion of social belonging bore traces of the normative, juridical presumption of social assimilation and integration inherited from the "Italian model." Yet it more closely resembled modern citizenship as a form of social belonging and a cultural identity, of shared values and customs and even (although the cases are few) the French language.

From 1660 to 1790, grants of citizenship contained a tension, expressed by petitioners within the letters themselves, between a voluntary affiliation to the king and kingdom and a "natural" condition—although hardly a biological or racial one—of citizenship. In a manner similar to those seeking ennoblement, petitioners for naturalization and declaration developed arguments about family "stock" and French "nature." Unlike ennoblement, however, Frenchness could be acquired by birth within the kingdom as well as by biological descent from French parents, but it did not formally require the "civil transfiguration" of a foreigner into a citizen (above, chapter 2). Yet ennoblement and naturalization converged theoretically, just as they converged as administrative practices, in the ability of the king to change the "nature" of a subject, and in specific letters of naturalization of foreigners also seeking nobility. Thus the request for a declaration of naturalization in October 1777 by Jean Evangeliste Louis Adam, the comte de Joyeuse, member of the imperial household and councillor in the Austrian Estates General. After a detailed genealogy of his family that demonstrated his profoundly French roots, the comte de Joyeuse excused his father's naturalization by the Austrian crown, claiming that his "filiation proves that he is of French origin, and even though his father and grandfather had renounced their fatherland, they have no right to deprive him of being reinstated; that his return [to the kingdom] of the petitioner would seem to give him the quality of being French, and would reestablish him in the rights attached to this quality." There was some juridical foundation to this claim, since Chancellor d'Aguesseau himself had once argued that "it is not within the power of a father to refuse his children the inestimable advantages of their origins" and that having returned to France and established themselves, the children could rightly claim their "original" nature, even if their fathers had expressly lost it.[80] As for the comte de Joyeuse, the chancellery (and no doubt, the council of dispatches) awarded him naturalization and ennoblement, duly recorded by the Chambre des aides.[81] Nothing was remarkable about the procedure except for the rhetoric of his letter, which identified both the status of nobility and nativeness as "natural qualities" passed through descent.

Foreigners seeking to become French, or French descendants seeking to restore their status as "natural Frenchmen," believed it best to "naturalize" their desires, identities, and emotional attachments—to claim that they were "naturally" inclined to be, if they were not already, French. Turning their interests and those of their families into facts of nature, they nonetheless expressed the will and desire to become, or to be recognized as, French. The tension between the expression of will and that of the natural order was best exemplified in the stories of children born abroad of French parents, within the idea of a "spirit of return." Other foreigners resolved the opposition between a juridical identity founded on birth and the act of naturalization founded on will by insisting on their natural desires and their naturalized links to France.

In both cases, the expression of will was largely determined by family ties and by a strategic and instrumental claim of nationality that rendered the foreigner capable of bequeathing and of inheriting property, or of holding offices and benefices in the kingdom. Such expressions of will were rarely anchored in an abstract political and modern notion of the citizen, who expressed undying loyalty to the fatherland (*patrie*) before and during the Revolution through the passions and interests of their families. The idea of will also mediated, especially in the case of female petitioners, the opposition between the family and the king; and, for dozens of other foreigners, the notion of will helped resolve the tension between the private interests of the claimant in becoming a citizen and his normative devotion to the public good.

In the stories of belonging, the "bosom of the family" remained the most evident space of the socialization—or even of integration—of foreigners resident in the kingdom, as well as descendants of Frenchmen and women born abroad who returned to France and sought to have their citizenship "declared" and re-instated. They were, through or despite their families (in the cases of abandonment and orphanage) already French by nature, and the act of naturalization or declaration merely affirmed by privilege what already existed in fact. In some ways, the vernacular fictions of naturalizations returned to the "Italian model" of the Commentators, and its idealization in France by the jurists of the sixteenth century. In other ways, the vernacular fictions anticipated the constitutional requirements of naturalization during and after the French Revolution, when periods of prior residency on French territory was proof of social assimilation. In the New Regime, however, especially in the Third Republic, socialization was to be assured by the state itself, through primary schools, military conscription, and political suffrage. Beyond that, the modern French "republican model" was to rest on the assumption, despite the formal and abstract formulas of civic identity, that the nationality of France's citizens was culturally specific—and that national groups had different degrees of potential assimilability.[82] In striking contrast, although the official model of the absolute citizen never invoked the criteria of language, ethnicity, or cultural identity as markers of belonging, the vernacular making of absolute citizens revealed how foreign citizens in the seventeenth and eighteenth centuries, including French descendants, anticipated this more "essentialist" understanding of identity.

PART TWO

A SOCIAL HISTORY OF
FOREIGN CITIZENS, 1660–1789

⊰ CHAPTER FOUR ⊱

STATUS AND SOCIOPROFESSIONAL IDENTITIES

The juridical, royal, and vernacular models of the absolute citizen emanated from the royal council and chancellery, the sovereign courts, and foreign citizens themselves. These discourses framed the social history of foreign migration and settlement in the kingdom until the French Revolution. Using the two overlapping sample populations of foreign citizens—the voluntarily naturalized foreigners (from 1660 to 1789) and the collectively taxed and naturalized foreigners (from 1697 to 1707)—the following three chapters turn to social history. The social and professional identities of foreign citizens are the subject of chapter 4; their countries and regions of origin and, less consistently, their place of settlement in the kingdom are the focus of chapter 5; and the timing of citizenship grants between Louis XIV and French Revolution is the concern of chapter 6. These chapters look through the lens of naturalization, focused on the national level, to make sense of a broad range of what social scientists call variables—law, politics, geography, and economy—that converged to produce general patterns of naturalization in the kingdom as a whole and among different social, professional, and "national" groups. Although this approach can explain much about foreign France in the Old Regime, it ultimately cannot account for the specificity of the thousands of individual decisions to become citizens or the single decision of an absolute monarch to forcibly tax and naturalize the foreign population of the kingdom.

Gender, Family, Age, Wealth: Citizenship as a (Relatively) Socially Inclusive Category

The absolute citizen was, in the theory of Bodin and the jurisprudence of the courts, a socially inclusive category: early modern jurists made a central distinction between citizen and foreigner, native subject and alien, founded on the droit d'aubaine. Yet just how inclusive socially was the category in practice, as revealed by the profile of voluntarily naturalized foreigners and those taxed in 1697?

Women represent more than a tenth of the foreign population forcibly taxed and naturalized in 1697 (including the heiresses of foreigners who settled in the kingdom after 1600); among the immigrants taxed in 1697, nearly 15 percent were women. The figures accord, grosso modo, with the proportion of women among individually naturalized foreigners from 1660 to 1790, when 13 percent were female, a figure that remained astonishingly consistent from one end of the period to another, across all different groups of foreigners, and among different kinds of naturalizations (letters of declaration, letters of naturalization).[1] For not only were women capable of becoming French citizens—unlike in Spain, late medieval Italy, or during the New Regime—but, in many cases, it was necessary for them to do so.[2] The category of citizen in France trumped that of women: even if women were in many ways the obverse of foreigners—they had inheritance rights but few property rights, and were required in every other aspect of civil law to follow the condition of their husbands (on this, the jurists were clear). A woman's marriage to a French native did not entail naturalization as a Frenchwoman under the Old Regime. The tax rolls between 1697 and 1707 contain numerous examples of foreign women required to pay the Naturalization Tax even though "married to a Frenchman," and the tax was also imposed on foreign men married to French women natives. In contrast to the New Regime, in which marriage was one of the mechanisms of attributing (or disqualifying) women from citizenship, Old Regime law disengaged marriage and citizenship.[3]

Among the 893 women naturalized from the Age of Louis XIV to the French Revolution, the greatest proportion were married, and their formal grants of naturalization named their spouse and, much more rarely, their children not born in the kingdom. One hundred of these women were widows, and another two dozen were fathers and other kin who sought citizenship for young girls.[4] Including the women and dependent minors named as beneficiaries in their fathers' or relatives' letters of naturalization, the proportion of women would increase to one in six, the same as among the taxed foreigners in 1697 (13 percent).

In juridical theory and the practice of naturalization, French citizenship was modestly inclusive, but not according to standards of absolute gender parity. The relatively small proportion of women naturalized reflected, if not the reality of immigration patterns in the early modern period, then at least the normative stigma that early modern lawyers (and others) attached to female immigrants. According to the jurist Papon, for example, women without husbands who left their homes abroad to come to France "are reputed to be whores and lecherous."[5] Still, it is worth underscoring that in the Old Regime, unlike the New Regime—and especially after the adoption of the Civil Code in 1803—foreign women frequently enough became French citizens by naturalization.

Likewise, foreigners of all ages could acquire the legal qualities of French natives, especially their capacity to inherit or devolve property according to the principles of French civil law. In this way, naturalization was not conditionally limited to the adult population, even though, in practice, most naturalized foreign citizens were adults. In fact, we know relatively little about the age of foreigners seeking citizenship (age appears in only 7 percent of the longitudinal data sample), but the statistical evidence suggests that most were mature adults: the median age was forty years old. Anecdotal evidence suggests that some were quite mature indeed. Jean Antoine Thuret, born in Puget-des-Theniers in the county of Nice, claimed to be eighty years old, having lived in Aix-en-Provence for fifty years, thirty of them as a priest in the parish of Cadenet (certainly with royal permission, although he only sought naturalization in 1722). But at least 5 percent of the beneficiaries of naturalization were quite young, legally minors and underage children whose parents or other relatives—especially those seeking to profit from an inheritance—sought naturalization or declarations on their behalf. Such was the case of Marie-Catherine Baudouin, whose Protestant father had been born in France but took refuge at the age of sixteen in the Low Countries ("Les Pays"), where his daughter was born in 1716. Seven years later, he returned with her to Metz, abjuring his Protestant faith, "to raise her in the Catholic religion." His daughter received letters of declaration on 11 September 1723.[6]

Relatively few petitioners for citizenship listed the number of years they had resided in France—most were content to rest with the formulaic phrase that they had been in France "for several years," a phrase that at least once, in the case of the *Gumpp v. Joner* and consorts in Alsace, became a relevant issue within the litigation.[7] In practice, approximating modern requirements of naturalization, most foreign citizens were long established in their local communities. Twenty years in the kingdom was the average length of residence (among the small percentage of naturalized foreigners about whom such things can be known). In social terms, voluntary naturalizations tended to come after a long period of residence, of "integration" and "assimilation" (and the acquisition of interests) in the community. Everything happened as if, in the practice of naturalization, the jurists' xenophobic strictures, articulated in the 1570s, occurred naturally: foreign petitioners were already longtime residents of the kingdom, socially assimilated and integrated into their local communities.

The crown did not impose a priori conditions of social status and integration on those who sought citizenship—there were no statutory requirements based on gender, prior residence, or religious faith (although Muslims were de facto excluded). But as a norm, foreign citizens of the Old Regime were long established in the kingdom, had reached a certain age, and—given the nature of the privilege—acquired a certain amount of property or goods that they sought to protect (or a professional office or benefice that they sought to acquire or guarantee).

Even in the absence of statutory limitations on who could become a citizen, there were de facto limits on the social inclusiveness of naturalized foreigners. Wealth and status, for example, clearly mattered—although in this case, the social variation of foreign citizens was surprisingly extensive, especially in relation to early naturalization practices of the fifteenth and sixteenth centuries. Those who were forcibly and collectively naturalized in 1697, of course, tended to be quite wealthy, at least in the eyes of the tax-farmers. Their median tax assessment was three hundred livres, roughly three years of income for a skilled mason in Bayeux or a tailor in Amiens under Louis XIV. (The median tax assessment of already naturalized immigrants in the data from 1697–1707 was even higher, at six hundred livres.)[8] But such fantastical assessments, not actual taxes levied, recall the political and economic project at the heart of the 1697 naturalization tax: to tax foreigners with movable and highly visible wealth who actively participated within the France of "movement" (including the service sector). Similarly, among those who sought citizenship for themselves and their families, the cost of the procedure alone, from three hundred to six hundred livres or more, meant that only foreigners with a certain level of income, property, and status would bother to seek naturalization.

Just how wealthy were the individually naturalized foreigners? Their income and assets are not disclosed in the texts of naturalization, and indices can be found only in the few extant records of verification and registration of naturalizations in certain jurisdictions of the Chambres des comptes and the royal treasury bureaux.[9] Anecdotal evidence from their inquiries of foreigners' net worth reveals a surprising range, from the very rich to those of far more modest means. Isaac-Pierre Boissière, a royal official in Brittany, was born in Geneva, the son of French parents. A treasury councillor in Brittany, his wealth was publicly known upon the registration of his declaration of naturalization on 31 January 1756 at the Nantes Chambre des comptes. He had purchased his office for sixty-eight thousand livres the year before, and upstanding members of the community—lawyers, gentlemen, and clergy—attested to his ownership of property and movable wealth in the town of l'Orient worth another ten thousand livres.[10] No wonder that he probably spent more than five hundred livres getting letters of naturalization, the cost of his "insurance policy" that guaranteed (perhaps) that his heirs would benefit from his wealth.

Boissière's case was unusual: few foreigners—much less French natives—had achieved quite that level of economic and social success. Although many enjoyed inherited wealth and advantages, the population of foreigners naturalized forcibly in 1697 or voluntarily during the Old Regime was not a group exceptionally dominated by the nobility. Certainly this was true in contrast to sixteenth century naturalizations, when the nobility accounted for nearly half of the foreigners granted citizenship. Among those forcibly and collectively naturalized between 1697 and 1707, a mere 2 percent were members of the titled nobility—still at least double the proportion of French natives in the kingdom. In the longitudinal database of individual naturalizations, only a maximum estimate of some 5 percent were titled nobles. By the late seventeenth century, and until the end of the Old Regime, naturalization was not only routinized, it was democratized as well.[11]

These nobles often stuck out with their elaborate claims and the self-evident way in which they supposed the existence of connections at court. Foreign princes (such as the duke and duchess of Savoy and their children in 1702) and the high-ranking foreign nobles at times occupied a disproportionate place in the archives, just as their narratives in the expository statements within the actual grants of naturalization tended to be more elaborate. Moreover, foreign nobles claiming citizenship were also more likely to receive dispensations of residence, and sometimes the king's recognition of their nobility. But as far as can be known statistically, the titled nobility (which did not, of course, include those "living nobly") did not amount to more than some three hundred cases among over six thousand. Far from being monopolized by either money or inherited privilege, the naturalized foreigners were an inclusive "sample" of the foreign population (albeit not as "inclusive" as those subject to the forcible collective naturalization of 1697).

A surprisingly large number of petitioners for naturalization made claims not only of their common and humble status but even, and especially, their outright poverty. Jeanne-Baptiste Beddat, born in Chambéry (Savoy), the daughter of a notary, came to France for the first time in 1738, at the age of twenty-three. She stayed four years before returning to her native town to marry a peddler from Bourg-en-Bresse. They returned to Lyon together in 1745, where she worked as a dressmaker, but at the time of her petition to become French she was "very uncomfortable" financially, without any real or movable property. Her father, she claimed, had "entirely wasted" her mother's inheritance.[12] Other examples abound, and these claims were often substantiated by the attorneys and other royal officials who verified and registered the letters at the provincial Chambres des comptes and the financial bureaux. At the Chambre in Normandy, a royal solicitor concluded that Elizabeth Morey, who had come to France at the age of six from Portsmouth, England, had lived thirty-three years in Cherbourg "on alms, having no wealth of any kind, and being without any goods or revenue, she had only sought letters of naturalization to be able to make a will to benefit the poor of the little she could collect by her work and savings." Priests and other clerics, gentlemen and municipal officers, and leading inhabitants of Cherbourg together underscored her poverty and the fact that she had "always worked."[13] To the financial bureau in Lyon at which his naturalization was registered, Antoine Pascal, a textile shearer from Sardinia, claimed that the one hundred livres he had spent so far to get his letters registered did not include the 120 livres for the registration fees at the financial bureau. The financial officers stated that he had even "borrowed the remainder which he could only do by selling part of his household goods which were already insufficient to pay for the dowry of his two wives," assuming that he was referring to consecutive marriages.[14] Of course, these are rhetorical claims: because the cost of naturalization—especially the "tax" levied by the Chambre des comptes—depended on the perceived wealth of the petitioner, the tendency was to exaggerate poverty. But when such overstatements are justified by the formal inquiry of the provincial Chambre, we are forced to take notice.

Thus Joseph Porter was no doubt poor, although he might have hidden the real interests behind his acquisition of French citizenship. Born in Warwick, England, Porter was, according to the verification of his letters by the Nantes Chambre des comptes in 1749,

> a young man, unmarried, and owning no immovable goods, and having no other goods than his clothing and attire kept in a trunk which he opened in our presence and in which there were, in effect, no other things except those that he declared, and for which we judge not worthy of a detailed description, given their little value.[15]

Other examples might be cited from elsewhere in the kingdom, wherever the verification records survive.[16] Anecdotally if not statistically, they point to a notable presence of an unexpected element of relative poverty within a wide range of wealth among foreign citizens in the Old Regime.

Within the "France of Movement" and the Service Economy: Socioprofessional Identities of Foreign Citizens

More can be known about the socioprofessional status of foreign citizens from the evidence of the expository narratives of naturalizations and declarations. The profiles of both the individually naturalized foreigners between 1660 and 1790 and the "foreign" population placed on the Naturalization Tax rolls of 1697–1707 were distorted mirror images of the native population of France. Both groups were predominantly urban, mobile, and (apart from the individually naturalized clerics) engaged in commerce and manufacturing, as merchants or artisans. A large number were part of what economists call the service sector, engaging in activities from royal officeholding to innkeeping and laundry work. The immigrants taxed at the beginning of the eighteenth century especially took part in the "France of movement"—that France of free commercial exchange and recruitment of foreigners on which Louis XIV had turned his back in 1697. Among them, a third were merchants, a third were artisans, and another fifth together were clergy, nobles, officeholders, and practitioners of the liberal professions. In a kingdom where nearly nine-tenths of the population was rural, a "peasant kingdom" with its enduring and stable structures of constraint and tradition, the immigrants were largely concentrated in the France of movement, the secondary (commercial and manufacturing) and tertiary (service) sectors of the Old Regime economy (table 4.1).

TABLE 4.1.
Socioprofessional Identities of Naturalized Foreigners (1660–1789) and
Immigrants Taxed (1697–1707)

	Naturalized Foreigners 1660–1789		Immigrants Taxed 1697–1707	
	Number	Percent	Number	Percent
Clergy	1090	39	231	7
Merchants	537	19	1145	34
Artisans	284	10	1125	34
Liberal professions	237	8	163	5
Military personnel	235	8	—	—
Officeholders	223	8	169	5
Servants	134	5	—	—
Agricultural workers	9	0	369	11
Others	27	1	67	2
Total	2776	100	3269	100

In the Paris region, for example, with its relatively high level of urbanization (including the capital city of nearly half a million), Jacques Dupâquier has shown that 38 percent of the male population in 1717 was concentrated in the secondary and tertiary sectors of economic activity. By contrast, among the taxed immigrant population on the tax rolls of 1697–1707, 98% held professions identifiable as commercial and service-oriented, while only 2 percent were engaged in rural, agricultural activities.[17] It was the same in other provinces, even if there were large concentrations of German and Flemish agricultural workers taxed in the province of the Three Bishoprics of Metz, Toul, and Verdun, and significant concentrations of sailors from Italy and the Mediterranean in Provence. But rural (and maritime) workers tended to be exceptions. In general, foreigners taxed in 1697–1707 were found not in the countryside but in the city: the small towns and the capital cities of the provinces, the coastal cities (Toulon, Bordeaux, Saint-Malo), and parts of the Mediterranean and the Atlantic, in the frontier towns of the east, a line stretching from the Channel to the Mediterranean, and of course in Paris. The urban framework of Old Regime France structured the reception of immigrants to the kingdom. In all these cities, the foreigners inscribed on the tax rolls played essential parts in commerce, in the manufacture of ordinary products and luxury goods, as well as in the service economy.[18]

The population of naturalized foreigners and descendants of French immigrants between 1660 and 1789 had a different profile than that of the immigrant population taxed between 1697 and 1707. For one, the mercantile and artisanal elements were much less present among the individually naturalized foreigners, among whom only one in five was a merchant and one in ten an artisan. Officeholders and practitioners of the liberal professions represented a slightly larger proportion of the longitudinal sample (8 percent each) than they did among the taxed immigrant population in 1697 (5 percent each). Military personnel, absent from the 1697 tax rolls because they were formally exempted by the royal edict of 1697, represented another 8 percent of the sample of foreigners who sought citizenship. Servants, absent in 1697 because largely ignored by the tax-farmers, made up 5 percent of the individually naturalized foreigners sampled, while agricultural workers were significantly less present among the foreigners who sought citizenship than they had been within the forcibly naturalized population in 1697: only nine can be found among the data set of individually naturalized foreigners, while they made up 11 percent of the taxed population of immigrants with known professions.

But the single greatest difference was the significantly more visible presence of clergy: of the 2,779 naturalized foreigners between 1660 and 1789 for whom professions are known (41 percent of the total number), more than a third of these (1,090, or 39 percent) were clergy. We begin therefore, and by convention, with the First Estate.

Clergy

That the largest single group of petitioners for naturalization were clergy is not surprising: an increasing number of them combined their requests for French citizenship with the request for a royal privilege to hold benefices (*congé de tenir bénéfices*). In jurisprudential theory and in royal edicts since the fifteenth century, foreign clerics were forbidden from holding either spiritual or temporal benefices in the kingdom. In practice, however, there were multiple ways in which foreigners could come to preach, and even hold benefices, without having been naturalized, much "to the detriment of true Frenchmen, to whom these dignities are due, which is a scandalous thing," wrote a frustrated Jean Papon in the late sixteenth century. Foreign clerics could acquire, some through court connections, simple permissions (*brevets*) to do so; more disturbing, according to Papon, they sometimes held benefices under someone else's name. Or, according to the barrister and aspiring jurisconsult Héricourt de Vautier, they might receive royal dispensations to hold benefices independent of their naturalizations.[19] But by the late seventeenth century, when the constant interdictions against foreigners holding ecclesiastical office became less frequent, foreign clergy increasingly sought a formal privilege to hold benefices within a letter of naturalization. Moreover, a consistent jurisprudence of the eighteenth century required clerics to be naturalized, and to be resident in the kingdom, if they sought to devolve their accumulated property to heirs.[20] Permission to hold benefices was not the same thing as naturalization. The jurisprudential consensus about foreign clergy was not entirely unchallenged into the eighteenth century, and there were always specific privileges (such as those accorded the English Benedictines in 1736) that exempted particular groups of foreign ecclesiastics from the droit d'aubaine, although without naturalizing them explicitly.[21]

The naturalized foreign clergy was almost evenly divided between "secular" (those in possession, at least theoretically, of cures of souls) and "regular" clergy (who took formal vows to enter religious orders), resulting in a much larger ratio of tonsured foreign clergy than among French clerics. Most curators of souls were identified as priests or curates (*vicaires, secondaires*), many of whom sought to be naturalized in order to take possession of their parishes.[22] Among them was Honoré Autheman, born in St.-Martin-d'Entraunes in the county of Nice (Savoy). According to his letter of naturalization, Autheman's uncle, also a priest, had resigned the presbytery of Glandève in Provence in his favor, and despite having obtained a papal permission, Honoré had deferred taking possession "in the fear that, having been born in the county of Nice, reputed to be a foreign country, he might be bothered in doing so, which obliged him to have recourse to the king to obtain his letters of naturalization." He became a citizen, with permission to hold benefices, in July 1753.[23] Others had long been in possession of their cures, and were at the end of their careers as priests before they sought to assure their succession. Jean Collin, born in 1676 in the Spanish Low Countries, had lived thirty-three years in Lille, where he had been in possession of his cure for over twenty-four years. In 1737, at the age of sixty-one and considering retirement, he sought to be naturalized with permission to hold benefices, "in the hope of finding under our dominion another benefice that would require less work, there being no other obstacle than his birth outside the kingdom, where he intends to pass the rest of his days and wishes to participate in the advantages that our true subjects and natives enjoy."[24]

Other noncloistered clergy, besides those several hundred in charge of the care of souls, included academics: sixteen theology students, eight bachelors of theology, and fifty-seven doctors of theology. Among the latter was François-Joseph Collignon, born in the village of Verton, in Trier (county of Luxembourg), who had gotten letters of naturalization ten years earlier, but did not receive his permission to hold a benefice until 1772. At that point, he sought—unusually, but in a way that revealed the citizenship revolution of the time—"all the rights of a Citizen and subject of the king of France."[25] There were also four cardinals, all high-ranking members of the nobility, including Ferdinand, cardinal of Furstemberg in the Holy Roman Empire, who was naturalized in July 1688 (with permission to hold benefices), and Louis and Jacques Gaulterio, Roman cardinals who also received a dispensation of residence in 1724.[26]

Among the regular clergy, who had taken vows to enter religious orders—especially in the French–Low Countries borderland, and in Alsace—nearly one-quarter were novices in a wide variety of monastic orders and institutions on French territory. The vast number of them were born in border territories that had shifted allegiances. In the seventeenth century, especially under Louis XIV, people crossed boundaries, and boundaries also crossed people. In the late eighteenth century, as states began to delimit their territorial boundaries, incidents of accidental foreignness were again important. Jean Glorieux, novice in the Capuchin Convent in Valenciennes, was born in Dottighiers in Flanders at a time when the parish was part of the French kingdom and the jurisdiction of the châtellenie of Lille. "But now [1773] by the delimitation arrangement of boundaries this parish is under the obedience of the empress, the claimant, although born our subject and regnicole fears that his accidental quality of being a foreigner will create obstacles in allowing him to make his vows in the convent." He received a declaration of naturalization on 23 June 1773.[27] Not all regular clerics were from the borderlands. Celia Celina Moor, born a Protestant in Chelsea (England), became a novice in the convent and monastery of the Capuchin nuns in Saint-Omer because, as she explained, "Divine Providence has granted her the grace of leaving her place of residence and calling her to the Catholic, Apostolic, and Roman religion, which she now professes." After expressing the formulaic desire to "finish her days in the kingdom," she became a citizen in March 1772.[28]

The regular clergy, among individually naturalized foreigners, was weighted toward the top of the First Estate's traditional hierarchy. Among them were sixty-three cathedral canons, an often-lucrative post, including one canoness (*chanoinesse*), the noblewoman Marie-Louise Saint Mart de Wassigny, born in French Flanders of a Flemish father and a French mother. In 1748, at the age of thirty, she was "nominated for a prebend of canoness in the county of Namur; she was obliged to move to this country to take possession of it and to complete her training," after which she came back to live in the château at Wassigny. Arguing that she needed to leave the kingdom in order to discharge her office for six weeks every year, she vowed that she nonetheless wished to continue living in France, where she intended to finish her days. This apparently presented no problem to the Great Chancellery, which in January 1755 issued her a grant of citizenship.[29]

The First Estate was in many ways an artificial unity, especially in social and economic terms. Just as the tax rolls of 1697–1707 reveal a foreign clergy that included the very rich (and privileged) and the poor, so too did individual naturalizations suggest an ecclesiastical population that mirrored the social hierarchies of the Old Regime, from abbots and cathedral deacons to the struggling parish priests who eked out a living from the modest benefices attached to their parishes. The data set of individual naturalizations between 1660 and 1790 reveal none of the very poor, the down and out clerics and monks so well known to historians of the eighteenth century; nor do the voluntarily naturalized priests of the Old Regime resemble the clerics that were taxed in 1697. Those tax rolls included large numbers of poor parish priests, or heirs of priests, who found themselves subjected to impossible levies, especially in Paris, the Three Bishoprics, Provence, and the Dauphiné, and most were too poor to seek recourse at the royal council. The individually naturalized foreign clergy in the

Old Regime, like the rest of the foreign citizens, had something at stake in the state of France—along with the foreign merchants and artisans who became French citizens.

Merchants and Artisans

In the 1690s, a debate raged, at least within the confines of Versailles, over whether to pursue the Dutch model, and encourage the movement of foreigners and their commercial wealth into the kingdom, or to revert to a xenophobic—at once mercantilist and absolutist—prohibition of foreigners, especially merchants. In 1697, the "traditional" vision triumphed. In 1697, over two-thirds of the immigrants taxed were merchants and artisans. Between 1660 and 1790, the proportion of merchants and artisans among individually naturalized foreigners was substantially smaller: about eight hundred became citizens, a fifth of the cases. Their proportions in the collective and individual naturalizations nonetheless reveal the contradictions of the absolutist policies of immigration built around the droit d'aubaine.

On the one hand, the absolutist monarchy, drawn to the energy of those who came to work, proffered exemptions and collective naturalizations to encourage them. On the other hand, Louis XIV perfected a tendency to discriminate against foreigners within "merchant France" by using the droit d'aubaine to draw the boundaries, especially in the economic realm, between foreigners and citizens. On this score, invoking an inheritance disability, Louis XIV was hardly unique—he was just several centuries outdated, at least with respect to England and Europe more generally.

The jurisprudence on merchants followed the conflicting leads of royal policy. On the one hand, Lefebvre de la Planche put forth a position of compassionate conservatism, acknowledging the subjection of merchants (whether established or passing through) to the droit d'aubaine, but urging leniency in its application: "There is no ordinance in favor of merchants in general, the rule is enforced against all of them and in all circumstances where the ordinances haven't exempted them; but it would mark the goodness of our kings to restrain the droit d'aubaine in this case."[30] No general set of privileges or exemptions existed for merchants or artisans established in France. Practices varied: there were numerous exemptions written into peace and commercial treaties (where the distinction between movables and immovables was sometimes invoked, especially in the case of England), and exceptions were part and parcel of the royal policies that encouraged migration and settlement, particularly in French border regions. Moreover, merchants might enjoy local privileges in a specific town, as Jean Baptiste Ghiringbelly did as a Swiss native in Lyon in 1686, but still seek to be naturalized "to better assure his estate."[31] The jurists tended to generalize the distinction between the immovables (including property and constituted annuities) and the movables of the unnaturalized foreigner, but the differences between goods, and the status of merchants more generally, were questioned in particular and often complex court cases. Two separate incidents of Spaniards who died in the early eighteenth century having recently returned to French ports, loaded with wealth from the New World, are good evidence of the jurisprudential confusion over the status of merchants—and in this case, over the status of Spaniards as well.[32]

Of course, the group of foreign merchants and artisans naturalized from 1660 to 1790 was extremely diverse: as among the clergy, social and economic hierarchies were marked, although it is sometimes difficult to tell because nearly a third of the merchants were simply identified as such (*marchands* or *commerçants*), while wholesalers (*négociants*) made up another fifth of the group. The latter tended to be drawn from the wealthier strata of the mercantile classes, and they often came for economic reasons. Jean Baptiste Marie Romald Fagnani, born in Rome, went to live in Paris with his uncle Philippe Fagnani, a "merchant jeweler, to assist him as best he could in his business of selling all sorts of haberdashery, paintings, stamps, porcelain works, and other precious items from China, in the interest of which commerce he wished to establish himself in Paris to finish his days in the kingdom and to assure his condition and that of his offspring."[33] But those identified as merchants did not always come to France solely to gain a livelihood. Nicolas Mogaillas from Greece, for example, who fled to France to escape religious persecution in the Ottoman Empire, eventually set himself up as a wholesale merchant. Swindled out of a fortune of thirty thousand livres, he had reestablished his business, become a local citizen of Marseille, and was naturalized in 1765 at the age of eighty with his thirty-six-year-old son.[34]

The tax rolls of 1697–1707 reveal the tendencies of social ascent in seventeenth-century "generations" of immigrants as a movement from mercantile and artisanal activities into the ranks of officeholders.[35] But several of the wealthier merchants naturalized individually were descendants of the nobility, such as those who turned to trade, among the descendants of the Jacobite refugees in Saint-Germain-en-Laye in the 1690s. In welcoming the Jacobites, Louis XIV exempted them from the droit d'aubaine by the fiction that they were not permanently settled in the kingdom. Indeed, most of them returned to the British Isles in the early eighteenth century, although many families left grown children in France who sometimes sought citizenship and who revealed in the process a trajectory of social declension. Jacob Sandilands, born in Bordeaux in 1719, issued from an ancient noble family from Scotland, and his father had followed the Stuarts to France in 1688. Despite his birth in the kingdom, and his marriage to a French native, Sandilands became a French citizen at the age of forty-three "wishing to prevent difficulties concerning his succession that might be made in his regard or that of his children and heirs if his quality of native and French natural (*naturel français*) were to be contested under the pretext that his father died in Scotland during his last trip there."[36] Finally, among this elite were a small number of merchants identified as commercial agents (*courtiers*), bankers, or brokers, wealthy financiers such as the brothers Diego and Antoine Martin de Moura de Mireta from Portugal, naturalized in January 1687, then taxed twenty thousand livres in 1697 (later reduced to three thousand livres) as two of the twenty foreign bankers taxed in the city of Paris.[37]

Below the elite of the mercantile professions, constituting a middling group of merchants, were the foreign grocers, innkeepers, and wine merchants who became citizens, a group of some seventy-nine individuals (16 percent of the merchants within the sample). The latter included poor Henri Piron, wine merchant from Bergue in the Low Countries, who had lived for eighteen years in Paris and in 1699 had paid his assessment of the Naturalization Tax of 1697, three hundred livres. By the letter of the law, the payment technically naturalized him, and normally he would not have had to go through the expense of an individual petition to the chancellery. Despite having paid his tax and "tasted for several years the sweetness of our domination," as he wrote (ironically?), his naturalization was registered in 1701 at the Paris Chambre des comptes.[38] Another sixty-one merchants (11 percent) were in the clothing, textile, or accessories trades: cobblers, haberdashers, tailors, hatmakers, weavers, and carders. These men were probably wealthier, especially if one includes the seven merchant jewelers such as Orthodox Christian Cyriac Chammas Cazadour. Born in "Mesopotamia" in the Ottoman Empire, Cazadour fled from religious persecution in the 1740s, and his naturalization case between 1760 and 1785 involved the first legally documented instance of "family reunification" in France. The case of Anne Bornevat, born in Annecy (Savoy) in 1682, is more banal, and certainly less fortunate. She came to Lyon in 1702 and had lived there twenty years, where "she succeeded in being accepted as a merchant linen-draper. . . . She continues to work in this profession to the great satisfaction of the public; she has always lived with great honor and integrity; and she wishes to remain in France and finish her days in our states as one of our subjects and natives."[39]

Such merchants, some of quite humble standing, hardly dominated the known professions of foreign citizens, but they were not at all uncommon, especially among foreigners involved in the commerce of primary materials or in the transport and delivery professions, among them barrelmakers, coachmakers, potters, ironmongers, and miners. The stereotypical images of the Savoyard wood-seller or the Flemish potter must certainly take their places alongside that of the Portuguese banker in Paris. The former could be a certain Anselme Coste ("called in the Piedmontese language Contaz"), a wood merchant who received a declaration of naturalization on 24 March 1718 at the age of thirty-one "because of the scruples of those with whom he worked and to establish himself and reside in France in the greatest security."[40] In fact, Coste's condition was far better socially than those of the bottom of the hierarchy of merchants, the two dozen peddlers and traveling merchants (*colporteurs, porteurs de balle, marchands ambulants*), nearly all of them from the Savoy, just as the eighteenth-century stereotype would suggest. Some, like Jean-Pierre Fournier, had stopped their itinerant lifestyle. Fournier "had begun a business of haberdashery carrying a trunk; he passed through the Franche-Comté and then came to our duchy of Burgundy; having married in the town of Suerre, he established himself and fixed his residence there for over eighteen years." Fournier became a citizen in 1714 to "assure his widow and heirs the goods he owns and that he could eventually acquire."[41]

Finally, in this foreign contribution to a "merchant France," a small but not insignificant percentage of foreign citizens were involved in the trades of maritime commerce. One in twenty foreign merchants naturalized between 1660 and 1790 engaged in maritime activities, a far greater proportion than among the French merchant population in the Old Regime. By the royal edict of 1715, foreign maritime merchants (*gens de commerce maritime*) were exempted collectively from the droit d'aubaine. But that did not stop Gaultier Archer from Ross County, Ireland, "captain of a merchant vessel in the [jurisdiction] of the admiralty of la Rochelle," from becoming a citizen in October 1735, bragging that "he had acquitted himself with such honor and fidelity that he had acquired the confidence of the inhabitants and merchants of the said town who had confided to him on many occasions their maritime interests, and he had made many voyages on our seas to the complete satisfaction of the public." His marriage in La Rochelle the previous year, Archer claimed, "had confirmed his plan to finish his days in our kingdom."[42] Most of the "sea people" (*gens de mer*), true to their stereotypical reputation, hailed from Italy, and especially the republic of Genoa: Cristoffe [Christopher] Colomb, among them, described at length how his father had come to France from Genoa, settled in the Provençal town of Arles, and had become a ship's captain. His son,

> inspired by the great name of Cristoffe Colomb that he has the good fortune of carrying, perfecting himself in the arts of navigation, he came several years ago to our kingdom and had already sailed three times on ships of this nation. With the knowledge he acquired of the mores and customs of our kingdom, joined to the temperate climate and welcome that he found here, he decided to establish himself in order to pass the rest of his days in the city of Arles.

He was received as an "inhabitant of the city of Arles" on 4 October 1754, and two months later he petitioned for citizenship.[43]

Maritime commerce apart, though, the distinction between merchants and artisans was sometimes difficult to draw in Old Regime France, where the store and workshop were often the same. Nonetheless, among those naturalized individually from Louis XIV to the French Revolution were some 282 artisans, 10 percent of the foreign citizens with professions. The artisanal classes included a range of groups from mere workers (*ouvriers*) and journeymen (*garçons*) outside (or at the very bottom of) the structured hierarchies of the workplace, to master craftsmen at the heart of the guild system (even at a moment when the title of guild "master" was falling into disuse, especially in Lyon).[44] Artisans, like merchants, tended to be dominated by the luxury and clothing trades: two-thirds of the artisans were jewelers, watchmakers, perfumemakers, on the one hand; and tailors, hatmakers, braidsmiths, and lacemakers, on the other. Their concentration in luxury production was far more notable than among the artisanal population living in the cities of the kingdom, and equally distinctive in relation to the 1,125 foreign artisans (34 percent of the immigrant population) taxed in 1697, whose ranks included many more poor artisans. If the individually naturalized foreigners were not all doing well in the luxury trades and crafts, many of them had made enough profit in their activities to seek out the status of citizen.[45]

There were, as we shall see below, curious concentrations of merchants and artisans from particular geographic regions and places. Fourteen of the forty jewelers were from Lorraine, all naturalized in the late seventeenth century as the duchy become de facto, then de jure, part of the kingdom; and another twenty came from the Germanies, from the principalities of the Rhineland and further afield. Jean Philippe Birnstible, a stone-setter from the Rhineland established in Paris for two years, described how he had "learned the art of setting stones under Jean Henri Furste, stone-setter of the prince of Baden; he lived in Augsburg and exercised his craft for some time until the zeal that he always had to excel gave him the resolve to go to Paris to learn new things from the greatest masters."[46] Other artisans were manual workers exercising a range of urban professions, from mason to plasterer to the "poor tailor's apprentice" (*pauvre garçon tailleur*) Alexandre Praimsendorf, a Protestant who had abjured his faith, and who by the age of thirty-five had "worked seventeen years in Paris without amassing any goods." He nonetheless sought citizenship at the demand of his future father-in-law.[47]

A Service Elite? Officeholders, Liberal Practitioners, and Military Officers

Following the groups of clergy, merchants, and artisans in numerical importance among the individually naturalized foreigners from 1660 to 1790 was a grouping of foreigners with professions and statuses that identify them as a service class, if not (in the context of a largely rural population of the Old Regime) a service elite: officeholders (royal, seigneurial, local), members of the "liberal professions," and military men, mostly officers. Together, these three categories made up nearly a quarter of the sample population of foreign citizens with professions or statuses; by contrast, they make up 10 percent of the collectively naturalized immigrants with professions in 1697–1787.[48]

Among the naturalized foreigners whose professions appear in the longitudinal dataset, a group of 223 officeholders made up something less than a tenth of foreigners with professions. The very existence of these foreign born municipal, seigneurial, and royal officeholders seems to run counter to the strictures of the absolutist monarchy, although, it will be recalled, foreigners could hold offices with simple permissions that did not make them citizens.[49] Some high-ranking ministers and officers were naturalized, such as John Law and the duke of Berwick, even if Protestants.[50]

So were a wide range of other officeholders. Among them were the Swedish ambassador to France, an Italian named Alphonse Marie Louis de Saint Severin d'Aragon, who, as a member of the diplomatic core, should not have needed naturalization,[51] and the bailiff of the seigneurial court of the count of Mérode, in Trélon near Lille. (Jacques Philippe Bonnain, the man in question, was born in the town of Mons, the son of an iron merchant, at a time when Mons was under French domination; he, too, should not have needed a grant of naturalization.)[52] Twenty-seven of the naturalized "officeholders" were actually high-ranking officials at foreign courts who continued to hold offices in other countries, which prevented no obstacle to their naturalization in France. These included noblemen such as Marie Claude Joseph de Raison de Freyberg, grand marshal of the court of Bavaria (naturalized in 1738); François Maximilien Issolinsky, count of Tekin, grand treasurer of Poland (1736); Jean Frédérique Karg de Robenberg, grand chancellor of the electorate of Cologne (1703); and Dom Philippe des comtes de Saint Martin d'Aglie, minister of state and grand master of the house of the duke of Savoy (1660). Nor were all foreign officeholders noble: another six held seigneurial offices abroad. Because none of these naturalization drafts included the clause of dispensation of residence, and all included the provision that the petitioner "finish his days in the kingdom," it is to be assumed that either these officeholders resigned their positions upon receiving naturalization, or that—more likely—they were able to exercise their offices while (fictionally) residing in France.[53]

Foreign citizens holding offices within the kingdom were dominated by royal officeholders: more than four of five petitioners were employed, in a wide variety of capacities, by the state. This is not surprising, given the proliferation of venal offices in Old Regime France and the notorious importance of officeholding to social mobility among French natives and foreigners alike.[54] As evidence, consider the office of "chief alternative and mid-triennial clerk" (*greffier en chef alternatif et mi-triennial*) of the financial bureau in Toulouse, evocative of the frequent doubling and tripling up of ordinary positions by the financially challenged monarchy. In 1775, Jean-Baptiste Lavedan, born in Madrid of a French father (who had held the office before him), moved to France and was declared a "natural Frenchman" in order to take possession of that charge. Many such descendants of expatriate French natives born in Spain, alongside the offspring of French Huguenots settled in northern Europe, returned to

France to become officeholders.[55] Twenty-three of these royal officeholders were lawyers at the sovereign courts, most of whom held the title of "barrister at parlement" (*avocat au parlement*), and were in the process of seeking other, higher-ranking offices. A typical case was that of Joseph Barbarin, also born in Spain of a French father, a barrister at the Aix parlement who sought the office of secretary-councillor of the chancellery at the Cour des comptes, aides, et finances in Provence. To take possession of that post, he was declared a French native.[56]

There were dozens of foreigners employed within the various "branches" of provincial and municipal financial administrations and tax-farms, including thirteen officeholders within the royal treasury. Some were admittedly of relatively low rank (*receveurs, procureurs fiscaux*) and often seeking higher offices; others already held high-ranking posts, officials such as Jacques de Vanolles, "royal councillor and treasurer-general of the navy." Vanolles, born Jacques Vanholt in the town of Orléans of a Dutch father and French mother, had changed his name by a royal declaration of 1697, the same year that he and his sister had paid the Naturalization Tax. Yet seven years later, he requested and received an individual declaration of naturalization, registered in the Paris Chambre des comptes on 17 September 1704.[57] Holding such a high (and visible) royal office required extra protection from the avarice of the tax-farmers, as well as from enemies and competitors for even higher offices. Dozens of other foreigners were employed in various capacities, from clerks to secretaries, in the royal administration, in the municipalities and cities of the kingdom, and in the tax-farms. Among the royal officers could be found, ironically, at least thirteen royal secretaries (*secrétaires du roi*)—the officials formally charged with drafting the letters of naturalization presented to the royal council and the chancellery—who were born in foreign lands, and another twenty-eight from Avignon.[58]

Equal in proportion to officeholders among the foreign citizens were the 236 claimants (8 percent of the sample) who exercised what anachronistically can be called the "liberal professions." Unlike offices and benefices, the monarchy rarely prohibited foreigners from practicing medicine of various kinds or from the "intellectual" professions in the schools and universities of the kingdom. Judges in the sovereign courts even tended to favor, on occasion, the claims of foreigners embroiled in professional disputes with native claimants for honors, as was the case when a foreign-born law professor at the University of Poitiers in 1610 was awarded a chair, in competition with a French native, only when he was naturalized.[59] This explains the statistically insignificant but nonetheless notable slippage between the proportion of individually naturalized foreigners practicing the "liberal professions" in Old Regime France (8 percent) and those caught in the tax rolls of 1697 (5 percent of all taxed immigrants with professions). In both cases, the category of "liberal professions" includes a certain concentration of artists, sculptors, and translators, some called to the court by the king and lodged in the royal palaces, others from the provinces or from Paris who held official patents (as marblers, painters, or sculptors).[60]

Among both immigrants forcibly and collectively naturalized in 1697 and foreigners who chose to become citizens between 1660 and 1789, the largest concentration of "liberal professionals"—nearly a third—were in the medical profession: twenty-three doctors of medicine, eleven doctors, twenty-three surgeons (*chirurgiens*, with several specializing in hernias), and eleven pharmacists (including Jean Guillaume Louis, born in the Palatinate, a Lutheran pharmacist who lived several months in Landau [Alsace] before he was naturalized in 1751).[61] Another quarter of the professionals came from the university and other teaching institutions, divided equally between teachers and students, even though students—and, according to some jurists, professors and principals as well—theoretically enjoyed a special exemption from the droit d'aubaine.[62] At the border of these two groups stood Louis Berthollet, who was born in the parish of Talloire near Annecy (Savoy) and had been received as a professor at the medical school at the University of Turin in 1770. Having come to France "to perfect the knowledge that he had acquired," he lived seven years in the kingdom. Enrolled again as a student, he sought French citizenship, arguing, in what became a contested claim of contemporary jurisprudence, that according to the "regulations which make up the law, it is not sufficient to enjoy the advantages of native subjects by means of treaties between sovereigns, but one must be either born French or naturalized explicitly by royal letters."[63] The picture of the "liberal" professions is filled out when the other "intellectual" professions, including six interpreters (men such as Jean-Baptiste Keyaert, who was a translator of the northern, commercial languages of English, Dutch, and Flemish in the Mediterranean port city of Cette in Languedoc),[64] several "scientists" (the trade listed on Jean Dominique Cassini's letter of naturalization in 1673), and a handful of architects (all but one from Italy). Their profile does not differ significantly from that of foreign practitioners of the liberal professions captured in the 1697–1707 rolls of the Naturalization Tax.[65]

Military men, most of them officers, constitute a third group of the "service elite," in roughly the same proportion as officeholders and the "liberal" classes and professions, although they were exempted from the forced naturalization of 1697 because of their service to the crown.[66] Military service was, of course, distinct in kind from the other "service professions" staffed by foreigners, whether in the church, the state, or the city. Foreigners served as officers and soldiers in the royal armies, and their increased participation in the age of Louis XIV and after is evident in the trail of privileges and exemptions from the droit d'aubaine given to foreign mercenaries.[67] Article 8 of the royal declaration of 1715, for example, gave foreign soldiers and officers who wished to remain in France the same status as "French naturals," a fact noted by Vincent Millanouits, a lieutenant colonel from the German regiment of Greder, born in Venetian Dalmatia on the Adriatic, when he petitioned for naturalization in

May of the following year.[68] But royal decrees were superseded by jurisprudential reason, politics by the law, and in the eighteenth century, the jurists were largely in accord that foreign-born officers, even having served twenty years under the king and having been named to the Military Order of Saint Louis, were not to be reputed French. An unusual case, summarized by the Alsatian barrister de Boug, involved Sr. Jean Frédéric Koesterich, born in Brandenberg, who died in March 1750, whose bequest to a fellow military officer was contested by a collateral relative. Other cases throughout the eighteenth century occasioned the intervention of ministerial officials, and no less than war minister comte d'Argenson, commenting on another case in 1749, claimed that an unnaturalized military officer was still to be considered an alien, and "the goods that he leaves are without question acquired by the domainial tax-farmers as escheat [à titre d'aubaine]."[69]

It is thus no surprise that many military officers failed to trust in the royal privileges exempting them collectively from the droit d'aubaine. Significant numbers of foreigners who had served in France's armies sought to become citizens, their petitions frequently wrapped in the patriotic language of service. Even as high ranking an officer as the comte de Mérode (from Malines, in Austrian Flanders) sought to be naturalized. The comte had been a lieutenant general in the king's service, after which he was given a pension, lodging at Versailles, and a title for his wife ("lady of the Queen's palace"). Although he argued that by his "birth, or by his residence in the kingdom where he will finish his days in the royal service, he should by the terms of the peace treaties be considered our true and original subject," he nonetheless took a grant of naturalization in 1727.[70]

A list of the foreign military officers who received individual naturalizations after having served in the French armies of the Old Regime reads like a table of ranks itself: eight lieutenant generals, thirty-four colonels and lieutenant colonels, five majors, fifty-six captains, twenty-three sergeants and corporals, as well as the eighteen naval officers, thirteen holding foreign military charges, and other officers who made up more than four-fifths of the military men. In certain cases, such as that of Jean-Marie de la Batoche, from the val d'Aosta in Piedmont (Savoy), naturalization capped a nearly fifty-year career in the military that saw service in every rank up to that of captain.[71] The nonofficers were simply identified as "soldiers" in specific regiments, or engaged in a variety of military employ, usually as cashiers, concierges, or employees in the garrison of troops. Some of the military officers became citizens to pursue other employ: after all, there were many merchants and officeholders who at one time had been military professionals. Such was the case of Jean Holker, who had been captain of the Oglivi Regiment, but by 1766 had lived in Rouen for twenty years where he had established a factory of cotton velours. For his efforts to introduce the "secret of a way of preparing different cloth which wasn't yet used in France," he had been given the commission of inspector general of manufacturers in that city.[72] Such was also the case of Joseph Jacob Auberjonnois, a former Swiss Guard, and an ex-Protestant. Abjuring his faith in 1744, he petitioned five years later for citizenship, intending "to procure for himself the office of clerk in our Chambre des comptes in Paris." His fear was that he could not do so without being naturalized because he was a "reputed alien," even though the Swiss Guards themselves, and later Swiss natives more generally, were exempted by an accumulation of royal privileges.[73]

Finally, overlapping at times with the category of officeholders were the 137 naturalized courtiers and servants. At least a fifth of these held ceremonial offices serving the king and the royal family, among whom were Jean-François Beccarie, born in Piedmont, "officer of the small apartments of the king" (1754); André Caterby, from Pezzaro, "regular chef of the king's goblet" (1664); Pierre Del, from Lorraine, "grand valet of the king's foot" (1733); Jacques Iwinski, from Warsaw, "queen's cook" (1748); Joseph Missilier, from Geneva, "inspector of the king's mouth and of the count of Artois."[74] Evidently, their service within the royal household and at court placed them in an excellent position to petition for citizenship, even if, as we have already seen, such connections were hardly necessary in order to be naturalized. Three members of the entourages of French ambassadors abroad were also among those naturalized, including Augustin Malo, whose son was born in Portugal while he served the ambassador in Lisbon. Arguing, correctly, "that the children of ministers that we have in foreign courts, and those of their servants born there, are reputed to be regnicoles," he sought French citizenship for his son in 1704 "to avoid any difficulties that could arise" from his birthplace.[75] Most of the other servants were simply identified as servants (*domestiques*), although some were clearly liveried servants in the households of noblemen and women, and represent what Daniel Roche has called the "wealthy poor."[76] Others had left domestic service for a variety of reasons. Jacques Agnellet, for example, born in Geneva, had been a servant and became a citizen in 1766 in order to acquire an office. Michel Miguet, also from Savoy, had served for twenty years as the lackey of the marquise of Rochebaron but had left his service two years prior to petitioning for naturalization in 1759 to live with his second wife in her "small household" in Lyon where they sold tobacco.[77]

The socioprofessional profile of the naturalized foreigners and children of French immigrants thus suggests the primacy of service: service to the church and the crown, of course, but also the service economy, the provision of necessities and perhaps especially luxuries in the towns and cities of the kingdom. The immigrant population taxed in 1697 was more firmly located within the "merchant kingdom"—and the "France of movement" more generally—than the foreigners naturalized between 1660 and 1790, even if more than 10 percent of those collectively naturalized in 1697 came from the "primary" economic sector (itself an inverse proportion to the tremendous weight of the rural world in Old Regime France). But the individually naturalized foreigners were even less a part of the "peasant kingdom," because almost none of them had professions that identified themselves as rural dwellers—no peasants, no agricultural laborers, no shepherds can be found among the individually naturalized foreign citizens in the Old Regime. The category of the citizen, acquired through naturalization, was socially inclusive of women, dominated by commoners, and even encompassed minor children. If in practice there were no a priori social restrictions, there were nonetheless social limits to the category of foreign citizens, for only those with material interests in the kingdom would seek the benefits of French citizenship.

CHAPTER FIVE

GEOGRAPHIC ORIGINS AND RESIDENCE

From where did they come, and where did they settle, these foreigners naturalized, either voluntarily or against their will, during the course of the Old Regime? The answers are not immediately obvious: the administrative sources at the level of the kingdom, reflecting premodern notions of belonging and invested in political projects of state building, do not provide transparent windows onto the geography of naturalizations. The cultural and political biases of the sources from which statistical series can be constructed force the abandonment of a "positivist" social history and require continuous interrogation of the sources themselves. At the same time, a social history of naturalized foreigners, at once statistical and anecdotal, must take into account the jurisprudence of nationality law, and in particular the frequently contested and constantly changing exemptions from the droit d'aubaine of specific foreign groups resident in the kingdom, as well as the state policies that shaped the decisions to naturalize.

A simple example can illustrate the nature of the problem. In the 1697 Naturalization Tax, the clerks and secretaries of the financiers who contracted to collect the tax in the généralité of Metz (on the borders of the duchy of Luxembourg, the diocese of Trier, and the Holy Roman Empire), uncovered some five hundred "Spaniards" in the region, a third of the resident population of taxed foreigners—and a fifth of the foreigners in the kingdom. The financiers and their clerks paid a great deal of attention to the identification of "foreigners" in the province, a set of strategic towns (Verdun, Metz, Thionville) that provisioned the French offensive in Alsace and beyond. The "Spaniards" caught on the tax rolls included Henri Thibourg, tunnel-maker in Longwy; Jean Esselbourg, carpenter in Bresitroffe; Nicolas Vatard, cook in Toul; Gaspard Vandenbosch, Joacques Hoc, Lambert Houbat, and others. Their names betrayed their northern and, for the most part, Flemish origins, as did their socioprofessional profile (a higher proportion of artisans and agricultural workers, more like those in neighboring Liège than in Spain). They were Flemish subjects of the king of Spain, hence "Spaniards" (as were many of the Neapolitans taxed in 1697, such as Jean Arfoux, a sawyer born in "Naples kingdom of Spain"). In fact, the clerks and financiers did not distinguish between an "ethnicity" (whether Neapolitan or Flemish, Spanish or German) and a place of origin (from Naples, Flanders, Spain, Germany). But they did pay attention, although not always with great accuracy, to a foreigner's political dependence.[1]

Concerning foreigners born close to the borders of French territory, the clerks had a tendency to fix on a place name, and especially a parish or bishopric of birth. Such ecclesiastical records, after the Council of Trent, were official markers of identification on the basis of birth. Invoked in letters of naturalization, they were also used by foreigners who had been forcibly taxed and naturalized to make arguments about their existing French identities.[2] Because ecclesiastical provinces rarely overlapped with the political boundaries of the kingdom, endless confusion was possible. Moreover, not all modes of identification were ambiguous in the same way. The example of "nations" (the word was itself rarely used) constitutes a different kind of fuzziness. In all the tax rolls drawn up for the kingdom, three-quarters of the taxed "Germans" were identified as "Germans" or "from Germany," but the same cannot be said for "Italians." Precision concerning the identity of residents from the Italian Peninsula was in direct correlation to geographic distance. In Mediterranean Provence, only thirteen of the 465 taxed families were qualified as "Italians": rather, they were identified by a specific town, parish, or political jurisdiction. But in Paris, half of the Italians were identified only by their hometown, parish, and polity. And in Brittany, the four taxed "Italians" had no more specific identity than as "Italians." Because political affiliation was the principal framework of identification, the naming of "Germany" and "Italy" in the tax rolls of 1697–1707 had the effect of superimposing a unified political frame on what can only be called "nations avant la lettre." These were not defined by ethnicity or language or even religion. The mental geography of the clerks identified foreigners in relation to political authority. This will explain, as we shall see, the peculiar patterns of taxation in Metz and Provence.[3]

To locate the geographic origins of individual foreigners who became French citizens between 1660 and 1790 presents different challenges. As Papon had shrilly noted, it was essential in principle to specify "national" origins. Such was not always the case in practice during the Old Regime, although individual letters are generally more revealing than the collective tax of 1697 about the actual origins of foreign claimants. Of course, the same structure of knowledge was evident: there was generally more specificity given to origins of foreigners in regions close to France's borders than in distant lands. And categories such as "Flanders" remained elusive, especially in the seventeenth century as the aspirations of Louis XIV's expansionist policy stretched from Dunkirk to Amsterdam.

Similar reflections might be offered about settlement patterns in the kingdom. Here the tax rolls of 1697–1707 are of great accuracy, since the tax was collected by financiers in each généralité, under the watchful eye of the intendant. But for individual letters of naturalization, residence in the kingdom cannot be consistently traced beyond the registration address of the Chambre des comptes and other sovereign courts, and sometimes that of the financial bureaux.[4] And because the Paris chambre covered two-thirds of the territory and at least half of the population, the results are only partially revealing at best. Despite these limitations, and at times because of them, we can compare the geographic origins and, to a lesser extent, the patterns of settlement of the two distinct populations of foreign citizens of Old Regime France: those who sought individual naturalizations (for themselves and their families) between the reign of Louis XIV and the French Revolution; and those who were forcibly and collectively taxed and naturalized between 1697 and 1707. A global perspective, taking cardinal points of geography that reflect the cultural landscape of Europe, reveals that the profiles of these two groups converged to a surprising degree (table 5.1 and map 2).

Foreigners from northern Europe—including the Flemings from Liège and the Low Countries, Germans from Alsace and the Rhineland, and the Dutch— were equally represented among the two populations, making up a little less than a third of each group of foreign citizens. True, there were differences among the proportions from specific places. The duchy of Lorraine, incorporated into the crown during the late seventeenth and early eighteenth centuries, produced few foreign citizens in the eighteenth century. And there are differences, too, within the Rhineland states and principalities, each of which had a different legal standing with respect to the collection of the droit d'aubaine, as well as the capacity to hold benefices—the principal motivations for individual naturalizations. Yet overall, the two profiles of foreigners from northern Europe converge significantly.

They converge much less in the case of the British Isles—England, Scotland, and Ireland—for a very specific reason: religion. The importance of religious refugees in France, especially the Jacobites installed in Saint-German between 1698 and the 1720s and their descendants in the eighteenth century, raised the rate of individual naturalizations from the British Isles significantly. Irish clerics constituted an important grouping of foreign citizens by choice who were not as targeted and taxed by the financiers and their clerks under Louis XIV. Again, the politics and jurisprudence concerning specific groups of foreigners shaped the patterns of individual naturalizations in the kingdom.

Nowhere is this clearer than among southern Europeans. In this instance, the two populations diverged significantly, although both reveal a higher proportion of southern Europeans than northern Europeans in the kingdom. Rural and regional historians of early modern France, from Emmanuel Le Roy Ladurie to Pierre Goubert, have occasionally taken note of the presence of foreigners in Languedoc and the Beauvaisie as they appeared in hospital registers and other sources. Migratory movements to France in the sixteenth and early seventeenth centuries tended to be dominated by an immigration of relative poverty from the north, including Flemish, English, and Irish.[5] This may have been true in many rural regions and small towns of rural France, including the

TABLE 5.1.
Geographic Origins of Foreign Citizens in the Old Regime

	Naturalized Foreigners (1660–1789)		"Foreigners" Taxed (1697–1707)	
	Number	Percent	Number	Percent
Northern Europe	1937	30.9	2142	28.7
"Flanders"	53	.8	181	2.4
Duchy of Lorraine	163	2.6	332	4.4
Rhineland states	282	4.5	94	1.3
Bishopric of Liège	260	4.2	299	4.0
Low Countries	845	13.5	916	12.3
Dutch Republic	285	4.6	287	3.9
Kingdom of Sweden	29	.5	14	.2
Kingdom of Denmark	20	.3	19	.3
British Isles	978	15.6	346	4.6
England	270	4.3	154	2.1
Scotland	30	.5	20	.3
Ireland	678	10.8	172	2.3
Southern Europe	2147	34.3	3976	53.3
Spain	193	3.1	212	2.8
Portugal	75	1.2	188	2.5
Italian states	723	11.5	759	10.2
Duchy of Savoy	1103	17.6	2754	36.9
Malta	53	.8	63	.8
Central Europe	1032	16.5	917	12.3
German states	712	11.4	795	10.6
Swiss Cantons	213	3.4	90	1.2
Poland	74	1.2	15	.2
Russia	6	—	12	.2
Hungary	27	.4	5	.1
Peripheries	169	2.7	89	1.1
Ottoman Empire	97	1.5	80	1.0
Africa	4	—	5	—
European colonies	60	1.0	3	—
Asia	8	.1	1	—
Total (known origins)	6263	99	7470	100

center. Among foreign citizens of the Old Regime, Italians and Savoyards far outnumbered the naturalizations from the north. Looking at hospital registers, one is more likely to find the "immigration of poverty" described in sixteenth-century Languedoc. Looking at tax rolls that tried to capture the wealth of foreigners, or at letters of naturalization of foreigners with stakes in the kingdom, one is more likely to find a different, more urban, and more economically established population. The northern populations on the tax rolls, were hardly dominated by the working poor, although the largest proportion of agricultural and urban workers in the kingdom came from the borderlands of Flanders and the Holy Roman Empire. But northern Europe rivaled England as a source of

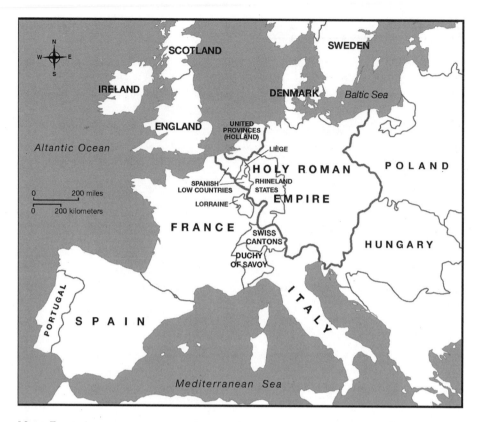

Map 2. Europe in 1700

the wealthiest (most heavily taxed) immigrants at the turn of the eighteenth century.[6]

Still, southerners were numerically dominant, although among them, the difference between the two sets of foreign citizens was notable. The tax rolls of 1697–1707 reveal more dramatically the politics of state building under Louis XIV, especially in border regions. More than a third of the "foreigners" taxed under Louis XIV came from the neighboring duchy of Savoy (and especially the county of Nice). In this Alpine borderland, the financiers and their clerks were complicit in the crown's political projects, in the midst of the long wars of the Sun King, of identifying the territorial extension of the kingdom and the boundaries of "citizens" and "foreigners."[7]

Between 1697 and 1707, the duchy of Savoy, and especially the districts bordering the county of Nice called the "New Lands" (Terres Neuves)[8] were at the center of the king's gaze, and that of the tax-farmers. These lands were subjected to rapid shifts of territorial control in the rivalry between Louis XIV and Victor Amadeus II of Savoy. Occupied by the French from 1691 to 1696, they were returned to the duke of Savoy until 1702, when they were again occupied by French troops, before being restituted once again to Savoy, minus the Barcelonnette valley, in the 1714 Treaty of Utrecht.[9] In 1697, shortly after the French had retaken possession of the districts, Louis XIV and his tax-farmers enacted in the tax rolls a veritable registry of "foreigners" in the towns and cities of Provence, with a detailed documentation of their places of origin and identities. Most were from peasant and artisanal classes that had been impoverished by the economic and demographic crisis of the seventeenth century. This migratory current had its sources in specific districts, villages, or even families in the county of Nice. The baronnie de Beuil, with its population of 750 in the mid-eighteenth century, had sent fifty-three migrants to France before 1700. More dramatic is the case of Saint-Martin-d'Entraunes, in the viguery of Puget-Théniers, with a population of three hundred or so, and 107 taxed in France.[10]

The migratory and settlement patterns of these shepherds, peddlers, small shopkeepers, and agricultural workers were utterly conventional. Traditional forms of out-migration typical of Alpine communities in the Old Regime more generally became in this context an international migratory flow, and one that was policed in 1697.[11] France and Savoy did not delimit their territorial boundary until the 1760s. Rather than impose a territorial identity on the kingdom, the tax-farmers under Louis XIV identified the boundaries of citizenship. They located, assessed, and named an extraordinarily large number of "Savoyards" within the taxed population of foreigners: over one-third of all foreign citizens taxed in the kingdom hailed from the lands of the duke of Savoy (37 percent of the 8,200 names of immigrants and their heirs who had settled in the kingdom since 1600).[12] Two-thirds of these settled in the neighboring French province of Aix, a third of them before the economic crises of the 1690s. When taxed in 1697, they were established in family and institutional networks in the towns and coastal cities of the province: Toulon (526 taxed "foreigners"), Arles (343), and Aix (250), a series of towns bordering the county of Nice, and the small port towns such as La Ciotat (225) and Antibes (111), where some turned from peasants into fishermen and merchants.

Among the voluntarily and naturalized foreigners during the Old Regime, the Savoyards were less numerous, although migrants from Nice and the Terres Neuves, Savoy, and Piedmont nonetheless constituted one in five naturalizations during the period. Among the other populations of southern Europe, only the profile of the Portuguese diverges significantly between the two data sets—largely explicable by the fact that in 1697, Jews were simply named "Portuguese," while in the individual letters of naturalization, as we have seen, they were not.[13]

Foreigners coming from central Europe—the Germanies beyond the Rhineland, the sprawling territories of the Austrian monarchy, the languishing republic of Poland, and distant Russia—were more comparably represented among taxed and naturalized foreigners. The vast peripheries of Europe—the Ottoman Empire and the North African protectorates, Europe's colonies in the New World and India, and the independent kingdoms of Persia and China—produced relatively few individually naturalized foreigners, less than one in fifty. Still, despite the statistical insignificance of peripheral foreigners, it is important to make sense of the logics and patterns that shaped their immigration and settlement in the kingdom.

Concentric Circles and Special Exemptions

In a premodern world, where movement by land was arduous (although less difficult for people than for goods and merchandise), it is not surprising that the vast majority of foreign citizens, like the immigrants and travelers who settled in or passed through France, came from the borderlands of the kingdom. The geographic patterns of origin, for both individually and collectively naturalized foreigners, vary in inverse relation to geographic distance from France. Everything happened as if France sat at the center of a set of widening geographical circles, with fewer immigrants coming from proportionally more distant lands. Most, then, came from the borderlands of the kingdom—from Flanders and the Rhineland, Savoy and northern Italy. A second circle of countries and provinces included Spain, Italy, Germany, Holland, and the British Isles. The fewest numbers of foreigners came from a third and fourth circle, from Hungary, Russia, Poland, the Ottoman Empire, the European colonies of the Americas and the Indian subcontinent, and as far afield as China and the "kingdom of Siam" (which produced only one naturalized foreigner, Constance Faulcon, identified in his letter as "first minister of the king of Siam").[14] Of course, terrestrial geography was not destiny in this premodern world, where it was often easier to move across bodies of water (such as the Mediterranean) than land, thus accounting for the geographically disproportionate number of Ottoman subjects settled in the kingdom, especially in the port cities of Provence and in the capital city of Paris. Distant geographically but linked by maritime transport, the colonial world came home as well: approximately 1 percent of the individual grants to foreigners came from the French and other European colonies thousands of miles away, in the Americas and the Indian subcontinent.

We begin with the "inner circle"—that is, with foreign citizens of the French kingdom itself, both those caught on the tax rolls and those who sought letters of naturalization and declaration. In this case, I am not referring to the descendants of foreigners born abroad who returned to the kingdom to claim their French citizenship, nor to the hundreds of native subjects of the crown caught in the nets of the tax-farmers, and who petitioned the royal council, at times successfully, for their removal.[15] Rather, the exceptional jurisdictions and shifting boundaries of France from the reign of Louis XIV to the French Revolution resulted in the inclusion of many subjects with varying kinds of "native" status among the population of naturalized foreigners: the "Portuguese Jews" in Bordeaux; the inhabitants of Comtat Venaissin and Avignon (the Papal enclaves on French territory); and the "foreigners" gradually or abruptly absorbed into the French kingdom from the conquered territories of Artois, Hainault, the Franche-Comté, the duchy of Lorraine, Alsace, and Roussillon.

The Portuguese Jews who had settled in Bordeaux, and especially the Bayonne suburb of Saint-Esprit, were taxed on the naturalization rolls between 1697 and 1707—but not as Jews. About half of the 188 "Portuguese" taxed by Louis XIV had names that identified them as Sephardic Jews, and a few were unambiguously "called the Jew" or "the Jewess," like Marie Diez, "merchant of Biarritz," taxed seven hundred livres in 1700. In the course of the eighteenth century, more Sephardim arrived in Bordeaux, and increasing numbers of families moved on to Paris.[16] Along with a handful of families from Avignon and even from Metz, they were naturalized—in letters that often omitted mention of their religion—after the mid-eighteenth century.

The first to do so were members of the Dalpuget family, merchants from Avignon who settled in Bordeaux. After having been denied the right to participate in the privileges of the "Portuguese" in the jurisdiction of the Bordeaux parlement, they became citizens by letters of naturalization in 1759, in which their religion went unmentioned.[17] A decade letter, Calmer Liefman, a German Jewish banker and army munitioner, born of a wealthy merchant family in the Hague "in Germany" [sic] and who purchased the baronnie de Pecquigny and acquired the title of Vidame d'Amiens, received a similar letter of naturalization in which his religious faith and cultural identity were omitted.[18] At the death of Louis XV, the advent of Louis XVI brought the renewal of the collective privileges of the "Portuguese merchants" in Bordeaux, and many Jews received individual naturalizations, or at times their doubly fictional equivalents.

In 1775, during the first months of Louis XVI's reign, several Jewish families from the Alsace and Franche-Comté, petitioned for naturalization and were granted citizenship in letters that also avoided mentioning their religious identities.[19] Cerf Berr, "merchant and supply contractor for the king's troops" was naturalized in March 1775, and the brothers Homberg and Lallement, Jewish merchants living in Havre de Grace, received their letters in September. The next year, Israel Bernard de Valabrègue, a Jew from Avignon established in Paris as a merchant and royal interpreter, received for himself and on behalf of his family a doubly fictional naturalization.[20] The same year, Jacob Perpignan and Moïse Castro Solar and their families, Portuguese Jews who had also settled in the capital city, became citizens by a somewhat simpler fiction. Such grants of citizenship despite the religious identity of the Sephardim were made, not coincidentally as the Ashkenaz Jews in the south and southwest achieved their commercial freedom in the kingdom.[21]

As for the non-Jewish foreigners born in the Papal enclaves in France (the counties of Avignon, Comtat Venaissin, and Orange): since the patent letters of May 1470, the inhabitants of Avignon were considered native-born subjects, a status universally affirmed by the jurists, but never as consistently articulated by the royal council. Monarchical policies toward the pope informed the treatment of the Avignonnais, who were at times but not consistently named aliens exempted, by the discretionary authority of the crown, from the droit d'aubaine.[22] Nonetheless, if only a handful of Avignonnais had found themselves placed on the tax rolls after 1697, some three dozen papal subjects living within the enclaves of Avignon, Comtat Venaissin, and Orange themselves sought citizenship between 1660 and 1790.[23]

Finally, there were the so-called conquered provinces—including Artois, the Franche-Comté, and Roussillon—acquired by Louis XIV in the early peace treaties of his reign. By international public law, as well as by an established French tradition of state building, the inhabitants of the conquered provinces were recognized as having the same legal status as native-born residents in the kingdom. This was the secret of French state building, the "automatic" legal assimilation of new subjects on the same terms as French natives, even as the conquered province acquired additional privileges. Some jurists believed that newly conquered inhabitants ought to take individual naturalization grants to affirm their commitment to their new country, and if this was not jurisprudential norm, it was sometimes local practice.[24] The jurisprudence defining citizens and foreigners within the conquered territories during the too-long reign of Louis XIV was divided enough so as to justify the efforts by foreigners, technically exempted from the droit d'aubaine, from seeking citizenship, or at least a declaration of naturalization.

This was true even among foreigners from the Franche-Comté, whose status was rarely contested by the jurists. Until 1678, when the Franche-Comté was officially ceded by the Spanish Habsburgs to Louis XIV, the subjects of the Spanish king were considered aliens, although they had been exempted from the droit d'aubaine in the neighboring French province and county of Burgundy.[25] After 1678, they were not required to seek naturalization, but many of them, especially in the first generation, did so anyway, and many sought out letters and more took declarations of naturalization (that recognized their existing condition). As late as 1720, Franche-Comtois such as Pierre Claude Morelli and his two brothers were declared, at some expense, to be the same as native-born residents of the realm. In this case, the fact that their father had been naturalized by the Spanish king, Charles II, in 1669 (even if the letters had not been registered at the Cortes), and that they themselves had been born in the Franche-Comté before 1672, no doubt inspired them to seek additional assurances. To justify their claim, they narrated at length the family's military service to the crown and to France.[26]

Individual examples apart, the patterns of geographic origins that emerge from the statistical databases of foreign citizens from beyond the boundaries of the kingdom reveal how the proportional presence of specific "national" groups depended at once on their geographic proximity to the kingdom, on their legal status, and on royal policies undertaken between the reign of Louis XIV and the French Revolution. Even a cursory overview of the patterns of geographic origins from the borderlands of the kingdom to the far peripheries of Europe, beginning this time in Flanders, shows how geography, law, and politics converged to shape the patterns of naturalization in Old Regime France.

The Northeastern Borderlands

The consensus of the jurists was that a good portion of Low Countries in the most expansive sense, from Artois to Holland, had once been a possession of the French crown, and after their cession to the emperor by the Treaty of Cambrai in 1529, the "right and custom of escheat or alien-ness" (*droit et coutume d'aubaine ou aubaineté*) was abolished for all Flemish subjects: they were considered capable of bequeathing and inheriting property from other Flemings in France.[27] The general principle that the droit d'aubaine was mutually and reciprocally abolished for subjects of the Low Countries and France was confirmed by international treaties throughout the early modern period, including Rastadt (1714), but it was also denied each time war broke out between Spain (and after 1714, Austria) and France. For subjects of the Low Countries settled in Mons in Hainault, a special and reciprocal jurisprudence applied, following a decision of the Paris parlement in 1741 that judged them not subject to the droit d'aubaine, and even permitted them to inherit during times of war.[28]

In general, during the Old Regime, Flemings from the Low Countries were twice as likely to take simple letters of declaration rather than full grants of naturalization. The preambles of declarations of naturalization from the late seventeenth century sometimes recognized that foreigners from the neighboring northern districts of Flanders, Hainault, and Brabant had a special status, because these provinces had previously been part of the royal domain. This status—of "near foreigners"—was also recognized in the application of the Naturalization Tax of 1697, when immigrants and their descendants from the Low Countries who had settled in Artois and Lille received, at their request, a special exemption from the tax rolls.[29] For petitioners seeking naturalization during the next century, such a privileged status of near foreigners, who had once been under French dominion, meant they did not technically need to be naturalized, a position affirmed by jurists in the eighteenth century.[30] "Even though [the inhabitants of] this part of Luxembourg bordering France, and which in the past was part of the kingdom, had the ancient rights of nativeness [*droits de regnicole*]," claimed François-Joseph Collignon, a doctor of theology and a priest, he nonetheless petitioned for citizenship in February 1772.[31] "Because in the past treaties drawn up between France and Spain, the subjects of His Most Catholic Majesty born in the Low Countries under Spanish domination are to be considered and reputed to be native subjects in the French kingdom," argued Jean Fontaine in his own letter of 1703, "as a result the said Fontaine does not need to be naturalized at all. Nonetheless, to further mark his attachment to [the king's] service, he very humbly pleads that he be accorded, not a declaration of naturalization, but a complete letter patent naturalizing him and his family."[32]

Whether to assure their inheritances or to qualify for offices or benefices, foreigners from the Low Countries, alongside numerous others from the northeastern borderland of the kingdom (including descendants of French emigrants and those caught between moving boundaries), did acquire grants of citizenship. These jurisdictions just beyond the kingdom's borders, themselves often ill-defined and largely unmarked by natural frontiers, were dominated in the northeast by important French commercial and economic centers (Maubeuge, Douai, Lens, Calais, and eventually Lille and Dunkerque). They included districts and their dependencies that frequently changed hands during the long wars of the seventeenth century, and to a lesser extent through the 1740s. The efforts to "rationalize" and to delimit the boundaries of the kingdom in the northeast also turned many French natives into foreigners, as we have seen.[33] It is therefore not surprising that the Low Countries were to provide such a large proportion of the naturalized foreigners in the Old Regime, especially of the foreign clergy who sought benefices or offices in France.

More than half of the identifiable foreign citizens from the northern and eastern borderlands were clerics, especially among those from the predominantly Catholic Low Countries, where 61 percent of the individual naturalizations and declarations were given to clergy. Not only was this substantially

TABLE 5.2.
Naturalizations from the Northeastern Borderlands, 1660–1789

	Number of Individual Naturalizations	Percent of All Naturalizations	Percent of Foreign Population Taxed (1697–1707)
Low Countries	845	13	12
Bishopric of Liège	260	4	4
Duchy of Lorraine	163	3	4
Rhineland principalities	282	4	1
Swiss Cantons	213	3	1
Total	1763	27	22

higher than the already large proportion of clergy among the voluntarily naturalized foreigners more generally (39 percent), but it was significantly larger than the proportion of clerics from the Low Countries among the taxed foreigners in 1697 (14 percent, still double the proportion of clerics among collectively naturalized immigrants more generally). From the predominantly Catholic provinces of Hainault and Brabant, and from the bishopric of Liège (with its special religious ties to the kingdom), France drew a notable number of clerics to staff the parishes of Champagne and the convents of Lille, reputed to be one of the most religious provinces of the kingdom, at least according to the intendant in 1698.[34] In addition, as we shall see, the reciprocal requirements of the Austrian and French courts to grant permission for religious officeholding in their respective territories in the second half of the eighteenth century motivated an increasing number of naturalizations to clerics in that period.

If the northeastern borderlands produced more clergy than among the general population of foreign citizens in the Old Regime, they also sent far fewer merchants (only 10 percent of those with known statuses or professions), compared to nearly double that percentage among individually naturalized foreigners in the Old Regime. Such a figure collates with the proportion of merchants among the taxed population in 1697–1707 (itself a lower proportion than the mercantile population of taxed foreigners).

The merchants from the Low Countries and Liège taxed at the end of the seventeenth century were quite wealthy, at least according to their assessments, and included a large number of international bankers alongside highly successful merchant brewers. Artisans, by contrast, were relatively few among the foreigners naturalized from the Low Countries and the rest of the northeastern borderlands, in striking contrast to the tax rolls of 1697–1707, which recorded an important cheap labor market in the border districts.[35]

From the cities and petty principalities of the Rhine River valley came some 282 foreigners and descendants of French emigrants seeking naturalizations and declarations between 1660 and 1790. Significant concentrations of them came from the electorate of the Palatine (43), the electorate of Cologne (33), the duchies of Breisgau (22) and Franconia (29), the imperial city of Mainz (19), and the electorate of Trier (18). Until the treaties of the 1760s and 1770s, few of these jurisdictions within the Holy Roman Empire were exempted from the droit d'aubaine. Lawsuits had periodically challenged the application of the droit d'aubaine, and there was clearly some divergence of opinion between the sovereign courts in the bordering provinces and the appellate courts of the Paris parlement.[36]

The socioprofessional profile of naturalized foreigners from the Rhineland was similar to the sample of foreign citizens more generally: it included members of the highest nobility, who received special treatment and exemptions, such as Louise Bénédicte de Bavières, Princess of Palatine, in 1668. Dame Bavières received not a naturalization but a special "permission to inherit the succession" of Dame Anne de Gonzagues de Clèves, widow of the Prince Palatine of the Rhine, notwithstanding her marriage to the duke of Brunswick and Lunenberg. She claimed that without the special permission, she would have lost the "rights and privileges of native subjects because of the said marriage" that took place in a foreign country. Although technically false, the claim revealed a vernacular model of citizenship that may have shaped the decision to award her a "doubly fictional" letter with a special dispensation of residence, given that neither she nor her children lived in the kingdom.[37]

Also naturalized among those born in the Rhineland were a number of seigneurs with lands in the French kingdom; merchants (generally of a modest caliber, including shopkeepers and grocers); clergy (although proportionally fewer than among naturalized foreigners generally, and far fewer than among the naturalized foreigners from the Low Countries); military officers; and artisans. The latter represented more than a quarter of the Rhinelanders with professions, a fact that dovetails, as we shall see, with the artisanal preponderance of foreign citizens from Germany more generally. The vast majority of Rhinelanders settled (or had their letters registered) in the sovereign councils of Alsace and in eighteenth-century Lorraine.

Finally, included in the districts making up the northeastern borderlands were the Swiss cantons (more closely linked to the Germanic and Flemish worlds than to Savoy or Italy), which produced 213 naturalizations between 1660 and 1790. More than a third of the letters taken by the Swiss were addressed to or registered at the sovereign councils of Strasbourg and Nancy, pointing to the importance of proximate migrations of the Swiss to France, and their settlement in the border regions of Alsace and Lorraine, as well as in Burgundy and Provence.[38] Since the late fifteenth century, the king periodically exempted his Swiss Guards and their families from the droit d'aubaine in a series of letters patent. Until 1715, with the treaty of alliance signed on 9 May at Soleure, the jurisprudence about the other Swiss was uncertain, and many Swiss who had not served the king claimed (often, according to the chief clerk of the foreign office in 1734, with the use of falsified privileges) to be exempt from the droit d'aubaine.[39] The Genevans, meanwhile, had their own exemptions, but the jurisprudence was often not in their favor.[40] Among the naturalized Swiss in the seventeenth and eighteenth centuries, more than half were clerics, underscoring their origins in the Catholic cantons of the Swiss Confederacy—even though subjects of the Catholic cantons had, by the treaty of 1715, been declared "deemed native and exempted from the droit d'aubaine."

The Southeastern Borderlands

As we have seen, more than a third of all the immigrants and others taxed at the turn of the eighteenth century were from the duchy of Savoy, and especially the county of Nice and its adjacent territories. The result of a conjuncture of geography and politics, the proportion radically skews the profile of taxed foreigners from the southeastern borderlands on the tax rolls of 1697–1707 (table 5.3).[41]

In the jurisprudence of the Old Regime, Savoyards were considered aliens, and were subjected to the droit d'aubaine unless they were born when the French king had controlled their native villages or towns and had settled permanently in France when their homelands had been returned to Savoy by formal peace treaty. In the Treaty of Lyon in 1601, Henry IV offered a special exemption from the droit d'aubaine for the districts of Bresse, Buget, Valromey, and Gex that had been ceded to France. In 1669, Louis XIV and the duke of Savoy agreed to mutually exempt Savoyards and Dauphinois from the droit d'aubaine, and to permit them to hold religious benefices in that province.[42] But the other subjects of the Savoyard state who settled in the province of Dauphiné and in the rest of the kingdom were subjected to the droit d'aubaine, even if typical borderland exemptions existed for the Niçois settled in Provence. (This was deftly elaborated in 1751 by baron Ripert de Monclar, a royal solicitor at the parlement of Provence, who himself had been born in Nice and was naturalized in 1749.)[43]

Most of the Savoyards and Niçois taxed at the turn of the eighteenth century were relatively poor, constituted by a group of lesser merchants in the cattle trade, peddlers, kettle-makers and ironmongers—all professions linked to an Alpine ecology and a mountain economy, and all professions unlikely to produce a high rate of naturalization.[44] Voluntarily naturalized Savoyards in the Old Regime did include a larger proportion of merchants (more than a third) than among the foreign citizens more generally (less than a tenth). There were relatively few bankers and wholesale traders among the Savoyards, while large numbers of peddlers as well as merchants involved in the sale of drink and foodstuffs (nearly 20 percent of those with professions) predominated among naturalized Savoyards in the Old Regime. Savoyards were also three times as likely to be servants and valets than the naturalized foreigners more generally in this period; it was a "profession" only partially illustrated by the case of

TABLE 5.3.
Naturalizations from the Southeastern Borderlands, 1660–1789

	Number of Individual Naturalizations	Percent of All Naturalizations	Percent of Foreign Population Taxed (1697–1707)
County of Savoy	837	13	15
County of Piedmont	152	2	2
County of Nice	97	2	21
Principality of Monaco	12	1	—
Republic of Genoa	174	2	3
Total	1272	20	41

Michel Miguet, born in Savoy and living in Lyon, who had been a liveried servant of the marquise de Rochabaron's household before opening a modest tobacco shop.[45] Among the Genoese petitioning for naturalization, there was also a predictably high concentration of sailors and others involved in maritime commerce.[46]

Compared with foreign citizens from the northeast, there were fewer clergy, artisans, officeholders, and members of the liberal professions among the naturalized foreigners originating from the southeastern borderland of the kingdom. And by the indices of their professions and statuses, they tended to be less wealthy, a fact confirmed by the tax rolls of 1697–1707. The rolls also reveal how the two border regions can stand in for a broader set of contrasts between immigrants coming from southern Europe (who were generally poorer and less devoted to the artisanal trades than to small commercial enterprises), and northern Europe (with its immigrant population made up of a wealthier mercantile class and a large labor pool of artisans and workers). The patterns of individual naturalizations from the borderlands reflect less this general contrast, in large part because the rate of naturalizations depended as much on the legal status of each foreign group as it did on their individual wealth.[47]

A comparison of the two borderlands shows a simple opposition between two Europes, north and south; but the model of concentric circles reveals more about the global patterns of migration to and settlement in the kingdom. If the proportional origins of foreign citizens in the Old Regimes stands in inverse relation to geographic distance, and the first concentric circle represents naturalized foreigners from the borderlands in the northeast and southeast,[48] a second concentric circle, to which we now turn, included the British Isles, the United Provinces, the southern European states (on the Italian and Iberian Peninsulas), and the Germanies beyond the Rhineland. The countries within this second circle produced half of the naturalizations and declarations between 1660 and 1790.

A Second Circle: The British Isles, the United Provinces of the Netherlands, the Italian and Iberian Peninsulas, and the Germanies

From the british isles . . .

Separated by the English Channel, and increasingly during the eighteenth century by a "natural enmity" that opposed the interests of the French and English states (in a political and economic struggle in the colonies and on the continent), many foreigners from the British Isles nonetheless sought French citizenship. Some had long resided in the kingdom; others included descendants of French Protestant refugees who returned to France in order to collect their inheritances. Nearly a sixth (978 cases) of the naturalized foreigners between 1660 and 1789 came from the constituent parts of what, after 1704, was Great Britain, compared to less than 5 percent of the immigrants naturalized by Louis XIV in 1697.

In theory, by established royal traditions and international treaties beginning in the sixteenth century, the English, Irish, and Scots were exempted from the droit d'aubaine. In practice, the juridical status of subjects of the English king was confused by the fact that the English themselves were only exempted for their movables, as per the commercial accords of 1610, 1629, 1632, 1655 and 1714. These consistently gave the subjects of the English king complete freedom to dispose and to inherit "although they are not considered citizens," with a conditional clause of reciprocity. The eighteenth-century commercial treaties continued to exempt the English for movable goods: those of 1748 and 1763 marked the end of specific wars, and that of 1786 was signed in conjunction with abolition the droit d'aubaine, and was followed by the letters patent of 1787 that specifically permitted subjects of the English king to inherit from French nationals, without a quid pro quo from England. Yet the eighteenth-century jurisprudence was divided on the thorny question of English succession in the kingdom, complicated by the fact that the droit d'aubaine itself was not known, although somehow presumed to exist, in the British Isles.[49]

The ambiguous legal status, privileges, and exemptions of English subjects, in an uncertain and frequently hostile political climate, no doubt impelled many to seek French citizenship, with the capacity to inherit property from French natives and the ability to hold religious benefices and offices in the kingdom. The ambiguities of the English privileges was complicated by the fact that Louis XIV had renounced the droit d'aubaine on the goods of the English and Irish Jacobites. These thirty thousand souls, including families and servants, arrived in France in 1688, under the legal fiction that they maintained their domicile in, and a desire to return to, England. Most of them, in the end, did return, although some, and their descendants, settled in the kingdom and left traces of their assimilation in letters and declarations of naturalization.[50]

The invocation of religious motives was explicit in a number of Jacobite requests, including that of Tobias Duigin, from County Kilkenny, a priest established in the town of Le Mans in 1703. Duigin stated that

> having left the said country of Ireland with no other goal but the hope of finding in this kingdom an asylum that we have always accorded those who like him professed the Catholic faith and sought refuge in order to devote themselves solely to pious acts; and having lived here for several years, he was so grateful to see peace, concord, and charity reign among our subjects that he formed the project of finishing his days here, provided that it would please us to accord him permission and dispensation to hold and possess any benefices which might be conferred on him in the future, he has humbly requested that he be given our letters to that effect.[51]

France was a land of religious refuge, especially for the Irish, two-thirds of whom were clerics, and many were from Jacobite families.[52] That the Irish were, theoretically, exempted from the droit d'aubaine in 1684, did not prevent dozens from seeking citizenship in order to acquire clerical benefices. The Irish settled in Paris but especially in the parishes of the Bordelais, in the southwest, a traditional site of the Irish religious refuge.[53]

Among the voluntarily naturalized Irish, two other groups of Irish stand out: soldiers and merchants. The former were made up of officers and soldiers of the "Wild Geese" regiments who fought in the armies of Louis XIV, and the dozens of conscripted Irish soldiers who in 1702 had been required to enroll in the Irish regiments (but without, this time, the promise of exemption from the droit d'aubaine).[54] The Irish were also prevalent among merchants (14 percent of all naturalized foreign merchants were Irish). Irish traders and their families tended to settle in Paris and in the cities of the western seaboard, in ports such as Nantes, Rouen, and Bordeaux. They were commonly wholesale traders (négociants) and merchants involved in the commodities trade that linked France to the Baltic, the Mediterranean, and the New World.[55] The triple face of the Irish—merchant, soldier, cleric—is confirmed and revealed in the portraits of Irish settlers who became citizens in the course of the Old Regime.

In Protestant and capitalist England, by contrast, there were far fewer clerics and soldiers and inevitably more merchants. Some were quite wealthy, engaged in the high finances of the French crown and Parisian society. In 1697, the tax-farmers targeted these milieus, and a quarter of the taxed English were bankers, brokers, and their agents. Within the longitudinal sample of individual naturalizations, more modest merchants predominated (wine-sellers or innkeepers, for example), although as in the case of the Naturalization Tax, they appear to be of a higher social status and wealthier than other taxed foreign merchants from the rest of Europe.

Given the historical strength of the "Auld Alliance" it is surprising, perhaps, to note the radical decline of naturalized Scots since the sixteenth century: a mere thirty cases could be identified for the period between Louis XIV and the French Revolution. Both the Scots in military service to the king as well as others had been exempted from the droit d'aubaine in 1558, although Bacquet warned that this privilege "was not perpetual, but only for a limited time and conditional" upon the kingdom of Scotland remaining within the "submission, confederation, and friendship of the king." Obviously, the condition no longer held once Scotland was legally assimilated to the English crown in 1704, as a decision of the French council of state was to affirm on 14 January 1727, and as Bacquet's editor of the 1744 edition of his works was to underscore.[56]

From the United Provinces of the Netherlands . . .

The largely Protestant United Provinces ("Holland" in the administrative language of the Old Regime) produced some 285 foreign citizens and their families between the reign of Louis XIV and the French Revolution. Approximately one in twenty cases were declarations of naturalization, offspring of French refugees born in the United Provinces but resettled in France to collect inheritances. The legal status of Protestant refugees before and after 1685 was shaped by the crown's episodic attempts to attract both foreign Protestants (and their commercial wealth) back to the kingdom, and to resolve the status of the sons and daughters of the Huguenot diaspora. The latter, in turn, produced a diplomatic struggle between the Netherlands and France, as they staged a competition to attract the wealth and dynamism of the French Protestant diaspora.[57] For the Dutch in France, meanwhile, their fate varied according to whether or not they had been naturalized before the revocation of the Edict of Nantes in 1685: those naturalized before were forced to convert, while those who settled in France after 1685 could be naturalized, although still Protestants, through a set of legal fictions.

The question of refugees apart, the ambiguous status of Dutch citizens in the kingdom—for the Netherlands developed, like France and England in the early modern period, the legal status of the citizen—was likely to inspire the Dutch settled in France to become French. In theory, they were often exempted from the droit d'aubaine by a long string of diplomatic and commercial treaties during the seventeenth century (1634, 1636, 1637, 1641, 1642, 1644, 1646, and 1662, 1678, and 1697). The monarchy's recurrent revocations, in times of war, of such exemptions was not the only motive that drove Dutch immigrants to seek naturalization. Like other foreigners, they did so to assure the transmission of their estates across generations. But the wealthy Dutch produced more litigation and legal division, and an increasingly confused jurisprudence, especially during the dismantling of the droit d'aubaine in the late eighteenth century.

Settled in Paris and especially in the port cities of the Atlantic seaboard, the Dutch under the Old Regime came largely from mercantile communities with economic interests that placed them near the top of a hierarchy of foreign wealth and commercial influence—at the center of a broader "merchant France" and a "France of movement."[58] According to the Naturalization Tax rolls of 1697–1707, the Dutch were far more likely than other foreigners to have become French. Such painstaking and costly procedures, executed to guarantee their families the fruits of their commercial enterprises, did not prevent them from being struck twice: first by the revocation of the Edict of Nantes in 1685 (which authorized the monarchy to confiscate the goods of Protestants who fled the country, or who relapsed from their forced conversions), and then by the Naturalization Tax of 1697.[59]

Among the individually naturalized Dutch during the Old Regime, there were few Roman Catholics, and most were clergy (the Dutch were four times less likely to be clerics than other naturalized foreigners). Those Dutch-born clerics that became citizens were, with only one exception, tonsured clerics in religious houses in Paris, Bordeaux, or Flanders, men such as Gerard Hoffman, a Carmelite in Paris, naturalized in 1786.[60] Protestants for the most part, the Dutch were unlikely to hold public office, and relatively few practiced in the liberal professions. By contrast, they were twice as likely as the rest of the foreign citizens to be merchants. Most of the thirty-seven Dutch merchants naturalized between 1660 and 1790 were identified only as merchants, but another fifth were clearly drawn from the elite of wholesalers, bankers, and commercial entrepreneurs. Among them was Jacob van Walendal, a wholesale merchant from Amsterdam living in la Rochelle who became a citizen in 1672 . . . but whose estate was confiscated by the fisc at his death in 1696 and given as a gift to the marquis de Villette. (Like many naturalized Protestants, Van Walendal was in a worse condition after the withdrawal of the Edict of Nantes than before: by not converting to Catholicism, he was once more considered an alien.)[61] The naturalized Dutch were also far more likely to be artisans—and a third of these were tailors, including Jean Toumis Palmarid, a Catholic from the province of Zeeland who was working as a "master tailor of women's clothing" in Paris when he was naturalized in 1688.[62] Finally, the naturalized Dutch included thirteen military officers such as Pierre d'Herault, born in The Hague, who in 1693 explained in his letter that "he passionately preferred over all the opportunities that he could claim in his country of origin, given that his father is commander of the Honor Guard of the Prince of Orange, to continue the service that he has given [us] over the last ten years as captain in the German regiment of Greder, and to spend his days in the kingdom as would a native-born subject, having married, to that effect, the Dame Marquise de

Monferrer," the daughter of the lieutenant general of the French armies in the province of Roussillon.[63]

Holland and England, true to their status as the economic centers of European capitalism in the seventeenth and eighteenth centuries, tended to send wealthier migrants than other countries, also within the second circle, which by the eighteenth century had become more marginal economically: Italy, Spain, and Portugal.

FROM THE ITALIAN PENINSULA . . .

The Naturalization Tax rolls of 1697–1707 distinguish between the population of taxed immigrants and their ancestors who arrived in the kingdom after 1600 but died before 1697. Measuring the proportion of immigrants within each national group and from different regions of Europe, we concluded in our earlier book that by the early eighteenth century newer migratory flows of foreigners to the kingdom were more likely to have arrived from the north rather than the south. Yet the persistent numerical superiority of southern Europe in the quantification of individual naturalizations points not only to the importance of Savoy as a land of emigration to France, but also to the Italian Peninsula. After all, the Italians of the late seventeenth and eighteenth centuries inherited a long and celebrated tradition of settling in France. Following the immigration of "Lombards" in the thirteenth and fourteenth centuries, that of the merchant-bankers of Florence, Genoa, Milan, and Lucca took shape in the fifteenth and sixteenth centuries, at the moment when the northern Italian Peninsula was the economic center of Europe. Lyon became an Italian city, economically and culturally; and Italians flocked to the court in response to French immigration policy shaped by both political and cultural recruitment. The French court in the sixteenth century gave a privileged place to Italian artists and artisans, the reflex in part of the crown's foreign policy interests in the region, where France was engaged with the Habsburgs in a struggle for hegemony on the peninsula. For all these reasons, the Italians who settled in France in the sixteenth century, especially in Paris and Lyon, constituted generally a "luxury immigration": gentlemen, courtiers, bankers, and financiers rubbed shoulders with master artists and artisans—silk weavers, master glazers, painters, sculptors, architects, and engineers—employed at Versailles, in Paris, and in Lyon.[64]

The social history of naturalized Italians during the sixteenth and seventeenth centuries shows that more than two-thirds of them belonged to socially or economically dominant groups. In contrast to the migratory flow of cheap labor from the north, Italian immigration to the kingdom reveals a marked contrast between a wealthier and higher-status group of emigrants from southern Europe and a poorer migration flow to the kingdom fed from the north by the Irish, the Germans, and the Spanish subjects in Flanders. In the course of the seventeenth century, with the arrival in France of Italians that were poorer and of more modest social status, the situation changed slightly. The Naturalization Tax of 1697 records the presence of the wealthy strata of Italian immigrants, including a significant number of nobles, alongside a group of painters, sculptors, and musicians often attached to the court. But it also reveals the presence of a petty merchant class and a large number of poorer Italian artisans in less than prestigious trades, especially in construction and transport. Finally, the tax rolls illuminate a pattern of migration from the peninsula dominated by Italians from the northern principalities, although the rolls also reveal an increasing movement of foreigners from Venice and Naples in seventeenth-century France. In the course of the early modern period, as Italian migrants to the kingdom became less wealthy, the zones of departure on the peninsula tended to move toward the east and the south.[65]

The geographic and socioprofessional identities of the 723 Italians naturalized between 1660 and 1790 confirm this image while slightly modifying it.[66] One hundred and five naturalized Italians came from the southern kingdom of the Two Sicilies, including Naples, and another 87 came from the Papal States in the center of the peninsula. But most of the Italians whose origins are known came from the north, a quarter of them from Genoa (including the island of Corsica), and another fifth from the swath of territory between the tiny republic of Lucca to the Venetian possessions on the Dalmatian coast of the Adriatic.

Unlike the profile of taxed foreigners with professions listed on the rolls of 1697–1707, there were relatively few Italian artisans naturalized between 1660 and 1790 (only nine of 234 with known professions). There were also relatively few clergy (20 percent), especially in comparison with the broader data sample of foreign citizens, and officeholders tended to be rare. By contrast, about a quarter of the voluntary grants of French citizenship to Italians in the Old Regime concerned merchants, and this group was dominated by the commercial and financial elite (with more than half of them bankers, wholesale traders, brokers, and agents). But the largest single concentration of naturalized Italians between 1660 and 1790 can be found among practitioners of "liberal" trades, including nine medical practitioners, fourteen musicians, ten painters and sculptors, and eighteen actors—the Old Regime inheritance of a sixteenth-century "luxury immigration."[67]

Many of these artists and artisans had close connections to the court. Joseph Nicolas Pancrace Royer, who received a declaration of naturalization on 10 July 1751, was "music teacher of the [royal] children of France." Born in Turin of a French father, he had been trained in mathematics and "hydraulic science," and "had given proof of his knowledge in the construction of the gardens and fountains of Versailles under Sr. de Franeine, to whom he was related." Royer related his story almost entirely in terms of his father's achievements. Sent to

Turin on the French king's orders to work on the gardens of the regent, he there became "gentleman of the artillery and intendant of wars and fountains" before returning to Paris with his wife and young child.[68] Louis-André Riccoboni made no reference to his ancestors, but presumably and perhaps unnecessarily used his connections at court to be naturalized. After all, he had been brought to court by the duc d'Orléans from Italy as a member of an Italian theater troupe. In 1722, he was left a very modest estate by a friend, Jean Bissoni, who was born in Florence but had become a French citizen, and as such was capable of drawing up a last will and testament. But Riccoboni had no ability to receive the bequest, as he explained in the grant of naturalization dated July 1730 for himself, his wife, and child: "Even though the little inheritance bequeathed to him by the said Bissoni consists only in a few goods among which there are no state or landed annuities, he could not legally accept the inheritance in the terms of [Bissoni's] letters of naturalization which do not permit Bissoni to bequeath his goods except to native and resident heirs."[69]

FROM SPAIN AND PORTUGAL . . .

Surprisingly few foreigners from the Iberian Peninsula settled in France, despite their geographic proximity to the kingdom: they made up only 3 percent of the taxed foreigners in 1697, and a similar proportion of the individually naturalized foreigners between 1660 and 1790. Far more Frenchmen settled in Spain than Spaniards (including Catalans, Aragonese, and Basques) settled in the kingdom.[70] A fifth of the 193 naturalized Spaniards and their families acquired declarations of naturalization for sons and daughters of French emigrant families who sought to "recover" their native identities in order to inherit property in the kingdom. Obviously, Spain and Portugal were Catholic strongholds, and these French descendants were not part of the Huguenot diaspora. Some were the children of French merchants who established residence in Spain, especially in Seville and Madrid. Others were the product of the early years of the Bourbon alliance, and included the sons and daughters of French nobles and officials who had served Philip V in Madrid after the Bourbon king came to the Spanish throne in 1700. Those who had gone to serve the Bourbons—as lawyers, doctors, and royal officials—were considered, according to custom and law, not to have lost the "spirit of return" (even when they occasionally were naturalized in Spain) and were thus exempted from the droit d'aubaine.[71] So too were the Catalans, who in 1659 received the right to inherit estates in the neighboring county of Roussillon and half of the county of Cerdagne, ceded to France by the Peace of the Pyrenees.[72]

Other Spaniards, except for those from Lower Navarre, were considered subject to the droit d'aubaine until the second half of the eighteenth century.

The major peace treaties of Vervin (1598) and the Pyrenees (1659) exempted them from taxes only, while the Treaty of Ryswick (1697) stipulated that subjects of the two crowns would be reciprocally permitted to inherit. These international treaties—like the others of the Old Regime—were not specific about the exemption from the droit d'aubaine, and were in any case subject to abrupt withdrawal at the first signs of diplomatic conflict.[73] The first Bourbon Family Compacts only extended "most favored nation" status on the subjects of the two crowns, but the subsequent accord of 1762 mutually exempted the subjects of France, Spain, and the Two Sicilies from the droit d'aubaine, although it did not explicitly permit respective subjects to inherit from nationals. Yet French case law tended to deny the exemptions from the droit d'aubaine—especially after the "great example" in 1702 of Don Gaspard de Arcdondo, the Spanish-born ex-governor of Puerto Rico, who came back from America "with great riches on a French boat," and died twelve days after disembarking. His estate was seized by the tax-farmers as if he had been an alien, and the heirs of the Spanish governor finally lost their case on appeal to the Paris parlement.[74]

Most Spaniards naturalized in the Old Regime can be identified only as coming from Spain, although fifty-six were born in the lands of the crown of Aragon, including thirty-five in Catalonia. More than a fifth of the Spaniards, and two-thirds of the Catalans, settled in the provinces of southern France, especially Roussillon, that were annexed by the crown in 1659. The socioprofessional profile of these Spaniards is similar to that of foreign citizens more generally, although among the subjects of the Spanish king could be found a slightly higher proportion of clergy, military officers, and practitioners of the liberal trades, and proportionally fewer servants (in fact, only one Spanish domestic servant can be identified: Martin de Moiselle, maître d'hôtel of the marquis of Lionne, born in Aragon and naturalized in 1675).[75] Moreover, among the naturalized Spaniards, there were fewer merchants and fewer artisans—less an affirmation of the stereotypical aversion of Spaniards toward the commercial and mechanical trades than an indication that most Spaniards who contributed to movement and commerce tended to sail to the Indies.[76]

We have seen that at least half of the "Portuguese" taxed in 1697 were Jews. In striking contrast, none of the naturalized Portuguese families before the 1770s were Jews; until that moment, Jews were generally not considered "aliens" in the Old Regime, and thus not subject to the droit d'aubaine.[77] The "true" Portuguese, subjects of the king of Portugal, did not enjoy any exemptions from international treaties with France, and were thus not exempted from the droit d'aubaine. Three-quarters of them declared themselves merchants (*marchands*), although little is known about their places of origin or settlement, except that a third of them lived in the Paris region, with a smaller concentration in the Atlantic port of Nantes.[78]

Moving, within the second concentric circle of countries from which foreign citizens originated, from the south to the east: a total of 712 foreigners (including descendants of French emigrants who were "declared" French natives) came from the German states (11 percent of the individual naturalizations), a figure that does not include the 282 (another 4 percent) who were born in the principalities and jurisdictions of the Rhineland. Although fewer could be identified as coming from the Rhineland among the Germans naturalized in 1697–1707, the proportion of Germans in the two samples of individually and collectively naturalized foreigners is essentially the same. The convergence stems from the fact that nearly all of the subjects of constituent principalities and jurisdictions of the Holy Roman Empire who settled in the kingdom, at least before the 1760s, were subjected to the droit d'aubaine.[79]

The specific origins of less than half of the Germans are known, given the tendency of clerks to consistently use the term "Germany" in a relatively undifferentiated way.[80] But a significant concentration came from the Catholic lands of the Austrian Empire, including Bohemia, Silesia, and Moravia (102 total). A smaller group originated in the Protestant states of Prussia, including Brandenburg (47 cases) and other northern German states (10 from Hamburg, 28 from Saxony). Some of these were sons and daughters of French Protestants who had taken refuge before and after the withdrawal of the Edict of Nantes in 1685, who themselves were born abroad, but returned to claim their often-contested family inheritances. Given the presence of Protestants more generally among the naturalized Germans in the Old Regime, it is not surprising that only slightly more than a quarter were members of the clergy, compared to 39 percent of the foreign citizens with known professions or statuses. The mercantile classes were also less likely to be found among Germans, but more than a fifth of the Germans were artisans. Such a finding diverges significantly from the tax rolls of 1697–1707, where more than 60 percent of the Germans practiced artisanal trades, but that proportion was inflated partially by the nearly one hundred workers in the building trades who came originally from the Alpine district of Tyrol—a specialized but impoverished migratory stream into the kingdom.[81]

According to the rolls of the Naturalization Tax levied between 1697 and 1707, a third of the Germans—not including those in the Rhineland district— settled in the provinces of Alsace and Lorraine in the east, while nearly half were established in the city of Paris and its region. This pattern of settlement was reproduced among foreigners who sought citizenship. The latter nonetheless had a stronger presence, during the eighteenth century, in the city of Paris and its suburbs, where German artisans and craftsmen dominated the furniture and cabinet trade, and played an important role in the jewelry markets and as tailors in the century before the Revolution. Another important concentration of Germans was long-established in Bordeaux, merchants and artisans active in the Baltic grain and merchandise trade.[82]

A Third Circle: From the Peripheries of Europe and Beyond

The final concentric circle of countries and regions from which naturalized foreigners originated includes those most distant geographically from the kingdom, both in Europe, and across the globe (table 5.4). These foreigners do not represent a highly significant proportion of the naturalizations between 1660 and 1790 (6 percent), although their presence in the longitudinal data set is double that among the forcibly and collectively naturalized "foreigners" in 1697. The numbers may be statistically without value, but the stories that they conceal reveal a broad range of patterns, and a convergent set of motives, among foreign citizens from the European peripheries settled in Old Regime France.

We begin with the northern edge of the European continent, with the forty-nine foreigners from the Lutheran countries of Sweden and Denmark who took letters of naturalization between 1660 and 1790. It is not surprising that the group includes a higher than average number of "French" children born of the Protestant diaspora who, like those in England, Holland, or part of Germany, converted to Catholicism and returned to the kingdom in order to inherit. Such was the case of Pierre Suchon, born in Gutenberg of a Lutheran family established there after the withdrawal of the Edict of Nantes in 1685. Having abjured the errors of his parents in 1721, he was declared French six years later. Among the twenty petitioners from the kingdom of Denmark, two were women married to Frenchmen, further evidence that marriage did not entail naturalization in the Old Regime. Catherine Brun, born in Hesflud, on the island of Zeeland (off the province of that name in Holland), received a grant of citizenship in August 1717. She was the wife of Pierre Hodecam, "poor journeyman wigmaker of French origin," by whom she had two children in Denmark, named in her letters, and a third in Nogent-le-Rotron in the province of Perche.[83]

The eastern reaches of Europe produced 107 naturalized foreigners—the lands identified in the grants as "Moscovy" or "Russia"; Hungary (part of the Ottoman Empire until 1697; most naturalizations from Hungary were given during the eighteenth century); and Poland (which was to be virtually dismantled by Russia, Austria, and Prussia in the late Old Regime, but from where seventy-four naturalized foreigners originated). There were, of course, among them a handful of descendants of French nationals—an armorer born of an Alsatian father in Hungary; the son of another Alsatian living in Danzig; the son of French parents in Warsaw, who sent him back to France at a young age "as much for the religion as for good customs." He received a declaration of his cit-

TABLE 5.4.
Naturalizations from the European Peripheries, 1660–1789

	Number of Individual Naturalizations	Percent of All Naturalizations	Percent of Foreign Population Taxed (1697–1707)
Kingdom of Sweden	29	.5	.2
Kingdom of Denmark	20	.3	.3
Russian Empire	6	.1	.2
Kingdom of Poland	74	1.2	.2
Kingdom of Hungary	27	.4	.1
Order of Malta	53	.8	.8
Ottoman Empire	97	1.5	1.1
"Africa"	4	.1	.1
European colonies	60	.4	0
Persia, India, China	8	.2	0
Total	378	5.5	3

izenship in 1750.[84] But at least nine out of ten foreigners from these regions received full naturalizations, even though the letter of the law might not have been required them to do so. For the seventy-four Poles who dominated the group of east Europeans, this was hardly an immigration born of poverty: in the 1697 tax rolls, Poles were assessed at double the tax rate as the "foreign" population more generally. Among individually naturalized Poles, one-third were state and private officeholders, and another third were clergy, testifying to the special relationship between France and Poland born of French king Henry III's reign as king of Poland.[85] Of the Hungarians naturalized, more than a third—and half during the eighteenth century—were military officers in the Hussards Regiments of France.[86] More generally, naturalizations from the eastern peripheries of Europe reproduced a global pattern of individual naturalizations between 1660 and 1790: most foreign citizens in the Old Regime came to France to serve—whether in the Church or the army, as officeholders or in the liberal professions—and less frequently as merchants.

Farther south on the peripheries of Europe, the Ottoman Empire, whose subjects were unexempted from the droit d'aubaine despite some vague invocation of privileges in the commercial treaties of the 1690s, was well represented in the population of foreign citizens. The story is less exotic than it might at first seem. Their large representation in the Naturalization Tax of 1697 (eighty, or 1 percent of the taxed population of immigrants and heirs of immigrants) speaks to the relative case of maritime transport. So too does the profile of their settlement in the kingdom: a quarter of them were established in the coastal cities and ports of Provence, where they practiced maritime professions, and many in Paris, where they tended to specialize in cafés and refreshments (*marchands limonadiers*). Most of the Ottoman subjects taxed were "true" foreigners—half of them of Greek origin, who came from what the clerks of the tax-farmers simply called "the Archipelago" (*l'Archipel*).[87] But nearly a quarter of the ninety-seven individual naturalizations of subjects from the Ottoman Empire were either declarations given to descendants of emigrant families from France, or were naturalizations conferred on other Europeans born or living in the lands of the Sultan. Some were even given to French natives who had been naturalized elsewhere, as was François Bres, the son of a Marseille merchant who had been received as a citizen by the magistrates of the republic of Venice after he worked in his native Cyprus to "attract, for the benefit of the French nation, a portion of the commerce that the Italians control in the Levant seaports."[88] But others were clearly native non-Europeans, born Muslims or Jews, who had converted to Catholicism before seeking citizenship. These included Lucie Esmer Fontana, an Armenian naturalized in April 1719 after having been brought to Paris by Sr. Fériol, then ambassador of Louis XIV to Constantinople, after being baptized there on Easter Sunday in 1697; and also Jean-Baptiste Diodet, born in Constantinople, who became French in February 1750 after his conversion to Catholicism.[89]

The case of the Maltese was distinct: participation in the Order of Malta—as the religious order of Saint John of Jerusalem was known after its installation on Malta in 1530—"serves as a rampart of Christianity against the assaults of infidels," as was argued in the case of Charles Verany. He considered himself a French native, born in Malta of a French father, and received a declaration of naturalization in 1727 because "our subjects who have entered the order were reputed our true and original subjects and native-born residents notwithstanding the fact that they are often obliged to reside on the isle of Malta for their service to the Order."[90] In this sense, Malta was a hybrid juridical entity, not quite an extraterritorial part of the kingdom, but not truly a foreign land from which subjects were unexempted from the droit d'aubaine. The uncertain status of the "province" (in its ecclesiastical and territorial senses) helps to account for the not insignificant numbers of Maltese, members of the religious order but not born in France or even of French parents, who sought declarations and naturalizations during the Old Regime (fifty-three, nearly 1 percent of the individually naturalized foreigners between 1660 and 1790).[91]

In the case of citizenship grants to foreigners originating in Europe's colonies in both the New World and East India, very few if any appear to have been given to indigenous peoples of non-European descent—although the nature of the data used in this book does not always disclose that fact.[92] It is true that the Black Code of 1685, Louis XIV's colonial law code that sought to stabilize the slave system in the Caribbean, permitted the manumission of slaves and their exemption from the droit d'aubaine, provided that they converted to Catholicism. Although such an "open" and "liberal" policy toward manumission in the Caribbean was reversed in the revision of the Black Code in 1724 for Louisiana, the 1685 Code seems to have been indebted to earlier colonial policies in North America that had exempted indigenous peoples from the droit d'aubaine, provided that they convert. Thus the royal charter of the

Compagnie des Cent Associés in 1634, given by Louis XIII at the instigation of Samuel Champlain for the "colonization" of North America, which specified that "the savages [*sauvages*] who have been brought to know the faith and have professed will be deemed and reputed to be French naturals, and as such can come live in France whenever they please and there acquire, bequeath, inherit, and accept donations and bequests in the same ways as true native-born residents and original Frenchmen without being required to take any letters of declaration nor of naturalization." Such a policy, however, proved difficult to adapt to the slave societies of the Caribbean.[93]

A number of legal cases involving slaves claiming French freedom preoccupied the admiralty courts and the royal council during the eighteenth century, leading to the royal ordinances concerned with the "regulation of black subjects" (*police des noirs*) in 1776–77.[94] But none of these involved claims to be exempted from the droit d'aubaine, and I have found few traces of indigenous inhabitants from the New World who sought French citizenship, although the data set is hardly exhaustive. Among the sixty individual naturalizations between 1660 and 1790, registered and verified either by the local sovereign councils in the French Antilles or the appropriate fiscal courts in the metropole, the vast majority were Europeans—English, Irish, Italians, Spaniards, and Germans—living in the Caribbean, or in other distant lands of the French empire in the Far East where the French lawyers believed that the droit d'aubaine was applied, in theory, until the French Revolution.[95] They were often the product of a European Creole environment, like Catherine Sylvester, the wife of Nicolas Boileau, "native [born on] the Isle of Santo Domingo, belonging to the king of Spain," daughter of a Spanish father and an English mother, who became a French citizen in 1718. Some considered themselves already French: François Baugras, "born under the French king's domination in a port of Mississippi belonging to the king, of parents originally from Guinea." Although he had his baptismal certificate, from the town of Montauban (Languedoc) from 1736, Baugras did not feel secure, and "to assure his condition and prevent all difficulties, he was counseled to have recourse to our letters of declaration of naturalization," which he received in 1742.[96]

A similar story about the ethnic identity of foreign citizens could be told of the small number of "Africans": all were Europeans from North Africa, the Barbary Coast and its islands. They included men such as Jean-François Aubry, the son of a French merchant from Rheims who was "sent to the Island of Tarques *en Affrique* [*sic*] for the Compagnie de Marseille to handle their affairs" and there he married the daughter of a Genoese woman of which union was born the petitioner; Emmanuel Taboada, who had been a colonel in the Ceuta regiment of the king of Spain, but who had settled and married in Lower Languedoc; and Philippe Vidary, born in Tripoli "on the Barbary Coast" who had been sent to study in Marseille and stayed twelve years before seeking naturalization.[97] Those from the Indian subcontinent were Europeans as well, men such as the Portuguese merchant Alexandre Carvalho who settled in Bengal in 1764, whose sister was married to the French governor of Calcutta, and who received a declaration of naturalization eight years later.[98]

The five naturalized "Persians," by contrast, do not seem to have been Europeans, and at least two were connected in some way to state service. Other than Constance Faulcon of Siam, with whom this chapter began, Gabriel Dolver, naturalized in 1720, had a father who was an "an important officer in the bodyguard of the king of Persia holding similar functions to those of our bodyguards which can only be exercised by nobles of the country." The claimant himself was a Muslim page brought to France in 1714 by Mahomet Rizabeg, extraordinary ambassador of the king of Persia; years later, he converted to Catholicism and eventually acquired a modest royal pension of six hundred livres.[99]

And in the odd and original case of Carlos Felix *dit Ahoye*, born in "Canton, Land of the Gentiles in China, baptized a Catholic in Macao in 1760, then aged six or seven," we cannot be sure either of his ethnicity or of his national origin, only that in April 1785 he became a French citizen somewhere in the jurisdiction of the Paris Chambre des comptes.[100]

The patterns of geographic origins among naturalized foreigners between 1660 and 1789 thus privileged the borderlands of the kingdom, although less than within the group of foreigners taxed in 1697. These patterns have been described, with important exceptions, as a series of concentric circles emanating from the kingdom where the number of foreign citizens decreased in direct relation to geographic distance. Such global patterns of naturalization were shaped not only by geography but by the legal status of specific foreign groups and the policy directives of the monarchy itself. More, as the following chapter seeks to demonstrate, the variations over time of foreigners seeking citizenship were significant, and these reflect the importance of the changing legal and political frameworks that governed the status of aliens between the Age of Louis XIV and the French Revolution.

CHAPTER SIX

TEMPORAL PATTERNS OF NATURALIZATION

B y the early reign of Louis XIV, the practice of naturalization had become a routinized and relatively automatic bureaucratic procedure. The Great Chancellery issued letters and declarations of naturalization to foreigners established in the kingdom and with interests to protect—an inheritance, an office, or a benefice—from either the voracity of the tax-farmers or from collateral heirs. Yet, the variation over time of individual naturalizations from 1660 to 1789 was considerable. This chronology of naturalizations was a response to the changing politics of the monarchy, the shifting jurisprudence of nationality law, and long-term trends in the kingdom's economic development.

Annual fluctuations in the number of naturalizations (or even five-year averages) only rarely correlate with single policy initiatives of the French monarchy concerning its international relations or its treatment of specific "national" groups. Nor were there inevitable links between case law concerning foreign inheritance and the reductions or increases in rates of naturalization among affected groups. Nonetheless, from a deeper historical perspective, decade-long fluctuations in the numbers and origins of foreign citizens did correspond to consistent jurisprudential trends, to evident political reorientations of the French crown, and to cyclical shifts in the French economy. Taking into account all known naturalizations and declarations between 1660 and 1789 (including those culled from inventories, both contemporaneous and contemporary), the tendencies appear self-evident, permitting the division of the Old Regime into three distinct phases.

The 130 years before the French Revolution are marked by three phases that echo what economic historians recognize as cyclical phases of commercial and economic movement (fig. 1). Counting the average number of naturalizations and declarations by decades, the first phase (1660–1709) was one of dramatic and precipitous decline, a consistent downward trend in individual naturalizations from an average of fifty-two a year in the 1660s to thirty-four a year in the first decade of the eighteenth century. The phase corresponds neatly, but not

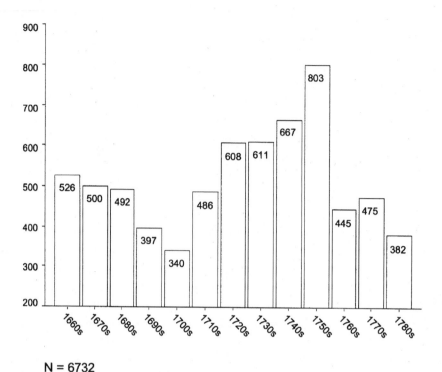

N = 6732

Fig. 1. Naturalizations, 1660–1789

exactly, with the too long and bellicose personal reign of Louis XIV (r. 1661–1715), when the monarchy's attitude toward the foreigner was one of marked ambivalence. On the one hand, the crown redeployed and amplified the droit d'aubaine as part of the fiscal politics of absolutism, culminating in the collective Naturalization Tax of 1697 that withdrew all prior naturalizations. On the other hand, the absolutist monarchy, in discretionary acts of sovereignty but also as part of international diplomatic settlements, continuously exempted particular "national" and professional groups of foreigners from the droit d'aubaine. At the same time, during this period of uninterrupted warfare between France and most of Europe, international treaties were torn up by the sword, only to be re-signed after great hardship and devastation. In this climate, and given the ambiguous signals coming from the monarchy, it is no surprise that individual naturalizations declined precipitously in the Age of Louis XIV. This was especially the case after the 1680s, when the fiscal impact of warfare was to be most harshly experienced in the French kingdom itself, and its material effects were evident in its borderlands.[1]

Louis XIV died in 1715, after fifty-four years of personal rule, but the apex of absolute citizenship—the unintended consequence of the 1697 Naturalization Tax—had already been reached. Not surprisingly, following the Naturalization Tax of 1697, citizenship grants reached their five-year nadir between 1700 and

1705. Thereafter, anticipating the great European peace treaties of Rastadt (1713) and Utrecht (1714), the average number of foreigners naturalized per half-decade began to grow in a marked fashion. Between 1710 and 1759, naturalizations increased from an average of thirty-four a year in the decade of 1700–1710 to more than eighty a year in the 1750s. This second phase of consistent and general growth coincides with, even if it anticipates slightly, the end of the wars of Louis XIV and the beginning of a "New European Order" after the Treaty of Utrecht in 1714, a new political and military context in which Louis XV and his ministers no longer aspired with abandon to European hegemony.[2] Moreover, the growth of naturalizations in the first half of the eighteenth century, especially after the 1730s, reflected and partially informed a period of renewed economic expansion in the kingdom and in Europe more generally. Economic historians have long noted the growth of population and agricultural prices, the upturn in indices of aggregate and per capita industrial output, and the overall commercial expansion of this period, at least before the economic conjuncture coinciding with the Seven Years War.[3] The less bellicose climate, in a favorable economic context, shaped the increase of naturalizations during this second phase of the Old Regime: in the early 1750s, grants of citizenship reached an annual apex of eighty-three a year.

Thereafter, in the third and final phase of the Old Regime (1760–89), naturalizations dropped once again, this time even more dramatically. By the early 1760s and well into the 1770s, the number of foreigners annually naturalized was reduced by half, to about forty-five; the five-year averages of new grants then dropped precipitously again in the 1780s. The third phase corresponds less to an economic downturn (breaking any strict correlation between naturalizations and the business cycles of wages and prices) than it does to the dramatic mutation of political culture that makes up the citizenship revolution of the eighteenth century. That revolution was constituted in the public refashioning of the political category of the citizen, but most importantly in the abolition of the principal juridical distinction between foreigners and citizens: the droit d'aubaine. In some threescore treaties and international conventions signed between 1765 and 1782, the French foreign ministry dismantled systematically if in a piecemeal and reciprocal fashion the principal juridical difference between French citizens and foreigners. This revolutionary refashioning of the meaning and boundaries of citizenship is the subject of the third section of this book. It is important to invoke it here, although not because the abolition of the droit d'aubaine *caused* the decline of naturalizations at the end of the Old Regime. Rather, the declining numbers of naturalizations, beginning in the early 1760s, *anticipated* the diplomatic requests and negotiations to abolish the droit d'aubaine—even if, in the end, the decline of naturalizations from 1759 to the outbreak of the French Revolution was profoundly shaped by the changing and contested legal status and definitions of the foreigner.

These three phases—of decline during the wars of Louis XIV (1660–1709),

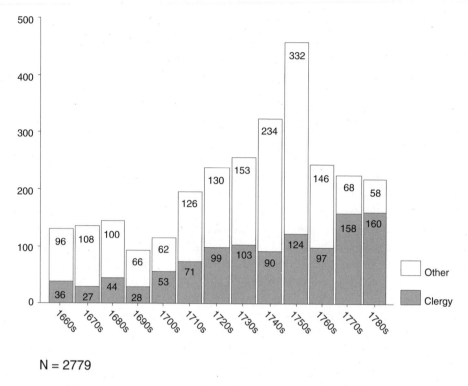

500 —

400 —

332

300 —

234

200 —

153

130

126

146

100 —

96 108 100

62

66

99 103 90

124 97

68 58

36 27 44 28 53 71

158 160

0 —

1660s 1670s 1680s 1690s 1700s 1710s 1720s 1730s 1740s 1750s 1760s 1770s 1780s

☐ Other

▨ Clergy

N = 2779

Fig. 2. Naturalizations of Clergy and Others with Professions, 1660–1789

growth after the wars and during the economic upswing of the first half of the eighteenth century (1710–59), and precipitous slump in the last decades of the Old Regime (1760–89)—unevenly distribute the data set of individually naturalized foreigners. Thirty-five percent of the total number of individual naturalizations or declarations were given in the forty-nine-year span of the first phase; 45 percent were given in the same number of years during the second; but only 20 percent of the data set of individual naturalizations were conferred in the last thirty-nine years of the Old Regime. These proportions, in fact, make even more evident the trends of the Old Regime: a period of long, slow decline under Louis XIV; a rapid period of expansion ending approximately with the Seven Years War (1756–63), and a sharp drop in naturalizations during the last decades before the French Revolution.

Before examining the variables informing these patterns, it is important to stress that the three phases correspond only to the total population of individually naturalized foreigners, including those receiving declarations. If the nearly 40 percent of the foreign citizens who were clerics (and who thus sought religious benefices attached to cures of souls as well as monastic offices) are considered apart from those other naturalized foreigners with known professions or statuses, the clerical counterexperience is immediately revealed (fig. 2).

Although the temporal pattern of naturalized foreigners practicing other "professions" continued to follow the three basic phases of the Old Regime, the pattern of foreign clerics seeking citizenship with clerical benefices was remarkably different. Measured by decades, or even by half-decades, the clergy, until the 1760s, was not a mirror image of the temporal shifts among foreign citizens. Rather, there was a gradual and persistent increase in clerical naturalizations from the early years of Louis XIV's personal reign to the outbreak of the French Revolution. This pattern can only be explained by the crown's growing efforts under the Old Regime to authorize and "police" the foreign clergy of the kingdom, and especially in the borderland provinces of the north and east, where the boundaries of bishoprics failed to coincide with those of the kingdom and where state concerns about political reciprocity dictated an increasing number of clerical naturalizations. At each moment of the three phases of the Old Regime, the distinct counterexperiences of the clerics are dramatically revealed.

The Age of Louis XIV (1660–1709)

From an initial decade-long total of 526 naturalizations in the 1660s, the numbers dropped slightly to 500 in the 1670s and to 492 in the 1680s; a decade later, they dropped more precipitously to 397, falling to a nadir of 340 in the ten years from 1700 to 1709. But separating the clerical naturalizations from those of foreigners with known professions or statuses, a less even and more contradictory movement can be demonstrated using five-year averages (fig. 3).

In fact, "secular" naturalizations (of foreigners with known professions other than the clergy) tend to *increase* in the first decade of Louis XIV's reign, while naturalizations and declarations of citizenship for foreign clergy drop until the 1680s.[4] The pattern is explained, in part, by the timing of warfare during the Sun King's reign. On his assumption of personal rule in 1661, Louis XIV first negotiated a series of international alliances and diplomatic accords with much of Europe, including the United Provinces, which was to become his nemesis by the 1670s.[5] In this more irenic atmosphere, naturalizations of foreigners from specific "nations," including Holland, increased slightly: from three naturalized Dutch a year in the early 1660s, for example, the rate increased to eighteen a year by 1670. The Dutch were likely to seek citizenship, even if many of them, both long settled and recently arrived in the kingdom, benefited from royal policy that conferred naturalization to attract their talent and wealth. Such a pro-immigration stance was both part of official policy (found, for example, in the collective exemptions from the droit d'aubaine given to Dutch engineers who drained the swamps of Versailles) and unofficially acknowledged (in the special treatment of wealthy merchant financiers, in Bordeaux and Paris, from whom the crown borrowed freely).

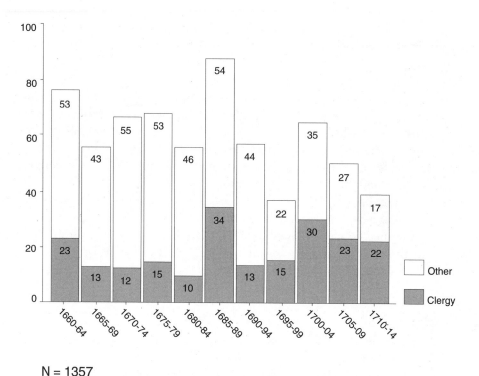

Fig. 3. Naturalizations of Clergy and Others with Professions, 1660–1714

N = 1357

Already by the early 1670s, however, the treaties and alliances of Louis XIV proved to be a hindrance, as the Sun King swapped the "prudence" of Richelieu and Mazarin for the pursuit of his own glory. Louis XIV put his personal hatred of the Dutch into practice, and the monarchy embarked on an aggressive and expansionist foreign policy. Naturalizations of foreigners from across Europe dropped noticeably as France entered into a period of sporadic and then sustained warfare. The War of Devolution (1667–68) against Spain and especially the Dutch War (1672–78) launched an economic and military war on land and at sea, part of the struggle for mercantilist precedence in the emerging global markets. Foreign-born residents of the kingdom settled in the northern and eastern borderlands felt the impact of these wars most keenly. Many, it shall be recalled, had long been settled in the kingdom, while others found themselves under French rule as a result of France's territorially ambitious military operations. French expansion in Flanders yielded the commercial and military strongholds of Lille, Tournai, Ypres, and Cambrai; in the east, Louis XIV acquired during the first half of his rule large parts of Alsace (officially conquering Strasbourg in 1682), the Franche-Comté (annexed in 1678), and the duchy of Lorraine (controlled by French troops for most of his reign). By the 1680s, France had established a military frontier (Vauban's "iron curtain") and political authority in the newly acquired territories, assisted by the legal apparatus of the "Chambers of Reunion" in Metz, Besançon, and Brisach that yielded to France many "dependencies," including such relatively large territories as the duchy of Luxembourg.[6] After the 1680s, it was open warfare, of Europe against France, in the War of the Augsburg League (1690–97) and the War of the Spanish Succession (1701–13). The results were disastrous for a kingdom already devastated by the demographic and economic crises that punctuated these decades. In the context of widespread fiscal crisis, aggravated by a remarkable series of military defeats, Louis XIV not only made fiscally and politically unwise choices (such as that of taxing "foreigners" in 1697), but was forced to settle diplomatically in the treaties of Rastadt (1713) and Utrecht (1714), in which France returned most of the territories conquered in Flanders since 1678 (map 1).[7]

During this disastrous second half of the reign, in a bellicose climate and within prolonged economic crisis singularly unfavorable to the presence of foreigners, the policy of the monarchy wavered. On the one hand, informed by the precepts of mercantilism, the crown continued to favor specific groups of foreigners (Irish and German mercenaries, Flemish tapestry workers, Venetian glassblowers, pilots, sailors, and other "sea folk") by offering them exemptions from the droit d'aubaine or naturalization in exchange for their labor power. On the other hand, war clearly suspended the modest increase of naturalizations during the 1660s when France reverted to more xenophobic and traditional policies of suspending privileges and expelling foreigners during wartime. Long established within international law, such practices converged with French policies. Already in the late sixteenth century, French lawyers and jurisconsults had insisted on the suspension of the "rights" of foreigners during and even beyond periods of war. "At the heart of any foreigner, there is always the suspicion of some hidden poison, I dare say treachery" wrote the jurist Jean Bacquet in 1577. He had in mind the Flemings, especially during times of war:

> And when there is open warfare, the inhabitants of these districts are the first who most enthusiastically take up arms, the first to make incursions into, to ravage and oppress the kingdom of France, such that *vere hostes appelari possune* [they can justly be called enemies].

No surprise, then, that the normal practice was for "the king to seize all the fiefs, lands, seigneuries, and estates within the kingdom that belong to foreigners and rebels."[8] The early modern jurists, from the learned humanist jurisconsult Jean Bodin to the legal hacks who compiled dictionaries of court decisions and royal decrees, concurred. "The foreigner can be chased from the kingdom, not only in times of war . . . but also in times of peace, to prohibit subjects from being spoiled and altered by vicious foreigners. . . . And during open warfare against the Prince, the foreigner can be detained as an enemy, following the law of war," wrote Bodin. The Parisian barrister and redactor of customary law Laurent Bouchel (1559–1629), whose *Bibliothèque du Trésor du Droit français* (1615) was reprinted several times in the seventeenth century, repeated the exact statement (although he did not cite its source).[9] During the long wars of Louis XIV, the practice of seizing the properties of France's "enemies" was revived and amplified. Specific "national" enemies were given notice to leave the country: the English in 1666, the (unnaturalized) Dutch in 1672 (even if Colbert sought to protect those in Bordeaux from the edict's full force), the "rebels" against the alliance of 1718.[10]

The inherited sixteenth and early seventeenth-century judicial xenophobia came in handy as the war clouds gathered after the first decade of Louis XIV's reign—Bouchel's text was republished in 1671—and the state attempted to sharpen the distinction between French subjects and foreigners. Foreigners were required, although hardly consistently, to hold passports when they came into the kingdom.[11] Periodic efforts to police the movement of vagrants and gypsies in the kingdom often gave them the same marginal status as aliens under Louis XIV.[12] Meanwhile, French subjects were prohibited from marrying outside the kingdom, or—in the famous ordinance of 1669 that was later applied to the French Protestant diaspora—from living in foreign countries without royal permission and from participating in foreign commerce, navigation, or industry.[13] War was bad for resident foreigners in France, and the long wars of Louis XIV were far more conducive to forced collective naturalization than to individual grants of citizenship. The imposition of the Naturalization Tax in 1697 drew a boundary between French citizens and foreigners, especially in the borderlands of the kingdom, justified by the royal prerogative of the droit d'aubaine. But even before the French monarchy redeployed this final, muscular extension of the droit d'aubaine in the Naturalization Tax, individual immigrants and their families were less likely to settle in France and become citizens.

The first significant drop in the numbers and rate of naturalizations occurred in the years after 1685, coinciding with the French king's withdrawal of the Edict of Nantes. The Edict of Fontainebleu proscribed Protestant worship in France, including among naturalized foreigners, but subsequent decrees, countering rumors that foreign Protestants were banished from France, encouraged the settlement of (unnaturalized) Protestants in the kingdom.[14] As might be expected, rates of naturalization among predominantly Protestant countries, including the United Provinces, England, and the states of northern Germany, tended to decline. After all, the onerous status of Protestant foreigners once naturalized outweighed the royal privileges granted to them collectively, as foreign national or professional groups in the kingdom. In the decade after 1685, even Catholic naturalizations, including those of foreign clergy, consistently declined. The steepest overall drop in all naturalizations and declarations occurred in the 1690s, during the War of the Augsburg League (1690–97), which ended with the collective Naturalization Tax imposed between 1697 and 1707. It is not surprising, then, that individual grants of citizenship reach their lowest annual number (nineteen) in 1699.

In the northeastern borderland, where the military acquisition of territories and jurisdictions had been particularly intense, the decline of naturalizations from the bishopric of Liège and the Spanish Low Countries was slow but certain, despite a clear increase of Flemish natives seeking French citizenship around 1682, the date when the first effects of the Chambers of Reunion were felt. Foreign clergy naturalized in the 1680s were most often from jurisdictions ceded or seized by France in what might be called the juridical conquest of the borderland. Charles Petit, who received a declaration with permission to hold benefices in 1687, after recounting how his natal village, Falais, in an enclave within Liège, had been under French dominion only since 1681.[15] Since the inhabitants of the conquered and "reunified" territories and jurisdictions were given the same rights and privileges as the king's true and natural subjects, there was little need, according to the letter of the law, for individuals to seek individual letters of naturalization or declaration. But many of them did so anyway, especially if they sought to conform to the royal prohibition of unnaturalized foreigners accepting benefices in the "newly conquered territories or those ceded by the peace treaties of Münster, the Pyrenees, Aix-la-Chapelle, and Nijmegen," as the royal declaration of January 1681 was to proclaim.[16] This singular royal act helps to account for the dramatic increase in clerical naturalizations after 1681—in fact, they tripled to over thirty a year in the 1680s, even if they were to drop off again in the 1690s.

The pattern of naturalizations from the duchy of Lorraine during the wars of Louis XIV is a special case (fig. 4). In the context of the lengthy French military occupation of the region, Lorraine was slowly integrated, juridically and politically, into the French kingdom. From its conquest by Louis XIII in 1632, the duchy of Lorraine—entirely within French territory—remained largely under French domination and tutelage until the end of the century. After 1670, French armies occupied Nancy, the capital city, and used Lorraine as a military base (assuring direct communication between the Low Countries, Luxembourg, and the Franche-Comté, and a staging ground for the eventual invasion of Holland). The marquis de Louvois had remarked in 1672 that "the king doesn't at all consider Lorraine as a country [pays] that he should give up, and there is reason to believe . . . that he is seeking the means to keep it." But the question was not even resolved in the Treaty of Ryswick in 1697, which returned the duchy to an independent status but only momentarily. The French occupied Lorraine again between 1702 and 1714, during the War of the Spanish Succession.[17]

The inconstant if successful military acquisition of the duchy of Lorraine resulted in an ambiguous juridical status in the seventeenth century. A century earlier, the Lorrains had been subjected to the droit d'aubaine, according to

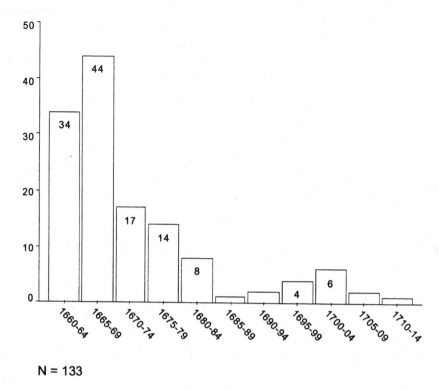

Fig. 4. Naturalizations from the Duchy of Lorraine, 1660–1714

Choppin, Bacquet, and other sixteenth-century jurists. Under Louis XIV, the jurisprudence still tended to lean toward treating the Lorrains as aliens. But an important dissenting interpretation argued that Lorrains who had died "since the conquest" were not to be subject to the droit d'aubaine. The legal problem then became one of determining the exact timing and nature of the conquest itself.[18] Even if international treaties had not recognized (and legally validated) the conquest, the French government began to treat its natives as if they were natural Frenchmen and women. In 1702, in recognition of this de facto legal practice, the king issued a declaration establishing the right of succession reciprocally between the subjects of the king and those of the duc de Lorraine. After that edict, citizenship grants to Lorrains became extremely rare, even before 1738, when the royal marriage alliance of Louis XV and the daughter of the Polish king, Stanislas I, gave Lorrains the status of French natives, and well before 1766 when Stanislas died and the French crown took full legal title, by inheritance, to the duchy.[19]

In fact, the pattern of naturalizations of subjects born in the duchy of Lorraine in the late seventeenth century reflected the gradual assimilation of the province into France—what might be called the naturalization of Lorraine itself.

Legal assimilation—the practice of nationality law as naturalization, in this context—actually preceded the political and institutional integration of the duchy into the kingdom. Moreover, the evidence from the Naturalization Tax rolls of 1697–1707 suggests that Lorrains in France included an unusually high concentration of practitioners of liberal trades and especially of officeholders, signs of the relative social assimilation of the duchy's inhabitants, or at least the local ruling elites, into French society by the turn of the eighteenth century. The tax rolls reveal that the Lorrains behaved more like a provincial, as opposed to a foreign, elite, drawn by the proximity of French towns and the opportunities of service and professional life in the capital city. Although some subjects of the duchy sought naturalization after the 1702 declaration made it unnecessary, the far larger portion of naturalized subjects of Lorraine became citizens before the end of the reign of Louis XIV in a pattern that dovetails with and identifies the social and legal assimilation of the province into France.[20]

Among foreigners coming from the southeastern borderlands, the trajectory and timing of citizenship grants were different, and the rate of naturalizations did not drop off until the 1690s—that is, at the moment when Louis XIV and the duke of Savoy began to exchange in rapid succession their control over the Alpine frontier, especially the so-called Terres Neuves in the county of Nice. The duchy of Savoy joined the coalition of Austria, the United Provinces, England, and Spain against France in October 1690, the year of fewest naturalizations of Savoyards and Niçois. Naturalizations from these counties increased slightly as the two powers exchanged control of the borderland, but remained low during the imposition, by the tax-farmers, of the Naturalization Tax between 1697 and 1707. A few subjects of Savoy, perhaps thinking to escape the tax, became citizens just after France had reconquered Nice in 1702 (and remained in possession of the county until 1711, in a conquest not sanctioned by treaty). But overall, naturalizations from the entire duchy of Savoy dropped off after 1685. Unlike in the English or Dutch cases, the decline was not motivated in the least by religious reasons. Instead, it was the experience of warfare and its attendant costs and anxieties in the borderland that formed the context of the decline from forty-nine naturalizations in the five-year period beginning in 1685, to forty in 1690, thirty-three in 1695, seventeen in 1700, and twelve in 1710 (fig. 5).

In the midst of the tax-farmers' attempts to collect taxes from the "foreigners" forcibly naturalized in 1697, individual grants reached their annual low, while the five-year nadir was in 1705–09, the beginning of the last, horrible war of the Spanish Succession (1704–14), which ended with the defeat of Louis XIV at the hands of the European coalition. That the number of naturalizations began to increase even before the full effects of the end of the wars and the subsequent peace treaties were felt remains something of a mystery. The worst of France's final wars with Europe were less centered in the borderlands of the kingdom, with notable exceptions in Catalonia and, further afield, in the Low Countries. More important, perhaps, were the effects of the Naturalization

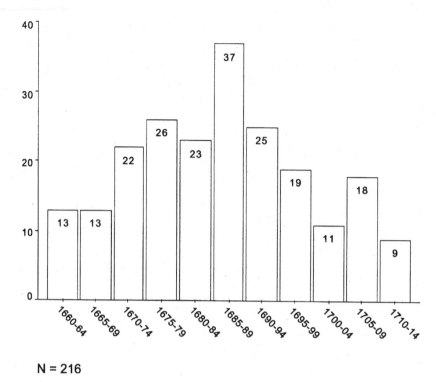

N = 216

Fig. 5. Naturalizations from the Duchy of Piedmont-Savoy, 1660–1714

Tax in 1697. That the tax withdrew all former individual naturalizations of foreign citizens of the kingdom and collectively naturalized all foreigners might lead us to expect *fewer* naturalizations after 1707. But just the opposite occurred.

As was obvious to a handful of foreigners taxed in 1697, the collective naturalization of 1697 did not have the intended effects, or at least the desirable ones from their perspective. Some foreigners and their families, despite having been taxed, sought citizenship: they recognized the political fictions of the 1697 law that promised them the status of native-born French residents but still made them liable to being discriminated against as foreigners (as the monarchy's subsequent efforts in 1709 to renew the tax affirmed). Jean Delcourt, born in Liège, had paid three hundred livres in tax in June 1697, but he invested at least as much in his subsequent naturalization of April 1699. Jean-Pierre Fournier, haberdasher from Savoy living in Dijon, received his declaration of naturalization on 22 March 1714, even though he had already been taxed by the 1697 declaration and was subsequently discharged by the edict of August 1700, which exempted foreigners established in Burgundy. And in August 1714, Severin Kragh, a native of Copenhagen who had been living in Paris since 1656 and was taxed in 1697, became a French citizen.[21] These foreigners were perhaps too cautious because they should not have had to seek naturalization once they were taxed; or they might have been the victims of aggressive tax-farming inspired by the 1697 tax. In whatever case, these several naturalizations were evidence of a more general trend of increased naturalizations that began as the long wars of Louis XIV came to an end.

The "New European Order" (1710–1759)

France signed the Treaty of Utrecht (1713) with Spain and the Netherlands, and the Treaty of Rastadt (1714) with the Holy Roman Empire and England; the following year, Louis XIV died, after reigning sixty-one years, and Europe breathed a sigh of relief . . . as, apparently, did foreigners resident in France and their families who once more sought to become citizens. Over the next five decades, the average number of naturalizations rose slowly but steadily from 486 in the 1710s to 608 in the 1720s, 611 in the 1730s, 667 in the 1740s, reaching a ten-year average of 803 in the 1750s, and their highest annual number (85) in 1759. Framed by the War of the Spanish Succession (1704–14) and the Seven Years War (1757–63), this period of relative peace for the French monarchy coincided, especially after the 1720s, with a period of economic recovery from the disastrous last decades of Louis XIV's reign. Not that warfare disappeared in the first half of the eighteenth century: the treaties and settlements following the wars of Louis XIV were to be dismantled, partially, by the Wars of the Polish Succession (1733–37) and of the Austrian Succession (1740–48). But unlike the wars of Louis XIV, the battles tended to take place farther afield—mostly in Italy and, to a lesser extent, in northern Flanders. Even when warfare approached the French borderland, it had far less of an impact on civilian populations, including on foreigners already resident in France. Eighteenth-century warfare was not only more "professionalized," in the sense of being provisioned and controlled by the state, but it was also strikingly "ritualized" or, as historians would call it, "domesticated" within the practices of siege warfare. Moreover, the principal conflagration involving France during the eighteenth century was its engagement in the Seven Years War with England (1756–63), in which most of the fighting took place far from the kingdom's borders.[22] Foreigners established in the kingdom, as well as French born abroad who returned to inherit, increasingly sought citizenship in this period—although the pattern was clearer in the case of lay foreigners who sought naturalization than it was among ecclesiastics, whose overall number of naturalizations in phase two were not to increase as dramatically (fig. 6).

In truth, the initial surge of naturalizations during the decade of the 1710s was fueled by two groups. On the one hand, fueling the initial increase in naturalizations after 1715 were the children of the Protestant diaspora who returned to claim their "natural" rights as Frenchmen. We have already encountered many of them from England, the Netherlands, and Prussia. In truth, their

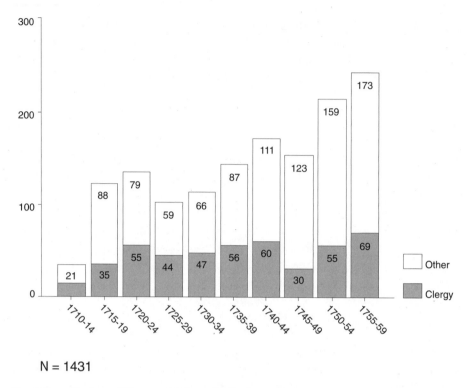

N = 1431

Fig. 6. Naturalizations of Clergy and Others with Professions, 1710–1759

presence was to be felt (especially among the jurists) only in the 1720s and 1730s, as they came of a certain age when properties are inherited and contested. The second group that fed the increase in citizenship grants were the foreigners born during the conquests of Louis XIV in territories annexed by France and subsequently lost, who sought naturalizations and declarations to assure their status and interests in property and benefices, often against competing claims.[23] Louis XIV had specifically exempted the inhabitants born in any part of the bishoprics of Metz, Toul, and Verdun, and others born in parts of the duchy of Luxembourg, the county of Chiny, Lorraine, and the Barrois that had been ceded to the king by the Treaty of Ryswick in 1697, but others born across the boundaries who had come to live in these districts sought to assure their status as French natives. The sovereign courts also debated extensively the circumstances and status of other border inhabitants, especially the Savoyards, who had been conquered by Louis XIV, but subsequently returned to foreign rule.[24] Many foreigners, including clergy born during the wartime years when France was in control of foreign territory, did not wait for the jurists to decide, and went ahead and sought citizenship. Thus the case of Pierre Joseph Wandermesche, born in 1703 when the town of Ypres was French and who stayed when the town was abandoned to the emperor by the Treaty of

Utrecht. In 1731, "in the perspective of benefiting from the advantageous arrangements of his maternal great uncle who decided to resign in his favor a prebend and canonry of the collegiate church of Saint-Pierre de Cassels in France, he has the project of establishing his residence there" and sought a declaration with permission to hold benefices.[25]

In the 1720s and 1730s, a period marked by the attenuation of seventeenth-century demographic and economic crises, naturalizations and declarations, both clerical and secular, experienced a persistent upswing, reaching an annual average of over eighty a year by the beginning of the 1750s. Of course, the overall growth in the annual number of naturalizations and declarations in this second phase masks the peaks and troughs of the trajectories and timing of specific "national" groups who sought to be naturalized. The rates of naturalization among the inhabitants of the northeastern borderlands, especially the Austrian Low Countries, increased in the 1720s, but dropped during the War of the Polish Succession (1733–37), which involved a return of military operations in the Rhineland and Luxembourg (fig. 7). They rose again in the last years of the 1730s, only to drop again with the outbreak of the War of the Austrian Succession (1740–47). The inverse correlation between warfare and citizenship grants, found in the first period, is not initially reproduced in the second. Rather, the decline of naturalizations among subjects of the Low Countries might be the result of the favorable decisions of the royal council (declaration of April 1737) and the Paris parlement (decision of 11 July 1741) that the inhabitants of Mons in Hainault and others from the Austrian Low Countries were not to be subjected to the droit d'aubaine, and allowed them to inherit "even in times of war."[26] After 1745, however, and especially after 1748, naturalizations of Flemings and others more generally rose dramatically again. Among Flemings, this was largely because of clergy seeking religious benefices at a moment of concern, in diplomatic circles, about reciprocal arrangements in the borderland. For the others, it may well have been in response to Louis XV's public emphasis on his pacific intentions and the abandonment of the "traditional schemes for Valois and Bourbon dynastic aggrandizement."[27]

Meanwhile, in the southeastern borderlands, naturalizations from Nice and Savoy rose dramatically after 1710, but dropped again after 1725, only to continue to grow, doubling to some twenty a year in the 1750s. The same pattern, but even more notable and precisely determined, can be found among subjects of the republic of Genoa, whose naturalizations jumped from four in 1717 to eight in 1718 then to thirty-eight in 1722 and then back to seven in 1723, remaining at a low level thereafter (fig. 8). In this instance, the correlation between royal policy and social patterns of naturalization is most evident. What began as a minor contestation between the French consul in Genoa and the magistrates of that town, when the former wanted to exercise jurisdiction over a naturalized Genoese, led to a series of royal declarations in 1718 and 1719 in which Louis XV withdrew all naturalizations from Genoese who did not reside in the

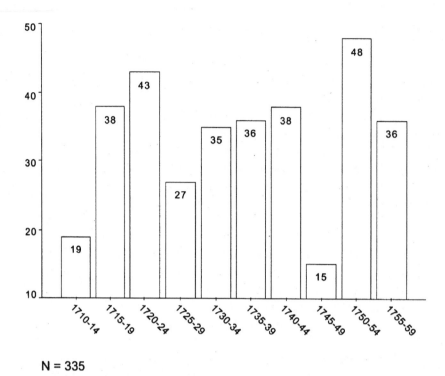

N = 335

Fig. 7. Naturalizations from the Austrian Low Countries, 1710–1759

kingdom. These decrees required the Genoese to sail only under their own flags unless they had resided four years in the kingdom. A more general royal ordinance of February 1720, naming the Genoese as examples, revoked and annulled all previous naturalizations of foreign citizens who failed to reside in the kingdom, and specifically those who undertook maritime commerce and "enjoyed the privileges accorded to our true subjects and native subjects, while navigating their ships, with permission of the French admiralty."[28] In fact, it was only after 1720 that the real effects of these edicts was seen in the timing of naturalizations among the Genoese established in France (most in the coastal cities of Provence): twenty-seven sought naturalization in 1721, and thirty-eight in 1722, before dropping off precipitously after. The pool of Genoese mariners in France was exhausted.

The case of the Genoese, however, was unique. In cases of other "national" groups of foreigners, patterns of naturalization did not seem to respond directly to either royal edicts or judicial decisions of the Paris parlement concerning inheritance rights of foreigners. For example, a decision of the Paris parlement in 1715 that allowed the Dutch to inherit in France, even from Frenchmen, did not produce any downturn in the number of naturalizations among citizens of the United Provinces of the Netherlands. Nor did the council of state's decision in 1727 against the Scots (despite their prior privileges),

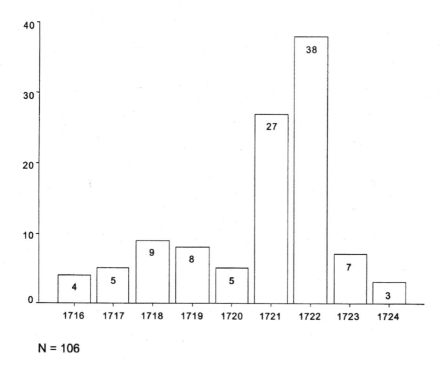

N = 106

Fig. 8. Genoese Naturalized in France, 1716–1724

subjecting them to the droit d'aubaine, produce any increase in the annual rate of naturalizations from that country (which were truly few).[29] A royal declaration in 1739, upheld in 1754 by the sovereign council of Alsace, affirmed the right of English subjects, following the Treaty of Utrecht, to transmit movables upon their death in France to legitimate heirs whether or not they were "citizens of our states," but this jurisprudence did not notably inflect the pattern of demands from that country.[30] The different groups of foreign citizens tended to follow trajectories that were relatively independent of the shifting jurisprudence or even of royal policy but reflected economic, geographical, and historical trends.

For example, immigrants from the Italian Peninsula, apart from the Genoese, did not dramatically increase their rates of naturalization in the first half of the eighteenth century. "Italian France" had reached its height in the sixteenth century; the eighteenth century, cosmopolitan, was also the century of "German France," at least concerning the growing numerical importance of German naturalizations. German naturalizations (including from Rhineland) went from one a year in the five-year period beginning in 1710 to seven a year in the early 1730s, nine a year in the early 1740s, and fourteen a year in the 1750s.

Although clerical naturalizations increased slightly in the period, the more important source of the growth in citizenship grants between 1710 and 1759 were from foreigners responding to France's (relative) decline in territorial ambitions, and to a more favorable economic climate especially after the 1720s. As the French economy developed both in its commercial and agricultural sectors, increasing numbers of immigrants arrived in the kingdom, especially in the capital city of Paris.[31] Given that the average length of residence before naturalization was twenty years, it is not surprising that the peak number of naturalizations overall occurred in the 1750s, when foreigners from both border regions (Savoy and the Low Countries), from Germany and Ireland, and from elsewhere in Europe increasingly sought French citizenship.

Toward the end of this second period, France became embroiled in the Seven Years War with England, a critical experience in the French construction of the nation—the invention of French nationalism itself, according to David Bell. In both official propaganda and unofficial pamphlets, iconography, poetry, and literature, an elaborate discursive patriotism cast the nation of France in opposition to the "English."[32] More pragmatically, the French government confiscated the estates of English landowners in France, and after the war it forced the English, Irish, and Scots, whether naturalized or not, to pay the *capitation* (the poll tax originally instituted in 1694).[33] Against the backdrop of such xenophobia, both official and vernacular, it is perhaps not surprising to learn that the number of naturalizations, already quite low among British subjects, fell off dramatically during and after the Seven Years War (fig. 9).

The decline was particularly notable among Irish clerics and merchants, especially with the expulsion of British subjects at the beginning of the Seven Years War, including those settled in Bordeaux.[34] The English were less affected by the law, for they enjoyed a more privileged status and tended to be exempted from the droit d'aubaine, according to the jurisprudence of the Old Regime, for their movable properties, even in times of war. Thus the apparent stability of the English (and Scottish) patterns of naturalization. Largely unaffected by the international struggles of midcentury, the English in France were paradoxical exceptions among other groups of foreign citizens. But in the 1760s, they became far more typical, as their naturalizations and declarations dropped precipitously alongside those of all foreign citizens in the third and final phase of the Old Regime.

The "Age of the Citizenship Revolution" (1760–1789)

After 1759, the drop in citizenship grants was nothing short of spectacular: from 803 naturalizations and declarations in the 1750s (peaking at eighty-five in the single year of 1759), naturalizations in the following decade dropped to half (445 in the 1760s), where they stabilized in the 1770s (475), before declining in the 1780s to a mere 382, or slightly over thirty-eight a year. Overall, naturalizations declined from an average of over eighty a year in the 1750s to only forty-two a year in the half-decade before the French Revolution, and this during a

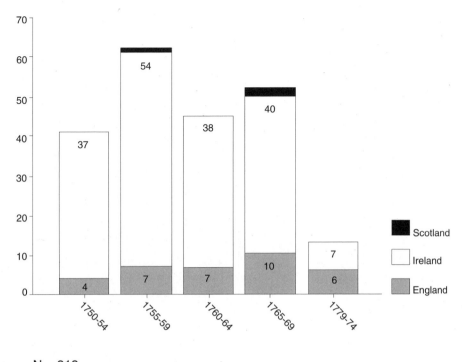

70

60
54

50

40
40
38
37

30

20

10
7
4
7
7
10
6

0

1750-54 1755-59 1760-64 1765-69 1779-74

■ Scotland
□ Ireland
▨ England

N = 213

Fig. 9. Naturalization of British Subjects, 1750–1770

period when the French economy was suffering from the toll of the Seven Years
War and the immigrant population of France was multiplying rapidly. Especially after the 1750s, despite the periodic economic crises of the late Old Regime, France became a cosmopolitan magnet for foreigners, both immigrants
and travelers, their presence increasingly known in Paris through the surveillance techniques of the foreign ministry.[35]

Such an abrupt decline in the numbers of new foreign citizens represented
nothing less than the social manifestation and perhaps cause of the critical
turnabout of royal policy. Beginning in 1765, Louis XV and his ministers began
to systematically dismantle the droit d'aubaine within a series of international
treaties of conventions and conventions, an essential component of the "citizenship revolution" that is the subject of the next chapter. As we shall see in detail, twenty-one bilateral treaties and collective dispensations were negotiated
between 1765 and 1769. By then, naturalizations and declarations had already
begun to drop: they went from seventy-eight a year in the late 1750s (1755–59),
to forty-three a year in the early 1760s (1760–64), before treaties were negotiated or signed. The dramatic drop in the rate and total number of naturalizations seems thus to have *anticipated* these treaties, rather than to have been a result of and reaction to them (fig. 10).

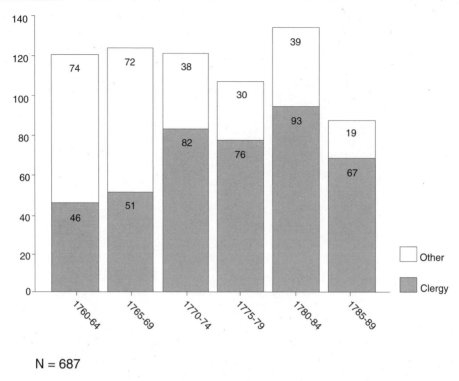

N = 687

Fig. 10. Naturalizations of Clergy and Others with Professions, 1760–1789

Why did the decline in annual naturalizations precede the citizenship revolution? There are no easy answers to the question. Certainly not because resident foreigners anticipated the signing of the conventions abolishing the droit d'aubaine. These were negotiated outside of the public view, and in any case, as some jurists were to argue, the abolitions of the droit d'aubaine did not necessarily, in themselves, entail naturalization, and particularly the right to inherit property. Rather, although the decline may have been the social expression of the broader mutation in French political culture after the 1750s, it was also the direct expression of France's involvement in the Seven Years War. Beyond the particular condition of British subjects in France at that time, war more generally was not conducive to naturalizations. Such had been the case under Louis XIV, and it was repeated under Louis XV, even as the theaters of warfare from 1756 until 1763 took shape far from France's immediate borderlands. The hypothesis linking the renewal of warfare to the decline of naturalization is partially confirmed by the fact that after the Peace of Versailles in 1763, the overall rate of naturalizations did pick up slightly, and naturalizations in the 1770s were, on average, slightly more frequent than in the 1760s. That war trumped the international accords in accounting for the decline is demonstrated by the increase in citizenship grants during the 1770s, precisely at a moment when

Louis XV and then his son, Louis XVI (r. 1774–92) signed more than twenty conventions, treaties, and patent letters that abolished or exempted foreigners from the droit d'aubaine with states ranging from the small German principalities to Poland (1777) and the United States (1778). By the 1780s, however, the treaties must have affected the rate of naturalizations, as these dropped to their lowest level (382 per decade) since the beginning of Louis XIV's reign.

And yet: if we separate out the clerical naturalizations (which included permissions for regular clergy to hold benefices or offices) from the citizenship grants to foreigners with other professions or statuses, the counterexperience of the clergy again becomes apparent.

Unlike the overall shape of naturalizations between 1660 and 1790, the patterns of clerical and nonclerical naturalizations and declarations appear in this period as near mirror images of each other. Both groups of foreigners did increasingly seek citizenship in the late 1770s, the first years of Louis XVI's reign, and both drop off synchronously in the last years of the Old Regime. Yet, overall, the clergy in the period between 1759 and the outbreak of the French Revolution made up 60 percent of the naturalized or declared foreigners with a known socioprofessional status, and a quarter of the entire population of foreign citizens, between 1660 and 1790. In the 1760s, the clergy made up 40 percent of the total population of naturalized foreigners (the same proportion as, on average, during the Old Regime). Yet by the 1770s, they made up 70 percent of the naturalizations, and three-quarters of the new foreign citizens whose professions are known were clerics during the last decade of the Old Regime. What was driving the foreign clergy in such numbers to seek French citizenship?

The answer, as always, was interest: fiscal and religious interests in cures and benefices, prebends, canonicats, monastic offices, and other stipends or honors of the French Catholic Church. It was still possible, although less and less likely, for a foreign cleric to gain possession of a benefice without being naturalized beforehand. But the foreign clergy, like other aliens settled in the kingdom, were still subject to the droit d'aubaine unless they had been specifically exempted. Moreover, even the mutual and reciprocal abolitions of the droit d'aubaine during the age of the citizenship revolution did not guarantee the ability of any given foreigner to inherit from a French native. So for the foreign clergy, especially, it made sense to become citizens as both a professional and family strategy, guaranteeing their ability to hold benefices and to bequeath their accumulated capital to heirs, although evidently not direct ones, born in the French kingdom.

The presence of such high proportions of clergy among the foreign citizens was also the effect of the crown's increasingly strict enforcement of the interdictions of holding benefices without royal permission, especially in the so-called conquered provinces. Since 1681 foreign clerics were required to seek special dispensations to hold cures and benefices. In Alsace and in other borderlands including Hainault and along the eastern Spanish frontier foreign clerics were especially likely to seek citizenship because ecclesiastical and political boundaries failed to coincide. Diocesan seats, such as Trier in the east or the Seu d'Urgell in the south, were sometimes located beyond the boundaries of the realm, and foreign bishops sought to control the appointments of parish priests who were frequently aliens not born in the kingdom.

The struggle between the French monarchy and such "foreign" bishops was, by the late eighteenth century, already well rehearsed. In the Catalan borderland of the Cerdagne, an agreement had been reached with the Bishop of Urgell in the 1730s whereby the French intendant of Roussillon approved the nomination of "Spanish" priests appointed by the bishop to local parishes. Required to speak French, these priests were forbidden in the 1740s from professing the Jansenist creed, part of the broader confessional struggle against Jansenism in Paris and the kingdom. In the decades that followed, several of the priests nominated and approved to serve in the parishes of the French Cerdagne sought citizenship, in part to guarantee that their collateral heirs could inherit their accumulated savings.[36]

The case of Alsace was different: although one of the "conquered provinces" of Louis XIV where foreign clergy needed special dispensations, the province contained a number of districts where Protestants were allowed to practice their faith. The monarchy had its hands full regulating the conditions of Protestant worship in Strasbourg and the towns of Alsace where the Reformed religion had been practiced before the conquests of Louis XIV. And the crown was increasingly concerned to staff adequately the Catholic parishes, interspersed among the "Lutheran" ones, with Francophone priests.[37] Following the January 1681 edict that formally excluded foreigners from the parishes as well as the higher offices in the abbeys and monasteries of the province, a further ordinance of 5 March 1703 forbade unnaturalized foreign novices from entering the religious orders of the province. Many Catholic clergy from the opposing bank of the Rhine—including from the Austrian Low Countries and Liège as well as those from the German principalities—and Ireland subsequently became citizens so as to assume their positions and cures.[38] Indeed, nearly a fifth of the clerical requests for citizenship in the last phase of the Old Regime were for clergy seeking benefices in Alsace. This posed a problem to royal officials, just as it did to German princes such as Charles of Lorraine, who requested a dispensation from the foreign ministry in 1763 in order to take possession of his two benefices in Alsace that belonged to the Order of Teutonic Knights. A local French official from the intendancy opposed the exemption, and concluded—reviving an old sixteenth-century argument— that even naturalized foreign clergy should not be in charge of the "cure of souls."

> There reigned such an abuse in this province; the best cures were given to foreign
> clergy by means of letters of naturalization permitting them to hold benefices,

from which two difficulties were born. One was the danger of such an abuse with respect to the influence that pastoral functions have on the spirit of peoples. The other is the chagrin of the local clergy that could only drive them away from training and study.[39]

By the end of the Seven Years War, the royal council as well was concerned that such foreigners, even when naturalized, were not "always well trained and that they not be entirely stripped of their prejudices, and should not be selected over other clergy whose birth and education has transmitted in their tender years the love and knowledge of their obligations toward Us and Our State." In its royal declaration of 11 February 1763, the crown judged that "it is essential for the good of our service and more that the positions that offer the greatest influence over learning and the behavior of peoples, such as benefices and the cure of souls, should only be given in this province to our natural subjects." The Old Regime monarchy used the Catholic Church as part of its enforcement of the political order, just as the late eighteenth-century state was to model its nation-building projects on the linguistic and cultural policies of the Counter-Reformation Church.[40]

The edict of 1763, however, did not stop foreign clerics in Alsace from seeking citizenship. The problem lay in one of recruitment: in this predominantly Protestant province, the French crown had a hard time staffing the Catholic parishes with native-born Frenchmen. By the 1780s, the problem had been resolved, at least according to a royal official in the sovereign council in Strasbourg, who penned a memorandum on the subject in 1785:

> The priesthoods were exempted from the general law [that required them to be French natives] during a certain time, because in this almost entirely Lutheran province it was not possible to find an adequate number of subjects to fill the positions . . . but since its establishment, the seminary at Strasbourg furnishes a sizable number of priests for the needs of this province, and this indulgence is no longer necessary.[41]

Even so, the "indulgence" was practiced until the Revolution: at least five clerics from the Rhineland and the Low Countries in the 1780s were made citizens with permission to hold benefices in Alsace.

To the north, in Metz, Hainault, and Artois—the bishoprics of Metz, Toul, Verdun, Nancy, and Saint-Dié, which depended on the diocese of Trier, with its seat outside the kingdom—the question was even more complex. Here, the monarchy's principal concern was that of reciprocity, and the French foreign ministry sought, from the 1750s onward, to assure parity between French-born clergy who took benefices in the provinces of the Austrian Low Countries and Flemings and other natives of the Low Countries who held ecclesiastical offices and benefices in France. At the same time, the foreign ministry maintained its official line, developed from the 1681 royal ordinance, of giving French natives preference among the lower clergy, or at least of requiring that foreign-born clergy be naturalized before taking possession of their benefices in the formally conquered provinces. The question was further complicated by the fact that the local parlements and sovereign councils, particularly that of Metz, often took action against foreign clergy, as in 1749 when a decree expelled all nonnative members in the religious orders of the Three Bishoprics. The Metz parlement had been moved to act at the end of the War of the Austrian Succession, when the empress had not gone back to the status quo before 1740 in allowing French clerics to hold benefices in the neighboring convents of the Low Countries.[42]

Within its portion of the diocese of Trier (divided between France, Lorraine, and the Holy Roman Empire), the French royal administration sought preference in the 1760s for French natives over foreigners. The result was a series of diplomatic struggles with the court in Vienna and the Austrian provincial council in Brussels, occasioned especially by the fact that the Austrian government refused to allow either French or Lorrains to hold benefices in the Low Countries.[43] In May 1769, France and Austria reached an agreement, but it was not to last. For one, opinion was divided within the French government. The duc d'Aiguillon, the minister of state charged with foreign affairs, argued with Chancellor de Maupeou over the protocol of reciprocity. Such disagreements emerged from contestations with the Viennese court over specific cases. Chancellors, ministers, and ambassadors thus spent inordinate time arguing about the naturalization of Jean Tassart, chaplain and musician, who petitioned for a residence dispensation in 1771 after having been given some nonresident benefices (*bénéfices foraines*) that depended on the cathedral chapter of Tournai de la Chapelle de Sainte-Catherine. France would be obliged, wrote the foreign minister, to allow him to take possession if Brussels were to offer the same conditions to French subjects, which hadn't been the case yet.[44]

By the 1780s, long after the mutual and reciprocal abolition of the droit d'aubaine with Austria, Louis XVI and the empress—or rather, the French foreign office now in agreement with the Chancellery in opposition to the Austrian ambassador—were arguing mightily over the mutual and reciprocal rights of their subjects to hold benefices in the borderland. Again, it was the sovereign court at Nancy that, in an administrative decision of 6 February 1782, declared that foreigners needed to be naturalized for at least a year before they took possession of their benefices. The solicitor-general of the Paris parlement took the occasion to elaborate, once again, on the boundaries of French citizenship founded on birth in the kingdom.[45] The royal council's concern, however, was more about reciprocity: by edicts of 18 June 1775 and 14 November 1776, the king formally forbade naturalizations with permissions to hold benefices to clergy born in the Low Countries, with the goal of "assuring reciprocity on the part of this government not only with reference to simple letters of naturalization, but also with respect to those involving the permission to hold benefices."[46]

Royal interdictions against foreign clerics holding benefices, and against those entering the religious orders in this borderland diocese with Austria did not discourage foreigners seeking just those things. To the contrary, the contested claims of citizens and foreigners resulted in increased requests for naturalization among subjects of the Austrian monarchy in the late eighteenth century, especially among clerics who already served parishes and monasteries on French territory. Jean-Baptiste Picard, born in the Austrian province of Luxembourg, had been a vicar in Longwy since 1770. In 1783 he was named to the collegiate prebend of that town and sought French citizenship after the sovereign council of Nancy required him to have letters. That same year, Marie-Antoinette Jonquée, born in Bruges, requested a naturalization in order to enter the Ursuline convent in the town of Saint-Omer. The chancellor wrote to the foreign minister asking whether she needed a recommendation from the Austrian government, and was told that because women could not own benefices, "the king can give letters of naturalization without requiring the nomination of the government of the Low Countries."[47]

But it was not enough for others—men—to simply get recommendations and permissions from Brussels to establish themselves in France, as Sr. Hougrand learned painfully in February 1783. The intention of the king, wrote Foreign Minister Vergennes to the chancellor,

> was not to make the concession of a grace depend on a foreign [government's] permission; the king's concession alone, in the end, always results in the conferral of the benefits that the kings of France and wise policies have reserved only for subjects of His Majesty. We know that these sorts of recommendations [by a foreign government] are not very hard to obtain, and the means that were most likely employed to have them accorded would in themselves suffice to have the recommendations rejected.[48]

The crown denied Hougrand his citizenship, and that of several others, in this exceedingly rare instance in which politics trumped the law in the practice of naturalization. Using its discretionary authority, the king's council determined, in the interest of diplomatic reciprocity, when and whether to confer citizenship on foreign clerics.

The diplomatic and political struggles over the authorization of foreign clergy in the borderlands goes far to account for the overall increase in the number of naturalizations from the Austrian Low Countries in the third and final phase of Old Regime, despite the formal abolition of the droit d'aubaine between the two countries in June 1766 (fig. 11).[49] Indeed, the divergent pat-

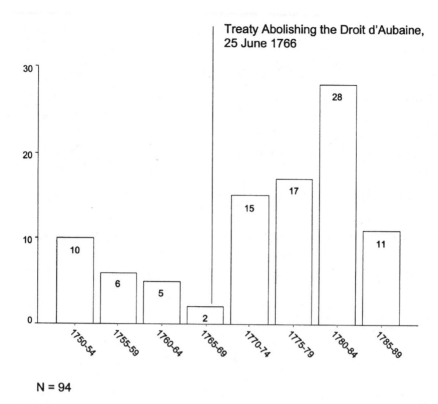

Treaty Abolishing the Droit d'Aubaine, 25 June 1766

N = 94

Fig. 11. Naturalizations from the Austrian Low Countries, 1750–1785

terns of naturalization from the Low Countries, compared to citizenship grants in the period as a whole, can only be explained by the concern for reciprocity in the borderland.

More typically, in all countries where clerics dominated the foreigners with professions—the Low Countries, Ireland, and Spain—the number of naturalizations tended to increase in the third phase of the Old Regime, at least until the very last years before the Revolution. And in countries or "nations" where clerics were a smaller proportion, such as Savoy or the United Provinces of the Netherlands, citizenship grants during this age of the citizenship revolution decreased consistently.

In some cases, notably that of the duchy of Savoy, the diplomatic treaties abolishing the droit d'aubaine had an immediate and notable impact on individual naturalizations. The duke of Savoy, king of Sardinia since 1718, signed a treaty in March 1760 with Louis XV that, citing prior letters patent from 1566 to 1674, ordered the delimitation of their territorial boundary and mutually exempted citizens of France and Savoyards from the droit d'aubaine "and all other [dues] which would contradict the freedom to inherit or devolve property [la liberté des successions]." Naturalizations from Savoy dropped from twenty-two

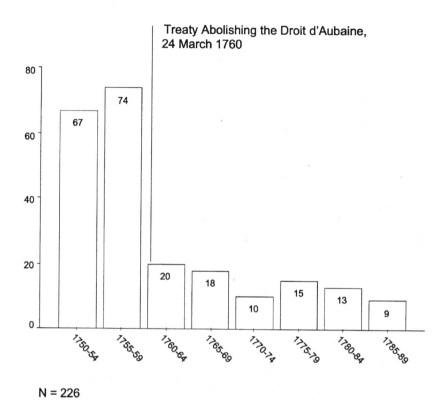

Fig. 12. Naturalizations from the Kingdom of Piedmont-Savoy, 1750–1789

in 1759 to eleven in 1760 to four in 1761, and remained at a relatively low level until the end of the Old Regime (fig. 12).

Among the Savoyards naturalized after 1761, at least two made reference to the treaty, acknowledging that they were no longer required to become French, but insisting that they wanted to "assure their estates." In other cases—Holland, for example—the numbers of foreign citizens had dropped to very low levels by the time of the international convention (1773), dropped slightly afterward, but rose again in the late 1770s. The total numbers are small, but the pattern is distinctive.

The reasons for this pattern remain obscure. A legal decision of the Paris parlement in 1761 recognized the ability of Dutch citizens to inherit from French natives, which might have caused naturalizations to decline after that, but the jurisprudence can hardly account for the steep rise in the late 1760s and again in the late 1770s. A glance at the international context of the late Old Regime provides a better framework of explanation. France's diplomatic and military involvement in the United Provinces—a twisted plot of international alliances and conflicts among France, the Netherlands, and Austria—represented a momentary return to seventeenth-century patterns, when warfare and diplomatic decisions became the most important contributing factor, before breaking with the inherited pattern that linked warfare to the decline of naturalizations. Britain's declaration of war on the United Provinces in 1780, and the growing rivalry between the Austrians and the Dutch, led to a crisis of French foreign policy that surfaced in the conflicts over the River Scheldt and Austrian domination of the Rhine in the mid 1780s. France was inevitably involved, and forced to take sides against the Austrians in the context of growing civil war after 1783 in the Netherlands. At the end of the Old Regime, even before Dutch patriots fled to France following the Prussian intervention in 1787, requests for French citizenship tended to increase.[50]

This counterexperience of the Dutch at the very end of the Old Regime is a sobering reminder that patterns of naturalization among foreigners can only be approximated in a study of the various factors and contexts—economic, legal, and especially political—that shaped the timing of naturalizations in the Old Regime. State policy, legal jurisprudence, or the economic context did not always determine the timing of the likelihood that foreigners would seek French citizenship, although three distinct phases between the reign of Louis XIV and the outbreak of the French Revolution were framed, grosso modo, by patterns of state building in France. The first coincided with a period of excessive warfare and economic downturn, lasting from the 1660s through the first decade of the eighteenth century. The second phase, anticipating slightly the "New European Order" established by the Treaties of Utrecht (1713) and Rastadt (1714), was marked by a consistent growth of naturalizations during a period of economic expansion that lasted until the first part of the Seven Years War. After 1760, however, the annual numbers of new foreign citizens dropped precipitously except for foreign clerics, whose distinctive counterexperiences set in relief the more general patterns of naturalization in the Old Regime. Embroiled in diplomatic disputes over contested religious jurisdictions in the eastern and northern borderlands, clerics tended to seek French citizenship with greater frequency at a moment when naturalizations from other foreign groups, both professional and "national," were in decline. The drop in grants during the third and final phase of the Old Regime did anticipate slightly the revolution of citizenship; yet that revolutionary mutation, to which I now turn, was to shape decisively the nature of naturalization and of citizenship in the Old Regime.

PART THREE

THE CITIZENSHIP REVOLUTION
FROM THE OLD TO THE NEW REGIME

CHAPTER SEVEN

FROM LAW TO POLITICS BEFORE THE FRENCH REVOLUTION

The absolutist model of the citizen that took shape in the collusion and slippage between French jurists and the crown during the sixteenth and seventeenth centuries perdured in the practice of naturalization until the French Revolution. Foreigners, albeit in declining numbers, continued to be granted French citizenship until the first years of the French Revolution in the routinized and bureaucratized protocol established by the late seventeenth century. At the same time, the citizenship revolution of the eighteenth century broke the absolute citizen apart. On the one hand, the citizen passed from law to politics, from a legal membership category of juridical and administrative discourse to a political category within an emerging public sphere of the mid-century monarchy. On the other hand, the central juridical marker of national difference—the droit d'aubaine—was systematically dismantled in the treaties and conventions that began in the mid-1760s and continued until 1782. Nearly simultaneous, these two dimensions of the citizenship revolution produced the conditions of the postabsolute citizen before 1789, although they did not formally fix the distinction between legal nationality and political citizenship that took shape after the Revolution itself, nor did they yet spell the end of the French droit d'aubaine.

To Enlightenment and Beyond: The Public and Political Citizen

In the framework derived from J. G. A. Pocock, the place of the citizen within the first moment of the eighteenth-century citizenship revolution shifted from law to politics, from a legal subject to a political being. This philosophical movement, from Gaius back to Aristotle, reversed the tendencies of the crown within the consolidation of absolute citizenship and of sixteenth-century and seventeenth-century French jurists. But liberated from the rhetoric and practice of civil law and litigation, the citizen after the 1750s recovered a political and public role within and beyond the political theory of the Enlightenment. What Daniel Gordon has called the Enlightenment "enrichments" of citizenship took place principally as an oppositional discourse and practice against monarchical "despotism." Expressed in the more abstract theoretical reflections of Rousseau, Diderot, and other versions of eighteenth-century republican discourse, they were also enacted in the more concrete political struggles for religious toleration and tax exemptions at the end of the Old Regime. More than simply returning to the political citizen of Aristotle, republican Rome, or the medieval city-states of Italy, the eighteenth-century citizenship revolution involved, in this first instantiation, a fundamentally novel and essentially modern construction of the citizen as a public and political being distinct from the citizen as a legal member of the polity.[1]

Perhaps no single document better summarizes and reveals this displacement of the absolute citizen and the enlightened enrichments of the category than the *Remonstrances* drafted in 1775 on behalf of the magistrates of the Cour des aides by the ex-director of the libraries (and treasurer of the famous *Encyclopédie* of Diderot and d'Alembert), Chrétien Guillaume Lamoignon de Malesherbes. Chancellor Maupeou had dismissed the venal officeholders of that court and the parlements in 1771 in what is often termed the Maupeou "revolution" or "coup," and this was their response.[2] Malesherbes wrote that early in the history of the monarchy, a code of written laws on which the "rights of citizens" could be more securely based had already made its appearance. This "code" engendered the professions of jurists, "magistrates, jurisconsults, and graduates in the law," whom he called a "new order of citizens." Thereafter, "justice" was divorced from "administration": the latter fell to the king, who was free to act, in the name of royal secrecy, independent of any restraints from the "representative assemblies" made up of magistrates. The result was a tyranny that threatened the structure of the monarchy itself. The only solution was to restore the traditional rights of representation of the sovereign courts, in the persons of the citizen-magistrates, and through them to establish a direct link between the king and the "nation." And the only way to do so, he wrote, was to introduce, through the printed word, "publicity" into every aspect of government.[3]

The result is what Keith Baker has termed "a vision of the traditional constitution restored and revivified in the light of new conditions," and nowhere is the mixture of traditional and contemporary so evident as in Malesherbes's use of the term "citizen."[4] His pamphlet reveals not only the structural crisis of the absolute monarchy in mid-century but also the place of the "citizen" in the debates over the nature of public authority in the 1770s. As "public law" was reborn in the second half of the eighteenth century, as the "public sphere" made its appearance, Malesherbes's idea of "publicity" had begun to take hold.[5] Within this rhetoric, the "citizen" moved beyond the narrow discourse of legal specialists to broader arenas of political debate. Malesherbes called the former a "new order of citizens," but in the Old Regime, most legal practitioners— apart from the handful of vocal pamphleteers attached to the parlements—were largely uncontaminated by the new rhetoric of the political citizen.[6]

This new citizenship emerged first in the classically Enlightened thought of the philosophes such as Diderot, and especially within a resurgent and opposi- tional strain of French republicanism (from Rousseau to Mably and beyond) that invested the term with new social dimensions and political valances. From a legal being who had the capacity to inherit property and to act freely in all civil matters, the citizen was turned into a public being, one whose political rights were often associated with the possession of property. Definitively eman- cipated from the narrow and technical language and practices of civil law, an emerging republican discourse turned the citizen into a gendered and proper- tied being, no longer simply a legal subject whose capacity to transmit property defined his citizenship. The citizen became the central rhetorical and political actor in the late eighteenth century, laying the ideological foundations of the French Revolution, French revolutionary citizenship, and the patterns of natu- ralization in France between 1789 and 1819.

During the Old Regime, pamphleteers, philosophes, and politicians dis- puted and discussed the nature of citizenship in a public sphere, a far more ex- pansive arena than the law courts and more limited print culture of the jurists, magistrates, and legal practitioners. Yet if this debate reached a broader audi- ence, the passage from law to politics expanded the ethical and political charac- ter of the citizen and shrank the category socially. Such a transformation can be seen in a reading of key Enlightenment texts, and most centrally in Denis Diderot's dictionary entry on the "citizen" in that vast, collaborative Enlight- enment project he edited with Jean d'Alembert, the *Encyclopédie, ou Dictionnaire raisonné des sciences, des arts, et des métiers, par une société des gens de lettres* (1752–77).[7]

All previous dictionaries, both famous and obscure of the late seventeenth and early eighteenth centuries, began their entries on the "citoyen" with the shrunken ideal of municipal citizenship, and focused their attention on what Jean Bodin had called its purely "honorary" dimensions. Such was the case in Antoine Furetière's and César de Rochefort's dictionaries of 1685, that of Pierre Richelet in 1705, the first edition of the dictionary of the Académie Française in 1694 (and subsequent editions until the fourth in 1762), and the first volume of the *Dictionnaire de Trévoux* in 1734.[8] Instead, Diderot followed Bodin in assum- ing that the French citizen was something other than the "honorary citizen" of a particular town or city, and could be identified at the level of the polity itself. But unlike Bodin, Diderot did not frame his argument around the legal distinc- tions between citizens and foreigners. Although there were short entries in the *Encyclopédie* for the "droit d'aubaine" and "naturalization," the entry on the "citizen" barely touched on a definition that presumed a socially inclusive category of "nationals" that stood opposed to "aliens." Diderot identified a more narrow category of rights-bearing subjects, members of civil society: "He who is a member of a free society [made up] of several families; who partakes of the rights of society, and enjoys its liberties [*franchises*]." If the first part of the definition, underlining the union of families as the basis of citizenship, recalls the "Renaissance model" of Jean Bodin, Diderot in fact broke dramatically with traditional French legal culture. The king was no longer cast as a paternal or absolutist source of citizenship: rather, it was society itself—technically, "civil society"—that conferred rights and obligations on its members. In his passing remarks on naturalization, Diderot argued that "naturalized citizens," and not "naturalized foreigners," were defined as "those to whom society has accorded participation in its rights and liberties, although they are not born in its midst."[9]

Diderot invoked briefly but quickly distanced himself from the idea of the citizen in natural law theory of the seventeenth century, the treatises of Samuel Pufendorf and Thomas Hobbes. He agreed with the precepts of early natural law theory that all citizens should be equal in claims and in wealth but posited the citizen as a creation of civil society, not of natural law. Moreover, Diderot distanced himself from the limited and subjugated character of the citizen in early natural law theory. Attacking Hobbes, he argued that "the name of citizen is not appropriate for those who live in a subjected condition, nor those who live in isolation." Attacking Pufendorf, he criticized the restriction of the title to a first union of families that founded the state. But despite his more universal claims about the formal equality and lack of subjugation of citizens, Diderot's own definition was restrictive both socially and politically.

For if the citizen, according to Diderot, was something other than the "honorary citizen" of towns defined in earlier dictionaries, he was also no longer coterminous with the socially inclusive "citizen" of the civil law jurists following Bodin, subjugated politically and defined negatively in opposition and contrast to the foreigner. Rather, Diderot's citizen was a rights-bearing subject with civil and political rights, albeit still vaguely defined. The category of the citizen was restricted, in comparison to civil law definitions, in two distinct ways. First, Diderot excluded, albeit with some ambivalence, women, servants, and children, who are only given the title of citizens "as members of the family of a citizen properly speaking; but they are not true citizens." Secondly, the "quality of citizen" was to be politically restricted as well. Echoing in this context the claims of late sixteenth-century jurists, Diderot favored the example of the Athenians, who preserved the dignity of the citizen by recognizing only the offspring of parents who were citizens, over the Romans, who gave away the "privilege" too freely. Only under restrictive conditions, demonstrating merit and honor, could citizenship be conferred. Nor was the citizen considered a private individual, as in the English republican tradition. As Diderot summed it up, the citizen "must be a public man," and this in the broadest and most gen-der-precise terms.[10]

Despite these echoes of early modern judicial xenophobia, Diderot, deeply critical of the French legal tradition, played an important role in the development of late eighteenth-century French republican thought.[11] Rousseau's *Social Contract* (1762) was a more dramatic and self-conscious break with the absolutist model of the "citizen," and more explicitly republican in its claims. In his famous footnote on the citizen, Rousseau positioned himself outside of common usage: "For the French . . . the name citizen expresses a virtue and not a right." He dismissed Bodin, as we have seen, and other French authors who "denatured" citizenship by ignoring its active, participatory, and political character.[12] Rousseau broke radically, explicitly, and abstractly with the absolutist model of the citizen by reintroducing the "people" as the source of sovereignty. The "association" of individual citizens is a condition of the General Will. Citizens, he continued in the text, are the individual designations of the "people" who participate in the sovereign authority, but these citizens are also subjects, "insofar as they are subjected to the laws of the state."[13]

Rousseau's *Social Contract* teetered on the brink of "modern" republican theory, in which political representation is founded on reason and experience, even as it owed much to an "ancient" republicanism and its discourse of political will and civic virtue. More concretely, Rousseau's apparently radical inversion of the absolutist model of the citizen was partly a retrieval of an ancient citizenship, and certainly modeled on his native Geneva. In that surviving city-state on France's borderland, four distinct classes of inhabitants (five, including foreigners) lived in the city, and only two "composed the Republic"—that is, belonged as citizens to the *res public*, the "public thing." Citizens were part of a restricted membership category. In this sense, Rousseau too recovered from within the tradition of the city-state the republican and ultimately Aristotelian notion of *zoon politikon*, the citizen as political being, who rules and is ruled in turn. Only certain classes of residents in the city would be citizens: excluded were men of lesser means, women, and servants, as well as minors, criminals, prisoners, the insane, and others suffering civil incapacities from their conditions of dependence.[14]

Enlightened republicanism, in the writings of Rousseau, was more a prescriptive model than an oppositional language, and the *Social Contract* itself hardly circulated before the French Revolution, although Rousseau's novels and other writings were best-sellers. Yet even before Rousseau, a strain of distinctively French republicanism served to critique the administrative and increasingly "despotic" monarchy. Its origins can be traced back to aristocratic critics of Louis XIV, including comte Henri de Boulainvilliers (1658–1722) and Henri-François d'Aguesseau. Historians have found in their writings from the 1690s to the 1710s not only the reconfiguration of classical republicanism (in dialogue with but quite distinct from Anglo-American thought in the eighteenth century) but also the origins of modern nationalism in France.[15] Yet it was only with later eighteenth-century republicans, notably Gabriel Bonnot de Mably (1709–85) and the barrister Guillaume Joseph Saige (1735–1812), that republicanism as an oppositional discourse to royal despotism came to the fore. Both authors penned republican responses to the Maupeou "revolution" of 1771 that endlessly reiterated the notion of a "good citizen" as an established male head of household and a political actor motivated by notions of virtue and the public interest. Initially, at least, such a concept did not even necessarily imply or engender social equality: rather, the citizen was defined foremost by "civic-minded disinterestedness and a primordial concern for the welfare of the nation."16

This new citizenship was socially and sexually exclusive. In the republican model, as more broadly in the Enlightenment enrichment of the citizen as a public and political being, women were considered incapable of citizenship understood as political action in the public sphere, and so too were the poor, the servile, and economically dependent members of civil society. But the republican exclusions of citizenship went beyond those of gender or wealth, or even those of civil capacity. Rather, for those writing in a republican tradition (adapted, of course, to the conditions of France during the crisis of the monarchy, beginning in the 1750s), the title of citizen could be denied all those within society who dissented politically. In Rousseau's case, this meant, abstractly, that those who did not obey the sovereign expressions of the General Will were excluded from citizenship. More concretely, Guillaume Joseph Saige not only elaborated on the "common rights of citizens" to liberty (including the freedom of movement and of publication) and to property (the right to consent to taxation), but he also enumerated the different exercise of citizenship rights among different social groups (identified, conventionally, as the clergy, nobility, and the Third Estate). Although explicitly defending the privileges of citizenship among members of the first two orders, Saige nonetheless anticipated aspects of the Abbé Sieyès's *Qu'est ce que le Tiers-Etat?* (1789) in the latter's claims that the first two estates represented "particular associations whose interests are, by the very constitution of the civil state, really subordinate to that part of this numerous order." It was not much of a leap to the point where these "privileged orders" could be excluded from the rights of the citizen, as was to happen during the Revolution. Such would be the logical consequence of the Enlightened and republican rethinking of the citizen, its reduction and reformulation from civil subject to political actor, in the eighteenth century.17

Citizens in Public Life

Beyond the radical philosophical critiques of republican intellectuals and pamphleteers and other Enlightenment enrichments of the citizen, the changing meaning of the citizen can be found more generally in the political debates of a nascent public sphere. "Everyone parades the name of citizen these days," sneered the abbé Bougniol de Montégut in 1756.[18] The public debates of the early 1750s through the mid-1770s over religious toleration and taxation took place before a rapidly growing audience and a diversifying print culture. In these debates, the "citizen" became a keyword of French political culture. Beyond even its Enlightened reworking, among opponents and apologists of the monarchy alike the citizen—especially the virtuous citizen—became an increasingly public and political subject whose interests were identified with those of the "nation," even if the citizen was not yet universally presumed to be the ultimate source of sovereignty.

In the printed remonstrances of the sovereign courts, in newspapers, gazettes, and a vast pamphlet press, and in a wide range of literary texts, the "citizen" gained center stage. Authors and readers gave different valences to the term, but all shared in a project that framed citizenship as something distinct from an inclusive grouping (as a legal category of "nationality," the contrasting identities of citizens and foreigners). The citizen, limited socially by gender and wealth, was a political being who participated in the public good—itself an eternally contested claim. The citizen acted in the name and interest of "society" (*la société*), of the "fatherland" (*la patrie*), and even of the "nation" (*la nation*). Such terms had, of course, existed under the absolute monarchy, but they were subsumed within the person of the king. Beginning in the 1750s, and especially by the 1770s, the use of these terms increased dramatically, and their referents shifted to imagined entities beyond the monarchy. Within this slippage, the language of the "citizen"—and more often, the "good" and the "virtuous citizen"—became diffused within a broad lexical field of "social theory," in France and elsewhere in Europe. As Pierre Rétat has shown,

> The concept "citoyen" was integrated into the conceptual field of the neighboring terms "patrie," "patriotisme," "intérêt," "vertu," and "bonheur," where it took on a new meaning and centrality. With this new meaning the "citoyen" became a fixture of social theory in the second half of the eighteenth century, and was revalorized, elevated to the level of the socialized individual.[19]

In this brave new world, the citizen became more clearly distinguished from the subject, although the subject (distinct from the slave), also took on new connotations, especially in parliamentary discourse: both terms were "put to work in opposing royal absolutism" and explicating the parliamentary version of the unwritten constitution. More broadly, the "citizen" was identified as a useful individual who organized his ethical and political life around the social good, not his private interest.[20] It is important to stress that such was not simply a republican language, nor even solely part of an oppositional rhetoric. By the 1770s, the king himself was identified, at least by royal apologists, as a citizen, if not a patriot: indeed, one of the eulogies to Louis XV upon his death in 1774 remembered him as a "citizen-king" (*citoyen-roi*), underscoring the late-monarch's devotion to the welfare of his people.[21]

Two pressing political debates of the day engendered such a revalorization of the citizen. The first was the question of religion in the public order. Since the withdrawal of the Edict of Nantes in 1685, France was officially a Catholic country. By a royal declaration of 18 March 1715, the monarchy decreed that there were no more Protestants in the kingdom, introducing the administrative fiction of religious and national conformity. In its further declaration of 14 May 1724, the crown affirmed the civil nonidentity of non-Catholics, requiring all French subjects to be baptized, married, and buried according to the rites of the Roman Catholic Church. But the Jansenist struggles over confessional tickets (*billets de confession*) in the 1750s, and especially the pamphlet wars over the question of toleration for Protestants in the next decade, engaged a political debate that ultimately led to what Jeffrey Merrick has called the "disjunction of Catholicity and citizenship." The culmination of this process before the Revolution was the royal Edict of Toleration, drafted by Malesherbes in 1787, that offered civil status to those of the so-called Reformed Religion, if not yet to Jews.[22]

The struggle for religious toleration in Old Regime France has been amply documented, and there is little point in rehearsing the details here. Scholars have shown how the draconian measures of Louis XIV were rarely applied to foreign Protestants in the kingdom. The practice of toleration treated the laws proscribing the Reformed Religion as a set of juridical fictions, just as I have demonstrated how many foreign Protestants were naturalized through a series of administrative fictions, including that of living in Alsace.[23] It is significant, however, that the idea of the citizen in the vast pamphlet debates over the civil status of Protestants carried a double meaning. On the one hand, it identified the common civil status of all French men, women, and children, noble and commoner, bourgeois and peasants. Those in favor of toleration—of disentangling "citizenship" and "Catholicity"—used the term "citizen" in this way, as a socially inclusive membership category of civil law. If Protestants were not recognized in civil law, argued a sympathetic pamphleteer, a half million Protestants living in the "wilderness" would remain "subjects of the king without being citizens." Those opposed to toleration could also identify the "citizen" as an inclusive category of French men and women, even if they upheld the official myth of religious conformity. As the staunchly conservative Claude Fauchet was to proclaim, it was necessary to be a Catholic in order to enjoy "the prerogatives of French citizens in their full measure."[24]

On the other hand, within the debate on religious toleration, the "citizen" was construed as a political actor: a 1780 pamphleteer in favor of toleration, for example, wrote how "the cause of the Protestants has become that of all good citizens." Of course, those on different sides of the politico-religious struggles could disagree over the meaning of citizenship itself. If an apologist for the refusal of sacraments in 1753 wrote that "every good citizen must respect by his silence the important affairs of state which do not concern him," a magistrate writing at the time of the assembly of the clergy in 1765 claimed that "there are no discussions more interesting for every good citizen than those concerning public affairs."[25] In this case, it was the latter position that came to dominate: the idea that a "good" or "true" citizen was a person devoted entirely, and publicly, to the public good.

Beyond this ethical behavior, the citizen also became understood as the subject of rights, including the right to the security of their persons and their property. Such rights "makes of a man a citizen," declared the Paris magistrates in a remonstrance of 1770 over clerical taxation, "and of all citizens a state."[26] At that moment of the Maupeou "revolution" that was to dismiss the venal officeholders of the Paris parlement, such a language had been current for nearly twenty years. The "sacred rights of citizens" had been invoked in the early 1750s, as when Louis XV had dismissed the magistrates of the Châtelet court over the sacraments controversy, and the court's apologists, although intent on defending corporate prerogatives and privileges, made general arguments defending the "rights" of the "citizen" and the "nation."[27] From Jansenism to the Protestant question, the language of citizenship and rights became part of public and political debate.

The second context in which a revitalized and politicized vocabulary of the citizen made its appearance, especially in the 1760s, was within the questions of universal taxes and particular tax exemptions. These were by far the most pressing concerns of a fiscally strapped and financially indebted state engaged in colonial and European struggles, primarily against England. In this mundane yet critically important debate over privilege, magistrates and lawyers, pamphleteers and publicists came to elaborate a postabsolutist language of the citizen and his rights. They did so especially in the 1750s and 1760s, overlapping with the debates on religious toleration. According to Michael Kwass, the crown's continuous efforts to impose taxes that did not recognize the privileges of the nobility (and many of the Third Estate) led to an unintended consequence: When nobles and privileged officeholders were faced with the necessity of paying taxes such as the income-based *vingtième*, the debate over royal finance became linked to the resurgence of the notion of citizenship as political participation. In the 1760s, tax disputes turned into political and polemical debates that took on the central question of political representation. If men of wealth and privilege were to be taxed, they had the right and obligation to represent themselves as "citizens" who spoke for the interests of the "nation."[28]

The new public and political citizen, increasingly (but not exclusively) conceived as an opponent of royal despotism, was thus identified with the cause of the fatherland and of the French "nation" itself. During and after the Seven Years War, French publicists, pamphleteers, and reformers conceived of a multitude of projects to "construct" or "invent" the French nation. Although the "nation" had long existed, as politicians, writers, and apologists across an array of ideological persuasions recognized, it was nonetheless necessary to actually "build" the ties of loyalty and identity to France, to compose a political nation of "patriots" from the cultural, linguistic, and political diversity of the kingdom. Louis XV and his ministers supported large parts of this pedagogical enterprise, ironically modeled on the success of the French Catholic Church, whose Counter-Reformation pedagogical projects, especially in reference to the linguistic diversity of the kingdom, shaped the state's nationalism in often-unacknowledged ways. Inventing a national "canon" of great Frenchmen, constituting a (diverse) literary definition of French national character, and especially, during the Revolution, defining and imposing a national language, were critical features of the French origins of modern nationalism.[29] The renovated language of the citizen occupied a central, if underexplored, place in this French "nationalist" project that began in the 1750s and 1760s.

At the same time, Enlightened enrichments of the citizen as public and political actor, especially within a discursive field opposed to the crown, began to conflict in the second half of the eighteenth century with equally Enlightened traditions of cosmopolitanism. Voltaire still gave expression to the latter in his *Dictionnaire philosophique* of 1762 when he followed Cicero and Cato in arguing that the best patriot would be a "citizen of the world." This cosmopolitan citizenship was that of intellectuals and men of letters, and it bound individuals into a universal society through the ideal and practice of "sociability." At the same time, Fougeret de Monbron's *Le Cosmopolite*, printed three times between 1750 and 1761, caricatured a "mainstream cosmopolitan ideal," tainting the latter with "cynicism, unmitigated skepticism, and naked self-interest," according to Daniel Gordon. The citizen, came to mean something quite different from the cosmopolitan ideal. Nowhere was this more unequivocally stated than in the 1762 edition of the dictionary of the French Academy, which defined the cosmopolitan (*cosmopolite*) as "one who does not adopt his homeland [*patrie*]. A cosmopolitan is not a good citizen."[30]

As a political being acting within an increasingly national arena, the citizen was a rights-bearing member of society who eventually became the source of sovereignty itself. In this movement, the category was restricted both socially and politically. The new citizenship passed from a legal membership category, encompassing the totality of the French population, to a limited membership category: only a portion of the population (excluding women and others) would be citizens, and among them, even fewer would be "good citizens." This rupture with the absolute model was thus a rejection of the legal conception that had dominated the practice of citizenship law since Bodin. As the notion of citizen passed from the more technical and arcane language of the law to the broader philosophical and literary discourse of the public sphere, it entered the world of politics. Citizens were political beings, even if the exercise of sovereignty was not yet consistently invoked as one of the "rights of the citizen."

Commerce and Reciprocity: The State Dismantles the Droit d'Aubaine

While the public debate of the citizenship revolution raged in the 1750s and 1760s, a more silent revolutionary movement took shape in civil law. The droit d'aubaine, amplified and made into a pillar of the absolute monarchy, was the vehicle and the object of this far more invisible revolution. Between 1765 and 1769, under the direction of foreign ministers duc de Praslin (1761–66) and duc de Choiseul (1766–70), the French crown signed twenty-one separate treaties and patent letters abolishing the droit d'aubaine, mostly under conditions of reciprocity. Before Louis XV died in 1774, the French foreign office had negotiated another eleven such conventions, and under Louis XVI, Foreign Minister Vergennes (1774–87) negotiated some twenty-five more in the first six years of the new king's reign. In all, the foreign office negotiated some sixty-six treaties and collective grants between 1765 and 1787.

The series of international conventions, bilateral treaties, and collective letters patent that dismantled the absolutist droit d'aubaine has not been the subject of serious attention since 1819, the date of the final abolition of what by then was universally condemned as the historical detritus of a "feudal" institution. In the half century between 1765 and 1819, however, at least six "experts," both jurists and employees of the French foreign ministry, drew up elaborate tables classifying the treaties according to a varying set of principles. Appendix 2 is the most recent, although far from the most comprehensive, of such efforts. By their quantity alone, but also in their legal and political implications for the French monarchy, these treaties and accords might have been more systematically studied by modern historians, but few have paid attention to the making and especially the implications and unintended consequences of this seemingly insignificant and marginal detail of foreign and domestic policy history.

A case could be made against such studied neglect: the series of some sixty-six treaties and grants that abolished piecemeal the droit d'aubaine between 1765 and 1787 had important and unintended results in the domain of French nationality law. Debates over the droit d'aubaine, its abolition, and the effects of its disappearance preoccupied the royal law courts, and even on occasion the offices of ministers and royal councillors. In their conception, negotiation, and justification, the treaties tacitly produced a countermodel to the absolute citizen. As the crown had used the droit d'aubaine to build an absolute citizen, so did the abolition of the droit d'abaine inevitably lead to a postabsolute citizen— whose identity before the French Revolution, however, was hardly fixed. In the aftermath of these treaties, and until the revolutionary reforms of citizenship and nationality, lawyers and men of state harshly contested the need for and the manner of drawing the legal boundaries between aliens and Frenchmen and women.

The French abolitions of the droit d'aubaine in the later eighteenth century tended to bring the monarchy in line with the more "progressive" states of eighteenth-century Europe, notably England. Since the 1660s, English politicians and a growing pamphlet press had been boisterously and publicly debating whether to naturalize all foreigners, a debate that was to continue through the experiments and failures of legislation that liberalized immigration in 1709 and the "Jew Bill" of 1753. Only in the 1760s did England finally adopt a cheap, easy, and "open door" policy on immigration and naturalization.[31] At that very moment, when England ended its debate, France began to abandon the inheritance of absolutism and the model of the absolute citizen. In the space of a decade, the monarchy reversed its long-standing policies of anti-immigration grounded in a renovated application of an amplified droit d'aubaine, and, with little public debate, began to systematically exempt and abolish a perceived "obstacle" inherited from the feudal world.

The movement to dismantle the absolutist model of the citizen can be traced to the aftermath of the 1697 Naturalization Tax: because the crown founded that levy on a maximum, muscular extension of the droit d'aubaine, it might be expected that the reaction to it would be equally strong.[32] In fact, the only juridical reactions to the tax occurred in the province of Lorraine, which had been returned to the status of an independent duchy in 1697, after more than a generation of military occupation by France. Louis XIV was to renew his conquest of Lorraine during the War of the Spanish Succession, but the juridical assimilation of Lorraine—its "naturalization," as described above—was launched through an abolition of the droit d'aubaine. When France reoccupied the duchy in 1702, the crown responded to the request made by representatives of the Lorrains and passed a declaration on 15 March to "extinguish and suppress the droit d'aubaine" between French subjects and Lorrains. The spirit was clearly to juridically assimilate Lorrains and French men and women, giving them all the "rights, honors, and privileges of our natural subjects" by abolishing the incapacity of the former to devolve property to other foreigners or to inherit from a French national. (The further edict of 1738, with the marriage of Maria Leczinski to Louis XV, abolished all the remaining civil incapacities of foreigners, effecting the juridical assimilation of Lorraine before its formal political incorporation in 1766.) The universal character of the droit d'aubaine's abolition in 1702, which gave Lorrains rights to inherit throughout the kingdom, salvaged the absolutist principle, but at the cost of the domanial right of the droit d'aubaine that the crown (and its apologists) had held so dearly. In short, while conferring a new role on the droit d'aubaine, the 1697 Naturalization Tax launched an inverse evolution that was to end in the de facto dissolution of the droit d'aubaine before the Revolution.[33]

The declaration in favor of the Lorrains thus opened another chapter in the history of the droit d'aubaine, and more generally, in the relations between the French monarchy and foreigners. But it was not a linear movement from the last years of the reign of Louis XIV until the French Revolution, despite the arguments that politicians and lawyers were to make during and after the Revolution. Indeed, the treaties signed between France and the European powers during the first half of the eighteenth century tended to resemble conventional and traditional treaties of commerce and alliance; these treaties merely exempted the respective subjects of a foreign power and the French from the droit d'aubaine, and usually they did so in limited ways. Thus the treaty of commerce between France and the cities of Lübeck, Bremen, and Hamburg in 1716 reciprocally exempted the French and the "subjects" of the three towns from the droit d'aubaine, and allowed them to "dispose by last will and testament, gift, or otherwise, their movable and immovable goods, in favor of whichever persons they please." The treaties signed between France and Denmark in 1742, France and Sweden in 1752 (only concerning movable goods), and France and Prussia in 1753 (only for ten years) did not constitute unilateral abolitions of the droit d'aubaine, only specific exemptions.[34]

The distinction between exemption and abolition became much fuzzier beginning in the 1760s, however, as a range of conventions, treaties, and royal letters patent reconfigured the relations of aliens and the French monarchy. What appeared to be "traditional" exemptions continued to be accorded, either by international treaties (with the kingdom of Piedmont-Savoy in 1760, or with Spain and the Two Sicilies in 1761) or by collective grants amounting to a collective naturalization (in the case of the inhabitants of Aix-la-Chapelle in 1764, the Order of Malta in 1765, the imperial free town of Frankfurt in 1767, or the imperial cities in 1770 and 1774). But a series of international conventions and collective letters patent mutually and irrevocably abolished the droit d'aubaine, either unilaterally or with concern for differing degrees of reciprocity. These exemptions and collective grants after the mid-1760s, the earliest of which concerned the principalities in the Rhineland in 1765–66, were fundamentally different in spirit from those of the seventeenth and eighteenth centuries. They occurred in a new political climate and within a broader movement to abolish the droit d'aubaine that challenged the foundations of absolutism itself.

Such international conventions, by all appearances, were nothing but collective naturalizations parading as public law. In fact, like individual naturalizations, they were not initiated by the French monarchy. Rather, dozens of independent principalities, petty bishoprics, cities, and noble orders of the Holy Roman Empire and beyond demanded them. This vast movement in the mid-1760s occurred at a low-water mark for the authority and international reputation of the French crown. In 1763 France signed the humiliating Treaty of Versailles, which marked the end of its North American colonial aspirations, and turned its attention to eastern Europe, where it was excluded as a major player in the great diplomatic struggles of the late eighteenth century, such as the partitions of Poland. Domestically, most of the French government's energy was directed toward problems at home. In those years, Louis XV was occupied by the expulsion of the Jesuits (1763), and then the Brittany Affair, which forced the famous confrontation between the parlements and the crown in the 1766 "whipping session" (*séance de flagellation*), when Louis XV articulated most explicitly the absolutist model of the social and political orders.[35] There were far more important issues, it would seem, than France getting involved in the affairs of the petty German principalities and others. In the French foreign office, the margrave of Baden-Baden was occasionally confused with the neighboring margrave of Baden-Durlach.[36] Yet in their requests to the French foreign ministry these otherwise insignificant principalities basically dictated the timing, if not always the terms, of the abolition of the droit d'aubaine. As an anonymous commentator remarked during initial negotiations with Baden-Baden in 1761, it was increasingly ridiculous that "France wanted to dispute, not only with an elector, but with the smallest imperial town the right to levy the droit d'aubaine," but such was in fact the case.[37]

There is a direct correlation between the dealings of France with the minor European powers and the monarchy's project, after the 1750s, to formally delimit its territory with its German and other neighbors. Indeed, the first conventions abolishing the droit d'aubaine were signed with the margraves of Baden-Baden, Baden-Durlach, and others that bordered—and whose holdings were interspersed within—the eastern reaches of the kingdom. More generally, the period in which the threescore treaties were signed also included a dozen delimitation treaties signed between France and its neighbors. In only a few cases— that of Savoy in 1760, the duchy of Deux-Ponts in 1766, the electorate of the Palatinate in 1766, or the county of Leyen in 1781—were the two projects the aim of a single treaty. But in many other cases (the Austrian Low Countries, the bishopric of Liège, the principalities of Nassau-Saarbrücken and Nassau-Weilburg, the canton of Berne, the electorate of Trier, and others), treaties of delimitation appeared within a year or two of treaties mutually abolishing the droit d'aubaine.

These delimitation treaties and the diplomatic accords abolishing the droit d'aubaine suggest a convergence between the construction of a territorial state and the abolition of the principal legal distinction between foreigners and nationals. After the 1750s, the French foreign office created specialized bureaux to delimit and demarcate the kingdom's boundaries. In this project, the notion of natural frontiers—boundaries that followed a natural feature of the landscape such as a waterway or mountain range—served the crown in its efforts to draw up a clearly delimited and demarcated boundary. Defined by its territorial extension, this more modern form of the state abandoned the feudalizing tendency of absolutism to restrict the inheritance rights of foreigners and to impose other civil incapacities on immigrants. In the process of abolishing the droit d'aubaine, the late eighteenth-century state effaced the principal legal distinction between foreigners and nationals.[38]

The modalities of this shift, if not about-face, of royal policy are revealed in the negotiations surrounding the margrave of Baden-Baden. In this tiny principality, which extended to both banks of the Rhine River below Strasbourg, "the subjects of the right bank are in relations of kinship, commerce, and interest with those on the left bank in Alsace," as described by the director-general of finance in a memorandum to the foreign minister in 1766.[39] In fact, the treaty with the margrave of Baden-Baden resulted from a petition of the margrave's representatives as early as 1761. At stake was the abolition of the droit d'aubaine and the right of their mutual subjects to inherit or devolve property only in the two neighboring provinces. In this, the agreement would have been no different from an accord conceived as early as 1719 concerning inheritance disabilities in the provinces of Alsace and Brisgau between France and the Austrian Netherlands (represented by the regency of Fribourg in this instance). It would have been no different from the special borderland regimes that were put in place during the seventeenth century—the parallel and mutual exemptions of the inhabitants of Savoy and the Dauphiné (1666), the Catalans on both sides of the boundary in the eastern Pyrenees (1659), or concerning Flanders and the Spanish Low Countries.[40] Already, nobles with fiefs in Alsace had been exempted from the droit d'aubaine, as were the bourgeois of Strasbourg as late as 1692.[41]

The 1719 talks broke down over reciprocity, although negotiations were revived in 1722 and again in 1737. A modus vivendi developed in which both courts agreed to relax the application of the droit d'aubaine and its German counterpart, although French tax officials continued to force foreigners from the Low Countries to take individual letters of naturalization "to prevent all difficulties, either from the [tax-]farmers, or from their kin."[42] Thus, the small but regular number of naturalizations from Baden-Baden in the middle of the eighteenth century, the last one in 1762 (anticipating the eventual accord reached in 1765 that abolished reciprocally the droit d'aubaine).

The negotiations in 1761 between Sr. Luce and the margrave's representatives began with a proposal for a similar bilateral provincial exemption. But as negotiations moved to the French foreign office, there was good support for a broader exemption from the droit d'aubaine to assure "communication and commerce" between the inhabitants of Alsace, Lorraine, the Three Bishoprics, the margrave of Baden-Baden, and the county of Sponheim.[43] The result, however, expanded in another, unexpected direction: a general abolition of the droit d'aubaine between French subjects throughout the kingdom and those of the principality of Baden-Baden, and this despite the even more ambitious vision of the French foreign office:

It should be added that since the king has wished to reach accords to abolish the droit d'aubaine with respect to most foreign nations, out of concerns about commercial relations and proximity [voisinage], it would be just for the king, and in the interest of his subjects to confer the same treatment on the German nation, where both concerns are relevant: a neighbor of France along a space of more than one hundred leagues, Germany also has important commercial relations with France that are to the latter's advantage, given the considerable wealth that enters the kingdom from Germany.[44]

But, of course, there was no "German nation," much less a German state, with which to negotiate, so the French foreign office entertained a series of distinct and piecemeal diplomatic initiatives with the constituting principalities and jurisdictions of the Holy Roman Empire.

The foreign ministry's vision, however, was accomplished through different means. France's convention with Baden-Baden, signed on 10 October 1765 (ratified by the Paris parlement on 27 December, then registered by that body on 20 February 1766), touched off a wave of mutual and reciprocal abolitions and conventions. Within two years after the Baden-Baden accord, a dozen other Rhineland principalities had mutually and reciprocally abolished the droit d'aubaine with France, largely under the same conditions, and the pace of abolitions continued full force into the 1770s. By then, the distinction between "exemptions" from the droit d'aubaine and "complete and total abolitions," already murky, became completely obscure. Some of the smallest jurisdictions of the empire sometimes received "exemptions" not as part of an international convention but as collective naturalizations issued as letters patent of the king. Two sets of patent letters seem to make use of the strongest possible language to effectively "naturalize" the particular group of foreigners in question. The "citizens and residents" of the imperial free city of Frankfurt were declared in 1767 "absolved and exempted" from the droit d'aubaine, and given the capacity to inherit all successions, with wills or ab intestat, movables as well as immovables, "like native residents and our own natural subjects." And the patent letters issued to members of the Order of Malta in June 1765, months before the accord with Baden-Baden was signed, used the exact formula of an individual naturalization, followed to the letter.

The reciprocal abolitions by international treaty were sometimes worded slightly differently, but often they were just as forceful in their language: the accord with the electorate of Cologne (modeled on that of Baden-Baden) announced that "there will be henceforth a complete and reciprocal abolition of the droit d'aubaine" between the two states. That convention, however, did not add the specific claim to treat the foreigners by the legal fiction that they were "natural subjects," but it did effectively abolish conditionally and reciprocally the droit d'aubaine, the principal civil-law distinction between foreigners and citizens.[45]

The treaties, nonetheless, can be classified into four types in a schema that draws distinctions between kinds of reciprocity. In 1801, the revolutionary jurist Roederer did just that, as did the lawyer Jean-Baptiste Gaschon in 1818, at the moment of the droit d'aubaine's abolition. These were efforts to classify the treaties based on the kind of inheritance capacities that subjects of the two states were reciprocally given: did the treaty confer on foreign nationals the ability to inherit in the kingdom? To inherit from French citizens? Reciprocally? But the French monarchy was initially uninterested in the details of inheritance capacity: rather, political reciprocity in the levy of taxes and dues on property successions, especially those that leave the kingdom, was its central concern.

A similar schema is the basis of the classification in appendix 2, but this is not simply a historian's conceit. The first attempts to classify the treaties, in Denisart and Bardet (both in 1773, at a moment when more than fifty-five had been signed), relied precisely on the question of political reciprocity. Moreover, the schematization corresponds to historical practice. For much like the model letter of naturalization available in the Great Chancellery under Louis XIV and after, something of a boilerplate accord—or rather, a series of templates—circulated in the diplomatic bureaux of the French foreign ministry.[46] And just like the last model letters of naturalization under Louis XV, these templates were not platonic models but concrete precedents. Thus, the exact text of the convention with Baden-Baden was used, over the next three years, as a template for the treaties with the margrave of Baden-Durlach (1765), the duchy of Deux-Ponts (1766), the electorate of the Palatinate (1766), the principality of Nassau-Usingen (1766), and others.

The accord with Baden-Baden exemplifies a type II treaty: it declared the reciprocal abolition of the droit d'aubaine, but made the case conditional, for, this entire class of treaties stated, "if there were to be levied by the prince any tax concerning successions that befall the subjects of the king, or their export," then "the same duties would be levied by His Majesty." The phrase was repeated, with some variations, in all type II treaties, with Nassau-Saarbrücken, Hungary, the hereditary states of Austria, the Palatinate, Hesse-Cassel, Hesse-Darmstadt, Nassau-Weilburg, Nassau-Usingen, Saxe-Gotha, Saxe-Saalfeld-Coburg, Saxe-Hildburghausen, Portugal, and Münster. By contrast, type I treaties—those signed with Savoy, Spain and the Two Sicilies, Frankfurt, Tuscany, Parma, Monaco, the United Provinces, the republic of Ragusa (Italy), and the United States of America—had no conditional clauses about other rights or duties, other than insisting on the general principle of reciprocity itself. Type III treaties, increasingly used in the accelerating trend of abolitions during the late 1770s (there were four in 1776, the same number in 1777, eleven in 1778, and five more before 1782) involved the reciprocal abolition of the droit d'aubaine, but specified a fixed rate of taxation on what was by then universally identified, in the French version of the treaties, as the *droit de détraction* (emigration tax).

The droit de détraction, among French commentators, administrators, and diplomats in the eighteenth and early nineteenth centuries, was a translation and gloss of the German *Abzug*. The term first appeared among French jurisconsults in the sixteenth century to describe a specific tax levied by some of the constituent towns and jurisdictions of the Holy Roman Empire on all personal property of emigrants. As mentioned by René Choppin in the 1570s,

> The custom in several cities of Germany is that those who change residence are obligated to leave to the town and city that they abandon a certain portion of their goods, which tax of departure is called in their language *Abzug* as is written by Zafius Alleman, native of Constance, in his commentaries on the law 2 *ff. de orig. iu.*[47]

But by the eighteenth century, both French lawyers and diplomats recognized that the Abzug could refer to different kinds of local taxes and customary levies, including those on property transfers at the time of succession (sometimes glossed as the *droit de rétorsion*) and an export duty on movable goods (sometimes referred to as a *droit d'émigration*). An anonymous memorandum from the French foreign ministry, written in the 1750s, produced a complex genealogy of the Abzug and its variants that went back to Rome, if not to Julius Caesar himself.[48] In fact, the Abzug like the droit d'aubaine had its origins in the feudal Germanic customs and seigneurial practices of the Holy Roman Empire. By the sixteenth century, fiefholders and the principalities themselves levied the duty, which was hardly analogous to the droit d'aubaine. According to the most learned of French commentators, the Abzug was an inheritance tax (of 5 or 10 percent) collected ostensibly for the "conservation of roads in good and secure condition, and the expenses incurred by the jurisdiction."[49] Even as the foreign ministers sought to equate this with the droit d'aubaine, French lawyers and bureaux secretaries recognized the difference. The droit d'aubaine, as an anonymous official in the foreign ministry put it sometime after 1756, "takes away the entire inheritance [and thus] supercedes the [Abzug] *droit de détraction*."[50]

In practice, the accords and conventions with France's neighboring principalities across the Rhine, and especially those bordering or interspersed in the French province of Alsace, sometimes mentioned the "droit de détraction" by name. More often, they glossed a formal nomenclature with a vague invocation of local and customary law, as stated, for example, in the fifth article of the 1767 convention between the king of France and the elector of Bavaria: "Laws, statutes, and local customs will be respected in relation to the dues levied under the title of *détraction*, or under any denomination in relation to succession or to the export of goods from an inheritance." On occasion, the droit de détraction was understood as a private right (*droit particulier*) in the possession of local French fiefholders that was levied, especially in the northeastern borderland, as a reciprocal response to the exercise of the German Abzug. Thus the treaty between France and the bishopric of Liège signed in December 1768 noted that the droit d'aubaine was abolished excepting dues which might legitimately be due in virtue of whatever titles or an immemorial possession by specific seigneurs and towns of the king's obedience, and notably the *droit de détraction*, called in German *Abschluss* or *Abzug*, which is levied in Germany on the export of goods and the sale price of immovable property deriving from bequests.

In both cases, type II treaties imposed the strict condition of reciprocity between two fiscal practices of radically different natures.[51]

France signed type II (and III) treaties with states—principally those of the Holy Roman Empire—that had a variety of surviving "feudal" practices, restrictions on inheritances as well as on the passage of property out of a particular jurisdiction, but none were fully equivalent to the droit d'aubaine. In fact, the foreign ministry's insistence on reciprocity, as we shall see, was grounded in an essential (and international) legal fiction that treated the varieties of German Abzug *as if* they were equivalent to the French droit d'aubaine. But because the droit d'aubaine was a uniquely French institution, reciprocity was inevitably unattainable as a goal of foreign policy.

Although the French crown signed the treaties and conferred the letters patent exempting and abolishing the droit d'aubaine at the demand of foreign delegations, it is important to stress that the foreign ministry did not extend these without due consideration, especially of the question of reciprocity. Such is revealed in the most cursory glance at the surviving archives of the county of Montbéliard, a largely Protestant jurisdiction of the duke of Württemberg, whose territories were administered by a regency council in the town of Montbéliard.[52]

An enormous jurisprudence surrounded the exercise of the Abzug by the duke of Württemberg. The state archives in this Francophone administration speak of the *droit d'abzug ou d'émigration* and occasionally refer to it as the droit de détraction, suggesting its lesser meaning as a tax pertaining to succession. Specific exemptions existed (or were claimed) for the neighboring canton of Berne, the republic of Geneva, the Grison valley, the county of Neufchâtel, and the republic of Mulhouse: these exemptions produced vast litigation and diplomatic contention in practice. Much of it revolves around individuals claiming specific exemptions by treaty or custom, but the Württemberg archives document the complex negotiations with France that took more than a decade to produce, on 14 April 1778, a mutual and (fictionally) reciprocal abolition of the droit d'aubaine, fixing the droit de détraction at 10 percent.

The negotiations had begun in the spring of 1766, in the context of the treaties recently signed with neighboring principalities in Germany. The problem was brought to the table by the Alsatian intendant de Luce (who had been instrumental in the negotiations with Baden-Baden in 1761), now supported by the city council of Strasbourg. The municipality wished to see an accord concerning Montbéliard linked to the treaty being negotiated with the margrave of Baden-Durlach, with which Montbéliard did not share a border, but with which there existed a "considerable commerce." The Strasbourg municipality, pushed by the regency council of Montbéliard, supported a convention that "followed word for word and mutatis mutandis the convention signed on this subject with the margrave of Baden-Durlach." Foreign Minister duc de Choiseul hesitated, arguing for linking the mutual exemption of the droit d'aubaine to a territorial delimitation between Burgundy and the principality of Montbéliard. In August 1766, when Choiseul agreed to the formal delimitation of the two territories, he also proposed a convention that differed significantly, however, from that signed with Baden-Durlach, particularly in an additional clause that prohibited Lutherans to emigrate. The French insistence on what became called "transmigration" drew on an interpretation of the law of 1669, in practice largely lapsed elsewhere in the kingdom, that forbade French subjects from leaving the kingdom without royal permission. Only in Alsace was the law revived, as the religious administration of France's only multiconfessional province became increasingly concerned with the potential "contamination" of the kingdom by Protestant immigrants. Choiseul invoked the 1669 ordinance, disingenuously claiming that the subsequent kings of France had never abolished "a political law that has always been observed by which it is forbidden for subjects of His Majesty to leave the kingdom without his permission."[53]

As time passed, baron de Thun, Württemberg's ambassador at the French court, exchanged angry if polite letters with the French foreign minister about the "transmigration" clause. De Thun grew impatient as France concluded treaty after treaty with nearby principalities (Deux-Ponts, Cologne, Spire, Liège), none of which, he argued, had as proximate economic relations with France as did Montbéliard, but all of which signed (according to the regency council of Montbéliard) "treaties beneficial to their states."[54] The negotiations dragged on (and off) until the end of the reign of Louis XV.

In December 1774, following the succession of Louis XVI in France, the regency of Montbéliard again took this "pressing matter" before their own prince. The duke again pressed the foreign minister—now the comte de Vergennes—for the abolition of the droit d'aubaine, and, once more, questions about the relation between the abolition of the droit d'aubaine and the delimitation of limits were raised. But it was France's insistence that the abolition pertain to Montbéliard alone, and not to its dependencies, that stalled the signing of the accord. Vergennes held firm, and was close to getting approval for a text that was based on that signed with the principality of Hesse-Darmstadt in 1767, when the Montbéliard regency council raised two other obstacles.

First, the council was concerned about language that failed to adequately address the question of the droit de détraction; and second, it feared that in using the language of the Hesse-Darmstadt treaty, subjects of Montbéliard would be restricted in their capacity to inherit. Concerning the latter, as the Württemberg ambassador de Thun reported in August 1777 to the regency council of Montbéliard, everything depended on the "meaning that can vary in the way future ministers might see things."[55] Vergennes, on his side, was growing increasingly impatient with a negotiation "which has taken all too long," but baron de Thun blamed Vergennes, saying he had "important and pressing business" that kept him from "looking after our droit d'aubaine." In the end, Vergennes offered as his ultimatum a text modeled on the treaty just signed, on 7 April 1778, with the elector of Saxe-Gotha (a classic type II treaty): the "transmigration clause" was gone, the dependencies were included, and a conditional 10 percent droit de détraction was named. On 15 April 1778, after almost thirteen years of negotiation, baron de Thun reported to the regency council of Montbéliard that a convention with Paris had finally been signed.[56]

The twisted, convoluted, and constantly delayed negotiations reveal much about the process of abolishing piecemeal the droit d'aubaine, and especially the overriding concerns of the French foreign ministry. These turned on the question of "reciprocity," understood in two senses, one political, the other social. In the first instance, Choiseul and then Vergennes were determined to assert France's interests by arguing for parity: although the droit d'aubaine was a uniquely French institution, these ministers and their offices claimed the Abzug or other droits de détraction as its equivalent. By the time Vergennes began negotiating with the Württemberg ambassador in 1774, France had signed a series of treaties (types III–IV) conditionally permitting the continued and reciprocal collection of such taxes.

The result was two unintended consequences for France. Because the Abzug and other related customary rights were affirmed in principle by international treaties, several German lords with territories or jurisdictions in Alsace went so far as to introduce its use in the kingdom. Empowered by the conventions that gave them the right to levy a new tax, they collected revenues on properties leaving their seigneuries (including in cases of succession) that they had previously ignored. To the French crown, this was an obvious assault on royal sovereignty, exacerbated by the purported identity of the droit d'aubaine and the droit de détraction. Only the king could exercise the droit d'aubaine, yet a series of borderland princes—notably, the counts of Hamau, the bishop of Spire, and the marquis of Rosen—had received patent letters confirming their legal right to the Abzug before the 1760s. It took a series of intellectual gymnastics for an anonymous commentator of the late eighteenth century to reassert royal sovereignty, but at the expense of equating, once again, the droit d'aubaine and the droit de détraction.[57]

A second unintended consequence flowed from what one official in 1783 called "the just law of reciprocity." Even though the French king had never previously recognized the existence of such a tax, the "law required that imperial subjects be subjected to this law in France," wrote the anonymous official. In fact, it was the local judiciary (the *bailliages*) in Alsace and Lorraine that took it upon themselves to try to collect the tax. Lacking precedents, they demanded clarification from the foreign ministry. Antoine, a royal attorney for the bailliage in Nancy, wrote to the foreign ministry that

> This tax is new [in France and] no one has yet taken any care with respect to it, for no official has yet been charged with collecting it. To nominate such officials would be useless unless they were to be properly instructed. . . . A circular memorandum would itself be insufficient; a decree of the royal council is necessary, endowed with patent letters addressed to the Chambre des comptes to be registered there, and sent not only to the bailiwicks but also to all the communities of the jurisdiction.[58]

But at this late date, however desperate it was for additional fiscal resources, the royal council was preoccupied with far more pressing fiscal questions about the nature of the royal debt in 1783, the result of France's military support of the United States in its colonial revolt. The fiscal significance of the droit d'aubaine and the droit de détraction remained marginal, and the government was not about to introduce that which it sought to abolish in the interests of commerce.

This was the second problem of reciprocity, a social and economic one in the case of Montbéliard, as with other bordering principalities and jurisdictions. The motives of the French government, as evident in the 1766 draft proposal offered by Choiseul, were to assure "reciprocal and free commerce between their respective subjects." Regarding Montbéliard's dependencies, "the relations of kinship, of commerce, and of proximity" and the "mutual needs of subjects" required "a free communication [among them], and the king himself is interested in favoring this with regard to the population." Local "rights of reciprocity," as the intendant Turgot had described them in the *généralité* of Metz in 1697, were ancient and made it impossible for states to "govern . . . absolutely as if the states were exactly delimited and different."[59]

France's official justification in the nearly six dozen treaties and conventions also turned on the keywords of "commerce" and communication." Every treaty signed between 1765 and 1787 contained the phrase, or some variant, "to promote and facilitate reciprocal commerce and communication between our subjects and the members, vassals, and subjects of" the prince or jurisdiction in question. Those negotiated with the borderland principalities of the Rhineland, which sometimes included calls to delimit boundaries, often further specified "good neighborliness and relations" (*bon voisinage et bonne correspondence*), as well as kinship and property ownership in the borderland (as was the case, beyond Montbéliard, in the treaties signed with the Palatinate, Deux-Ponts, and others). Recognizing the "reciprocal interest of being able to have commercial relations between them, and to contract [marital] alliances without being submitted to the rigors of the droit d'aubaine," as stated in the treaty with the duchy of Deux-Ponts, the treaties insisted on abolishing the obstacles—most centrally, the droit d'aubaine—to the free circulation of goods and people between the two states.

In these texts, as in the letters, memos, and commentaries on these accords, French foreign ministers and their staffs built their policies around the idea of "commerce," never quite realizing the loaded charge the word was to take on during the second half of the eighteenth century. Principally, they understood and developed the term in a strict economic sense: the state's interests lay in attracting the greatest flow of wealth and economic activity, and that included the principle of encouraging foreigners to settle in the kingdom. In the hands of the crown's financial ministers and the foreign office, the droit d'aubaine represented a symbolic and practical obstacle to the movement of people and goods into the kingdom. In their writings, they drew on a range of critiques of the droit d'aubaine that had suddenly appeared in the 1750s, including that of baron de Montesquieu.

In the third volume of the *Spirit of the Laws* (1755), Montesquieu—a moderate monarchist with a deep fascination for classical republicanism—had identified the droit d'aubaine with the right of salvage (*droit d'épave*), both of which he characterized as barbarian remnants put in place at the end of the Roman Empire. "At that time the senseless *droit d'aubaine* and salvage were established; men thought that, as foreigners were not united with them by any communication or civil rights, they did not owe them, on the one hand, justice of any sort or, on the other, pity of any sort."[60]

With this single philosophical intervention, Montesquieu overturned the absolutist model of the droit d'aubaine that tended, at least in the hands of the jurists, to derive its legitimacy from Rome. The connection with Rome was irretrievably broken by the Enlightenment: no longer could the droit d'aubaine be justified as having Roman origins, as sixteenth-century practitioners of "scholarly law" were to argue. Rather, it originated among the Germanic tribes after the fall of the Roman Empire, when commerce and civil law were virtually nonexistent. The *droit civil* in question was not the narrow idea of civil law that stood opposed to the *droit des gens*, as many eighteenth-century jurists were to understand the terms. Rather, it was constituted in the social and civil condition engendered by the "spirit of commerce." The principles of civility, cosmopolitanism, and sociability led Montesquieu, despite his ostensible monarchism, to give commerce an emancipatory role that could liberate society from the "Machiavellianism" of princes.[61]

But the "commerce" identified by the French foreign office and financial ministers in the 1750s owed far less to Montesquieu and his invocation of a classical republican tradition than to the first physiocratic writings of the 1750s. Physiocracy, an expression coined in 1767 by Pierre-Samuel Dupont de Nemours (as he was known after 1789), was the "rule of Nature" founded on property as natural right and natural law (*droit naturel*). In a global sense, Physiocracy formed part of a broader critique of mercantilist thought and practice in mid-century France, England, and Scotland, a breakthrough moment of economic liberalism and the invention of political economy.[62]

Historians have not always acknowledged the international dimensions of physiocratic thought and policy in France, no surprise given the relative neglect with which the Physiocrats treated international trade, and indeed all "commerce" other than the "good commerce" of agricultural products. Nor have they considered its consistent condemnation of the droit d'aubaine as part of a broader citizenship revolution in the period. But the crown's abolition of the droit d'aubaine and its reconfiguration of the absolute citizen between 1765 and 1787 was founded on a particular reading of physiocratic doctrine.

Unlike mercantilism, much more a practice than a theory of economic development, Physiocracy was very much conceived as a school, a "catechism" in the self-conscious practices of Victor Riquetti, marquis de Mirabeau, an early convert.[63] The separate publications and often-unacknowledged collaboration of Mirabeau (L'Ami des hommes, ou traité de la population, 1756) and François Quesnay (whose article on tax-farmers [fermiers] appeared the same year in Diderot and d'Alembert's Encyclopédie) conventionally mark the beginning of the movement. In a short time, the "Economists" or "citizens-philosophers" had their own journal, entitled the Ephémérides du Citoyen, published between 1765 and 1772 by Abbé Nicolas Baudeau. (In this, they took part in the discursive and political revolution of citizenship.) Mirabeau held a regular Tuesday dinner meeting at his house beginning in 1767, attended by, among others, the king's attorney and great popularizer of the "economists," Guillaume-François Le Trosne. Also in attendance at these organized dinner-assembly-classrooms were the princes and margraves of the Rhineland, all disciples of the "doctrine," who returned periodically to Paris ("mouths watering" at the prospect, according to the margrave of Baden-Baden in 1770) to take philosophical vacations from their largely unsuccessful experiments with liberalizing the grain trade in their own territories.[64]

What was the "doctrine" that informed these and later discussions? In the broadest sense, the renewed emphasis on "commerce" in French domestic and foreign policy in late 1750s turned a minor heresy, as it had been developed by Fénelon and Boisguillebert in the 1690s, into a major orthodoxy. The heresy was a pure form of economic liberalism, especially with respect to the grain trade. As official policy, economic liberalism predated the Physiocrats in the experiments of Controller-General of Finances Machault d'Arnouville. Machault's responsibility for the first edict that freed the grain trade, decreed on 17 September 1754, was in response to famine and high prices, especially in southern France, but the experiment was not to last, and Machault was disgraced in 1757.[65] The physiocratic notions of wealth and commerce that emerged at that time owed a debt to Machault's valuation of the agrarian world.

Plans by Quesnay and others for a single property tax were devised to increase agricultural revenue and capital investment, and were to be accompanied, in the words of historian Mario Einaudi,

> by a sweeping grant of economic freedom and by a complete abolition of trade restrictions, farm servitudes, and petty feudal privileges. The restoration of an unhampered circulation of goods, including the free export of agricultural products, constituted the logical conclusion of a process aiming at the reconstruction of the economic order on a foundation, not artificial and capricious, but natural and permanent. That the new economic order was to be in direct relation to natural law was a strongly embedded belief of the physiocrats.[66]

It is true that their fixation with agrarian wealth led the Physiocrats to distinguish between "productive" classes (of which only landed proprietors could be "essential members") and "sterile" classes comprised of not only rentiers and financiers but also wholesale merchants and the commercial classes.[67] But while Quesnay may have downplayed the significance of international trade, most of the physiocratic school believed deeply in the extension of "the regime of commercial liberty" to the national economic barriers and systems of tariffs that had constituted the mercantilist and absolutist precepts and practices. According to Mirabeau, relations between bordering "nations" were to be the same as those among provinces, because

> What are nations if not large families? The duty of legislators is to unite them; to dismantle first concerning their members, then for the territory, these repugnant distinctions of native residents and foreigners. The entire world is contiguous: all countries are neighbors; all men are brothers.

Yet despite such universalist and cosmopolitan claims, Mirabeau never swayed in his belief in the principle of reciprocity: if free exchange were to occur between neighboring states, the abolition of tariffs and dues would have to be reciprocal. In this sense, his position was more adaptable to the "new diplomacy" of the eighteenth century, itself informed by physiocratic precepts.[68]

The dominant physiocratic position, while it recognized the principle of commercial freedom, paradoxically rested on the centrality of the "productive" classes of landowners and cultivators who were stable, established, and unlikely to be displaced. In this sense, Physiocracy continued to underscore the normative ideal of an absolutist "peasant France" against the "merchant France" of commerce and movement. Indeed, as appropriated by government officials in the last decades of the Old Regime, the pure agrarian roots of Physiocracy increasingly combined with the contrary belief that "commerce" formed, in the words of the professor of natural and international law at the Collège royal, Michel-Antoine Bouchaud, "not only the link that unites all peoples and all climates [but] also the soul, the support, and the wealth of the state, a wealth that can only come from that of individuals . . .."[69] Such an emphasis on "commerce" formed the basis of what one might call the monarchy's project of "practical cosmopolitanism," at the center of which was the abolition of the droit d'aubaine.

The Physiocrats were content to dismiss the droit d'aubaine without elaborate philosophical condemnation: its existence was self-evidently against the interests of reason and state. The marquis de Mirabeau briefly referred to the "wretched droits d'aubaine," which he linked to a "blind barbarism" that self-evidently ought to be abolished.[70] As elaborated by the royal barrister and reformer Le Trosne, the droit d'aubaine "comes from feudal tyranny; this royal right is a residue of our ancient barbarity softened by civilization and converted to fiscal dues." Le Trosne tacitly followed Montesquieu in tracing its origins back to "barbaric times," but he went further in arguing that since property rights emanated from "natural," not "civil," law, the droit d'aubaine and any restrictions on the possession or transmission of property were unconscionable. That "aliens" could not hold office without being naturalized was one thing, but the right to property is "a natural right, not a concession of the Sovereign. It precedes civil societies, which are only formed for and by [natural right]; and if the capacity of deeding property is indeed a civil right, which remains a question in itself, the right to bequeath one's goods to one's heirs is a natural right, a sequel and consequence of property itself."[71]

Among publicists and commentators, as among ministers and their secretaries, the condemnation of the droit d'aubaine spread far more widely than the circles of Physiocracy. "The droit d'aubaine is a vestige of the barbaric institutions dating from the early times of the French monarchy," wrote the marine minister in charge of colonial affairs in 1771, and only recently had "the system of commerce begun to prevail over fiscal principles."[72] At stake were basic policy orientations of French commercial and immigration policy that, for the first time in French history, were beginning to be debated publicly if obliquely and circuitously within the condemnation of the droit d'aubaine. This was part of a broader and emerging orthodoxy that, to a large degree, turned to England as a model, despite the great rivalry between France and England in the late eighteenth century.[73] England had adopted by the 1760s an "open door" policy on immigration and foreign participation in commerce that seemed to be achieving its expected effect as England emerged triumphant, despite the loss of its North American colonies, in 1776. French commerce seemed to languish, and contemporaries widely perceived a population decline despite the significant demographic growth that marked the second half of the eighteenth century.[74]

The decline of the French population was due not so much to a failure of birth rates, according to the reformers, but to the fact that emigration was hardly compensated by an influx of foreigners. Such was the "national illness" described in Jean-Baptiste Moheau's *Recherches et considérations sur la population de la France* (1778). "The countryside has almost no foreigners, the great cities have a few, only manufacturers give us some," Moheau wrote. More precisely, although his numbers were sometimes implausible,

> fifteen or twenty years ago, there were 30,000 French established in London; many fewer were the number of English established in Paris, or even in the kingdom. It was estimated that the number of French established in Spain was 8,000; there are not even 800 Spaniards in France. One could count five or six hundred French in Portugal, not including the ambassador's household and the Jews, and only 50 Portuguese in France. It is said that there are 15,000 French living in Italy, and that there are not even 3,000 Italians living in France. Holland is full of French, born in France or descended from French families, and one finds few Dutch in France. In 1738, there were 10,000 French living in the States of the Great Lord [the Ottoman Empire], and perhaps only 50 of his subjects in the entire kingdom. . . . No large state in the world has more of its inhabitants living in France than it has Frenchmen established in its country.

The reason, quite simply, was the droit d'aubaine, "a truly uncivilized, barbarous, and absurd right . . . that repels foreigners from our districts and places, and in the name of the king, erects great barriers to the increase of his subjects."[75]

Moheau's condemnation of the droit d'aubaine as an outmoded royal prerogative that impeded population growth and commerce echoed, beyond Physiocracy itself, a broader Enlightened critique of the institution. The droit d'aubaine was, after Montesquieu, indelibly linked to "feudalism" and the historical detritus of barbarian times. At stake was the notion that the development of civilization was coterminous with commerce itself, and that a state's attitude toward foreigners was an index of its degree of advancement. This had been the position taken by Grotius, and reiterated by Emmerich de Vattel and other theorists of the "law of nations" in the Enlightenment.[76] And it was part of the broader expressions of cosmopolitanism in public law as well. The Chevalier de Jaucourt's entry "foreigners" (*étrangers*), a term of public law in the 1752 edition of the *Encyclopédie*, denounced the Scythians, who sacrificed and ate the unfortunate foreigners who came to visit. Sparta fell because of its rigorous persecution of foreigners, and—in the classical world—only Alexander the Great had set an example for the modern world:

> Now that commerce has united the entire world, that the interests of polities have become enlightened, that humanity extends to all peoples, there is not a single sovereign in Europe who does not think like Alexander. The question, greatly debated, is whether hard-working foreigners should be permitted to settle in our country, submitting themselves to the laws. Nobody denies that nothing contributes more to the grandeur, the power, and the prosperity of a state than the

free access it gives to foreigners who wish to come and settle. . . . The United Provinces [of the Netherlands] saw the happy results of such wise behavior.[77]

The *Encyclopédie*'s reference to Holland was the same as Fénelon's in the 1690s. Sixty years later, the encouragement of enterprising foreigners as an important means of promoting "commerce" became an organizing ideal of the late absolutist state. Within this shift, the droit d'aubaine, previously an uncontested mark of royal sovereignty, was condemned as a barbaric remnant of uncivilized times.

After mid-century, the financial ministry of France consistently proposed the universal abolition of the droit d'aubaine. In November 1755, the marquis d'Argenson reported in his journals that Controller-General of Finances Séchelles "is currently working on removing the droit d'aubaine entirely and making a general exemption, which would draw here many foreigners."[78] But it was only after France's disappointing and costly participation in the Seven Years War that the financial administration began to take seriously the project of abolishing unilaterally the droit d'aubaine as an obstacle to commerce and communication. In this, a succession of controllers-general and directors-general of finance locked horns with the foreign ministry, which accepted the critique of the institution but sought to proceed piecemeal, in the interests of reciprocity, with its abolition.

In 1774, with Anne-Robert-Jacques Turgot, the provincial magistrate who took the office of controller-general of finance at the accession of Louis XVI, the "doctrine" of Physiocracy experienced a modest revival. Physiocracy became associated with "enlightened despotism," the ministerial efforts of Turgot and Necker to homogenize the rule of absolutism by breaking with reliance on privilege in classical or first absolutism. Turgot's inspired if unsuccessful efforts to free the grain trade, and to reorganize the guild system, dovetailed with his outspoken efforts to abolish the droit d'aubaine. His overall goal was much the same as that of Colbert a century earlier: to encourage wealthy foreigners to settle in France. But unlike Colbert and all of mercantilist doctrine, there was no ambiguity in his welcome of foreigners, for whom the obstacles to property inheritance should also be eliminated.

Upon assuming office in 1774, Turgot argued insistently with his rival, foreign minister comte de Vergennes, to abolish with a general law the droit d'aubaine. Citing the authority of his friend and Physiocrat Dupont de Némours, Turgot believed that the institution "repels a relatively large number of skillful men and useful artists, of capitalists and merchants, from settling in France, who otherwise would want nothing more than to establish their businesses here, and even dissuades rich individuals, drawn by the charms of our customs and society, and by the pleasant climate and the governance" of France, from coming to the kingdom.[79] But while he argued more publicly for a general abolition of the institution, Turgot acted quietly to put pressure on the foreign minister to sign as many individual and reciprocal accords as possible. His project of unilaterally abolishing the droit d'aubaine was inherited by none other than Jacques Necker, the Swiss Protestant banker turned controller-general from October 1776 to May 1781, who was returned to office on the eve of the Revolution.[80]

In his public life, Necker inherited Turgot's position on the droit d'aubaine, even though he was not, strictly speaking, a Physiocrat.[81] In his 1784 tract on *L'Administration des Finances de France*, he invoked the broader, "enlightened" position, calling the droit d'aubaine an "ill-advised and barbaric right." Yet his real condemnation was directed toward its fiscal failure and counterproductive effects. Not only did the droit d'aubaine discourage wealthy foreigners from settling in the kingdom but it produced a dysfunctional financial state. "The revenue is almost entirely consumed by the costs of formalities, and by the attributions which belong to judicial officials," he wrote. Moreover,

> Often our fiscal officials, not having been instructed quickly enough as to the true fatherland of foreigners who died in the kingdom, begin their inquiries and disquieting procedures that a more enlightened examination later obliges them to abandon; thus unexpectedly, against our will, contestations and complaints abound. Such unfortunate consequences can only be prevented by a general abolition.

He proposed the general abolition of the droit d'aubaine in 1780, the first draft of which invoked the principles of enlightened administration, justice, and hospitality: "We have thus thought that it would be worthy of our sense of justice and hospitality to wipe out entirely the traces of a law that no longer seems applicable to the present, which is in contrast to French mores, and is a shock to the principles of enlightened administration."[82]

Necker fell from power before seeing the law through, but it was a testament to the strength of the idea that his rival and successor, Charles Alexandre de Calonne, took over the project in 1783. In consultation with Foreign Minister Vergennes and Chancellor Miromesnil in the spring of 1786, Necker's ordinance was redrafted, but largely unchanged. It laid out the principles as follows:

> Having seen that the droit d'aubaine established in our kingdom disrupts the relations that commerce, as well as the sciences and the arts, establishes between our subjects and those of other princes and states of Europe, we have decided to follow the example [of specific agreements] and to abolish totally, by a general law for all nations, this right, the exercise of which is repugnant in the context of the benevolent policies that we have always tried to pursue.[83]

But despite Calonne's best intentions, the project was not to come to fruition under the Old Regime, and in the spring of 1787, the edict was still held up by the chancellor, who was understandably "occupied with other things" at the time, according to Calonne.[84] It is true that other, more pressing matters of the prerevolutionary years—the fiscal crisis and the opposition of the parlements, the failure of Calonne's Assembly of Notables, the convocation of the Estates General, for example—help to explain why the droit d'aubaine was not abolished before the French Revolution. But it is also important to underscore the rather different agendas of the foreign ministry and the controllers-general, divided over the question of reciprocity.

Controllers-general and directors-general of finance, as had already been clear when Turgot and Vergennes locked horns in 1774, wanted to abolish the droit d'aubaine in a general fashion and without concern for reciprocity. Foreign Minister Vergennes "thought, to the contrary, that it should only be abolished piecemeal, and to use these abolitions as an enticement to obtain some commercial advantages from other nations that so desired to be exempted." Vergennes was later to dismiss Necker's "English and Genevan" principles because they were "incompatible with the French monarchical tradition."[85] The entrenchment of the principle of reciprocity especially in the hands of a powerful foreign minister such as Vergennes helps to account for the failure of a general ordinance. The 1786 draft of the general abolition of the droit d'aubaine was unilateral and unconcerned with reciprocal abolitions by neighboring powers, as was its "final" abolition in 1790 (albeit cast in more Enlightened terms). But as the Old Regime came to an end, Chancellor Miromesnil continued to express concerns about the absence of reciprocity in the draft edict of 1786 that had been taken up by Calonne, which probably led him to delay enactment of the law. His concerns were countered by the not very convincing claims that "the failure of reciprocity on the part of the other courts turns essentially to our advantage" because it imposed obstacles to French emigrants settling abroad.[86] Calonne's proposal—and those of finance ministers stretching back to the 1750s—were a dead letter in 1789.

Still, if Vergennes was wedded to the notion of reciprocity, in one specific instance he favored a more "universal" and distinctly unreciprocal abolition of the droit d'aubaine: the case of England in 1787. By the early 1780s, the series of conventions and treaties abolishing or mutually exempting foreign subjects from the droit d'aubaine had come to a close. After 1782, only Russia and Great Britain signed general treaties of commerce and alliance with France that included, more incidentally and like the earlier seventeenth-century treaties, the abolition of the droit d'aubaine. Controller-General of Finances Calonne had already urged Vergennes in 1785 to abolish the droit d'aubaine in the treaty with England, in order to attract English capital to the kingdom. The commercial treaty of 1786, strongly influenced on the French side by physiocratic doctrines, included the reciprocal abolition of the droit d'aubaine. But it did not go far enough.[87] The following year, just before his death, Vergennes produced an unprecedented piece of legislation, unique with respect to the sixty-six reciprocal agreements and collective exemptions negotiated since 1765. By patent letters registered on 19 April 1787, Louis XVI gave the subjects of the English crown a unilateral and unconditional exemption from the droit d'aubaine in France. This break with the Old Regime practice of reciprocity, specifically negotiated by Foreign Minister Vergennes, was, however, less surprising than it might at first appear.

England had, of course, been the bane of France's existence since the latter's defeat and reduction of its colonial territories in North America at the end of the Seven Years War. In the oppositional construction of French nationalism, England functioned as France's "Other," around (or rather, against) which a patriotic pamphlet literature, partly sponsored by the government, found expression.[88] Such Anglophobia was to resurface with a vengeance during the French Revolution, even if the Enlightened philosophes and the urbane world of fashionable French "society" had upheld the model of England as a constitutional and liberal counterexample to France.[89] France, of course, supported the North American colonies in their emancipation from the yoke of English tyranny in 1776, and indeed throughout the 1780s. But when it came to commercial policy, at least late in his life, Vergennes combined crucial elements of Colbert's mercantilism (notably, the encouragement of wealthy foreigners) and certain parts of the economic liberalism of the Physiocrats in his English wager. Although he did not live to see the results, he believed that a free trade agreement with England would lead to the dismantling of the prohibitive English tariffs on French products, especially those on luxury goods such as silk.[90]

After the 1786 treaty was signed, and just before his death, Vergennes pushed for royal letters patent that unilaterally abolished the droit d'aubaine for English subjects. Contemporaries were to question his motives. At the Academy of Amiens, a certain Claude-Joseph de Mayer gave a eulogy that insisted how, unlike previous ministers "who believe that they have nothing to do once they have finished with what are called the great operations," Vergennes pushed for a general abolition of the droit d'aubaine, because he didn't believe "that a minister should perpetuate laws that nature and humanity abhor."[91] But Vergennes had opposed such a universal abolition of the droit d'aubaine. His subsequent critics, including those who successfully reintroduced a redefined version of the droit d'aubaine in 1801, later claimed that the foreign minister had only granted the collective exemption on the expectation that the English Parliament would follow suit: Vergennes had been duped when the English failed to act reciprocally. But supporters of the revolutionary status quo before 1801 cited verse and text from archival sources in the foreign ministry to prove Vergennes's true motives. There they found evidence that Vergennes had merely reasoned diplomatically about the problem of reciprocity, and found it, in this instance, to be dysfunctional. The 1787 letters patent for the English were hardly an act of pure philanthropy, as would be the universal and unilateral abolition instituted by the French revolutionaries three years later. As Vergennes himself had argued,

> It is not at the demand of the English minister that the abolition of the droit d'aubaine be proposed; it is despite him that it must be done. This suppression must not be considered an act of condescension, but from a political perspective. . . . If this right were to be levied on French [nationals], it would not be motive enough to do the same to others. For reciprocity is never a reasonable thing except when it can be done without damage to one's country, and the droit d'aubaine is even more harmful to nations that collect it than to foreigners whose wealth it usurps.[92]

In the end, Vergennes, like Necker before him, condemned the unproductive effects of the droit d'aubaine: an obstacle that discouraged wealthy foreigners and especially English manufacturers from settling in the kingdom, it ran counter to diplomatic and commercial policies that should strive to produce exactly the opposite.

Vergennes never went as far as his opponents and rivals, the financial ministers from Turgot to Necker to Calonne, who proposed the unconditional and unilateral abolition of the droit d'aubaine. The difference was not one of goal but of method: all believed that the droit d'aubaine was a remnant of barbarian times—in this, they all took their cue from the Enlightened critics of the institution—and should be abolished when faced with the commercial and social relations of the "modern" world. Vergennes wanted to decide on a case-by-case basis, maintaining the principle of reciprocity while his rivals were convinced of the universal good that would result from a general and unconditional abolition.

No one was more keenly aware than Vergennes, himself the great-grandson of a barrister, that the attack on the droit d'aubaine amounted to nothing less than a revolutionary rejection of the "ancient jurisprudence" of the lawyers, and also of the royal model of the absolute citizen. For centuries, the monarchy had worked in collusion with the jurists and magistrates to turn the droit d'aubaine into a mark of royal sovereignty. As late as 1749, the monarchy produced a "project for a declaration" on the droit d'aubaine that, although it no longer survives intact, clearly pointed to an amplified royal droit d'aubaine as an amplified and absolute right of sovereignty.[93] But after the 1750s, jurists and the crown struggled to dismantle the absolutist model of the droit d'aubaine and of citizenship itself in the aftermath of its piecemeal if consistent and reciprocal abolition.

Legal commentators after the 1750s who reedited earlier texts of absolutist theory ironically spent much ink deconstructing the long-standing monarchical project of turning the droit d'aubaine into an essential element of sovereignty. Lefebvre de la Planche, the royal solicitor-general of the Chambre du domaine in the early eighteenth century, had been the last great commentator who identified the droit d'aubaine with a "fundamental law" of the kingdom and a "mark of royal sovereignty." His editor in the 1760s, Paul Charles Lorry, a professor of Roman law in Paris, performed feats of legal gymnastics in arguing that although collecting the droit d'aubaine might be a royal prerogative, and issuing letters of naturalization was certainly as well, these were acts of "power" (*puissance*), not "domainial authority" (*domaine*), and thus the crown was acting "absolutely" in offering collective exemptions and abolitions.[94] But Vergennes himself, however deeply conservative he was in his views on royal authority and religion, nonetheless rejected the absolutist model, and the jurisconsults who had constructed it, in his claim to (reciprocally) abolish the droit d'aubaine.[95] The "old jurisprudence," he admitted, had simply been wrong. In a memorandum of 11 December 1785 to the council of state, he denied that the droit d'aubaine contained "the very essence of our constitution. We began to be enlightened on this matter only under the reign of Louis XIV. But the few exceptions conferred by this king were only temporary. . . . Louis XV gave a greater development to the principles. This monarch accorded exemptions to the droit d'aubaine to all nations that asked for it."[96]

Vergennes, like other foreign ministers and controllers-general since the 1760s, overturned the "ancient jurisprudence"—and, with it, the absolutist model of citizenship. The foreign office and the finance ministries differed over the procedures for abolishing the droit d'aubaine, but both parties shared a notion that the droit d'aubaine was a remnant of barbarian times. The result was a kind of practical cosmopolitanism that sought to liberate property and trade from the constraints of inherited legal traditions and, more precisely, to abolish the droit d'aubaine as the principal obstacle to free trade and commercial interests.

If such were the central claims of the French ministries in the latter half of the eighteenth century, it is nonetheless important to stress that the condemnations and proposals for a universal or a reciprocal and conditional abolition of the droit d'aubaine did not explicitly make use of the renovated political language of the "citizen" that formed part of the first instantiation of the citizenship revolution, the invention of the citizen as public and political actor. But physiocratically inspired reformers of the late eighteenth century did use this enriched notion of the citizen in another context: in their proposals to create assemblies of citizen-landowners who participated in the assessment and collection of taxes. The fiscal origins of representative government emanated, in part, from Enlightened philosophes sympathetic to the Physiocrats such as the baron d'Holbach ("It is property that makes the Citizen"). But mostly they came from apologists for royal reform, from Le Trosne to Necker to Turgot. Le Trosne, who was to voice a powerful condemnation of the droit d'aubaine in his physiocratically inspired 1779 treatise on provincial administration, also argued strongly for representative assemblies of proprietary "citizens" four years after the first calls to convoke the Estates General had been made by the Cour des aides.[97] The 1770s saw a spate of similar proposals, including that of the Director General of Finances Necker, who experimented with representative assemblies in Berry in 1778. Meanwhile, Controller-General Turgot's *Mémoire sur les municipalités* (written in 1775, but published in 1788) linked land ownership indelibly with "the true right of citizenship" (*le véritable droit de cité*). Turgot had envisaged a new kind of "citizen": the male adult landowner of independent means who took on modest powers of self-representation in assessing and levying direct taxes. Property, in this sense, became a prerequisite for citizenship. As stated baldly by Dupont de Nemours, "Whatever the constitutions say, the only complete citizens are the owners of the land, those whose revenues truly contribute to the maintenance of the public good [*la chose publique*]."[98]

As such, the late monarchy's reforms unwittingly followed, if only distantly and partially, the enlightened and republican critics of absolutist monarchy, and especially the parliamentary milieu that opposed the imposition of universal taxes that attacked their privileges. Magistrates and their apologists, critics of royal despotism, had turned taxpayers into citizens (including the members of the legal and fiscal *corps* and corporations of the Old Regime state) as early as the 1750s. Of course, they—alongside more explicitly republican pamphleteers—took a predictably dim view of the idea of representative assemblies proffered by the ministries, and informed by physiocratic ideals. It was hardly enough, in the minds of Mably or Rousseau, to be a proprietor, nor was the self-assessment of taxes sufficient to constitute true citizenship. For the magistrates and others, as more generally for the majority of taxpayers "who wanted an immediate and thorough redistribution of the tax burden," according to Michael Kwass, "the experience of the provincial assemblies was disappointing."[99]

Nonetheless, both the crown and its critics came to rely on a "political" and exclusive idea of the citizen, in opposition to the legal and inclusive membership category of the jurists. Pamphleteers and philosophers opposed to "royal despotism" turned the citizen from a legal being into a political actor, and thus narrowed significantly the social and gender boundaries of the category. The late absolutist monarchy under Louis XVI also moved the notion of citizen from a legal subject to a political actor, founding limited rights of "citizenship" on landownership. In this public discourse after the 1750s, the (political) citizen became identified, in different ways, with the possession of property. The citizen, defined as an independent male property owner and no longer in opposition to the foreigner by a capacity to devolve or inherit property, passed definitively from the legal to the political sphere.

The ministerial projects and treaties abolishing the droit d'aubaine, the second moment of the citizenship revolution, were part and parcel of this shift from law to politics, and from property succession to property ownership, even though they never resorted to the new language of the citizen in French political culture. In signing the sixty-odd treaties abolishing or mutually exempting foreigners from the droit d'aubaine, the crown dismantled the central institution that defined the absolute citizen. What then was to mark the legal and political differences between Frenchmen and women, on the one hand, and foreigners, on the other? The early Physiocrats implied that such distinctions had become irrelevant, and ministers, reformers, and pamphleteers engaged in discussions and actions to abolish the droit d'aubaine rarely paused, at least until the 1780s, to consider the legal and political ramifications of these abolitions. Instead, that problem was left to the jurists, the courtroom lawyers whose arguments sought to clarify the meaning of the postabsolute citizen in the decades before the French Revolution.

King versus Civil Society: The Trials of the Droit d'Aubaine

Amid the obscure diplomatic struggles to abolish the droit d'aubaine and the public debates over the political rights and identity of the citizen, the practice of naturalization (and the absolute citizen within the private law) continued unreconstructed. Although naturalizations decreased precipitously after the 1750s, except for those given to foreign clerics, the routinized procedure and commentaries of the jurists who litigated disputes between native residents and aliens continued to reproduce the absolutist model. Most civil law practitioners, in fact, stayed out of the public light of the citizenship revolution. Few of the jurists who figured in the elaboration of a judicial "doctrine" of citizenship—professors of French law, arrestographes, or practicing barristers—were inclined to emphasize their public or political roles as citizens.

The jurists responsible for the continuing jurisprudence about aliens in the late eighteenth century were hardly the same lawyers who conceived of their world outside the Palais de Justice along a central political axis, believing that "they held an honorable and indispensable position within the constellation of estates and institutions that made up the French polity." David Bell has studied a particularly vocal group of such barristers who, under the influence of Jansenist doctrine and practice in the mid-eighteenth century, challenged the authority of the monarchy through the publication of the parliamentary remonstrances and judicial memoirs (*mémoires juidiciaires*). These were men who conceived of themselves as forming the "sort of absolutely independent little republic at the center of the state," as the Order of Barristers was described in the eighteenth century.[100]

Only a handful of such legal publicists were involved, even indirectly, in fundamentally reformulating the jurisprudence of nationality law, although among the activists were several of the shining lights of the Paris Bar Association, including Antoine-Gaspard Boucher d'Argis, Armand-Gaston Camus, and Pierre Bayard. These three Parisian barristers extensively reedited the seventeenth and eighteenth century legal dictionaries, Argou and Denisart among them, responding to a growing market, and contributing to the making of a modern legal instrument, the alphabetical repertoire. In their annotated editions of legal dictionaries, they sometimes introduced a new language of citizenship that was in keeping with their authorship of judicial memoirs attacking the monarchy and defending the rights of the nation. Camus and Bayard, for example, in their new edition of Denisart, provided an extended legal treatment of laws on aliens. They also produced an entry on the *cité/citoyen* that began with a practically verbatim statement of Rousseau—an indication of how nationality was to become an exclusive quality in the brave new world of nations founded on the General Will: "The essential condition of the social contract [*pacte social*] being to put in common the person and all his powers under the supreme direction of the General Will [*volonté générale*] and this contract requires consequently the total alienation of each associate of all his rights to the entire community, it follows that it is impossible for any individual to be simultaneously a member of two polities."[101]

Most practicing lawyers, by contrast, did not engage in the rhetoric of the citizenship revolution, and some even took refuge in the more technical and arcane language of alien, native resident, and natural Frenchman (and woman). It is significant that Pierre-Antoine Merlin's vast dictionary, taken over from Guyot, relied on this more technical lexicon, although it is also true that neologisms occasionally crept into the administrative vocabulary, and several lawyers and even petitioners for naturalization very occasionally had recourse to a more overtly "political" language about the "rights of citizens." But most of the technicians of civil law, those who argued or compiled case law on aliens at the end of the Old Regime, were deeply conservative and not, by any means, the producers or even the consumers of texts elaborating enlightened enrichments of citizenship.[102] Nonetheless, these technicians of the law offered a formidable critique of the late absolutist monarchy that dovetailed, however unintentionally, with the new political culture of late absolutism and the "enlightened" enrichments of the language of citizenship. They, too, invented "civil society."

The eighteenth-century lawyers consistently introduced a new distinction, largely ignored by their sixteenth- and seventeenth-century predecessors: between the droit d'aubaine as a royal right and prerogative (that could be or was abolished by treaties) and the capacity of foreigners to inherit, especially from French natives. From Bosquet to Ricard, the jurists developed this legal distinction that was founded on the ancient Roman division of the "law of nations" (*droit des gens*) and "civil law" (*droit civil*). The distinction ran parallel and overlapped with the natural law philosophers, and especially the Physiocrats, but the lawyers grounded their ideas of civil law less on principles of nature and natural rights. Instead, they drew on classical distinctions of Roman law that marked the boundaries of a "national" civil society around the question of property transmission.[103] According to the eighteenth-century jurists, the droit des gens, founded on natural law, gave all men the capacity to own or acquire property, to gift and to receive it among the living. But the capacity of members of a society to inherit property, especially from fellow "nationals," was independent of international law. Succession and inheritance were instead part of a narrower "civil law" as it had been defined by Justinian, "which each people constitutes for itself, which is unique to each."[104]

In the sixteenth and seventeenth centuries, Roman law provided the materials to fill the gaps and dissonance left by customary law and royal ordinances: it provided the "written reason" to justify specific decisions, even as jurists declared that "French law" was to be formally distinguished from Rome. In that period, learned jurists also derived the origins of the droit d'aubaine from Roman legal practices toward the peregrinus, even as they insisted on its functional value in drawing the boundaries between French citizens and foreigners. But in the eighteenth century, things changed. On the one hand, Roman law—poorly taught in the universities, and increasingly abandoned by professors of French law in the south—ceded primacy in the works of Domat, Bourjon, Pothier, and Portalis to "nature" and "reason" as the basis of a single common law of the kingdom.[105] On the other hand, jurists increasingly recognized the utility of the general framework of Roman law as a template for rethinking and codifying French civil law. Such was already the case with the Jansenist jurist Jean Domat, and it was increasingly the case among legal reformers of the eighteenth century. Roman law distinctions, then, but not Roman origins: historians have long noted the importance of Roman law in the making of the French Civil Code (1803), but they have not paid sufficient attention to the eighteenth-century debate over the complex relations between Roman law and the "common law" of France.[106]

The juridical redeployment of the Roman law distinction between the "law of nations" and "civil law" had profound implications in the legal struggles over the status of aliens and the droit d'aubaine. In a series of lawsuits that took shape after (and often as a result of) the French monarchy's abrupt dismantling of the droit d'aubaine beginning in the 1760s, jurists put forth a distinctive model of the droit d'aubaine that formally broke with the absolutist construction of their professional ancestors. If the droit d'aubaine was abolished (as a royal prerogative that ran counter to the "law of nations"), they argued, some form of incapacity would still persist on foreigners who sought to devolve or inherit property in the kingdom (as part of a "civil law").

Even the most royalist of the crown's apologists came to recognize the distinction. The king's solicitor in the Chambre des comptes during the 1730s, Lefebvre de la Planche, commenting on prior privileges and exemptions issued by French kings to specific national groups, underscored that the droit d'aubaine was a "right that belongs to the king on the inheritance of foreigners. Independent of this right, foreigners are incapable of receiving inheritances in

France. The letters are silent on this incapacity, which is an altogether different matter than the droit d'aubaine."[107] Practicing barristers, especially those arguing against the cases of reputed "foreigners" in civil lawsuits, went even further. They underscored how the collective exemptions and abolitions of the droit d'aubaine never amounted to naturalization itself. Bosquet glossed the conventions of the late 1760s, noting how they only provided a

> remittance that only concerns the king's right, and in no way includes anything that has not been expressly accorded. The capacity to inherit is one of the principal effects of civil law, which is specific to each nation, and affects only the members of that nation, such that the foreigner is not capable of exercising the civil law of another nation except by a special privilege through which the defect of foreignness [*vice de pérégrinité*] is effaced in him.[108]

Lefebvre's editor, the Roman law professor Paul Charles Lorry, who frequently disagreed with the author's absolutist inclinations, was in this case to amplify the author's discussion with an entire discourse about the varieties and gradations of inheritance capacities within French civil law. In his long footnote concerning the Dutch exemption from the droit d'aubaine, Lorry argued that the exemption from the droit d'aubaine had to be considered as a matter of degrees: there was a fundamental distinction between the capacity to inherit and to devolve property; the capacity to devolve property could involve either a French native or a foreigner; property could be either movable or immovable . . . [109] In short, he organized a system of classification, clearly inspired by the spirit of Roman law, that revealed at once the complexity of the question and the simple fact on which most eighteenth-century lawyers were to insist: faced with the abolition of the droit d'aubaine, they renewed the distinction, justified in Roman law, between a royal fiscal prerogative and the civil capacity of a foreigner to inherit or devolve property.

The juridical differentiation of the droit d'aubaine as royal prerogative from the question of inheritance predated the political conventions and treaties beginning in the 1760s. In fact, in a deeply ironic twist of legal and political history, this disassociation emerged within the "return" of Roman law in the eighteenth century, especially in the provinces of written or Roman law (*droit écrit*) in the south (and in the eastern provinces annexed from the Holy Roman Empire) where the absolute application of the droit d'aubaine had never fully succeeded. Such is revealed in the 1730s, when the lawyers of the Roman-law jurisdictions responded to a royal questionnaire intended to lead toward a formal legal codification of civil law. Chancellor d'Aguesseau's ambitious project to create positive statutes governing civil law, in order to limit the judicial discretion of the parlements and to create a "national" code of private law, was inscribed in a long monarchical tradition of legal codification and unification.[110] The project produced, after years of delay, only three general ordinances governing deeds (1731), wills (1735), and trusts (1747). The attempt to unify civil law failed in large measure because of the judicial resistance and foot-dragging of the provincial parlements, but also because of the impressive diversity of practices revealed in the questionnaire on disabilities sent to the sovereign courts of the kingdom in 1728.[111]

The first question of this fifty-two–point interrogation about "incapacity" was whether the droit d'aubaine was practiced in the jurisdiction, and the second was intimately related: "If bequests [*dispositions à cause de mort*] by an unnaturalized foreigner in favor of children or kin living in the kingdom are valid."[112] Unfortunately, only the responses from the Roman law provinces have survived; yet these are the most revealing, for they show how the lawyers and magistrates in Bordeaux, Grenoble, Pau, Toulouse, the Franche-Comté, and Alsace insisted on drawing a distinction between the royal droit d'aubaine and the civil capacity to inherit or devolve property—a distinction not made by sixteenth- and seventeenth-century legal apologists of the absolute citizen.[113]

The responses, of course, differed greatly in detail, but they were remarkably convergent: the lawyers who responded in the names of their respective parlements traced the origins of the droit d'aubaine directly to Roman civil law, at the same time that they distinguished the king's right to confiscate property from a dead alien from the capacity of a foreigner to inherit or devolve property in the province. Thus, like Jean Bodin and other sixteenth-century jurists, they continued to invoke the authority and origins of Rome, unlike the Enlightened critique of the droit d'aubaine that had squarely placed its origins in "feudal," customary law.

But the barristers who spoke for the magistrates of the provincial courts were caught in a legal conundrum. The droit d'aubaine derived from Rome, and their own legal culture, taught at the universities and produced in treatises and case-law compilations of decisions, was shaped by Roman law. But the droit d'aubaine, as a royal right of escheat, was never universally levied in their provinces, and thus was distinguished from the ability to deed or inherit property. Citing the early seventeenth-century jurisprudence of the Grenoble parlement, for example, the lawyers speaking for the Toulouse parlement argued that in their province as well the "droit d'aubaine is not levied," and the foreigner could will property and be instituted as an heir.[114] But other parlements that resisted the application of the droit d'aubaine, such as the Franche-Comté (annexed to France in 1678), still insisted that foreigners did not enjoy full civil rights, because they could not gather inheritances, either by will or otherwise, from French natives. As a lawyer for the Bésançon parlement wrote: "The king willingly does not take in escheat the goods of a foreigner; he abandons [his right], he gives the goods back. But if he renounces the droit d'aubaine, it is necessarily in order to favor his own subjects."[115] One lawyer for the parlement of Aix, where the droit d'aubaine did admittedly exist (despite the case he made for its exemption), argued that "the political interest worthy of the attention and the wisdom of our kings" was the true motive in collecting it. In particular, the purpose of the droit d'aubaine, in this jurisdiction of port cities and commercial centers more attuned than most to the flight risks of capital, was to "forbid the export of money, to attract citizens, to retain or recall natural Frenchmen to their fatherland: these are the principles that one should follow in this area of public law." Not surprisingly, then, even the lawyers who recognized the droit d'aubaine insisted that nonnaturalized and foreign children could not inherit, except by the "grandeur and generosity of a pure favor bestowed by the king" in the letter of naturalization.[116] However much they differed on the subject of monarchical generosity or natural right, all made the distinction between a fiscal prerogative of the monarchy and the ability of foreigners to inherit or devolve property.

There were two responses from the parlement of Aix to d'Aguesseau's questionnaire of 1728 that anticipated claims made several decades later within the citizenship revolution—that the abolition of the droit d'aubaine should also confer on foreigners the capacity to inherit property, even from French citizens. The lawyer Pazéry wrote that "it would be desirable, for the interest of the State and the glory of the King, that this fiscal law be restrained, and that the native-born and resident kin be allowed to inherit: this favor would invite and attract foreigners." The counsellor Montvalon of the Aix parlement went even further, arguing that "the interest of commerce" and the state should authorize bequests for foreigners "in favor of children, brothers, uncles, and nephews living in the kingdom even if not naturalized, and allow for no distinction between French and naturalized foreigners."[117]

Such anticipations of what the foreign ministry was actually to accomplish in the treaties from 1765 to 1782, the second volley of the citizenship revolution, were few and far between. In the early 1740s, when the parlements in the districts of written law finally got around, after great delay, to responding to d'Aguesseau's questionnaire, they generally distinguished the droit d'aubaine from the civil capacity to gather or devolve an inheritance, and their arguments amounted to the claim that even should the former be abolished, the latter still had the force of law.

Twenty years later, in the midst of the treaties and conventions abolishing the droit d'aubaine or exempting specific groups of foreign subjects, a series of lawsuits brought on appeal before the Paris parlement—whose jurisprudence was founded on customary law, but acknowledged the role of royal statutes and case law—sought to clarify the meaning of the droit d'aubaine's abolition and the nature of French nationality. Lawyers argued, obviously, on both sides of the question, for and against the distinction between a royal prerogative and a civil incapacity to inherit. But the magistrates of the Paris parlement tended to rule in favor of reputed foreigners who, exempted from the droit d'aubaine by international treaty or convention, were thereby allowed to inherit, even from French natives. In this way, the dominant jurisprudence offered an interpretation of the meaning of citizenship that was not to be found in the initial governmental justifications but that the government was eventually to accept.

Beginning in the early eighteenth century and running parallel to the monarchy's first piecemeal attempts to dismantle the droit d'aubaine in specific cases, parliamentary jurisprudence tended to favor the inheritance rights of foreigners. The Paris parlement ruled precociously in 1715 in favor of the Dutch (the case of *Marguerite de la Cherois v. Marie and Jeanne-Catherine Vekems*, born in the Netherlands), disallowing the claims of a collateral heir born in France, over a direct one born in Holland. But the subsequent jurisprudence of the Paris parlement, although occasionally favorable to future Dutch claims of a similar nature in the eighteenth century, was resolved only after the international convention was signed with the United Provinces (23 July 1773).[118] For the Dutch, as for other foreigners, the Paris parlement conclusively ruled in the 1780s in favor of the foreigner's ability to inherit from a French kinsman, even a collateral one.

One of the more important cases of the 1780s that touched on what, exactly, had been accomplished by the treaties of the citizenship revolution was that of the Sieur d'Ellevaux et consorts, from the bishopric of Liège, who appealed to the highest court in 1786 against the Chevalier d'Estres, a native-born Frenchman.[119] The case dated from the death in 1778 of the French widow of a liégeois seigneur, and pitted five French collateral maternal relatives, all first cousins, against her daughter Madeleine d'Estres, who had been born in Liège, and eventually her grandson, also born in Liège. In fact, until her own death in 1781, the daughter had "enjoyed her succession," but at that moment the maternal first cousins filed a lawsuit against her son, claiming that he was Liegeois, and that they were French. As usual, there were several related questions to decide, but central to these was the juridical status of the 1768 treaty with the "State of Liège." Did it allow Liégeois to inherit from their French kin? And were native-born Liégeois, but children of a French woman, to be excluded from the conditions dictated by the treaty?

Concerning the first question, lawyers for the Chevalier d'Estres argued that the treaty represented the "simple remittance of the fiscal right of escheat, since the motives of the convention were to firm up, to multiply the relations of friendship and kinship between the respective subjects." But since it did not explicitly permit Liégeois to inherit from French natives, the second question was, in their argument, moot.

In response, the defendant—the lawyer of Sieur d'Ellevaux—argued in the first instance that Madeleine d'Estres had never abandoned her identity as a Frenchwoman, even though her ancestors had been born abroad. For one, the 1669 anti-emigration statute did not apply to foreigners who chose to live abroad, and Maître Molé cited Cardin Le Bret's maxim, an interpretation of the French freedom principle: "The French are free, not slaves." He pointed out that the edict of 1669 concerned Protestants during the civil wars, whereas

Madeleine d'Estres was a good Catholic. More important, the "presumption of the law" (itself a juridical fiction) was that she did not establish herself in Liège without the king's permission, and that she continued to "belong" (*faire corps*) to her family in France. In a remarkable argument, Maître Molé echoed the Old Regime jurists more generally in their opinions about descendants of expatriate French nationals who had left the kingdom, whether for reasons of religious persecution or otherwise: their descendants did not inherit the disabilities that may have been incurred by their parents, or grandparents, according to the 1669 ordinance. This argument could be read as a claim against the "principle" of descent, what the nineteenth century would somewhat misleadingly call the *droit de sang*. But Molé put it in a way that emphasized the notion of lineage. Echoing d'Aguesseau, he argued that the incapacities of the father cannot detract from the rights of children, "from the right that blood has transmitted to them, that they hold from their ancestors." Sr. d'Ellevaux had never lost his French identity, because his mother had been born of French parents in Liège and he had returned to the kingdom of France.

Maître Molé's first argument, then, was conventional and in keeping with jurisprudential tendencies of the eighteenth century. But it also reflected, however dimly, an Enlightenment view of "rights," and he even used the language of an "international community" of rights, pontificating about how "nations have recognized that it would be absurd to establish an indefinite right against emigrants and their descendants."[120] Molé then produced a second and contradictory argument: as was common in the rhetorical strategies of lawyers in the Old Regime (and indeed, today), Molé argued that *even if* Madeleine d'Estres was to be considered as a native of the bishopric of Liège, her son would still have the capacity to inherit her property. As proof of this argument, he cited at length the Paris parlement's decision permitting the Dutch to inherit from the French in 1715; a 1781 decision by the Paris parlement permitting an English woman to inherit from her brother, who had died in France, against the claims of French kin (who argued that she should have been excluded as a religious refugee). He also invoked the Châtelet's 1784 decision in favor of the daughter of a French woman married to a Portuguese man who claimed, not her maternal filiation, but her paternal origins. And he invoked the cause célèbre of the *Comtesse Doria v. Marie Jeanne Bellow* and heirs that was decided on appeal at the Paris parlement on 3 April 1784. The case was important because it began in 1775, with the Portuguese comtesse Doria's death, and was initially decided by the Paris parlement in 1781 in favor of the French-born Bellow (herself descended from an Irish gentleman who died shortly thereafter). Before the liquidation of the estate, Marie Jeanne Bellow died, and two of her heirs forced the case to be reopened. When it was, Maître Polverel for the comtesse Doria took note of the 1778 convention with Portugal, and argued that the treaty rendered her capable of inheriting from a French woman. The Grand 'Chambre of the Châtelet in Paris heard arguments on both sides; these turned on the very definition of the "droit d'aubaine." Was it a mere fiscal right of the king, or was it a generic incapacity "attached to the vice of foreignness" that included the inability to gather an inheritance in the kingdom? The court thought the former, and decided in favor of Doria. On appeal to the Paris parlement, Joly de Fleury, as solicitor general, upheld that decision. The abolition of the droit d'aubaine definitively entailed the "right to inherit among kin without regard to nation."[121]

In the case of d'Ellevaux, the question of Portugal opened Maître Molé's proof in his second argument: France's 1768 treaty with Liège was identical to that with Portugal in 1778, on the basis of which the magistrates of the Paris parlement had ruled that Portuguese nationals could inherit the estates of French kin and citizens.[122] Molé glossed the question as a general principle: the ability to inherit, far from being a "rare privilege," was "the common law, the original law of Nations," and all incapacities were exceptions "against the law of nature and of hospitality." The distinction between fiscal privilege and native right was false. He admitted to two original meanings of the droit d'aubaine, but the efforts of the absolutist monarchy had borne fruit: the authorities Molé cited—Vattel, Claude de Ferrière, Chancellor d'Aguesseau (although misquoted)—had all defined the droit d'aubaine as a general incapacity to inherit, not simply as a "fiscal law" (*droit du fisc*). In all the treaties signed between France and the German principalities, the droit d'aubaine was understood in its "general and unlimited exceptions." "Not a word," he argued in a close reading of the 1768 text, "as can be seen in this convention, which limits the abolition of the droit d'aubaine to a purely fiscal law." Although Molé offered a literalist reading of the treaties, he did not argue original intention, and offered to the crown the final decision in the matter: "Only sovereigns themselves can interpret their treaties; they alone can declare what they wanted, what they promised."[123] In the end, the court ruled in favor of Sieur d'Ellevaux, as Molé's arguments proved persuasive.

Lawyers continued to litigate the estates claimed by French native heirs, who tended to be less closely linked by kinship ties, against the presumptive claims of "foreign" collateral heirs. Jurisprudential arguments did, in fact, interpret royal policy. Lawyers tended to argue successfully that the political abolitions of the droit d'aubaine amounted to the effacement of the principal juridical distinction between citizens and foreigners. The citizenship revolution had abolished the legal framework of French nationality.

Perhaps the most important of these lawsuits was the collective grievance against the Abbé Lemmens, born in Maastricht, a town of divided jurisdiction between Liège and the United Provinces. Lemmens stood to inherit a valuable estate, part of which was in the Caribbean colony of Saint-Domingue, worth the princely sum of 640,000 livres (not including the 53 slaves [*têtes de nègres*], worth another 150,000 livres). The object of several published *factums*, the case pitted the claim of a paternal uncle of two insane children, the last of whom had died in 1780, against three maternal first cousins. The latter, represented by Rousseau des Fontenelles, *conseiller au parlement de Bretagne*, argued that the town of Maastricht was not, technically, included in the treaties with the Dutch. Even if it were, he reasoned, Lemmens would have no right to inherit the properties. Lemmens was legally "incapable": he had no permanent domicile in France (Brabant was his "real" one); he was a foreigner (proven by his having posted bond, the *judicatum solvi*, for this very lawsuit), but most of all, the treaties between Holland and France "only contain a simple remission of the droit d'aubaine; none of them mention the abolition of foreignness [*pérégrinité*]."124

Moreover, a careful reading of the treaty with Holland convinced Rousseau that it contained no such clause specifically permitting foreigners to inherit. On the other side of the aisle, Lemmens and his lawyer argued that a phrase in Article 1 of the treaty, "that the French and the Dutch will be treated in every way and everywhere as natural subjects of the authority of the country where they would reside," in fact allowed Dutch to inherit from French natives. They also cited the earlier court decisions of 1715 and 1760 in their favor. The 1760 decision by the Paris parlement had coincided with the Dutch Estates General's declaration that the French could inherit from its own natural subjects of the United Provinces. According to Rousseau des Fontenelles, it was the spirit of this act, and the court decision itself, that led to the 1773 treaty.125

The Paris parlement ruled in favor of Lemmens in 1781, and continued to rule consistently until the French Revolution that the abolition of the droit d'aubaine in the international treaties of the eighteenth century gave foreigners the capacity to inherit from French citizens. Having helped to construct the droit d'aubaine as a tool of absolutism that served to distinguish "French" from "foreign," the lawyers at parlement were complicit in the eradication of this juridical difference, claiming that the foreign ministry had put "native-born subjects" on the same footing as "aliens." In 1801, when the droit d'aubaine was partially reinstituted, and again in 1819, when the final debates raged about its abolition, lawyers and politicians who favored drawing a clear legal distinction between citizens and foreigners were less certain about what the eighteenth-century treaties had accomplished. The jurist Jean-Baptiste Gaschon, for example, whose compilation and commentary informed the parliamentary opposition to the final abolition of the droit d'aubaine in 1819, was convinced that without an explicit mention of "positive" inheritance rights, the conventions exempting or abolishing foreign subjects from the droit d'aubaine did not permit them to inherit from French nationals.126 It is true, as Gaschon underscored, that the treaties were largely silent about the possibility of foreigners inheriting from French citizens, and vice-versa, between countries where the droit d'aubaine had been mutually abolished or exempted. But, as the lawyer Molé was to point out in 1786, "whatever the talent, the enlightenment of a jurisconsult, his counsel is but an opinion, and the declaration of the Sovereign is a Law."[127] So what *had* been the intention of the sovereign, the king, and especially that of his foreign ministers who negotiated the treaties?

The crown's clarification of its intentions—or perhaps, its post-facto justifications for earlier decisions written into the bilateral accords—took shape within diplomatic debates that centered on the relations between France and the Austrian Low Countries. In fact, French-Austrian discussions that helped to crystallize French intentions occurred with reference to two distinct geographic arenas of contestation. The first involved France's northeastern borderland with the Low Countries, when the arguments of ordinary litigants passed into the mouths of the French foreign minister Vergennes and the imperial ambassador comte Florimond de Mercy-Argenteau. The other was in France's colonies, and once again, it was Mercy-Argenteau who unwittingly helped to solidify a French consensus on the nature of the droit d'aubaine and its abolition.[128]

Mercy-Argenteau paid a lot of attention to the question of the droit d'aubaine in the early 1770s: unlike the French foreign minister, who was preoccupied with what a French publicist called "the great undertakings," the problem was quite high on the list of diplomatic priorities established by the court at Vienna. In response to a series of incidents involving the inability of Austrian subjects to inherit from their French kin, but also the question of Austrian clerics who held benefices and offices in the French kingdom, the comte de Mercy-Argenteau insisted on the "maxim" that in light of the 1766 treaties, the respective subjects of the two crowns would be treated in all manners "as if" they were natural subjects of their respective realms. The treaties, in effect, required that "the respective subjects" of the two monarchies "be considered from here on as a single nation," thus allowing nonnative (and unnaturalized) heirs to inherit, according to the same kinship rules in force, as native subjects.[129]

In fact, it was in ministerial debates and judicial lawsuits over the question of France's overseas colonies—the second arena of contention—that the crown's policy finally crystallized. Before the exemptions of the 1760s, official policy and French jurisprudence concurred that, unless specifically exempted, foreigners in the colonies were subject to the droit d'aubaine just as they were in the kingdom itself. In the case of the colonies, however, the monarchy's (and tax-farmer's) insistence on collecting this royal due was strengthened by the more general prohibitions of foreigners trading in the colonies. In royal letters patent of October 1727, the crown reiterated the prohibition of trade between colonial subjects and foreigners (including those with letters of naturalization).[130] Even after the commercial impact of the American Revolution in the Caribbean prompted the French monarchy to gradually dismantle the scaffolding of mercantilism, resulting in the trade edict of 1784 that opened the ports of Saint-Domingue and other Caribbean possessions to "foreign" trade, foreigners were still prohibited from deeding or inheriting property from other foreigners or French natives.[131]

The "colonial question," at least as it concerned the droit d'aubaine, thus went largely uncontested before the 1760s. But in that decade, and especially after the treaties with Spain (1762) and Austria (1766) abolishing the droit d'aubaine, the question of the colonies came to the fore. In the broader context of debates over what Malick Ghachem has called the principle of "interiority" (the separate civil law of the colonies, founded on local knowledge and in tension with the aspirations of uniformity in the colonial Enlightenment), a series of specific cases in the late 1760s and early 1770s brought the colonial question to the attention of the foreign minister and the royal council itself.[132]

The claims of Sr. Tosgobby, an archpriest born in Masslingo, in the northern diocese of Lodi in Italy that depended on the Austrian monarchy, was the subject of a specific diplomatic disagreement from which a general resolution was taken. Tosgobby claimed the inheritance of his brother who had died in Saint-Domingue, and whose will was contested by the tax-farmers of the king because he was a foreigner, a subject of the imperial empress. France and Austria had agreed in 1766 to mutually and reciprocally abolish the droit d'aubaine, and the exact meaning of that abolition was now brought into question. Once again, it was the indefatigable ambassador of the empress who produced the arguments that led the French monarchy to articulate its intentions in abolishing the droit d'aubaine. Ambassador Mercy-Argenteau held to the strict principle of complete reciprocity in the 1766 treaty. There was no disaccord in theory: the French foreign ministry too argued that the "basic principle" was one of reciprocity. Rather, the disagreement was over its application. According to the marine minister, the marquis de Boynes, extending the abolition of the droit d'aubaine to the colonies could only be done in a reciprocal manner. Austria, however, was a ramshackle, largely landlocked kingdom without colonial possessions of any importance. No reciprocity was therefore possible, and France could continue to collect the droit d'aubaine from Austrian subjects in the colonies, including those of the archpriest Tosgobby.[133]

In fact, the colonial droit d'aubaine became, for several years, a rather urgent matter of state, and dozens of memoranda were drafted and exchanged between the ministries of the marine and foreign affairs, and with the court at Vienna. In these writings, it was clear to all parties that Spain was the only country with which France had signed an accord (in 1762) that specified that the exemption from the droit d'aubaine would take place only with respect to possessions in Europe. For the French, the omission of any mention of colonial possessions had been deliberate and intentional; for the Austrians, the omission of such a clause in their own treaty implicitly extended the abolition of the droit d'aubaine to all territorial possessions of the respective monarchs. But the French government held to an ironclad rule of reciprocity concerning England and Spain (which still prohibited foreigners from trading in their possessions, even if they were naturalized). In the case of Austrian subjects in the colonies, marquis de Boynes argued, the crown should in principle enforce the droit d'aubaine—even if royal practice was more lenient. Writing in 1772, Boynes noted:

> If, on the one hand, the courts of the French colonies have exactly maintained the droit d'aubaine, when such occasions were presented, the king, on the other hand, wished in several cases to abandon this right and remit to foreign heirs the bequests that belonged to them. I have found, on this point, a rule consistently followed with respect to Spaniards on the island of Saint-Domingue who, being drawn daily into commercial operations on the French part of this island, have disposed of their goods by last will and testament and whose [Spanish] heirs have gathered their inheritances.[134]

He went on to cite a half-dozen cases where the king had offered remissions, without ever endangering the principle of the application. Still, the question continued to plague the authorities in the 1770s—especially because the royal official charged with collecting the droit d'aubaine in the colonies (where tax-farming was not practiced) continued to seize the properties of foreigners who died in Saint-Domingue.[135]

But the local sovereign courts of the French Caribbean tended to overrule the fiscal courts, and by the late 1770s the magistrates of Saint-Domingue were acting as if the abolition of the droit d'aubaine actually extended to the colonies, ruling consistently in favor of foreigners who inherited from French natives. On 4 June 1777, the minister of the marine wrote to underscore official policy that "these treaties should never be extended to the Americas," but the question was hardly resolved. Two years later, the Spaniard Buondia died in Saint-Domingue and his heirs cited the patent letters of July 1766 in their favor. Again, the minister of the marine stepped in to clarify the situation, and on 25 July 1779 decreed once more that the abolition of the droit d'aubaine did not include the colonies.[136]

Yet even if this was not the final word from the French government, the argument had clarified the nature of the droit d'aubaine itself. For the lawyers arguing in favor of "foreign" claimants to successions opened in France, the droit d'aubaine was more than a royal and fiscal prerogative: it included the inability to inherit as well. The abolition of the droit d'aubaine may not have extended to France's colonial possessions, but it did entail, at least in the metropole, the ability of foreigners to inherit from French natives, and vice versa. Not successoral capacity but political reciprocity lay at the heart of the foreign ministry's concerns about abolishing the droit d'aubaine. Constructed in the sixteenth and seventeenth centuries as a pillar of absolutism that included the incapacities of foreigners to inherit in the kingdom, the droit d'aubaine came tumbling down in the late eighteenth century, and with it fell the principal legal distinction between citizens and foreigners.

It was the simple obstinacy of Austrian ambassador Mercy-Argenteau that forced Foreign Minister d'Aiguillon to seek further clarification from Chancellor Maupeou, who was otherwise occupied in his dismissal of the venal judges of the French parlements from their offices. In May 1773, the French chancellor ruled as forcefully as he had when he had spoken to the magistrates themselves:

> The droit d'aubaine, Monsieur, having been abolished between the subjects of the King and those of the Empire, they must be seen, concerning their right to inherit, as the true and natural subjects of their respective States. Towards them, as towards others, the ordinary rules of inheritance apply, and I do not see on what basis any difference toward them could be argued. . . . Only their successoral proximity must matter in all cases. . . . On this matter, Monsieur, this is the rule which it seems to me must be followed in the respective states concerning the droit d'aubaine, and if some of our courts diverge in this regard, the king shall not forget to remind them of it.[137]

This unflinching interpretation of the treaties abolishing the droit d'aubaine was reiterated in subsequent cases by subsequent ministers. In the words of the marquis de Boynes, who had disagreed with the intent of the international accords, the letter of the treaties required that "foreigners must be treated in every respect as native residents."[138] Postrevolutionary jurisprudence, reconsidering the abolitions of the droit d'aubaine in light of their partial restoration in 1801, was not to agree. Ultimately, the courts were to side with the lawyer Gaschon, who argued in 1819 that the Old Regime's multiple abolitions of the droit d'aubaine did not entail the capacity of foreigners to inherit from French citizens. In decisions of 1801 and 1825, the Paris court of appeals turned away from the dominant jurisprudence of the eighteenth century.[139] It also ran counter to the political consensus of the French government before 1789: the abolition of the droit d'aubaine necessarily entailed complete inheritance rights for foreigners.

The distinction between the alien tax and the civil capacity to inherit or will property was therefore not part of the state's vision. Absolutism had sealed the fate of the droit d'aubaine, linking a royal right of confiscation to the inheritance capacities of the foreigner. The international conventions, treaties, and royal letters patent that during the mid-eighteenth century abolished or exempted specific groups of foreigners from the droit d'aubaine were largely silent about specific inheritance rights, but in the 1770s, the government made it clear that it had been the king's intention had been, at least in retrospect, to efface the inheritance restrictions on foreigners in the kingdom.

An Incomplete Revolution: Politics, Police, and the Postabsolute Citizen

"The spirit of conquest and the spirit of commerce are mutually exclusive in a nation," wrote Jean-François Melon, close friend of Montesquieu, in his 1734 *Essai politique sur le commerce*.[140] He was reiterating what had been a commonplace to the critics of Louis XIV during the difficult years of the 1690s, when the Sun King turned his back on the "France of movement" and attempted to tax the foreign population of the kingdom. By the middle of the eighteenth century, however, the crown's position was reversed: the era of annexations was over, and commerce, taxation, and administration became the primary concerns of the modernizing state. "This is no longer a time of conquests," the marquis d'Argenson famously wrote in his memoirs after he was disgraced in 1747 as foreign minister of Louis XV. "France must be satisfied with its greatness and extension. It is time to start governing, after spending so much time acquiring what to govern."[141] Indeed, in a period of relative international weakness, and as part of the last phase of absolutism, France's political modernization amounted to a "practical cosmopolitanism" partially inspired by the physiocratic reform movement of the 1750s and 1760s. The ministers and officials of Louis XV and Louis XVI came to insist on the freedoms of "commerce" and "communication" among European states, and especially on the abolition of the droit d'aubaine as a "feudal" obstacle to the progress of civilization. Although the language of citizenship never appeared in these negotiations, subsequent jurisprudence made it clear that in the period of late absolutism, the crown had, at times unwittingly, abolished the central legal distinction between Frenchmen and women, on the one hand, and foreigners, on the other.

Having abolished such legal distinctions, however, the crown hardly effaced the political ones. The foreign ministry's concern for parity and reciprocity in diplomatic negotiations offers a hint that the assimilation between citizens and foreigners was far from complete. Indeed, in an entirely different context, the failure to assimilate the status of foreigners and French nationals is revealed most dramatically. At the same moment that France abolished, piecemeal and conditionally, the droit d'aubaine, at a time when the rhetoric of the political citizen became central to French political culture, the foreign ministry in Paris perfected its bureaucratic and routinized administration of policing the foreign population of the capital city. The late eighteenth-century monarchy, and especially the foreign ministry in collusion with the Paris lieutenant general of police, refined this more political definition and mechanism of policing foreigners.[142] Just as the monarchy developed administrative tools to police the black population in Paris in 1776, and just as the provincial administrations put in place similar mechanisms to police Muslims in Provence and Protestants in

Alsace, so too—and more elaborately—did the royal council perfect in the 1770s the administrative institutions with which to police foreigners, at least in Paris.[143]

Indeed, the citizenship revolution of the second half of the eighteenth century—the rhetorical and political construction of the "citizen" in public debates, alongside the elimination of the principal legal distinction between citizens and foreigners in international law—could even be said to have included a third dimension: a renewed emphasis on the "police" of the foreign population. This was especially the case in Paris, at a time when perhaps two-thirds of the city's residents were "foreigners"—from the provinces and beyond.[144] At the center of the non-French population were the diplomatic milieus so closely watched by the spies and informants of the lieutenant general of police in Paris, the archival traces of which date back to the 1720s.[145] But the monarchy's administrative gaze came to extend far beyond such milieus, eventually monitoring all foreigners *de passage* in the capital city. Of course, the municipal policing of foreigners was an ancient preoccupation: the registers of the Paris administration reveal the collaboration of the municipal elite with the crown in registering foreigners from the early fourteenth century and throughout the early modern period (edicts of 1577, 1584, 1617, 1620, 1632, 1693, and 1707 although none of the actual records have been found).[146] But after the middle of the eighteenth century, coinciding with the multiple and reciprocal treaties that abolished or exempted foreign subjects from the droit d'aubaine, the foreign ministry paid a renewed attention to policing foreigners, especially in the capital city.

The administrative history of policing foreigners in Paris was one of increasing specialization, with the responsibility resting first with the lieutenant general of police under Louvois (1667), then with an *inspecteur de police* with other responsibilities, such as the *police des moeurs* (1708). In 1752, an inspector was named whose only task was to "police all the foreigners, especially the ambassadors and ministers, to arrest undesirables and suspects, and to keep the seals placed on all their papers and effects." Officially called an *inspecteur de police chargé de la partie des étrangers*, he took responsibility for the administrative inspection of boardinghouses and rented rooms, and for the surveillance of the ambassadorial milieu, in which a large network of his own spies and informants (*mouches*) were employed. Lieutenant General of Police Gabriel de Sartine, who held the office from 1759 to 1774, put the finishing touches on this administrative machinery.[147]

This administrative practice of policing foreigners reached its fullest extent in the 1770s, during the last years of the reign of Louis XV, and at a time when most of the conventions abolishing the droit d'aubaine had been put in place. The surviving registers of the "lodging control" (*contrôle des garnis*) and of the "neighborhood surveillance of foreigners" (*surveillance des étrangers par quartiers*) date precisely from this period. These biweekly reports on all the foreigners lodged in Paris were sent directly to the minister of foreign affairs. Jean-François Dubost has presented a complete portrait of the transient foreign population, tourists and merchants, aristocrats and peddlers who passed through Paris during the 1770s and 1780s. Vincent Millot has detailed the notions of "public security" and the "police" implicated in the practices. What is important here is the timing: Was it a mere coincidence that this uninterrupted paper trail of registering foreigners begins only in the 1770s? Perhaps, but the 1770s were critical in all sorts of ways: at the moment that the state was effacing the *legal* distinction between foreigner and national, the *administrative* and *political* apparatus of identifying foreigners in the capital became fully functional.

Thus, the unfinished revolution of citizenship. Unfinished, because when the French Revolution broke out in 1789, the postabsolute model of the citizen had still not acquired a definitive shape. On the one hand, in the public arena, the citizen was increasingly an (adult, male, property-owning) actor in pursuit of the public good, if not a patriot, one willing to be taxed but demanding political representation as its cost. At the same time, the very fact that citizenship was premised on the possession of property, as opposed to the inheritance of property across generations, in and of itself signified the shift of the citizen from the world of nationality law to politics.

In the domain of French private or civil law, and in what can only be called private international law, the identity of the citizen, as distinct from the foreigner, was not resolved before the French Revolution. Universally, the droit d'aubaine had been condemned, and politically, in the international conventions from 1765 to 1782, it had been dismantled in a piecemeal fashion, even if a general abolition was not to appear before 1790. Forced by the lawyers litigating cases between French and foreign heirs, the Paris parlement, the foreign ministry, and the royal chancellery of the late eighteenth century admitted that the government had eliminated the principal legal distinction between citizens and others, which was the incapacity of foreigners to inherit. Yet neither the government nor the lawyers elaborated on the resulting significance of the new citizen.

There were important and unintended consequences to the dismantling of the absolute citizen at the end of the Old Regime. The crown had used the droit d'aubaine to build absolute authority; the feudal due became a juridical marker of national difference but also an unquestioned mark of sovereignty. The abolition of the droit d'aubaine inevitably put into question the nature of absolutism itself, and in the decades before the Revolution, the crown struggled to redefine its political authority on a new foundation. More precisely, the removal of the droit d'aubaine from royal policy left the legal boundaries of citizenship undefined.

What, after the abolitions and conventions from 1765 to 1782, would ultimately distinguish the "citizen" from the "foreigner"? Lawyers turned their attention, in practice, to the legal incapacities of foreigners to inherit. The foreign ministry turned its attention to the administrative policing of the foreign population, especially in Paris. But the public debate in which the citizen had become primarily an actor in the political arena, and in which, collectively, citizens came to constitute the nation as the source of sovereignty, burst its bounds to create a series of unanticipated consequences with the outbreak of the French Revolution of 1789.

NATURALIZATION AND THE DROIT D'AUBAINE FROM THE FRENCH REVOLUTION TO THE BOURBON RESTORATION

T he Revolution of 1789 marked a profound rupture in the political life of France, and nowhere is this more evident than in the history of citizenship. The *Declaration of the Rights of Man and the Citizen* of August 1789 empowered citizens individually, as the equal subjects of rights, and collectively as the nation, the source of sovereignty.[1] From the Estates General to the Constituent Assembly, in the process leading to the radical Republic of 1792, deputies elected by voters with varying degrees of property qualifications were the active citizens shaping the new political order. Amplifying and putting into practice the new political citizen of the late eighteenth century, but rupturing with the Old Regime in proclaiming the principle of equality and in making the nation and its citizens the locus of sovereignty, the revolutionaries perfected the modern citizen as political actor.

Of course, such a universal and democratic citizenship was socially and politically limited in practice. Sociologically, citizenship ran on two tracks. From the beginning, "passive citizens" (women, children, and other legally incapable persons) were distinct from "active" ones (male, independent property holders) with the right to participate politically. Written into the 1791 Constitution, the distinction was temporarily elided in constitutional law and political practice. During the first radical republican experiment with popular government amid war and terror, at the rhetorical height of the Revolution itself, citizenship became foremost a claim about the boundaries of political loyalty to the New Regime, and not about the legal difference between French and foreigner. Jean-Lambert Tallien, ex-fiscal clerk and radical deputy to the Convention, epitomized the revolutionary idea of the citizen in his oft-cited remark that "the only foreigners in France are bad citizens."[2] Legal and political foreigners—émigrés, refractory priests, aristocrats, and geographical foreigners—were to be lumped together as enemies of the nation. Before the end of the radical Republic in thermidor year III (July 1794), according to most historical accounts, the French Revolution affirmed citizenship as a category of political loyalty while effacing the legal boundaries of French nationality. It was only with the enactment of the first article of the Civil Code in 1803 that a distinction between citizenship and "nationality" (what contemporaries called the *qualité de français* [quality of being French]) was to be clearly articulated.[3]

Attention to the legal and political history of the droit d'aubaine and naturalization in these years brings a different perspective to the problem of revolutionary citizenship. It offers a different lens to examine the ruptures and continuities between the Old Regime and the French Revolution, and helps to revise our understanding of nationality law and practices in 1789 and after. Between 1789 and 1819, the regime governing the droit d'aubaine changed four times: the institution itself was in constant mutation.

The revolutionaries continued the project of the late absolutist monarchy in abolishing the "feudal" remains of a barbaric past. But they went further, stressing not the state's commercial interests but the philosophical fraternity and unity of peoples as the rationale of its abolition. In fact, abolished in four different ways in 1790–91, the "droit d'aubaine" was rhetorically and conceptually reconfigured. A much reduced version, understood as a successoral incapacity alone, was restored in the Civil Code, on a limited and conditional basis; parliamentarians and peace treaties after the defeat of Napoleon affirmed the continued practice of this new and limited "droit d'aubaine" in 1814, which was finally abolished in 1819 after extensive debate. In its reformulations, the droit d'aubaine took on a radically different form and function than under the Old Regime: it became uncoupled from the practice of naturalization. In the period from 1789 to the Bourbon Restoration, naturalization also changed in meaning and functions, losing its strong tie to inheritance and property, and eventually becoming ineffably linked to political participation.

In 1790 the Constituent Assembly abandoned the practice of conferring individual grants of citizenship and established an "automatic" naturalization of foreigners who met the statutory requirements of public law. In revolutionary France, naturalization was no longer a discretionary intervention of the sovereign (despite the symbolic and honorary naturalizations of 1792); it was no longer a "grace" or a "favor" of the king or the representatives of the nation. Especially in the early years of the French Revolution, an unprecedented number of foreigners (men and women) became French nationals not because the state forcibly naturalized them, as in 1697, nor because they sought to become citizens for reasons of property, office, or benefice, as in the Old Regime. "Naturalization" (involving differing degrees of automaticity and requirements of voluntary declarations) took place without the discretionary intervention of the revolutionary state.

But the New Regime turned Old: after 1799, Napoleon Bonaparte, the military hero turned French emperor in 1804, reinstated the discretionary practices of naturalization (by laws of 1802 and 1808) that permitted foreign men of service to the state or society to become citizens. In 1814–15, the restored Bourbon monarch Louis XVIII became the authoritarian but constitutional ruler of a bicameral government, and the administrative and legal practices of naturalization were reaffirmed. Much had been changed by the revolutionary experiments in law and politics between 1789 and 1815: although the vocabulary, and often the texts themselves, of naturalization underscored an apparent continuity with the Old Regime, the meaning of citizenship, naturalization, and the droit d'aubaine itself were transformed. Citizenship became identified exclusively with the right of political participation; the Civil Code was to formally distinguish the exercise of political rights from civil ones. But until the Civil Code, and even afterward, the imbrication of "nationality" and "citizenship" was a highly complex experiment, subject to contradictory and conflicting political ideals beginning with the legislation of 1790 that automatically naturalized foreigners in the kingdom.

Society over the State:
Automatic Naturalization in the New Regime

The citizenship revolution of the eighteenth century shaped (even if it was anticipated by) the consistent decline of individual naturalizations at the end of the Old Regime. This decline, especially in the 1780s, was reversed slightly in the tumultuous year of 1789, when thirty-seven foreigners—no doubt anxious to protect their properties and offices from the impending storm—sought naturalizations or declarations of naturalization. In substance, the naturalizations of 1789 and 1790 hardly seemed inflected by the revolutionary upheavals. In February 1789, as the Abbé Sieyès drafted *Qu'est ce que le Tiers-Etat?*, and as all of France drew up statements of grievances (*cahiers de doléances*) to be presented to the Estates General (within which the occasional denunciation of the droit d'aubaine could be heard),[4] Frédéric Desforges received the more prosaic and self-interested grant of a declaration of naturalization. Born in Hamburg of French stock ("established for over three hundred years" in the kingdom), he had grown up in Rouen, but sought a career as a cleric that took him to Rome and then, in the service of the French ambassador, to Russia. Clearly, he thought himself in line for a major benefice, a world apart from the ideas and practices fermenting throughout the kingdom.[5] Others who became citizens remained equally oblivious to the political events around them. Thus, as the Estates General met in Versailles in May 1789 and the Third Estate took on the title of the National Assembly, Pierre Chomel received his recognition of citizenship. A descendant of Huguenot refugees who fled to Berlin in 1684, Chomel resorted to the then formulaic claim about how he was "recalled to our state by the love of his old fatherland, wishing to establish himself [in France] and to finish his days under our dominion."[6] His letter testifies to the continuing problem of Huguenot refugees more than a century after the Edict of

Fontainebleau. The National Assembly eventually debated and resolved the Protestant diaspora question, one element in the relation between religion and citizenship, by the law of 9–15 December 1790. "All persons who, born in foreign countries, descend in whatever degree from a Frenchman or woman who expatriated for reasons of religion are declared to be French natives [*naturels français*] and to possess the rights attached to this quality, if they return to France, establish their domicile, and give the civic oath." The law reestablished the right of Protestant descendants who returned to the kingdom to become French citizens while implicitly emphasizing the legal principle of descent.[7]

In 1789, as in the last decades of the Old Regime, most of the foreigners seeking French citizenship were clerics motivated by a desire to hold benefices and to assure that their estates could be inherited by their kin. Jean Ambrois Parin received a declaration of naturalization with permission to hold benefices in August through the intervention (unnecessary but useful) of the foreign ministry, days before the night of 4 August when the National Assembly dismantled, in a stroke, the "feudal regime" (and abolished, simultaneously but only in part, the droit d'aubaine).[8] In October, as the market women of Paris marched on Versailles to return triumphantly with the king and his family, Maurice Ferris, a priest from Lille, received a letter in which the salutation of the king was unchanged. Only late in 1789 did the formula of the letters begin to acknowledge the revolutionary rupture, and the salutation was changed to a more constitutional formula: "Louis, by the Grace of God and by the Constitutional Law of the State, King of the French" [*Roi des Français*].[9] Individual naturalizations, repeating that formula, were reduced to a trickle but continued as late as July 1790, when Jacques Vincent, a monk from Chambéry in Savoy, received his letter of naturalization, addressed to the Paris parlement and French treasury officials at a time when those institutions were already being dismantled.[10]

Poor Jacques Vincent, who had gone to great efforts to secure his privilege in 1790: by then, individual naturalizations were no longer necessary. French citizenship became a condition acquired by the fulfillment of statutory requirements. Naturalization became automatic, no longer a privilege issued by the discretionary authority of a sovereign power. Nor did naturalization depend on a resident foreigner's will or desire to become French; in principle, the law of 30 April 1790 conferred the quality of citizenship and its rights on thousands of foreigners already established in the kingdom.[11]

The law was introduced by the Old Regime barrister and elected Third Estate representative Guy Target, who was to play an important role in the elaboration of the 1791 Constitution, that incorporated the law of 30 April–1 May with slight but significant modifications. Target pointed out that the law was concerned principally with the frontier departments and maritime ports, "full of married men, landowners of longstanding, or owners of commercial establishments, born in foreign countries." Such men, "an eighth, a seventh, a sixth of the population," had served in the municipalities and in the National Guard since the Revolution, and all had sworn the civic oath of loyalty. The proposed text of the law conferred on them the status of French "citizens," although the language did not quite break with the Old Regime.

> All those who, born outside the kingdom of foreign parents, who are established in France, are reputed to be French; with the civic oath, they are permitted to exercise all rights of active citizens after five years of continuous residence in the kingdom, or if they have or have acquired immovables, or have married a French woman, or have formed a commercial establishment, or have received from a town letters of bourgeoisie; and this, notwithstanding all contrary laws, which are hereby annulled. But it cannot be understood in the present decree that any election already held must be redone, nor by this do we wish to resolve the question of the Jews, which has been and remains adjourned.

The decree was then issued as a patent letter by the king, on 2 May 1790, that appeared, ironically, as one of the last naturalizations of the Old Regime monarchy.[12]

On close reading, Target's proposed law described two kinds of statutory conditions that we distinguish as "nationality" and "citizenship." The first was cast in the idiom of the Old Regime: a foreigner was "reputed to be French" if, born outside the kingdom of foreign parents, he had established residence in France. This applied to all men, women, and children of foreign origin. The second was fundamentally novel: it was based on the Abbé Sieyès's idea of "active citizenship" and represented the revolutionary invention of political rights. These were conferred on foreigners only after they had met one of several statutory requirements, each of which was a sign of their social integration and assimilation into their local communities. But the justification is revealing: "married men, landowners of longstanding, owners of commercial establishments. . . ." The foreigners who could claim French citizenship were presumed to become citizens of a certain kind: male and active.

The distinction between "active" and "passive" citizens was a critical one in the first years of the Revolution, when it represented an amplification and clarification of the political and rhetorical distinctions within the eighteenth-century citizenship revolution. "Active" citizens were (political) men, while "passive" citizens were (legal) nationals. First introduced by the Abbé Sieyès, the distinction became part of the vocabulary of the committee on the constitution, and the Constituent Assembly more generally, in its debates over the adoption of the 1791 Constitution in September.[13] Title II ("Of the Division of the Kingdom and the Condition of Citizens") of the constitution defined the citizen in its most general and inclusive meaning, as "passive," or what was sometimes referred to—though not in the text of the law—as "simple citizenship," according to a formula that institutionalized the criteria of belonging in Old Regime jurisprudence: "French citizens are those who are born in France of a French father; those who, born in France of a foreign father, have fixed their residence in the kingdom; those who, born in a foreign country of a French father, have returned to establish themselves in France and have given the civic oath." The revolutionaries thus adopted a complementary set of conditions of "soil," "blood," and "residence," although the subsequent constitutions of 1793, 1795, and 1799 were to insist more pointedly on the guiding principle of *ius soli*. The civic oath, in the revolution, was a ritualized enactment of the Old Regime notion of residence, a sign of loyalty, commitment, and social assimilation.[14]

Title III ("Of Public Powers") of the constitution defined the quality of "active" citizen in a positive and general statutory fashion:

> To be an active citizen, one must be born or have become French; be at least 25 years old; be domiciled in a city or canton for as long as stated by the law; pay, anywhere in the kingdom, property taxes [*contribution directe*] at least equal to the value of three days of work, and have a receipt thereof; not be in a condition of servitude, that is, a wage servant; be registered on the books of the National Guard in the municipality of domicile; have given the civic oath.

The conditions were cumulative, and the status of active citizen was thereby exclusive of a significant portion of the population. Women, not specifically excluded from citizenship in the language of the law, were in fact like children, the very poor, and others in a position of dependence, only capable of enjoying "the quality of being French" (*qualité de français*), and its attendant civil rights, but not the rights of political participation.[15] Adult men who demonstrated not only their devotion to the new political order (through the civic oath and by participation in the National Guard) but also their social insertion and economic integration into a local community (through payment of taxes) could qualify as "citizens" in a more narrowly political sense. Pierre Rosanvallon has argued that such a citizenship was not founded on a regime of property ownership, as the Physiocrats and reforming ministers had proposed in the Old Regime or like that which emerged in the early nineteenth century. Rather, revolutionary citizenship was cast in terms of independence—the reversal of a notion of incapacity inherited from the Old Regime. All those in a dependent position (children, women, servants, the poor) were not capable of representing the nation, although they were nonetheless included among its citizens.[16]

The case of Jewish emancipation is illuminating in this regard. Target's law of 30 April 1790 tabled the Jewish question, commensurate with his own claims that "we have more important matters with which to deal." But already on 28 January 1790, the National Assembly had broached the question when it granted "the rights of active citizen" on 28 January 1790 to the so-called Portuguese Jews of Bordeaux and the Sephardic communities of Avignon. The former had been the most assimilated of the Jews by their collective naturalization from Henry II in 1552, but their acquisition of citizenship in 1790 applied only to Jewish men who could meet the requirements of "active" citizenship in France. In other words, the presumption was that the entire Sephardim in the south could already be considered citizens, albeit passive ones. As for the Jews of Lorraine, Alsace, and Paris: their claims for emancipation were effectively tabled until two weeks after the Constitution of 3–15 September 1791. At that point, and in response to much public pressure and debate, the Assembly decreed that they, too, could become active citizens by conforming to the public law of the constitution. After 1789, then, Jews in the kingdom were presumed to be "passive citizens," not "foreigners," and later some of them were granted active citizenship status.[17]

Target's law of automatic naturalization adopted without debate on 30 April 1790 also seems to make the same distinction, presuming different kinds of citizenship ("passive" or "simple" and political citizenship). The first clause—"All those who, born outside the kingdom of foreign parents, established in France, are reputed to be French"—naturalized all foreigners, men and women, rich and poor, adult and child. The second clause, under which a foreigner would be "permitted to exercise the rights of active citizens," detailed the conditions of social integration and insertion for independent, male foreigners.

But the Constitution of September 1791 did not state things exactly the same way, even if its reporter claimed that Target's law had been included "textually, such as it was decreed long ago." Two things changed in the 1791 text: first, the foreigner was now required to express his will and volition by taking the civic oath—an ephemeral requirement that disappeared in the more radical Constitution of 1793.[18] Second, Article 3 of Title II listed a set of *possible* criteria by which a foreigner could become a French citizen: "Those who, born outside the kingdom of foreign parents and who reside in France become French citizens after five years of continuous residence in the kingdom if they have, beyond that, acquired immovables or married a French woman, or formed an agricultural or commercial establishment, and if they have given the civic oath."

At stake was the notion of "active" citizenship: although the text of the constitution did not spell this out, foreigners became French nationals by fulfilling criteria that were equivalent to those conferring political rights to participate in the governance of the country. It would seem, then, as if becoming French meant becoming capable of political action: that nationality was conferred in the process of acquiring citizenship. In any case, such citizenship was conferred, not by the state in its exercise of discretionary authority, but on the local municipality that verified whether a foreigner met the statutory requirements (although such verification was never the subject of explicit instructions on the part of the government). In the early years of the Revolution, local communities, and not the state itself, became the border guards of French citizenship.[19]

How exclusive was this new citizenship? In social and gender terms, it is easy to imagine, especially for France's frontier provinces and its capital city, how many foreign-born day laborers and working men and women might not have qualified to become citizens. It is true that those settled in France before the law of 1790 would already have acquired the status of French nationals, and that the jurisprudence of the courts in the 1790s sometimes conferred on women the "quality of being French." In local communities, such as those of Alsace studied by Jennifer Heuer, municipalities occasionally recognized foreign-born women as "citizens," although the conflation of nationality and citizenship in the single term of "citizen," especially after 1791, makes ambiguous the nature of their newly acquired status. But the difference from Old Regime practices of naturalization is apparent. Before 1789, foreign men, women, and children of all ranks and statuses could acquire the privilege of citizenship. After 1791, the automatic naturalization of foreigners tended to exclude in practice foreign women and dependent persons from simple citizenship, since the constitution of that year—and those of 1793, 1795, and 1799—only provided the possibility of citizenship to established male property holders who fulfilled the statutory requirements.[20]

Honorary Citizens and Philosophical Politics in the New Regime

In some sense, the 1791 Constitution represents a partial triumph of Diderot's vision of the citizen and the citizenship revolution of the eighteenth century more generally. In his *Encyclopédie* article of 1752, Diderot had noted how "society" alone (civil society), as opposed to the discretionary will of kings, had the authority to admit foreigners to the status of citizens. But Diderot had adopted elements of the old juridical model, since he considered the act of naturalization as a species of honor, to be conferred on those who contributed to the proper functioning of society, who were rewarded on the basis of their merit. If the French revolutionaries moved away from the idea of naturalization as a special honor in 1791, retaining the notion that "society" itself, and not the government, could naturalize foreigners, the constitution nonetheless permitted (Title II, Article 4) "the legislative power to, for important considerations, give an act of naturalization to a foreigner with no other conditions than he fix his residence in France and take the civic oath." A discretionary judgment of the sovereign, located in the legislative body of the nation, could thus confer citizenship on resident foreigners. From the handful of grants made by the Legislative Assembly in 1791–92, it is clear French citizenship given to foreigners attributed French nationality and included the political rights of participation.

The debates about naturalizing foreigners in the early revolution give shape to a new kind of naturalization, albeit one inspired by older models. The Assembly voted that the quality of citizen be given in a political act that recognized the foreigner's political and philosophical loyalty to the revolution itself. In this way, revolutionary citizenship, as seen through naturalization, completed the slow but certain transformation of the citizen from a legal to a political being. Where Jean Bodin had dismissed the "honorary" political citizen from the "true" legal one, the Revolution, drawing on the citizenship revolution of the Old Regime, completed the revalorization of the citizen principally as a political actor.

Before August 1792, only a few foreigners sought the title of French citizen by decree of the Legislative Assembly. On 9 September 1791, even before the final vote on the constitution, the Corsican-born administrator and reformer Philippe Buonaratti petitioned to become a French citizen. Buonaratti, later to become famous as a revolutionary in his own right, had fled Florence in 1789 "as soon as the sun of liberty began to shine in France" in order to be "the witness and comrade [*compagnon*] of our struggles against despotism." No action was taken on his written request. Then, shortly after the vote on the constitution, on 26 September 1791, the Italian reformer Giuseppe Gorani also petitioned the Assembly "to obtain the quality of [an] active French citizen." The petition was sent to the diplomatic committee but languished in its archives. Seven months later, in May 1792, Gorani wrote to the Assembly's president, requesting a follow-up, but his case was not considered until the collective and honorary naturalizations of August 1792—even as he published, that very year, a treatise on the "science of government" that argued strenuously against inheritance restrictions on foreigners.[21]

That same month, in May 1792, Sieur Frédéric-Guillaume-Conrad de Hobes, the son of a noble, wealthy, and well-connected family at the Swedish court (where his father was chamberlain), requested to speak to the Assembly to explain why he wished to be "adopted by the French Nation in the name of its children, to live freely and die for her." He was the first foreigner to address the Assembly publicly with a claim to participate, as a citizen, in the political life of the nation, but the language of his petition reeked of the Old Regime. He emphasized that he was requesting a favor and not invoking a right, and he offered—to the loud applause of the assembled representatives—to exchange his vain, inherited nobility for the "nobility of carrying the name of a Frenchman." President Koch then spoke on his behalf, reading a letter from General Luckner, who attested to the man's remarkable virtues and his civic devotion. The Legislative Assembly celebrated, with the naturalization of a foreigner, the universal principles of the Revolution. The Assembly ordered the legislation committee to draw up an act of naturalization within a week . . . although none was presented to the Constituent Assembly that spring or summer.[22]

The next to be heard from was William Priestley, son of the famous scientist, who also went before the Assembly on 8 June 1792 in a performance of his request to be naturalized. The deputy François recommended Priestley, and read a letter from his father who expressed his undying gratitude for the honor that might be accorded to his son, and who intimated that his own political views might force him to flee England before too long. The deputy François made a passionate speech before the Assembly, explaining the moral worth of the son by the virtues of his father. The elder Priestley was to be considered a "defender and apostle of our Revolution"; his support had led to his persecution and denunciation by Edmund Burke ("just like Aristophanes had done to Socrates"). The Assembly should undertake the act of "national gratitude" toward the son, and thus become known as "the asylum of virtue proscribed and persecuted genius." To great applause, the Assembly ordered the committee on legislation to draw up the decree within three days.[23] A report, finally produced sometime before 10 August 1792 by Claude Bernard Navier, a moderate ex-barrister from Burgundy, included the requests of Hobes, Priestley, and Philippe Buonarotti (but not Gorani). The report encouraged the Assembly to admit these three foreigners, and any others who sought French citizenship, stressing "how advantageous it is for the French Nation to have [them] to oppose the critics of the constitution."[24]

But there was a problem in the cases of Hobes and Priestley, both of whom were under the age of twenty-five, the age of majority. As such, they became test cases for whether the Assembly viewed citizenship as legal nationality or as a political right. The answer was . . . both. The well-rehearsed distinction between "simple" (or "passive") and "active" citizenship framed the debate. Navier proposed to resolve the issue in a general way, arguing that it might not be unreasonable to naturalize these foreigners as simple citizens as opposed to active citizens (even though the two young men could have obtained the consent of their fathers, which seemed important to Navier). There was some debate, but in the end the draft decree did suggest a more "simple" citizenship, admitting all three "to the name of French citizens, to exercise these rights from the day that they fix their domicile in France and take the civic oath before the municipality where they reside." In fact, the exact nature of their citizenship was never explained, and it never mattered: although sent to the legislation committee, the decree was never published.[25] In the interim, the tumultuous events of 10 August 1792—the "Second French Revolution"—soon overcame the Legislative Assembly, and on 22 September, the newly elected members of the convention proclaimed the First French Republic.

If these individual cases went unresolved, the more general philosophical and political problem of naturalization was placed before the deputies of the convention two weeks after the events of 10 August 1792. On 24 August, the playwright Marie-Joseph Chénier (himself born in Constantinople, and closely tied to Danton) led a Parisian delegation before the Assembly with a request to follow the Roman example and to "bestow an illustrious and worthy reward on talent and love of liberty, that the benefactors of humanity be declared French citizens." The petition included the names and exploits of fourteen courageous philosophes, including two Americans (Paine and Madison), seven Englishmen (among them, Joseph Priestley) and an Irishman (Naper-Tandi), the Italian Gorani ("honored by the hatred, illuminated by the persecution of the House of Austria"), two Germans (both writers), a Swiss citizen, and a Pole (the maréchal Malakouski, "a grand example to his compatriots who stands alone on top of the ruins of Polish liberty").

> Such men, fellow legislators, are worthy of France; they are apostles, supporters, and martyrs of liberty. We ask for them the rights of French citizens. . . . If the choice of the people carried these illustrious men to the National Convention, what an imposing and solemn spectacle they could offer to this assembly that shall decide such a great destiny! Would not the elite of men from all parts of the globe seem like a congress of the entire world?

The decree was adopted on 26 August 1792, naming for inexplicable reasons a slightly different group of foreigners, just days after the Prussian army forced the eastern stronghold of Longwy to capitulate.[26]

Although there had been much enthusiasm for the measure, a number of dissenting voices were heard. Two issues came to the fore. First, some members of the Convention wondered whether these foreigners shouldn't be required to make the request themselves. This was the position of the former Protestant pastor Lasource from the Tarn, who, while not opposing the collective grant, believed that writers and others needed to make their own requests. The second issue was about their political participation: did the bestowal of citizenship in the spirit of what Adrien Lamourette, the former grand vicar of Arras, called the "philosophical consanguinity" with these illustrious foreigners permit them to be elected to the nation's primary assemblies? Were they political actors, as Chénier implied? One deputy proposed that a commission draw up a list of all foreigners who had celebrated the French Revolution in print, and that these be declared French citizens, with the ability to serve as representatives in the primary assemblies. But others dissented, resisting the attribution of political rights to foreigners that would allow them to participate in the governance of the nation, even if these illustrious foreigners were to establish residence in the republic.[27]

When the project was put to a vote, the Convention decreed, to booming applause from the Assembly and the galleries, that "the title of French citizen shall be given to all philosophes who have the courage to defend liberty and equality in foreign countries." Some deputies pointed out the need to reconcile the opinions of different committees on the matter, and the matter was sent to the public education committee "to put forth the names of those who are worthy of this honor." But, in all likelihood, that committee never reported. In part, the call for the new constitution, in the shadow of European warfare, occluded the philosophical politics of naturalization. Similarly for the case of individual demands to be naturalized. On 8 November 1792, the committees on civil and criminal legislation and the committee on feudalism stated their joint opinion concerning the petitions of several "foreign citizens who seek to obtain letters of naturalization in France," most probably the three mentioned (Hobes, Priestley, and Buonoratti). That committee observed that "it would be inconvenient to give [grants of naturalization] until the Constitution is written and accepted in the place of the one rejected."[28]

In fact, the collective, honorary, and philosophical naturalizations did not represent, even in principle, an application of Title II, Article 4 of the 1791 Constitution, which stressed the conditions of a fixed domicile and civic oath. The deputies in the convention made occasional reference to examples from ancient Greece and especially Rome, but not to the similar conferral of citizenship of the medieval city-states in their grants of the citizen *ad honorem*, or to General Lafayette's honorary naturalization by the Congress of the United States of America.[29] In any case, the philosophical naturalizations of 1792 had dubious legal value: most of the writers, politicians, and reformers named did not reside in France, and their attribution of citizenship was purely symbolic. Only two of those mentioned—Thomas Paine and Anacharsis Cloots—fulfilled the criteria of the 1791 Constitution, and both were elected to the Convention before being purged, as foreigners, by the decree of 5 nivôse year II (25 December 1793). As for individual naturalizations that conformed to Title I, Article 3 of the 1791 Constitution, only three seem to have been approved by the National Convention after September 1792: that of Buonarotti on 27 May 1793; the Belgian Pierre Plouvier on 10 June 1793; and that of Joel Barlow, who was to become the United States ambassador to France during the empire, and who by a decree of 17 February 1793—several weeks after the trial and execution of Louis XVI—was given "the title and rights of a French Citizen" with a simple and unelaborated decree bearing the seal of the Republic.[30] In sum, although the 1791 Constitution provided for the discretionary legislative conferral of naturalization, the attribution of French citizenship—apart from the philosophical politics of honorary citizenship in September 1792—symbolically ruptured with Old Regime royal authority and jurisprudence. Naturalization took place at the municipal level, with the enforcement and verification of the constitutional conditions that automatically conferred citizenship on foreigners—even as the exact relation between citizenship and nationality remained unelaborated.

The Quadruple Abolition of the "Droit d'Aubaine," 1790–1791

In the same years that the French revolutionaries broke with Old Regime jurisprudence and invented statutory naturalization, the Constituent Assembly also moved to unilaterally abolish the droit d'aubaine. The two events or processes, closely linked temporally, were not causally related, even if the droit d'aubaine was the principal reason foreigners became citizens under the Old Regime. But they were linked by affinity and within a political framework: both reforms of the Constituent Assembly—like all of its work—were committed to dismantling the Old Regime institutions of "feudalism." And there was perhaps no better example of "feudalism" in the early 1790s than the infamous droit d'aubaine, already understood as such after the middle of the eighteenth century. The Constituent Assembly in 1790 and 1791 consciously followed the precedent of the Old Regime monarchy, while at the same exceeding it by abandoning the principle of reciprocity and abolishing the droit d'aubaine in universal and unilateral terms, and in the spirit not of commerce but of fraternity.

In the first years of the Revolution, the Assembly abolished the droit d'aubaine not once but on three separate separate occasions (or four, if one counts the specific positive law on the inheritance rights of foreigners of 1 April 1791). The apparent redundancy in fact testifies to the ways in which the "feudal" right was interpreted: as a royal prerogative, a seigneurial right, a marker of French territory, and a civil law incapacity to either devolve property to other foreigners or to inherit property from French natives.

The first abolition of the droit d'aubaine began on 1 May 1790, the day after the Assembly debated and approved Target's project on the "laws and forms" of naturalization, suggesting the intimate linkage between the two. Appropriately, perhaps, in the same spirit as the August decrees of 1789 that had abolished the "feudal regime," a titled nobleman elected to the Estates General from the Dauphiné, Jean Marsanne, comte de Fontjulianne, introduced a decree to abolish the droit d'aubaine, which he called the "sole remaining vestige of the feudal regime."[31] The project was continuous with the ministerial and governmental proposals of the 1780s. The report of 6 August 1790 by Bertrand Barère de Vieuzac, previously a lawyer at the Toulouse parlement, explicitly established this linkage.[32] Barère quoted Montesquieu describing the right as a vestige of barbaric times without "communication or commerce" between nations; he paraphrased Necker on the sparse revenue it produced (40,000 livres); and he invoked the populationist argument of the reformer Moheau. The proposal, in a language that nonetheless exceeded that of the Old Regime in its invocation of the "rights of man and the citizen," was adopted with little debate on 6 August. The preamble of the law introduced the general principles of freedom and humanity:

Considering that the droit d'aubaine is contrary to the principles of fraternity that should link all men, whatever their country and government; that this right, established in barbarian times, should be proscribed among a people that has founded its Constitution on the Rights of Man and of the Citizen; that a free France should open its heart to all peoples of the earth, inviting them to enjoy, under a free government, the sacred and inalienable rights of humanity . . .

The National Assembly thus unilaterally abolished, "forever and definitively," the droit d'aubaine.[33]

If the first elimination of the droit d'aubaine ended a royal, domanial practice that had been attacked by the monarchy itself in the second half of the eighteenth century, the second abolition of the droit d'aubaine on 22 February 1791 addressed the fact that, as a seigneurial right, the droit d'aubaine was still officially "on the books." It took a proposal from the committee on feudalism, charged with making practical sense of the grandiose rhetorical claims advanced in the decrees of August 1789, to abolish the droit d'aubaine, alongside the rights of bastardy, abandoned or unclaimed objects (épaves), "found treasure" (trésor trouvé), and the right to appropriate abandoned land. Again adopted without apparent debate,[34] the second abolition of the droit d'aubaine thus completed symbolically the monarchy's appropriation of the right from seigneurs, a process that had begun in the thirteenth century.

The third abolition of the droit d'aubaine amplified and modified the decree of August 1790. It was approved in April 1791, and contributed to a debate over the legal status of France's overseas territories, its colonies in the Caribbean. Distant events from Saint-Domingue provided the motive and occasion of the law, after treasury officials in Port-au-Prince seized a ship upon the death of its captain, a citizen of the United States. The decree of 6 August 1790 had specifically ordered that "all procedures, pursuits, and inquiries which would have these rights as their object are extinguished," but the continued efforts of the royal fisc in France's largest Caribbean possession to confiscate the properties of dead foreigners assured the survival of the droit d'aubaine in the colonies. Or so reported Barère de Vieuzac, again, to the Assembly, this time in the name of the committee on domains, on 12 January 1791. Blaming the need to act not only on the fisc but on the "too vague disposition of the decree" of August 1790, he proposed that the formal abolition of the droit d'aubaine be extended to France's colonies. Moreau de Saint-Méry, the lawyer and member of the superior council of Saint-Domingue before 1789 who later became a deputy to the Constituent Assembly, supported the law. Projects for suppressing the droit d'aubaine in France's colonial possessions had failed previously, he had argued even before the Revolution, for not taking into consideration the fact that foreign commerce itself was prohibited, according to royal patent letters issued in 1727 and never rescinded. France should have abolished long ago, and unilaterally, all such prohibitions, including the droit d'aubaine.[35] The problem was not in itself complex, but the jurisdictional questions were confused, reflecting the multiplicitous status of the droit d'aubaine, and the colonies themselves, in Old Regime law. Thus the Assembly required reports from the committees on the colonies, the constitution, diplomacy, agriculture, and commerce. Barère de Vieuzac finally reported for all of them on 13 April 1791, and the Assembly adopted, without apparent discussion, the third and final abolition of the droit d'aubaine, this time specifying that it would take place "in all French possessions, even in the Two Indies."[36]

Yet even after the triple abolition of the droit d'aubaine, some of the most pressing questions of the eighteenth-century jurists remained unanswered. During the first debate to abolish the droit d'aubaine, François Andrieu, an Alsatian lawyer originally elected to the Third Estate, argued for the need to distinguish between the droit d'aubaine as a royal right and the ability of foreigners to dispose of their property, for without such a restriction, "foreigners will come en masse to acquire in our fatherland national goods whose revenues they will consume in their own."[37] And Barère de Vieuzac himself, in the name of the committee on domains in January 1791, returned to the new Old Regime distinction between civil law (*droit civil*) and international law (*droit des gens*), itself a retrieval in eighteenth-century legal culture of the Roman law divisions. Had the Assembly, he queried, meant to allow foreigners the ability to inherit from their French relatives, without having to reside in the kingdom? To answer the question, he divided the eighteenth-century treaties abolishing the droit d'aubaine into two classes: in the first, an explicit concession allowed foreigners to inherit indiscriminately (following local law and custom), just as native-born residents; in the second, far larger class of treaties, no explicit claim allowed foreigners to inherit from French kin. This was the first "revisionist" classification of the treaties abolishing the droit d'aubaine, following the efforts of several jurists and clerks in the 1780s. Unlike the earlier attempt to classify the treaties by the French foreign ministry in 1781, the concerns of Barère de Vieuzac were not about the reciprocity entailed by treaties with foreign powers concerning the droit d'aubaine (or other inheritance rights), but about whether the treaties were explicit in permitting foreigners to inherit from French citizens.[38] Barère himself was in favor of abolishing this "odious difference established by our laws between the strictly called droit d'aubaine and the vice of foreignness [*vice de pérégrinité*] or capacity to inherit." Urging the Assembly to go beyond the simple remission of a fiscal right, he argued that the law courts of the Old Regime had already recognized the right of foreigners to inherit, even from French men and women, and he cited extensively the opinions of Lemmens case in 1781. It was not legal precedent, however, but philosophical principles that were at stake: "The true legislator can accord this right by the great principles of liberty, of reason, and of the fraternal spirit which must unite all peoples."[39]

On 1 April 1791, the radical deputy Antoine Merlin, called Merlin de Thionville (Metz), in the name of the committees of alienation and of the constitution, proposed Article 3 as an amendment to the decree on successions ab intestat: "Foreigners, even if established outside the kingdom, are legally capable of gathering in France the inheritances of their kin, even French; they can in the same way inherit and bequeath by all means authorized by law."[40] The proposal, like Barère's, was quite radical in the context of the late eighteenth-century debates about whether foreigners had the right to inherit from French natives. After all, even if the Paris parlement had upheld such a right in a number of key cases (especially the Lemmens affair of 1781), it had still presumed that the foreigner receiving a bequest reside within the kingdom. Since much legal opinion had opposed the abolition of inheritance restrictions on foreigners, the issue was far from resolved when the Revolution broke out in 1789.

It is no surprise, then, that although the *Archives parlementaires* recorded that Merlin's amendment was adopted "without debate," subsequent accounts suggested otherwise. In particular, the account of this vote ten years later by the lawyer Pierre-Louis Roederer, charged with writing the report that was to re-institute a form of the droit d'aubaine in Title I of the Civil Code, suggests that a great deal of debate took place. According to Roederer, there had been opposition in the Assembly to such a unilateral and unreciprocal act. The deputy Loys, in particular, was concerned "that foreigners could enrich their country with our spoils, without French being able to take their revenge." But it was none other than Maître Martineau, the lawyer who had unsuccessfully argued *against* Lemmens in the 1781 inheritance dispute, opposing the right of foreigners to inherit, who gave a convincing oration that France should proffer the example of "universal fraternity" and permit such an inheritance right to foreigners.[41] A man—especially a lawyer—could easily change his mind and his arguments, especially during a revolution. The amendment was then adopted in its proposed form, and eventually incorporated into the Constitution of 1791 and then the Constitution of 1793—although the principle came into conflict with the radical republican law of inheritance, passed early in 1794 in the middle of war with Europe, that gave inheritance rights in France only to citizens of nonenemy states.[42]

By the spring of 1791, then, the droit d'aubaine—as royal prerogative, as feudal due, in its colonial incidence, and in relation to inheritance restrictions—had been formally abolished, as had all other obstacles to foreigners devolving or inheriting their property, and foreigners were not even required to reside in the kingdom! This was radical. Within the politics of inheritance law, the National Assembly had neatly inverted the project of the absolute citizen, and the attendant policies against foreigners under Louis XIV, who had favored "war" over "commerce" (and "immobile France" over the "France of movement"). Moreover, the Assembly went far beyond the "enlightened" or late absolute monarchy that had, beginning in the 1760s, systematically dismantled the droit d'aubaine through bilateral treaties and collective privileges. Turning from specific abolitions or exemptions to a general principle, the Revolution succeeded where the Old Regime had failed in all but the case of England in 1787, and it did so, replacing the concerns of commerce and reciprocity with universal claims of natural law and human rights.

Politics over Law in the Revolutionary Constitutions of 1793, 1795, and 1799

The National Assembly had acted somewhat haphazardly in the dismantling of the droit d'aubaine, but had done so with an evident self-righteousness: the droit d'aubaine was the last remnant of the feudal era, and was ideologically intolerable in an age of self-conscious rupture with the past. Impelled by the "cosmopolitan spirit" and the ideal of "fraternity," the French revolutionaries thus abolished the principal legal distinction between French natives and foreigners within "private" or "civil law."[43] Yet just as it finished that task, the Revolution began its radical slippage, as the French Republic went to war against the "despots" of Europe, and the revolutionary government (increasingly dominated by Maximilien Robespierre and the Committee of Public Safety) sought to rescue the Revolution from its foreign and domestic enemies.

The declarations of war in the spring of 1793 led directly to the extensive legislative proscriptions against foreigners, as the figure of the "foreigner" became, in the revolutionary imagination, the enemy, the traitor, or the spy.[44] The old monarchical tradition of confiscating the properties and expelling "enemy foreigners" combined with the eighteenth-century administrative policing of foreigners in Paris to produce, in a bellicose and revolutionary climate, an overtly political identification of foreigners as enemies of the republic. The decrees of 26 February and 21 March 1793 required foreigners to register their presence with the authorities. By 16 October, the Convention decreed that foreigners from countries with which France was at war were to be declared prisoners. On 5 nivôse year II (25 December 1793), foreigners were excluded from the right of representing the French nation, a law of Robespierre directed specifically at the elected foreign deputies Anacharsis Cloots from the duchy of Clèves and the American Tom Paine. The next day, the Convention extended the prohibition of foreigners participating in political life to all French descendants born abroad: only those born in France could represent the nation. A week later, the Convention clarified its "fourth" abolition of the droit d'aubaine, specifying in the law of 17 nivôse year II (6 January 1794) on succession that only foreigners from states with which the Republic was not at war could enjoy the right to inherit.[45] The next spring, on 26 germinal year II (15 April 1794), the radical revolutionary Louis Saint-Just proposed a general project and decree identifying foreigners with ex-nobles, barring their presence in key towns, and excluding them from popular societies, surveillance committees, and communal or sectional assemblies.[46]

The French historian Albert Mathiez, writing at the end of the First World War, saw in these measures a historical shift from the universal "cosmopolitanism" of the early Revolution to the fiery "nationalism" of the radical republic, an inevitable by-product of the revolutionary wars against England and Europe.[47] Yet it was less a temporal shift than the working out of an ideological tension inscribed at the heart of republican citizenship in revolutionary France. The republican citizen was, first and foremost, a political actor who supported the revolutionary government: the boundaries between "citizen" and "foreigner" in political discourse, as the decree of 26 germinal year II suggests, were drawn not on the basis of legal membership in the polity but on political grounds. "The only foreigners in France are bad citizens," Tallien's remark, articulates the preeminently political citizenship of the radical republic.[48] At the same time, the Constitution of 1793 defined the "citizen" in terms of public law, incorporating in unexpected and unintended ways a definition of French "nationality."

The distinct revolutionary constitutions—1793, 1795 (after the dismantling of the radical republic), 1799 (before Bonaparte's coup d'état)—were more or less radical in their definitions of the "active" citizen. But how did they define the relation between nationality and citizenship, and the distinctions between French citizens and foreigners? The constitutions, especially that of 1793, have recently become the subject of extensive commentary as scholars attempt to interpret the nature of "citizenship" inscribed in public law, and the relation between "cosmopolitanism" and "nationalism" in the intentions of their framers. According to the legal historian Vanel, writing in the 1940s, the constitutional texts were concerned exclusively with public law, the distribution of powers and political rights, and only the political quality of citizenship entered into discussion. More recent readings of the texts and contexts, based in part on contemporary commentary and subsequent jurisprudence, have put such a claim into doubt. For legal historians and scholars such as Vida Azimi and Patrick Weil, the "failure" to distinguish definitions of French nationals from citizens follows logically from the approach of Condorcet, the author of the 1793 Constitution. Like his contemporaries, Condorcet was fully aware of the distinction between simple and political citizens but chose to articulate their relationship as a rebus or puzzle: in the constitutional text, the condition of a citizen followed logically from the first clause, nonbinding in gender terms, of Article 4, "All men are French." The Constitution of 1793, like those of 1795 and 1799, thus embedded a specific legal category of "nationality" within a definition of "citizenship" that was principally a political one.[49]

The question, however, might be differently resolved by exploring the multiple and overlapping meanings of the "citizen" and the "foreigner" at the height of the French Revolution, and in its immediate aftermath. Both keywords were largely unstable in their meanings; among their many uses, they formed the rhetorical weaponry of the National Convention deputies. Conceiving of radical republicanism in largely universal terms, politicians at the height of the Revolution struggled to exclude their political enemies, universally identified as "foreigners" in both literal and metaphoric senses. The legal definition of foreigners and of citizens, like the process of naturalization itself, was largely displaced in favor of a political one. Revolutionary citizenship expanded the category of "foreigners" beyond national boundaries while it shrank the category of "citizens" within them.[50] The political deputies to the Convention and their successors in the Directory who framed and approved the Constitutions of year III (1795) and year VIII (1799) established the criteria by which foreigners could become citizens with varying degrees of automaticity and varying markers of social assimilation. But those who argue that "nationality" was completely effaced by political citizenship must confront the fact that, between 1793 and 1796, the revolutionary deputy Jean-Jacques Cambacères, in three separate projects to codify French civil law at very different moments in the revolutionary process, never deemed it necessary to define the conditions or quality of what it was to be (or to become) French. That was, according to Cambacères and his committee, a question of public law, which the revolutionary constitutions had already defined.[51]

Still, although the 1793 Constitution, approved on 24 June then suspended on 10 October "until the peace" in the name of "revolutionary government," did define French "nationality," it did not do so to everyone's satisfaction. Conceived in the midst of war, its final form was the product of the ascendancy of Robespierre and the Montagnards (who eliminated the Girondin opposition just before voting in the constitution). Although its first articles were concerned with the definition of the French citizen, as both legal and political being, the constitution paradoxically presented a strikingly cosmopolitan and universalist set of claims about the republican revolution. And this from its inception: on 19 October 1792, in the aftermath of the proclamation of the French Republic in September, it was again Barère who reported, in the name of the committee on the constitution, on the "invitation to be extended to friends of liberty and equality, to present their views on the Constitution to be given to France." For him, as for the other newly elected members of the Convention, the call for universal participation was self-evident: "The Constitution of a great Republic cannot be the work of several souls; it must be the work of the human spirit." The decree that followed authorized the committee to translate and publish the works sent in by foreigners.[52] More than eighty such projects were received, many of them commenting on the first Girondin proposal introduced in February 1793, and many were incorporated into the debates on the Convention floor. These interventions provide a fine sample of political opinion, both in the Convention and beyond, about what it meant to be, and to become, a French citizen.

Most of the constitutional projects, including the first Girondin proposal by Condorcet and Barère, abandoned the effort to define explicitly a notion of "nationality" that stood distinct from the condition of a "citizen" holding political rights. Despite their differences over how to attribute the quality of citizenship to foreigners, the constitutional proposals shared what Jean Lanjuinais, analyzing them in the spring of 1793, described as a "confusion." Lanjuinais had been a professor of ecclesiastical law at the University of Rennes before the Revolution, and later fled the Montagnard persecution only to emerge as the royalist-leaning president of the Convention after Thermidor. (A survivor, Lanjuinais went on to become a senator under Napoleon Bonaparte but later opposed the empire, for which he was rewarded in 1814 with membership in the newly formed Chamber of Peers.) Reviewing the projects, Lanjuinais noted that at the center of this confusion was a double meaning of the word "citizen." It is worth quoting his report at length:

> The general idea revealed by the word citizen is that of member of a city, of civil society, of the nation. In a strict sense, it means only those who have been permit-ted to exercise political rights, to vote in the assemblies of the people, those who can elect and be elected to office; in a word, the members of the sovereign body. Thus children, the insane, minors, women, persons condemned to punishment or infamy, until their rehabilitation, would not be citizens. But, in common usage, this word is applied to all those of the social body, that is, who are not foreigners nor civilly dead, whether or not they have political rights, who enjoy full civil rights, and whose persons and goods are governed by the general laws of the country. This is the citizen in ordinary language.

Pamphleteers and legislators, including the authors of the 1791 Constitution, confused the two different meanings, and from there, "the confusion and ap-parent incoherence of certain proposals"—including the draft of the 1793 con-stitution presented in February by his fellow Girondins.[53]

To resolve the confusion, Lanjuinais proposed a return to Sieyès's distinc-tion between "active" and "passive" citizens, and to introduce a notion of for-eigners who possessed all the civil rights of French citizens, including the right to inherit and devolve property, but not political rights of self-governance. He further recommended an emendation of the articles of the 1791 Constitution, omitted entirely in the 1793 projects, that formally permitted foreigners ("whether or not established in France") to inherit property from French citi-zens, even as they were to be subject, in their persons and goods, to the same laws as Frenchmen and women.[54]

Lanjuinais's commentary that the constitutional project should regulate the civil condition of persons, as opposed to public powers, was to fall mostly on deaf ears, although the naturalized citizen Joel Barlow criticized the 1791 con-stitution on the same grounds.[55] The debates, instead, turned on the question of how to attribute the French citizenship, without explaining what it meant. Some proposals presumed that citizenship was conferred automatically by birth and residence in the kingdom. At one extreme stood the radical republican projects, such as that of Cherhal Mont-Réal, whose *Constitution republicaine* stated unequivocally that "French citizens are all those who breathe on Republican soil, and who are irreproachable."[56] The addition of this last characteristic points not only to the air and earth but especially to the political definition of citizenship that encompassed those who supported the revolutionary regime.

Most proposals did seek to reduce the length of residence required of a foreigner before acquiring citizenship, without insisting on the "irreproachable" quality of foreign citizens but still presuming the nature of citizenship as political participation. Durand Maillane, in support of the project of Montagnard constitution, argued the principle that "one should deprive as little as possible citizens born [in France] from the exercise of their political rights and we should also make our association more accessible to foreigners. The soil of France is open to all men, and it will bring, for all French, only the fruits of liberty." He proposed to add an article, adapting the Old Regime "freedom principle" to the new revolutionary conditions, that "the French Republic, founded on the natural and reasonable principles of liberty, equality, and fraternity which should unite all men, declares that its territory is open to all foreigners and that it shall never see either serfs or slaves."[57] The radical Montagnard Louis Saint-Just was less ambitious, rhetorically at least, and proposed simply that: "1. All men aged 21 and living a year and a day in the same municipality have the right to vote in the assemblies of the people. 2. All men aged 25 are eligible for all offices."[58] (Inherited from Old Regime jurisprudence, the notion that a year and a day residence was enough to assure social assimilation was echoed in proposals by Jean-Antoine Debry [an ex-barrister], Nicolas [an ex-doctor], and many others.) The less radical Boissy d'Anglas, a descendant of Protestants who held venal office in the household of the king's brothers and who was later to play an important role in defining the status of foreigners in the Civil Code, insisted that the residence be a minimum of two years, and posited a large number of conditions under which citizens might lose their status.[59] Others sought to increase the length of established domicile to four or five years. But very few made an effort to distinguish between a political and a civil status of the citizen, and most discussed citizenship exclusively as political rights.

A number of projects did worry about the inclusion of foreigners as citizens with political rights.[60] Antoine-Joseph Thorillon, the Parisian deputy and justice of the peace in 1793, wrote that it would be "impolitic and even absurd to let foreigners take part in making our laws," echoing the complaints of the sixteenth-century jurists in his emphasis on the lack of "good faith" among foreigners and their potential for treason. Jacques Rouzet, an ex-noble from Quercy elected to the Convention from the Haute-Garonne, also invoked the Old Regime, wishing that they be called "recognized foreigners" who would still suffer incapacities. These would include the inability to "participate and deliberate in the primary assemblies and to be elected as national representatives."[61] But other deputies, in a spirit of pure universal republicanism (so different from that of the Old Regime) argued that the conferral of citizenship required the ability of the foreigner to exercise political rights in France. Although opinions differed, the presumption was that foreigners would acquire citizenship according to its constitutional conditions, not subject to legislative or executive discretion.

In the end, as the Montagnards seized power, a modification and radicalization of the original Girondin proposal was adopted in June 1793: Title II, Article 4 defined the political citizen as an adult ("All men born and domiciled in France, over the age of 21"), and immediately stated the conditions through which foreigners could become citizens: "All foreigners over 21 who, residing in France at least a year, live there by their own work, or who acquire properties, or who marry Frenchwomen, or who adopt a child, or who feed an old person."[62] The foreigner who became a French citizen would most likely be male, independent, socially assimilated, and offering some visible expression of his contribution to the public good. (The requirement of public service thus made explicit the faint echo of such that was found in the transmutation of registration fees for Old Regime naturalization into charitable donations.) Certainly these were the most generous conditions of naturalization since 1790, when the Constituent Assembly had simply decreed that foreigners resident in the kingdom were to be "reputed to be French." Unlike the 1791 Constitution and the original Girondin proposal, no formal civic oath was required. And although the legislature reserved the discretionary right to naturalize, to "permit foreigners who benefited humanity to exercise the rights of the French citizen," there is no evidence that the Convention systematically undertook to do so.[63]

But the actual meaning of citizenship in the 1793 Constitution was severely put to the test by the subsequent legislation that identified foreigners with ex-nobles and other enemies of the Revolution, especially the law of 26 germinal year II (15 April 1794).[64] Hundreds of surviving petitions sent to the Convention reveal the essential confusion, both official and vernacular, over the meaning of citizenship at the heart of revolutionary France. A large number of foreign-born individuals—men and women, nobles and commoners—thought of themselves as "citizens" of France, and found themselves unjustly forced into exile. Their plaintive, handwritten petitions to the Convention constitute a reasonable sample of everyday claims about French citizenship at the height of the radical Revolution.

Why should "Citoyen Belz," born in England of a French father and established in France since 1788, employed as a postal worker, have been subjected to the decree and considered a foreigner? How could Jean Baptiste Vermeulan, born in Berg-op-Zoom in Holland but living in France since 1787 and naturalized in 1788, who since 1793 was a furrier in a Belgian batallion, be considered a foreigner? How could the Jew "Citoyen Lallemand," a drink merchant from Trier living in France since 1766, and married to a Frenchwoman, be considered anything but a citizen? Why should Colin Campbell, born in Jamaica who in 1790 became a citizen "using the power given to me by the decrees of the

Constituent Assembly," have been placed on the lists? And so forth. Women, too, placed on the lists felt themselves to be "citoyennes françaises," even if they knew they had no right to participate in politics. Thérèse Bernard wrote to the Convention seeking to remove herself: born in the Hague in Holland, she had married a Prussian and come to Paris in 1770 to work as a chamber-maid, and although she had periodically left the country since then (notably be-tween 1772 and 1775, when she went to care for her grandmother), Bernard had lived in France since the outbreak of the Revolution, working as a washer-woman. Or Marie Deschamps, born in Brussels of two French parents, who had lived in Paris since 1784, "mother of a republican child, son of an excellent patriot," and now forced to flee France because she was declared a foreigner?[65] No formal decisions about any of these cases survive in the archives, but it is clear that if the jurisprudence of the French courts would likely have recog-nized these men and women as having attained the qualité de français, their persecution as foreigners suggests, at the very least, how political definitions of citizenship overshadowed legal ones at the height of the radical Revolution.

In the aftermath of Thermidor and the dismantling of the radical republic, the new Constitution of 5 fructidor year III (22 August 1795) abandoned the philosophical politics of the radical Revolution and the possibility of honorary and political naturalization as a special reward or compensation for service to the nation. Pierre-Claude-François Daunou, the Norman deputy who with Lanjuinais authored the 1795 Constitution (and who would go on to become a member of the Tribunate before being stripped of his position by Napoleon), still insisted in the face of debate within the Convention that naturalization could not result from the discretionary authority of the executive. Instead, only the legislative body could state, in constitutional terms, the conditions for the acquisition of French citizenship.[66] This renewed insistence on "automaticity" was tempered and eroded by the inclusion of a clause that required the for-eigner to formally make a voluntary declaration of his intention.[67] At the same time, the 1795 Constitution was far more "conservative" than the 1793 Consti-tution, or even that of 1791, by increasing the duration of residence to seven years—and there were objections on the floor of the Convention that, even so, the acquisition of the "title of French citizen" was far too easily achieved. The deputies Lakanal and Mailhe, in particular, pointed out that France's premier enemy, the British government, could easily "in the space of seven years and at very little cost populate France with troublemakers always ready to disturb, to rip, and to dissolve your society." Daunou dismissed their fears, responding that it would be extremely difficult for any foreign government to support a foreign agent for seven years in France, and ultimately his judgment prevailed.[68]

In addition to the shortened residence, however, the Constitution of 1795 in-cluded the earlier clauses that were indices and proof of social integration, including the minimum age of 21, the payment of direct taxes, property ownership, the establishment of an agricultural or commercial enterprise, or marriage to a French woman (Title II, Article 10). To become French, a foreigner had thus to fulfill requirements that were nearly identical to those of an active citizen, a male, tax-paying French man, as defined in Article 8: the acquisition of citizenship was tantamount to the acquisition of political rights. The addition of gender-specific language ("marriage to a French woman") alongside the requirement of seven-year residence and property ownership points to the exclusive nature of this largely political citizenship in the aftermath of the radical republic.

The Constitution of year VIII (1799) increased the residency requirement to ten years (Title I, Article 3), while retaining the requirement that the "title of French citizen" be the result of a voluntary request on the part of the foreigner; yet it eliminated all mention of the explicit signs or indices of social integration and assimilation. In this way, the Constitution of 1799 represents a marked break with the constitutional legislation of the republic, and signals a partial return to Old Regime practices.[69] Residence, once more, was presumed to assure both social assimilation and political loyalty, the latter affirmed in the voluntarism of the petitioner's request (much as the Old Regime jurists were to understand the act of petition and registration of letters of naturalization before 1789). At the same time, the Constitution of 1799 marked a continuity with its revolutionary predecessors. Like the Constitutions of 1793 and 1795, it permitted foreigners to acquire political rights (*droits de cité*), that is, to become members of political society but it offered no formal mechanism by which a foreigner could become a French national—to acquire the qualité de français—without becoming a citizen endowed with political rights.

Although absent from constitutional law, the distinction between legal citizenship and political rights began to take shape after Thermidor, then during the Directory (1795–99). The republican revolutionaries had occasionally made reference to the legal category of French nationals in the use of a neologism, first introduced in 1792, of *républicole* (modeled on the Old Regime *regnicole*). But with the dismantling of the radical republic, administrators and publicists increasingly distinguished between those with the "quality" or "title" of Frenchman or woman (*qualité* or *titre de français*) and citizens who qualified to exercise political rights (*citoyens*). In 1798, some Knights of Malta claimed not to be subject to the general laws on emigration, carefully distinguishing between their political rights given up when joining the order, and their legal identity as Frenchmen that they retained. Similarly, returning Protestants were entitled to the "quality of being French" but were to be barred from political citizenship for at least seven years.[70] Both cases highlight the growing distinction between civil status and political rights.

Yet only in the discussions leading toward the Civil Code between 1801 and 1803 was a formal distinction between French "nationality"—the civil rights of

Frenchmen and women—and citizenship consistently invoked by legislators and jurists. Better put, it was only after the Revolution that jurists and politicians sought to distinguish "citizens" from "French nationals."[71] French constitutional law had identified French nationality, still avant la lettre, but submerged its definition within one of political citizenship. As the republican experiment fell apart under the Directory, and as political citizenship became discredited, so it was left to the codification of private law, in the battles over the Civil Code of 1803, to identify the boundaries of French nationality.

Continuity and Rupture in and around the Civil Code (1803)

The discussions and debates among jurists and politicians beginning in July 1801 and leading to the adoption of Title I of the Civil Code ("On the Enjoyment and Privation of Civil Rights") on 18 March 1803, mark a two-fold rupture with revolutionary practices. First, the debates and the final text of the Civil Code explicitly distinguished between civil and political rights (Article 7), and provided a juridical and administrative mechanism by which foreigners could legally acquire the former through the government's authorization of their residence in France (Article 13). Second, the Civil Code broke with revolutionary practices in reinstituting, albeit reciprocally, what contemporaries were to call the "droit d'aubaine" (Article 11). In fact, the "droit d'aubaine" in this context referred only to the reciprocally imposed restrictions on the ability of foreigners to inherit property from French nationals. It did not include the right of the sovereign to confiscate the property of an alien who died in the republic. Drawing on a distinction that originated with the citizenship revolution of the eighteenth century, the jurists and politicians of the Directory broke with the absolutist droit d'aubaine but revived the Old Regime concerns of political reciprocity. Although they recognized the "feudal" nature of the institution, they reinstituted reciprocally, but not without debate, the thin version of the "droit d'aubaine" as inheritance rights.

A third rupture with the Old Regime coincided with the debates leading to the Civil Code: the reintroduction by Napoleon of the discretionary authority of the executive to confer on foreigners the status of French citizens (law of 26 vendémiaire year XI [18 October 1802]). In this way, the legal treatment of foreigners and naturalization at the beginning of the First Empire signal a partial if limited return to many of the inherited but reconfigured practices of Old Regime naturalization, as was the case in so many aspects of French public and political—as well as social—life.[72]

On 22 frimaire year VIII (13 December 1799), shortly after the adoption of the 1799 Constitution and Napoleon Bonaparte's coup d'état of 9 November that led to the establishment of the Consulate, the French government, under the close supervision of First Consul Napoleon Bonaparte, began work on the elaboration of a civil code. The first three projects of the revolutionary government, between 1793 and 1796, were stillborn, in part because they were the work of parliamentary commissions of elected politicians, and were subjected to sharp political debate both in the commissions and in the assemblies themselves. This time, the Consulate ordered a commission of professional jurists to establish the fourth and what was to become the definitive project of a civil code to be presented to the upper parliamentary chamber, the Tribunate, and then to the lower Legislative Corps.[73] None other than the aged jurisconsult François Tronchet was designated president of the commission. (Napoleon, despite his disagreement with Tronchet over the very definition of a Frenchman, called him "the soul of the Civil Code.") Tronchet's own trajectory since the Old Regime exemplifies the means through which "new law" both ruptured and conspired with "intermediary" revolutionary law and with "ancient law" concerning the legal definitions of the citizen and the ways in which that condition was acquired. Born in Paris in 1726, scion of a parliamentary attorney, Tronchet passed the bar in 1745, and over the next decades produced more than three thousand written consultations as a practicing barrister. In public life, he had been most insistent on the acquisition of French nationality based on the principle of descent, but also on the distinction between the droit d'aubaine (as royal tax) and the capacity of a foreigner to inherit in the kingdom. The positions he developed under the Old Regime were formative in his subsequent contributions to the making of civil law in the New Regime.[74]

In the first project of Title I, Tronchet argued—not unexpectedly—for the principle of filiation and descent as opposed to birth on French territory in defining French nationality (*qualité de français*). A preference and prejudice inherited from the Old Regime, the principle was affirmed in Tronchet's experience during the radical Revolution, which led him, like many others, to insist on family descendance as the most secure criteria for assuring the loyalty of French citizens. Tronchet's vision, however, was opposed by First Consul Bonaparte himself, who insisted on the simple formulation that "every individual born in France is French." At stake was more than the question of which "principle" would be primary: contra Tronchet and the jurists, who in the Old Regime had founded the attribution of nationality on the rights of French offspring to inherit, Bonaparte responded that "the question must be understood in relation to the interest of France," that is, the French state.[75] By 1802, the determination of nationality, like the acquisition through naturalization of French citizenship, was to be a function of state policies and interests and not the result of an individual's capacity to inherit.

Napoleon's first project, however, was defeated when presented to the Tribunate on 1 January 1802. He reacted swiftly, purging the Tribunate of twenty of his harshest critics and political enemies. "Domesticated," writes Weil, "the Tribunate then approved the ensemble of 37 projects that constitute the Civil

Code, and made no more modifications." But Tronchet's original propositions concerning nationality law survived the purge, despite Bonaparte's opposition, and the new Tribunate definitively adopted Tronchet's terms on 27 ventôse year XI (18 March 1803). The resulting definition of French nationality depended principally on filiation (*ius sanguinis*), a definitive rupture with the constitutional law of the Revolution as well as the jurisprudence of the Old Regime. The principle was to remain in place, with minor modifications, until 1889. Nationality became a status of persons, no longer derived from principles of territoriality.[76]

The presence of figures such as Tronchet helps to explain how the Civil Code broke with revolutionary practices of nationality law, and often returned to the same arguments of Old Regime jurisprudence on the matter.[77] But the continuity of personnel cannot by itself account for the most important rupture with both revolutionary practice and with Old Regime jurisprudence: the key claim of Article 7 that "the exercise of civil rights is independent of the quality of the citizen, which can only be acquired and preserved in conformity with constitutional law." The statement had no precedent in the jurisprudence of the Old Regime, as the jurists themselves recognized.[78]

But the distinction between citizen as political actor and citizen as member of civil society—the disengagement of the political citizen from its jurisprudential definition as nationality—originated during the citizenship revolution of the eighteenth century. The Abbé Sieyès's distinction between "active" and "passive" citizenship took up the terms in a revolutionary context, valorized in the Constitution of 1791, but abandoned in public law until the Civil Code. If the public and constitutional law of the revolutionary regimes had momentarily amalgamated the two, the distinction between "civil rights" and "political rights" reappeared and crystallized in the council of state debates beginning in July 1801, in which Sieyès was an active participant.

The distinction was uncontested—although the lawyers were to disagree among themselves and with the first consul over whether territoriality (*ius soli*) or descent (*ius sanguinis*) was to take precedence. But the difference between being French and being a citizen was universally accepted as a foundational principle of French public and private law. As summarized by Boulay, who presented the first project to the Legislative Corps in December 1801: "The exercise of political rights presupposes that of civil rights; but the exercise of civil rights does not presuppose that of political rights: thus one cannot be a citizen in France without being French, but one can be French without being a citizen in France [*être Francais sans être citoyen en France*]." Indeed, the most recent restatement of Article 7 in the 1994 Civil Code repeats the phrasing of the 1803 Code practically verbatim.[79]

As a necessary counterpoint, the Civil Code of 1803 defined without precedent in either revolutionary or Old Regime law the conditions under which it was possible for a foreigner to reside and take part in French civil law, but without becoming naturalized. Article 13 formalized the notion of "domicile," by which a foreigner requested permission to reside in France and was given by public powers full "civil rights." (The administrative and jurisidictional modalities of attribution were not yet defined, but fell logically to the municipalities in the first instance).[80] The article included two significant departures from both Old Regime jurisprudence and revolutionary legislation. No previous jurisprudence permitted an intermediary status for a foreigner who wished to reside in the kingdom without seeking citizenship, a status akin to the English denizen. The novelty of Article 13 was, in this sense, incontestable, although contemporary jurists glossed the relation between the Civil Code and the Old Regime by arguing that "naturalization" before the Revolution was functionally equivalent to the permission to reside in the kingdom.[81] The second implication was even more novel: for if foreign women were able to be naturalized in the Old Regime, and recognized as French until 1803, the Civil Code was to formally exclude them from the category of citizenship, permitting them only to enjoy, as foreigners, civil rights acquired by the permission to establish residence in the kingdom.

Articles 7 and 13 of the Civil Code of 1803 thus marked a rupture in nationality law; at the same time, the Civil Code conjointly marked a rupture in the legal status of resident foreigners—and more specifically, the legislation concerning what contemporaries still called the "droit d'aubaine." In the midst of the first discussion of the council of state on 25 July 1801 about the attribution of French nationality, Tronchet began to discuss Article 4 of the initial project: "The foreigner will exercise in France the same civil rights accorded to the French by the nation to which the foreigner belongs." Although not named in the article, subsequent debate within the commission was about the "droit d'aubaine." Tronchet was strongly in favor of reciprocally reimposing this droit d'aubaine, and in response to Bonaparte's query about the changes introduced by the Constituent Assembly, he set the terms of the debate.

Should the Civil Code follow the revolutionary assemblies, which had abolished the droit d'aubaine without any concern for reciprocity? Or should the principle of reciprocity be reinscribed into international law such that diplomatic conventions would regulate the question of a foreigner from a specific nation's ability to inherit in France and a Frenchman's ability to inherit in a particular foreign country? Bonaparte ordered the barrister Pierre-Louis Roederer, one of the architects of Bonaparte's own coup d'état of 18 brumaire year VIII (9 November 1799), to draw up a report.[82]

Roederer swiftly produced his summary report for the council of state on 24 thermidor year IX (12 August 1801), but First Consul Napoleon demanded an amplification of and detailed commentary on the legal abilities of foreigners from each nation to inherit, which took Roederer somewhat longer. Only on 8 frimaire year IX (29 November 1801), after consultation with the personnel of the foreign ministry, was he able to present his lengthy and learned disquisition on the droit d'aubaine, drawing on what was the third official compilation and classification of the treaties and conventions of the late eighteenth century.[83] In his report, he began with two significant moves. First, like other members of the council of state, Roederer identified the droit d'aubaine not as the right of the king to seize the property of a foreigner who died in the kingdom without a native heir but exclusively as the juridical incapacity that refused foreign heirs the right of succession in the kingdom. (Roederer further distinguished the capacity of the latter to do so—which he understood to be the object of the decree of 6 August 1790—from the ability of foreigners to inherit from French natives in the legislation of 1 April 1791.) From this point forward, almost all participants in the debates about the abolition of the "droit d'aubaine" that were to last until 1819 understood it as an inheritance restriction, not as a sovereign right. In this sense, the eighteenth-century revolution in citizenship that had abolished piecemeal the droit d'aubaine, and had led lawyers to distinguish a regal privilege from a national inheritance restriction, had completed its work. The droit d'aubaine had become definitively fixed as civil law, and not as a sovereign privilege or prerogative.

The second claim with lasting consequences lay in Roederer's rewriting of the history of the droit d'aubaine. Following Montesquieu and other Enlightened thinkers, Roederer traced its origins to barbarian times, before civilization softened mores, when Scythians ate foreigners. . . . But Roederer, like the eighteenth-century philosophes, did not simply identify the "feudal" origins of the droit d'aubaine. He also pointed to the political (and reciprocal) origins of the royal right as a solitary act of reprisal in the succession disputes of Edward III of England and Philip VI of France.[84] In the centuries that followed, the French kings had taken an opposite tact, continuously exempting foreigners and abolishing the droit d'aubaine for specific national, professional, or geographically defined groups. In this prism, the French Revolution appeared, on the one hand, as the culmination of a longstanding royal tradition identified with civilization itself and, on the other hand, as a rupture with the royalist tradition that had insisted on the principle of reciprocity.

Reciprocity once again was at the heart of the question: should France return to a system abolished in 1790 and 1791 in which the ability to inherit was tied, in the diplomatic sphere of international relations, to the principle of "perfect reciprocity"? Roederer argued that it should, but he did so only after undertaking a lengthy investigation of both fact and political theory. In empirical terms, he established the identities of states with which France had not signed treaties that reciprocally abolished the droit d'aubaine (and the droit de détraction). This made him the most recent but hardly the last in a long line of lawyers, administrators, politicians, and academics who generated massive tables of the eighteenth-century treaties that abolished, with or without restrictions, reciprocally or not, the droit d'aubaine and droit de détraction. Among his more than seventy treaties divided into six classes, Roederer noted that only for the English, by the patent letters of 18 January 1787, was the droit d'aubaine abolished without reciprocity, and that the only states for which no treaties existed were Prussia, the Papal States, the Ottoman Empire, Genoa, and (only concerning immovables) Sweden.

After establishing the facts, Roederer advanced a question of principle: Was it in the interest of France to revoke the benefits accorded to those few nations that had been without exemptions at the time of the laws of 1790 and 1791? More generally, should France extend to the larger states, Europe as a whole, or the entire world the right of foreigners to inherit without requiring reciprocity? Roederer argued that France should not, in any of these cases. Although it might be in the nation's general interest to attract immigrants who brought their talents and wealth to France, there were occasions—such as times of war—when it was not in France's interests to do so, and so it was best to abolish the droit d'aubaine only reciprocally and by diplomatic treaty. More important, the abolition of the droit d'aubaine (understood as an inheritance restriction on foreigners) represented a chimerical means of attracting foreigners to France, unless it was valid reciprocally and included the right of foreigners to inherit from native Frenchmen or women who had only foreign heirs. Roederer further argued that without the clause of reciprocity, the French who emigrated and became wealthy, spreading French culture and civilization along the way, would remain at the mercy of countries that continued to exercise the droit d'aubaine. Finally, and in perhaps his most compelling claim, Roederer pointed out that abolishing the droit d'aubaine without reciprocity destroyed any motivation of other nations to abolish it in favor of France, "and even authorizes those that had partially done so to take a step back toward barbarism."[85]

Roederer's report apparently produced little debate within the council of state, and the article was adopted as it had been presented.[86] The entire law of thirty-seven articles was presented to the Legislative Corps on 11 frimaire year X (2 December 1801) by Boulay. His exposition of the motives for the law sought distance from the example of Rome, where foreigners were excluded entirely from civil rights, and from the French Revolution, which had abolished the droit d'aubaine without reciprocity. An "intermediary solution" was required, founded on the principle of commerce and civilization that brought the world together in "a kind of general community." The "philanthropic" perspective of the Revolution had gone too far, and the wager that the unilateral abolition of the droit d'aubaine would engage other nations to do the same was deemed a complete failure. The only solution was to return to the principle of reciprocity whose "advantages had been felt in the last period of the monarchy."[87] The Legislative Corps adopted the article without debate, then transmitted that same day the first draft of the first article to the Civil Code back to the Tribunate.

At that moment, the relative unanimity of the jurists who drafted the first article broke down. A commission of the Tribunate (made up of Siméon, Boisjolin, Boissy d'Anglas, Chabaud, Caillemer, Roujoux, and Thiessé) reported on 25 frimaire year X (16 December 1801). It not only rejected the articles of the law touching on the definition of what it meant to be French (insisting, rather, that the principle of territoriality stand on an equal basis with that of filiation), and those concerning the withdrawal of civil rights (especially the articles on civil death), but also took a diametrically opposed stance on the droit d'aubaine, arguing in favor of the Revolution's unilateral abolition of inheritance restrictions.[88]

The Tribunate was ultimately to reject the proposed first article of the Civil Code principally on the basis of its formulations of Article II (on the loss of civil rights), and in the context of a widespread opposition to Napoleon's recently proposed concordat with the pope that revealed the ancient Gallican instincts of men previously of the Third Estate. Nonetheless, the specific debate over the droit d'aubaine—beginning 29 frimaire year X (20 December 1801) and lasting for ten days—demonstrated the depth of opposition to the "monarchical" principle of reciprocity reiterated in Roederer's report, and the surprisingly strong support for the Revolution's unilateral abolition of inheritance restrictions.

The opposition was led by the lawyer François Boissy d'Anglas, president of the Tribunate, whose career since 1789 revealed that he had, despite his modest radicalism during the Convention, "the heart of royalist, even in the darkest hours of the Revolution."[89] Yet his "royalism" hardly prevented him from supporting the revolutionary reforms. Three years before the Constituent Assembly's abolition of the droit d'aubaine in 1790, the monarchy had unilaterally abolished inheritance restrictions on subjects of the king of Great Britain. "Public opinion" supported this decision, he declaimed, as well as "the writings of the most enlightened men in this truly enlightened century." Louis XVI had not acted out of pure philanthropy in doing so; rather, he had acted out of interest, that of increasing French prosperity. Reciprocity would not, in this case, have advanced the interest of the state. With respect to England, a strict reciprocity would have required France to adopt the English system, an even harsher system of disallowing simple foreigners ("aliens") from owning land; disallowing permanent residents (whom he called "denizens"), naturalized by the king, to transmit an inheritance; and only allowing naturalized foreigners (through an act of Parliament) to inherit land. In the case of Spain, where the droit d'aubaine (he argued) was abolished in 1266, and where foreigners enjoyed even greater privileges than Spaniards, it would require France to treat foreigners better than French nationals. The only way to achieve a positive flow of population into France, to increase its wealth and prosperity, would be to make it as attractive as possible, and to uphold the Constituent Assembly's dismantling of the droit d'aubaine. Not only was it in France's interest, but reciprocity would soon follow: the failure of other nations to adopt similar laws removing inheritance obstacles was the result of the war against Europe, "this cruelly prolonged war that only ended with the victory" of France.

The debate thus slipped imperceptibly into one about France's immigration policy. As the marquis de Carrion Nisas, a great defender of Napoleon, argued, this was "the original question: Is it good to call forth the foreigner, to privilege him, to engage him by all means necessary to come and live on French territory?"[90] The transformation of the debate over a reestablished droit d'aubaine into one about French immigration policy was recast in terms more fitting of a nascent bourgeois and manufacturing society, and it was this discourse that came to fruition in the final abolition of the droit d'aubaine in 1819. But already in 1801, France had "caught up" to the English debate about immigration: discussions of the droit d'aubaine no longer turned on royal authority, nor even on the acquisition of French citizenship, but rather on the state's own immigration policies and on the best ways to encourage the settlement of wealthy foreigners (and not the "scum of nations") in France.[91]

Members of the Tribunate elaborated on the commercial importance and political interests of France in recruiting wealthy foreigners. Granlh returned to the arguments of the Enlightenment, if not Physiocracy, in invoking the "science of political economy" and the "ideas of commerce, its means, and its advantages" as the source of a law on foreigners. After twelve terrible years of war, France was in desperate need of foreign capital, and exponents of reciprocity—what he called the "Roman system"—misjudged the extent to which the "droit d'aubaine" would repel future immigrants. Moreover, Article 4 reestablishing reciprocity would be a retrograde step because, even before its suppression in 1790, "the droit d'aubaine only existed as exceptions, and immunity was the natural state." If adopted, Article 4 would reestablish the droit d'aubaine "not as it existed in the last days of the monarchy, limited and restrained by a wealth of exemptions in favor of industry, commerce, and capital, but as it existed in the times of superstition and barbarism, without exceptions or restrictions."[92] Others concurred, citing the usual suspects, Montesquieu, Adam Smith, Jean-Jacques Rousseau, Jacques Necker, the Physiocrats Le Trosne, Turgot, Mirabeau, and others. They denied the Roman origins of the droit d'aubaine, and linked it, following Montesquieu, to the epoch of barbarism. The droit d'aubaine, in a poignant metaphor that all would have accepted, was a "languishing branch of the old tree of feudalism: it should follow the destiny of the trunk, without apparent usefulness, to which its frail existence is linked."[93]

There were, to be sure, other arguments against the proposed Article 4 besides that of encouraging wealthy foreigners to settle in France. Among those who pointed out the difficulties involved in the article's implementation was Camille Saint-Aubin, who was born in the duchy of Deux-Ponts in the Rhineland, had come to France during the Revolution and had benefited from an "automatic" naturalization by the time he began his political career in 1794.

In allowing the status of specific national groups of foreigners to be defined by diplomatic relations, Saint-Aubin argued,

> It would not only be necessary to create an ad hoc diplomatic office which would examine the thousand and one ways in which foreigners are treated, in relation to civil rights, in the different states of Europe, and in the different provinces of each of these states; but also, the courts and administrations charged with the daily application of this law of reciprocity on foreigners in their jurisdictions would be obliged to consult at all times this Code, which would be far more voluminous than the customal of Brittany and its commentaries ever were.

Low-level administrators would be required to find out about the status of movable and immovable property in Wertheim, Wales, Livonia, South Carolina, and everywhere else, he continued. "What chaos! What a labyrinth!": such would be the inevitable consequences of a system of pure reciprocity.[94] Other opponents sought to counter the nationalistic claims made in favor of the return of the droit d'aubaine, such as those of the conservative comte de Curée. Member of the Tribunate and then the Conservative Senate, Curée had argued that the dignity, respect, and love for the land, "the defense of which cost the blood of a million brave men," would be sacrificed to the interests of powerful foreign capitalists on whom entire families within French cities depended, and who would maintain complete control of their immense revenues and properties. Although grounded in the language of patriotism and nationalism, the position recalls the physiocratic antipathy toward merchants and industrialists, and their exclusion from the citizenship of proprietors and cultivators.[95]

Obscure as the droit d'aubaine might have been, the debate and opposition in the Tribunate to the proposed Article 4 of the Civil Code thus became an occasion to continue some of the ideological struggles of the French revolutionaries against feudalism while transforming the debate about the droit d'aubaine into one about French immigration policy. Not all those who spoke against the principle of reciprocity were bitter opponents of Bonaparte, however, or even of the monarchical tradition. And none of the more outspoken opponents of the article were targeted in the purge of the Tribunate in March 1802, following the defeat of the legislative package in January.

That purge led to a far more accommodating Tribunate, which listened respectfully to a new proposal for Title I of the Civil Code, presented on 5 March 1803. Article 11—corresponding to what had been Article 4—reestablished what contemporaries and recent historians have misleadingly called the "droit d'aubaine" by stating that "the foreigner will possess in France the same civil rights as are or will be accorded to the French by the treaties of the nation to which this foreigner belongs." Accepted without debate, the article was included in the law that was approved by a vote of 52–2. The droit d'aubaine— now understood as restrictions on the capacity to inherit property, including the incidental taxes on property passing outside the jurisdiction known as the droit de détraction—was thus reintroduced, and was later affirmed tacitly in Articles 726 and 912, which confirmed the right of foreigners to inherit on the basis of reciprocity. This "droit d'aubaine" did not include the state's right to confiscate the estate, nor even the incapacity to make a will or to transmit a succession ab intestat, but only the capacity to inherit from a French native.[96]

Thus was a decision about the civil status of foreigners turned back into an issue of international private law and diplomacy. The meaning of the relevant articles of the Civil Code, however, was not at all obvious to the baron de Talleyrand, minister of foreign relations and future plenipotentiary at the Paris and Vienna peace conferences of 1814–15, who sought clarification on the question of reciprocity. Was a formal treaty absolutely necessary, or could a simple convention suffice? Or could a foreigner be allowed to reclaim an inheritance "by proving in an authentic way that the same possession [of rights] is accorded to Frenchmen by the law of his country?" In a letter of 14 floréal year XII (4 May 1804), Minister of Justice Claude-Ambroise Reignier, an ex-barrister of Nancy in the Old Regime who had participated in Napoleon's coup d'état of 1799, sent a clarification in response to his colleague's queries. The highest judicial authority in France answered clearly: Article 11 used the word "treaty" in its most rigorous sense, but the goal of reciprocity was its endgame. "When this reciprocity is constant, when the proofs that establish it are authentic and cannot be placed into doubt, it seems to me that the foreigner should be admitted [to inherit], since the goal of the law is accomplished." The proof of reciprocity could lie in "treaties, specific conventions, or the dispositions of territorial laws": what mattered was that the principle of reciprocity be at all times respected.[97]

As the republic became an empire in fact then in name, Napoleon's armies marched across Europe, defeating allied powers with relative ease. "La Grande Nation" was to eventually stretch from Hamburg to the Adriatic and to include 130 departments by 1812. The Low Countries, including the Netherlands, and much of northern and central Italy became French, as did the Illyrian provinces. In their formal annexation, following the Old Regime principles of conquest, their inhabitants suffered no further inheritance restrictions as foreigners—although their status was to be further debated in 1814, once those territories were returned.[98] As for the allied states, several of the previously named "sister Republics," including those established by Napoleon on the Italian Peninsula, were transformed into "kingdoms" (as France shifted its political vocabulary back to that of the Old Regime) and were granted remission and exemption from inheritance restrictions. Such was the case for the subjects of what became in late 1805 the "Kingdom of Italy," for whom the droit d'aubaine and all other inheritance restrictions were abolished by imperial decree of 19

TABLE 8.1.
Abolitions of the *Droit de détraction,* 1811–1813

Country	Date of Treaty	Object	French Abolition
Duchy of Anhalt-Bernburg	24 December 1812	Droits d'aubaine and détraction	18 March 1813
Kingdom of Denmark	30 December 1812	Droit de détraction	10 July 1813 (treaty)
Free City of Frankfurt	15 January 1812	Droit d'aubaine	25 April 1812
Principality of Lippe-Detmold	7 December 1812	Droits d'aubaine and détraction	18 March 1813
Lucca and Piombino	23 January 1811	Droit d'aubaine, with reciprocal inheritance rights	?
Duchy of Mecklenburg-Schwerin	13 March 1812	Droit d'aubaine and détraction	28 May 1812
Duchy of Mecklenburg-Strelitz	10 December 1812	Droits d'aubaine and détraction	18 March 1813
Kingdom of Prussia	6 August 1811	Droits d'aubaine and détraction	2 December 1811
Principality of Schwarzburg-Sondershausen	12 December 1812	Droits d'aubaine and détraction	18 March 1813
Principality of Schwarzburg-Rudolstadt	7 December 1812	Droits d'aubaine and détraction	18 March 1813
Principality of Waldeck	20 January 1813	Droits d'aubaine and détraction	15 May 1813

Source: C. De Martens and F. de Cussy, *Recueil manuel et pratique de traités, conventions et autres actes diplomatiques . . . depuis l'année 1760 jusqu'à l'époque actuelle,* 4 vols. (Leipzig, 1846); and J.-B. Gaschon, *Code diplomatique des aubains* (Paris, 1818).

February 1806 (a decree that also included the annexed territories of Parma, Piacenza, and Guastalla), and foreigners were specifically given the ability to inherit property from French natives.[99] Other smaller European states, especially in the Rhineland, remained nominally independent, although closely allied with France. The minor inheritance restrictions that subsisted among them, the droits de détraction or succession, had been reciprocally maintained in the eighteenth-century treaties, and were subjected to Article 11 of the Civil Code. In response to a wave of decrees by the rulers of these smaller principalities in 1811 and 1812, the French Empire formally acknowledged the elimination of the droit de détraction in a series of "letters to ratify compromises" (*réversales*) (table 8.1).

Many of these international accords acknowledged in their preambles the conventions and treaties of the eighteenth-century citizenship revolution. They stated that the residual inheritance restrictions had been reciprocally maintained in those treaties or that the droit d'aubaine had been subsequently reintroduced. Either way, the Old Regime principle of reciprocity, eliminated during the Revolution, triumphed again under Napoleon. It was not the only dimension of nationality law that suggested a return, however incomplete and distinctive, to the Old Regime.

Return of the Old Regime? Naturalization from the Napoleonic Empire to the Bourbon Restoration (1803–1814)

The Civil Code's rupture with revolutionary legislation in Article 7 (distinguishing civil and political rights), Article 13 (permitting foreigners to enjoy civil rights having requested of the government a permission to reside in France), and Article 11 (the restoration of the "droit d'aubaine") marked three different instances of rupture with Old Regime jurisprudence. The fourth case of rupture was the reinstitution of the exclusive, discretionary authority of the executive to naturalize foreigners. Contemporaneous with the passage of the Civil Code, this legislation bore the mark of Napoleon's authoritarian hand and represented an even more formal return to the older, prerevolutionary models. Yet in practice naturalization under Napoleon differed substantially in legal, social, and administrative terms.

The absence of the sovereign's discretionary authority to naturalize after the Constitution of 1791 did not mean that individual "foreigners" were without recourse to the central executive in seeking affirmation of their status as "French citizens." Dispersed throughout the archives of the revolutionary governments are a handful of cases involving foreigners who requested naturalization from the government, despite the fact that they had fulfilled all the statutory requirements, put in place by the revolutionary governments, that assured them of their French citizenship. Revolutionary law and the practice of automatic naturalization left many interpretive gaps into which foreigners fell. To take but one example: the case of Louis Benell, a Danish subject of the Swedish king, already settled in France before the Revolution. Benell had lived in the towns of Chartres then in Saint-Germain-en-Laye since August 1786, where he had acquired property and annuities worth twenty-seven hundred francs annually, and where he had served in the National Guard during the Revolution. In his request to the interior minister on 27 messidor year V (15 July 1797), he sought to be "naturalized as a French citizen." According to the ministry, he had brought a certificate of the municipality of Saint-Germain declaring his acceptance of the constitution, and local testimony that he had in fact participated in the primary assemblies during the Revolution (thus proving that he already exercised the "rights of the citizen"). The ministry reported that, having lived in France for eleven years, having acquired property and exercised his political rights, he could be declared a French citizen, and ordered his name "inscribed on the civic register."[100] But the case was to prove exceptional, as the government subsequently made clear, that naturalization could occur only *after* the acquisition of a formal permission to reside.[101] The council of state was to affirm on 20 prairial year XI (9 June 1803) that a prior "permission to reside" under Article 7 of the Civil Code was an essential condition of subsequent naturalization, which would then result from a decree on the basis of a report of the minister of justice and the opinion of the council of state. The appellate courts were subsequently to assert, in decisions of 1825 and 1829, that a foreigner could not become French no matter how long his residence, or how great his taxes, without a prior authorization fixing his domicile in France. But the council of state refused in the same decision to formally regulate the validity of past acts, noting in 1803 that "these permissions [to reside in France] are subjected to modifications, restrictions, even revocations, depending on circumstances, and should only be determined by rules or general formulas."[102]

The administrative confusion stemmed from the fact that none of the revolutionary constitutions, including that of 1799, had created the administrative protocol of discretionary naturalization. Only as a result of a proposal presented to the Senate by the government on 16 vendémiaire year XI (8 October 1802), voted into law ten days later, was such a mechanism—including the reestablishment of a Conseil du sceau des titres, under the chancellor—reinvented.[103] The official motivation behind the law was to encourage immigration: the need to call foreigners "to the heart of a pacified and triumphant France" (after the peace treaty with Great Britain). The law's preamble continued: "Some, drawn only by the desire to see the Great Nation victorious by its own forces against almost the entire universe allied against her, take back to their own countries astonishment and admiration; others make the vow to associate themselves to so many advantages, to share such a destiny rich in reality and hope: they desire to become French."[104] The government saw that Article 3 of the Constitution of 1799 provided a general rule, but that there could be exceptions "motivated by circumstances, founded on the public interest, authorized by justice, even required as reward." It had in mind wealthy and enterprising foreigners, especially those talented with manufacturing "secrets," artisans, and soldiers who had already demonstrated, at the risk of life and limb, their devotion and loyalty to the French nation. Criticizing the provisions of Article 4 of the 1791 Constitution that had given such a prerogative to the legislature, the government argued that only the executive—in this case, the council of state—could guarantee that the "favor" accorded would be done with justice and prudence.[105]

The law of 1802 was approved for a five-year period. Its enactment immediately required clarification and amplification after a handful of foreigners—including a Danish military captain, a Neapolitan chemistry professor, and a Greek naval captain—quickly stepped forward seeking to be naturalized. The council of state decided that they would be naturalized only after a minimum one-year period following their declared residence.[106] More than a year after the law's expiration in 1806, a *sénatus-consulte* of 21 February 1808 institutionalized the practice of the executive and discretionary conferral of naturalization, providing both ideological justification and administrative protocol, which had hitherto remained unregulated.

Article 1: A foreigner who renders or has rendered important services to the state, or who brings to it talents, inventions, or useful industries, or who establishes large enterprises, can, after a year of residence, be admitted to the possession of the right of a French citizen.

Article 2. This right shall be conferred by a special decree, rendered on the basis of a report of a minister, with the accord of the Council of State.

Article 3. An executionary act of the said decree will be delivered to the claimant, endorsed by the Justice Minister.

Article 4. The claimant, supplied with this execution, will present himself before the municipality of his domicile and take the civic oath of obedience to the constitutions of the Empire and of fidelity to the Emperor. A register and verbal proceeding of this oath-swearing will be drawn up.[107]

Still, the protocol was not transparent, especially because the law did not fully curtail the devolution of authority over citizenship to the municipalities.

From the beginning of the French Revolution until 1808, mayors of communes (towns, cities, and villages) held an unusual authority as the gatekeepers of nationality law: their declarations and statements were proof of a foreigner's length of residence, social integration, and political behavior.[108] A report to the emperor on 30 June 1808 by the interior minister noted that "until now, those foreigners who acquired [naturalization] by statute, had their title validated by the mayors of their communes in their respective domiciles, and the title that they thus obtained can only have been a certificate of their inscription on the civic register." That practice, however, was "too simple" and left too much discretion to "the lowest functionary of the administrative order." Instead, the importance of naturalization was such that only the emperor himself should be able to "pronounce" the acquisition of the title of citizen. Thus the decree of 17 March 1809 that suppressed the "automatic" acquisition of nationality entirely, and established the administrative procedures to be followed: once the "conditions required to become a French citizen" were met, "his naturalization would be pronounced by Us," that is, the emperor himself.[109]

In practice, however, even if the effective power to naturalize was centralized in the person of the executive, the administrative procedures through which foreigners proved either their residence (according to the Constitution of 1799) or their exceptional merit (by the laws of 1802 and 1808) remained confused. This is revealed in a limited sample of the incomplete, surviving dossiers involving foreigners' requests for permission to reside in France or to be naturalized before 1814.[110] Before 1810, it was unclear exactly how municipalities receiving requests to establish domicile from foreigners would proceed, and whether the minister of justice or the interior would make the report and recommendation to the emperor.[111] The council of state turned down quite a few initial requests because the petitioners had not first established their legal domicile in France, as was the case of Matthias Mazaneque, an Austrian prisoner of war, who requested naturalization on 22 July 1811.[112] Most petitions for naturalization (although exactly what proportion cannot be known) were put forth by foreigners who were technically "prisoners of war," their status defined by a series of decrees in 1802 and 1803 that identified foreigners from enemy countries. These were men who had often legally established their residence in France (and sang in their petitions of their great contributions to the nation's commerce and industry). Thus the case of George Hards, an English mechanic living in Saint-Quentin, who made his original request for naturalization, as a prisoner of war, on 28 December 1806. It was a request without immediate issue, and on 19 March 1808 he wrote again, this time to the comte de Montalivet, minister of the interior. In his request for naturalization, he described his plans for a sewer system in Paris, and offered to construct "in front of your own eyes" an alarm clock for the emperor that would allow him "to learn, every morning, whether a sentinel was absent or had fallen asleep the previous night." More than three years after this second request, War Minister Berthier, prince of Neuchâtel and Wagram, wrote that there was no reason to remove him from the list of war prisoners because "he has established no business of his own, and does not give any guarantee, by his wealth, of the sincerity of his declarations." (Such a judgment was made despite the recommendation of the subprefect to the justice ministry in July 1811 that Hards, since his residence in Saint-Quentin, "had rendered his services essential to the merchants who are owners of the cotton mills," a fact attested by the "landowners of the town" in their own letter that summer.) The justice minister overruled the war minister, however, and authorized a naturalization on 4 October 1811.[113]

It should be apparent that such requests for naturalization, unlike those for legal domicile in France, were exclusively accorded to men. Such was the logical implication of the Civil Code's distinction between "civil" and "political" rights, the former pertaining to participation in the political sphere, which excluded women (and other incapable persons). Before 1803, we have seen, women might seek to confirm their "quality of Frenchwomen," as passive or simple citizens, in the courts or at the level of local communities. But after 1803, as was clarified in the several requests from or on behalf of women to the council of state, foreign women no longer had any claims to French citizenship.

Thus the Irishman Robert Beeby, who had been accorded on 11 April 1807 the "title of French citizen," and who believed—until doubts had been cast— that the privilege would extend to his daughters, two of whom were under age. His concerns were obvious, and they were ancient: he wanted to assure that his large fortune in France could be inherited, and petitioned in 1806 for their rights of citizenship "in all that can concern a person of her sex." The response of Minister of Interior Crétet, comte de Champmol, on 31 December 1807 was unequivocal: citing the Civil Code, he wrote that "French women possess civil rights and not political rights. Foreign women cannot claim the same rights . . . they follow the condition of their husbands when they are married, and will be considered either French or foreigners when their husbands are either French or foreigners."[114] When women requested naturalization—such as the English women Louise Stephens and Anne Bradshaw—they were informed in no uncertain terms that they could legally establish domicile only and thereby lay claim to enjoy the civil rights authorized by the Civil Code, but could not be naturalized as citizens.[115]

Nor was the procedure for naturalization by any means automatic. Unlike the Old Regime, even a proper completion of the confusing administrative protocols was no guarantee that naturalization would be granted. The ministries of interior and justice, along with those of police and war, scrutinized carefully all of the requests, and although there were often disagreements among them, the general tendency was to refuse naturalization by the laws of 1802 and 1808 for any number of often undisclosed reasons. Some dossiers, of course, were fully in order, and gained approval with relative expediency. Jean Charles Burckhardt, born in Leipzig (Saxony), was admitted to the exercise of the rights of a French citizen on 18 thermidor year XI (6 August 1803) by means of the law passed less than a year earlier because he was a "distinguished astronomer, the author of numerous treatises on different scientific matters, an adjunct member of the Longitude Bureau at the Collège de France," even though he had lived in France for only five and a half years. More common were the requests, expeditiously denied by the council of state, that did not merit "the honor of naturalization."[116]

Among those seeking naturalization before 1814, several were foreigners for whom, technically speaking, naturalization was not necessary, as they had already fulfilled the statutory requirements and gained automatic naturalization from the revolutionary constitutions. Thus Isaac Brown, a tobacco and arms manufacturer from England resident in Dunkerque since 1783 who had five children, all of whom had been born in France. According to his petition of 5 November 1807, he already considered himself a French citizen, and had been exempted from the precautionary and police measures taken against foreigners. But his request for an official affirmation of his citizenship was turned down, first by the prefect (because the five-year law of 1802 had already expired), and then by the council of state on 18 April 1809 (because, in its reasoning, the dispositions of the new law of 19 February 1808 were not applicable, and Brown produced no evidence that he had ever requested a legal domicile such as was required by Article 3 of the 1799 Constitution!).[117] In several cases an earlier document issued by a municipality provided the claim of prior citizenship, as was the case of Michel Busnah, who came to Marseille in 1795 to start a business, and who in 1809 provided a document signed by the municipality on 1 frimaire year V (21 November 1796) that recognized his "quality as a citizen" (*qualité de citoyen*). He requested that the government "recognize [him] as French and allow him to possess all the advantages attached to this quality." Although the outcome is not known, a marginal note in his petition stated that although, admittedly, he had acquired the title of citizen, "it is necessary that he ask the Emperor to accord him the act."[118]

In short, the government reinstituted in 1802 and 1808 the practice of discretionary naturalization abolished after the 1791 Constitution, although its procedures were hardly as routinized or "automatic" as those of the Old Regime. Part of the project involved the imperial government's retrieval of the authority to confer citizenship from the hands of the municipality. Everything happened as if the revolutionary experiments with automatic naturalization had sent France down a "Spanish road," where communities retained the authority to naturalize foreigners. The empire quickly wrested the authority from local communities and officials, restoring aspects of a distinctively French monarchical model of exclusive and discretionary naturalization. More important, the revolutionary definition of citizenship as political participation, social assimilation, and moral virtue continued to exact its price. Beyond simple membership in the polity, citizenship was a reward for "virtue" and "public service" conferred on a male, established landowners or merchants, who thereby acquired the right of political participation. The empire replaced the revolutionary practices of naturalization by statute, and reconceived the "honor" as a reward for service and contribution to the public good. France had come full circle, returning to a version of the sixteenth-century juridical model of citizenship as merit and virtue, now conceived largely in the language of social utility.

What happened to naturalization and citizenship in 1814, when the empire finally collapsed? Napoleon's first abdication in April led quickly to the restoration of the Bourbon monarch, Louis XVIII, and the negotiation of the first Treaty of Paris, signed on 30 May 1814. By that treaty between France and the allied powers, France was brought back to its 1792 borders (for which the treaty announced the imminent delimitation), conserving several of its revolutionary conquests and most of its colonial possessions. Article 28 expressly upheld the reciprocal abolition of the droits d'aubaine, détraction, "or others of the same nature."[119] Napoleon was to return, memorably, during the One Hundred Days (March–June 1815), and the second restoration of Louis XVIII was accompanied by the much harsher Treaty of Vienna (9 June 1815). Now France's boundaries were reduced to those of 1789 (but including Avignon), and the country suffered an indemnity of seven hundred million francs. Yet in the domain of naturalization and legislation concerning foreigners, it was the Treaty of Paris in 1814 that unleashed a debate within the new bicameral French parliament—the Chambers of Peers and Deputies—that restored and distorted an Old Regime vocabulary and set of practices.

In the first instance, Louis XVIII proffered a royal ordinance to the chambers, passed without debate on 4 June 1814, specifically benefiting foreign members of the imperial nobility—seven senators, ministers (including the prince of Essling and the count of Belderblusch, minister of the electorate of Cologne) and military generals (including Maréchal Massena)—all of whom had voted for the removal of the emperor after the One Hundred Days, and whose reward came in the form of naturalization. These men were not explicitly named in the general ordinance of 4 June, but the resulting individual letters of naturalization issued in August reveal that they were indeed the object of the decree.[120] The law cited ancient royal ordinances dating to the fourteenth century that prohibited "at the demand of the Estates General" foreigners from possessing offices or benefices, or holding any public function in France. "We have not sought to reproduce the severity of these ordinances," read the decree, "but it is above all necessary to see seated in the chambers only men whose birth guarantees their devotion to the sovereign and the law of the state, and who were raised, from childhood, with the love of their fatherland." The ordinance affirmed the emperor's "privilege" to accord letters of naturalization, while nonetheless assuring that the dispositions of the Civil Code concerning naturalization be executed. No mention was made of Napoleon's laws of 1802 and 1808 concerning discretionary naturalization: the point of reference, in the absence of provisions in the Civil Code or the Constitution of 1799, was exclusively the Old Regime.[121]

On 30 August, the king presented the letters to both chambers, and in December the Chamber of Peers acted, in the name of a special commission that included Boissy d'Anglas, to approve that legal privilege now called "letters of great naturalization" (lettres de grande naturalisation). The continuity with the Old Regime, at least regarding the protocol and the text itself, was uncanny: not only did the chambers act on 13 December 1814 as if they were simply "registering" the king's privilege, as the Chambres des comptes had done in the Old Regime, but the texts of these letters were a verbatim reproduction of the royal privilege of naturalization under the Old Regime. Clearly, the crown had either relied on one of the model texts in circulation during the eighteenth century or chosen a particular example of prerevolutionary naturalization to serve as a model. Indeed, there was only one sentence in the 1814 letters that differed from an Old Regime letter of naturalization: the naturalized foreigner was given not only the capacity to devolve and inherit property, as one of the "privileges, franchises, and liberties" that he was to enjoy, but specifically received "the right to sit in the Chamber of Peers and that of Deputies."[122]

Between the ordinance of 4 June 1814, which set forth the principle of great naturalization, and the "registration" of specific instances by the Chamber of Peers that December, a second, and far more contentious, debate echoed through the French parliamentary chambers. That debate concerned the thousands of "foreign" men who had served the French government at the height of its imperial expansion "through their talents, their enlightenment, and their services" as soldiers, officials, or merchant suppliers in territories that had been annexed to the empire but which by the Treaty of Paris were returned to foreign powers. On 9 August 1814, Sieur Dembray, chancellor and president of the Chamber of Peers, presented a draft law proposing that "letters of declaration of naturalization" (*lettres de declaration de naturalité*) be given to the inhabitants of the departments united to France since 1791 who either resided on French territory or who did not meet the requirements of Article 3 of the 1799 Constitution, which required a demonstrable and uninterrupted residence of ten years. The draft law also stated that other individuals born and resident in departments that were no longer part of France could ask for permission to establish themselves, and would receive (as by the Constitution of 1799) "civil rights" without exercising the "rights of the citizen." This meant, according to the chancellor, the existence of two kinds of letters. "The first are reserved for eminent services rendered, and submitted to the two Chambers, that confer the full rights of the citizen, only excluding those reserved in the ordinance of 4 June [1814] to participate in the making of laws in the Chambers of Peers and Deputies." The second were the "letters of declaration of naturalization" that conferred "ordinary," or civil, rights. The distinction, according to the chancellor, was necessary "to reconcile the care of our glory and our security with proper measures due to new Frenchmen."[123]

The distinction between "letters of naturalization" and "declarations of naturalization" reproduced the terms, without duplicating the meaning, of the Old Regime instruments, masking the radical ruptures of the revolutionary and Napoleonic decades. Part of the rupture can be seen in the abbreviated debate of the Chamber of Peers on 9 August 1814. Begun at four in the afternoon, the debate briefly raised the question of whether declarations of naturalization were "favors" or "rights," and the chancellor quickly silenced proponents of the second position in stressing the former, that declarations of naturalization were to be interpreted above all as a discretionary act of royal authority. Although no further substantive comments from the chamber followed, a number of voices nonetheless fixed on the formula of the proposed law, claiming that the legislative authority of parliament (and not the executive authority of the king) was paramount. But after a brief debate, the royalists surfaced: worried about raising delicate constitutional matters, they argued that in agreeing to the law the legislature would be participating in the conferred adoption by the two chambers, and thus involved in citizenship. By voice vote, and then by counted ballots, the law was approved by an "absolute majority" and sent to the Chamber of Deputies.[124]

The lower house formed a special commission charged with examining the law, and it reported, in the person of Augustin Ollivier (grandson of a grocer, and ex-regent of the Bank of France) on 16 September 1814. The commission proposed an amendment to the third article because of the equivocal status of the inhabitants of ex-departments of the empire. According to Ollivier, "They have almost ceased to be French, although they cannot quite be assimilated to true foreigners, or at least not all of them." Not all foreigners were in the same position: some had lived in France ten years, others had lived less than that in the empire, but had expressed their desire to become French citizens, while still others had stayed in their native land. Ollivier's amended Article 3 was very much a compromise position from a royalist perspective, allowing the king to give inhabitants of the "separated departments, when judged necessary, letters of declaration of naturalization before the completion of ten years of residence."[125]

A second position on Article 3 was staked out by the playwright, philologist, and sometime political deputy (he was to shortly renounce all political activity) Just-François-Marie Raynouard. According to the record of his intervention, the question of residence was irrelevant, because these inhabitants were not by any stretch of the French language "foreigners." Relying on what he called an "essential principle of public law," he argued that once incorporated into France by an international treaty, they became members of that state, forming part of its "great family." His amendment to Article 3 was based on Old Regime precedents, corresponding to the historical and philological interests expressed in his tragic poems. In the Chamber, he cited as precedents and models the royal edicts of 1687 and 1715, and proposed that soldiers, public functionaries, and manufacturers who come to settle in France be "reputed to be French natives" (réputés naturels français) without having to take letters of naturalization, and without having established a prior ten-year residence in the kingdom.

A lively debate ensued over the next two weeks in which more than thirty deputies intervened in lengthy speeches, all of them published as pamphlets, as a broader debate within print culture. A more radical opinion was voiced by Pierre Glaugergues, a lawyer from Toulouse who had lived his professional life in the regions of Roman law, which may have led him to argue for fewer obstacles to the assimilation of foreigners. Emphasizing the tenets of public international law—inherited from the Old Regime—he insisted that the inhabitants of the "separated departments" were equally French. The "de-unification" of French territory did not take away their Frenchness, and they did not require any state intervention to be "declared" French. Their own expressions of will— as evidenced in their resettlement within France's boundaries—was enough. No further law was necessary, he continued, since Article 27 of the Paris treaty of May 1814 had provided a six-year period in which "native inhabitants and foreigners from whatever nation" could resettle in the country they chose.[126]

The debate was spirited, enough so that by late September the Chamber of Deputies decided to create a "secret committee" to further discuss the project. Its opinion was swiftly presented by baron Claude-Pierre Bouvier, trained under the Old Regime as a barrister and law professor at Dijon, who had survived as a staunch royalist under the republic and the empire. Not surprisingly, then, he took on the more absolutist-derived model and supported the original bill: these men from the foreign territories of France were foreigners, he stated unequivocally. They required the government's authority to reside in France, and a completion of the Civil Code provisions to become naturalized (unless their residence requirement was shortened by royal decree). In proffering such an opinion, Bouvier offered a strange gloss on the Old Regime and on the jurists who commented on the Civil Code. The latter had equated Old Regime naturalization with the state's conferral of the right to reside in the kingdom, and to enjoy all the civil rights of natives, according to Article 13. Bouvier equated "nativeness" (*naturalité*) with the "title of citizen" (*titre de citoyen*), as distinct from the status of "native-born resident" (*regnicole*). The latter provided all civil rights enjoyed by Frenchmen, but that did not give a foreigner the right to political participation. This bizarre equivalency, which retrospectively turned Old Regime naturalization into a capacity for political action, prompted yet a third version of an amendment to Article 3, put forth by deputies Pompières and Labbey. The amendment stated that a simple declaration and residence in France on the part of inhabitants of the separated territories would suffice to give them civil rights, but to exercise political rights, they would be required to request "letters of naturalization."[127]

The debate continued until 29 September 1814, when, at the urging of the president and despite several objections from the floor, the chamber voted on the original amendment to Article 3 proposed by the commission. Each article was read and adopted in succession, and a final secret ballot produced a clear majority in favor of the law: of 193 votes cast, 139 (72 percent) of the deputies approved the measure. The result was a bill that reintroduced the possibility of declarations of naturalization for those who did not fulfill the conditions of Article 3 of the Constitution of 1799, and reaffirmed that others could establish themselves in the kingdom without exercising the prerogatives of French citizens while nonetheless enjoying the civil rights outlined in Article 11 of the Civil Code of 1803. At the same time, it produced a jurisprudential controversy that lasted until the 1840s over whether letters of declaration acquired after the law of 1814 were retroactively effective or not.[128]

By the end of the Napoleonic Empire, then, the Old Regime categories and practices of naturalization had been reconceived in light of the Civil Code. On the one hand, the restored monarchy had affirmed the code's elimination of the revolutionary reforms that had unilaterally abolished the droit d'aubaine, restoring a "droit d'aubaine" redefined narrowly as the residual inheritance incapacities not reciprocally abolished by diplomatic treaties. On the other hand, the new Bourbon king and his royalist parliamentary bodies had explicitly returned to Old Regime practices of naturalization, while modifying these substantially. Three kinds of "naturalization" were put into place. "Great naturalizations" were reserved for a small political elite who sought the highest political offices in parliament. "Naturalizations" entailing political rights (such as they existed in the Restoration) were given to meritorious foreigners who had previously been granted permissions to establish their domicile in France. And "declarations of naturalization" were to be conferred on "useful" foreigners—soldiers, manufacturers, and property owners—born in territories detached from the empire who subsequently settled in France and sought to enjoy the civil rights of French nationals. It is perhaps not surprising that the restored monarchy made little overt reference to the practices of the imperial government, although in the second case, the 1814 laws reproduced the intentions of Napoleon in his laws of 1802 and 1808.

Nonetheless, despite such apparent continuity, a profound rupture had taken place. The invention of a distinction between "civil" and "political" rights was the result of the revolutionary affirmation of citizenship as political participation. Citizenship became the domain of male property owners, distinguished from the broader and socially more inclusive definition of who was a French national, who shared the (legal) "quality of a Frenchman." Most foreigners in France, who settled with the permission of the government, became much like the denizens of England: enjoying most civil rights, they were treated like French nationals in civil law, but they could not without naturalization participate in the political life of the nation. Thus, as we shall see in conclusion, naturalization became a largely unattractive procedure for most foreigners, even before the final abolition of the droit d'aubaine in 1819.

CONCLUSION
ENDING THE OLD REGIME IN 1819

The story that frames this book ends in 1819, when the French government formally and definitively abolished what was still called the "droit d'aubaine" as the last, feudal vestige of a premodern world. But 1819, by any other standard, is a date without apparent significance in the social, political, or legal histories of French immigration, citizenship, or nationality.

The social history of foreigners in France is not inflected, even symbolically, by the droit d'aubaine's demise in 1819. After the European peace settlements following the fall of Napoleon in 1814 (and 1815), migratory flows to France did not grow or change their nature substantially in the course of the nineteenth century. France was an asylum for political refugees, a "land of liberty" (but also internment of Spanish, Italian, and German liberals), and the country continued to attract foreigners of all social statuses (although far fewer than the French who emigrated during the nineteenth century). Patterns of immigration did not shift until the mass arrival of foreign laborers towards the end of the century, after the first wave of "industrial migration" in the 1870s that so fundamentally reshaped the practices of citizenship and naturalization in republican France.[1]

In the political history of citizenship itself, 1819 changed nothing. The Charter of 1815 had created suffrage and representation of a highly limited nature, a regime of male property owners and, increasingly after 1830, manufacturers and industrialists. Although a great change from the "democracy without citizenship" of the First Empire, formal political participation was limited in the nineteenth century until the expansion of male suffrage during the Second Republic (1848–51). Although citizenship was democratized, it was only after the end of the Second Empire that it became a republican practice socially inclusive of all men, independent of their access to property, while French women did not become political citizens until 1947.[2]

Legally, according to older and more recent accounts of French nationality law, 1819 is a date without apparent meaning. The framework of nationality defined by the first article of the Civil Code (1803), with its emphasis on *ius sanguinis*, dominated the mode of attributing French nationality in the nineteenth century. Despite modest returns to *ius soli* in 1831 and 1851, it was not until the celebrated Nationality Law of 1889 that France "returned" to republican territorial principles. More central to this story, the Nationality Law of 1889 ended the need for an intermediary status of resident foreigners who enjoyed civil but not political rights (although Article 13 of the Civil Code was only abolished in the law of 1927), and it created the modern bureaucratic protocol, and the demand, for naturalization. Between 1889 and 1896, the annual requests for naturalization increased nearly tenfold over what they had averaged before the Third Republic. Driven by industrial migration and colonial questions, thousands of foreigners were required to be naturalized to gain access to the benefits of citizenship in the nation-state.[3]

In so many ways, the 1880s—and perhaps even 1889—thus mark the real termination of a period that opens, not as has conventionally been claimed, with the French Revolution of 1789, but with the citizenship revolution of the 1750s. The period of experimentation and change in nationality law and naturalization, with its constant ruptures and reconfigurations between the Old and New Regimes, ended with the installation of democratic institutions and republican nationality law in the Third Republic. If the absolute citizen crystallized under Louis XIV and was dismantled after the mid-eighteenth century, postabsolutist citizenship took its final shape only at the end of the nineteenth century. The citizenship revolution—which was, in fact, a dual revolution of both "citizenship" and "nationality"—ended four generations after the 1750s, under new conditions of democratic participation, republican government, and mass migration.

Beyond the revolutionary experiments, during most of the nineteenth century, there was more continuity than rupture in the history of naturalization. Naturalization became (except during the Second French Republic, 1848–51) a limited practice that conferred on wealthy adult men the rights of political participation. It involved small numbers of foreign manufacturers, soldiers, and men who aspired to political office.[4] For even before the final abolition of the droit d'aubaine in 1819, naturalization had become a rather unattractive procedure for most foreigners. Immigrants to the kingdom were content with the acquisition of civil rights guaranteed by their formal permission to reside in the kingdom (*admission à domicile*), including their exemption from the remnants of the droit d'aubaine. The number of foreigners who actually became citizens annually during the nineteenth century was smaller than under the Old Regime, for nineteenth-century patterns of naturalization were no longer framed by the droit d'aubaine (or its abolition in 1819). Nor was French citizenship, as a consequence, tied to the ability to transmit property across generations. Instead, political participation in the New Regime was initially grounded on the *ownership* of property, at least until the advent of universal male suffrage. More importantly, citizenship was defined exclusively as a *droit de cité*, the political right to participate in the business of governing the nation, and nationality became its necessary but insufficient precondition.

What was debated in 1818 and finally abolished on 14 July 1819 was hardly the droit d'aubaine of absolutism. Beginning in the thirteenth century, the crown identified and began to confiscate from the lords a feudal right of customary law by which the crown claimed the property of aliens who died in the kingdom without native heirs. Turned into a mark of sovereignty, the droit d'aubaine became a foundation of absolutism, and was expanded to include a host of other civil incapacities, from the inability to inherit in the kingdom to the prohibition of foreigners holding political offices and ecclesiastical benefices. The jurists of the sixteenth century contributed to the definition of the droit d'aubaine and the absolute citizen in their writings and through the accumulated prohibitions decreed in the sovereign law courts. The absolute definition of the droit d'aubaine and of the citizen found its highest expression in Louis XIV's Naturalization Tax, the forcible collective naturalization of foreigners in 1697 justified by the droit d'aubaine. This robust redefinition of the droit d'aubaine as a mark of sovereignty and a totalizing definition of foreigners' disabilities was a long cry from the highly circumscribed "droit d'aubaine" finally abolished in 1819.

Between 1697 and 1819, the droit d'aubaine was dramatically transformed. It shrank in scope and definition: already the eighteenth-century jurists had turned their backs on the monarchy's absolutist amalgamation of incapacities, although they inextricably unlinked the king's right of escheat to the foreigner's inability to inherit. The droit d'aubaine shifted its locus from the state to society, becoming an inheritance disability under Napoleon and after.

In the middle of the eighteenth century, a final version of French absolutism—variously called "ministerial," "enlightened," or "despotic"—abandoned its earlier tendency to shore up individual and collective privileges and tax exemptions. The late Old Regime monarchy resolved the inherent contradictions of absolutist rule that, with respect to the droit d'aubaine, had both exempted individuals and collectivities as part of its exercise of sovereignty (and its recruitment of skilled foreign labor), and had attempted to impose a totalizing and homogeneous droit d'aubaine on the entirety of the kingdom and all its foreign inhabitants. The droit d'aubaine was a victim of this fundamental shift in state building: in the 1760s the crown began the piecemeal abolition of a "feudal" institution that had so disturbed the Enlightened critics and apologists of the monarchy. Such an understudied aspect of the history of citizenship and nationality law before 1789 had unintended results. Lawyers arguing the cases of "foreigners" claimed that the treaties signed by Louis XV and Louis XVI abolished not only a right of the fisc but also the juridical distinction between citizens and foreigners. The effacement of national differences led to a variety of lawsuits and ministerial interventions whereby the crown, which had amalgamated a royal right and a civil incapacity, was forced to deny its control of both.

The French Revolution abolished the "droit d'aubaine" not once but three times (as a royal prerogative, a seigneurial right, and a marker of colonial identity). But it was the fourth abolition of the droit d'aubaine, in the legislation that removed obstacles to the foreigner's capacity to inherit (even outside the kingdom) that bequeathed a working definition of the droit d'aubaine to the commissions that drafted Napoleon's Civil Code, to the diplomats that signed the peace treaties in 1814 and 1815, and to the politicians who finally abolished the feudal institution in 1819. The droit d'aubaine as the reciprocal incapacity of French citizens and foreigners to mutually inherit represented a diminished and "thin" version of a right universally denounced as a residue of feudalism. When the Chambers of Peers and Deputies began to debate the abolition of the droit d'aubaine in the winter of 1818–19, few contested the judgment that the practice represented the historical remnants of a "feudal" practice (although fewer still distinguished among its diverse aspects, as a mark of sovereignty or kind of inheritance incapacity).

More than a simple history of the expansion and then reduction in the scope and definition of this minor feudal right, the trajectory of the droit d'aubaine from the sixteenth to the early nineteenth centuries encapsulates nothing less than the history of citizenship in France from the Old Regime to the New. This history, I have argued, took shape in the movement of the citizen from politics to law in the sixteenth century, and its shift back to a new political sphere as part of the citizenship revolution of the eighteenth century. The movement of the citizen from political being to legal subject in the sixteenth century was coterminous with the general construction of absolutism as the rule of law, defined as the juridical supremacy of the sovereign over his subjects. Not surprisingly, the retrieval and invention of political citizenship by participants in an emerging public sphere after the 1750s took place "under the brief" of legal challenges to absolutism, especially in the realm of family law.[5] But absolutism itself was transformed by the ministerial reform projects of the period. In its desperate search for revenue, especially after the Seven Years War, the reforms of the crown came to identify "citizens" as a class of male property owners who participated, albeit in restricted ways, in the business of governance. Enlightened reformers and thinkers, republican critics of the monarchy among them, went much further in reversing the model of the absolute citizen while preserving the integrity of sovereignty. In these ways, the first public expressions of the citizenship revolution—the Enlightenment enrichments of the citizen in political discourse—placed the citizen at the center of the public and political life of the nation.

The citizenship revolution sealed the fate of the droit d'aubaine and of citizenship, and the French Revolution of 1789 was to deepen the critique of the droit d'aubaine as it amplified the political identity of the citizen. The twisted and complex history of the droit d'aubaine between 1789 and 1814 reaffirmed its status as a feudal hangover as well as the socially and politically limited identity of the French citizen. In 1818, when the parliamentary chambers under

Louis XVIII began to consider its final abolition, politicians understood the "droit d'aubaine" not as a legal practice but as an element of public policy. Around the question of the droit d'aubaine, the chambers debated not French citizenship or nationality law but the immigration policy of the French state, and especially the settlement of foreigners and investment in the kingdom emanating from France's rival and notable industrial power, England. Not lawyers in their briefs, but politicians acting in a public sphere (however limited and institutionalized), set out in their speeches, printed pamphlets, and treatises the virtues and liabilities of the droit d'aubaine in relation to French immigration policy. Such political discussions took place in the guise of a debate surrounding the persistence of an "archaic" and "feudal" legal practice—the "justice of barbarian times"—that had doggedly persisted at the heart of modern France.

Naturalizations before and after 1819

Thanks to the painstaking efforts of two graduate students, we have a global sense of the numbers of individual acts of French nationality law between 1814 and 1848.[6] The researchers count 11,490 published legal acts in those years—some 383 a year, a far superior number to the acts and declarations of naturalization located for the period 1660–1790 (some 52 a year). But around 4,050 (42 percent) of these "naturalizations" were in fact official permissions to reside in France (and thus to enjoy all civil rights, including inheritance rights), and the remaining 6,800 or so "naturalizations" were unevenly distributed in time, space, and in their fundamental identity. Most of them were in fact "declarations of naturalization" (déclarations de naturalisation or déclarations de naturalité) and were made before 1819 in the wake of the empire's demise: nearly 2,800 cases—around 41 percent of all the naturalization acts issued between 1815 and 1848—were of this nature and from this period.

In fact, the statistics mask the fact that practices of naturalization, like those registering civil status (état civil), had hardly stabilized by 1815.[7] The law of October 1814, we have seen, allowed the king to issue "letters of declaration of naturalization" to former residents of the French Empire whose departments were returned to foreign rule. Singled out specifically were the manufacturers, property owners, and soldiers who had served the interests of the Great Nation and now served France. A further law of 17 February 1815 left no choice to the soldiers serving in French armies if they wished to enjoy their pensions: they were required to declare, after ten years of residence, their desire to remain in France, and those born outside the existing boundaries of French territory to obtain "letters of naturalization."[8]

Note the difference of the term from the 1814 law. The government showed significant indecision about the vocabulary of naturalization in the early years of the Restoration, and a fundamental ambivalence about the relation of contemporary practices to Old Regime precedents. First, the monarchy continued to issue letters of "great naturalization" (*grande naturalisation*) to foreigners aspiring to be seated in parliament: in addition to the eleven grants to foreign-born loyalists of the Bourbon monarchy at the moment of Napoleon's fall in 1814, the monarchy issued some forty others over the course of the first half of the nineteenth century.[9] Second, and far more common, were the "declarations of naturalization" issued to former soldiers and local politicians and merchants born "abroad" (in the territories previously annexed by France) and who were living in France. Like their homonyms of the Old Regime, these "declarations" did not fictionally transform foreigners into French citizens; rather, they were retroactive recognitions of the existing quality of Frenchness. (Unlike the Old Regime, they did not automatically include the wives and children of the petitioner, nor were they issued as letters patent from the royal chancellery).[10] Third, actual grants of "naturalization" proper were given only to several dozen foreigners a year, most of whom had been born in Switzerland, in England, or (after 1867) in the Austro-Hungarian Empire, who were mostly settled in the border departments of the Moselle or the Ardennes, and who met the statutory residence requirement of the Constitution of year VIII (1799). These foreign citizens acquired the rights of political participation.[11]

The New Regime thus stumbled toward four categories of discretionary grants concerning the status of foreign-born residents in the kingdom: permissions to reside, declarations of naturalization, naturalizations, and great naturalizations . . . not to mention permissions to be naturalized abroad, a category of acts that is equally revealing of the changing meaning of naturalization.[12] In the language of the law, these were very different, but in the language of vernacular practices they were sometimes confounded, as a sample of dossiers suggests. In fact, only naturalizations themselves, including great naturalizations, restored many of the protocols of the Old Regime. For these, the sovereign—through the royal *commission du sceau* (established in 1814, replacing Napoleon's *conseil du sceau des titres*), and independent of the ministry of justice—issued "patent letters." Claimants paid substantial "rights of the seal" (*droits de sceau*), as established by Napoleon in 1808 and clarified in the royal ordinance of 5 June 1816.[13] These were the only "naturalizations" that had to be "registered" after 1815; concerning naturalization proper, the Chamber of Peers played the role of the Chambre des comtes under the Old Regime. Declarations of naturalization for the former inhabitants of the empire required a much simpler administrative procedure involving requests, first at the municipal level (for proof of residence) and then at the ministry of justice. The process was not fully transparent, however, and admitted to many aborted requests.[14]

Those who petitioned for the quality of French citizen often invoked the different categories of discretionary acts. For example, Alonzo de Viado, a Spanish Austrian nobleman who had sided with the French and took refuge in Toulouse, requested a permission to fix his domicile in France and to be naturalized in October 1814. (He was eventually "admitted to establish his residence in France, and to possess all civil rights, as long as he shall reside there.")[15] Many others, especially from Belgium and the Rhineland states, asked for "letters of naturalization" and received "declarations of naturalization" following the provisions of the laws of 14 October 1814 and 5 June 1816. Most requests from the ex-departments of France involved claimants seeking to keep their pensions or offices, as was the case of Pierre Sybertz, a customs official born in Gladbach, Germany (in the French department of Roër under the empire).[16] In the case of foreigners born beyond the ex-boundaries of the French Empire, the government only slowly developed consistency in granting "naturalization" (but not "great naturalization") to foreigners who demonstrably but not retroactively fulfilled the ten-year residence requirement of the 1799 Constitution. In these years, the government itself hesitated between the Old Regime usage, *lettres de naturalité*, and what was to become the standard term by the late 1820s, *lettres de naturalisation*.

The dossiers of foreign claimants are far from complete, and it is difficult to know what percentage of requests for declaration or naturalization were actually granted. In the early years of the Restoration, thousands of declarations were issued—more, it seems, than simple permissions to reside in the kingdom. There were relatively few naturalizations proper, perhaps some thirty or forty a year in the decade after the Napoleonic Empire, and decreasing numbers as the nineteenth century wore on (except for 1848–49).[17] Not all letters patent of naturalization, however, were withdrawn from the appropriate authorities by their beneficiaries (just as not all had been "withdrawn" and registered in the sovereign courts of the Old Regime). An average of ten a year between 1815 and 1821 were not picked up, and this for a variety of reasons. Some foreigners, like the priest d'Estala in 1816, could not pay the apparently elevated duties (which the ministry of justice was unwilling to reduce); others, like that of Georges Platz in 1818, were lost in a disorganized bureaucracy; while still others, such as a certain Bernard in 1819, claimed not to know that he had to go through that formality.[18]

In truth, neither former residents of the French Empire who were restituted in their quality of Frenchmen by "declarations of naturalization" nor foreigners who became naturalized were much motivated by the problem of inheritance law. A simple act of government that admitted a foreigner to reside in France was sufficient to guarantee him or her all the "civil rights" of a French national, including that of inheriting property from another French national in instances where the droit d'aubaine was still in existence until 1819. Instead, naturalization and declarations were generally consistent with attempts to hold on to pensions and offices, and mattered less in family inheritance strategies as they had under the Old Regime, when the droit d'aubaine was a consistent motive in the desire to become naturalized. In short, naturalization—and citizenship—lost their strong link to the transmission of property, although they did not lose their strong link to the pragmatic and calculating interest of foreigners. At the same time, in the first half of the nineteenth century, citizenship as political participation deepened its linkage to property, because only male taxpayers of a high level of wealth could become electors or representatives.

When the French parliament began to debate the final abolition of the droit d'aubaine in 1818, the ancient feudal due became a vehicle for a revisionist retelling of French history and an argument in the construction of a politics of immigration in France.

"La justice des temps barbares": The Political Demise of a Legal Tradition

The final abolition of the droit d'aubaine by the law of 8 July 1819 occurred in the Restoration government's continuing construction, under the shadow of conservative reaction, of the "New Regime." In the end, a reactionary government formed against the revolutionary movement ended up borrowing the Revolution's "liberal and humanitarian" legislation toward foreigners.[19] In truth, the droit d'aubaine was not a high priority, and the debate and passage of the law were delayed by attention to laws concerning censorship and the creation of a "Holy Alliance" of France, Austria, and Russia that emerged from the Congress of Aix-la-Chapelle at the end of 1818. The government's hesitancy was further revealed in the way it tested the waters: Louis XVIII's first proposition, sent to the Chamber of Peers in April 1818, was only to consider *whether* the king should make a law to abolish the droit d'aubaine. The vociferous debate of the first part of 1819 was focused on this proposal, not on a specific text of a law.

The comte de Lévis, a strong supporter of the "Aristocratic party" in the upper chamber who favored extending the privileges of the English in France and was the author of several tracts on French finances, introduced the legislation in April 1818. In his opening speech, he offered a comprehensive history of the droit d'aubaine that was simultaneously a history of France and of the progress of civilization. Taking up (and citing directly) the language and arguments of the Enlightenment, Lévis observed how "this right, remnant of the barbarism of the Middle Ages, is repugnant to the natural beliefs of justice and humanity."[20] Lévis and all the others inherited the conclusions of the debate of the Tribunate in 1801–2, namely, that the droit d'aubaine was not at all a Roman inheritance, but a peculiar "feudal" custom that had been introduced into France "in the spirit of reprisals" against acts of the English king Edward III in the fourteenth century. Lévis recognized that the earliest version of the droit d'aubaine coincided with a generic escheat (*droit de déshérence*), by which the king inherited from those without known heirs. And such a custom made a certain amount of sense at a time when there was no "communication" or "commerce" among peoples.

> But since civilization and commerce have brought men closer together, since swift and regular communications have been established between even the furthest countries, since regular mail service and even newspapers guarantee certain and not costly communication . . . the droit d'aubaine has no more excuse for existing.

More, the comte de Lévis outlined a history of this commercial progress that ran parallel to, if it was not directed by, the development of the French monarchy. Saint Louis was not the king who consolidated the crown's hold on this seigneurial right, but the first who sought to attenuate the effects of the droit d'aubaine. The story of his successors involved exemptions given freely one after another: Louis XIV stood not as the embodiment of an absolutist model that was to give way in the eighteenth century to the final if not quite "enlightened monarchy" (as this book has argued), but as a midpoint in the continuous "softening" of the droit d'aubaine, a process supplemented by the authors of the Enlightenment (quoting le Trosne, Necker, and Montesquieu) and by the international treaties of Louis XV.[21] If, for Lévis and others, there was a rupture in this tradition, it was not the patent letters signed in favor of the English on 18 January 1787 that abolished unilaterally the droit d'aubaine, nor even the Revolution of 1789 that decreed its abolition in the spirit of cosmopolitanism and fraternity. Rather, the rupture was found among the lawyers who, under Napoleon, insisted on the principle of reciprocity and reinstituted the droit d'aubaine. Lévis sought clearly to identify reciprocity in this instance not with French interests per se but with the survival of an "ancient system of reprisals," if not with the feudal regime itself. "The principle of reciprocity then held, but equity was only superficial. Retaliation is the justice of barbarian times; political reciprocity is hardly more reasonable, for the parity of situations is never found among civilized peoples."[22]

Other histories of the droit d'aubaine were proffered in both chambers, but they did not differ significantly from that rehearsed by the comte de Lévis. The marquis de Clermont-Tonnerre, an ardent royalist and military colonel, one of the members of the special commission named at the end of the 1818 session to study the question, saw Charlemagne's exemptions in favor of the Scots as the origins of an attack on this "law invented by stupidity . . . this tyrannical right." And rather than Louis XI, it was in fact Francis I who "began the march that would strike the mortal blow to the droit d'aubaine," an unintended praise of the French Revolution. Even the royalists linked the "march of civilization" to the dismantling of this abuse: thus at the moment of the French Revolution, "the triumph of civilization over the droit d'aubaine approached, but was not yet completed."[23]

Other royalists opposed the law, including Gilles Porcher, comte de Richebourg, whose own narrative converged with supporters—until the moment of the French Revolution. They shared the foundational judgment that the droit d'aubaine itself was a "barbaric custom," and that the history of the monarchy, from Charlemagne forward, was a history of progress.[24] They disagreed, however, on the question of reciprocity, and especially on the purported "mistakes" of the revolutionaries in breaking with French tradition. Instead of seeing reciprocity as indelibly tied to feudalism, opponents of the bill saw in the principle of reciprocity the only means to ensure that French interests were safeguarded, especially concerning wealthy foreigners. On 26 January 1819 the marquis de Maleville (who had replaced Tronchet as president of the court of appeals) argued that the existing articles of the Civil Code, especially Article 13, would guarantee that "useful" foreigners could enjoy all civil rights as authorized residents. The abolition of the droit d'aubaine, he predicted, would open the door to foreigners to invest without residing in France and allow them to withdraw their profits from the country in complete liberty. Instead, he insisted, the principle of reciprocity should prevail.

In his argument, Maleville drew freely on the treatise and compilation of the droit d'aubaine laws published in 1818 by the lawyer Jean-Baptiste Gaschon, the *Code diplomatique des aubains*. Gaschon had indeed claimed that only a few eighteenth-century treaties had specifically authorized foreigners to inherit from French natives, while the majority of international accords did not. (Others who intervened in the debate, including the comte des Richebourg and Maleville, also cited Gaschon's treatise in their opposition to the unilateral abolition of the droit d'aubaine, although it is unlikely that they had read it).[25] Precisely because the principle of reciprocity was so central, Maleville considered it possible to generally suppress "this barbarian right" among the members of the Holy Alliance, or by specific laws with England, but the general principle of reciprocity was all that would protect French wealth from leaving the country.[26]

At stake for both supporters and opponents of the law was the case of England. In the political debate, the legal status and transformations of the droit d'aubaine were never questioned, only its purported implications with respect to immigration and to foreign investment by the English in France.

The English question was raised specifically in relation to the letters patent of 1787 that abolished unilaterally, with explicit reciprocity, the droit d'aubaine with respect to the English. Opponents such as the marquis de Marbois went to great length to demonstrate that those letters had involved "the interests of great families" in England and that the Paris parlement and Chambre des comptes had only registered them without reservations because "we were counting on a reciprocal act on the part of the British Parliament. I would be on solid ground in claiming that reciprocity was promised," he declaimed, but "events of another order" had overtaken both sides in 1789.[27] The situation was only rectified by the return of reciprocity in 1803. When the deputy Siméon reported to the Chamber in March 1819, he too focused on the letters patent for the English in 1787, citing archival evidence to prove that the ministers of Louis XVI had *not* anticipated a reciprocal act from the English Parliament, and had no interest, in fact, in getting one.

More generally, the pressing question of the day was foreign investment, and especially English investment in the kingdom. Proponents of the law argued persuasively, citing the "science of political economy," that the droit d'aubaine was an obstacle to this highly desired goal.[28] The opposition, while not disagreeing that the droit d'aubaine was a "barbaric law whose abolition is generally desired," also recognized that the English problem was the only relevant one. As deputy de Bonald argued,

> The droit d'aubaine is irrelevant to the Spaniard, who does not leave his country; to the Swede, so far from us; to the Turks, separated from us by their mores even more than by distance. But the English are still somewhat nomadic, especially the wealthy; England is closer to the center of our government than many English provinces [are to each other]; England is more often our enemy than our ally, and her children are naturalized among other peoples with far more difficulty than all other Europeans; England, finally, is cunning in her policies, and can put much money behind them. It is therefore prudent to maintain the droit d'aubaine, and even England itself would not wish to see it disappear.[29]

The concern with English immigration and investment, expressed in a debate over the abolition of the droit d'aubaine in 1818 and 1819, were not entirely without precedent, in part because of the continuity of actors who engaged in the discussion. Boissy d'Anglas, the neoroyalist revolutionary who helped abolish the droit d'aubaine in 1791 and had so strenuously argued the losing proposition against the principle of reciprocity before the Tribunate in 1801, revived and deepened his argument that the abolition of the droit d'aubaine would encourage the best kind of immigration and investment. It would be interesting to know if Boissy d'Anglas had kept notes; in any case, his speech of 1818 was even more emphatic than his intervention of 1801 in stressing the positive role that the abolition would play in calling "rich and industrious capitalists of all countries" to dig France's canals, clear its lands, and increase its overall prosperity. Boissy also repeated his arguments of 1801 that the abandonment of reciprocity would not call to France those foreigners who were to be feared, "this class of men without means, talent, or industriousness; this scum of nations that goes everywhere there is trouble with the hope to commit crimes." Those foreigners were indifferent to the droit d'aubaine, whereas wealthy and interested foreigners would, should it persist, avoid investing or settling in France.[30]

Opponents of the proposition recommended that the droit d'aubaine, however barbaric a custom, ought to be maintained, and that the English and other foreigners who sought to protect their investments, especially in property, either establish their authorized residence in the kingdom (as per Article 13 of the Civil Code allowing them to enjoy all civil rights), or seek naturalization.[31] In this way, they echoed the old mercantilist interest in ensuring that wealth would remain in the kingdom. Boissy d'Anglas countered that to ask wealthy foreigners to give up their nationality would present an insurmountable obstacle to their establishment in the kingdom.[32] Others, such as the marquis de Pastoret, one of the authors of the Charter of 1814, more strenuously sought to separate the practice of naturalization from the debate over the droit d'aubaine. Naturalization conferred not a "right of property" (*droit de propriété*), referring to civil law, but a political "right of citizenship" (*droit de cité*). Pastoret equated the meaning of "nativeness" (*naturalité*) used among "the old jurisconsults" with the political rights of the *droit de cité*, just as Bouvier and others had done during the debate over naturalization in 1814.[33] The politicians thus contributed to the myth that Old Regime France knew no category approximating "nationality," and that "citizenship," if it existed before 1789, was necessarily a political category.

Ultimately, the politicians were unconcerned with the past: their questions were immediate, policy ones: "Money! Money! Capital! Interest rates! Industry!, these are the words that echo in this Chamber," noted the marquis de Marebois.[34] The question was how to encourage the investment and immigration of foreigners in order to ensure that the economic interests of France were served. Proponents and opponents of a law that would abolish the droit d'aubaine differed in their answers, but both agreed that the droit d'aubaine was a remnant of feudalism and barbaric times that French governments since Charlemagne (or Saint Louis) had sought to "soften," through unilateral abolition or reciprocal treaties. This was a political discussion, and neither side made much attempt to make sense of the diverse and distinctive aspects of the practice—as sovereign right of escheat, as a prohibition of offices and benefices, as a civil incapacity to inherit, or as the capacity of a foreigner to inherit from a French national, not to mention any applicability of the "droit d'aubaine" to the colonies. Some members did signal the complexity of the task of simply abolishing the droit d'aubaine. The marquis de Clermont-Tonnerre, although not trained in the law, noted in January 1819 how the question was not a simple one:

> That to the contrary it contains in relation to law and legislation a great number of questions which the legislator, acknowledging this principle, should examine most profoundly. Thus, Messieurs, he should set out, in all instances, the exact relations of inheritance between foreigners and native inhabitants [*regnicoles*]; thus, he would determine up to what point the full abolition of the system should be applied. . . . These are serious questions which require of the legislature the most mature deliberations.[35]

But until the law was actually introduced, the legislators did not offer "profound meditations," and tended to debate the proposal to present such a law and assume a unitary and reified "droit d'aubaine" directly related to English immigration and investment.

Things changed slightly when the government of Louis XVIII introduced the proposed law in May 1819. Although the title of the law "relative to the abolition of the droit d'aubaine" seemed to point in the same direction, the law itself, significantly, did not mention the droit d'aubaine at all. Instead, it was an abrogation of articles 726 and 912 of the Civil Code that argued in Article 1 that "as a result, foreigners shall have the right to inherit, to bequeath, and to dispose of their goods in the same way as the French, in the entire extension of the kingdom."

Although harshly contested, significant majorities in both houses approved the proposition that the king draw up a law on the droit d'aubaine.[36] The final law, introduced in May and approved in July 1819, differed significantly from the political discussion of the droit d'aubaine: it simply abrogated Articles 726 and 912 of the Civil Code, and thus gave foreigners the right (with one exception) to inherit, to deed, and to otherwise acquire property in the same manner as French nationals. But the law also introduced a second article anticipating the case of divided successions between foreigners and French natives. In that case, Article 2 stated that the French heirs "would receive a portion of the goods in France equal to the value of goods from which they are excluded situated in foreign countries . . . in virtue of laws and local customs."[37]

No mention of this second article had appeared in the previous debates in the two chambers. Indeed—although further research is needed to fully justify the claim—it seems as if the chancellery had once more turned to the opinions of lawyers, not politicians, in drafting the act. Certainly, as the keeper of the seals argued in submitting the legislation to the Chamber of Peers, His Majesty had reviewed the discussion of the two chambers and acted not out of generosity but of calculation (*calcul*) in claiming to "erase the differences in relation to inheritance and the transmission of goods."[38] But it appears that jurisconsults urged the adoption of the second article, which maintained a faint echo of reciprocity in specific cases, with the purpose of "privileging the foreigner, but not to the detriment of nationals [*nationaux*]." In any case, when the Chamber of Peers debated the proposition beginning on 22 May 1819, although many of the older arguments were once again rehearsed, the comte de Lévis—the original sponsor of the 1818 legislation—noted with respect to article 2 that "it is up to the enlightened jurisconsults who sit in this chamber to fix our opinion on a delicate and thorny question, as with all those involving the regulation of rights among several heirs."[39] He was content to rehearse what he called the "principle of the law," by which he meant its political role in encouraging foreign investment and immigration.

The result was that much of the debate evaporated: although the comte de Cornudet proposed an additional amendment, fearing that the second article would abrogate the reciprocity of Article 11 in the Civil Code, his opinion was overruled by the keeper of the seals. Without further debate, the Chamber of Peers adopted the law by a majority of 84 to 33. As for the Chamber of Deputies, to whom the law was presented on 29 May 1819, the baron de Pasquier only noted how the second article, on the equal division of inheritances between foreigners and French nationals, was added so as not to "sacrifice the true rights of Frenchmen and women." Some members protested, claiming that the second article contradicted the first. No doubt many representatives in both chambers failed to follow the subtleties of the legislative proposal, nor did they bother to concern themselves with these refined points of inheritance law. On 8 July, the Chamber of Deputies adopted the abrogation of Articles 726 and 912 of the Civil Code "without discussion" by an overwhelming vote of 133 to 19.[40]

At the very end of the process of abolishing the droit d'aubaine, legal language and concerns had seemingly trumped politics. Or rather, the legal definition of a much reduced and reconfigured droit d'aubaine—a mere shadow of its former, absolutist self—had resisted the political slippage that had turned a thin version of the droit d'aubaine into a debate over France's immigration and investment policies toward the English. This thin version of the droit d'aubaine, before and even after 1819, had been defined first by jurists during the citizenship revolution of the 1750s and 1760s as an inheritance obstacle to foreigners in the kingdom. The impoverished juridical definition, momentarily effaced in the Revolution's unilateral abolition of the droit d'aubaine and inheritance restrictions, was restored partially in the Civil Code and upheld in 1814. Even in the "final" abolition of the droit d'aubaine, a trace of the late-absolutist concerns of the jurists could be found in the desire to not completely efface the distinction between "nationals" and "foreigners."

The law of 13 July 1819 was hardly the last word on the droit d'aubaine.[41] For one, it required clarification by the justice minister a year later. In response to an inquiry from the son of the famous barrister and redactor of the Civil Code, Portalis, the justice minister argued that the law brought a "complete assimilation of foreigners and nationals, founded on the desire to attract foreign capital to the kingdom," and that the principle of reciprocity had been completely extinguished.[42] Yet lawsuits over what was still called the "droit d'aubaine" were to continue in the 1820s and 1830s, and to reappear in one form or another until the middle of the twentieth century. In 1824, the "droit d'aubaine" was at the center of litigation in an inheritance contested between a Dane and a Frenchman, and in 1825, the Paris court of appeals returned to the question of whether the Old Regime treaties, in particular that with Spain in 1761, had intended to abolish civil law distinctions on the successoral incapacity of foreigners to inherit. It decided, in the tradition of the Old Regime Parisian magistrates, that the droit d'aubaine was distinct from the capacity to inherit.[43] And in 1829, the courts and government invoked the "droit d'aubaine" in a case involving a certain Louis Duran, "presumed to be Spanish who died in Paris without known heirs." As such, failing diplomatic treaties to the contrary, the inheritance fell to the state "in virtue of article 768 of the Civil Code." But the courts insisted this ancient right of escheat—the right to "vacant goods" of feudalism—was nothing less than the droit d'aubaine, and on the eve of the July Revolution that was to push France forward toward a liberal nation-state, ministers again reinvented the droit d'aubaine in its most "feudal" definition.[44] Beyond this palest of definitions of the droit d'aubaine, the question of reciprocity and parity in international private law, including the problem of inheritance taxes, continued well into the twentieth century.[45]

Rights of and to inheritance had been, from the late sixteenth century until the French Revolution, the foundation and substance of citizenship in France, defined primarily in the domain of law, not politics. The citizenship revolution after the 1750s marked a watershed shift in emphasis toward political citizenship, which until 1803 left the question of nationality implicit and harshly contested in practice. In fact, the citizenship revolution only ended with the establishment of the Nationality Law of 1889. The final abolition of the droit d'aubaine in 1819, then, was but a passing episode in this longer history. Yet the episode is telling: the politicians and governmental officials who eliminated an enduring feudal remnant in modern France reiterated and affirmed the distinction between the civil rights of inheritance (accessible to resident foreigners) and the political rights of the French citizen. It may have appeared incidental, but the end of the droit d'aubaine capped a long history of the making and unmaking of citizenship under absolutism, just as it announced the eventual birth of modern citizenship in France.

SOURCES OF THE STATISTICAL STUDY OF NATURALIZATIONS, 1660–1790

T his study is based on a partial, incomplete, and (in the end) random sample of letters of naturalization and declarations of naturalization, or official mentions of such letters, issued between 1660 and 1790—roughly from the personal reign of Louis XIV (1661) to the French Revolution (1789)—and located in the national and provincial archives of France. The sample is random because of the partial survival of diverse series in the archives that have suffered from the vagaries of history. It is incomplete because I have not attempted to collect all letters or mentions of letters that can be found in the National Archives, the sources for which have been usefully inventoried by Jean-François Dubost;[1] nor those dispersed widely throughout the provincial archives, especially in the archives of the sovereign courts responsible for their verification and registration (the eight Chambres des comptes of the kingdom); and those in the archives of the royal financial bureaux. Instead, I have constructed a database from the principal sources and collections of letters expedited by the secretary of the royal household and sealed at the great chancellery, and the principal records of registration of these letters by the Paris fiscal courts (whose jurisdiction covered almost two-thirds of the kingdom's territory, and at least half its population) and those of the provincial sovereign courts.

The compilation of this statistical series of letters (and what I shall call "traces" of letters) rests on a fundamental paradox: very few *original* grants of naturalization survive in the French public archives. Once issued, sealed, and registered, the letters were returned to their petitioners and remained in the hands of the foreigners naturalized or of their families. By definition, then, original letters of naturalization found in the crown's archives were those of beneficiaries who, for one reason or another, never collected their letters. Still, because of the complex bureaucratic process that a petitioner was required to follow, including the different registrations that were to be made, a relatively comprehensive record of the naturalizations survives at both the national and provincial levels.

This study is based on a collection of 6,732 "naturalizations" and "declarations of naturalization" over 140 years—including drafts of naturalization letters presented to the king in his council, and mentions of naturalization in the different inventories (both contemporaneous and contemporary) of the secretary of the royal household, the chancellery, the fiscal courts, and the various treasury bureaux of the kingdom. It is worth recalling here the procedure for naturalization, described in more detail in chapter 2. A petitioner would engage the offices of a royal secretary; the letter would be drawn up by his clerk, then processed in the machinery of the great chancellery, expedited by the secretary of state of the royal household, and then returned to the chancellery for the seals. Except for cases involving ennoblement and a few others, described in the text, the procedure did not involve the intervention of the king or any of the councils, and only in exceptional cases—involving, for example, Flemish priests in the eastern border regions after the 1760s—did it involve other royal ministries. I argue in chapter 2 that nearly all demands for naturalization that reproduced model texts and followed the proper protocol, including the correct "address" to the relevant courts, were granted and returned to the petitioner. The applicant was charged with ensuring the letter's verification in the relevant Chambre des comptes and then registering it (but not to the exclusion of other sovereign courts) in the Chambre du trésor (after 1693, the Chambre du domaine).[2] Letters were sometimes registered again, with dubious juridical value, in other sovereign courts (the sovereign parlements, the Cour des aides, and the sovereign councils of the provinces). After 1693, the letters also had to be registered at the local offices of the royal treasury; and after 1703, the grants were formally required to be insinuated as well (like all other civil actions) at the treasury bureaux in the provincial généralités (as explained in chapter 2).

In this study, for nearly one-third of the 6,732 naturalizations or mentions of naturalizations gathered from the archives of the royal household and other central administrative sources, no record of registration in the provincial Chambres des comptes was found. This does not mean that they were incomplete naturalizations, however. The archives of the Chambre des comptes de Paris were destroyed by fire in 1737, and its records were only partially reconstructed. And because this study relied in some cases on inventories, it was not possible to trace the trajectory of all grants once they had been expedited by the secretary of the royal household. Certainly a small number of naturalization letters received the expedition of a royal secretary of state but were for a variety of reasons never sealed at the chancellery. Quite a few others were sealed by the chancellery but never registered at any of the Chambres des comptes or other sovereign courts of the kingdom. Exactly how many remains uncertain, although particular cases are discussed in the text. But because there is no evidence that anything approaching a statistically significant portion of naturalizations were denied to petitioners—except for those who failed to follow proper administrative protocol, and more rarely, for reasons of religious difference—

for the purposes of a descriptive statistical profile, the "incomplete" naturalizations and mentions of naturalizations are grouped with those registered at the sovereign courts to constitute a single database. All duplicates were then eliminated, a less than self-evident process when taking into account the highly variable orthography of family names, and the multiple renewed demands, amplifications, and surannuations (requests for new letters because of delays, wrong addresses, and so forth).

The majority of naturalizations and mentions of grants (4,813, 71 percent) were collected from the archives of the secretary of state of the royal household. Twenty volumes of secretarial "drafts" (*minutes*), copies, and occasional annotations of letters and declarations bound in double folio volumes (probably collected as early as the 1670s, but likely rebound in the late nineteenth century) were systematically exploited and coded in the principal database prepared for this study.[3] An additional 540 letters were extracted from the twenty-three volume index of the O series (that of the royal household, containing, not incidentally but not systematically studied here, the records of donations by the king of properties of "aliens" that had been confiscated and then distributed through patronage networks at the court).[4] To these may be added the copies of naturalizations and declarations culled from several smaller series in the royal administration, such as the remnants of the chancellery archives that contain eighty-six drafts of letters issued between 1673 and 1718, and copies of letters salvaged from the Paris Chambre des comptes.[5]

An additional source of naturalizations and declarations are the tax rolls drawn up by the tax-farmers contracted to collect the 1697 Naturalization Tax. The tax rolls (1697–1707) of this forced, collective naturalization of foreigners—which targeted wealthy, mobile foreigners who contributed to the "France of movement"—constitute a distinct database on which I have drawn to describe the social history of naturalized foreigners at the turn of the eighteenth century.[6] Among 8,153 cases of "foreigners" and their families (including the heirs of foreigners who settled in France after 1600), some 760 foreigners or descendants of foreigners had already received individual letters of naturalization (9 percent of the taxed population), many of which dated from before Louis XIV's personal rule. Those given to immigrants between 1660 and 1707, however, were folded into the database of individual naturalizations of the Old Regime, eliminating duplicates.

A few drafts, copies, and inventories of naturalizations and declarations of naturalization were gathered from other archives and ministries. The archives of the Order of Malta list eight letters issued within the dates of this study (1660–1789), while thirty-three cases can be found in an archival depot of the ministries involved in colonial affairs ("naturalizations of foreigners in the colonies of Saint-Domingue, Martinique, Guadeloupe, and the Ile Bourbon, 1711–1785"). From the papers of the Joly de Fleury dynasty of royal attorneys and prosecutors at the Paris parlement, deposited in the National Library, nineteen letters were reproduced (generally as a result of their contested juridical status), and I added seventy-three cases found in the archives of the ministry of foreign relations that involved clerics in the late eighteenth-century Austrian borderland. In these instances, however, most of the letters turned out to be duplicates, having been mentioned in other collections and inventories of the royal household and the Chambre des comptes.[7]

In addition to copies and drafts of letters, I have relied extensively (although, in retrospect, perhaps not enough) on the registers of verification and registration by the various Chambres des comptes and other sovereign courts of the kingdom.[8] The most important of these courts was the Paris court, whose jurisdiction covered a large part of the kingdom (see map 1). In 1737, the archives of this court burned, and a partial reconstruction was attempted during the reign of Louis XV: from this, 255 letters issued between 1660 and 1766 can be found in the National Archives.[9] For the period after 1737, twelve registers of the Paris Chambre des comptes contain all the letters mentioned in the official *plumitif* or registry of that body between 1737 and 1789 (3,069 cases of naturalization and declarations were collected for this database).[10]

Registers and inventories of registers of the other provincial Chambres des comptes and other sovereign tribunals yield far fewer letters (most of them registrations of letters already collected from other series), underscoring the centralization efforts of the monarchy, as well as the ample jurisidiction of the Paris Chambre des comptes. Most of the surviving records of verification and registration date from before the reign of Louis XIV, and were thus not systematically consulted. For the period 1660–1789, the Chambre des comptes at Nantes (Brittany) yielded 183 naturalizations for the period under study[11]; the Chambre at Aix (Provence) registered 209[12], while smaller numbers of letters were found in the Chambre des comptes (and their inventories) at Rouen (43)[13]; Montpellier (72)[14]; Grenoble (22)[15]; Pau (14)[16]; Dijon (78)[17]; Besançon (Dole) (38)[18]; Nancy (53); and Metz (129).[19] In addition, letters of naturalization were registered in other sovereign courts but not the Chambres des comptes. For example, among the cases collected for this database, 182 letters (mostly of clerics) were addressed to be registered in the Paris parlement, but not in the Paris Chambre des comptes. To the sovereign court (*conseil souverain*) at Colmar (Alsace), 531 were registered; between 1685 and 1706, twenty-seven letters were addressed to the conseil souverain at Tournai, and after 1700, 224 were addressed to the parlement at Douai.[20]

This incomplete and partially random database is thus without "organic" foundation in the French archives. It nonetheless comprises some 6,372 naturalizations and declarations of naturalizations that left their traces in the official minutes, expeditions, verifications, registrations, and inventories thereof, and that sometimes appear only because requests were superannuated and redone, or even occasionally duplicated, in the complex but surprisingly functional and bureaucratic machinery of the monarchy between 1660 and 1790.[21]

In 1790, individual naturalizations were abolished alongside the droit d'aubaine (although, as I show in chapter 8, a statistically insignificant but politically meaningful number of grants and demands took place during the Revolution). After the adoption of the first article of the Civil Code in 1803, and the reintroduction of the discretionary sovereign procedure of naturalization that same year, it becomes possible—at least in theory—to systematically collect naturalizations again, including official permissions to establish residency.[22] In the last chapter, I have only sampled requests and grants of the diverse and not yet stabilized practices of naturalizations and permissions to live in France given during the Napoleonic Empire and early in the Bourbon Restoration.[23] But the statistical sources on which I rely for the social history of foreign citizens, framed by the legal and administrative orders of absolutist and postabsolutist governments, are those of the Old Regime, from the advent of Louis XIV to the first years of the French Revolution.

TREATIES WITH FRANCE ABOLISHING OR EXEMPTING FOREIGNERS FROM THE DROIT D'AUBAINE, 1753–1791

	Country	Further Procedures	Group/Conditions[a]	Sources[b]
1753 14 February	Kingdom of Prussia	treaty of commerce; ratified 2 March 1753	IV. Reciprocal exemption only for 10 years	Gaschon 110–12
1754 24 December	Kingdom of Sweden	patent letters, registered 11 March 1755	IV. Reciprocal exemption only for movable goods	Gaschon 341–43
1760 24 March	Kingdom of Piedmont-Savoy	ratified 24 August; registered 6 September 1760	I. Reciprocal abolition, treaty of limits	BN F-20090(66); Gaschon 76–78
1761 15 August	Kingdom of Spain and the Two Sicilies	patent letters of July 1762, registered 3 September 1762	I. Reciprocal abolition, art. 23 of the Family Compact	BN F-21709(1)
1764 May	Town of Aix-la-Chapelle	patent letters, registered Flanders 6 July 1766, Paris (by further letters) 26 November 1766	I. Reciprocal exemption	BN F-21169(47); Gaschon, 118–22
1765 June	Order of Malta	patent letters registered 12 July 1765	I. Reciprocal abolition, recognizing the Maltese as regnicoles	BN F-21171(26); Gaschon 118–21
1765 10 October	Margrave of Baden-Baden	ratification on 27 December; registration on 20 February 1766	II. Reciprocal abolition, conditional droit de détraction	BN F-21247(38); Gaschon 214–19
1765 20 November	Margrave of Baden-Durlach	patent letters of 23 December 1765; ratification of convention, 23 April 1766	II. Reciprocal abolition, conditional droit de détraction	BN F-23627 (493); Gaschon 219–23; AN AD XV 1
1766 15 February	Principality of Nassau-Saarbrücken	ratified 11 March 1766; abolition and conditional droit de détraction only concerned Lorraine, Alsace, and Three Bishoprics; extended to the kingdom by convention of 26 April 1774, registered on 30 July	II. Reciprocal abolition, conditional droit de détraction; treaty of exchange and limits	Gaschon 136–39; Martens 1: 324–53

	Country	Further Procedures	Group/Conditions[a]	Sources[b]
1766 10 May	Duchy of Deux-Ponts	ratification of convention, 29 May; registration 26 November 1766	II. Reciprocal abolition, with conditional droits sur les successions	BN F-23627 (546); Gaschon, 166–68;
1766 16 June	Electorate of the Palatinate	confirmed by patent letters of 16 November 1781	II. Reciprocal abolition, with conditional droit d'aubaine; treaty of limits between bailliage of Seltz and Haguenbach	4-BN F-4347(34); Koch 2: 145; Gaschon 227–31
1766 24 June	Austria (Hereditary Lands)	ratified 3 August, registered 29 November 1766	II. Reciprocal abolition with conditional droits sur les succession; recognizes existing status et usages in different provinces	BN F-21247(51); Gaschon 96–102; Martens I:402–407
1766 2 December	Principality of Nassau-Usingen	ratified 22 December; registered 2 April 1767; abolition and conditional droit de détraction between province of Alsace and seigneurie of Lahr; extended to France and Nassau-Usingen by convention of 7 May 1777, ratified 16 May, registered 30 June	II. Reciprocal abolition, conditional droit de détraction	Gaschon 136–39; 283–86; Martens 1:324–53
1767 March	Free Imperial Town of Frankfurt	patent letters registered 9 February 1767	I. Reciprocal exemption	Gaschon 299–305
1767 19 March	Bishopric of Strasbourg	ratified 27 March 1767; registered 9 February 1768	II. Reciprocal abolition, conditional droit de détraction	BN F-21247(59); Gaschon 235–36; BN O/1/112, fol. 775
1767 31 March	Landgrave of Hesse-Cassel	ratified 24 April; registered 9 February 1768	II. Reciprocal abolition, conditional droit de détraction	4-BN F-4347(53); BN O/1/112, fols. 809–10, 815–16
1767 15 April	Electorate of Trier	ratified 8 May; registered 9 February 1768	II. Reciprocal abolition, conditional droit de détraction	4-BN F-4347(58); BN O/1/112, fols. 821–22; 827–28; Gaschon 132–36
1767 14 August	Electorate of Bavaria	ratified 6 September; registered 9 February 1768	II. Reciprocal abolition; conditional droit de détraction as established by local "lois, statuts, coutumelles"	4-BN F-4347(69); Gaschon 146–51
1767 7 September	Principality of Hesse-Darmstadt	ratified 26 September; registered 9 February 1768	II. Reciprocal abolition, conditional droit sur les successions	BN F-23627(698); Gaschon 247–49

Year	Date	Party	Treaty details	Cat.	Description	Source
1768	16 August	Prince-Bishop of Spire	ratified 23 August; registered 14 April 1769	III.	Reciprocal abolition, droit de détraction maintained	4-BN F-4348; 35 Gaschon 231–
1768	6 October	Electorate of Cologne	ratified 12 October; registered 14 April 1769	III.	Reciprocal abolition, droit de détraction maintained	4-BN F-4348(37); Gaschon 123–26
1768	6 December	Prince-Bishop of Liège	follows a treaty of limits of 9 October 1767	III.	Reciprocal exemption, conditional droit de détraction	4-BN F-4348(42); Gaschon 24–30
1768	6 December	Grand Duchy of Tuscany	ratified 10 January 1769; registered 6 July 1769	I.	Reciprocal abolition	4-BN F-4348(44); Gaschon 89–93
1769	23 February	Duchy of Parma	ratified 18 March; registered 6 July 1769	I.	Reciprocal abolition	4-BN F-4348(53); Gaschon 84–86
1769	February	Equestrian Circles of the Imperial Nobility of Swabia, Franconia, and the Rhine	patent letters registered 14 April 1769	I.	Reciprocal exemption (affranchissement et exemption)	Gaschon 329–35
1769	March	Free Imperial Town of Hamburg	treaty of commerce ratified 12 April; registered 6 July 1770; renewed by convention of 17 March 1789	IV.	Reciprocal abolition, 10% détraction and only for 20 years	Gaschon 305–10
1770	July	Principality of Monaco	ratified 18 August, registered 7 May 1771	I.	Reciprocal exemption	Gaschon 81–83
1770	July	22 Imperial Cities	patent letters, registered 6 September 1770	III.	Reciprocal exemption, 10% droit de détraction	BN F-23628(74); Gaschon 316–20
1771	26 February	Grand Duchy of Saxe-Weimar	ratified 19 March 1771; registered 13 August 1771	III.	Reciprocal abolition, 5% droit de détraction	4-BN F-4349(77); Gaschon 179–82
1771	7 December	Swiss Protestant Cantons and Towns of Saint Gall, Mulhouse, and Biel	ratified 20 January 1772; registered 16 march 1772; treaty of alliance with the ancien corps helvétique specifies the continued validity of abzug	II.	Reciprocal exemption, with conditional droit de détraction	4-BN F-4351(9); Gaschon 56–65
1773	1 June	Prince-Bishop of Bamberg and Würzburg	ratified 22 June 1773; registered 28 August 1773	II.	Reciprocal exemption, with conditional droit de dfraction	4-BN F-4352(20); Gaschon 152–56
1773	23 July	Estates General of the United Provinces	ratified 1 September 1773; registered 28 March 1774	I.	Reciprocal exemption	4-BN F-4352(27); Gaschon 36–39
1774	18 February	Principalities of Neuchâtel and Valangin	patent letters; registered 30 July 1774	II.	Reciprocal abolition, same conditions as Saint Gall, Mulhouse, and Biel	BN F-23628(879); Gaschon 66–68
1774	28 February	Republic of Venice	ratified 30 March 1775; registered 16 December 1776	II.	Reciprocal exemption	BN F-21300(310); Gaschon 102–6

	Country	Further Procedures	Group/Conditions[a]	Sources[b]
1774 14 April	States of the Teutonic Order	ratified 27 April; registered 30 April 1773	II. Reciprocal abolition, conditional droit de détraction or others in lois, statuts, et coutumes locales	4-BN F-4352(40); Gaschon 208–13
1774 26 April	Principality of Nassau-Saarbrücken	above, 1766	II. Reciprocal abolition, conditional droit de détraction	4-BN F-4352(39)
1774 November	23 Imperial Cities	patent letters, registered 7 January 1775	III. Reciprocal exemption, 10% droit de détraction	BN F-23628(955); Gaschon 320–24; Martens 2:326
1776 24 January	Principality of Nassau-Weilburg	ratified 7 February, registered 17 August 1776	II. Reciprocal abolition, conditional droit de détraction	BN F-23629(181); Gaschon 281–83; Martens 2:429
1776 16 July	Electorate of Saxony	ratified 20 July; registered 16 December 1776	III. Reciprocal abolition, 10% droit de détraction	BN F-23629(166); Gaschon 173–78
1776 September	Principality of Schwarzenberg	patent letters, registered 12 May 1777	III. Reciprocal exemption, 10% droit de détraction	BN F-23629(299); Gaschon 162–65
1776 29 October	Republic of Ragusa	patent letters; registered 16 December 1776	I. Reciprocal exemption	BN F-23629(320); Gaschon 106–9; Martens 2:474–77
1777 16 March	County of Wied-Neuwied	patent letters, registered 12 February 1778	III. Reciprocal exemption, 10% droit de détraction	BN F-23629(386): Gaschon 127–32
1777 16 March	Principality of Furstemberg	patent letters, registered 12 August 1777	III. Reciprocal exemption, 10% droit de détraction	BN F-23629(384); Gaschon 223–26
1777 7 May	Principality of Nassau-Usingen	above, 1766	II. Reciprocal abolition, conditional droit de détraction	BN F-23629(422); Gaschon 283–97
1777 9 November	Kingdom of Poland	patent letters, registered Besançon 27 January 1778	III. Reciprocal exemption, 10% droit de détraction	BN F-23629(535); Gaschon 349–56
1778 6 February	United States of America	treaty of commerce; confirmed by patent letters of 26 July 1778, registered 4 August 1778	I. Reciprocal exemption	BN F-21725(54); Gaschon 376–86; Martens 2:628–31
1778 19 February	Margrave of Anspach and Bareith	registered cour des aides de Paris 24 May 1786, and Sovereign Council of Alsace, 17 August 1786	III. Reciprocal abolition, 10% droit de détraction	BN F-21216(76); Gaschon 157–62
1778 7 April	Duchy of Saxe-Gotha and Altenburg	ratified 20 April, registered 4 August 1778	II. Reciprocal abolition, conditional droit de détraction	4-BN F-4354(14); Gaschon 187–91

Year	Date	State	Registration/ratification	Type	Provisions	Reference
1778	7 April	Duchy of Saxe-Saalfeld-Coburg	ratified 20 April, registered 4 August 1778	II.	Reciprocal abolition, conditional droit de détraction	4-BN F-4354(15); Gashon 197–201
1778	14 April	Duchy of Württemberg	ratified 20 April, registered 4 August 1778	III.	Reciprocal abolition, 10% droit de détraction	4-BN F-4254(13); Gaschon 202–7; Martens 2:628–31
1778	21 April	Kingdom of Portugal	ratified 21 June, registered 23 April 1779 and at Nancy on 15 April 1779	II.	Reciprocal abolition, conditional droit de détraction	BN F-21249(60); Gaschon 50–55
1778	29 April	Duchy of Mecklenburg-Schwerin	ratified 16 May, registered 4 August 1778; confirmed by the treaty of commerce of 18 September 1779	III.	Reciprocal abolition, 10% droit de détraction	BN F-23629(623); Gaschon 264–73
1778	29 April	Duchy of Mecklenburg-Strelitz	ratified 16 May, registered 4 August 1778	III.	Reciprocal abolition, 10% droit de détraction	BN F-23629(624); Gaschon 273–80
1778	20 July	Duchy of Saxe-Hildburghausen	ratified 28 September, registered 15 December 1778	II.	Reciprocal abolition, conditional droit de détraction	BN F-23629(652); Gaschon 192–96
1778	29 August	Principality of Fulda	patent letters, registered 23 April 1779	III.	Reciprocal exemption, 10% droit de détraction	BN F-23629(653); Gaschon 253–57
1778	16 October	Duchy of Brunswick-Lüneberg	ratified 8 November	III.	Reciprocal abolition, 10% droit de détraction	BN F-21249(61); Gaschon 258–63
1779	12 March	Duchy of Saxe-Meiningen	patent letters, registered 6 September 1779 and at Metz, 22 November 1779	III.	Reciprocal exemption, 10% droit de détraction	BN F-21726(70); Gaschon 183–87
1779	6 July	Landgrave of Hesse-Homburg	patent letters; registered at Besançon, 10 January 1780	III.	Reciprocal exemption, 10% droit de détraction	Gaschon 250–53
1780	13 June	Bishopric of Münster	ratified 11 July 1780; registered 28 April 1781	II.	Reciprocal abolition, conditional droit de détraction	BN F-21250(11); Gaschon 114–17
1780	20 June	Bishopric of Basel	ratified 11 July 1780, registered 28 April 1781	II.	Reciprocal abolition, conditional droit de détraction	BN F-23620(74); Gaschon 68–70; Martens 3:317–34
1781	27 September	County of Leiden	patent letters of November 1782, registered at Alsace 13 December and Paris on 31 January 1783	III.	Reciprocal exemption, 5% droit de détraction; treaty of limits	Gaschon 168–82; Martens 3:354
1782	February	Principalities of Salm-Salm and Salm-Kyrburg	patent letters; registered 28 April 1782	III.	Reciprocal exemption, 10% droit de détraction	BN F-23630(289); Gaschon 141–45
1787	11 January	Russia	treaty of commerce, ratified 15 March 1787, registered 22 April 1788	III.	Reciprocal exemption, 10% droit de détraction	BN 4-Lg6-511; Gaschon 344–47
1787	January	Great Britain	patent letters, registered at Alsace, 19 April 1787	III.	unilateral abolition	BN F-217343(17); Gaschon 11–17

Country		Further Procedures	Group/Conditions[a]	Sources[b]
1790	6 August	all	General unconditional abolition of the droit d'aubaine and the droit de détraction in France	AP I 17, 628–29
1791	22 February	all	General unconditional abolition of the droit d'aubaine as a "feudal" right	AP I 23, 329
1791	1 April	all	Unconditional rights of succession and inheritance given to all foreigners	AP I 24, 496
1791	13 April	all	Extension of abolition of the droit d'aubaine to France's colonies	AP I 15, 11

[a] I. Reciprocal and unconditional exemption or abolition
II. Reciprocal exemption or abolition with conditional *droit de détraction*
III. Reciprocal exemption or abolition with a *droit de détraction* fixed at a given rate (identified in table)
IV. Reciprocal exemption or abolition with other restrictive clauses

[b] M. Rémy-Limousin, ed., *Traités internationaux de l'Ancien Régime* (Paris, 1997) catalogues the holdings of the Bibliothèque Nationale (BN). Additional sources are J. B. Gaschon, *Code diplomatique des aubains* (Paris, 1818); and C. De Martens and F. de Cussy, eds., *Recueil manuel et pratique de traités, conventions, et autres actes diplomatiques ... de l'année 1760 jusqu'à l'époque actuelle*, 4 vols. (Leipzig, 1846).

NOTES

The abbreviations used in the notes can be found in the bibliography.

Preface

1. For example, see the collected studies in J. Bottin and D. Calabi, eds., *Les Etrangers dans la ville* (Paris, 1999); and for Spain, the work of T. Herzog, "Municipal Citizenship and Empire: Communal Definition in Eighteenth-Century Spain and Spanish America," in *Privileges and Rights of Citizenship: Law and the Juridical Construction of Society*, ed. J. Kirshner and L. Mayali (Berkeley, 2002), 147–68. Herzog's book, *Defining Nations: Immigrants and Citizens in Early Modern Spain and Spanish America* (New Haven, 2003), appeared too late to be considered here.

2. AN E 3706[11–12].

3. *La France italienne, XVIe–XVIIe siècle* (Paris, 1997).

4. J.-F. Dubost and P. Sahlins (Paris, 1999).

5. Cf. C. Wells, *Law and Citizenship in Early Modern France* (Baltimore, 1995); older French legal histories, including those provoked by the war and Vichy, are generally more useful in this regard: J. Boizet, *Les Lettres de naturalité sous l'Ancien Régime* (Paris, 1943); M. Vanel, *Evolution historique de la notion de français d'origine du XVIe siècle au Code civil: Contribution à l'étude de la nationalité française d'origine* (Paris, 1945); M. Folain-Le Bras, *Un Projet d'ordonnance du Chancelier Daguesseau: Etude sur quelques incapacités de donner et de recevoir sous l'Ancien Régime* (Paris, 1941). For a recent and definitive account of French nationality since the Revolution, see P. Weil, *Qu'est-ce qu'un Français? Histoire de la nationalité de la Révolution à nos jours* (Paris, 2002); on the history of the word, see his remarks, 388–89, and below, chap. 1.

6. On the history of political citizenship since the eighteenth century, see the insightful readings of published texts in P. Rosanvallon, *Le Sacre du citoyen: Histoire du suffrage universel en France* (Paris, 1992). For the French Revolution (below, chap. 8), see inter alia O. Le Cour Grandmaison, *Les Citoyennetés en Révolution (1789–1794)* (Paris, 1992); R. Waldinger, P. Dawson, and I. Woloch, eds., *The French Revolution and the Meaning of Citizenship* (Westport, Conn., 1993); S. Wahnich, *L'Impossible citoyen: L'Etranger dans le discours de la Révolution française* (Paris, 1997); M. Rapport, *Nationality and Citizenship in Revolutionary France: The Treatment of Foreigners, 1789–1799* (Oxford, 2000); and J. Heuer, "Foreigners, Families, and Citizens: Contradictions of National Citizenship in France, 1789–1830" (Ph.D. diss., University of Chicago, 1998).

Introduction: Citizenship, Immigration, and Nationality Avant La Lettre

1. For some reflections on these different and interlocking aspects of contemporary citizenship in France and elsewhere, see E. Balibar, *Les Frontières de la démocratie* (Paris, 1992), 109–23; S.

Bouamama, "Nationalité et citoyen: Le Divorce inévitable," in S. Bouamama, A. Cordeiro, and M. Roux, *La Citoyenneté dans tous ses états: De L'immigration à la nouvelle citoyenneté* (Paris, 1992), 145–70; C. Wihtol de Wenden, "Citizenship and Nationality in France," in *From Aliens to Citizens: Redefining the Status of Immigrants in Europe*, ed. R. Baubock (Aldershot, 1994), 85–94; and P. Costa, "The Discourse of Citizenship in Europe," in *Privileges and Rights of Citizenship: Law and the Juridical Construction of Society*, ed. J. Kirshner and L. Mayali (Berkeley, 2002), 199–225. On the renewed scholarly attention, especially among sociologists, to the theoretical problems, see W. Kymlicka and W. Norman, "Return of the Citizen: A Survey of Recent Work on Citizenship Theory," in *Theorizing Citizenship*, ed. R. Beiner (Albany, 1995), 283–322. The invocation of "imagined communities" is of course a reference to B. Anderson, *Imagined Communities: Reflections on the Origin and Spread of Nationalism* (London, 1983).

2. There is a remarkable consensus on this point within a seventy-five-year historiographical debate over French and European "absolutism"; for recent historiographic syntheses of the concept, see D. Parker, "Absolutism," in *Encyclopedia of European Social History*, 6 vols. (New York, 2001), 3:439–48; and F. Cosandey and R. Descimon, *L'Absolutisme en France: Histoire et historiographie* (Paris, 2002).

3. R. Brubaker, *Citizenship and Nationhood in France and Germany* (Cambridge, Mass., 1992), 39; see also C. Tilly, "The Emergence of Citizenship in France and Elsewhere," *Citizenship, Identity, and Social History*, ed. C. Tilly, *International Review of Social History* 40, supplement 3 (1995): 223–36; and G. Bossenga's review of recent literature, most of which underscores the dramatic mutation of 1789, "Rights and Citizens in the Old Regime," *French Historical Studies* 20, no. 2 (1997): 217–43.

4. *The Social Contract*, trans. M. Cranston (London, 1968), esp. 61–62. A fuller discussion of Rousseau appears below, chap. 7.

5. Reflections on the distinction between ancient and modern citizenship include E. Balibar, "Is a European Citizenship Possible?" *Public Culture* 8 (1996): 355–76, esp. 358; Costa, "Discourse of Citizenship," and especially J. G. A. Pocock, "The Ideal of Citizenship since Classical Times," in *The Citizenship Debates: A Reader*, ed. G. Schafir (Minneapolis, 1998), 31–42.

6. General works on late medieval Italy include W. Ullmann, "The Rebirth of the Citizen on the Eve of the Renaissance Period," in *Aspects of the Renaissance: A Symposium*, ed. A. R. Lewis (Austin, 1967), 5–25; and W. M. Bowsky, "Medieval Citizenship: The Individual and the State in the Commune of Siena, 1287–1355," *Studies in Medieval and Renaissance History* 4 (1967): 195–243; and the works discussed below, chap. 2.

7. For J. G. A. Pocock, seventeenth-century England was key in the transmission of republican thought from the city-states of Renaissance Italy to the American Revolution: *The Machiavellian Moment* (Princeton, 1975). For the standard view of the subjected citizen on the Continent, cf. C. Wells, *Law and Citizenship in Early Modern France*, chaps. 1–2, and 96: "The rising sun of absolutism led inevitably to the eclipse of the autonomous citizen as an actor on the political stage." For a critique of this "too simple alternative" posed through an excessive attention to the English and American liberal traditions, see L. Jaume, "Citoyenneté et souveraineté: Les Poids de l'absolutisme," in *The Political Culture of the Old Regime*, ed. K. Baker (Oxford, 1987), 515–34.

8. Sir Henry Maine, *Ancient Law* (London, 1878), 170; T. H. Marshall, *Citizenship and Social Class and Other Essays* (Cambridge, 1950); on the revival of Marshall's work in the 1980s and 1990s, see Costa, "The Discourse of Citizenship," esp. 202–10. For a critique of Marshall's plan in the case of eighteenth-century England, see M. R. Somers, "Citizenship and the Place of the Public Sphere: Law, Community, and Political Culture in the Transition to Democracy," *American Sociological Review* 58 (1993): 587–620; for critiques of the model applied to France, see D. Lochak, "La Citoyenneté: Un Concept juridique flou," in *Citoyenneté et nationalité*, ed. D. Colas, C. Emeri, and J. Zulberg (Paris, 1991), 89; P. Rosanvallon, *Le Sacre du citoyen*, 16. Lochak and Rosenvallon suggest, differently, how the French Revolution produced all three stages simultaneously. Others have pointed to the distinction between an English liberal tradition of "rights" and a French model of "civic republicanism" that lead to vary different expressions of citizenship: see, for example, D. Marquand, "Civic Republics and Liberal Individualists: The Case of Britain," in *Citizenship: Critical Concepts*, ed. B. S. Turner and P. Hamilton (London, 1994), 238–50; and A. Oldfield, *Citizenship and Community: Civic Republicanism and the Modern World* (London, 1990).

9. M. Foucault, *The Order of Things: An Archaeology of the Human Sciences* (New York, 1970), 144 (my translation from the French, *Les Mots et les choses* [Paris, 1966], 157).

10. The centrality of the droit d'aubaine in the premodern history of French nationality law has not escaped the attention of previous historians, but they have not always been attuned to the multiple and contested meanings, and their transformations over time, of this strange institution. Reflective of different periods of historical inquiry, see previous scholarship by J. C. Demangeat, *Histoire de la condition civile des étrangers en France* (Paris, 1844); J. Boizet, *Les Lettres de naturalité*; M. Vanel, *Evolution historique*; R. Villers, "La Condition des étrangers en France dans les trois derniers siècles de la monarchie," *L'Etranger/Foreigner: Recueil de la Société Jean Bodin pour l'histoire comparative des institutions* (hereafter cited as *RSJB*) 10 (1958): 139–50; Wells, *Law and Citizenship*. Two exceptions to this inattention: the older legal dissertation by Pierre Lainé, *Etude sur la capacité successorale des étrangers en France* (Paris, 1900), 10 et seq.; and the recent work of B. d'Alteroche on the origins of the droit d'aubaine as a royal prerogative: *De l'Etranger à la seigneurie à l'étranger au royaume, XIe–XVe siècle* (Paris, 2002). I am indebted to Bernard d'Alteroche for his willingness to share a copy of his impressive dissertation before its publication. Cf. M. Rapport, " 'A Languishing Branch of the Old Tree of Feudalism': The Death, Resurrection, and Final Burial of the *Droit d'Aubaine* in France," *French History* 14, no. 1 (2000): 13–40, which outlines this story but fails to interrogate the multiplicity of its object.

11. See the collected essays on the legal and social incapacities of foreigners in comparative perspective, *RSJB*, and the introductory essay by J. Gilissen, "Le statut de l'étranger à la lumière de l'histoire comparative," *RSJB* 9 (1958): 1–57. On English notions of allegiance, see J. Kettner, *The Development of American Citizenship, 1608–1870* (Chapel Hill, 1978), esp. 3–130.

12. A. de Tocqueville, *The Old Regime and the Revolution*, ed. F. Furet and M. Melonio, trans. A. S. Kahn, 2 vols. (Chicago, 1998–2001).

13. G. Pagès, *La Monarchie française de Henri IV à Louis XIV* (Paris, 1928); R. Mousnier, *The Institutions of France under the Absolute Monarchy, 1598–1789*, trans. B. Pearce, 2 vols. (Chicago, 1979–84); see also D. Richet, *La France moderne: L'Esprit des institutions* (Paris, 1973); D. Bien, "Offices, Corps, and a System of State Credit: The Uses of Privilege under the Ancien Régime," in *The Political Culture of the Old Regime*, ed. K. Baker (Oxford, 1987), 89–114; and for a general historiographic account, Cosandey and Descimon, *L'absolutisme*, 131–32 and passim.

14. See below, chap. 7.

15. J. Garrisson, *L'Edit de Nantes et sa révocation: Histoire d'une intolérance* (Paris, 1985); E. I. Perry, *From Theory to History: French Religious Controversy and the Revocation of the Edict of Nantes* (The Hague, 1973).

16. On the French Huguenots in England and Holland, see C. B. Gibbs, "The Reception of Huguenots in England and the Dutch Republic, 1680–90," in *From Persecution to Moderation: The Glorious Revolution and England*, ed. O. P. Grell, J. I. Israel, and N. Tyake Grell (Oxford, 1991), 275–306; P. L. Nève, "Le Statut juridique des réfugiés français huguenots; quelques remarques comparatives," in *La Condition juridique de l'étranger, hier et aujourd'hui*, Actes du Colloque organisé à Nimegue, 9–11 May 1988 (Nijmegen, 1988), 223–46; and R. Feenstra and H. Klompmaker, "Le Statut des étrangers aux Pays-Bas," *RSJB* 10 (1958): 333–73. On the French Protestants in Germany, see E. François, "L'acceuil des réfugiés huguenots en Allemagne," in *La Révocation de l'Edit de Nantes et les Provinces Unies, 1685*, International Congress of the Tricentennial, Leyden, 1–3 April 1685 (Amsterdam, 1986), 207–16. On the 1753 "Jew Bill" in England, see T. W. Perry, *Public Opinion, Propaganda, and Politics in Eighteenth-Century England: A Study of the Jew Bill of 1753* (Cambridge, Mass., 1962).

17. D. Statt, *Foreigners and Englishmen: The Controversy over Immigration and Population, 1660–1760* (Newark, Del., 1995).

18. M. Antoine, "La Monarchie absolue," in *The Political Culture of the Old Regime*, ed. K. Baker (Oxford, 1987), 10. The concept of the "administrative monarchy," originally formulated by Georges Pagès, has long been debated among historians of French absolutism: see Cosandey and Descimon, *L'absolutisme*, esp. 137–66 and 202 n. 19.

19. For some reflections on this historiographical lacuna, see A. Limousin, "L'histoire de l'immigration en France: Une histoire impossible," *Pouvoirs: Revue francaise d'etudes constitutionnelles et politiques* 47 (1988): 5–22; and G. Noiriel, *The French Melting Pot: Immigration, Citizenship, and Na-*

tional Identity, trans. G. de Laforcade (Minneapolis, 1996), esp. 1–90, 189–226. More generally, French historians have tended to ignore population movement, the subject of relatively few pages, for example, in Fernand Braudel's massive reflections in *L'identité de la France*, 3 vols. (Paris, 1986) [an English edition appeared as *The Identity of France*, trans S. Reynolds, 2 vols. (New York, 1988–90)]. For a different perspective that emphasizes mobility in early modern France, see J. B. Collins, "Geographic and Social Mobility in Early-Modern France," *Journal of Social History* 24 (1991): 563–577; and on Europe more generally, J. Lucassen and L. Lucassen, eds. *Migration, Migration History, History: Old Paradigms and New Perspectives* (Bern, 1997), esp. the article by N. L. Green, "The Comparative Method and Poststructural Structuralism: New Perspectives for Migration Studies," 41–56; and L. Moch, *Moving Europeans: Migration in Western Europe since 1650* (Bloomington, 1992), esp. chap. 2.

20. Pierre Nora, who edited the massive seven-volume collection of essays about France's "realms of memory," (*Les lieux de mémoire*, 7 vols. (Paris, 1984–92]), wrote in 1986 that immigration was "a novelty of the country's present day situation," and only after a public debate with the sociologist Gérard Noiriel did he include Noiriel's essay, "Français et étrangers," in the third installment of the series (*Les Frances*), 2:2433–66. Two compilations in translation of Nora's project are published: *Realms of Memory: Rethinking the French Past*, trans. A. Goldhammer, 3 vols. (Columbia, 1996–98); and *Rethinking France: Les Lieux de mémoire*, vol. 1: *The State* (Chicago, 2001). Nora is quoted in Noiriel, *French Melting Pot*, 3; Noiriel's contribution to the debate is "French and Foreigners," in *Realms of Memory*, 1:145–78. For a critique of Nora's project, see S. Englund's review, "The Ghost of Nation Past," *Journal of Modern History* 44, no. 2 (1992): 299–320; some criticisms of Noiriel's own approach are made by D. A. Bell, "Forgotten Frenchmen," *Times Literary Supplement*, 24 January 1997.

21. T. Hampton, *Literature and the Nation in the Sixteenth Century: Inventing Renaissance France* (Ithaca, 2001) and more generally, A. Khatibi, *Figures de l'étranger dans la littérature français* (Paris, 1987); on foreigners in the thought and practice of Enlightenment culture, see especially D. A. Bell, L. Pimenova, and S. Pujol, eds., *La Recherche dix-huitièmiste: Raison universelle et culture nationale au siècle des Lumières / Eighteenth-Century Research: Universal Reason and National Culture during the Enlightenment* (Paris, 1999); and also the fine social and cultural history of the "foreign" element in French freemasony during the Enlightenment: P.-Y., Beaurepaire, *L'Autre et le frère étranger, la franc-maçonnerie au XVIIIe siècle* (Paris, 1999). On the history of foreign troops in the service of France, a topic that still awaits its modern historian, see J. Mathorez, *Les Etrangers en France sous l'Ancien Régime*, 2 vols. (Paris, 1919), 1:110 et seq; the groundwork laid by A. Corvisier, *Les controles de troupes de l'Ancien Régime*, 4 vols. (Paris, 1968); and the older study of E. Fieffé, *L'histoire des troupes étrangères au service de France*, 2 vols. (Paris, 1854). On foreigners among retired soldiers, especially in Paris, see J.-P. Bois, *Les anciens soldats dans la société française au XVIIIe siècle* (Paris, 1990), 191–201. On the movement of foreigners in Paris, see D. Roche, ed., *La ville promise: Mobilité et accueil à Paris (fin XVIIe–début XIXe siècle)* (Paris, 2000); and for France more generally, J.-F. Dubost and P. Sahlins, *Et si on faisait payer*, esp. chaps. 5–8 ; on the settlement of foreigners in Provence, see P. Echinard and E. Temime, *Migrance: Histoire des migrations à Marseille. Vol. 1: La Préhistoire de la migration (1482–1830)* (Aix en Provence, 1989).

22. See the (incomplete) synthesis by J. Mathorez, *Les Etrangers en France*, and the specific sources cited in discussions of the different "national" and "professional" groups below, chap 5.

23. For a general overview of the demographic profile of foreigners in the Old Regime, see J.-P. Poussou, "Mobilité et migrations," in *Histoire de la population française*, vol. 2: *De la Renaissance à 1789*, ed. J. Dupâquier (Paris, 1988), 124–137, and his other syntheses, "Migrations et mobilité en France à l'epoque moderne," in *Les Mouvements migratoires dans l'Occident moderne*, Civilisations, no. 19 (Paris, 1994), 39–62; and "Les mouvement migratoires en France et à Partir de la France du XVe au début du XIXe siècles: approches pour une synthèse," *Annales de démographie historique* 1970: 11–78.

24. The proportion of naturalized foreigners among those from whom the tax-farmers attempted to collect the 1697 Naturalization Tax was undoubtedly exaggerated by the fact that these earlier, individual grants of naturalization left traces in the royal archives to which the employees of the tax-farms had access: see Dubost and Sahlins, *Et si on faisait payer*, 112–15.

25. *Annales de la Cour et de Paris, 1697–1698*, quoted in Mathorez, *Les Etrangers en France*,

1:109, who quotes Dulaure, *Nouvelles description des curiosités de Paris*, vol. 1 (Paris, 1785), 327. Using notarial and police archives, A. Thillay counts far fewer foreign artisans in the district: 2875 cases between 1690 and 1780: "Les artisans étrangers au faubourg Saint-Antoine à Paris (1650–1793)," *Les Etrangers à la ville*, ed. Bottin and Calabi, 264; the figures for foreign travellers in Paris are from Dubost, "Les étrangers à Paris," 236.

26. On the statistical importance and character of migration to eighteenth-century Paris, see D. Roche, "Nouveaux Parisiens au XVIIIe siècle," *Cahiers d'histoire*, no. 3 (1979): 3–20; L. Henry and D. Courgeau, "Deux analyses de l'immigration à Paris au XVIIIe siècle," *Population* 6 (1971): 1073–92. Important and underexploited statistical sources and descriptive sources measuring foreign movement into Paris include the extensive dossiers at the Archives des Affaires Etrangères (Quai d'Orsay) on the "Police des étrangers" (usefully exploited by several authors in *La Ville promise*, ed. D. Roche; and the police spy reports beginning in the early eighteenth century found at the Bibliothèque de l'Arsenal, Paris (partially used by L. Bély, *Espions et ambassadeurs au temps de Louis XIV* [Paris, 1990]). An unexamined source of foreign migration in Paris can be found in the eighteenth-century hospital registers at the Archives de la Santé Public, where the proportion of foreign-born inmates was surprisingly high.

27. The decline of naturalizations in the latter half of the eighteenth century, just as migration to the capital city was increasing dramatically, anticipated as it confirmed the systematic abolition of the droit d'aubaine through international treaties and collective privileges: see below, chap. 7.

28. Herzog, "Citizenship and Empire," and " 'A Stranger in a Strange Land': The Conversion of Foreigners into Members in Colonial Latin America (Seventeenth–Eighteenth Centuries)." *Social Identities* 3 (1997): 247–63.

29. See below, conclusion. This chronology would dovetail, although it does not reproduce exactly, recent historiographical choices to define "revolutionary France" more generally as the continuing history of republicanism in the nineteenth century: see F. Furet, *Revolutionary France, 1770–1880*, trans. A. Neville (Oxford, 1995); most recently, see the edited collection of essays by M. Crook, ed., *Revolutionary France, 1788–1880* (Oxford, 2002).

30. My distinction between the legal and political dimensions of the citizen, elaborated in chap. 1, takes its cue from Pocock, "Ideal of Citizenship."

31. For a recent overview of the postrevisionist shifts to the study of political culture and beyond, see V. R. Gruder, "Whither Revisionism? Political Perspectives on the Ancien Régime," *French Historical Studies* 20 (1997): 245–85. Significant work includes K. Baker, *Inventing the French Revolution* (Cambridge, 1990), R. Chartier, *The Cultural Origins of the French Revolution*, trans. L. G. Cochrane (Durham, 1991); R. Darnton, *The Literary Underground of the Old Regime* (Cambridge, Mass., 1982); D. Van Kley, *The Damiens Affair and the Unraveling of the Ancien Régime* (Princeton, 1983); D. Gordon, *Citizens without Sovereignty: Equality and Sociability in French Thought, 1670–1789* (Princeton, 1994); S. Maza, *Private Lives and Public Affairs: The Causes Célèbres of Prerevolutionary France* (Berkeley, 1993); D. A. Bell, *Lawyers and Citizens: The Making of a Political Elite in Old Regime France* (New York, 1994); and more recently, his *Cult of the Nation in France: Inventing Nationalism, 1680–1800* (Cambridge, Mass., 2001).

32. See the synthesis by J. Van Horn Melton, *The Rise of the Public in Enlightenment Europe* (Cambridge, 2001), esp. 1–15, which summarizes historiographical approaches to the "public sphere" and "public opinion" since the translations of J. Habermas's *Structural Transformations of the Public Sphere: An Inquiry into a Category of Bourgeois Society*, trans. T. Burger (Cambridge, Mass, 1989).

33. The struggles between the parlements and the crown have been a mainstay of French historiography: see J. Swann, *Politics and the Parlement of Paris under Louis XV, 1754–1774* (Cambridge, 1995), who usefully surveys the historiographic debate; my remarks on the meaning of citizenship in the "politico-religious" politics of the eighteenth century is indebted to the work of J. Merrick, especially *The Desacralization of the French Monarchy in the Eighteenth Century* (Baton Rouge, 1990).

34. E. Dziembowski, *Un nouveau patriotisme français, 1750–1770: la France face à la puissance anglaise à l'époque de la guerre de Sept Ans*, Studies on Voltaire and the Eighteenth Century, vol. 365 (Oxford: Voltaire Foundation, 1998); and Bell, *Cult of the Nation*, passim. Bell's argument, engaged below (chap. 7), considers how both official and unofficial France not only constructed the

nation (in patriotic literature, national language reform, or canons of French authors) but undertook and, under the Revolution, completed the political project of identifying the nation as a
source of sovereignty—hence the origin of nationalism itself. For a more conventional view of the
development of "nationalism" that nonetheless emphasizes the importance of the 1750s and the
Seven Years War, see R. R. Palmer, "The National Idea in France Before the Revolution," *Journal of the History of Ideas* 1 (1940): 95–111.

35. In the interim, see See D. Gordon, "Citizenship," in *The Oxford Encyclopedia of the Enlight-
enment*, ed. A. Kors et al. (Oxford, 2002); J. Merrick, "Conscience and Citizenship in Eighteenth-
Century France," *Eighteenth-Century Studies* 21 (1987): 48–71; J. Merrick, "Subjects and Citizens in
the Remonstrances of the Parlement of Paris in the Eighteenth Century," *Journal of the History of
Ideas* 51 (1990): 453–60; J. H. Shennan, "The Political Vocabulary of the Parlement of Paris in the
Eighteenth Century," *Diritto e potere nella storia europea: Atti in onore di Bruno Paradesi* (Florence,
1982) 951–64; and P. Rétat, "Citoyen-Sujet, Civisme," in *Handbuch politisch-sozialer Grundbegriffe
in Frankreich 1680–1829*, ed. R. Reichardt and E. Schmitt, 10 vols. (Munich, 1985–), 9:75–105; and
his "The Evolution of the Citizen from the Ancien Régime to the Revolution," in *The French Revolution and the Meaning of Citizenship*, ed. Waldinger et al., 3–15; A. Geffroy, "Citoyen/citoyenne
(1753–1829)," in *Dictionnaire des usages socio-politiques (1770–1815)*, vol. 3: *Designants socio-politiques*,
part 2, Société française d'étude du 18e siècle (Paris, 1989), 63–86; and S. Branca-Rosoff, "Les
Mots de parti pris. *Citoyen*, *Aristocrate* et *Insurrection* dans quelques dictionnaires (1762–1798),"
ibid., 47–73. Paris, A crude but revealing measure of the increasing use of the noun *citoyen* can be
found in the largest digital database of French-language texts of the period, mostly but not exclusively literary, the ARTFL database (humanities.uchicago.edu/ARTFL). In the second half of the
eighteenth century, the frequency, per 100,000 words, of *citoyen* tripled, from 3.8 to 14.8; the critical decade in which the number of total citations doubled was the 1750s (303 citations, up from 153
citations in the 1740s), a total that was relatively stable in the 1760s, then increased to over 450 in
the 1770s.

36. On the "diplomatic revolution," see L. Bély, *Les relations internationales en Europe,
XVIIe–XVIIIe siècle* (Paris, 1992), chap. 17; J. Black, *From Louis XIV to Napoleon: The Fate of a Great
Power* (London, 1999), chap. 4; and the older but still useful R. Waddington, *Louis XV et le renversement des alliances* (Paris, 1896); on the transformation and "enlightenment" of eighteenth century diplomacy, see F. Gilbert, "The 'New Diplomacy' of the Eighteenth Century," *World Politics*
4, no. 1 (1951): 1–38.

37. Although these treaties (appendix 2) were often listed in collections of international
treaties in the eighteenth and nineteenth centuries (e.g., Koch, Märtens), the diplomatic correspondence has not been published (e.g., J. Flammermont, *Les Correspondances des agents diplomatiques étrangers en France avant la Révolution conservées dans les archives de Berlin, Dresde, Genève,
Turin, Gênes, Florences, Naples, Simancas, Lisbonne, Londres, La Haye et Vienne* [Paris, 1896]). The
treaties go unmentioned in near contemporaneous histories of foreign policy (e.g., Flassan, *Histoire générale et raisonné de la diplomatie française; ou de la politique de la France; depuis la fondation de
la monarchie jusqu'à la fin du règne de Louis XVI* [Paris, 1811]), and also modern manuals and text-
books of historical scholarship, from G. Zeller, *Les Temps Modernes: II. de Louis XIV à 1789*, vol. 3
of *Histoire des Relations internationales*, ed. P. Renouvin (Paris, 1955) to Bély, *Les relations internationales*, including recent biographies of the French kings under whose watches the droit d'aubaine
was abolished: see, for example, M. Antoine, *Louis XV* (Paris, 1989). Cf. the brief and inadequate
treatment by Rapport, " 'A Languishing Branch of the Old Tree of Feudalism.' "

38. A typical example: that great chronicle of public opinion, E.-J.-F. Barbier's *Chronique de la
Régence*, vol. 8 (1763; Paris, 1857), 56, notes laconically on 5 September 1762 the registration of
the patent letters giving privileges to the subjects of the kingdom of Spain and the Two Sicilies
("the subjects of the kings of Spain and Naples") and France abolishing the droit d'aubaine, immediately after disclosing gossip about local real estate (M. le duc de Bedfort "is going to take, it
is said, a magnificent lodging in the faubourg Saint-Germain, and will have it well equiped.") Such
accounts of international accords differed little from those of the chroniclers of Louis XIV, for example, Ph. de Dangeau, whose *Journal* in 1684 recorded, after noting the sudden death of
the abbé de Sainte-Geneviève and an "Italian comedy" played at Versailles, the royal declaration

concerning the subjects of the United Provinces, by which they could gather successions in France without being naturalized (Paris, 1845–60), 116.

39. For example, see the memoires of Carlo Goldoni, the Venetian ambassador to France who negotiated the abolition of the droit d'aubaine in 1778, and who mentions fleetingly his efforts: Carlo Goldoni, *Memorie*, ed. Guido Davico Bonino and trans. Eugenio Levi (Turin, 1993 [orig. French ed. 1787]), 539. Thanks to Jim Amelang for this reference. On the "secret du roi," a historiographic term that has fallen out of disfavor, see the still useful study by the duc de Broglie, *Le Secret du Roi. Correspondance secrète de Louis XV avec ses agents diplomatiques, 1752–1774*, 2 vols. (Paris, 1878), which fails, however, to treat the abolitions of the droit d'aubaine.

40. Below, chap. 7; for a major reconsideration of French political culture in the late absolutist state, see M. Kwass, *Privilege and the Politics of Taxation in Eighteenth-Century France: Liberté, Egalité, Fiscalité* (Cambridge, 2000); and his synoptical treatment, "A Kingdom of Taxpayers: State Formation, Privilege, and Political Culture in Eighteenth-Century France," *Journal of Modern History* 52, no. 2 (1998): 295–339; on the bureaucratic revolution, J. Bosher, *French Finances, 1770–1795: From Business to Bureaucracy* (Cambridge, 1970).

Chapter 1: The Making of the Absolute Citizen

1. Rousseau, *Social Contract*, 62.

2. Jean Bodin, *Les Six livres de la république* (Paris, 1583). All citations of Bodin, unless otherwise noted, are my translations from the fourth edition (1583), where his argument on the nature of citizenship was expanded (and subsequently published in the "definitive" Latin edition of 1584).

3. The traditional view of Bodin is represented by J. H. Franklin, *Jean Bodin and the Rise of Absolutist Theory* (Cambridge, 1973) and J.-F. Spitz, *Bodin et la souveraineté* (Paris, 1998), who disagree, however, on just how absolutist he was. On Bodin's conception of "order," see R. A. Vernon, *Citizenship and Order: Studies in French Political Thought* (Toronto, 1986), chap. 1; and W. H. Greenleaf, "Bodin and the Idea of Order," in *Jean Bodin: Proceedings of the International Conference on Bodin in Munich*, ed. H. Denzer (Munich, 1973), 23–38. For reevaluations that focus more attention on Bodin's understanding of the citizen, see K. Kim, "L'Etranger chez Bodin, l'étranger chez nous," *Revue de l'histoire de droit* 76 (1998): 75–92; and the important article by D. Quaglioni, "Les Citoyens envers l'Etat: L'Individu en tant que citoyen de la *République* de Bodin au *Contrat social* de Rousseau," in *L'Individu dans la théorie et dans la pratique*, ed. J. Coleman (Paris, 1996), 311–21.

4. Bodin, a legal humanist, was not a follower of the *mos gallicus*, the late fifteenth and early sixteenth century French school, best represented by Jacques Cujas (1522–90), that sought to recover the purity of the *Corpus* and other ancient sources, breaking with the tradition of the Commentators: see D. R. Kelley, *Foundations of Modern Historical Scholarship: Language, Law, and History in the French Renaissance* (New York, 1970); and P. Ourliac and J.-L. Gazzaninga, *Histoire du droit privé français de l'an mil au Code civil* (Paris, 1985), esp. 155.

5. Quoted in Wells, *Law and Citizenship*, 31. On Bodin's "Romanism" with respect to civil law, see. W. Wolodkiewicz, "Bodin et le droit privé romain," in *Jean Bodin: Actes du Colloque Interdisciplinaire d'Angers, 24 au 27 mai 1984* (Angers, 1985), 303–10; and on Bodin's juridical sources more generally, see M. Reulos, "Les Sources juridiques de Bodin: Textes, auteurs, pratique," in *Jean Bodin*, ed. Denzer, 187–94.

6. Bodin, *Les Six livres*, 71.

7. C. Parry, *Nationality and Citizenship Laws of the Commonwealth and the Republic of Ireland*, 2 vols. (London, 1957), 1:3–4 et seq., who argues that the legal concept of nationality was a nineteenth-century development "contingent on the introduction of compulsory military service upon a totalitarian [*sic*] scale, and the universalisation of national political rights"; cf. the works of Statt and others cited in note 44, below.

8. M. Walker, *German Home Towns: Community, State, and General Estate, 1648–1871* (Ithaca, 1971), esp. chap. 2, "The Civic Community"; on the creation of Neapolitan citizenship, see M.

Peytavin, "Españoles e italianos en Sicilia, Napoles y Milan durante los siglos XVII y XVII. Sobre la oportunidad de ser nacional o natural," *Relaciones* 19, no. 73 (1998): 85–114. On Spain, see the works of Herzog, op. cit.

9. For the emblematic status of the "bourgeois de Paris," see J. di Corcia, "*Bourg, Bourgeois, Bourgeoisie de Paris* from the Eleventh to the Eighteenth Centuries," *Journal of Modern History* 50, no. 2 (1978): 207–33; and for an interpretation of the changing social profile of the "bourgeois" in Paris, R. Descimon, " 'Bourgeois de Paris': Les Migrations sociales d'un privilège, XIV–XVIIIe siècle," in *Histoire social, histoire globale? Actes du colloque des 27–29 janvier 1989*, ed. C. Charles (Paris, 1993), 173–82. On crown-city relations in the seventeenth and eighteenth centuries, see G. Bossenga, "City and State: An Urban Perspective on the Origins of the French Revolution," in *The Political Culture of the Old Regime*, ed. K. M. Baker (Oxford, 1987), 115–40.

10. C. Loyseau, *Cinq livres du droit des offices* (Paris, 1613 [1610]), 200.

11. Bodin, *Les Six livres*, 76.

12. Ibid., 82, 91.

13. Brubaker, *Citizenship and Nationhood*, 21–34.

14. Bodin, *Les Six livres*, 68.

15. Pocock, "Ideal of Citizenship," 31–41.

16. Y. Thomas, *"Origine" et "Commune Patrie": Etude de droit public romain (89 av. J.-C. — 212 ap. J.-C.)*, Collection de l'Ecole Française de Rome 221 (Rome, 1996). On Gaius and the "fundamental division" of Roman society into legally free men and slaves, see M. Ducos, *Rome et le droit* (Paris, 1996), 32–49; and on the linkage between manumission and citizenship in Rome, see A. Watson, *The Spirit of Roman Law* (Athens, Ga., 1995), 45–51. For overviews of Roman citizenship and the treatment of foreigners before and after 212 c.e., I have relied on C. Nicolet, *The World of the Citizen in Republican Rome*, trans. P. S. Falla (Berkeley, 1988; and A. N. Sherwin-White, *The Roman Citizenship* (Oxford, 1973). Of course, Roman citizenship was itself transformed by the end of the Republic, as the "civic structure" changed through the abandonment of direct taxation, citizen militias, and the correlatedly diminished participation of citizens in political decisions: see Nicolet, *World of the Citizen*, 385–86; and also F. de Visscher, "La Condition des pérégrins à Rome, jusqu'à la Constitution Antonine de l'an 212," *RSJB* 9 (1958): 195–208. These changes marked the passage of citizenship from "politics" to "law" that culminated in the jurisprudence of Gaius.

17. Alternatively, "Licet liber vivat," in Bacquet, *Oeuvres* 1:53; on Bodin's resulting opposition to slavery within the ideology of absolutism, see M. W. Ghachem, "Sovereignty and Slavergy in the Age of Revolution: Haitian Variations on a Metropolitan Theme," Ph.D. diss., Stanford University, 2001, 5–17; and on the "freedom principle" in France, see S. Peabody, *"There Are No Slaves in France" The Political Culture of Race and Slavery in the Ancien Régime* (New York, 1996), 26–37.

18. Bacquet authored six "little treatises" on the king's domanial rights, beginning with the one on the droit d'aubaine, justifying his choice as follows: "And it seemed to me that the treatise on the droit d'aubaine should come first as it is the least known, but the most frequent because of the great multitude of foreigners that, for some time, have settled in the kingdom and are subjected to the alien law [*loi d'aubaine*])": *Les Oeuvres de maistre Jean Bacquet, Advocat du Roy en la Chambre du Trésor. . . .* , 2 vols. (Lyon, 1744), 2:1–144 ("Traité du droit d'aubaine"); quote, 2.

19. R. Choppin, *Oeuvres*, 5 vols. (Paris, 1662), 1:94–124. For brief sketches of these "theorists" of citizenship in the 1570s, see Wells, *Law and Citizenship*, 58–87. Additional biographical and bibliographical information on these and other jurisconsults of early modern France can be found in A. Rodière, *Les Grands jurisconsultes* (Toulouse, 1874); P. Taisand, *Vie des plus celebres jurisconsultes* (Paris, 1837); and J. Balteau, M. Barroux, M. Prévost, and R. d'Amat, ed., *Dictionnaire de biographie française* (Paris, 1933–42); and L. G. Michaud, *Biographie universelle ancienne et moderne*, 45 vols. (Paris, 1854–65). For other propospographical indications as well as some important reflections, especially on the growing gulf between university instruction and legal practice in the Old Regime, see J.-L. Gazzaniga, "Quand les avocats formaient les juristes et la doctrine," *Droits* 20 (1994): 31–41.

20. J. H. M. Salmon, *Society in Crisis: France in the Sixteenth Century* (Toronto, 1975) and H. A. Lloyd, *The State, France, and the Sixteenth Century* (London, 1983) provide thorough syntheses of the period.

21. On the pamphleteers' accusations that French ills resulted from foreign imports, see M. Yardeni, *La Conscience nationale en France pendant les Guerres de Religion (1559–1598)* (Louvain, 1971), 38–42; on the protests of the Third Estate at Orléans in 1560 against the economic advantages given to foreigners, see G. Picot, *Histoire des Etats-Généraux considérés au point de vue de leur influence sur le gouvernement de la France de 1355 à 1614*, 5 vols. (Geneva, 1979 [Paris, 1872]), 2:253–55; on anti-Italian diatribes in the sixteenth century, culminating in the "ritual murder" of Concini in 1617, see Dubost, *France italienne*, chap. 11; and on the images of the Concini themselves, see H. Duccini, "L'Entourage des Concini: Les Étrangers et leur image entre 1610 et 1617," in *Le Sentiment national dans l'Europe moderne*, Association des historiens modernes, Actes du colloque de 1990, bulletin 15 (Paris, 1991), 25–52. On anti-Spanish sentiment especially after the accession of Henry IV, see Yardeni, *La Conscience nationale*, chap. 10; and J. Mathorez, "Notes sur les Espagnols en France depuis le XVIe siècle jusqu'au regne de Louis XIII," *Bulletin Hispanique* 16 (1914): 335–71. During the Revolution, G. Brizard continued to blame "foreigners" for the disorders in sixteenth-century France: *Du Massacre de la Saint Barthélémy et de l'influence des étrangers en France durant la Ligue. Discours historique*, 2 vols. (Paris, 1790).

22. "Jurisconsultus hoc est Homo politicus," quoted in D. Bell, *Lawyers and Citizens*, 9; more generally, on the role and activity of lawyers in the construction of the early modern European culture and political orders, see W. Bouwsma, "Lawyers and Early Modern Culture," in W. Bouwsma, *A Usable Past: Essays in European Cultural History* (Berkeley, 1990), 129–53.

23. C. Wells, "The Language of Citizenship in the French Religious Wars," *Sixteenth Century Journal* 30, no. 2 (1999): 441–56; Yardeni, *La Conscience nationale*, 183–200, on the Protestant rhetoric of patriotism and the citizen.

24. Argou quoted in A. Watson, *The Making of Civil Law* (Cambridge Mass., 1981), 156; M. Fumaroli, *L'Age de l'éloquence* (Paris, 1980), esp. 585–612; W. F. Church, "The Decline of the French Jurists as Political Theorists, 1660–1789," *French Historical Studies* 5 (1967): 1–16, who argues that after the "generation of the 1560s," and especially between the reign of Louis XIV and the French Revolution, barristers and magistrates tended to function as legal technicians, not political theorists; but cf. below, chap. 7, on the eighteenth-century revival of public law and the political role of some jurists.

25. Quoted in D. Richet, "La Monarchie au travail sur elle-même?" in *Political Culture of the Old Regime*, ed. Baker, 28.

26. Bacquet, *Oeuvres*, 1:2. The traditional view of France's nonreception of Roman law, its relegation to secondary status, is rehearsed by B. Barret-Kriegel, "La Politique juridique de la monarchie française," in *L'Etat moderne: Le Droit, l'espace, et les formes de l'etat*, ed. N. Coulet and J.-P. Genet (Paris, 1990), 91–108. For more nuanced synthesis, see Cosandey and Descimon, *L'absolutisme*, 27–49.

27. The notion of "written reason" (*ratio scripta*) in French classical law was best formulated in Jean Domat's *Les Loix civiles dans leur ordre naturel*, 1689; see A. Watson, *Sources of Law, Legal Change, and Ambiguity* (Philadelphia, 1984), 51–77; P. Dubouchet, *La Pensée juridique avant et après le Code civil* (Paris, 1991), 80–85; and Vanel, *Evolution historique*, 34, 58, 67, et seq. But according to the "school" of customary law, in the work of Charles du Moulin (1500–1566) and Guy Coquille (1523–1603), Roman law was only invoked when "neighboring customs" failed to fill the gap.

28. Gazzaniga, "Quand les avocats," 31 et seq.; J.-C. Garreta, "Les Sources de la législation de l'Ancien Régime," *Mémoires de la Société pour l'histoire du droit et des institutions des anciens pays Bourguignons, Comtois, et Romands* 29 (1968–69): 275–364.

29. C. Chêne, "L'arrestographie, science fort douteuse," *Recueil des mémoires de la Société d'histoire du droit et des institutions des pays de droit écrit* (1985): 179–87, quoting Berroyer and Jean Catellan, himself the author of the *Arrêts remarquables du Parlement de Toulouse* (1723). Catellan protested against "the bad effects that these collections produce in the spirit of lazy people who think themselves dispensed from studying the principles and searching in the true sources of Roman and French jurisprudence as long as they have imperfect but facile definitions in the collections of decrees."

30. Boissy, *L'Avocat, ou reflexions sur l'exercice du barreau* (Paris, 1777), cited in Bell, *Lawyers and Citizens*, 224; see his useful guide to research on Parisian barristers, "Les Avocats parisiens d'ancien régime: Guide de recherches," *Revue de la Société internationale d'histoire de la profession d'avo-*

cat 5 (1993): 213–54. See also L.-R. Berlanstein, *The Barristers of Toulouse in the Eighteenth Century, 1740–1793* (Baltimore, 1975); and R. Kagan, "Law Students and Legal Careers in Eighteenth-Century France," *Past and Present* 68 (1975): 38–72. In discussing the French jurists, I focus on the opinions of barristers: judges themselves did not give justifications for their court decisions, and the winning pleas of the barristers provided de facto juridical "doctrine": see Gazzaninga, "Quand les avocats," 32–33 and passim.

31. Pierre-Jacques Brillon (1671–1736), lawyer at the Paris parlement and later the general intendant of the duc de Maine's household, recalled how his colleagues "sacrificed ten years and more in making extracts from their books and putting them on cards." He himself was the author of an influential *Dictionnaire des arrêts* (1711) of the French parlements and other courts that expanded through three editions before 1727 (and was later pirated in 1781). It was an unwieldy work, which may explain the success of a less prolix author such as Barthelemy-Joseph Bretonnier (1646–1727), whose *Recueil par ordre alphabétique des principales questions de droit qui se jugent diversement dans les différens tribunaux du Royaume* was first published in 1718 and reedited five times before 1783.

32. See the bibliography for a complete list of titles, publication dates, and editions consulted.

33. The *Collection* was originally published in three volumes between 1754 and 1756; the ninth edition of 1783 was dedicated to the Keeper of the Seals Miromesnil, and acknowledged his role in developing a "public" repertoire of court decisions and in directly supporting the enterprise of gathering more than six thousand court decisions for the publishers. The four-volume eighth edition of 1783, however, only reached the letter "C"; by 1807, 14 volumes had been published, but stopped at the letter "I." I have relied mostly on the eighth (1783) and ninth (1784) editions.

34. P. A. Merlin et al, *Répertoire universel et raisonné de jurisprudence. . . .*, 5th ed., 18 vols. (Paris, 1827–28 [1812–15]); see also L. Rondonneau, *Table générale, alphabétique, et raisonnée des matières contenues dans le répertoire de jurisprudence et dans le recueil des questions de droit de M. Merlin* (Paris, 1828). On Boucher d'Argis in his roles as editor of repertoires and pamphleteer in the struggle against royal despotism, see below, chap. 7.

35. On the teaching of "French law" in the universities during the seventeenth and eighteenth centuries, see L. W. B. Brockliss, *French Higher Education in the Seventeenth and Eighteenth Centuries: A Cultural History* (Oxford, 1987); A. De Curzon, "L'Enseignement du droit français dans les universités de France aux XVIIe et XVIIIe siècles," *Revue historique de droit Français et étranger* 42 (1919): 209–69, 305–64; F. Olivier-Martin, "Les Professeurs royaux de droit français et l'unification du droit civil français," in *Mélanges juridiques dédiés à M. le Professeur Sugiyama* (Paris, 1970), 263–81; and esp. the works of C. Chêne, "La Politique royale de l'enseignement du droit en France au XVIIIe siècle: Les Survivances dans le régime moderne," *Revue d'histoire des facultés de droit et de la science juridique* 7 (1988): 21 et seq.; "Les Facultés de droit françaises du XVIIe siècle à la Révolution, éléments de bibliographie," *Annales d'histoire des facultés de droit* 3 (1986): 199–242; and *L'Enseignement du droit français en pays de droit écrit (1679–1793)* (Geneva, 1982).

36. Quoted in Gazzaniga, "Quand les avocats," 39. François Bourjon (d. 1751), lawyer at the Châtelet court in Paris, also drew on customary law in his compilation of *Le Droit commun de la France et la coutume de Paris réduite en principes*, 2 vols. (Paris, 1747), reprinted for a third time in 1773, and traditionally described as the source of the French Civil Code in 1803—although opinion of his work has suffered in recent years: see R. Martinage, *Bourjon et le Code Civil* (Paris, 1971), who traces the composition of the Civil Code of 1803 directly to Bourjon's texts; more recently, Ourliac and Gazzaniga call him a "mediocre lawyer at the Châtelet," *Histoire du droit privé*, 159.

37. J.-J. A. Lefebvre de la Planche, *Mémoires sur les matières domaniales, ou Traité du domaine*, 3 vols. (Paris, 1764–65); on Lorry, see G. Antonetti, "Traditionalistes et novateurs à la faculté des droits de Paris au XVIIIe siècle," *Annales d'histoire des facultés de droit* 3 (1986): 49–50.

38. It is no accident that d'Aguesseau's writings, apart from his legal opinions, tended to develop precociously the more political language of the "citizen" that was to become central in the public sphere after 1750. On d'Aguesseau's inauguration of "the beginning of a new era in French political culture and cultural politics," see Bell, *Cult of the Nation*, esp. 52–53. For a recent biography of d'Aguesseau that situates his liberalism in context, see I. Storez, *Le Chancelier Henri François d'Aguesseau (1688–1751): Monarchiste et libéral* (Paris, 1996).

39. D. Gordon, "Citizenship," in *The Oxford Encyclopedia of the Enlightenment*, ed. A. Kors et

al. (Oxford, 2002). A cursory examination of the largest literary database of electronic texts, the ARTFL project, reveals Bossuet's typical usages of the term in his published works from the *Discours sur l'Histoire Universel* (1681) through his *De la connaisance des Dieux* (1704), among his other ecclesiastical writings published that year.

40. Weil, *Qu'est-ce qu'un Français?* 398–99, correcting the more limited investigation of literary sources by G. Noiriel, "Socio-histoire d'un concept: Les Usages du mot 'nationalité' au XIXe siècle," *Genèses* 20 (1995): 4–23, reprinted in *Etat, nation, et immigration: Vers une histoire du pouvoir* (Belin, 2001), 147–65.

41. J. Krynen, " 'Naturel': Essai sur l'argument de la nature dans la pensée politique française à la fin du Moyen Age," *Journal des Savants* (1982): 169–90, quote 169; Bell, *Cult of the Nation*; and for a more conventional view of the history of the word "nation," emphasizing the medieval uses of the word to denote communities of foreigners, see G. Zernatto, "Nation: The History of a Word," *Review of Politics* 6 (1944): 351–66.

42. Originally, the "alien" was one without a personal allegiance to a lord: see M. Boulet-Sautel, "L'aubain dans la France coutumière au Moyen Age," *RSJB* 10 (1958), 70; on the more plausible etymology of aubain derived from *ali ban*, see A. Lefebvre-Teillard, *Introduction historique au droit des personnes et de la famille* (Paris, 1996), 24–25. The definitive discussion of the etymology of aubain is d'Alteroche, *De l'Etranger*, 11–24 and passim. The "false etymology of the *aubain* ("born elsewhere") is rehearsed in Bacquet, *Oeuvres*, I, 3–4; A. Loysel, "Du droict d'aubaine et des étrangers," in *Divers opuscules tiréz des mémoires de M. Antoine Loisel. . . .*, ed. Claude Joly (Paris, 1652), 151; and Denisart, *Collection* (1773), 1:164; by contrast, Ducange derives the term from *albanus*, the name given to Scotch and Irish settlers in the kingdom: *Le Grand dictionnaire historique de Moréri*, 9 vols. (Paris, 1759), s.v. "aubain"; and C. Demangeat, *La Condition civile des étrangers*, 67–68, who follows the same etymology. In 1606, Jean Nicot's *Thrésor de la langue française* derived the "droit de Hobaine" from the verb "*hober*, meaning to leave a place and transport oneself to another one." On the appearance and meaning of the word in the redacted customals, see F. Ragueau, *Glossaire du droit francais, contenant l'explication des mots difficiles qui se trouvent dans les ordonnances roys de France, dans les coustumes du royaume, dans les anciens arrests et les anciens titres*, ed. E. de Laurière (Paris, 1882 [1583]), 45–48.

43. Bacquet, *Oeuvres*, 1:3, 102–3; d'Alteroche, *De l'Etranger*, 88–89.

44. Bacquet, *Oeuvres*, 1:14–34; F. De Maisons, *Nouveau traité des aydes, tailles et gabelles*, 4th ed. (Paris, 1666 [1622?]), 85–102. See Dubost and Sahlins, *Et si on faisait payer*, 65–66. A. Lefebvre-Teillard notes the convergence of the terms *citoyen* and *regnicole* at this same moment: "Citoyen," *Droits* 17 (1993): 38.

45. *Oeuvres complètes du Chancelier d'Aguesseau*, 16 vols. (Paris, 1819), 2:131.

46. This was the consensus of most jurists, although the best-selling text of Argou, *Institutions du droit françois* (Paris, 1787), defined the aubain as "living in the kingdom," and not necessarily a native subject (1:75).

47. For some general remarks on Roman law as "common law" (*ius commune*) in early modern Europe, see R. C. Van Caenegeam, *An Historical Introduction to Private Law* (Cambridge, 1992), 45–85; Watson, *Making of Civil Law*; and P. Stein, *Roman Law in European History* (Cambridge, 1999). On the king's sovereign removal of the "vice" through naturalization, see below, chap. 2.

48. The French *vice*, from the Latin *vitium*, meant fault, defect, or impurity, but also carried a moral judgment, the "habitual inclination of a soul toward evil," according to the *Dictionnaire de l'Académie française* (1694), s.v. "vice." For some uses among the jurists, see, e.g., Denisart, *Collection* (1773), 2:601–6; and d'Aguesseau, *Oeuvres* 3:133–34.

49. Bodin, *Les Six livres*, 93–94.

50. Bacquet, *Oeuvres*, 1:53–54; Choppin, *Oeuvres*, 2:98; on Italians in sixteenth-century France, see Dubost, *La France italienne*.

51. C. Storti-Storchi, "The Legal Status of Foreigners in Italy (XVth–XVIth Centuries): General Rules and their Enforcement in Some Cases concerning the *Executio Parata*," in *Of Strangers and Foreigners (Late Antiquity–Middle Ages)*, ed. L. Mayali and M. M. Mart (Berkeley, 1993), 97–135.

52. On the disabilities of foreigners in England, see D. Statt, "The Birthright of an Englishman: The Practice of Naturalization and Denization of Immigrants under the Later Stuarts and

Early Hanoverians," *Proceedings of the Huguenot Society of London/Great Britain and Ireland* 25 (1989): 61–74; Kettner, *Development of American Citizenship*, 29–43; A. H. Carpenter, "Naturalization in England and the American Colonies," *American Historical Review* 9 (1904): 288–303; and more generally, A. Dummett and A. Nicol, *Subjects, Citizens, Aliens, and Others: Nationality and Immigration Law* (London, 1990), esp. chaps. 1–4. The Enlightenment and revolutionary reinterpretations of the droit d'aubaine's origins located it within French king Philip IV's reprisals against Edward III during the Hundred Years War, see below, chaps. 8–9.

53. Herzog, "Municipal Citizenship and Empire," passim. On trade with the Indies in the sixteenth and seventeenth centuries, see R. Konetzke, "La Legislación sobre inmigración de extranjeros en América durante el reinado de Carlos V," in *Charles Quint et son temps* (Paris, 1959), 93–111; and A. Dominguez Ortiz, "La Concesión de 'naturalezas par comerciar en Indias' durante el siglo XVII," *Revista de Indias* 19 (1959): 227–39. For general if sometimes misleading overviews, see M. Alvarez-Valdès y Valdès, *La Extrangería en la historia del derecho español* (Oviedo, 1992); and R. Gibert, "La Condición de los extranjeros en el antiguo derecho español," in *RSJB* 10 (1958): 151–200.

54. M. Folain-Le Bras, *Un Projet d'ordonnance du Chancelier Daguesseau: Etude sur quelques incapacités de donner et de recevoir sous l'Ancien Régime* (Paris, 1941), 45; R. Laprat, "Les Aubains en droit canonique," in *Dictionnaire de droit canonique*, ed. R. Naz, 7 vols. vol. 1: 1332–46. (Paris, 1935–66), col. 1334. Walker, *German Home Towns*, passim, does not discuss the Abzug in Germany (below, chap. 7). The text of the *Omnes peregrini* read: "All pilgrims and immigrants shall freely lodge where they wish, and if the guest should wish to make a will for the orderly disposal of his possessions, it shall be kept undisturbed. If the guest should indeed die intestate, nothing shall come to his host, but rather the guest's goods shall be brought together by the hand of the bishop of the place for his heirs, if this can be done, or they shall be expended in pious causes," quoted and translated in Wells, *Law and Citizenship*, 23. The practice did not involve a right of lorship. More generally, see H. Thieme, "Dies Rechtsstellung der Fremden in Deutschland von 11. bis zum 18. Jahrhundert," in *RSJB* 10 (1958): 217–30. Significantly, only in limited parts of Hainault, Brabant, and Flanders did seigneurial prerogatives over the properties of aliens initially resemble what became the monarchy's initial definition of the "droit d'aubaine": see J. Gilissen, "Le Statut des étrangers en Belgique du XIIIe au XXe siècle," *RSJB* 9 (1958): 266–82; and more generally, on foreigners in Old Regime "Belgium," see B. Bernard, "Les XVIIe et XVIIIe siècles: Une hospitalité parcimonieuse," in *Histoire des étrangers et de l'immigration en Belgique de la préhistoire à nos jours*, ed. A Morelli (Brussels, 1992), 75–90.

55. Quoted in Wells, *Law and Citizenship*, 16, who also notes that Charles Loyseau, son of Antoine de Loysel, even linked the purchase by the *peregrinus* of the *droit de Cité* from the Roman emperor with the fees charged the aubain for naturalization in the kingdom. There were occasional dissenting opinions: Bernard Automne, *La Conférence du droit français avec le droit romain* (Paris, 1610), 4, who noted that the law *in orbe romano* was not observed in the kingdom. For an overview of the status of the Roman peregrinus, which of course shifted significantly over the five centuries from the republic to the empire, F. de Visscher, "La Condition des pérégrins à Rome," 195–208; and A. Weiss, *Traité théorique et pratique de droit international privé*, 6 vols. (Paris, 1908–1913), 2:27–45.

56. Domat, *The Civil Law in Its Natural Order*, trans. W. Strahan, 2 vols. (Boston, 1853 [1696]), 2:26 and passim.

57. D'Alteroche, *De l'Etranger à la seigneurie*; Boulet-Sautel, "L'aubain dans la France,"; also Wells, *Law and Citizenship*, 15–25, which closely follows Demangeat, who took his cue about the "Germanic" origins of the "right" from Enlightened thinkers during the eighteenth century (below, chap. 7).

58. Bacquet, *Oeuvres*, 1:4; G. Bouchel, *Bibliothèque du trésor du droit français*, 3 vols. (Paris, 1671), 1:286.

59. Quoted in F. Ragueau, *Glossaire du droit françois*, 79.

60. C. Beaune, *The Birth of an Ideology: Myths and Symbols of Nation in Late Medieval France*, ed. F. L. Cheyette, trans. S. R. Huston (Berkeley, 1991); see also the various contributions to the collective "monument" of French national identity, *Les Lieux de mémoire*, ed. P. Nora. T. Hampton has recently explored the literary construction of the nation and the simultaneous invention of

new literary genres: *Literature and the Nation in the Sixteenth Century: Inventing Renaissance France* (Ithaca, 2001).

61. D'Alteroche, *De l'Etranger*, passim; the cultural, theological, and symbolic construction of the "nation" (*natio*) and "fatherland" (*patria*) in the late medieval period has received greater attention than has the legal making of nationality in these same critical decades: on the latter, see E. H. Kantorowicz, *The King's Two Bodies: A Study in Medieval Political Theology* (Princeton, 1957); and his "Pro Patria Mori in Medieval Political Thought," *American Historical Review* 56 (1951): 472–92.

62. Boulet-Sautel, "L'aubain dans la France," 79.

63. See the list produced by the royal attorney of the Paris parlement, Joly de Fleury, in BN MS JF, 2393, fols. 246–329, which notes that the redacted customs of Sens, Hainault, Amiens, Maine, Auxerre, and Poitou, mostly in the northeast, attributed the droit d'aubaine to the lords, and that at the moment of their redaction, between the late fifteenth and late sixteenth centuries, a dozen other customary-law regions saw litigation between seigneurs and the crown over rights to the droit d'aubaine: "L'aubain dans la France," appendix, 97–100.

64. Denisart, *Collection* (1783), 1:579–80; AN AD XV I, decision of the council of state affirming the judgment of the Chambre du domaine of Bordeaux adjudicating the succession of Martin de Gathieres to the king "a titre d'aubaine" against the claims of the duc d'Aiguillon. The king's claims applied as well to parts of the "engaged royal domain" ceded by the king: ibid., decision of Paris parlement, 29 July 1706. See also J. B. Bosquet, *Dictionnaire raisonné des domaines et droits domaniaux*, 2 vols. (Paris, 1763), 1:181–83.

65. Bacquet, *Oeuvres*, 1:84–85; Lefebvre de la Planche, *Mémoires*, 2:5; Loysel, *Divers opuscules*, 72, 4 verso suppl. The identification of the droit d'aubaine with the "fundamental laws" of the kingdom seems to have first appeared in the secretarial summation of the legal claims of Anne d'Estes de Némour, around 1637: "The *loy d'aubeine* or the exclusion of foreigners from inheriting in France is a law of state, not introduced by edict or ordinance, but of the same origin and ancientness as the fundamental laws of the monarchy and other rights of the crown; and thus there can be no exceptions or derogations to the law in favor of any person whomsoever" (quoted in Wells, *Law and Citizenship*, 95; my translation). On the French Revolution's abolition of the droit d'aubaine, see below, chap. 7.

66. Argou, *Institutions*, 1:75–76.

67. Loysel, *Divers opuscules*, 471: "A l'estranger sois humain et propice / Et s'il plaint incline à sa raison / Mais lui donner les biens de la maison/ C'est faire aux tiens et honte et injustice" (my translation).

68. Papon and Maynard dissented on this regard, citing a case involving the Hôtel-Dieu des Pélérins du Saint-Jacques in Toulouse in 1567 (Maynard, *Notables et singulières questions de droit escrit et jugées par arrests mémorables de la cour souveraine du Parlement de Tholose* [Toulouse, 1638], 1259). D'Aguesseau's case as solicitor-general before the Paris parlement in 1695, however, resolved the question, and "charitable works" were not exempted from the prohibitions on aliens donating property: *Oeuvres*, 2:595–620.

69. Denisart, *Collection* (1773), 1:166.

70. The legal literature of the early modern period provides comprehensive lists of these incapacities and prohibitions, and a comparison between those announced by Bacquet (1578) and Lefebvre de la Planche (edited by Paul Charles Lorry, 1764–65) reveals the accumulation of prohibitions over the early modern period. Two useful eighteenth-century compilations, dating from just before the abolitions of the droit d'aubaine within the citizenship revolution of the 1760s, include the 1764 edition of Denisart's *Collection de décisions nouvelles* (usefully compared to the 1773 edition); and the manuscript memoranda prepared in the 1740s by the first secretary (*commis*) of the ministry of foreign affairs, Nicolas-Louis le Dran, dispersed throughout AAE MD. According to the foreign minister d'Argenson in 1744, Sr. le Dran "knows a lot and writes badly; nonetheless, you will get a great deal from his enormous work and his perfect obedience." Quoted in A. Baschet, *Histoire du département des archives des affaires étrangères* (Paris, 1875), 294, and 292–323 for more on Le Dran; and C. Piccioni, *Les Premiers commis des affaires étrangères au XVII et XVIIIe siècle* (Paris, 1928), 214–19.

71. Loysel, *Divers opuscules*, 72, 1 recto suppl.; Brillon, *Dictionnaire*, 2:776.

72. Bacquet, *Oeuvres*, 1:9. The seventh book of Lefebvre de la Planche's *Mémoires sur les matières domaniales* was devoted to the royal "Droit de batardise," *Oeuvres*, 2:254–640. For a definitive treatment of the legal status of bastards, see M. Gerber, "The End of Bastardy: Illegitimacy in France from the Reformation to the Revolution," Ph.D. diss., University of California, Berkeley, 2003, esp. chap. 1.

73. Bacquet, *Oeuvres*, 1:50–51; Denisart, *Collection* (1773), 1:166; P. Sueur, *Histoire du droit public français, XVe–XVIIIe siècle*, 2 vols. (Paris, 1989), 2:145. On the *cautio*, see G. A. Mandy, *La Cautio judicatum solvi: Les Étrangers devant la justice en droit international privé: Etude de législation comparée* (Paris, 1897); and Weiss, *Traité théorique*, 5:41–45.

74. Bourjon, *Le Droit commun*, 1:87; and Rousseau de la Combe, *Recueil de jurisprudence civile*, 107; and Lefebvre de la Planche, *Mémoires*, 2:122–23, on the *contrainte par corps*. See also J. C. Demangeat, *Histoire de la condition civile des étrangers en France* (Paris, 1844), 144–45. The 1737 parliamentary decision can be found in AN AD XV 1.

75. Wells, *Law and Citizenship*, 46, n. 56; on such metaphors more generally, see C. Wells, "Leeches on the Body Politic: Xenophobia and Witchcraft in Early Modern French Political Thought," *French Historical Studies* 22 (1999): 351–77. On the national preferences and economic protectionism of the sixteenth-century Estates and their denunciation of foreigners, see Picot, *Histoire des Etats-Généraux*, 2:253–55 (Orléans; 1560); 3:31–37 (Blois, 1574).

76. Dubost, "Les Étrangers en France," 519.

77. Dubost and Sahlins, *Et si on faisait payer*, passim. Nonetheless, foreigners were permitted to acquire annuities on the Paris municipality—in other, more limited cases, royal edicts explicitly prohibited unnaturalized foreigners from acquiring annuities on the Paris municipality: see, e.g., AN AD XV 1, edict of December 1674—which exempted foreigners from the droit d'aubaine for these purchased bonds, and after 1735 they were also relieved of the droit d'aubaine for bonds taken from the clergy's "free gift": see Lefebvre de la Planche, *Mémoires*, 2:131–33.

78. Papon, *Secrets*, 455–56; B. Honig, *Democracy and the Foreigner* (Princeton, 2001), esp. chap. 1.

79. Wells, *Law and Citizenship*, 23–25; Dubost, "Les étrangers en France," 520–21; C. Billot, "L'assimilation des étrangers dans le royaume de France au XIVe et XVe siècles," *Revue historique* 270, no. 2 (1983): 284–85.

80. F. Bourjon, *Le Droit commun de la France et la Coutume de Paris réduits en principes*, 2 vols. (Paris, 1770), 1: 86; Cardin Le Bret, *Les Oeuvres de Messire Cardin Le Bret, conseiller ordinaire du Roy en ses conseils d'état et privé, cy-devant Avocat Général en la Cour des Aydes, et depuis au Parlement de Paris* (Paris, 1689), 66; and more generally, Lefebvre de la Planche, *Mémoires*, 2:117. In the seventeenth century, the instances of the foreign born ministers and royal favorites, Concini and Mazarin, occasioned a parliamentary and public reaction that invoked the general prohibition on foreigners serving the crown: see for example the anonymous "Discours sur l'employ des étrangers aux charges et dignités de ce royaume," directed against Mazarin; in AN K 118, no. 1. For other Old Regime examples of foreigners holding high-ranking offices, see Boizet, *Les Lettres de naturalité*, 157–59; on Saxe, see G. Camon, *Maurice de Saxe, Maréchal de France* (Paris, 1934). On the inability of offices to confer citizenship in France, see Bacquet, *Oeuvres*, 1:40, 48–49; and Lefebvre de la Planche, *Oeuvres*, 2:188–90. The ambivalence about the faith of naturalized foreigners was shared by jurists (and politicians) of twentieth-century in France: see P. Duclos, "L'Accession des Naturalisés aux fonctions publiques," *Revue du droit public* no. 1 (1938): 5–86.

81. Pithou is quoted in Boizet, *Les Lettres de naturalité*, 150. The collective *Mémoires du clergé*, 14 vols. (Paris, 1716), 12:717 et seq., list the edicts and ordinances excluding foreigners from benefices; see also R. Laprat, "Les Aubains en droit canonique," 1:1332–46; Loysel, *Divers opuscules*, 471.

82. J. Papon, *Secrets du troisième et dernier notaire* (Lyon, 1578), 451–52; Boutaric is quoted in Boizet, *Les Lettres de naturalité*, 145; see Boizet's more general discussion, 145–55. On the status of foreigners in medieval canon law, largely uninflected by political considerations, see W. Onclin, "Le Statut des étrangers dans la doctrine canonique médiévale," *RSJB* 10 (1958): 37–64.

83. Bacquet, *Oeuvres*, 1:47–48; C. Blondeau and G. Gueret, *Journal du Palais, ou Recueil des Principales Décisions de tous les Parlements et Cours Souveraines de France sur les questions les plus important de droit civil*, 4th ed. 2 vols. (Paris, 1755), 1:789; Guy du Rousseau de la Combe, *Recueil de*

jurisprudence canonique et bénéficiale (Paris, 1755), 290–91; P. Bardet, *Recueil d'arrests du Parlement de Paris pris des Mémoires de feu M. Pierre Bardet, ancien avocat en la Cour avec les notes et Dissertations de M. Claude Berroyer, Avocat au même Parlement. Nouvelle edition . . . par M. C. N. Lalaure*, 2 vols. (Avignon, 1773 [1690]), 1:288–92. The 1681 declaration is reproduced in AN AD XV 1, no. 116. On the French crown's policies toward the conferral benefices in the border province of Alsace before and after 1681, see R. Metz, *La Monarchie française et la provision de bénéfices ecclesiastiques en Alsace de la paix de Westphalie à la fin de l'Ancien Régime* (Strasbourg, 1947).

84. L'Huillier quoted in Dubost and Sahlins, *Et si on faisait*, 95.

85. Another was the *capitation* or poll tax, introduced in 1695: S. Mitard, *La Crise financière en France à la fin du XVIIe siècle: La Première capitation (1695–1698)* (Rennes, 1934). Ultimately more productive, the tax represented what Kwass has called the first of the "universal taxes" (imposed, read the royal edict, "on all our Subjects without any distinction") that were to later produce the public debate on privilege and taxation that turned taxpayers into citizens: Kwass, *Privilege*, 34–35 and passim, and below, chap. 7.

86. Dubost and Sahlins, *Et si on faisait*, chap. 1, and 444–49 (reproduction of the royal declaration, 22 July 1697 [reg. Paris parlement, 21 August 1697]). Bouchel, *Bibliothèque*, 1:286, noting the Greek and Roman origins of *chevage*, claimed that "anciently" foreigners paid to the king twelve *deniers parisis* annually to the *collecteur des mortes main*. Baquet found evidence of these payments in the registers of the chambre des comtes, but these had been abandoned at least two and a half centuries before the Naturalization Tax. It is perhaps significant that the regulatory decree given a week after the 22 July declaration, on 30 July 1697, did not mention the right of *formariage*, and only vaguely invoked, without naming, the droit d'aubaine ("by means of a payment from which sums will be confirmed in their possession and enjoyment the goods which are due the said foreigners by rights of inheritance, succession, or donation"). The shift in language, we have argued, was perhaps the result of the reworking of the text by the treasury bureaux (*contrôle générale*), and may have also constituted an official response to the Dutch ambassador, independent of the sponsored pamphlets that responded to such complaints (see following note).

87. *Mémoire pour répondre au plaintes faites par MM. les ambassadeurs plénipotentiares d'Espagne, d'Angleterre, et d'Hollande contre la déclaration du roi du 22 juillet 1697*, BNF Lg(6) 338, fol. 2, written in apparent response to the printed *Mémoire sur la déclaration du roy contre les étrangers habituez dans le Royaume*, AN AD XV 1. In 1739, the bureau chief of the foreign ministry, Nicolas-Louis Le Dran, noted that Louis XIV's response was "very badly written, and contains unsustainable claims on the part of the king": see his memorandum "Sur les privilèges dont jouissent en France par rapport aux successions les sujets de la république des Provinces Unies," in AAE MD Low Countries, vol. 60, fol. 198–199v, quote 198v.

88. Details on the contracts can be found in Dubost and Sahlins, *Et si on faisait payer*, esp. 104–9; ibid., chap. 11, gives a financial assessment of the tax: of more than nine million livres imposed, 360,000 initially entered the royal treasury. It is impossible to know the total revenue produced by the tax (only the account books of the tax-farmers would have revealed the figures, and these do not survive), but calculations of about 600,000 livres appear most plausable: 363–65.

89. Argou, *Institutions*, 1:85–86; J.-P. Massaloux, *La Régie de l'enregistrement et des domaines au XVIIIe–XIXe siècles* (Geneva, 1988), 50–58; on the seventeenth-century treasurers-general, see J.-P. Charmeil, *Les Trésoriers de France à l'époque de la Fronde: Contribution à l'histoire de l'administration financière sous l'Ancien Régime* (Paris, 1964): 198–99. A handful of foreigners were naturalized before taking possession of their offices of treasurers-general (20–21), but such was not always the case (see below, chap. 3).

90. On patronage and clientage of the classical absolute state in France more generally, see the historiographical synthesis of A. L. Herman Jr., "The Language of Fidelity in Early Modern France," *The Journal of Modern History* 67 (1995): 1–24; and for a detailed examination, P. Campbell, *Power and Politics in Old Regime France, 1720–1745* (London, 1996). On the "dons d'aubeyne," see Boizet, *Les Lettres de naturalité*, 127–28, drawing on examples in AN KK 627. These were occasionally printed: see AN AD XV 1, *Arrêt du conseil d'état*, 3 November 1779. A statistical series of these gifts could be constituted using the inventories of the AN O/1 series ("Maison du roi").

91. The jurisprudential consensus since the late sixteenth century presumed that a person who died in the kingdom was French and not subjected to the droit d'aubaine, and it was up to the fisc to prove his or her alien status: Papon, *Secrets*, 244; Lefebvre de la Planche, *Mémoires*, 2:14–16; and Du Rousseau de la Combe, *Recueil de jurisprudence civile*, 206, who argued that the collection of the droit d'aubaine was "a simple enactment of fact," and nothing prevented the king from doing with it whatever he pleased. It was then up to the recipient of the king's largesse to prove, if litigation were pursued, the alien status of the deceased and/or the heir who might claim it.

92. *De Jure Belli ac Pacis Libri Tres*, trans. F. W. Kelsey et al., 2 vols. (Oxford, 1925 [1643]), 2:266 (bk. II, chap. VI). On the place of Grotius in the development of international public law, see W. G. Grewe, *The Epochs of International Law*, trans. and rev. by M. Byers (Berlin, 2000), passim.

93. Dubost and Sahlins, *Et si on faisait*, 77–78; J. S. Reeves, "The First Edition of Grotius' *De Jure Belli Ac Pacis*, 1625," *American Journal of International Law* 19, no. 1. (1925): 12–22, esp. 16.

94. D'Aguesseau, *Oeuvres*, 2:113.

95. Bacquet, *Oeuvres*, II:12; L'Huillier is the probable author of the memoir "Pour le droit d'aubaine contre ceux de Genève," in BN Collection Dupuy 854, f. 218; see also Bouchel, *Bibliothèque*, 1:286.

96. F. de Maisons, *Nouveau traité des aydes, tailles et gabelles*, 4th (?) ed. (Paris, 1666 [1622]), 86.

97. Loysel, *Divers opuscules*, 179

98. Ph. Bonolas, "La Question des étrangers à la fin du XVIe siècle et au début du XVIIe siècle," *Revue d'histoire moderne et contemporaine* 36 (1989): 304–317, who calls the treatise the "summit of mercantilist thought," 306; A. de Montchrétien, *Traicté de l'économie politique*, ed. T. Funck-Brentano (Paris, 1889 [1615]); B. de Laffemas, *Recueil présenté au roi de ce qui se passe en l'assemblée du commerce au Palais à Paris, fait par Laffemas, contrôleur-général dudit commerce* (1604), in *Archives curieuses de l'histoire de France*, 1st ser., vol. 14 (Paris, 1837). Some additional background is provided in G. Fagniez, *La Condition des commerçants étrangers en France au début du XVIIe siècle* (Paris, 1908). Classical studies of mercantilism include P. Harsin, *Les Doctrines monétaires et financières en France du XVIe au XVIIe siècles* (Paris, 1928); and C. Cole, *Colbert and a Century of French Mercantilism*, 2 vols. (New York, 1939), but see more recent work that emphasizes practice over theory: J. Morini-Comby, *Mercantilisme et protectionisme* (Paris, 1980); P. Dockès, *L'Espace dans la pensée économique du XVIe au XVIIIe siècle* (Paris, 1969), 99–123; and C. Larrère, *L'Invention de l'économie au XVIIIe siècle* (Paris, 1992), 95–134. On the relation of mercantilism and "reason of state" in France, see N. O. Keohane, *Philosophy and the State in France: The Renaissance to the Enlightenment* (Princeton, 1980), 151–73.

99. Bacquet, *Oeuvres*, 1:12; see also D. Le Brun, *Oeuvres*, 2 vols., 4th ed. (Paris, 1737), 1:10.

100. Bacquet, *Oeuvres*, 2:36.

101. P.-J. Brillon, *Dictionnaire des arrêts ou jurisprudence universelle des Parlements de France et autre tribunaux*. (Paris, 1727 [1711]), 1:314; oblique evidence of its application can be found in the small but consistent demands for naturalization in Provence, of which 209 were registered between 1660 and 1790 (see appendix 1).

102. On the late fifteenth-century exemption of Languedoc from the droit d'aubaine, see Picot, *Histoire des Etats Généraux*, 1:470–72; and P. Ourliac, "La Condition civile des étrangers dans la region Toulousaine au Moyen Age," *RSJB* 10 (1958): 101–8.

103. Lefebvre de la Planche, *Mémoires*, 2:35; indeed, sixteenth-century lawyers, at times torn between the defense of local privileges and collusion with the absolute monarchy, often contradicted themselves on this score. Thus the Toulousain barrister Maynard argued in the same text (*Notables et singulières questions*) that "foreigners were held to be native subjects in Languedoc" (628) and "foreigners who die in France without children have only the king as heir by the droit d'aubaine" (1259).

104. On the naturalizations registered in the Chambre des comptes of Languedoc (Montpellier), see M.-R. Santucci, "Devenir régnicole: Les Enquêtes de la Chambre des comptes," *Recueil de mémoires et travaux publiées par la Société d'histoire du droit et des institutions des anciens pays de droit écrit* 13 (1985): 129–51, who counts 124 individuals naturalized between 1541 and 1786. The significance of the 1697 Naturalization Tax in permitting the crown to impose the droit d'aubaine in Languedoc is detailed in Dubost and Sahlins, *Et si on faisait payer*, 85–87. The tax rolls drawn up for Languedoc in October 1698 coincided with the meeting of the provincial estates of Langue-

doc. The estates promptly protested, insisting on their privileges given by Louis XI and Charles VIII, and asserted that foreigners and their descendants and heirs not be taxed. The royal council's response was brief and to the point: "The king does not deem it appropriate to accord the request." Undismayed, the deputies of the provincial estates returned, in 1702, 1704, and 1705, arguing not only on the basis of their privileges but making use of the monarchy's own discourse about the economic and demographic utility of exempting foreigners. To settle the question, the affair was sent to the zealous intendant Basville, who suggested that the exemption be renewed for only twenty years, an accord adopted in 1706. (A year later, the estates made their final attempt: again citing how "one could retain in the province a great number of workers drawn by the manufacturers, which would replace the inhabitants lost," referring obliquely to the forced diaspora of the Huguenots, they requested that foreigners be allowed to freely settle in the kingdom without taking letters of naturalization or being subjected to the droit d'aubaine. The royal response, just as laconic, upheld the 1706 agreement: "His Majesty has not deemed it relevant to change anything." Twenty years later, "the privilege evaporated after the twenty year expiration," concluded Lefebvre de la Planche with evident satisfaction (Mémoires 2:87).

105. C.-J. Gabriel, Observations détachées sur les coutumes et les usages anciens et modernes du ressort du Parlement de Metz, 2 vols. (Bouillon, 1787), 1:110–35; on the case of Strasbourg, annexed by France in 1681, see S. Herry, Une Ville en mutation: Strasbourg au tournant du Grand Siècle (Strasbourg, 1996), 279–87; and Heuer, "Foreigners, Families, and Citizens," esp. 251–54. On local citizenship and aliens in neighboring Lorraine, see J. Imbert, "Les Rapports entre l'aubaine et la bourgeoisie en Lorraine," Annales de l'Est, 5th ser., no. 4 (1952): 349–64.

106. AN H1 1588⁵⁰: "Mémoire sur la généralité de Metz par M. de Turgot" [1698], fol. 11–14.

107. Ibid. On immigration in Metz, see J. Rigault, "La Population de Metz au XVIIe siècle: Quelques problèmes de démographie," Annales de l'Est 3 (1951): 307–15.

108. Dubost and Sahlins, Et si on faisait payer, 87–92. It is worth noting that two years later, the intendant of Bordeaux reported to the duc de Bourgogne that foreigners in the commercial center of the province had taken naturalizations before 1660 in order to enjoy the privileges of accountants (comptables), but since that date, when the privileges of the local bourgeoisie were taken by the king, "they are no longer taking letters of naturalization": AN H1 1588⁵⁰, fol. 24v.

109. Brillon, Dictionnaire des arrêts, 1:314; Gabriel, Observations détachés, 1:110–35.

110. Médéric Louis-Elie Moreau de Saint-Méry, Loix et constitutions des colonies françaises de l'Amérique sous le vent (Paris, 1785), 597 ff: "Mémoire et lettre du Conseil de Marine, au Sujet du Droit d'Aubaine, et de la nature mobiliaire ou immobiliaire des Esclaves, et Ordonnance des Administrateurs sur le même sujet," 20 October 1717, and 6 April 1718. Yet if the 1697 Naturalization Tax initially included foreigners resident in French colonies, a decree of the royal council in 1702 resolved that these foreigners would be exempted, thus giving a narrow (metropolitan) definition to the "countries, lands, and seigneuries of our obedience": see Dubost and Sahlins, Et si on faisait payer, 323–24.

111. H. Boniface, Arrests notables de la Cour du Parlement de Provence, Cour des Comptes, Aydes, et Finances du Meme Pais 5 vols. (Lyon, 1708), 2:59.

112. Older scholarly treatments of the condition of foreigners frequently list these privileges and exemptions as well: see C. Jandot-Danjou, "La Condition civile de l'étranger dans les trois derniers siècles de la monarchie"(thèse de droit, Université de Paris, 1939), pt. 2; and Demangeat, Histoire de la condition civile, 155–234.

113. Bosquet, Dictionnaire raisonné, 2:173–85; cf. the list in the 1773 edition of Denisart, Collection, 1:167–70.

114. The sixteenth-century jurists, including Bacquet, sought to prove that despite the cession of Avignon and the Comtat to the papacy by Philippe le Bel, they were nonetheless part of the royal domain, a position affirmed in patent letters of May 1470, confirmed in 1571, 1574, 1599, 1611, and 1643. The frequency of these edicts reveals the complexity and contention involving their status as regnicoles. Dubost and Sahlins, Et si on faisait payer, 67–68; and below, chap. 4.

115. On Colbert's efforts to attract foreign workers, see especially Mathorez, Les Etrangers en France, passim; and G. Martin, La Grande industrie sous la règne de Louis XIV (Geneva, 1978 [1899]), 60–83.

116. Contemporary lists of exemptions include: Merlin, *Répértoire*, 1:526–27; Bosquet, *Dictionnaire raisonné*, 173–74, 658, passim; Lefebvre de la Planche, *Mémoires*, 2:37–49, 87–94; see also Weiss, *Traité théorique*, 2:72–79; and Dubost and Sahlins, *Et si on faisait payer*, 40–63. For specific examples of foreign claims to these exemptions, see below, chap. 4.

117. Dubost and Sahlins, *Et si on faisait*, 72–75; contemporary lists include Denisart, *Collection* (1783), 1:591–92, and Lefebvre de la Planche, *Mémoires*, 2:33–37.

118. Thus, for example, the case of Marseille: see M. Christian, "Du Citadinage à la naturalité: L'Intégration des étrangers à Marseille (XIIIe–XVIe siècles)," *Provence historique* 49 (1999): 333–52; and Ch. Carrière, *Négociants marseillais au XVIIIe siècle: Contribution à l'étude des économies maritimes* (Marseilles, 1973), 7–8, who reproduces the terms of the 1669 edict: "His Majesty has wished that this famous town become the common fatherland of all peoples, even more than Rome was in its day. The most barbarous and backward nations will find an asylum there with no more of foreigness; the foreign merchant will bequeath his goods like a French native [*comme naturel français*], the foreign heir will gather his inheritance like a French native, all is free, all is reduced to the rules of the law of nations."

119. Bosquet, *Dictionnaire raisonné*, 1:175; Guyot, s. v. Aubaine, cited in Vanel, *Evolution historique*, 68; for the opposing doctrine, see Blondeau and Gueret, *Journal du Palais*, 2:739. Pothier's "Traité des personnes" gave the definitive gloss on Old Regime practices when he discussed the conservation of the "qualité et les droit de citoyens" of the inhabitants of a dismembered province who established themselves under French domination, cited in Weiss, *Traité théorique*, 1:610; see also F.-H. d'Orschwiller de Boug, *Recueil des édits, déclarations, lettres patents, arrêts du Conseil d'etat et du Conseil souverain d'Alsace*, 2 vols. (Colmar, 1775), 2:731–34; M. Augéard, *Arrests notables des différents tribunaux du Royaume*, 2 vols. (Paris, 1756), 2:52–55; and Lefebvre de la Planche, *Mémoires*, 2:18–22 et seq. On the claims of jurists in the conquered provinces, see Gilissen, "Etrangers en Belgique," 268–69. For a general discussion of the jurisprudence, see R. Sélosse, *Traité de l'annexion au territoire français et son démembrement* (Paris, 1880).

120. On Savoy and the Dauphiné, see Augéard, *Arrests notables*, 1:62; and J. G. Basset, *Notables arrests de la Cour de Parlement, Aydes, et Finances de Dauphiné* (Grenoble, 1730), 111–25, citing a royal decree confirming the parlement's jurisprudence in July 1669; see also Bosquet, *Dictionnaire raisonné*, 2:602, who notes that clergy could also hold benefices in Dauphiné and Savoy without receiving prior naturalization; on the Roussillon and Catalonia, see P. Sahlins, *Boundaries: The Making of France and Spain in the Pyrenees* (Berkeley, 1989), 77–80; on Flanders and Artois, see G. Louet, *Recueil de plusieurs arrests du Parlement de Paris contenant un grand nombre de décisions recueillies par Maître Julien Brodeau*, 2 vols. (Paris, 1742), 1:61–62, and AN AD XV 1, printed "Déclaration portant reglement pour le droit d'aubaine à l'égard des sujets du roi qui sont nés dans les évêchés de Metz, Toul, et Verdun, Pays messins et autres lieux qui faisaient parti du duché de Luxembourg, du comté de Chinay, de la Lorraine et du Barrois qui ont ete cédés au roi par les traités," 11 July 1741. On the lawsuit behind the Paris parlement's ruling, see J. Imbert, "L'exercise du droit d'aubaine à l'égard des habitants du Hainault à la fin de l'Ancien Regime," *Revue d'histoire du droit français et étranger* (1950): 548–59.

121. Lefebvre de la Planche, *Mémoires*, 2:102–111. Jordan argues that the Jews of France in the fourteenth century were legally aliens who could be naturalized, but the Jews of medieval and early modern France were not subjected to the droit d'aubaine: W. C. Jordan, "Home Again: The Jews in the Kingdom of France, 1315–1322," in *The Stranger in Medieval Society*, Medieval Cultures, vol. 12., ed. F. R. P. Akehurst and S. C. Vand'Elden (Minneapolis, 1997), 28–30; cf. Z. Szajkowski, "The Jewish Status in Eighteenth-Century France and the 'Droit d'Aubaine,'" *Historia Judaica* 19 (1957): 147–63; and P. Sahlins, "Fictions of a Catholic France: The Naturalization of Foreigners, 1685–1787," *Representations* 47 (1994): 96–102. Szajkowski has compiled the essential reference work on French Judaica: *Franco-Judaica: An Analytical Bibliography of Books, Pamphlets, Decrees, Briefs, and Other Printed Documents Pertaining to the Jews in France, 1500–1788* (New York, 1962).

122. A. Hertzberg, *The French Enlightenment and the Jews* (New York, 1968), 12–28, at 14; see the useful essays and collection by B. Blumenkranz, *Juifs en France: Ecrits dispersés* (Paris, 1980); and Blumenkranz, ed., *Juifs en France au XVIIIè siècle* (Paris, 1994). On the Jews in Lorraine, see also F. Job, *Les Juifs de Nancy* (Nancy, 1991).

123. Hertzberg has rightly pointed out that it is not always possible to identify the "New Christians" as "really marranos," and cites the case of the intellectual Isaac de la Peyrère, "most certainly of Jewish blood," but in turn a Protestant and a Catholic "whose theology contained both Christian and Jewish elements," in *French Enlightenment and the Jews*, 15. The privileged status of the Portuguese Jewish community of Bordeaux did not mean that their poorer members couldn't be exposed to periodic expulsion, such as that by decree of the royal council in 1684, reproduced in G. Nahon, *Les Nations juives du sud-ouest de la France (1684–1971): Documents*, Fontes Documentas Portugesas 15 (Paris, 1981), 317.

124. BN MS JF 461, fol. 46, "Mémoire intéressant sur les successions des Juifs à Paris," n.d.; J. Cavignac, "A Bordeaux et Bayonne: Des 'marchands portugais' aux citoyens français," in *Juifs en France au XVIIIe siècle*, ed. B. Blumenkranz (Paris, 1994), 53–72. For more detailed research on their local integration, see A. Zink, "Communautés et corps social: Les Juifs à Saint-Esprit-lès-Bayonne du XVIIe au début du XIXe siècle," in *Les Etrangers dans la ville*, ed. J. Bottin and D. Calabi (Paris, 1999), 313–28; and Zink, "Une niche juridique: L'Installation des juifs à Saint-Esprit," *Annales HSS* (May–June 1993), no. 3: 639–70. The language of the 1723 new patent letters for the Jews for the first time broke open the fiction and named the "Portuguese merchants" or "New Christians" as *Juifs*, and further gave them the right "to enjoy all their previous privileges, and especially that of disposing of their goods between living persons and at death." Their residence was restricted yet again. The only legal exception to the residence restriction was the case of the handful of Jews in the French Caribbean, who continued to be tolerated, especially after the issuance of patent letters in 1723. Juridically, these few families, especially the Gradis (who dominated the colonial trade after 1717), helped to establish the status of Portuguese Jews as regnicoles in the kingdom after they won litigation in the 1760s that exempted them from the droit d'aubaine, following the efforts of the comte d'Estaing, governor general of the islands, to tax them and impose the droit d'aubaine in the 1760s: see Hertzberg, *French Enlightenment and the Jews*, 54–55; and A. Cahen, "Les Juifs dans les colonies françaises au XVIIIe siècle," *Revue des études juives* 4 (1881): 132–39.

125. Below, chap. 2. On the Jews of Avignon, see R. Moulinas, *Les Juifs du Pape en France: Les Communautés d'Avignon et du Comtat Vénaissin aux XVIIe et XVIIIe siècles* (Toulouse, 1972); and on the Jews settled in Provence, see F. Hildesheimer, "La Présence juive en Provence à la fin de l'Ancien Régime: Sources et bilan," in *Juifs en France au XVIIIè siècle*, ed. B. Blumenkranz (Paris, 1994), 111–23.

126. Hertzberg, *French Enlightenment and the Jews*, 19–21; Z. Szajkowski, "The Jewish Problem in Alsace, Metz, and Lorraine on the Eve of the Revolution of 1789," *Jewish Quarterly Review* 44 (1954): 205–43; and her book, *The Economic Status of the Jews in Alsace, Metz, and Lorraine (1648–1789)* (New York, 1954); for a useful and more recent study of the seventeenth century, see G. Roos, *Relations entre le gouvernement royal et les juifs du nord-est de la France au XVIIe siècle* (Paris, 2000).

127. On the "freedom principle" that associated French liberty with emancipation from slavery, see Peabody, *"There Are No Slaves in France,"* passim; more generally, see J.-F. Dubost, "Refuge religieux et politique en France," in *Dictionnaire de l'Ancien Régime: Royaume de France, XVIe–XVIIIe siècle*, ed. L. Bély (Paris, 1996), 1061–63. The contradiction was made explicit in the work of the Parisian barrister François de Maisons, who wrote in 1622 that "France is the common asylum of all nations of the world . . . but following such a favorable treatment, it would not be fair that the goods that foreigners acquired here during their lifetime would be taken elsewhere by their heirs after their death, the law of the kingdom states that if a capable foreigner dies without being naturalized, that only the king can be his heir, by a right called the droit d'aubaine, which is a royal right and of the sacred domain of the crown": *Nouveau traité*, 87–88.

128. "The king's own mind was a battleground, in which two political conceptions fought each other," wrote Arthur Herzberg about Louis XIV's attitudes toward the Jews, in *French Enlightenment and the Jews*, 13. In fact, Herzberg captures beautifully the more general ambivalence of the monarchy toward its others, but also the shift in notions about the "economy" in the mid-eighteenth century that also informed the eighteenth-century citizenship revolution (see below, chap. 7).

129. For recent syntheses, see G. Chaussinard-Nogaret, *Gens de finance au XVIIIe siècle* (Paris,

1993); and J.-M. Constant, "Absolutisme et modernité," in G. Chaussinard-Nogaret, J.-M. Constant, C. Durandin, A. Jouanna, *Histoire des élites en France du XVIe au XXe siècle: L'Honneur—Le Mérite—L'Argent* (Paris, 1991), 145–214. Exhaustive monographic studies of the financiers include F. Bayard, *Le Monde des financiers au XVIIe siècle* (Paris, 1988); D. Dessert, *Argent, pouvoir, et société au grand siècle* (Paris, 1984). Among apologists of the financiers, men such as François de Maisons, a barrister at the Paris parlement and author of a *Nouveau traité des aydes, tailles et gabelles* (4th ed., 1622), this interest in the droit d'aubaine formed the basis of a broader xenophobia occasionally cast in terms of cultural difference. Taking up the sixteenth-century xenophobia of the lawyers, Maisons wrote: "In fact I find nothing more dangerous in a State, because Foreigners have different customs and live differently, that they make an unhappy mixture over time of the mores of their Fatherland and those where they go to live. This mixture produces most often a poisoned corruption from which is born much trouble, and sometimes the entire devastation of the country that had favorably welcomed them"(86).

130. Dubost and Sahlins, *Et si on faisait payer,* 142–44. On the fertile distinction between an "immobile" France and a "France of movement," see the typology developed by E. W. Fox, *History in Geographic Perspective: The Other France* (New York, 1971). This "France of movement" does not completely correspond to what Daniel Roche calls, metaphorically, a "merchant kingdom" (as opposed to the "peasant kingdom"), "the society born of exchange and of the commercial developments of great port cities and large cities of business and enterprise": *La France des lumières* (Paris, 1993), 100.

131. In their *mémoires* to the duke of Burgundy in 1698, the intendants of commercial provinces such as Bordeaux often sang the praises of foreigners and the commerce that they undertook, although they worried about the bullion leaving the kingdom: see "Mémoire concernant la généralité de Bordeaux, dressé en 1698," in AN H/1 1588/15. The intendants also found themselves opposed to the financiers over particular seizures: in 1696, the secretary of the controller-general claimed (on behalf of the beneficiary of the king's gift) the estate of a certain Duplaa, a trader from Béarn who died in Saragossa (Spain). The intendant of Béarn intervened, in a memoire to the controller-general, where he indicated that "for the Sieur Duplaa to be truly an alien (*aubain*), he would have had to obtain letters of naturalization in Spain; that he would have had to transfer his domicile there, to move his goods, and that he be *non solume peregrinans sed peregrinus* [not only traveling but established abroad]. But other than the fact that it is not proven that he was naturalized in Spain, we see a man who left the kingdom with his wife and almost no goods, who during the forty-four years he spent in Spain he had a very important commercial establishment, by means of which he acquired property in France and could give up to one hundred and fifty-eight thousand livres for the dowries of four of his girls who married French men": A.-R. de Boislisle, *Correspondance des contrôleurs-généraux des finances avec les intendants des provinces,* 3 vols. (Paris, 1874–97), 1:438.

132. F. Salignac de la Mothe de Fénelon's *Aventures de Télémaque* was composed between 1694 and 1696, before the July declaration of 1697, but first published in 1699; citation, vol. 1, bk. 3. More generally on Fénelon, see H. Sée, *Les Idées politiques en France au XVIIe siècle* (Paris, 1923), 209–33; and on the Burgundy Circle's opposition to Louis XIV and the policies of "mercantilism," see L. Rothkrug, *Opposition to Louis XIV: The Political and Social Origins of the French Enlightenment* (Princeton, 1965), esp. chaps. 5–8. H. A. Ellis, *Boulainvilliers and the French Monarchy: Aristocratic Politics in Early Eighteenth-Century France* (Ithaca, 1988), 57–64, criticizes Rothkrug's "oppositional" reading of the Burgundy Circle; but cf., on Boisguillebert, Dockès, *L'Espace,* 179–93.

133. For a historiographical overview, see Kwass, *Privilege and the Politics of Taxation,* 1–19.

134. In truth, the distinction between "public" and "private" law was not fully articulated until the middle of the seventeenth century: see G. Chevrier, "Remarques sur l'introduction et les vicissitudes de la distinction du 'jus privatum' et du 'jus publicum' dans les oeuvres des anciens juristes français," *Archives de philosophie de droit,* n.s. 1 (1952): 5–77; but cf. Watson, *Making of Civil Law,* 144–67, for a critique. On Roman law's lack of clarity about this distinction, see Watson, *Spirit of Roman Law,* 42–56. It is significant that the jurisconsult Jean Domat, inspired by and at the same time critical of Roman law in his synthetic treatments of "public" and "civil" law, divided

his discussion of the droit d'aubaine and the civil incapacities of foreigners to inherit between his separate treatises.

135. For example, in a long gloss on Lefebvre de la Planche's commentary about treaties of alliances exempting foreigners from the droit d'aubaine, Pierre Charles Lorry noted that "if the magistrates consider it necessary to believe that a nation is exempt from the droit d'aubaine, their judgments not contradicted by any claim of public power [*puissance publique*], will be the testimony that such [examples] are in effect the customs of the nation": Lefebvre de la Planche, *Oeuvres*, 1:85–86.

136. L. Soëfve, *Nouveau recueil de plusieurs questions notables tant de droit que de coutumes jugées par arrests d'audiences du Parlement de Paris depuis 1640 jusques à présent*, 2 vols. (Paris, 1682), 1:321–33. The highly publicized case involved the contested inheritance of Charles de Gonzague, duke of Mantua and Montferrat in Italy, whose family was connected by multiple marriages to the French Valois, and whose ancestors had become French citizens in 1559, assuming the titles of ducs de Never and de Rethel. When Charles died in 1637, the lawyers of his Italian aunts, including Louis Soëfve, attempted to block his French heirs from any part of the estate.

137. Vanel, *Evolution historique*, 70–71, also 8–9. Vanel thus follows the conventional, general claim, already made, for example, by the sixteenth-century jurist Guy Coquille, that the sovereign courts were established "for the cases of individuals and not for affairs of state," quoted in J. A. Carey, *Judicial Reform in France before the Revolution of 1789* (Cambridge, Mass., 1981), 10.

138. Vanel, *Evolution historique*, 9.

139. An exception is Bacquet, who reported the use of the Latin term *iura sanguinis* by the lawyers of Marie Mabile: *Oeuvres*, 1:141, mentioned again by d'Aguesseau, *Oeuvres*, 8:136. Of course, concerning the nobility, the "right of blood" was a common trope: see, e.g., C. Le Bret, *Recueil d'aucuns plaidoyez faict en la cour des aides* (Paris, 1604), 200–201, on "nobility as an illustration of lineage [*race*]."

140. Unlike the New Regime (see below, chap. 8), marriage had no part in the determination of "nationality."

141. Lefebvre-Teillard, *Introduction historique*, 25.

142. A. Lefebvre-Teillard, "Ius sanguinis: L'Emergence d'un principe (Eléments d'histoire de la nationalité française)," *Revue critique de droit international privé* 82, no. 2 (1993): 223–50. J. de Cambolas, *Décisions notables sur diverses questions du Droit jugées par plusieurs arrêts de la Cour du Parlement de Tolouse* (Toulouse, 1659 [6th ed., Toulouse, 1744]), 200–202: "Droit d'aubaine n'a lieu, s'il y a des enfans nés en France et regnicoles." Papon, *Recueil d'arrêts notables*, 242, cites the several decisions of the Paris parlement, in 1519, 1520, and 1548, in the Chambre du domaine, 1536. The editor of the sixth edition of Papon's compilation in 1603 cited Bodin, Choppin, and a court case of 1540 to prove that "this point is not required. For children born and living in France inherit completely from their foreign, unnaturalized fathers and mothers."

143. Bodin, *Les Six livres*, 70.

144. Lefebvre-Teillard, "Ius sanguinis," 237–28; on the jurist's "ideological" opposition to easy naturalization (with a lack of evidence of social assimilation), see below, chap. 2.

145. J.-P. Poussou, "Mobilité et migrations," in *Histoire de la population française*, vol. 2, *De la Renaissance à 1789* (Paris, 1988), 124–37. Poussou, citing the importance of the Huguenot diaspora, argues that emigration was more important statistically than immigration in the Old Regime (136).

146. For a recent sythesis of French emigration overseas, see R. Cornevin and M. Cornevin, *La France et les français outre-mer* (Paris, 1990), esp. chaps. 4 and 5.

147. AN O/1/220, fol. 406, declaration draft of October [?] 1715.

148. B. C. Poland, *French Protestantism and the French Revolution: A Study in Church and State, Thought, and Religion, 1685–1815* (Princeton, 1957), esp. chap. 1. On the Protestant diaspora in Europe, see M. Yardeni, *Le Refuge protestant* (Paris, 1985); on Protestants in Germany, see K. Voigt, "Huguenots et Vaudois en Allemagne à partir de 1685," in *Emigrés français en Allemagne, Emigrés allemands en France, 1685–1945* (Paris, 1983), 10–42. The French legislation has been usefully collected in *Edits, déclarations et Arrests concernans la Réligion P[rétendue] Réformée, 1662–1751*

(Paris, 1885); and selectively reproduced in C. Bergeal, ed., *Protestantisme et tolérance au XVIIIe siècle, de la Révocation à la Révolution (1689–1789)* (Carrièrs-sous-Poissy, 1988).

149. Wells, *Law and Citizenship*, 113–20, draws interesting parallels of identity between the Huguenots and aliens, although she does not explore the diverging identities in the cases of hundreds of children of the Protestant diaspora who returned to the kingdom to claim French citizenship.

150. Bacquet cited in Wells, *Law and Citizenship*, 98; Loysel, *Divers opuscules*, 153. On the 1669 edict, the subject of extensive jurisprudential commentary, especially as it concerned French "natives" in the bordering province of Alsace after the French conquest, see below, chap. 2.

151. AN O/1/220, fol. 306, declaration draft of June [?] 1714; Lefebvre de la Planche, *Mémoires* 2:23–26.

152. Vanel, *Evolution historique*, 53–54. There were precedents, of course, to the Paris parlement's solemn ruling in September 1576, not all of which had to do with religious emigrants. Royal privileges attributed French citizenship to princes, princesses, and their descendants who had married or ruled abroad: for Marguerite of Savoy in 1568, as for Henry duc d'Anjou in 1573 (elected king of Poland), patent letters declared that they and their children would maintain all the "rights of natural Frenchmen."

153. Ibid., 51–52.

154. The jurisprudence was divided: some judges upheld the position that children of the diaspora could inherit if they returned to France: see the arrêt of 12 March 1707, *Journal des principales audiences du Parlement*, 7 vols. (Paris, 1733–1754), 6:211 et seq.; and A. Lapeyrère, *Décisions sommaires du Palais*, 7th ed. (Bordeaux, 1808 [1749]), cited in Bourjon, *Le Droit commun*, 1:89. Others invoked the 1669 ordinance and denied the children of Protestants the right to inherit. For a summary account, see AP ACA Fonds Tronchet, vol. 15, n. 1418, "Notice d'arrêts sur la question quand le français se retire en pays étranger a perdu, ou conserver, le droit de cité [n.d. but ca. 1783]," listing decisions of 1514, 1554, 1556, 1605, 1647, 1667, 1743, 1752, and 1770 favorable to the claims of French emigrants abroad, but also decisions of 1565, 1582, 1647, 1660, and 1703 that denied the right of succession, especially to women, among French emigrants.

155. H.-F. d'Aguesseau, *Oeuvres complètes*, 16 vols. (Paris, 1819), 8:115–40.

156. Ibid.; Vanel, *Evolution historique*, 81–82; on the roman precedents, see J. Imbert, *Postliminium* (Paris, 1944). It should be noted, however, that d'Aguesseau's opinion was hardly definitive on this score. On the one hand, questions constantly arose around collateral issues. For example, if descended from a French father and foreign mother, could a foreign-born offspring returning to the kingdom claim his mother's inheritance? Sébastian Frain, *Arrests du Parlement de Bretagne . . . Troisieme édition, revue . . . par Pierre Hévin*, 3d ed., 2 vols. (Rennes, 1684 [1659]), 138–45, argued yes. On the other hand, litigation involving descendants of Protestants continued throughout the eighteenth century, for example, the case of the Anne Bloin, widow of Jean Bernard, against her daughters who returned to the kingdom in 1778 to claim an inheritance, and were denied (*Gazette des Tribunaux* 6, no. 27 [1778]: 296, 305). Another case, this one argued before the Grenoble parlement involved a Swiss Protestant, in which the defendants successfully argued their privileges as Swiss, not returned French Protestants, in being exempted from the droit d'aubaine: *Gazette des Tribunaux* 14, no. 27 (1785): 103–4. Only the French revolutionaries were to definitively settle the question of the offspring of Protestant refugees: see below, chap. 8.

157. Lefebvre-Teillard, "Ius sanguinis," 230–33; Vanel, *Evolution historique*, 77–80: at the end of the Old Regime, according to the jurist Pothier, such a "spirit of return" was a presumption that had to be disproved by "contrary facts" (quoted in Vanel, 79); see also below, chap. 3. On the medieval origins in Italian jurisprudence, see Gilli, "Comment cesser d'être étranger," esp. 76–77. The principle was upheld in provinces following Roman written law, such as Provence, where in this instance the Paris parlement's rulings had precedence, at least according to Boniface, *Arrests notables*, 1:58.

158. AP ACA Fonds Tronchet, vol. 15, n. 1441–42, "Question: si les enfants nés d'un français retiré en pays étranger peuvent succéder en France à leurs parents français," n.d. but ca. 1783–84; and the opinion of late 1783 on the same question, ibid., n. 1441–42 (case of Pierre le Blanc). Tronchet dismissed the 1669 ordinance as a "law of pure circumstance" and argued that France "always keeps her arms open to receive her children," and he created tabulations of court decisions

both in support of and in opposition to the claim. (It is notable that five of the seven court decisions that refused to recognize the right of citizenship among émigrés concerned women, in keeping with the growth of patriarchal authority within the renovation of Roman law, especially in the universities.) For a provincial perspective, see Boug, *Recueil des édits*, 2:658–59: "Arrêt du 16 janvier 1764 qui juge qu'un Père Français qui se retire et s'établit en pays étranger ne peut nuire au droit de son enfant, si celui ci vient en France pour y demeurer." At the end of the seventeenth century, d'Aguesseau, following Le Bret, Bignon, Choppin, and Bacquet, claimed that it was not necessary for the offspring of French citizens to claim declarations of naturalization, but "prudent" to do so (*ad majorem cautelam*): Vanel, *Evolution historique*, 54; and below, chap. 2.

159. The jurisprudential emphasis on claims of descent ran parallel to the changing notions of the nobility in the early modern period (below, chap. 2). Although historians disagree about the timing of the shift, most concur that the nobility—and especially the upper nobility—increasingly defined itself by blood and race, developing a biologically based argument about family "stock": see L. Schalk, *From Valor to Pedigree: Ideas of Nobility in France in the Sixteenth and Seventeenth Centuries* (Princeton, 1986); A. Devyer, *Le Sang épuré: Les Préjugés de race chez les gentilshommes français de l'Ancien Régime, 1560–1620* (Brussels, 1973); and A. Jouanna, *L'Idée de race en France au XVIe et au début du XVIIe siècle, 1498–1614* (Montpellier, 1981), esp. pt. 4.

160. Watson, *Evolution of Law*, 69.

161. Quoted in Vanel, *Evolution historique*, 58–59.

162. Bardet, *Recueil d'arrests*, 2:242.

163. Thomas, *"Origine" et "commune patrie,"* esp. 72–73; and Y. Thomas, "Citoyens et résidents dans les cités de l'Empire romain: Essai sur le droit d'origine," *Identité et Droit de l'Autre*, ed. L. Mayali (Berkeley, 1994), 1–56; Lefebvre-Teillard, "Ius sanguinis," 229–31; d'Alteroche, *De l'Etranger,* 80–87.

Chapter 2: The Letter of Naturalization in the Old Regime

1. According to Jean Papon, naturalization alone could "efface the stain, withdraw the mark, and abolish whatever is sordid": Papon, *Secrets*, 509; see also Lefebvre de la Planche, *Mémoires*, 2:150; and d'Aguesseau, *Oeuvres*, 3:133.

2. For comparative accounts of the cultural and moral requirements of naturalization in contemporary Europe, see P. Weil, "Access to Citizenship: A Comparison of Twenty-Five Nationality Laws," in *Citizenship Today: Global Perspectives and Practices*, ed. T. A. Aleinikoff and D. Klusmeyer (Washington, 2001), 17–35; D. Çinar, "From Aliens to Citizens: A Comparative Analysis of the Rules of Transition," in *From Aliens to Citizens: Redefining the Status of Immigrants in Europe*, ed. R. Baucock (Aldershot, 1994), 49–72; and C. Wihtol de Wenden, "Les Pays européens face à l'immigration," *Pouvoirs* 47 (1988): 133–44.

3. Bodin, *Les Six livres*, 70.

4. Although foreign naturalization might be invoked as an argument in favor of identifying a French citizen as an alien (see below, chap. 3), naturalization in Old Regime France did not exclude, especially for high-ranking foreign nobles and dignitaries, the ability to retain and acquire further privileges, dignities, benefices, and political offices abroad. The crown's position was made clear in the case of the cardinal de Furstemberg, naturalized in July 1688 (registered at the Paris Chambre des comptes in August). Aspiring to the electorate of Cologne, Furstemberg received a clarification from the French foreign ministry that, as far as the monarchy was concerned, his naturalization "was not for him an exclusion that should stop him from attaining other privileges to which he could legitimately aspire, and His Majesty consents to allow him taking the oath for these new dignities, relieving him as needs be of any past or future subjection or other specific of personal engagement that he might have with respect to His Majesty for whatever reason": AAE MD Germany 94, fol. 118.

5. The first example I found of a foreigner identified as "naturalized French" dates from 1782 (AAE MD France 1454, fol. 145). The first claiming "all the rights of the Citizen and subject of the king of France" dates from 1772: AN O/1/235, fol. 14. Although very occasionally during the reign of Louis XIV foreigners claimed to be "bon citoyens," the administrative language of the

law between 1660 and 1790 relied on the terminology of "natural subjects" and "native residents." The word "naturalization" was first introduced in 1566, around the time when the jurists had shaped an expanded set of alien incapacities (above, chap. 1), but was not commonly deployed in the juridical vocabulary until the late eighteenth century.

6. *Les Quatre livres du droit public* (Caen, 1989 [1697]), 122.

7. F. Roumy, *L'Adoption dans le droit savant du XIIe au XVIIe siècle* (Paris, 1998), 116–36, Pisoia quoted 123; R. Dekkers, *La Fiction juridique: Etude de droit romain et droit comparé* (Paris, 1935), 84–85; see also I. MacLean, *Interpretation and Meaning in the Renaissance: The Case of Law* (Cambridge, 1992), 138–42. On Roman precedents, see Dekkers, *La Fiction juridique*, 8 et seq.

8. For an overview, see the sources cited in chap. 1, n. 3, and the works of J. Kirschner, "Between Nature and Culture: An Opinion of Baldus of Perugia on Venetian Citizenship as Second Nature," *Journal of Medieval and Renaissance Studies* 9 (1979): 179–208; " 'Ars imitatur naturam': A *Consilium* of Baldus of Perugia on Naturalization in Florence," *Viator* 5 (1974): 289–331; and " 'Civitas sibi faciat civem': Bartolus of Sassoferrato's Doctrine of the Making of a Citizen," *Speculum* 48 (1973): 694–713.

9. P. Reisenberg, *Citizenship in the Western Tradition: Plato to Rousseau* (Chapel Hill, 1992), esp. 118–39; Riesenberg, "Civism and Roman Law in Fourteenth-Century Italy," in *Economy, Society, and Government in Medieval Italy: Essays in Honor of Robert L. Reynolds*, ed. D. Herliy, R. Lopez, and V. Slessarev (Kent, Ohio, 1969), 237–54.

10. Quoted in Wells, *Law and Citizenship*, 7; J. Canning, *The Political Thought of Baldus of Ubaldis* (Cambridge, 1987), esp. 169–84.

11. Wells, *Law and Citizenship*, 3, 6. The fusion of "true" or "original" citizens and naturalized urban citizens in Siena, and elsewhere, took place in the course of the fourteenth century, according to W. Bowsky, "Medieval Citizenship: The Individual and the State in the Commune of Siena, 1287–1355," *Studies in Medieval and Renaissance History* 4 (1967): 195–243, esp. 201, 205.

12. Kirshner, "Between Nature and Culture," 193 and passim; but cf. Canning, *Political Thought of Baldus*, 174–75, who disagrees with Kirshner on the interpretation of the legal fiction; see also Canning, "A Fourteenth-Century Contribution to the Theory of Citizenship: Political Man and the Problem of Created Citizenship in the Thought of Baldus de Ubaldis," in *Authority and Power: Studies in Medieval Law and Government Presented to Walter Ullmann on His Seventieth Birthday*, ed. B. Tierney and P. A. Linehan (Cambridge, 1980), 197–212. On the notion of "habitus" in Italian jurisprudence, see Wells, *Law and Citizenship*, chaps. 1–2.

13. Kirshner, "Between Nature and Culture," passim; see also Kirshner, " 'Ars imitatur naturam,' " passim.

14. In general, French discussions of naturalization rarely invoked such biological metaphors, nor was the Aristotelean notions of "habitus" and "second nature" the subject of direct commentary. The one counterexample is the barrister Emmanuel de Gama, arguing the case of an inheritance left by a Spanish officer coming from the West Indies on a French boat at the orders of the French king. De Gama cited René Choppin who had claimed the "denaturalization" of French citizens who established themselves abroad. Citing Plutarch in Solon, and using examples from Roman law, de Gama dwelled briefly on the simile of a tree: "The tree is planted on my grounds; if, nonetheless, it grows roots in the grounds of my neighbor, it is no longer mine, but belongs to the owner of the grounds where it took root. . . . And the same for a citizen who leaves his fatherland, and voluntarily goes and establishes himself in another kingdom: he is there subjected to the laws and customs of the country, however severe they may be for him, and does not keep the domicile of his birth [only] by his own willful declaration. That is why the example of a tree, even though it is a thing and not a person, is applicable." *Dissertation sur le droit d'aubaine* (Paris, 1706), 47, 49–50.

15. Bacquet, *Oeuvres*, 2:7; Papon, *Secrets*, 458.

16. Rebuffi is quoted in Wells, *Law and Citizenship*, 34–35; see also below, chap. 3, on the vernacular perceptions of such requirements among foreigners petitioning during the late seventeenth and eighteenth centuries.

17. *Oeuvres*, 1:121; on the Estates General, see Picot, *Histoire des Etats Généraux considérés au point de vue de leur influence sur le gouvernement de la France de 1355 à 1614*, 5 vols. (Geneva, 1979 [Paris, 1872]), 2:102–5.

18. Above, chap. 1. As late as the eighteenth century, lawyers like Brillon continued to argue that, in order for a foreigner to devolve property to a native resident (regnicole), the mother must be French, but he recognized that the jurisprudence, as early as 1518, did not concur with his opinion: *Dictionnaire*, 3:150.

19. Picot, *Histoire des Etats Généraux*, 2:538–39.

20. Above, chap. 1, n. 46. On naturalization in the kingdom of Aragon before the eighteenth century, see N. Sales, *De Tuïr a Catarroja: Estudis sobre institucions catalanes i de la Corona d'Aragó (segles XV–XVIII)* (Valencia, 2002), 95–126; and J. Lalinde Abadia, "De la nacionalidad aragonesa a la regionalidad," *Revista juridica de Cataluña* 72 (1973): 536–80. On seventeenth-century naturalizations, see Dominguez Ortiz, "La Concession de naturalezas" 227–39.

21. Herzog, "Municipal Citizenship and Empire," and " 'A Stranger in a Strange Land,' " passim.

22. D'Aguesseau, *Oeuvres complètes*, 3:130.

23. Le Bret, *Recueil*, 197–201.

24. Papon, *Secrets*, 480. For a description of early modern procedures of ennoblement, see J.-R. Bloch, *L'Anoblissement en France au temps de François I: Essai d'une définition de la condition juridique et sociale de la noblesse au XVIe siècle* (Paris, 1934), esp. 137–52; and D. Bien, "Manufacturing Nobles: The Chancelleries in France to 1789," *Journal of Modern History* 61 (1989): 445–86.

25. Lefebvre de la Planche, *Mémoires*, 2:151.

26. Denisart, *Collection* (1773), 3:344.

27. Bodin, *Les Six livres*, 90; Bacquet, *Oeuvres*, 1:74–76.

28. Bacquet, *Oeuvres*, 2:40.

29. Boniface, *Arrests notables*, 5:10. The idea had resonance in what Bartolus described as *civilitas contracta*, in which naturalization was a binding force "derived from natural as well as civil law": Kirshner, "Civitas Sibi Facial Civem," 707.

30. Quotes are from K. Gager, *Blood Ties and Fictive Ties: Adoption and Family Life in Early Modern France* (Princeton, 1996), 3, who documents the practices of adoption among Parisian artisan families. On sixteenth-century adoption practices in Lyon, see P. Gonnet, *L'Adoption lyonnaise des orphelins légitimes (1536–1793)*, 2 vols. (Paris, 1935); more generally, see J.-P. Gutton, *Histoire de l'adoption en France* (Paris, 1993).

31. Roumy, *L'adoption dans le droit savant*, passim; Kelley, *Foundations*, passim.

32. Quoted in Wells, *Law and Citizenship*, 6; see also Canning, *Political Thought of Baldus*, 180–81.

33. Lefebvre de la Planche, *Mémoires*, 3:74; Bacquet, *Oeuvres*, 1:3; Bourjon, *Le Droit commun de la France* 1:93.

34. Bodin, *Les Six livres*, 12; on the coronation and anointment, see R. Jackson, *Vive le roi!: A History of the French Coronation from Charles V* (Chapel Hill, 1984), 85–90; on medieval precedents, including the bestowal of a ring on the king's finger, see Kantorowicz, *King's Two Bodies*, 212–32. Kantorowicz argues that the earlier rituals, adapting episcopal ceremonies, did not imply a marriage between the king and the kingdom. For the sixteenth-century legal and political uses of the metaphor, see S. Hanley, *The "Lit de Justice" of the Kings of France: Constitutional Ideology in Legend, Ritual, and Discourse* (Princeton, 1983), 83–85 and passim; Hanley, "The Monarchic State in Early Modern France: Marital Regime, Government, and Male Right," in *Politics, Ideology, and the Law in Early Modern Europe*, ed. A. E. Bakos (Rochester, 1994), 111–13; R. Descimon, "Les Fonctions de la métaphore du mariage politique du Roi et de la République France, XVe–XVIIIe siècle," *Annales HSS* (November–December 1992), no. 6: 1127–47; and M. Borgetto, "Métaphore de la famille et idéologies," in *Le Droit non-civil de la famille* (Paris, 1983), 3–8. For a discussion of how the metaphor of the king as father functioned in eighteenth-century political life, see J. Merrick, "Fathers and Kings: Patriarchalism and Absolutism in Eighteenth-Century French Politics," *Studies on Voltaire and the Eighteenth Century* 308 (1993): 281–303.

35. Corcia, "Bourg, Bourgeois, Bourgeoisie de Paris," 208–10; C. M. Small, "The Royal Bourgeoisies in the Duchy of Burgundy," in *Proceedings of the Annual Meeting of the Western Society for French History* 13 (1986): 1–9. For early modern accounts of the status of the droit de bourgeoisie, see, for example, Loysel, *Divers opuscules*, 119–22, who claimed that the medieval monarchy acted *ad exemplum civium Romanorum* in making such grants; see also the important disquisi-

tion by the Burgundian lawyer Droz, *Essai sur l'histoire des bourgeois du roi, des seigneurs, et des villes* (Besancon, 1760).

36. D'Alteroche, *De l'Etranger à la seigneurie*, esp. 49–86, significantly revising the earlier accounts given in Boizet, *Les Lettres de naturalité* (privileges of the Lombards quoted 27) and the older but still useful studies of C. Chabrun, *Les Bourgeois du roi* (Paris, 1908) and the unpublished thesis of E. Babelon, "Les Bourgeois du Roi au moyen âge," Thèse de l'Ecole de Chartes, 1878. The latter, which discusses at length the "laboratory" of Champagne, can be consulted with permission in AN AB XXVIII 197.

37. The language of *bourgeoisie* very occasionally made its appearance in the letters of naturalization in the seventeenth century, until at least the 1690s: thus, for example, the naturalization of François Caron in July 1665 was called a "lettre de naturalité et droit de bourgeoisie," and registered at the Paris Chambre des comptes and Chambre du trésor, 9 February 1666: AN K 173, no. 160.

38. D'Alteroche, *De l'Etranger à la seigneurie*, 98–99 and passim.

39. J.-F. Dubost, "Signification de la lettre de naturalité dans la France des XVIe et XVIIe siècles," Institut Universitaire Européen Working Papers in History, no. 90/3 (Florence, 1990); and the older and often misleading work of Boizet, *Les Lettres de naturalité*, passim.

40. Dubost, *La France italienne*, 29–33, noting that the elevated rates in the mid-sixteenth century were an "exceptional situation" (31), a parallel for which can be found in the sharp increase of legitimations after 1565 (Gerber, "The End of Bastardy," chap. 2). During the reign of Henry IV, naturalizations stabilized to around forty a year, slightly less than the average for the period from 1660 to 1790, the basis of the statistical work of this book (appendix 1). It is interesting to compare these figures with England during the period corresponding to the reign of Louis XIV, when naturalization and denization acts together represent a similar number (but whose timing was subject to more abrupt mutation during experiments with general naturalization acts): see Statt, *Foreigners and Englishman*, 34–35.

41. Dubost, *La France italienne*, esp. 30 (tabulation of naturalizations from 1547 to 1681, based on catalogues of royal acts, inventories of registered letters at the courts, etc.). On Italians naturalized under Francis I, see C. Billot, "Les Italiens naturalisés sous le regne de François I," in *Struttura familiari, epidemie, migrazioni nell'Italia medievale*, ed. R. Comba, G. Piccini, and G. Pinto (Siena, 1984), 477–91.

42. Guyot, *Répertoire de jurisprudence*, 10:483; G. Lepointe, *Petit précis des sources de l'histoire du droit français* (Paris, 1937), passim. Letters patent with more transitory effects (including declarations of naturalizations, described below) were sealed with yellow wax, and were dated with the day and month, unlike perpetual patent letters, that were dated only by the month. On the diplomatics (the study of instruments and documents) of privileges more generally, see H. Michaud, *La Grande Chancellerie et les écritures royales au XVIe siècle* (Paris, 1967); G. Tessier, *Diplomatique royale française* (Paris, 1962); Sueur, *Histoire public*, 2:111–24.

43. D. Bien, "The *Secrétaires du Roi*: Absolutism, Corps, and Privileges under the Ancien Régime," in *Vom Ancien Regime zur Französischen Revolution: Forschungen und Perspektiven*, ed. E. Hinrichs, E. Schmitt, and R. Vierhaus (Göttingen, 1978), 153–68. For an institutional account of the royal secretaries, see P. Robin, *La Compagnie des secrétaires du Roi (1351–1791)* (Paris, 1933); and for a prosopography (including the several dozen foreign-born and naturalized secretaries), see C. Favre-Lejeune, *Les Secrétaires du Roi de la Grande Chancellerie de France: Dictionnaire biographique et généalogique*, 2 vols. (Paris, 1986).

44. S. de Dainville-Barbiche, "Les Archives du sceau," *La Gazette des archives*, nos. 160–61 (1993): 127–151; G. Tessier, "L'Audience du sceau," *Bibliothèque de l'Ecole des Chartes* 109 (1951): 51–95. The office of chancellor normally held the title of keeper of the seals (*guarde de sceau*), but the title was often revoked, and could be conferred by the king at will: see Barbiche, *Les Institutions*, 161–62, and the interesting historical note written to maréchal Pétain during his reorganization of the office, reproduced in Weil, *Qu'est-ce qu'un Français?* 401. On the reorganization of the sceau under the Revolution and Napoleon, see below, chap. 8.

45. On the *secrétaire d'état de la maison du roi*, sometimes called the *petit Département*, see the entry by R. M. Rampelberg, in *Dictionnaire de l'Ancien Régime*, ed. L. Bély, 1135–40; and more

generally, R.-M. Rampelberg, *Aux origines du ministère de l'intérieur: Le Ministre de la Maison du Roi, 1783–1788. Baron de Breteuil* (Paris, 1975).

46. A. Cans, "Les Registres d'expéditions du Secrétariat d'Etat et de la maison du roi," *Revue d'histoire moderne et contemporaine* 4 (1902–3): 257–61.

47. Weil, *Qu'est-ce qu'un Français?* 23–26, and below, chap. 8.

48. AN O/1/231, fol. 290, original petition (one of the only surviving examples) to the comte d'Argenson; and ibid., fol. 313, naturalization draft of January 1757. Perhaps more common were appeals for the "protection" of the foreign minister: thus the case of Jean Delevigne, a priest at Tournay, who "dared to ask" for such protection "to help the chancellor decide to give him [letters of declaration]": AN O/1/235, fol. 151, declaration draft of June 1773; AAE MD France 1454, fol. 60–63, including his petition to the duc d'Aiguillon, who sent on a copy to the chancellor, 29 April 1773.

49. AN O/1/226, fol. 315–19: the dossier is unusually complete; another unusually important dossier was constituted in the case of the baron de Thurn et Balsallin in 1782–83, and includes a letter of the baronne de Ferrette to the foreign minister asking for the young man's "protection" and for the minister to "employ the credit that you might have with the keeper of the seals to engage him to accord these letters," although such intervention was more than likely necessary given that the claimant sought to hold benefices in the jurisdiction of the parlement of Bésançon, possibly subject to the same restrictions as those in neighboring Alsace: see AN O/1/237, fol. 186, 191; MAE MD 1454, fol. 141, 149, 153, 156.

50. Ghezzi had appealed to the French ambassador in Rome, who wrote to the comte de Morville, secretary of state of foreign affairs, about his naturalization. The answer was that the request would be forwarded, exceptionally in this instance, to the royal council: see M. Antoine, *Le Conseil du Roi sous le règne de Louis XV* (Geneva, 1970), 501, n. 383.

51. Ibid.

52. Below, chap. 7 and appendix 1: thus the large collection of letters in the archives of the foreign ministry from the 1770s and 1780s.

53. BN MS 5085, fol. 328.

54. *Le Grand stile et prothocolle de la chancellerie de France. . . .* (1548), fol. iv. The 1532 edition did contain a model privilege accorded to an alien allowing him or her to make a will (fol. 238v.), but such an act was not named a letter of naturalization, and was omitted from the 1548 edition.

55. The formulas from the 1670s can be found in AN O/1/6, fol. 227–46; see also Cans, "Les Registres d'expéditions," 257–61. All the manuscript templates dating from the 1720s and 1730s, found in AN KK 627 (see E. Schwob, *Un Formulaire de Chancellerie au XVIIIe siècle* [Paris, 1936]), were drawn directly from specific letters of naturalization. Thus the 1723 naturalization of the Pole Albert Joseph Boupkiewicz (AN O/1/77, fol. 598) provided the "model text" of naturalization; the example of naturalization with benefices was that given to the Irish cleric Jacques Doudall in 1733 (AN O/1/225, fol. 107); the naturalization of a regular cleric with the right to participate in the benefits of his religious order reproduced the grant to the English Augustinian Jacques Duany in 1735 (AN O/1/235, fol. 345); and the model declaration of naturalization was based on the one given to Charles de Moracin and his family, from the Netherlands, in 1733 (AN O/1/225, fol. 149).

56. Sahlins, "Fictions of a Catholic France," passim.

57. More rare are letters of naturalization with an extended preamble, that "literary ornament" containing general considerations, "often of a moral order, that present themselves as the condition of the exception about to be granted" (Michaud, *La Grande Chancellerie*, 214). In the case of naturalization, the king might invoke the traditions of his ancestors in receiving foreigners: "The satisfaction that the kings, our predecessors, had in offering their protection and receiving into our kingdom foreigners who had requested from them the permission to establish themselves, drawn as they have always been by the peace and quiet which our subjects enjoy, engages us to offer the same grace to those who make the request and in whom we especially recognize good qualities which deserve such a grace; we have favorably listed to the petition which has been made in this way by our dear and good Jacques Forestal." (AN O/1/222, fol. 110, naturalization draft, November 1720)

58. These narratives will be read in the next chapter as constituting certain vernacular fictions of citizenship.

59. D'Alteroche, *De l'Etranger à la seigneurie*, 88–89.

60. Papon, *Secrets*, 461, emphasis in text.

61. For an account of the "mental geography" of the late seventeenth-century clerks who inscribed foreigners onto the tax rolls of 1697–1707, see Dubost and Sahlins, *Et si on faisait payer*, 161–71, and below, chap. 5.

62. By the seventeenth century, the language was consistent: the petitioner used "subjects and native born residents"; only in the late eighteenth century did references to the "citizen" appear. More generally through the Old Regime, examples (including model texts) are found where the exposition ends with an intervention on the part of the king, an exposition of a general set of motives that will justify the privilege of naturalization.

63. Papon, *Secrets*, 459. See below, chap. 3, on the limits of the discretionary intervention of the royal secretaries in their redaction of the expositions.

64. D'Alteroche, *De l'Etranger*, 11–15 and passim.

65. Don Fernando Altamiro of Lisbon in 1679 explained that he married a French woman in Portugal, and wanted to settle in France "which was his own desire and in order to give his wife a sign of the affection that he has for her" (AN K 174, n. 15); Elpidio Benedetty, a cleric from Rome who in 1661 claimed he didn't reside in France, but whose letter also included an exceptional dispensation of residence (AN o/1/218, fol. 160, draft of naturalization with permission to hold benefices up to three thousand livres in annual revenue, February 1661).

66. Despite the ideological biases of the sixteenth-century jurists, who believed that prior residence ought to be required of a foreigner, no jurists after that argued that in order for naturalization to be valid, prior residence in the kingdom was necessary. The single exception was the Parisian barrister Poulain du Parc in 1779, cited in Boizet, *Les Lettres de naturalité*, 75, n. 14.

67. Württemberg: AN O/1/220, fol. 299–304; AAE MD Germany 94, fol. 119, drafts and copies of naturalization of 1713; Tuscany: AN O/1/219, fol. 230, 239, 248, draft permission of January 1698; AN O/1/220, fol. 21, draft exemption, July 1702; AN MS JF 124, fol. 193–97. In fact, the letters given to the grand duke and his daughter were not initially called letters of naturalization, but simple permissions to reside and enjoy all rights with respect to property. The reason appears to lie in a marginal comment about naturalization, which was said to include access to "the greatest offices of the Crown and government or other ecclesiastic or secular dignities, without exceptions"—thus a counterpart or remedy to the most "absolutist" definition of the droit d'aubaine. But because the duchesse, Anne Marie Louise, was also named, the chancellery ended up issuing patent letters of exemption from the droit d'aubaine. For the duke and duchesse of Savoy, see the printed version in *Actes Royaux. Catalogue générale des livres imprimés de la Bibliothèque nationale*, ed. S. Honoré, 7 vols., n.d., n. 2649, "Lettres patentes de l'exemption du droit d'aubaine du duc et duchesse de Savoie," July 1702; for others, see Boizet, *Les Lettres de naturalité*, 76–77.

68. BN MS JF 306, fol. 218–51. The affair dragged on until 1758.

69. AN P 2596, fol. 8, registration of letters by the Paris Chambre des comptes, 8 February 1763.

70. AN o/1/225, fol. 102, draft naturalization of Ayme, February 1733; AN O/1/226, fol. 33, draft naturalization of Bockshammer, May 1736. Examples of ambiguous clauses include the letter issued in October 1756 to Jean-François Engel, a bourgeois merchant-cooper from Nassau in the Rhineland, that stated that he could live in the town of Bousservillier in Alsace, but neither restricted his residence to Alsace nor gave him permission to reside in the kingdom at large: AN O/1/229, fol. 277. Jean Adam Schneider too was given, in November 1750, a letter restricting his residence to Alsace, but the clause concerning being unable to leave without the king's permission was inexplicably dropped: AN o/1/229, fol. 279.

71. Protestants were not permitted in the previously Catholic districts, including Strasbourg. Within the Protestant districts (below, chap. 6), the crown increasingly sought to impose confessional uniformity: see M. de Roux, *Louis XIV et les provinces conquises: Artois, Alsace, Flandres, Roussillon, Franche-Comté* (Paris, 1938), 210–16; G. Livet, "Louis XIV et les provinces conquises," *XVIIe siècle* 22 (1952): 481–507. It is significant that in the struggle for religious toleration during the 1750s and 1760s, an anonymous memoir proposed that all Protestants be "naturalized" as "Al-

satians" as a means of preserving the legal fiction of Catholic uniformity. The anonymous memoir is cited in Merrick, *Desacralization*, 150, n. 28.

72. Arrêt du conseil, 28 June 1686, reaffirming the royal declaration of 25 January 1683, in *Recueil des Edits*, 387, 155; BN MS JF 42, fol. 83–87, "avis à M. le comte de Mouvelle sur un arrest pour permettre aux étrangers protestants de venir dans le royaume," 25 November 1725.

73. On the Lutherans around the Swedish embassy, see J. Driancourt-Girod, *L'Insolite histoire des luthériens de Paris, de Louis XIII à Napoléon* (Paris, 1992) and her fine study of Lutherans at the Swedish embassy, *La Chapelle de l'ambassade de Suède à Paris, 1626–1806* (Paris, 1976); on the Protestants around the British embassy during the Regency, see J. Gres-Gayer, "Le Culte de l'ambassade de Grande-Bretagne à Paris au début de la Régence (1715–1720)," in *Bulletin de la Société de l'histoire du protestantisme français* (hereafter cited as *BSHPF*) 130 (1984): 29–46. On Protestant cemeteries in Paris and elsewhere during the eighteenth century (where native French Protestants, despite their lack of a civil status, were buried after 1777), see the documents reproduced by Ch. Read, "Cimetières et inhumations des Huguenots, principalement à Paris, aux XVIe, XVIIe, et XVIIIe siècles, 1563–1792," *BSHPF* 11 (1862): 132–50, 351–59; 12 (1863): 33, 141, 143, 247, 367; 13 (1864): 224; 15 (1866): passim. On the Marseille Protestant cemeteries, where native Protestants could be buried following the royal declaration of 9 April 1735, see V.-L. Bourilly, "Les Protestants à Marseille au XVIIIe siècle," *BSHPF* 59 (1910): 518–53.

74. ADLA B 84, fol. 267; B 96, fol. 82r; significantly, because he was already naturalized and had converted, Pitters does not appear on the registers of the Protestant church in Bègles, outside Nantes: see C. Landré, "Les Protestants hollandais à Bordeaux, avant et après la révocation de l'édit de Nantes," *Bulletin de la Commission pour l'histoire des Eglises wallones* 2 (1887): 269–75.

75. The reverse administrative fiction can also be found: the case of Jean Balthazard Guthjar, who was identified explicitly as "professsing the Confession of Augsburg" in his letter of July 1750, was conferred the privilege of living in "Attemat or any other place in our kingdom, countries, lands, and seigneuries of our dominion that pleases him": AN O/1/229, fol. 247.

76. AAE France 1454, fol. 179, draft declaration of 18 September 1784.

77. AN M 1031, no. 140, copy of naturalization. On the distinction between residence and domicile in juridical discourse, see the clearly stated (but still contestable) assertions of Argou, *Institutions*, 1:81 et seq.

78. Du Sault, *Nouveau Stile des lettres des chancelleries de France* (Paris, 1666), 346–47; cf. the model text of the 1730s reproduced by Schwob, "Un formulaire de chancellerie," which rephrases the formula, dropping one of the redundant clauses about the right to inherit. See below, chap. 7, for a discussion of the renewed centrality of inheritance capacity as a marker of citizenship at a moment when the droit d'aubaine was beginning to be dismantled.

79. Papon, *Secrets*, 458. These three conditions were different from the specific category of privileges for foreign clerics who entered the regular monastic orders, and which permitted them the right not to hold benefices but to enjoy all rights, privileges, and material benefits that could accrue to them in their participation within the religious order. Thus, for example, the letter for a religious novice in the nunnery of the Aumonier de Cleste in Paris, Eleonor O'Farrel from Dublin, who was given the ability to accept "all gifts, bequests, and donations which would be given to the said convent and monastery, to possess and administer the goods and revenues of these following and conforming [to] the rules and institutes of the said congregation; to pass all acts and contracts necessary for the good of these as the law will permit": AN o/1/235, fol. 97, naturalization draft of January 1773.

80. AN V/1/542, copy of naturalization given to Francis Ernest Nitner, born in Hartenberg, cleric of the diocese of Olmuta in Moravia, December 1702.

81. AN O/1/229, fol. 141, draft naturalization of Frederic Saint-Séverin d'Aragon, from Plaisance [Italy], December 1749. According to L. de Héricourt du Vautier, the clause could be added at the discretionary judgment of the king: *Les Loix ecclésiastiques de France dans leur ordre naturel, et une analyse des livres du droit canonique conférés avec les usages de l'Église gallicane* (Paris, 1771), 428–29.

82. J.-F. Dubost, *Les Etrangers en France, XVIe siècle–1789: Guide des recherches aux Archives Nationales* (Paris, 1993), 44–46. These three conditions overlapped with more general formalities involving the collation and possession of secular and regular benefices in the French Catholic Church: for an overview of these, see J. Gérardin, *Etude sur les bénéfices ecclésiastiques au XVIe et*

XVIIe siècles (Geneva, 1971 [1897]). For examples of more specific overlaps—such as those requiring clergy in France to speak the language and not be followers of Jansenism—see below, chap. 6.

83. AN O/1/238, fol. 219, draft naturalization of September 1788; AN O/1/236, fol. 167, draft naturalization of February 1778.

84. Bayard, "Naturalization," 301. On the royal letters of legitimation, which enacted the "fiction that erases the irregularity of a bastard's birth and places him within the ranks of legitimate offspring," see Merlin, *Répertoire universel*, s.v. "légitimation," 263; L. Delbez, *De la légitimation par lettres royaux* (Montpellier, 1923); and most recently, Gerber, "The End of Bastardy," chap. 2.

85. BN MS JF 2401, fol. 4; 2494, fol. 4; and AN P 151. On Terwell's cartographic accomplishments, see the brief biographical sketch of L. André and E. Bourgeois, *Les Sources de l'histoire de la France. XVIIe siècle (1610–1715)*, vol. 5, *Histoire politique et militaire* (Paris, 1926), 94.

86. Loyseau, *Cinq livres*, 63; D'Alteroche, *De l'Etranger*, 222–23.

87. For example, AN O/1/219, fol. 196–207, draft naturalization, declaration of nobility, and dispensation of residence given to Arnold de Ville, an imperial baron from Liège (and "Governor of the [Water] Machine" at Marly), whose dispensation of residence was given in perpetuity to his heirs in May 1692, with address rectification of 2 January 1693 following registration at the Paris parlement on 13 September 1692.

88. BN MS JF 124, fol. 178–204, an important dossier based on the request of Hayes and his wife, Catherine Sorocold. The petition was supported by the solicitor general of the Paris parlement, Joly de Fleury, who wrote that "the favor asked here is not new, but it is true that it is rare, and one must not accord it without careful review, not only because it is regarded as a kind of singular distinction in favor of descendants of allied princes, but because if this favor is mixed with others, it would become so ordinary that one could not refuse it" (fol. 180).

89. Sahlins, "Fictions of a Catholic France," passim; and below, chap. 5. It is worth mentioning here the case of Chammas Cazadour, a Chaldean Christian born in Diabekir, in southeastern Anatolia, whose father sought religious refuge in France in 1732 and settled in Marseille. Joseph was naturalized by patent letters of May 1764. In 1760, he began what was to become, but only in 1785, a successful petition to bring over ten members of his extended family: the first case of "family reunification" in France. His family, however, received doubly fictional letters—actually dispensations from obtaining letters of naturalization. See BN MS 21714, fol. 96–109; BN MS JF 2494, fol. 14–37. The case involved an extensive inquiry into the identities and backgrounds of all the claimants, and was complicated by the fact that Chammas had changed his name to Hormis da Gallo, or Hormees Gallo.

90. Less than a tenth of the letters in the database are known to have been declarations of naturalization, but because more than half the data was collected from inventories, the proportion should surely be higher, as is suggested from soundings in the registration records of the Chambre des comptes and the O series of the Maison du Roi (appendix 1).

91. D'Aguesseau, *Oeuvres*, 3:133, citing Le Bret, Bignon, Choppin, Bacquet, and Brodeau, as well as "an infinite number" of decisions by the Paris parlement.

92. An occasional preamble in the letters of naturalized Flemings stated: "Although the lands [*pays*] of Flanders, Brabant, Hainault, Holland, Zeeland, and all other provinces composing the said Low Countries were of the ancient domain of our crown, and that the inhabitants of the said countries now living in our kingdom have always been deemed and reputed to be our true and original subjects and native residents [*regnicoles*], nonetheless because the great part of these countries is not at this time under our obedience . . .": AN V/1/542, 406, copy of declaration of naturalization of Jean Marie Tignobon (born in Mons), July 1696.

93. AAE MD France 1454, fol. 124, copy of naturalization of François de Meurisse, 1779, annotated and sent to the royal chancellor. On the persistence of the different legal status of "near foreigners" such as the Flemings in the late seventeenth century, see Dubost and Sahlins, *Et si on faisait payer*, 155–56 et seq.

94. AN o/1/224, fol. 7, draft declaration of 28 February 1727. In 1768, J.-L. Moreau de Beaumont wrote that the use of letters of declaration of naturalization for the Flemings "has become useless and superfluous to them by the disposition of different treaties that have fixed in a stable fashion the status of the inhabitants": *Mémoires concernant les impositions et droits en Europe*, 4 vols. (Paris, 1787), 4:629.

95. AN o/1/236, fol. 55, draft declaration of naturalization, 18 December 1776.

96. Marie Sophie and Hope Luther, born in St. Martin on the Ile de Ré of parents who had come from Ireland and Scotland, sought to be declared French naturals in 1771 so as to enjoy without problems "the privileges and exemptions enjoyed by our true subjects," even though she should have been considered French by her place of birth: AN o/1/234, fol. 299, draft declaration of naturalization, 7 August 1771; see also the case of Jacob Scandiland (a merchant, born in Bordeaux of a Scottish father, who had been among the Jacobite refugees): AN o/1/233, fol. 53, draft naturalization, December 1762; AN P 2597, fol. 50, registration at the Paris Chambre des comptes.

97. Argou, *Institutions*, 1:75, defined the term in its strict etymological sense, as "resident of the kingdom," but the dominant definition was that of Papon, *Secrets*, 465, where the *regnicole* was the "native subject."

98. BN MS 18,271, fols. 5–12, Fresnes Forget, secrétaire d'Etat, "Mémoire sur les Clauses qu'il faut observer aux Lettres qui se scellent en la Grande Chancellerie" (n.d., ca. 1637): "Naturalizations. There is nothing to note except [to insist on] the clause 'that the heirs be native-born residents,' and for the duchy of Milan, the marquisat of Saluce, and Artois, it is only necessary to have declarations [of naturalization] because these countries are part of France's dominion. And if there is a gift of the financial charge, it must be signed by a royal secretary" (fol. 5v).

99. Papon, *Secrets*, 466.

100. Papon, *Secrets*, 449; see J. B. Bosquet, *Dictionnaire raisonné des domaines et droits domaniaux*, 2 vols. (Paris, 1763), 1:18 et seq., who emphasizes the royalist position that such property fell to the king, "not the *haut justicier*, because the droit d'aubaine is levied in infinitum on persons descended from foreigners." Throughout the eighteenth century, the crown's right was often tested, by lords and by its own officers: see the case of the naturalized Englishwoman Hélène de Fleming, who died ab intestat with no apparent French heirs, in AN AD XV 1, decisions of council of state, 11 November 1749, 8 September 1750, and 13 February 1759. In the case of the Abbot Labiewsky, a naturalized Pole, the receiver general of domanial rights of the city of Paris (who claimed the property "by law of the alien") contested the claims of the royal tax-farmers who believed that the succession was due to them by right of escheat (*à titre de désherence*), and it was the royal tax-farmers who emerged victorious: Ibid., printed decision of 24 February 1748.

101. Denisart, *Collection* (1783), 1:577 et seq.

102. Boizet, *Les Lettres de naturalité*, 76–77.

103. The Parisian law professor Claude de Ferrière, in his *Les Instituts du droit français* (Paris, 1687), adopted such a "principle," which had precedents in the highly publicized lawsuit of Charles de Gonzague in the 1630s that had helped to establish the norm. Although the barrister Bignon successfully argued for the right of the duc de Mantua's French heirs to claim a portion of the estate, the necessity of residence in the kingdom had clearly become a central point of jurisprudential debate, as revealed in the losing lawyer's opinion: Soëfve, *Recueil*, 2:321–23; see the brief discussion of the case in Wells, *Law and Citizenship*, 106 et seq.

104. Lefebvre de la Planche, *Mémoires*, 2:74, 175; Bourjon, *Institutes*, 91.

105. Isambert, *Recueil générale*, 14:404–5; on medieval precedents, see d'Alteroche, *De l'Etranger*, 92–94 and passim.

106. Lefebvre de la Planche, *Mémoires*, 2:82.

107. AN O/1/236, fol. 287–92 (an unusually complete dossier, including his draft naturalization of June 1780).

108. ABA Recueil Gaultier de Breuil, vol. 57, no. 5 (1764): 7–9.

109. Vanel, *Evolution historique*, 59–61; Isambert, *Recueil général*, 17:366–70.

110. By edict of December 1689, such confiscations were no longer made for the "profit of the king" (for whom, in any case, it was common practice to gift the estate to the heirs), but specifically "to the benefit of paternal or maternal kin to whom, following the customs and usages observed in the kingdom, they would have belonged by the natural death of those who left the kingdom (art. 1)." The result was extensive litigation, over the next century, between direct heirs who returned to the kingdom and collateral French natives: see *Gazette des Tribuneaux et Mémorial des corps administratifs et municipaux* 7 (March-July 1793): 121 et seq.

111. Denisart, *Collection* (1773), 2:398–99. The mercantilist aspects of the original 1669 ordi-

nance were retrospectively illuminated by the royal decree of 1716 addressed to the French commercial consuls abroad that specifically excluded the offspring of fugitive French citizens from inheriting: the decree is cited in AN K 873, n. 39.

112. Lefebvre de la Planche, *Mémoires*, 2:209–53.

113. Above, chap. 1. Concerning Alsace, for example, the crown attempted in 1720 to prohibit the investment of its subjects "in foreign countries," but also encouraged foreign workers from the Alsatian borderlands to work in France by offering them free "certificates" to work wherever they wished: see Boug, *Recueil des édits*, 1:551–52.

114. L. Bély, *Espions et ambassadeurs au temps de Louis XIV* (Paris, 1990). AN AD XV 1, decree of 28 February 1765 reiterating "les défenses faites de tout temps en France, à tout sujets, d'entretenir aucune relation en matière d'affaires publiques avec les pays étrangers," without the express permission of the king.

115. Sahlins, "Fictions of a Catholic France," passim. Those who assume Catholicism as a condition of citizenship include R. Villers, "La Condition des étrangers en France dans les trois derniers siècles de la monarchie," *RSJB* 10 (1958): 147; and E. Glasson, *Histoire du droit et des institutions de la France*, 8 vols. (Paris, 1896–1903), 8:284. Boizet, *Les Lettres de naturalité*, does offer a more nuanced view, but without explicitly considering the legal and administrative fictions at work in the eighteenth century.

116. Lefebvre de la Planche, *Mémoires*, 2:151; Lefebvre's editor and glossator in 1765, Paul Charles Lorry, disagreed. On Lefebvre's anti-Semitism, see Sahlins, "Fictions of a Catholic France," 97–99.

117. AN O/1/225, fol. 89, draft naturalization of January 1733. In 1751, Antoine Fredy, born in Ragusa, Italy, but living in Martinique, received his letter, which also included the clause, "provided nonetheless that the said claimant, his children and heirs profess, live, and die in the Catholic faith." AN M 1031, no. 126, copy of naturalization, June 1751.

118. ADLA B 83, fol. 10, registration of 16 February 1666; the clause can also be found among letters issued immediately after the revocation in 1685: for example, AN V/1/542, naturalization draft of the Swiss Ghiringbelly.

119. "Discours à l'Assemblée de Saint-Germain," in *Oeuvres complètes*, ed. P. J. S. Dufey (Paris, 1825), 1:442: ". . . plusieurs peuvent estre *cives* qui non *erunt christiani*, même l'excommunié de laisse pas d'estre citoyen."

120. A draft of Law's letters can be found in AN o/1/221, fol. 31, 33; AN PP 151, which notes the existence of a "decision of the Chambre des comptes to make a representation to the king on the naturalization letters, not registered in the Chambre, obtained by Law," 10 January 1735; those of Berkeley and Fitz James, in AN K 175, no. 21; on these and Berwick, see Boizet, *Les Lettres de naturalité*, 80.

121. AAE MD France 1454, fol. 30.

122. AN O/1/231, fol. 397, corrected draft naturalization, August 1757.

123. *Mémoires*, 2:174.

124. Below, chap. 5. On Hayes, see above, n. 85, and BN MS JF 124, fol. 180, 184, 186; AN P 2595, fol. 9v., 11v.; on de Saxe, see AN P 2593, fol. 19. Another case, apparently not involving religious differences, concerned the comte de Hoym, Polish ambassador to the French court, who received a "doubly fictional" patent letter in 1727: AN K 175, no. 90; AN MS JF 124, fol. 190.

125. Billot, "L'assimilation des étrangers," 288; Papon, *Secrets*, 470; Bodin, *Les Six livres*, 83. The key dates between which the crown moved from collecting a "finance" and offering naturalization as a "gift" were 1550 and 1570. In 1549, the exemption from the tax seems exceptional; in the 1550s, naturalizations with exemptions correspond to more than a third of the total. The decisive turning point was the reign of Charles IX: see Dubost and Sahlins, *Et si on faisait payer*, 23.

126. Quoted in Dubost and Sahlins, *Et si on faisait payer*, 23.

127. A. Tessereau, *Histoire chronologique de la grande chancellerie de France*, 2 vols. (Paris, 1710), 1:703 et seq.; 2:341–53.

128. Le Chanteur, *Dissertation historique et critique sur la Chambre des comptes* (Paris, 1765); E. Lalou, "La Chambre des comptes de Paris: Sa mise en place et son fonctionement (fin XIIIe–XIVe siècle)," in *La France des principautés: Les Chambres des comptes, XIVe et XVe siècles* (Paris, 1996); comte H. Coustant d'Yanville, *La Chambre des comptes de Paris* (Paris, 1866–75); see

also *Le Cour des Comptes: Histoire de l'administration française*, Pref. A. Chandernagor (Paris, 1984), 4–313; and for the fate of the Chambres during the "bureaucratic revolution" of the late eighteenth century, see Bosher, *French Finances*, chap. 6 et seq.

129. Boizet, *Les Lettres de naturalité*, 93–96, usefully points out the difference between verification and registration; but cf. his more general account of the protocols and jurisprudence of the fiscal courts, 87–118.

130. Boizet, *Les Lettres de naturalité*, 96–100; d'Aguesseau, *Oeuvres*, 2:129.

131. The fiscal bureaux of the treasury appear to have been more consistent in making such formal inquiries, although there is no evidence of local financial officials denying naturalization: see Bayard, "Naturalization in Lyon," passim. For an excellent use of the sovereign court records in Montpellier, see Santucci, "Devenir régnicole," passim.

132. ADSM B 2B 361, patent letters of naturalization registered at the Chambre des comptes de Rouen, 1631–1789.

133. AN 0/1/229, fols. 104, 109, 116–31, 136, draft naturalization of April 1687 and inquiry; registration, 9 December 1687; see also AN V/1/542, 414.

134. AN 0/1/219, fols. 55–61, draft naturalization, March 1686, and dossier concerning the registration of his letters in the Chambre des comptes.

135. ADLA B 84, fol. 258; B 357, "Sans avoir à l'omission de la clause faisant profession de la R.P.R. on ait a proceder à l'enregistrement pur et simple desdits lettres": AN P 2671, registration of 5 August 1613.

136. Bacquet, *Oeuvres*, 1:74; Lefebvre de la Planche, *Mémoires*, 2:173, notes that "on regarde cet usage présentement comme de style."

137. Boizet, *Les Lettres de naturalité*, 92–94.

138. Lefebvre de la Planche, *Mémoires*, 2:175; BN MS 338501, no. 91, fol. 54: "Lettres patentes du roi par lesquelles Sa Majesté a confirmé celles qui ont été données par ses prédécesseurs, portant que la moitié de toutes les sommes de deniers qui seront converties et employées, in pios usus, adjugées par nos gens de la chambre des comptes, touchant les lettres de naturalité, légitimation et annoblissement seront données aux pauvres enfants de la Sainte Trinité de la ville de Paris" (n.p., 1574).

139. AN AD XV 1, no. 111, *Lettres patentes*, 17 September 1582. The practice served the monarchy well, especially with the imposition of the 1697 Naturalization Tax, when the tax-farmers and their clerks pursued already naturalized foreigners through these archives: see Dubost and Sahlins, *Et si on faisait payer*, 97–125.

140. Lefebvre de la Planche, *Mémoires*, 2:175.

141. Comte de Mortaigne: AN P 2593, fol. 26, registration of naturalization, May 1748; Lefebvre de la Planche, *Mémoires*, 2:182.

142. Bayard, "Naturalization in Lyon," passim.

143. The revival of Roman "insinuation" had begun in the sixteenth century, but reached its highest form under Louis XIV: see Massaloux, *La Régie*, 7–8. Article 17 of the edict of December 1703 is reproduced in Bosquet, *Dictionnaire raisonné*, 2:284–85. The edict established the cost to the beneficiaries at fifty livres, a sum restated in the royal declaration of 27 September 1707, but increased to one hundred livres by article 10 of the royal tariff of 29 September 1722.

144. Denisart, *Collection* (1773), 3:346, citing the case of an Italian, Borio, who successfully claimed the estate of a French native, Boulanger, decided by the Paris parlement in 1747.

145. Mathorez, *Les Etrangers en France*, 1:140; Boizet, *Les Lettres de naturalité*, 115, has argued that, in addition, the letter of naturalization, as a "contract signed between the king and the petitioner, is a favor or a grace that is essentially personal and precarious" and that it had to be renewed at the beginning of each reign, subject to a "right of royal advent." At the beginning of each reign, he claimed, "one had to purchase each time the sovereign's favor." Although it is true that many foreigners did pay the advent tax (as evidenced in the domanial tax rolls at the accession of Louis XV, for example, in AN Q/3/90–92), this confirmation of royal letters patent was never mentioned by the jurists, and the tax remained a singular fiscal expedient: on the tax, see M. Marion, *Histoire financière de la France depuis 1715*, 5 vols. (Paris, 1919), 1:122–23.

146. AN K 174, no. 40; the requirement was reiterated periodically through the eighteenth

century: see, e.g., the *arrest du Conseil* of 12 March 1735, in AN PP 151 and the jurisprudence cited in Bacquet, *Oeuvres*, 1:180–82.

147. Denisart, *Collection* (1773), 3:344.

148. Boizet, *Les Lettres de naturalité*, 104–7.

149. AN o/1/238, fol. 220, 229.

150. Tessereau, *Histoire chronologique*, 1:353, 703, 2:759–80. The secretary who drafted the letter received half the honorarium; the other half went to a *bourse commune* (341).

151. Michaud, *La Grande Chancellerie*, 263; Saint-Simon is quoted ibid., 219.

152. AAE MD France 1454, fol. 124, case of Pierre François de Meurisse, born in Bruges, whose letter was sent by the foreign ministry to the chancellery requesting that he be issued a declaration, "which costs half as much" as naturalization. The estimate of salaries is from M. Baulant, "Les Salaires des ouvriers du batiment de Paris de 1400 à 1726," *Annales ESC* (March–April 1971), no. 2: 480; and P. Goubert, *The French Peasantry in the Seventeenth Century* (Cambridge, 1989), 101.

153. For example, Pierre de Redmond described himself in his naturalization of July 1727 as having left Ireland "for religious reasons" and fled to Portugal where he had five children, all of whom came to France several years before. The letter was granted, but it had not been registered at the Chambre du domaine, which produced trouble for his heirs. When his widow, Dame Anne Parker, died in 1747, the district attorney of the Chambre du domaine obtained a decree from the Bureau des finances to confiscate the inheritance. Their children showed the letters of naturalization, but the fiscal officer challenged its validity, claiming that the letter hadn't been registered at the Chambre du domaine. To end all these difficulties, "because of the omission of this formality the necessity of which was unknown," the children successfully sought to register the letters, notwithstanding their surannuation: AN o/1/224, fol. 58, naturalization draft of July, 1727; ibid., fol. 60, patent letters for the registration of this naturalization, 22 July 1747. In another example, Jean Ferdinand de Poitiers, a military officer born in Liège, received in May 1740 letters that "maintained" his original letter of naturalization issued in 1703, which he had failed to pick up from the Chambre des comptes, the archives of which had burnt (he noted) in 1737: AN o/1/227, fol. 31.

154. To cite two examples: in 1736, Antoinette Constance Marie Therèse Treggius Dorival, a widow from Bologna living in Metz, sought a "reformation" of a set of original letters, already registered at the courts in Paris and insinuated at Metz, in which she was named "by mistake" Anne instead of Antoinette, Treggius was written Freggius, and she was born in 1695, not 1697. She received new letters in July 1757, but those still were full of errors, she claimed: AN O/1/226, fol. 53 (June 1736), 205 (July 1737); AN O/1/228, fol. 6, draft reformation of naturalization, March 1738. In another example, Dominique François Pou de Piefleury of Holland originally received letters of naturalization in February 1759, and his wife Amelie Thèrese got hers in March 1761, but since his name on both letters was spelled "Poe" instead of "Pou," and because of other errors of transcription, they feared "under the pretext of these errors and omissions of names they might be troubled in the possession of her privileges and advantages in which we had wanted them to participate." They received additional letters in October 1765, which were registered at the Paris Chambre des comptes the following May: AN O/1/233, fol. 301; AN P 2597, fol. 18v. On the use and abuse of "errors" within patent letters of naturalization, see below, chap. 3.

155. Lefebvre de la Planche, *Mémoires*, 2:174.

Chapter 3: The Use and Abuse of Naturalization

1. Michaud, *La Grande Chancellerie*, 251. Damour is quoted in AN E 675(B), fol. 274, arrêt of the council of state, 13 May 1698. That the preambles were not exclusively written by the royal secretaries themselves can be demonstrated by a sampling of 161 naturalizations and declarations in register AN O/1/234 (1767–71). These contain the signatures of seventy-three royal secretaries—of the three hundred or so attached to the Great Chancellery in Paris. More than two-thirds of the secretaries or their clerks authored only one letter; of the others, only a handful produced more than five, and a certain Domilliers signed off on twenty-six. The secretaries that

authored more than one letter did not consistently reproduce the same formulas, and the variations in the narratives can thus be attributed, in part, to the petitioners themselves.

2. For an inventive reading of the expository sections of letters of pardon and remission that explores the narrative and fictional elements of the law, see Natalie Zemon Davis, *Fiction in the Archives: Pardon Tales and Their Tellers in Sixteenth-Century France* (Stanford, 1987), to which this chapter is intellectually and methodologically indebted; for some reflections on the uses of "stories" in recent cultural history, see S. Maza, "Stories in History: Cultural Narratives in Recent Works in European History," *American Historical Review* 101 (1996): 1493–1515.

3. Davis, *Fiction in the Archives*, 3–6. For a set of philosophical and cognitive reflections on the "fiction and reality" of identity, see T. Kozakai, *L'Etranger, l'identité: Esssai sur l'intégration culturelle* (Paris, 2000), 89–137.

4. Only rarely were jurists specifically cited in narrative preambles; an example among the few instances that invoke legal treatises is the narrative exposé of Pierre François de Meurisse, born in Bruges and naturalized in 1779, who explicitly cites Jean Bacquet, among others (AAE MD France 1454, fol. 124). More rare still were developed legal arguments based on public international law and affirmed by royal letters patent, such as the narrative composed in the name of Hubert Charles le Roi, a Dutch Catholic merchant in France and Martinique, who invoked commercial treaties as far back as 1613 and letters patent of 1751 to justify the claim that he didn't legally need to be declared a natural Frenchman, but sought to do so anyway: AN O/1/238, fol. 99, draft declaration of 10 May 1786.

5. Vanel, *Evolution historique*, 54–55.

6. The estimated five hundred traces of naturalizations and declarations used in this sample of more than six thousand letters that contained stories, however abbreviated, of the petitioner's lives and intentions suggest that the different narrative choices and the language of citizenship in the narrative sections of the letters of naturalization were not linked to specific groups of foreigners. There is no distinctively "Flemish" claim, for example, beyond the invocation of geographic proximity and historical relations to the French crown, discussed below (chap. 5). Nor did these choices vary over the time period under consideration, from 1660 to 1790, with the exception of the very last petitions in the series, which show a distinct "contamination" by revolutionary language, occasionally invoking general principles of the "rights of the citizen" (below, chap. 7).

7. The case is reconstructed from the collection of printed pamphlets or *factum* found in BACA Collection Chanclaire, vol. 90, no. 50; vol. 92, nos. 43, 45–47, and vol. 93, no. 5. For background on the French conquest and incorporation of Alsace under Louis XIV, see R. Reuss, *L'Alsace au XVIIe siècle* (Paris, 1904); and more recently, J. Siat, *Histoire du rattachement de l'Alsace à la France* (Saint-Etienne, 1997). On the demographic mobility of the population in the province and the backdrop of the lawsuit in question, see J.-P. Kirtz, "La Mobilité humaine en Alsace, XVIe–XVIIIe siècle," *Annales de démographie historique* (1970): 157–83.

8. AN O/1/224, fol. 386, draft naturalization, October 1731; O/1/225, fol. 3, draft declaration, 28 January 1732.

9. BACA Collection Chanclaire, vol. 92, no. 45, "Mémoire (signifié) pour Dame Marie Jeanne Thanner, femme du sieur Leopold Wimpf, soneiller au Magistrat de Colmar, et Consorts," signed by the barrister Guisain d'Orsigny (1738). Vol. 92, no. 43, "Mémoire pour Joseph-Clerment Marie de Yonner . . . signifié le 25 mai 1739," signed by the barrister Charlet.

10. Maître Charlet argued the case against Dame Wimpf and consorts in terms of "public law" and the "interest of the nation." The invocation and appropriation of "national interests" was surprisingly rare in the jurisprudence of inheritance disputes involving foreigners—unlike, for example, in the administrative contention of rural communities in the French-Spanish borderland during the eighteenth century, which cloaked their local interests in the language of national difference: see Sahlins, *Boundaries*, esp. chap. 4. Even late eighteenth-century civil law practitioners rarely used the language of the "nation," unlike their more activist colleagues of the Paris parlement who used printed court cases (*factum*) involving "private lives" to make big arguments critical of the "public affairs" of the crown: see, e.g., S. Maza, *Private Lives and Public Affairs*; and below, chap. 7.

11. Parallel claims of "badly-obtained letters of naturalization" were put forth by descendants of French parents taxed in 1697. Their arguments before the royal council insisted that their par-

ents' grants were either not necessary, or (in the case of Louis Jourdan de La Salle, a commissioner at the Châtelet court, taxed in 1697 and who obtained a reduction) that his father's letters "were useless to him and had been obtained unscrupulously": see Dubost and Sahlins, *Et si on faisait payer,* 329.

12. M. Viroli, *For Love of Country: An Essay on Patriotism and Nationalism* (Oxford, 1995); Bell, *Cult of the Nation,* passim; and below, chap. 7.

13. AN K 174, registration at the Paris Chambre des comptes, 14 June 1673.

14. AN O/1/224, fol. 180, draft naturalization of February 1729; AN K 175, no. 117, registration at the Paris Chambre des comptes, 5 May 1729. The case concerned one Antoine Armand, born in the Tyrol, and working in the royal mint in Paris. He was being rewarded "for his work in discovering two very useful techniques currently being used, one for the smelting, and the other for metal refinery."

15. AN O/1/221, fol. 69, draft naturalization of 1716; see also the case of François Bocconi, brought to France at the age of four, who narrated expansively about his father's contribution to the service of Louis XIV as a general inspector of saltpeter and gunpowder, as already rewarded by numerous privileges: AN o/1/223, fol. 189, draft naturalization of June 1724; AN K 175, no. 48, registration at the Paris Chambre des comptes, 11 July 1724.

16. AN O/1/229, fol. 386, draft declaration, July 10, 1751; AN P 2594, fol. 51, registration at the Paris Chamber des comptes, August 1751. There were, of course, famous musicians and artists at the court of Louis XIV and after, including Vigarani and Lully: on these and other foreign artists at court, see M. Benoit, *Versailles et les musiciens du Roi, 1661–1733: Etudes institutionnelle et sociale* (Paris, 1971), 263–81; and for the earlier period more generally, see M. Paquot, *Les Étrangers dans les divertissements de la cour, de Beaujoyeulz à Molière, 1581–1673* (Brussels, 1933); and Dubost, *La France italienne,* passim.

17. AN K 173, no. 160, registration at the Paris Chambre des comptes, 9 February 1666. Caron had been in the Indies from 1619 to 1641. He only settled in France in 1665 with his wife, "Constancia Boudavent," and was subsequently to author a "True Description of the Mighty Kingdoms of Japan and Siam" (the first by a nonmissionary), before being accused of securing a false patent of nobility: see D. F. Lach and E. J. Van Kley, *Asia in the Making of Europe,* vol. 3, pt. 4: *Southeast Asia* (Chicago, 1993), 1855–68 et seq.

18. In the eighteenth century, the French monarchy rewarded foreigners who made industrial contributions with naturalization. Jean Holker, of Lancaster, England, had been settled in Rouen for twenty years when he sought naturalization in 1766. Holker's contribution was to give "the secret of an entirely new way of preparing cloth hitherto unknown in France, which gained him the commission of Inspector General of Manufacturers" in Rouen, where he had also established a manufactory of cotton velours: AN O/1/233, fol. 335, draft naturalization for Holker, his wife and son, 29 January 1766.

19. AN o/1/223, fol. 286, draft naturalization, July 1725. Gaultier Archer, born in Ross, Ireland, declared how he had "acquired the confidence of the inhabitants and traders of La Rochelle who several times confided in him their interest in our Oceans on which he made several voyages to the great satisfaction of the public": AN O/1/225, fol. 392, draft naturalization, October 1735, apparently registered in July 1739 [AN P 2592], although Archer renewed his demand in 1741: AN O/1/225, vol. 227, fol. 102.

20. AN O/1/227, fol. 362, draft naturalization of July 1743. In fact, Mainetto had requested letters in 1722, along with a large number of Genoese whose letters were revoked for nonresidence. His own claim was that he had "desired" to come live in France, but had not been able to move until later: ibid., fols. 362, 307. On the revocation of all letters in 1720, see the edict in AN AD XV 1, edict of February 1720.

21. AN Joly de Fleury 2494, fol. 38; Sahlins, "Fictions of a Catholic France," 100–102; on Cerf Berr's role as an "enlightened" part-time manufacturer and landowner, who bought feudal land on which he seems to have made a futile attempt to settle some poor Jews, see Hertzberg, *French Enlightenment,* 73 and passim. On the French intendancies' use of Jews in Metz and Alsace to supply grain in times of famine, see M. Lemalet, "Juifs et intendants au XVIIe siècle," *XVIIe siècle,* 183 (1994): 290–92.

22. AN O/1/238, fol. 281, draft naturalization of Sapin; O/1/221, fol. 311; AN PP 151, regis-

tration at the Paris Chambre des comptes, 23 March 1719. Elizabeth Morey, born near Portsmouth, England, and living in Cherbourg, sought naturalization in 1782. In the inquiry of the Chambre des comtes, local clergy, gentlemen, municipal officers, and others testified that she had no fortune at all, and only sought letters so as to bequeath her few goods "that she could save from her work" to the poor of Cherbourg: AN O/1/237, fol. 101, declaration draft, 30 January 1782; ADSM B 2B 361, inquiry of the Chambre, registered 5 August 1784.

23. AN O/1/223, fol. 138, draft declaration, 12 February 1724; AN K 175, no. 97, registration at the Paris Chambre des comptes, 23 April 1728. Other arguments based on medical contributions to the kingdom include Jean Batiste Dandora de Polemon, born in Constantinople and trained as a surgeon, who came to France at the age of twenty-four in 1724 in the entourage of the French ambassador, whom he then followed to Switzerland and later to Strasbourg. Serving in the hospitals of that town, then in various regiments, Dandora left his mark: "Given the reports that have been made to us on his experience with his art, of his good qualities and of his affection for our service, we then named him Surgeon General of the military hospital in Douai, where he has fixed his residence": AN O/1/228, fol. 373, draft naturalization, March 1748. Ernest Frédéric Pietsch, born in Brandenburg in 1723, not only translated German works on medicine and surgery into French but in 1761 began to train the surgeons and midwives of Alsace, and spent many years lecturing and demonstrating his skills. "Hoping he will continue to make himself useful," the king awarded him the qualities of "our true and natural subject and native resident": AN O/1/237, fol. 70, draft naturalization, July 1781.

24. AN O/1/230, fol. 316, draft naturalization, April 1754.

25. AN V/1/542, 446, copy of naturalization, April 1692; AN K 174, no. 55, registration at the Paris Chambre des comptes, 26 January 1693.

26. Viroli, *For Love of Country*, esp. 18–41.

27. AN O/1/236, fol. 354, draft declaration, 1779; another example is in AN O/1/220, fol. 9, draft naturalization of Jean-François Kiecler, 1701.

28. AN O/1/226, fol. 23, draft naturalization of November 1737; P 2592, fol. 9, registration at the Paris Chambre des comptes, 12 March 1738; another example of such "ancestor worship" that stresses family service to the kingdom is the letter given to Robert Dillon, a descendant of the Jacobite Arthur Dillon, who had worked as a banker in Bordeaux before purchasing an estate nearby, and among whose thirteen naturalized children were four who served in the Dillon Regiment or at the court of Louis XV: AN O/1/230, fol. 367, draft naturalization of June 1754.

29. AN P 2600, fol. 5, registration at the Paris Chambre des comptes of declaration of naturalization, 2 March 1775; his ancestor's grant can be found in AN O/1/218, fol. 204, draft naturalization and ennoblement, January 1665.

30. AN O/1/234, fols. 30, 32, draft naturalization, August 1767.

31. AN O/1/238, fol. 137, draft declaration of 28 February 1787. Other examples include Jean-Baptiste de Lavedan, who became a citizen in 1775 in order to inherit the office of his father, a royal officer in the financial bureau in Toulouse, which he had acquired after returning from Spain, where his son had been born: AN O/1/235, fol. 375; and Prosper Vincent, who had purchased the office of *huissier audiencier* at the financial bureau of Lyon, but in order to be received by the corporation, needed to be naturalized, which he was in December 1763: AN P 2597, fol. 14v, registration at the Paris Chambre des comptes, 10 April 1764.

32. AN O/1/223, fol. 283, draft naturalization, July 1725.

33. For example, Antoinette Andlau's father was born in Ensisheim, Alsace, but later moved to Basel, "a neutral country within the alliance of the Swiss cantons." In 1710, she sought French citizenship in order to be elected to administrative offices of the noble Abbey of Masmünster in Upper Alsace: AN O/1/220, fol. 160; Sophie Louise de Spak, a converted Catholic, born a Lutheran in Sweden, noted how "her zeal and passion for her estate had made her ecclesiastical superiors name her a prioress" in the Abbey of Panthemont, for which she needed letters of naturalization: AN O/1/235, fol. 38, draft declaration, 19 June 1772.

34. AN O/1/220, fol. 265, draft naturalization, March 1713.

35. AN O/1/219, fol. 149, draft naturalization, December 1688; a copy of the naturalization grant in AAE France 1454, fol. 13; O/1/221, fol. 232, draft confirmation of naturalization with surannuation, July 1718.

36. AN O/1/221, fol. 181, draft declaration of naturalization, 24 March 1718.

37. AN O/1/220, fol. 394, draft naturalization of Praisendorf, July 1715; O/1/220, fol. 237, draft naturalization of Hooghstoel, August 1712.

38. AN K 173, no. 129, copy of naturalization, February 1660; PP 151, registration at the Paris Chambre des comptes, 5 March 1660.

39. BN MS JF 306, fols. 252–56, copies of letters of April 1760 and declaration of 22 April 1760; AN P 2596, fol. 32, registration of letters at the Paris Chambre des comptes.

40. AN O/1/231, fol. 290, request of d'Argenson for naturalization, 10 November 1756; ibid., fol. 313, draft naturalization, January 1757.

41. AN O/1/225, fol. 357, draft declaration of 16 June 1735.

42. S. Hanley, "Engendering the State: Family Formation and State-building in Early Modern France," *French Historical Studies* 16 (1989): 4–27.

43. On nineteenth-century usages outside of the law, see Noiriel, "Socio-histoire d'un concept."

44. AN O/1/226, fol. 91, draft naturalization of Louis Palyart, January 1739; AN O/1/238, fol. 61, draft declaration of Ritte Palyart, 23 November 1785. On the Portuguese in Rouen, see F. de Vaux de Foletier, "Les Portugais à Rouen au XVIIe–XVIIIe siècle," *Revue des sociétés savantes de Haute Normandie* 7 (1957): 33–42. For an excellent example of the kind of local study that can address the question of social assimilation, here of Iberians in Rouen, see G. Brunelle, "Immigration, Assimilation, and Success: Three Families of Spanish Origin in Sixteenth-Century Rouen," *Sixteenth Century Journal* 20 (1989): 203–19.

45. AN O/1/230, fol. 235, draft declaration of 18 July 1753. Claude François de Lannoy provides another such example, when he argued in December 1708 that his birth in the Spanish Low Countries was "a pure accident" that occurred because his mother, when traveling to Spanish Flanders, had found herself "so burdened from her pregnancy" that she couldn't return to France: AN O/1/232, fol. 198, draft naturalization of June 1758; AN P 2595, fol. 49v, registration at the Paris Chambre des comptes.

46. AN O/1/232, fol. 198, draft naturalization of June 1759; AN P 2595, fol. 49v, registration at the Paris Chambre des comptes.

47. AN O/1/235, fol. 139, draft declaration, 23 June 1773.

48. Vergennes intervened in the case of Jean François de Caul, born of French parents in the comté de Chiny (province of Luxembourg), named to an ecclesiastical benefice on French territory, and "fearing trouble" because of his birth outside of France. Vergennes argued, citing d'Aguesseau, Le Bret, Bignon, and others, that the claimant did not need recommendation letters from the Brussels authorities, despite a recent agreement between France and Austria that required a mutual and reciprocal approval when foreign priests were nominated to cures of souls on French territory, even though this territory was under the jurisdiction of an ecclesiastical province of the Austrian monarchy: AN O/1/236, fol. 42; AAE MD France 1454, fols. 86, 99, 100–104, 106. For a more complete discussion of the complications arising from overlapping jurisdictions during the eighteenth century, see below, chap. 6.

49. AN O/1/221, fol. 128, draft naturalization, August 1717.

50. AN O/1/238, fol. 286; Parin had received earlier letters patent permitting him to hold ecclesiastical office with income up to twelve hundred pounds, in May 1782 (O/1/237, fol. 119); see also the commentary by the minister of foreign affairs, also part of French efforts to administer benefices in a region where foreign ecclesiastical jurisdictions and royal territory interwined: AAE MD France 1454, fol. 234.

51. AN O/1/220, fol. 179, draft naturalization, December 1710.

52. AN O/1/229, fol. 174, draft declaration, 15 February 1750. On the Irish in Bordeaux, see below, chap. 5.

53. AN O/1/223, fol. 207, draft naturalization, July 1724.

54. AN O/1/233, fol. 185, draft naturalization of June 1764.

55. AN O/1/222, fol. 329, draft declaration, 29 June 1722; copy of naturalization in AAE MD France 1454, fol. 16.

56. AN O/1/225, fol. 45, draft naturalization, June 1732.

57. AN O/1/219, fol. 285, draft naturalization, February 1700. Marie Joseph Poujol, born in Genoa of a French father, claimed to have kept "the natural inclination which she had for her

original country" given to her by her father. As evidence of this inclination, she returned to France and married a surgeon in Saint-Cloud. She was granted citzenship in May 1719: AN O/1/221, fol. 339, draft naturalization.

58. In fact, more detailed and local studies reveal the centrality of the family in practice as well: see, for example, C. Dolan, "Famille et intégration des etrangers à Aix-en-Provence au XVIe siècle," *Provence historique* 35, no. 142 (1989): 401–13; or Brunelle, "Immigration, Assimilation, and Success," passim.

59. After 1803, French law made nationality into a status of persons, and placed an emphasis (despite Napoleon Bonaparte's intentions) on the centrality of family descent; yet in the "republican model" put in place by the end of the nineteenth century, and especially in the 1889 nationality law, the attribution of nationality shifted back to territory, and the presumed socialization that would occur, through mandatory primary schooling and military service, growing up in France: see P. Weil, *Mission d'étude des législations de la nationalité et de l'immigration* (Paris, 1997), 19–20; and *Qu'est-ce qu'un Français?* passim.

60. d'Aguesseau, *Oeuvres* 2:595–620.

61. Above, chap. 1.

62. AN o/1/227, fol. 288.

63. AN o/1/238, fol. 156, draft naturalization of Jacques Antoine Reymond de Saint-Sulpice, a converted Calvinist from Lausanne (Switzerland), 23 June 1787.

64. AN o/1/230, fol. 389. Following the royal edict of 25 January 1683 directed against the Protestant "cult," "Mahométans et idolatres" could only convert to the Catholic faith: Isambert et al., *Recueil général*, 14:414–15. Accounts of Muslim baptisms appeared frequently in the quasi-official journals *Gazette de France* and the *Mercure Galant* during the 1680s against a backdrop of the crown's repression of Protestants and efforts to redeem French slaves in North Africa: on the latter, see G. L. Weiss, "Back from Barbary: Captivity, Redemption, and French Identity in the Seventeenth and Eighteenth Century Mediterranean World," Ph.D. diss., Stanford University, 2002.

65. AN o/1/222, fol. 19. Others brought involuntarily include Marie Julie Julistanne, a Muslim from Hungary, who was a daughter of a Turkish officer, taken at the age of two by the Imperial Army, then put under the protection of a French gentleman who brought her to France and had her baptized, and now at the age of twenty-nine she sought to "finish her life as a true subject and native resident": AN o/1/220, fol. 214; o/1/221, fol. 112; PP 151. Jean Baptiste Taha, naturalized in January 1711, was taken at the seige of Bude and brought to France at the age of six by the Marquis de Heron, who had him baptized in April 1689, after which Taha became his servant: AN o/1/220, fol. 183.

66. AN o/1/227, fol. 303.

67. AN o/1/236, fol. 242. The metaphor was frequently used in the sixteenth century: see Boniface, *Arrests notables*, 1:331–37, quoting its usage by the French legal humanist Jacques Cujas (1500–1590).

68. AN o/1/223, fol. 89.

69. AN o/1/220, fol. 320. Nor was it simply Muslims and Jews who told stories of family abandonment. Yves Knight, naturalized in August 1705, had been sent over by his family from England in 1680 "to learn the French language." After having embraced the Catholic faith and "renounced the heresy of the Anabaptists," he was "abandoned by his family such that ever since he has been supported by the alms of several charitable persons": ADLA B 92, fol. 369v.

70. AN K 174, no. 58, copy of naturalization and legitimation, 16 October 1693.

71. AN O/1/227, fol. 176, draft declaration of naturalization, 31 January 1742.

72. Bacquet, *Oeuvres*, 2:54. On the contested status of the law *unde vir et uxor* and its application to foreign widows, see G. Loüet, *Recueil de plusieurs arrests notables du Parlement de Paris contenant un grand nombre de décisions recueillies par Maître Julien Brodeau*, 2 vols. (Paris, 1742), 1:58–59, covering the seventeenth-century jurisprudence; and the commentary on the case involving the estate of the Dane Nonmacher, who died in Paris in 1777, by Jean-François Joly de Fleury, councillor of state: AN MS JF 543, fols. 343–46.

73. For example, see Augéard, *Arrests notables*, 1:161–65, on the marriage of Anne Meusnier from Savoy to Nicolas de Maisonneuve. Bacquet only considered how a married male foreigner and his wife (native or foreigner) could exchange goods by reciprocal donation, but never con-

sidered whether the marriage of a foreigner and a native would confer French citizenship: *Oeuvres*, 2:60.

74. AN O/1/222, fol. 384, draft declaration, 20 September 1722.

75. AN O/1/237, fol. 172, draft naturalization, 1782.

76. AN O/1/232, fol. 232, draft declaration, 10 August 1759; AN P 2595, fol. 47, registration at the Paris Chambre des comptes, 1 July 1760. In another case, Marie Antoinette de Leyonsted, born in Stockholm, had been married to a gentleman and seigneur from Perigord, who had been secretary to the French ambassador to Sweden, and subsequently minister of the Republic of Poland. Before he died, he "had inspired in her sentiments of faithfulness and attachment to our crown." Indeed, upon his death, she came to France to fix her domicile and end her days, receiving a letter of naturalization in 1755: AN O/1/231, fol. 82, naturalization of July 1755; AN P 2595, fol. 50, registration at the Paris Chambre des comptes. In another case, a woman abandoned by her husband petitioned the king to restore her "birthright." Marie Catherine Jaume, the abandoned wife of Antoine Ojardas, was born in Nice of a French merchant. She claimed in 1752 that because the attachment her father "had always kept for our kingdom had made him wish to see his children established here, he took care to raise the petitioner in France." Now abandoned by her husband, Marie Jaume sought to participate in the "rights that her father and ancestors had acquired by birth": AN O/1/230, fol. 71, draft declaration, 16 June 1752; AN P 2594, fol. 75, registration at the Paris Chambre des comptes. Note that the late seventeenth-century jurisprudence of the Paris parlement deprived a French woman of citizenship if she was married to a foreigner and remained abroad after the death of her husband: Vanel, *Evolution historique*, 79.

77. AN O/1/230, fol. 96, draft naturalization, July 1752.

78. AN O/1/231, fol. 196, draft naturalization, March 1756.

79. Kettner, *Development of American Citizenship*, 13–63; R. Kiefé, "L'Allégeance," in *La Nationalité dans la science sociale et dans le droit contemporain* (Paris, 1933), 47–68; and F. Terré, "Réflections sur la notion de nationalité," *Revue de droit internationale privé* 99 (1975): 197–214. For a development of the notion of will in Old Regime law, see R. H. Tison, *La Prise de l'autonomie de la volonté dans l'ancien droit français* (Paris, 1931).

80. D'Aguesseau, *Oeuvres*, 2:618.

81. AN O/1/236, fol. 128, draft declaration, 4 October 1777; ibid., fol. 151, 12 December 1777 (reissued because the first one had an error in his name); ibid., P 2601, fol. 24v, registration at the Paris Chambre des comptes, April 1778.

82. Weil, *Qu'est-ce qu'un Français*, pt. 2.

Chapter 4: Status and Socioprofessional Identities

1. Dubost and Sahlins, *Et si on faisait payer,* 129–30. The proportion accords as well with the several hundred foreigners who registered their letters with the tax bureaux in Lyon during the Old Regime: see Bayard, "Naturalization," 280–81.

2. On Spain, Herzog, "Communal Definition," 89; on Italy, Gilli, "Comment cesser d'être étranger," 59 and n. 1; on the New Regime, below, chap. 8. For an example of how marriage occasionally made it necessary, in the claimants' eyes, to seek naturalization: the case of Marie Philippes, born in Nevers in France, "even though a natural Frenchwoman, had married [Hyacinthe Bianky] and made her fortune in a long stay in Poland." Husband and wife both "feared that under this pretext, they would be prevented from enjoying their goods," and sought a joint naturalization: AN K 173, no. 165, copy of naturalization of January 1668, registered at the Paris parlement on 14 September of that year.

3. Dubost and Sahlins, *Et si on faisait payer,* 129–30; below, chaps. 7–8, on women and citizenship in the New Regime.

4. Widows often sought recourse before the royal council, claiming exemption from the tax on the basis of their not having community of property with a foreigner; their arguments were often successful. See Dubost and Sahlins, *Et si faisait payer,* 308–10.

5. Papon, *Secrets*, 447 (citing biblical texts). Such a bias was evident in the administrative documentation of naturalization, both in the tax rolls of 1697–1707 and in the individual naturaliza-

tions of 1660–1790. Although a few women were identified as members of the titled nobility (countesses, marquises, duchesses) and allied royal families, more rarely were women's identities disclosed except in relation to their husbands and families. Thus we can learn relatively little from the state's archives about their professions. Although we occasionally glimpse the identity of a "laundress" or a (female) "merchant" (*marchande*), most of their social identities remained unspecified—even though women tended to develop elaborate narratives justifying their naturalization (above, chap. 3).

6. Thuret: AN O/1/222, fol. 366, draft naturalization of July 1722; AN O/1/223, fol. 99, Badouin: draft declaration of 11 September 1723.

7. Above, chap. 3.

8. Dubost and Sahlins, *Et si on faisait payer*, 149. It should be recalled that the livre was a "money of accounting" that did not correspond to a set metallic value until 1726, and that its value varied after that in different provinces of the realm. The archives yielded no traces of a tax schedule, so these sums reflect state assessments (in the two senses of the word) and not the actual wealth of foreigners (or bastards) taxed.

9. Bayard, "Naturalizations," 306, basing her research on registrations at the treasury bureaux in Lyon, found that among 110 naturalized foreigners in the seventeenth and eighteenth centuries who declared their wealth, 13 percent claimed less than 100 livres; 21 percent between 100 and 499 livres; 21 percent between 500 and 999 livres; 27 percent between 1,000 and 4,999 livres; and 18 percent over 5,000 livres.

10. AN o/1/231, fol. 155; ADLA B 103, fol. 12r; the Nantes Chambre des comptes inquiry is in ADLA B 491.

11. For a succint account summarizing the numbers of nobles and patterns of ennoblement in the eighteenth century, see J. Meyer, "Noblesse française au XVIIIe siècle," *Acta poloniae historica* 26 (1977): 15–21. The democratization of naturalization since the sixteenth century ran parallel to the increasingly "popular" character of immigration more generally, already evident in the early seventeenth century among the Italians: Dubost, *La France italienne*, esp. chap. 12. On nobles taxed in 1697, see Dubost and Sahlins, *Et si on faisait payer*, 138–39, including sources (such as the capitation tax rolls of 1695) on the estimated proportion of titled nobility in the kingdom.

12. AN o/1/231, fol. 380, draft naturalization, July 1757; AN P 2596, registration at the Paris Chambre des comptes, 7 May 1760.

13. ADSM B 2B 361; AN O/1/237, fol. 101: draft declaration (?) of naturalization, 30 January 1782, registered at Rouen, 5 August 1784.

14. Bayard, "Naturalization," 308; AN O/1/232, fol. 139, draft naturalization, January 1759; AN P 2595, fol. 16v, registration at the Paris Chambre des comptes, 13 March 1759.

15. ADLA B 481: AN o/1/229, fol. 32, draft naturalization, March 1749; ADLA B 101, fol. 283r: registration at the Nantes Chambre des comptes, 24 April 1749.

16. Jacques Butler, a priest from Ireland holding a cure in Brittany, received his naturalization in January 1747, and the "inquiry into his life and mores" performed by the Nantes court found that "the said Butler currently has no movable property or furnishings, nor even a permanent residence in the city of Nantes nor elsewhere, and to survive he is obliged to be a vicar or chaplain on land or at sea," which didn't prevent the court from registering his letter: ADLA B 481, inquiry based on letters of January 1747 in AN O/1/228, fols. 211, 299 [redone in February 1749] and registered 8 February 1749 at Nantes, ADLA B 101.

17. J. Dupâquier, *La Population rurale du Bassin parisien à l'époque de Louis XIV* (Paris, 1972), 193–98, 205–10.

18. Dubost and Sahlins, *Et si on faisait payer*, esp. chap. 8, for a discussion of how the settlement of foreigners in the kingdom complicated the geographic and economic divisions of the kingdom into "several Frances" found within the work of F. Braudel, *Civilization and Capitalism, Fifteenth–Eighteenth Century*, 3 vols., trans. S. Reynolds (New York, 1986), 3:315–52; and I. Wallerstein, *The Modern World System*, 2 vols. (New York, 1974–80), 1:263–69. For an overview of the urban framework in the Old Regime, see E. Le Roy Ladurie, ed., *La Ville classique de la Renaissance aux révolutions*, vol. 3 of *Histoire de la France urbaine*, ed. G. Duby (Paris, 1981).

19. Papon, *Secrets*, 451–52; Héricourt du Vautier, *Loix ecclésiastiques de France*, 428–29.

20. Dubost, *Les Etrangers en France*, 44–46.

21. Blondeau and Gueret, *Journal du Palais*, 2:798–800; see also Bosquet, *Dictionnaire raisonné*, 1:171, citing an arrêt du conseil of 20 January 1728 that reiterated the prohibition, and formally underscored that simple permissions to hold benefices did not entail in themselves naturalization, "the right of the citizen" (*le droit de citoyen*), as he unusually called it. The case concerned a dispute between the king and the comte de Soissons, who was claiming the estate of sieur Bauban, a priest in Bregny, originally from Liège; the bailiff of the comte de Soissons had argued that Bauban did not die an aubain, and that therefore his estate could be confiscated by the count through his seignurial prerogatives. On the case of the English Benedictines, see Lefebvre de la Planche, *Mémoires*, 2:48.

22. On the functions and social status of French priests in the eighteenth century, see R. Simon-Sandras, *Les Curés à la fin de l'Ancien Régime* (Paris, 1988).

23. AN O/1/230, fol. 243, draft naturalization, July 1753.

24. AN O/1/226, fol. 221, draft naturalization, September 1737. Collin would have lived through the Dutch occupation of Lille in 1708 that so abruptly shifted allegiances of the city toward Louis XVI and France, at least according to L. Trénard, "La Notion de 'naturalité' à Lille au XVIIIe siècle," *Cahiers Plisnier* (Brussels, 1959), 87–93.

25. AN O/1/235, fol. 288, draft naturalization, February 1772; see also AAE MD France 1454, fol. 69, which involved correspondece with the foreign minister because of the diplomatic struggles over reciprocity in the French borderland with the Austrian Low Countries: see below, chap. 6.

26. AAE MD Germany 94, fol. 118, naturalization draft of July 1688, registered August 1694 in the Paris Chambre des comptes; AN K 175, no. 31; AN PP 151.

27. AN O/1/235, fol. 139.

28. AN O/1/235, fol. 18, draft naturalization, March 1722.

29. AN O/1/231, fol. 7; AN P 2595, registration in the Paris Chambre des comptes, April 1755. Other high-ranking regular clergy included one archdeacon (Joseph Alziary, born in the county of Nice, archdeacon of the Cathedral Church in Vence in Provence, naturalized with permission to hold benefices in 1763) and seventy deacons, as well as lower-ranked clerics who took religious vows (such as the Irish subsexton John Drady, working in the church of Angers, naturalized in May 1778 [draft, AN O/1/236, fol. 187]).

30. Lefebvre de la Planche, *Mémoires*, 1:34.

31. AN V/1/542, 403, copy of naturalization, April 1686. More generally, see Lefevre de la Planche, *Mémoires*, 2:37–41, 89–92 (including lists of the partial privileges given to merchants in Lyon); and Bosquet, *Dictionnaire raisonné*, 1:173 et seq. In the sixteenth century, Bacquet had argued that foreign merchants coming to France were not subject to the droit d'aubaine: *Oeuvres*, 2:44–45.

32. AN AD XV 1, "Ordonnance du Bureau des Finances de la Rochelle," 3 May 1702, involving the widow of the ex-governor of Puerto Rico, which eventually resulted in a general royal ordinance exempting Spaniards using French ships to come back to Europe from the Indies (BN NAF F338311685, 5 September 1709); and the case of a succession contested between the recipient of a king's gift of aubaine and the heirs of the Spanish merchant Esnos, who died in Saint-Malo in 1705: Gama, *Dissertation sur le droit d'aubaine*, passim; Dubost and Sahlins, *Et si faisait payer*, 81–82.

33. AN O/1/221, fol. 29, draft naturalization, May 1716; AN PP 151, registered at the Paris Chambre de comptes, 25 June 1716.

34. AN O/1/233, fol. 313, draft naturalization, November 1765; on the foreign merchants of Marseille, see Carrière, *Négociants marseillais*, esp. 272–90.

35. Dubost and Sahlins, *Et si on faisait payer*, 144–47.

36. AN O/1/233, fol. 53, draft declaration, 12 December 1762; AN P 2597, fol. 50, registration at the Paris Chambre des comptes. The Jacobite social trajectory of Sandilands, from nobility to commercial capitalism, was typical: see G. Chaussinard-Nogaret, "Une Elite insulaire au service de l'Europe: Les Jacobites au XVIIIe siècle," *Annales ESC* (September–October 1973), no. 5: 1097–1122.

37. Dubost and Sahlins, *Et si on faisait payer*, 271. Yet according to Lefebvre de la Planche, despite Moura's individual and forced naturalizations, when he died, his estate was nonetheless

confiscated by the king: *Mémoires*, 2:102. On foreign Protestant bankers in France, see H. Luthy, *La Banque protestante en France, de la révocation de l'édit de Nantes à la Révolution*, 2 vols. (Paris, 1961), 2:315–29.

38. AN K 174, no. 84, registration, 23 September 1701.

39. AN O/1/223, fols. 98, 117, draft naturalization, August 1723; AN PP 151, registration at the Paris Chambre des comptes, 16 November 1723.

40. AN O/1/221, fol. 181, draft declaration of 24 March 1718.

41. AN O/1/220, fol. 311, draft declaration of 22 March 1714; on peddlers from Savoy, and more generally, see L. Fontaine, *History of Peddlers in Europe*, trans. V. Whittaker (Durham, 1996), passim; on the stereotypical images and realities of the Savoyard "diaspora," see R. Devos and B. Grosperrin, *La Savoie de la Réforme à la Révolution française* (Rennes, 1985), 505–6 et seq.

42. AN O/1/225, fol. 392, draft naturalization, October 1735; apparently, Archer did not receive that letter, because another draft copy from 1741 can be found in O/1/227, fol. 102. Oddly, however, there is a record of registration in the Paris Chambre des comptes from 1739 (AN P 2592).

43. AN O/1/230, fol. 462, draft naturalization, December 1754.

44. M. Garden, *Lyon et les Lyonnais au XVIIIe siècle* (Paris, 1975), 213–25. For an impressionistic account of the world of artisanal work in the Old Regime, see A. Poitrineau, *Ils travaillaient la France: Métiers et mentalités du XVIe au XXe siècle* (Paris, 1992).

45. Dubost and Sahlins, *Et si on faisait payer*, 136 and passim.

46. AN O/1/229, fol. 94, draft naturalization, July 1749.

47. AN O/1/220, fol. 394, draft naturalization, July 1715.

48. Dubost and Sahlins, *Et si on faisait payer*, 138–40.

49. Above, chap. 1.

50. Boizet, *Les Lettres de naturalité*, 157–59; Lefebvre de la Planche, *Mémoires*, 2:188–90.

51. AN PINV registration of naturalization by the Paris Chambre des comptes, 12 March 1738; Lefebvre de la Planche, *Mémoires*, 2:41, 45, argues that "ambassadors are also exempt from the aubaine by virtue of their service and because of their long stay in France," but only for movable property, citing Lebret and Bacquet (41). The jurisprudence on ambassadors tended to converge in Bosquet's opinion that ambassadors (and their suites) "were not considered to have left their fatherland, and can dispose of their goods by last will and testament," citing the royal council's decision of 14 January 1727 "concerning the estate of Sr. Thomas Crawford, Scotch nobleman, ambassador of the king of England at the French court, in which, without deciding on the claims of Sr. Crawford his brother concerning the furnishings left in France by the deceased, it is ordered that the Chambre du domaine, which had declared the sucession escheated to the king by the droit d'aubaine, would be executed concerning the said immovable property," in Bosquet, *Dictionnaire raisonné*, 1:171.

52. AN O/1/227, fol. 247, draft naturalization of July 1742.

53. Freyberg: AN PINV, registration at the Paris Chambre des comptes, 23 May 1738; Issolinksy: ibid., 13 September 1736; Karg de Robenberg: AN K 174, no. 1, registration, 19 September 1703; Dom Philippe: BN MS JF 306, fol. 335, copy of naturalization of January 1660. The case of Don Josep de Mora, "permanent steward of the city of Barcelona," who purchased the baronnie de Lló in the French Cerdagne and claimed that he had "designs to stay and live there and finish his days in France," suggests that not all naturalized foreigners followed the letter of the law, because Mora continued to reside in Barcelona, despite his eventual naturalization in 1748. This case was the subject of lengthy exchanges between the Spanish ambassador, the French chancellor, and the intendant of Roussillon: see AAE MD France 1747, fol. 331–41, and AN O/1/228, fol. 438, draft naturalization of November 1748. In the case of a military officer, Antoine de Reynolds, who held the municipal office of "councillor of the great council of the town and canton of Fribourg in Switzerland," a specific clause dispensing the beneficiary of residence in the kingdom was added to the letter: see AN O/1/218, fols. 190, 194, draft naturalization, March 1663.

54. Dubost and Sahlins, *Et si on fasait payer*, 144–46.

55. AN O/1/235, fol. 375, draft naturalization (despite the fact that Lavedan's father was French), November 1775.

56. AN O/1/232, fol. 330, draft declaration, 11 July 1760.

57. AN K 174, no. 90. Note also the case of Antoine de Mouline Peronet, another royal councillor and French treasury official given his office on 12 July 1693, who had been in Spain twenty years earlier when war between the two countries broke out. He had been forced to seek naturalization in that kingdom, an act for which he received a royal dispensation in France. In November 1694, fearing that "the troubles that ill-willed people would give him concerning the possession of his goods," he petitioned for "letters of rehabilitation of nativeness" (*lettres de rehabilitation de naturalité*), which were issued and registered at the Paris Chambre des comptes on 26 November 1694 (AN K 174, no. 59). On foreigners naturalized before becoming royal treasurers, see J.-P. Charmeil, *Les Trésoriers de France*, 20–21.

58. Out of 2,050 royal secretaries who entered the chancellery between 1672 and 1789, according to Favre-Lejeune, *Les Secrétaires du Roi*.

59. Blondeau and Gueret, *Journal du Palais*, 325–27: "Sur un Appel interjetté de la reception d'un Docteur Regent en Droit en l'Université de Poitiers," decision of Paris parlement, 28 April 1610.

60. Dubost and Sahlins, *Et si on faisait payer*, 139–40 and chap. 8, passim. For a list of naturalizations given to foreign artists in the seventeenth century, see J. Guiffrey, "Lettres de naturalité accordées à des artistes étrangers pour les permettre de s'établir en France (1612–1699)," *Nouvelles archives de l'art français*, vol. 2 (Paris, 1873), 222–61; for a breakdown of the 275 foreign students at the Royal Academy of Painting in the late eighteenth century, see L. Dussieux, *Les Artistes français à l'étranger: Recherche sur leurs travaux et leur influence en Europe* (Paris, 1956): xcii.

61. AN O/1/229, fol. 412, draft naturalization, August 1751, which includes the clause restricting residence to Alsace: see above, chap. 2.

62. Lefebvre de la Planche, *Mémoires*, 2:87–88; Le Bret, *Oeuvres*, 68; Bosquet, *Dictionnaire raisonné*, 2, 10, 172, argued, citing Bacquet [who in fact dissented in part: *Oeuvres*, 1:43], that "doctors, school principals, and school children" are considered aliens regarding their movable goods, but foreign students in France "are not subjected to the droit d'aubaine for their books, apparel, and other furnishings that they possess; and as during the time of their study, it is rare that they acquire immovable property, the question of royal escheat is very rare. Nonetheless, if the case arises, it cannot be doubted that their goods would be adjudicated to the king." For a general overview, see M. Waxin, *Statut de l'étudiant étranger dans son développement historique* (Paris, 1939).

63. AN O/1/236, fol. 167, draft naturalization of February 1778; see below, chap. 7, on the contested juridical value of treaties abolishing the droit d'aubaine in the late eighteenth century.

64. AN O/1/226, fol. 448, draft naturalization of August 1739.

65. Dubost and Sahlins, *Et si on faisait payer*, 139–40.

66. Ibid. On the history of foreign troops in the service of France, a topic that still awaits its modern historian, see Mathorez, *Les Etrangers en France*, 1:110 et seq.; the groundwork laid by A. Corvisier, *Les Contrôles de troupes*; and his synthesis in *L'Armée française de la fin du XVIIe siècle au ministère de Choiseul*, 2 vols. (Paris, 1964), 1:543–65 and table. See also the older study of Fieffé, *L'Histoire des troupes étrangères*.

67. Lefebvre de la Planche, *Mémoires*, 2:44–45.

68. AN O/1/221, fol. 35, draft naturalization, May 1716; Lefebvre de la Planche, *Oeuvres*, 2:48, n.(a); Mathorez, *Les Étrangers en France*, 1:144.

69. Boug, *Recueil des édits*, 2:382–86; see also Denisart, *Collection*, 4:594–95.

70. AN O/1/224, fol. 11, draft declaration of 1727, ibid., fol. 164, draft declaration of May 1728; AN PP 151, registration at the Paris Chambre des comptes.

71. AN V/1/542, no. 404, naturalization of October 1685; registration at the Paris parlement, 15 January 1687.

72. AN O/1/233, fol. 335.

73. AN O/1/229, fol. 88, draft naturalization, June 1749, registered in the Paris Chambre des comptes, AN P 2593, fol. 50v. On the Swiss, see Dubost and Sahlins, *Et si on faisait payer*, 70; and below, chap. 5.

74. AN O/1/230, fol. 296, draft naturalization, 1754; AN E 370611; AN O/1/225, fol. 136, draft naturalization, 1733; AN O/1/228, fol. 432, draft naturalization, September 1748; AN 0/1/238, fols. 158, 164; and AN P 2601, fol. 9v, registration of naturalization, 11 July 1787.

75. AN O/1/220, fol. 58, draft naturalization, August 1704.

76. D. Roche, *Le Peuple de Paris* (Paris, 1981), 71, 76–77.

77. AN O/1/233, fol. 406; AN P 2597, registration of naturalization at the Paris Chambre des comptes, 1 October 1766; AN O/1/232, fol. 191, draft naturalization, April 1759. Bayard, "Naturalizations," 305, notes that Miguet owned no immovables and owed 240 livres to a daughter from his first marriage, and an increase of 220 livres for his wife's maintenance, but his trade and movable goods were valued at 2,000 livres, and according to his testimony before the financial officers, "he should also receive 300 livres [as inheritance] from his parents."

Chapter 5: Geographic Origins and Residence

1. Dubost and Sahlins, *Et si on faisait payer,* 161–71. Not to dismiss the possibility of "co-penetration" of Flemish and Spaniards in the seventeenth century: see J. Lefèvre, "La Compénétration Hispano-Belge aux Pays Bas Catholiques pendant le XVIIe siècle," *Revue belge de philologie et d'histoire* 16 (1937): 599–621. Individually naturalized foreigners sometimes had their origins corrected, in keeping with the dictates of Papon (above, chap. 2): for example, Jean de Castelberg, from the Grisons Valley, declared himself to be "of the German Nation" at one time and of the "Swiss Cantons" another: AN O/1/219, fols. 81–103 (including a copy of the inquiry), 106 (draft naturalization of August 1686), and 115. In the naturalization tax, foreigners disputed their identifications as well with the royal council, seeking relief and reduction in their tax assessments: Dubost and Sahlins, *Et si on faisait payer,* 310–19.

2. Dubost and Sahlins, *Et si on faisant payer,* 336–37.

3. Ibid., 167–68.

4. It is likely that the complete exploitation of the registration rolls of the surviving treasury bureaux would yield a much finer portrait of the settlement patterns of individually naturalized foreigners in the kingdom: see, for example, the kind of data generated in Bayard, "Naturalization."

5. In the southern province of Languedoc, E. Le Roy Ladurie, *Les Paysans de Languedoc,* 2 vols. (Paris, 1966), 1:99–100, noted that the hospital registers of Montpelliers at the end of the seventeenth century contained large contingents of Swiss, English, and Germans, but few Italians and, surprisingly, almost no Spaniards. Further north, in the Paris basin, P. Goubert, *Beauvais et le beauvaisie au XVIIe siècle* (Paris, 1960), 66–67, found a large number of Flemings, but virtually no southerners.

6. Dubost and Sahlins, *Et si on faisait payer,* passim, esp. chap. 8.

7. Ibid., 385–89 and passim.

8. Not the "New World," as many historians have thought, but the viguery of the valley of Barcelonette and Puget-Théniers, including the baronnie de Beuil, whose inhabitants had "left the domination of the counts of Provence in 1388 to submit themselves to those of Savoy": see E. Baratier, G. Duby, and E. Hidesheimer, eds., *Atlas historique: Provence, Comtat, Orange, Nice, Monaco* (Paris, 1989); and R. Demotz, "La Géographie administrative médiévale: L'Exemple du comté de Savoie, début XIIIe siècle-début XVe siècle," *Moyen Age* 1 (1974): 261–300.

9. P. Guichonnet, ed., *Histoire et civilisation des Alpes,* 2 vols. (Toulouse, 1980), 1:280–89; see also P. Sopheau, "Les Variations de la frontière française des Alpes depuis le XVIe siècle," *Annales de géographie* 3 (1893–94): 183–200.

10. Dubost and Sahlins, *Et si on faisait payer,* 253–55, map 8.7. Family traditions of emigration can be documented by the recurrence of the same names (Bellon, Antoine, Allard), especially in the valley of Barcelonette. A historical anthropology of the valley completes the picture from the other side: see H. Rosenberg, *A Negotiated World: Three Centuries of Change in a French Alpine Community* (Toronto, 1988).

11. H. Costamagna, "Notes sur les migrations dans le comté de Nice au XVIIIe siècle," in *Les Migrations dans les pays méditerranéens au XVIIIe et au début du XIXe siècle* (Nice, 1974), 80–89; M. Vovelle, "Gavots et Italiens: Les Alpes et leur bordure dans la population marseillaise au XVIIIe siècle," *Provence historique* 108 (1977): 137–69; and more generally, A. Poitrineau, *Remues d'hommes: Les Migrations montagnardes en France, 17e–18e siècles* (Paris, 1983). For a description and statistical account of the population of Provence at the end of the seventeenth century, see the

critical edition of the intendant's memoir "for the instruction of the duc de Bourgogne": F.-X. Emmanuelli, *L'Intendance de Provence à la fin du XVIIe siècle* (Paris, 1980).

12. Dubost and Sahlins, *Et si on faisait payer*, 168–71, 178–82, and 253–56. Savoyards born during the alliance of the two crowns who lived in France had been exempted from the droit d'aubaine and were considered native subjects by a decision of the Metz parlement on 20 March 1692 (Augéard, *Arrests notables*, 1:162), a jurisprudential opinion, among many others, trumped politically by the royal ordinance of 22 July 1697 that established the Naturalization Tax.

13. Ibid., 152, 205–6.

14. AN PINV, registration of naturalization by the Paris Chambre des comtes, 16 March 1689. His name derived perhaps from his craft as a breeder and trainer of hawks.

15. On the latter, see Dubost and Sahlins, *Et si on faisait payer*, 307–10.

16. Ibid., 203–5; see the excerpted names of the "Rolle concernant les Naturalitez" of 12 January 1700 for the province in Nahon, *Les "nations" juives portugaises*, 49–50; J. Cavignac, "L'Immigration des Juifs portugais a Bordeaux au XVIIIe siècles," in *Les Relations entre le Sud-Ouest et la péninsule ibérique*, Actes du XXXVIIIe congrès de la Fédération historique du Sud-Ouest, Pau, 5–6 October 1985 (Pau, 1987), 125–38. On the Jews in Paris, especially the Sephardim during the eighteenth century, see Z. Szajkowski, "Jewish Emigration from Bordeaux during the Eighteenth and Nineteenth Centuries," *Jewish Social Studies* 18 (1956): 118–24; and A. Burguière, "Groupe d'immigrant ou minorité réligieuse? Les Juifs à Paris au XVIIIe siècle," in *Le Migrant: "France, terre de migrations internes; France, terre d'immigration,"* Actes du colloque d'Aurillac, 5–7 June 1985 (Aurillac, 1986), 183–200.

17. BN 23626 (644): "Lettres patentes en faveur des Juifs . . . au mois de mai 1759." Jews in the Caribbean colonies of France were technically subject to civil incapacities elaborated in the Code Noir of 1685, but individual merchants, most of them originally from Bordeaux, received patent letters specifically removing these incapacities, without naturalizing them: see A. Cahen, "Les Juifs dans les colonies françaises au XVIIIe siècle," *Revue des études juives* 5 (1882): 80–81.

18. Sahlins, "Fictions of a Catholic France," 101–2; on the Dalpuget, see P. Hildenfinger, ed., *Documents sur les Juifs à Paris au XVIIIe siècle* (Paris, 1913), 23, n. 169.

19. On Liefman, see I. Loeb, "Un Baron juif français au XVIII siècle: Liefman Calmer," *Annuaire des archives israélites de France* 46 (1885): 188–90, 196–98; on the Valabrègue, see AAE MD France 1454, fol. 21; BN MS JF 2494, fols. 38, 163; and AN O/1/234, fol. 246.

20. AAE MD France 1454, fol. 21; BN MS JF 2494, fol. 38, 163; AN O/1/234, fol. 246; and Z. Szajkowski, *Franco-Judaica*, 471. Bernard de Valabrègue signed the printed *Odes prononcées par les Juifs d'Avignon et de Bordeaux résidants à Paris dans leur Assemblée à l'occasion du sacre de Louis XVI.*

21. Traces of Jacob Perpignan's naturalization can be found in AAE ADP France, fol. 10, 241; Szajkowski, *Franco-Judaica*, 470; BN MS JF 472, fol. 11; the draft of Solar's "naturalization" (including legitimation for his "natural son" born out of wedlock, but without his faith being mentioned in the letter, which apparently was not registered in the Paris Chambre des comptes, but probably in the Paris parlement) is in AN O/1/236, fol. 16 (reproduced in Nahon, *Les "nations" juives portugaises*, 18–19). On these and others, see Hertzberg, *French Enlightenment and the Jews*, 54–64 and 133–37.

22. Dubost and Sahlins, *Et si on faisait payer*, 67–68.

23. Other foreigners, living in Avignon, took letters of naturalization, revealing their susceptibility to political rumors of conquest or annexation: Jérôme Vanenbruge, born in Brussels, settled in Avignon with his wife and sister since 1760, was naturalized along with them eight years later "having reason to believe that by the reunion of Avignon to the French crown, they would themselves be subjected to the droit d'aubaine": AN O/1/234, fol. 69, draft declaration, 13 July 1768.

24. Sahlins, *Boundaries*, 113–14; Marquis de Roux, *Louis XIV*, chaps. 4–5; Bosquet, *Dictionnaire raisonné*, 2:21; see also Augéard, *Arrests notables*, 2:52–55.

25. Bacquet, *Traité du domaine*, 1:35–37; Boniface, *Arrests notables*, 2:53–62, decision of the parlement of Provence, 7 May 1665.

26. AN O/1/222, fol. 90, draft declaration of 29 September 1720. Concerning the subjects of the duchy of Lorraine, not technically a "conquered province," patterns of naturalization ran parallel to its gradual legal and administrative assimilation as French territory (see below, chap. 6).

27. Dubost and Sahlins, *Et si on faisait payer*, 155–57. Whether or not they could inherit from

French subjects became a more contested matter only in the second half of the eighteenth century (below, chap. 7).

28. AN AD XV I, *Arrest de la cour de parlement*, 11 July 1741; Denisart, *Collection* (1773), 1:165–66. See the useful account of the *mémoire* of 1741 at the origin of the decision: J. Imbert, "L'Exercise du droit d'aubaine à l'égard des habitants du Hainault à la fin de l'Ancien Régime," *Revue d'histoire du droit français et étranger* (1950): 548–59. The case involved François Brisard, born in Mons, who married a French woman in Brussels, and subsequently settled in France near Amiens. Marie de James, his wife, died having willed all her property to her husband, who himself died shortly thereafter, leaving the inheritance to be collected by the tax-farmers. Officials at the financial and domanial bureaux of Amiens upheld the seizure by the droit d'aubaine, but were overruled by the Paris parlement.

29. On the Flemish exemptions from the Naturalization Tax and the problem of "near for-eigners," see Dubost and Sahlins, *Et si on faisait payer*, 155–57.

30. AAE France ADP 1, 1, fols. 1–32v, [Le Dran], "Sur la question: 'quelles sont les nations qui en France sont sujettes au droit d'aubaine' . . .'"; see also Le Bret, *Oeuvres*, 67–68; and Lefeb-vre de la Planche, *Mémoires*, 2:53–58, all citing (with differing degrees of accuracy) the opinion of Bacquet, in *Oeuvres*, 1:25–30; see also the remarks by J. B. Gaschon, *Code diplomatique des aubains* (Paris, 1818), 30–33.

31. AN O/1/235, fols. 14, 288, draft naturalization, February 1722; copy in AAE MD France 1454, fol. 69.

32. AN O/1/220, fol. 51, draft naturalization, 1703.

33. Above, chap. 3. On the efforts to delimit France's boundaries in the region, see N. Girard d'Albissin, *Genèse de la frontière franco-belge: Les Variations des limites septentrionales de la France de 1659 à 1789* (Paris, 1970); and more recently, S. Dubois, *Les Bornes immuables de l'Etat: La Ratio-nalisation du tracé des frontières au siècle des Lumières (France, Pays-Bas autrichiens et principauté de Liège)* (Courtrai-Heule, 1999).

34. Trénard, "La Notion de 'naturalité,' " 87–93; quotation, 90.

35. Dubost and Sahlins, *Et si on faisait payer,* 184–91.

36. See, for example, the case of the comte de Linange-Dabo versus the comte de Hohenloe, grand chamberlain of the emperor, and the Princess Frederick of Hesse-Homburg, his wife, that resulted in a decision of the Colmar Sovereign Council in 1737 permitting the "Germans" to in-herit, but that was overturned the following year on appeal to the Paris parlement: AP BACA Re-cueil Chanclaire, vol. 83, nos. 60–61.

37. AAE MD Germany 94, fol. 117v; BN MS JF 306, fol. 338, copy of permission of Septem-ber 1668.

38. Gaschon, *Code diplomatique des aubains*, 55–65, on the treaty of 1715. On the settlement of the Swiss in eastern France, including Alsace, Burgundy, and Lyon, see the work of A. M. Burg, *Les Suisses et le repeuplement de Haguenau dans la seconde moitié du XVIIe siècle* (Paris, 1952); G. Livet, "Croissance économique et privilèges commerciaux des suisses sous l'Ancien Régime: Note sur les commercants suisses établis en France au XVIIIe siècle," in *Lyon et L'Europe: Hommes et Sociétés. Mélanges d'histoire offerts à Richard Gascon*, 2 vols. (Lyon, 1980), 2:43–63; and his "Une Page d'his-toire sociale: Les Savoyards à Strasbourg au début du XVIIIe siècle," *Cahiers d'histoire* 4, no. 2 (1959): 131–45; R. Lopez, "Les Suisses à Marseille: Une immigration de longue durée," *Recherches Regionales* 28, no. 1 (1987): 49–74.

39. AAE ADP France 1, fols. 22–23; AAE MD Geneva 1, fols. 72–76, note of Le Dran, 24 September 1734, "on the exemptions claimed by Sr. Possel, originally from Genoa, a merchant in Saint-Quentin"; and ibid., fols. 103–16, a note by Le Dran of 15 October 1738 on their obligation to provide bail when appearing before French courts; see also Lefebvre de la Planche, *Mémoires*, 2:41–44. For a contemporary history of the Swiss Guards by one of its distinguished members, see Anne de Zur-Lauben, *Histoire militaire des Suisses au service de la France* (Paris, 1751). On the set-tlement of the Swiss Guards in the Paris region, see the contributions to *Les Gardes Suisses et leurs familles aux XVIIe et XVIIIe siècles en région parisienne*, Colloque du 30 septembre et 1er octobre 1988 (Reuil-Malmaison, 1989); and the recent synthesis by J. Bodin, *Les Suisses au service de la France de Louis XI à la Légion étrangère* (Paris, 1988).

40. Lefebvre de la Planche, *Mémoires*, 2:67–71; the patent letters of Henry IV in 1608 ex-

empting those from Geneva from the droit d'aubaine are reproduced in Bacquet, *Oeuvres*, 1:19–20. The most famous Genevan to plead his privilege of "alien" was Jacques Necker, who in 1786 consulted the barrister Tronchet in an unsuccessful attempt to will to his daughter, Germaine de Staël, more property than was allowed by the Paris custom: AP ACA Fonds Tronchet, vol. 16, no. 1616, 15 April 1786, and below, chap. 7.

41. It is likely that a good many inhabitants of the county of Nice were also counted among these Savoyards, since the number of naturalized Niçois (ninety-seven) pales in comparison to the number of Niçois taxed between 1697 and 1707, although clearly the attempt to tax them responded to a political initiative of the French crown seeking control of the Alpine frontier. More generally, relying in part on the information constituted in the administration and police of foreigners during the Revolution, see M. Vovelle, "Piémontais en Provence occidentale au XVIIIe siècle," *Migrazioni attraverso le Alpi occidentali: Relazioni tra Piemonte, Provenza e Delfinato dal Medioevo ai nostri giorni*. Atti del Convegno Internazionale, Cuneo, 1–3 Giugno 1984 (Turin, 1988), 73–92.

42. AAE France ADP 1, 1, fol. 27; and J. G. Basset, *Notables arrets de la Cour de Parlement, Aydes, et Finances de Dauphiné* (Grenoble, 1730 [1676]), 111–25. At least twelve Savoyards living in the Dauphiné had letters registered at the Chambre des comptes in Grenoble.

43. Lefebvre de la Planche, *Mémoires*, 2:99–101; on Monclar and his memorandum, see F. Hildesheimer, "Aubains ou regnicoles: La Capacité à succeder des Niçois en Provence," *Nice historique* 83, no. 3 (1980): 122–26.

44. Poitrineau, *Remues d'hommes*, chap. 4. Of course, not all Savoyards were poorer: see the counterexample studied by J. P. Klintz, "Savoyards et Grand Commerce à l'aube du XVIIIe siècle: L'Exemple de la Compagnie des Trois Frères," in *L'Europe, l'Alsace et la France: Hommage à Georges Livet* (Strasbourg, 1986), 32–39.

45. AN O/1/232, fol. 191, draft naturalization, April 1759. On the settlement of Savoyards in Lyon, see A. Châtelain, "La Formation de la population lyonnaise: Apports savoyards au XVIIIe siècle," *Revue de géographie de Lyon* 25 (1951): 345–49; and for an earlier period, O. Zeller, "L'Implantation savoyarde a Lyon à la fin du XVIe siècle," in *Habiter la Ville, XVe–XXe siècle*, ed. M. Garden and Y. Lequin (Lyon, 1984), 25–35. On the Savoyards in the Franche-Comté, see G. M. Fournier, "L'Immigration savoyarde en Franche-Comté avant 1789," *Mémoires de la Société d'émulation du Doubs*, n.s. (1959): 1–99; and J. Michaud, "L'immigration savoyarde à Poligny [Jura] au XVIIe siècles," *Généalogie et histoire*, no. 62 (1990): 31–37; no. 63 (1991): 23–27. For the Savoyards settled in Alsace, see D. Ingold, "Note sur l'immigration marchande savoyarde à Thann [Haut Rhin] sous l'Ancien Régime," *Amis Thann* 3 (1988): 2–6; Livet, "Une Page d'histoire sociale," 131–45.

46. The obviously instrumental naturalizations of Genoese shipowners and captains around 1720, in the interest of enjoying the privileges of sailing under French flags, brought the wrath of the royal council, and led to the edicts of Louis XV in 1719 and 1729 that withdrew all naturalizations of nonresident foreigners in the kingdom (above, chap. 2).

47. On the relative wealth and the contrasting patterns of immigration over time of these two borderlands, see Dubost and Sahlins, *Et si on faisait payer*, chaps. 5–6.

48. But also from Spain, even though it is difficult to differentiate those who came from the immediate borderlands of the northern part of the peninsula: see below, this chapter.

49. Gaschon, *Code diplomatique des aubains*, 1–17; Lefebvre de la Planche, *Mémoires*, 2:72–76; Denisart, *Collection* (1783): 1:31–42; an example of a particularly contentious case in Dunkirk involved claims to the estate of Helen Jensen, who died in 1741, which turned on the interpretation of clauses in the international treaties: see A. Vandenbossche, "Contribution à l'étude des privilèges: Quelques problèmes posé par l'exemption du droit d'aubaine en Flandre Maritime au XVIIIe siècle," *Annales de la faculté de droit de l'université de Bordeaux, série juridique* (1955): 117–48.

50. G. Chaussinard-Nogaret, "La Diaspora jacobite et l'Europe moderne," *Revue de la Bibliothèque nationale*, no. 46 (1992): 2–3; and N. Genet-Rouffiac, "Les Jacobites à Paris et à Saint-Germain-en-Laye," *Revue de la Bibliothèque nationale*, no. 46 (1992): 44–49. For a case study of assimilation, see P. Clarke de Dromantin, "Condition juridiques et sociales de l'assimilation d'une famille jacobite réfugiée en France," in *L'Autre exil: Les Jacobites en France au début du XVIIIe siècle*.

Actes du Colloque "La Cour des Stuarts à Saint-Germain-en-Laye au temps de Louis XIV," February 1992. (Aubenas, 1993), 157–70.

51. AN O/1/220, fol. 42, draft naturalization, July 1703, registered at the Paris Chambre des comptes (PP 151).

52. Atypical in many respects was the case of Winifred Rakay [sic], 96, and her daughter, 50, who naturalized in January 1777. Winifred was the widow of Admiral Lamoke, who came to France "à la suitte du roy jacques," and whose wife had a daughter who, at the age of seventeen, went back to England "without royal permission." The daughter married and, at her death, left several children, including the petitioner. More, the case was complicated by the fact that Admiral Lamoke, after living some time in France, went to Spain where he was employed in the royal navy, and lived there about sixteen years, "after which they moved back to France and he died two years later, leaving the widow in France with her two daughters. The youngest has been for many years in a [religious] community in Rouen" and the eldest "stupidly" married a certain Bernard, but returned to her mother's household, with her own daughter, in the little town of Saint-Calais "where they live in the greatest mediocrity": AN O/1/236, fol. 62, draft naturalization, January 1777.

53. AN O/1/28, fol. 103, draft of patent letters, n.d. 1684; see also AAE ADP France 10, dossier 233, "Irlandais en France, 1702–1829," and the materials in ADLA IJ 266 (Irish in the Nantes region). Secondary sources include J.-P. Poussou, "Recherches sur l'immigration anglo-irlandaise à Bordeaux au XVIIIe siècle," in *Bordeaux et les Iles britanniques du XIIIe au XXe siècle* (Bordeaux, 1975); and R. Hayes, C. Preston, and J. Weygand, eds., *Les Irlandais en Aquitaine* (Bordeaux, 1971). On the Irish clergy, see Ph. Loupès, "Les Ecclésiastiques irlandais dans le diocèse de Bordeaux au XVIIe et XVIIIe siècles," in *Bordeaux et les Iles Britanniques du XIIIe au XXe siècle* (Bordeaux, 1975), 80–98; and on the Irish seminary (1603–1790) in Bordeaux, see L. Bertrand, *Histoire des séminaires de Bordeaux et de Bazas*, 2 vols. (Paris, 1894), 1:321–405. On merchants in western France, see L. M. Cullen, "The Irish Merchant Communities at Bordeaux, La Rochelle, and Cognac in the Eighteenth Century," in *Négoce et Industrie en France et en Irlande aux XVIIIe et XIXe siècles*, ed. L. M. Cullen and P. Butel (Paris, 1980), 51–64.

54. AN AD XV 1, no. 119, *Ordonnance du Roy*, 12 February 1702; more generally, J. McGurk, "Wild Geese: The Irish in European Armies (Sixteenth to Eighteenth Centuries)," in *The Irish World Wide: History, Heritage, Identity*, vol. 1: *Patterns of Migration*, ed. P. O'Sullivan (Leicester, 1992), 36–62; P. Gouhier, "Mercenaires irlandais en France, 1635–1664," *Revue d'histoire moderne et contemporaine* (1964): 612–90.

55. J. Mathorez, "Notes sur la colonie irlandaise de Nantes du XVIe au XVIIIe siècles," *Bulletin de la Société archéologique de Nantes et du département de la Loire-Inférieure* 53 (1912): 169–95; Hayes et al., *Les Irlandais en Aquitaine*; Poussou, "Recherches sur l'immigration anglo-irlandaise." For an overview, see L. M. Cullen, "The Irish Disapora of the Seventeenth and Eighteenth Centuries," in *Europeans on the Move: Studies on European Migration, 1500–1800*, ed. N. Canny (Oxford, 1994), 113–49.

56. Bacquet, *Oeuvres*, 1:22; AN AD XV 1, "Arrest du conseil d'état du Roy qui déclare un Etranger, Resident en France pour le Roi d'Anglettere, sujet au Droit d'Aubaine, nonobstant sa qualité, et les Priviléges accordés à la Nation Ecossoise," 14 January 1727; see also BN NAF 9801, fols. 174–201. W. F. Leith, *The Scots Men of Arms and Life-guards in France* (Edinburgh, 1882); and E. Bonner, "French Naturalization of the Scots in the Fifteenth and Sixteenth Centuries," *Historical Journal* 40, no. 4 (1997): 1085–1115, describe the earlier history of the Scots in France.

57. AAE MD Low Countries 60, fols. 178–211: note by the *premier commis* Le Dran in 1739, "Sur les privilèges dont jouissent en France par rapport aux successions les sujets de la république des Provinces-Unies." French Protestant refugees had been naturalized by the Estates of the Netherlands in 1709, "seeing that French refugees were not permitted to gather in France successions that might befall them, ordered reciprocally that subjects of France would be excluded from succession of their kin who found refuge in the United Provinces," fol. 202v; see also Lefebvre de la Planche, *Mémoires*, 2:58–64; and Feenstra and Klompmaker, "Le Statut des étrangers aux Pays-Bas," 333–73.

58. No comprehensive study of the Dutch has yet appeared, but see the many local studies including C. Landré, "Les Protestants hollandais à Bordeaux, avant et après la révocation de l'édit

de Nantes," *Bulletin de la Commission pour l'histoire des Eglises wallones* 2 (1887): 269–75; J. Augustin, "Trois familles hollandaises et protestantes à la Rochelle au XVIIe siècle," in *La Condition juridique de l'étranger,* 247–62; for the Dutch among other merchant communities in Bordeaux, see the work of P. Butel, *Les Dynasties bordelaises de Colbert à Chaban* (Paris, 1991), 39–45, and *Les Négociants bordelais, l'Europe et les Iles au XVIIe siècle* (Paris, 1974), 152–63 and passim.

59. The economic supremacy of Holland, especially under Louis XIV, helps to explain why the Dutch were dominant among the financial and capitalist classes; according to the tax rolls, they were among the wealthiest immigrants in France, and nearly three times as likely to be naturalized by the time that Louis XIV collectively naturalized foreigners in 1697: see Dubost and Sahlins, *Et si on faisait payer,* 207–11.

60. AN O/1/238, fol. 119, draft naturalization, September 1786.

61. AN PINV, registration of naturalization at the Paris Chambre des comptes on 5 April 1672; his estate was confiscated in 1696 and given as a gift from the king to the marquis de Villette.

62. AN V/1/542, 428, copy of naturalization, December 1688.

63. AN O/1/219, fol. 208, draft naturalization, February 1693.

64. The definitive study of Italians in sixteenth-century France is Dubost, *La France italienne;* see also his article, "Les Italiens dans les villes françaises aux XVIe et XVIIe siècles," in *Les Immigrants à la ville: Insertion, intégration, discrimination (XIIe–XXe siècles),* ed. D. Menjot and J.-L. Pinol (Paris, 1996), 91–105; and Billot, "Les Italiens naturalisés," 477–91. On the Lombards in France see R. S. Kohn, "Le Statut forain: Marchands étrangers, Lombards, et Juifs en France et en Bourgogne (deuxième moitié du XV siècle)," *Revue historique de droit français et étranger* 61 (1983): 7–24; and O. Morel, *Les Lombards dans la Flandre français et le Hainault* (Dijon, 1908). On Italians established in Lyon, see M. Morineau, "Lyon l'Italienne, Lyon la Grande," *Annales ESC* (July–August 1977), no. 6: 1537–50; and R. Gascon, *Grand commerce et vie urbaine au XVIe siècle: Lyon et ses marchands,* 2 vols. (Paris, 1971), passim.

65. Dubost and Sahlins, *Et si on faisait payer,* 199–203; on the more socially and economically modest currents of Italian migration in the seventeenth and eighteenth centuries, see Vovelle, "Gavots et Italiens"; C. Grimmer, "Juifs et Italiens dans l'Auvergne du XVIIIe siècle," in *Le Migrant: "France, terre de migrations internes; France, terre d'immigration,"* Actes du colloque d'Aurillac 1985 (Aurillac, 1986), 201–8; and J. Mathorez, "Petits métiers exercés en France par les Italiens au XVIIe et XVIIIe siècle," *Ethnographie* (1922–25): 65–71.

66. Because most Italians in France were unexempted from the droit d'aubaine, a comparison between migration and naturalization patterns is more easily justified. (Those exempted from the Italian Peninsula included the papal subjects inhabiting the Comtat Venaissin and Avignon and subjects of the duchy of Milan, which, according to Jean Bacquet, had once been a legitimate possession of the French crown, and whose subjects, as a result, were required only to take simple letters of declaration: see Bacquet, *Oeuvres,* 1:31.) Bosquet reported a decision of the royal council on 13 June 1741, confirming a decision of the financial bureau of Provence of 21 August 1739, which subjected the Tuscans and Florentines to the droit d'aubaine. The council adjudicated the estates of Marc de Boccony and his son, François de Boccony, against the claims of his other son, Jean, giving them to the crown "by the privilege of aubaine [*à titre d'aubaine*], notwithstanding the letters of naturalization obtained in June 1724 by the said François, after the death of his father, and the project of a treaty to be signed between France and the republic of Florence, invoked by Jean de Boccony": AN O/1/223, fol. 189, draft naturalization, June 1724; and AN K 175, no. 48, registration at the Paris parlement, 11 July 1724. Boccony's naturalization, the royal council ruled, did not allow him to devolve property to his brother Jean, who had not been naturalized, and was thus considered an "alien."

67. The exemptions that Italians sometimes received, such as for those recruited to work at the Gobelins tapestry under Colbert, hardly prevented them from seeking individual naturalizations: within five years of Louis XIV's ordinance of 1667, four Italian artisans sought individual naturalizations.

68. AN O/1/229, fol. 386, draft declaration, 10 July 1751; AN P 2594, fol. 51, registration at the Paris Chambre des comptes.

69. Riccoboni first received a permission to accept a "universal bequest" in 1722, registered at the Chambre des comptes on 14 March 1722 (AN K 175, no. 22), then was required to seek

naturalization, according to the correspondence with the solicitor-general of the Paris parlement: BN MS JF 124, fol. 20 et seq.

70. On French emigration to Spain, see the contributions to *Les Français en Espagne à l'époque moderne (XVIe–XVIIIe siècles)* (Paris, 1990), especially the articles by B. Bennassar, and (for the later eighteenth century) J. Antonio Salas Ausens; see also A. Girard, *Le Commerce français à Séville et Cadix au temps des Hapsbourgs: Contribution à l'étude du commerce étranger au XVI et XVIIe siècles* (Paris, 1932); and Sahlins, *Boundaries*, 105.

71. AAE MD Spain 51, fols. 320–322v, memorandum of Sr. Le Dran, at the request of the minister of foreign affairs, 2 March 1753. See the additional note by Sr. de Bernage, "chef du bureau des brêvets et passeports auprès de M. Amelot," 8 May 1740, noting that recently French subjects established in Spain had asked for certificates of permission (*brevets de permission*) to stay there, but the foreign ministry had not issued any. On French military officers in Spain, see the anonymous memorandum arguing that their exemption depended on whether they could prove the persistence of the "spirit of return": ibid., fols. 323–24, March 1743. The earlier jurisprudence tended to support Le Dran's argument: see P. Hévin, *Arrêts du Parlement de Bretagne* (Rennes, 1684), chap. 34, concerning the case of Jacques and Pierre Despinose.

72. Sahlins, *Boundaries*, 53–54.

73. AAE MD Spain 51, fols. 303–314, "Sur les privileges des sujets de la Couronne d'Espagne en France par rapport aux Successions, par M. le Dran," October 1743; ibid., fols. 316–319v, "Sur l'exercise du droit d'aubaine en France à l'egard des Espagnols décédés dans le Royaume," s.a., ca. 1750.

74. AN AD XV 1, printed Ordonnance du Bureau des Finances de la Rochelle, 3 May 1702, "which adjudicates to the king by the title of aubaine the goods of a foreigner, even traveling through," along with a contradictory decision of the royal council of state, 20 May 1704. A similar case involving another Spaniard, Dom Martin de Esnos, was heard before the Nantes Chambre des comptes in 1706: see the printed pamphlet by de Gama, *Dissertation sur le droit d'aubaine* (copies can be found in Bibliothèque municipale de Dijon MS vol. 8, no. 4861: 19718; and in BN MS 35311).

75. AN OINV, draft naturalization, n.d. 1675.

76. There were, of course, important exceptions of Spanish merchant families that had established themselves in France along the Atlantic seaboard, and particularly in Nantes. See J. Mathorez, "Notes sur les rapports de Nantes avec l'Espagne," *Bulletin Hispanique* 14 (1912): 119–26; 15 (1913): 383–407.

77. Sahlins, "Fictions of a Catholic France," 95–100; Dubost and Sahlins, *Et si on faisait payer,* 162–63, 203–4.

78. AAE MD Portugal 2, fols. 108–114, note of Le Dran, "Sur la question si les biens laissez en France par les Portugais décédés dans le royaume sont sujets au droit d'aubaine," October 1731; for Normandy, see Vaux le Foletier, "Les Portugais à Rouen," 33–42.

79. From the perspective of German emigration, see H. Frenske, "International Migration: Germany in the Eighteenth Century," *Central European History* 3 (1980): 332–47. On the legal status of Germans, see AAE MD Germany 94, fols. 121–145, note by Le Dran, "sur les privilèges des Allemands en France par rapport aux successions," 12 November 1730. The legal status and fate of these "Germans" established in the kingdom was to change dramatically in the citizenship revolution (below, chap. 7), once the French ministry of foreign affairs negotiated with the German principalities to mutually abolish the droit d'aubaine (and/or to preserve, by reciprocity, a German tax [*Abzug*] that would become known to the French as the *droit de détraction*).

80. Dubost and Sahlins, *Et si on faisait payer,* 162. On the increased frequency of official invocations (in peace treaties and diplomatic negotiations) of the "German nation" during the seventeenth century, see J.-F. Noël, "Le Concept de nation allemande dans l'Empire au XVIIe siècle," *XVIIe siècle* 44, no. 176 (1992): 325–44.

81. Dubost and Sahlins, *Et si on faisait payer,* 214–18.

82. Mathorez, *Les Étrangers en France,* 2:102–71; the predominance of Germans among cabinetmakers and woodworkers in Paris is evident in the various repertoires and dictionaries of eighteenth-century artisans, especially those established in the faubourg Saint-Antoine: see, for example, H. Vial, A. Marcel, and A. Girodie, *Les Artistes décorateurs du bois: Répertoires alphabétiques des ébénistes, menuisiers, sculpteurs, doreurs sur bois, etc., ayant travaillé en France aux XVIIe et XVIIIe*

siècles (Paris, 1912); and Thillay, "Les Artisans étrangers," 264, who notes that these dictionaries establish that the proportion of foreign woodworkers in Saint-Antoine was around 20 percent; see also Roche, *Nouveaux parisiens,* 10.

83. AN K 175, no. 180, draft declaration of Suchon, 10 May 1727; AN PP 151, registered in the Paris Chambre des comptes on 17 May 1727; AN O/1/221, fol. 129, draft naturalization of Brun, August 1717; AN PP 151, registered at the Paris Chambre des comptes. On the Germans in Bordeaux, see the older but useful study, A. Leroux, *La Colonie germanique de Bordeaux: Etude historique, juridique, statistique, économique d'après les sources allemandes et françaises,* 2 vols. (Bordeaux, 1917–18).

84. AN O/1/229, fol. 236, draft declaration of 10 July 1750; the other examples include AN O/1/235, fol. 339; AN O/1/224, fol. 365, and so on.

85. Dubost and Sahlins, *Et si on faisait payer,* 219–20.

86. See T. Ferenc, "Identité nationale en exile: Le Rôle du sentiment national hongrois dans la constitution des régiments de Hussards en France au XVIIIe siècle," in *La Recherche dix-huitièmiste: Raison universelle et culture nationale au siècle des Lumières / Eighteenth-century Research: Universal Reason and National Culture during the Enlightenment,* ed. D. A. Bell, L. Pimenova, and S. Pujol (Paris, 1999), 91–107; see p. 106 for a list of the fifteen naturalizations of Hungarians in the eighteenth century.

87. Dubost and Sahlins, *Et si on faisait payer,* 219–20.

88. AN O/1/231, fol. 124; draft declaration, 18 October 18 1734.

89. AN O/1/221, fol. 329, draft naturalization, April 1719; AN O/1/229, fol. 167, naturalization of February 1750, registered at the Paris Chambre des comptes: AN P 2594, fol. 17.

90. AN O/1/224, fol. 24, draft declaration, 15 April 1727; ibid., fol. 64, draft declaration, 29 August 1727.

91. On the Maltese Order, see the entry by M. Fontenay in *Dictionnaire de l'Ancien Régime,* ed. Bély, 937–38; and C.-E. Engel, *L'Ordre de Malte en Méditerranée (1530–1798)* (Monaco, 1957).

92. Far more revealing are the descriptive accounts of "others" in the kingdom, with which Mathorez opens his study, *Les Étrangers en France.* For a case study of exoticism under Louis XIV, see A. Lombard-Jourdan, "Des Malgaches à Paris sous Louis XIV: Exotisme et mentalités en France au XVIIe siècle," *Archipel: Etudes interdisicplinaires sur le monde insulindien* 9 (1975): 79–90.

93. Mathorez, *Les Etrangers en France,* 1:372–73 and passim; on the Code Noir, see the now classic study by L. Sala-Molins, *Le Code Noir, ou le calvaire de Canaan* (Paris, 1987); and Ghachem, "Sovereignty and Slavery," chap. 2.

94. Peabody, *'There Are No Slaves in France,'* passim.

95. Below, chap. 7. As already noted, the 1697 tax initially included foreigners resident in the colonies, but the royal council excluded them in 1702. The number of cases (those taxed before 1702) is certainly undercounted, as is the number of cases (60) of individual naturalizations undercounted, since archival research was not completed in the conseils supérieures of Guadeloupe, Haiti, or Martinique, where letters would have to be registered. Instead, for the latter, I relied on a list compiled by the ministry of the marine (AN M 1031) and the drafts collected in the O/1 series of the National Archives (see appendix 1).

96. AN O/1/221, fol. 264, draft naturalization of Silvester, September 1718; AN P264, registration at the Paris Chambre des comptes, 22 April 1719; AN O/1/227, fol. 201, draft declaration of Baugras, 29 April 1742.

97. AN O/1/220, fol. 46, draft declaration of Aubry, October 1706; AN O/1/230, fol. 59, draft naturalization of Taboada, May 1752; and AN O/1/229, fol. 163, draft naturalization of Vidary, January 1750. Even though his mother was French, Vidary received a naturalization, not a declaration.

98. AN O/1/234, fol. 330, declaration of naturalization, 4 December 1771; AN P 2598, fol. 4v, registration of naturalization by the Paris Chambre des comptes, 17 January 1772. That the claimant received a declaration, not a naturalization, was perhaps due to court influences.

99. AN O/1/222, fol. 98, draft naturalization, October 1720.

100. AN O/1/238, fol. 11, draft naturalization, April 1785; AN P 2601, fol. 7v, registration at the Paris Chambre des comptes.

Chapter 6: Temporal Patterns of Naturalization

1. For overviews of the political and international impact of Louis XIV's foreign policy, see L. André, *Louis XIV et l'Europe* (Paris, 1950), and *Le Règne de Louis XIV (1661–1715)* (Paris, 1998); and the useful chronology by J. Cornette, *Chronique du règne de Louis XIV* (Paris, 1997).

2. Bély, *Les Relations internationales*, 415 et seq.

3. See F. Braudel and E. Labrousse, eds., *Histoire économique et sociale de la France*, vol. 2: *Des Derniers temps de l'âge seigneurial aux préludes de l'âge industriel (1660–1789)*, 2 vols. (Paris, 1977), esp. the contributions by P. Léon and C.-E. Labrousse. C.-E. Labrousse's *Esquisse du mouvement des prix et des revenus en France au XVIIIe siècle*, 2 vols. (Paris, 1933), established the price series that provide the evidence for the (cyclical) upswing(s) of the French economy, especially beginning in the 1720s, although the Labroussian model has come under criticism in recent years. For a summary account of economic development in the first half of the eighteenth century, see J. C. Riley, *The Seven Years War and the Old Regime in France: The Economic and Financial Toll* (Princeton, 1986), 3–37.

4. In Lyon, the registration of naturalizations at the fiscal bureaux show a similar increase in total naturalizations in the 1660s and 1670s: see Bayard, "Naturalization," 287.

5. André, *France et L'Europe*, pt. 1, passim.

6. Sahlins, *Boundaries*, 68–70; D. Nordman, *Frontières de France: De l'espace au territoire, XVIe–XVIIe siècle* (Paris, 1998), esp. pt. 2 on the different "models" of the frontier in Alsace, Lorraine, the Pyrenees, and the northern territories.

7. G. Zeller, *Les Temps Modernes*, chap. 4; for a more recent synthetic assessment of French foreign policy under Louis XIV, see J. Black, *From Louis XIV to Napoleon: The Fate of a Great Power* (London, 1999), 33–69.

8. Bacquet, *Oeuvres*, 2:7, 26–30.

9. Bodin, *Les Six Livres*, 98; Bouchel, *Bibliothèque*, 1:1067–69; see also Boniface, *Arrests notables*, 2:53–62, on the specific question of succession rights of the Comtois during times of war; and, more generally, Lefebvre de la Planche, *Mémoires*, 2:83–85: "The right of war thus renders all goods and even persons of foreigners subject to seizures, both of movables and immovables, in the name of the king" (84).

10. BN MS 23612 (856–57), "Ordonnance portant que les Anglais qui se trouvent dans le royaume devront en sortir dans trois mois," 1 February 1666; on the Dutch, see Mathorez, *Les Étrangers en France*, 1:130; on the Spaniards in 1718, see AN AD XV 1, royal ordinance of 7 February 1720 against the "rebels" of the Bourbon alliance (other copies in BN MS 21085 [28], 21308 [136], 23622 [182]). For an eighteenth-century discussion of Germany, see AAE MD Germany 94, fols. 220–34, note by the first clerk Le Dran "sur la question comment on doit de la part de la France dans le cas de rupture avec l'empereur en user par rapport aux sujets de ce prince. . . . ," 28 September 1733.

11. AN F 5001 (401), ordinance of 2 November 1677, "pour empêcher qu'aucun étranger ne puisse entrer dans le royaume ou le traverser sans avoir passeport, et sans que SM en soit avertie." On the late medieval proliferation of signs, badges, and other modes of identification, see V. Groebner, "Describing the Person, Reading the Signs in Late Medieval and Renaissance Europe: Identity Papers, Vested Figures, and the Limits of Identification, 1400–1600," In *Documenting Individual Identity: The Development of State Practices in the Modern World*, ed. J. Caplan and J. Torpey (Princeton, 2001), 15–27. On the uneven development of the passport and related documents in France, see D. Nordman, "Sauf-conduits et passeports, en France, la Renaissance," in *Voyages et voyageurs à la Renaissance*, ed. J. Céard and J.-C. Margolin (Paris, 1987), 145–58, and his entry in the *Dictionnaire*, ed. Bély, 1122–24. For a statistical and administrative study of passports issued in 1712, see Bély, *Espions et ambassadeurs*, chap. 4. More generally, see J. Torpey, *The Invention of the Passport: Surveillance, Citizenship, and the State* (Cambridge, 2000), 4–20.

12. On the policing of movement under Louis XIV, especially the 1682 edict against gypsies and vagrants, see L. Lucassen, "Eternal Vagrants? State Formation, Migration, and Traveling Groups in Western Europe, 1350–1914," in *Migration, History, Migration History: Old Paradigms and New Perspectives*, ed. J. Lucassen and L. Lucassen (Bern, 1997), 225–51, esp. 235; and H. Asséo, "Le Roi, la marginalité, et les marginaux," in *L'Etat Classique, 1652–1715*, ed. H. Méchoulan and J. Cornette (Paris, 1996), 355–71.

13. On the 1669 ordinance, see above, chap. 2. The strictures against marriage outside the kingdom were particularly applied to the borderlands: in the case of Roussillon, the prohibition resulted from instructions of War Minister Louvois in 1678 (Sahlins, *Boundaries*, 116); in the case of Alsace, the strictures against emigration and marriage were reiterated throughout the eighteenth century, esp. in 1769 (e.g., Boug, *Recueil des édits*, 2:839).

14. Arrêt du conseil, 11 January 1686, reaffirmed 28 June 1686, in *Edits, déclarations et Arrests*, 270–71, 290–91.

15. O/1/219, fol. 132, declaration draft of November [?] 1687.

16. AN AD XV 1, no. 116: royal declaration of January 1681, registered 12 February 1681, added to the 1744 edition of Bacquet's *Oeuvres*, 47. For a detailed study of the provision of ecclesiastical benefices in Alsace, see R. Metz, *La Monarchie française et la provision de bénéfices ecclesiastiques en Alsace de la paix de Westphalie à la fin de l'Ancien Régime* (Strasbourg, 1947), passim.

17. Louvois is cited in André, *Louis XIV et l'Europe*, 128; see M. Parisse, ed., *Histoire de la Lorraine* (Toulouse, 1977), and J. Voss, "La Lorraine et sa situation politique entre la France et l'Empire vues par le duc de Saint-Simon," in *Les Habsbourg et la Lorraine*, ed. J.-P. Bled et al. (Nancy, 1988), 91–99.

18. Blondeau and Gueret, *Journal du Palais*, 1:383–87.

19. The edict of 1702 is reproduced in Bacquet, *Oeuvres*, 2:16–17. By an additional edict of 12 June 1738, the towns and bishoprics of Metz, Toul, Verdun, and others were given reciprocity with Lorraine with respect to the capacity of individuals to inherit. All these different dispositions "had begun to form a great alliance between these Peoples so close to one another, they did not suffice to erase the quality of foreigner in the person of the subjects of the duke of Lorraine, and to put them in the condition of enjoying the same rights and privileges as our subjects and native residents of the kingdom [*regnicoles*]." But now that they live as subjects of Louis XV's father-in-law, it was time to "abolish all the differences which can distinguish them, so that the subjects of the duke be considered just like ours," abolishing all the accumulated disabilities of foreigners, such as putting up bail, paying for the judge, and other laws. Boug, *Recueil des édits*, 1:199.

20. Dubost and Sahlins, *Et si on faisait payer*, 187–9. As illustrative, consider the cases of Claude Mathieu, who had been received as a barrister in the Paris parlement in 1692, was given patent letters for the function of "greffier en la maîtrise des Eaux et Forets d'Ensisheim" in Alsace, and became a royal solicitor in that administration before seeking his letters of naturalization in July 1725: AN O/1/223, fol. 283, draft naturalization, July 1725; and of Louis Ignace, comte de Sampigny, who was the seigneur of Dumesnil La Horgne, but who accumulated offices from both the French crown and the duke of Lorraine, holding the charge of *conseiller secrétaire de France et des finances* as well as *conseiller d'état* of the duke of Lorraine and governor of Villechateau. In 1723, having been in Paris for just a year, he sought a declaration of naturalization, even though, as he himself noted, by the declaration of 1702 the Lorrainois living in France had "all the rights, honors, and privileges of our natural subjects": ibid., fol. 58, declaration of 7 May 1723; AN PP 151, registration at the Paris Chambre des comptes, 24 May 1723.

21. Delcourt: AN K 174, no. 78, registered by the Paris parlement, 7 April 1699; Fournier: AN O/1/220, fol. 311; Kragh: AN O/1/220, fol. 351; on the August 1700 edict, see Dubost and Sahlins, *Et si on faisait payer*, chap. 10.

22. Black, *From Louis XIV to Napoleon*, 70–95; Zeller, *Temps modernes*, chaps. 5 and 7.

23. AN AD XV 1, printed decisions of the general commission of the royal council, confirming that of the Chambre du domaine of 1734, concerning the adjudication to the king of the succession of Anne-Claire Deinschs, born in the village of Croff in the electorate of Trier, which had been occupied by French troops.

24. AN X/50-1, 2686, Déclaration du roi, 24 May 1701, on the Three Bishoprics, Lorraine, and Metz; on the Savoyards, see Lefebvre de la Planche, *Mémoires*, 2:25, note (a) [25–28].

25. AN O/1/224, fol. 393, draft declaration, December 1731.

26. Bosquet, *Dictionnaire raisonné*, 2:179–85; AN AD XV 1, no. 18.

27. Black, *From Louis XIV to Napoleon*, 118–19.

28. AN o/1/221, fol. 238, draft of declaration of 1718; BN MS 2174, fol. 88, *Arrêt du Conseil*, 21 November 1718; AN MS 21082 (57), printed "édit en forme de lettres patentes sur arrêt" of 1719; AN XV/1, printed edict of February 1720 (other copies in AN F23622 [173]); see also AAE MD Genoa 21, fols. 37–38, note of Le Dran, "Sur les privilèges des Gênois en France par rapport aux successions," 11 January 1721; and Mathorez, *Les Etrangers en France*, 1:42. The February 1720 edict must be read in conjunction with the ordinance of 12 February 1720 "portant que les estrangers naturalisez francais faisant le commerce maritime ne seront point censez faire corps de la nation dans les Echelles de Levant et de Barbarie, ports d'Italie, et autres estrangers, s'ils n'en ont obtenu une permission particulière du roi": see AN F 20983 (41) and 23622 (183). The surge in Genoese naturalization was also occasioned by the periodic royal ordinances forbidding them mercantile relations with France: see, for example, AN F 5001, 458, royal ordinance of 15 May 1684.

29. AN AD XV 1.

30. Ibid.; Boug, *Recueil des édits*, 2:210.

31. Henry and Courgeau, "Deux analyses"; Roche, "Nouveau Parisiens."

32. Bell, *Cult of the Nation*; Dziembowski, *Un nouveau patriotisme français*.

33. AAE MD England 59, fol. 180: Controller-general to the duc de Praslin, "Contre la prétension des Anglais residents en France à l'exemption de la Capitation," 18 February 1764; ibid., fols. 186–193v, "Réponse aux mémoires de M. l'Ambassadeur d'Angleterre," n.d. [April 1765].

34. T. O. McLoughlin, "A Crisis for the Irish in Bordeaux: 1756," in *Nations and Nationalisms: France, Britain, Ireland, and the Eighteenth-Century Context*, ed. M. O'Dea and K. Whelan (Oxford, 1995), 129–45.

35. On the origins and (temporary) residence of foreigners in Paris after the middle of the eighteenth century, see J.-F Dubost, "Les Etrangers à Paris au siècle des lumières," and V. Milliot, "La Surveillance des migrants et des lieux d'acceuil à Paris du XVIe siècle aux années 1830," both in D. Roche, ed., *La Ville promise: Mobilité et accueil à Paris (fin XVIIe–début XIXe siècle)* (Paris, 2000), 221–90 (Dubost) and 21–76 (Milliot); and below, chap. 7.

36. On the Cerdagne, see Sahlins, *Boundaries*, 77–80. Examples from the Cerdagne include the cases of Simon Masfarner, born in the Spanish border town of Puigcerdà, "Cerdagne Espagnole," who took letters of naturalization in 1722. Having served for four years as a vicar in the town of Saint-Laurens de la Salanque, he had obtained the cure of neighboring Saint-Marie de la Mer, and "shortly afterwards brought his two sisters and brother, a priest who took his place as vicar of Saint-Laurents; such that at this time, his whole family is in the kingdom." For familial and "professional" reasons, he thus sought naturalization with permission to hold benefices (AN o/1/222, fol. 385). And Vincent Grau, born in the Spanish enclave of Llívia of French parents, who received a declaration in September 1767, registered at the sovereign council of Perpignan, to assure his possession of the cure of Targassona, left to him by his uncle (AN O/1/234, fol. 41).

37. Siat, *Histoire du rattachement de l'Alsace*, 139–62; on the crown's religious policies toward the "conquered provinces," see de Roux, *Louis XIV*, 203–50; on the regulation of foreigners in Alsace, esp. the two ordinances of May and June 1720, see de Boug, *Recueil des édits*, 1:551–52; on prohibitions of selling land in Alsace, see BN MS 21714, fol. 108, declaration of 10 July 1731.

38. Metz, *La Monarchie française*, passim. The 1681 and 1703 ordinances were sometimes paraphrased in clerical letters of naturalization more generally: for example, those of Corneille Lyon, born in Ireland: AN O/1/230, fol. 267; naturalization draft of October 1753, redrafted in September 1754 (ibid., fol. 431).

39. AAE MD France 1434, fol. 35, letter of baron de Chateul to Foreign Minister duc de Praslin, August [?] 1763.

40. Boug, *Recueil des édits*, 2:629; on the relation of state building and the church in Old Regime and revolutionary France, see Bell, *Cult of the Nation*, esp. chaps. 1 and 6.

41. Ibid., 2:13.

42. AAE MD France 1454, fols. 11–12r, "Mémoire sur le rétablissement de la réciprocité à

l'égard des lettres de naturalité nécessaires pour posséder bénéfices dans les Pays-Bas," n.d. but ca. 1750.

43. BN MS JF 443, fols. 112–21, "Mémoire des cures et vicaires de la partie du dioceze de Trêves située en Lorraine et dans le royaume," on the occasion of a collective petition of priests and vicars of Trier concerning the nomination of a certain Petrement to the cure of Villête by the abbot of Bernardins in Chatillon-en-Verdunois in 1769.

44. AAE MD France 1454, fols. 39–43.

45. BN MS JF 554, fols. 71–80, "Consultation de M. le Garde des Sceaux sur une lettre de M. l'Eveque d'Ascalon qui proposait trois questions relative à la nomination des étrangers à des bénéfices dans le royaume," 31 March 1785.

46. AAE MD France 1454, fol. 123, letter of Vergennes to Chancellor Maupeou, 14 November 1788.

47. AN O/1/237, fol. 214, draft naturalization of Picard, December 1783; ibid., fol. 230; AAE MD France 1454, fols. 160–62, copy of naturalization of Jonquée, 1783.

48. AAE MD France 1454, fol. 159, letter of 27 February 1783.

49. Occasionally, individual foreigners who sought naturalization in the aftermath of the 1766 treaty invoked it and the subsequent patent letters: for example, the draft declaration of baron de Mean, 28 August 1771: O/1/234, fol. 309.

50. M. Price, *Preserving the Monarchy: The Comte de Vergennes, 1774–1787* (Cambridge, 1995), 187–222; and O. T. Murphy, *Charles Gravier, Comte de Vergennes: French Diplomacy in an Age of Revolution, 1719–1787* (Albany, 1982), 459–72; more generally, on French foreign policy after the American War of Independence, see Black, *From Louis XIV to Napoleon*, 134–47.

Chapter 7: From Law to Politics before the French Revolution

1. Pocock, "Ideal of Citizenship"; Gordon, "Citizenship"; cf. C. Wells, *Law and Citizenship*, chap. 5, and Riesenberg, *Citizenship*, 253–66.

2. On the Maupeou reforms, see the classic work of J. Egret, *Louis XV et l'opposition parlementaire, 1715–1774* (Paris, 1970); and the reinterpretations by Carey, *Judicial Reform in France*, esp. chap. 4, and J. Swann, *Politics and the Parlement of Paris, 1754–1774* (Cambridge, 1995); on its repercusions in French political culture, see S. Singham, "A Conspiracy of Twenty Million Frenchmen: Public Opinion, Patriotism, and the Assault on Absolutism, 1770–1775," Ph.D. diss., Princeton, 1991.

3. *Très-humbles et très respectueuses remontrances, que présentent au roi notre très honoré souverain et seigneur, les gens tenants sa Cour des Aides à Paris* (Paris, 1778), published in Dionis du Séjour, *Mémoires pour servir à l'histoire du droit public de la France en matières d'impôts* (Brussels, 1779), 628–93, reprinted with a translation by G. Robinson, *Translations and Reprints from the Original Sources of European History*, vol. 5, no. 2 (Philadelphia, 1912).

4. K. M. Baker, "Political Thought at the Access of Louis XVI," *Inventing the French Revolution* (Cambridge, 1990), 109–27, quote 119.

5. On the instruction and development of "public law" in the eighteenth century, see J. Portemer, "Recherches sur l'enseignement du droit public au XVIIIe siècle," *Revue historique de droit français et étranger*, 4th ser., 37 (1959): 341–97; and Chaussinard-Nogaret, *Le Citoyen des lumières*, 69–100. On the "rise of the public" more generally, see the recent synthesis of Van Horn Melton, *Rise of the Public*, esp. chap. 1.

6. On the role of the Paris Bar Association lawyers in the development of a "public" and oppositional discourse, informed by Jansenist critiques of the monarchy, see Bell, *Lawyers into Citizens*, passim, and below, this chapter, for a discussion of the relations between civil law practitioners and judicial publicists within the citizenship revolution.

7. 23 vols. and 4 suppls. (Neufchatel, 1752–77), vol. 3 [1753], 488–89. See the digital version of the *Encyclopédie* on two CD-ROMs, including the 2,800 plates produced by Redon in 1999.

8. A. Furetière, *Dictionnaire universel, contenant généralement tous les mots françois tant vieux que modernes, et les termes de toutes des sciences et des arts . . .* (Paris, 1727 [1685]); César de Rochefort, *Dictionnaire général et curieux* (Lyon, 1684); P. Richelet, *Dictionnaire françois augmenté par Pierre*

Richelet (Amsterdam, 1706); *Nouveau dictionnaire de l'Académie française*, 2 vols. (Paris, 1718); *Dictionnaire de Trévoux: [Dictionnaire universel françois et Latin. . . .]* (Paris, 1734). Nor did the first edition of the abbé Prévost's more prosaic *Manuel lexique ou Dictionnaire portatif de mots françois dont la signification n'est pas familière à tout le monde* (Paris, 1750) even list the entry "citoyen." But in the 1771 edition of the *Dictionnaire de Trévoux*, the definition of the *Encylcopédie* had taken hold: the citizen, it read, had "a specific relation to political society."

9. *Encyclopédie*, s.v. "citoyen."

10. Ibid.

11. K. Baker, "Transformation of Classical Republicanism in Eighteenth-Century France," *Journal of Modern History* 73 (2001): 23–53. The essential work on classical republicanism is Pocock, *The Machiavellian Moment*, which, as Baker has pointed out (34 and n. 6), fails to consistently reflect on republicanism in eighteenth-century France.

12. As we have seen, the accusation is unfair: Bodin had deliberately distinguished the *ville* (its inhabitants) from the *cité*: "for the town does not constitute the city, as several authors have written, no more than the house is constituted by the family," *Les Six livres*, 72.

13. *Social Contract*, 61–62.

14. Ibid. In his footnote critizing Bodin, Rousseau also cited d'Alembert and his essay on "Geneva" in the *Encyclopédie* as the only French author to have gotten it right. On Rousseau's idea of citizenship, see Riesenberg, *Citizenship*, 253–66, who identifies Rousseau with the "final citizenship of the Old Regime," and not an expression of the modern (cf. Brubaker, *Citizenship and Nationality*, 42). On Rousseau's inspiration by his native Geneva, see O. Krafft, "Les Classes sociales à Genève et la notion de citoyen," in *Jean-Jacques Rousseau et son oeuvre: Problèmes et Recherches*. Commémoration et Colloque de Paris (16–20 October 1962) (Paris, 1964), 219–227; C. Eisenmann, "La Cité de Jean-Jacques Rousseau," in *Etudes sur le contrat social de Jean-Jacques Rousseau* (Paris, 1964), 191–201; and H. Rosenblatt, *Rousseau and Geneva: From the First Discourse to the Social Contract, 1749–1762* (Cambridge, 1997). On the unenunciated dialogue of Bodin and Rousseau, see Quaglioni, "Les Citoyens envers l'Etat," 311–21.

15. Baker, "Transformations," passim. On Boulainvilliers, see Chaussinard-Nogaret, *Le Citoyen des lumières*, esp. 17–40; and especially Ellis, *Boulainvilliers and the French Monarchy*. Liah Greenfeld has traced the social origins of French nationalism to the aristocratic politics of the high or blood nobility (*Nationalism: Five Roads to Modernity* [Harvard, 1992], esp. 145–56), but David Bell has convincingly dismantled this social interpretation: see his *Cult of the Nation*, introduction and passim.

16. M. P. Fitzsimmons, "The National Assembly and the Invention of Citizenship," in *French Revolution*, ed. Waldinger et al., 30; on Mably, Saige, and French republicanism in the eighteenth century, see Baker, "Transformations," and *Inventing the French Revolution*, esp. chaps. 5–6.

17. On Sieyès's ideas of the citizen, see esp. W. H. Sewell, *A Rhetoric of Bourgeois Revolution: The Abbé Sieyès and What Is the Third Estate?* (Durham, 1994), esp. chap. 5; more generally, on the exclusions of revolutionary citizenship, see below, chap. 8.

18. Quoted in Merrick, "Subjects and Citizens," 453.

19. "Citoyen-Sujet, Civisme," 9:83; on the German method of *Begriffsgeschichte* in relation to social history, see R. Kosselleck, *Futures Past: On the Semantics of Historical Time*, trans. K. Tribe (Cambridge, Mass., 1985), esp. 73–91. Less methodologically but equally illuminating, see D. Gordon, *Citizens without Sovereignty: Equality and Sociability in French Thought, 1670–1789* (Princeton, 1994), on the parallel development of "society"; and Bell, *Cult of the Nation*, on the eighteenth-century redefinitions of the "fatherland" and "nation." Parallel accounts for other European countries are lacking, but the material interspersed in Ferrone and Roche, eds., *Le Monde des lumières*, is useful. On the Dutch, see also W. Mijhardt, "The Batavian Citizen: Dutch Ideas on Moral Citizenship in the Batavian Period," in *Civisme et citoyenneté: Une longue histoire*. Journées scientifiques du Pôle Universitaire Européen de Montpellier et du Languedoc-Roussillon (Montpellier, 1999), esp. 151–52.

20. Merrick, "Subjects and Citizens," 458.

21. The reversed term *roi-citoyen* was already in use before the death of Louis XV. Josephe de Maistre, in his *Considérations de la France*, noted that "Racine the younger penned this fine poem for the king of France in the name of Paris, his hometown: 'Under a king-citizen, each citizen is a

king' [*sous un roi-citoyen, tout citoyen est roi*]," and before that Charles Favart (1710–92), in *Soliman Second* (1761) wrote: "No slaves among us; one breathes in France / Only the pleasures, liberty, and comfort / Each citizen is king under a king-citizen." Louis Philippe eventually took the official title of Citizen-King in 1830.

22. For an overview on the Jansenist question in eighteenth-century France, see D. Van Kley, *The Religious Origins of the French Revolution, 1560–1791* (New Haven, 1996); on the struggle for toleration, including for Jews, my remarks are heavily indebted to Merrick, *Desacralization*, and his "Conscience and Citizenship in Eighteenth-Century France."

23. Above, chap. 2; Merrick, *Desacralization*, passim, esp. chap. 6 (on the "fiction of uniformity").

24. Citations are from Merrick, *Desacralization*, 33, 178.

25. Citations are from ibid., 105–6.

26. Ibid., 134; on the development of a language of "rights" in the second half of the 18th century, see L. Hunt, "The Paradoxical Origins of Human Rights," in *Human Rights and Revolutions*, ed. J. N. Wasserstrom, L. Hunt, and M. B. Young (Lanham, Md., 2000), 3–7; and Shennan, "Political Vocabulary," 956, who documents the rhetorical shifts toward "rights" in the parliamentary vocabulary of the 1750s. On the developing discourse of the "nation" more generally, see the older studies of R. Bickart, *Les Parlements et la notion de souveraineté nationale au XVIIIe siècle* (Paris, 1932), and J. Egret, *Louis XV et l'opposition parlementaire, 1715–1774* (Paris, 1970).

27. Cited in Merrick, *Desacralization*, 86–87; Merrick, "Subjects and Citizens," 456–57, notes the insistence on this language in the "Great Remonstrances" of 9 April 1753 and especially the remonstrances of 27 November 1755 in defense of religious liberty.

28. Kwass, *Privilege and the Politics of Taxation*; and, in a convergent interpretation, the processes traced by G. Bossenga, "From *Corps* to Citizenship: The *Bureaux des Finances* before the French Revolution," in *Journal of Modern History* 58 (1986): 610–42. For an exemplary case study of how a new language of liberty (and equality and citizenship) appeared from within the corporative structure of the Old Regime, see David Bien's interpretation of the relations of taxation and debt management in "Old Regime Origins of Democratic Liberty," in *The French Idea of Freedom: The Old Regime and the Declaration of Rights of 1789*, ed. D. Van Kley (Stanford, 1994).

29. Bell, *Cult of the Nation*, passim. As its title suggests, Bell's argument gives primacy to religion: he follows the lead of Marcel Gauchet, arguing for a "disenchantment of the world" that opened a conceptual space to be filled by secular constructs such as the "nation"; and he links the official construction of French nationalism to the earlier efforts of the Counter-Reformation clergy in the kingdom (see esp. 1–21).

30. On Fougeret and the decline of cosmopolitanism after the 1760s, see D. Gordon, "The Origins of a Polarity: Cosmopolitanism versus Citizenship in Early Modern Europe," unpublished manuscript generously circulated by the author; C. Bruschi, "Note sur l'étranger et la nation au XVIII siècle," in *Nation et République: Les Éléments d'un débat*, Actes du colloque de Dijon (6–7 April 1994). Association française des idées politiques (Aix, 1995), 41–47; and J. Grieder, *Anglomania in France, 1740–1789: Fact, Fiction, and Political Discourse* (Geneva, 1985), 117–46. Synoptical treatments of the intellectual history of cosmopolitanism in France and Europe include P. Hazard, "Cosmopolite," in *Mélanges d'histoire littéraire générale et comparée offerts à Fernand Baldensperger*, 2 vols. (Paris, 1930), 1:354–64; and W. Frijhoff, "Cosmpolitisme," in *Le Monde des lumières*, ed. V. Ferrone and D. Roche (Paris, 1999), 31–40.

31. Statt, *Foreigners and Englishmen*; on the "Jew Bill" of 1753, see the classic study by Perry, *Public Opinion*; and, for the seventeenth-century background, D. S. Katz, *Philo-Semitism and the Readmission of the Jews to England, 1603–1655* (Oxford, 1982).

32. In our earlier work, Dubost and Sahlins, *Et si on faisait payer*, esp. 377–84, we perhaps exaggerated the importance of the 1697 tax specifically in the crystallization of a universal distinction between "citizens" and "foreigners," following a historiographical tradition that has often identified the 1690s as a moment when the language of "nation" and "citizen" was born (e.g., Chaussinard-Nogaret, *Le Citoyen des lumières*, 17 et seq.). Chaussinard-Nogaret's argument is partially supported in a crude statistical study of digitalized literary texts (the ARTFL project) that mark a notable increase in the use of the term "citoyen" during the 1690s, including (and especially) in the works of Fénelon. David Bell, however, has convincingly argued that modern expressions of "nationalism" (as the self-conscious political construction of national identity and self-gover-

nance) were a product of the period that only began during the Seven Years War (1756–1763): *Cult of the Nation*, passim; in tandem, the vocabulary of the "citizen" also appeared at this moment, within the citizenship revolution.

33. Dubost and Sahlins, *Et si on faisait payer,* 372–77.

34. Gaschon, *Code diplomatique,* 305–10 and passim. Unless otherwise noted, all citations from the treaties are from Gaschon's treatise, verified and complemented from the sources mentioned in appendix 2. Gaschon's was the last in a long line of compilations of and commentaries on these treaties that began in the 1760s. His text, as we shall see, was engaged in the political debates over the final abolition of the droit d'aubaine in 1819, and he argued that its "reciprocal abolition" in the treaties of the Old Regime (a principle that he supported) failed in all but a few cases to institute the positive civil right of foreigners to inherit from French nationals: see below, chap. 8 and conclusion.

35. On the consequences of the Seven Years War, see Riley, *The Seven Years War,* passim; on the declining role of France in the international arena, see, for example, Bély, *Les Relations internationales en Europe,* chap. 18; for an overview of the political struggles and fiscal crises in France during these years, see, for example, Swann, *Politics and the Parlement of Paris,* passim, and 27–44 for a fine historiographic survey of the problem.

36. AAE ADP France 1, no. 39, marginal annotation: "One only speaks of the margrave of Baden, such that it isn't clear which of the two princes made the request. One presumes it is Baden-Baden, because its prince has the greater interest in doing so."

37. France 1, no. 39, "Sur la lettre de M. le Contrôleur-Général et le mémoire qui est joint concernant la demande de Baden . . . ," 13 December 1761.

38. On the territorialization of the state in the eighteenth century, especially in relation to "natural frontiers," the subject of an extensive literature in recent years, see P. Sahlins, "National Frontiers Revisited: France's Boundaries since the Seventeenth Century," *American Historical Review* 95, no. 5 (1990): 1423–51, Table of Delimitation Treaties, 1439; Sahlins, *Boundaries,* chap. 5; J. F. Noël, "Les Problèmes des frontières entre la France et L'Empire dans la seconde moité du XVIIIe siècle," *Revue historique* 235 (1966): 336–37; Nordman, *Frontières de France,* esp. pt. 3, and sources cited above, chap. 5, n. 26. The foreign minsitry set up a "bureau des limites" initially in 1746, run by Nicolas Louis Le Dran, son of the first secretary of the foreign office who in the 1730s had developed the most elaborate apology of the droit d'aubaine as a right of royal sovereignty (above, chap. 1).

39. AAE ADP France 1, no. 39.

40. AAE MD Austria 7, fols. 188–224, "Mémoire sur la proposition faite par M. de Penterioter de suprimer réciproquement entre l'empéreur et le roy le droit d'aubaine sur les sujets de l'Alsace et sur ceux de Brisgau," 15 January 1719.

41. But in the 1680s French treasury officials in the province had begun to collect the droit d'aubaine as part of the extension and homogenization of the king's authority throughout the kingdom. BN MS 21754, fols. 43–45, exemption of bourgeois and inhabitants of Strasbourg, 15 December 1692 (noting earlier decrees of 1683 and 1684).

42. AAE MD Austria 7, fols. 194 et seq., 15 January 1719.

43. AAE ADP France 1, no. 74, letter of Intendant Luce of Alsace, November 1763.

44. Ibid., n. 39, esp. fols. 39–55, 13 December 1761.

45. The lawyers and politicians of the Napoleonic Empire and the Bourbon Restoration, from Roederer to Gaschon, were to make much of the fact that the language was ambiguous, but this did not stop them from distinguishing the few treaties or privileges that gave positive inheritance rights to foreigners from the bulk of the treaties that exempted, in varying degrees, subjects of other states from the droit d'aubaine.

46. No doubt, the first secretary (*premier commis*) was responsible for these: see Piccioni, *Les Premiers commis,* chap. 7; and more generally, J.-P. Samoyault, *Les Bureaux du Secretariat d'Etat des affaires étrangères sous Louis XV* (Paris, 1971). There is also no doubt about the involvement in the French foreign ministry of the so-called German Chancellery made up of Alsatian jurisconsults employed in the foreign ministry to "translate" the public law of the empire: on these clerks and officials, see A. Salomon, "Les Alsaciens employés au ministère des affaires étrangères au XVIIe et XVIIIe siècle," *Revue d'histoire diplomatique* 54 (1931): 449–72.

47. Choppin, *Oeuvres*, 2:118. *Abzug* was itself glossed in the Latin *ius detracta*.

48. On the *ius detractus*, see de Vattel, *The Law of Nations or the Principles of Natural Law Applied to the Conduct and to the Affairs of Nations and Sovereigns*, vol. 3 (Buffalo, 1995), bk. 2, chap. 8; and AAE France ADP 1, fols. 35–8, "Droit d'émigration: Quelle est sa nature . . ." n.d. [post 1756].

49. AAE France ADP 1, fol. 36. Such an interpretation served the French well, since the abolitions of the droit d'aubaine involved, precisely, the establishment of "commerce" and "communication."

50. AAE ADP France 1, fols. 92–97, anon. letter to Boislecompte, 27 November 1783.

51. Type I treaties did not mention such a right, nor did they invoke customary practices. Except for Savoy, the signatories of this group of treaties were not bordering states, nor states with developed feudal traditions in which taxes on the transfer of property were imbedded. The accord with the United Provinces makes no mention of the droit d'aubaine, nor does the collective exemption of the imperial nobility of the Swabian Circles (a variation on the 1783 type II).

52. Montbéliard's state archives survive in France because the duchy and its dependencies were completely surrounded by French jurisdictions in Alsace: "reunited" with France during the Thirty Years War and formally annexed in 1681, they were restituted in the Treaty of Ryswick (1713), and only definitively attached to France during the Revolution. The archives are in AN K 2043/2–3, 2044/1–3. See J. M. Débard, "La Principauté de Montbéliard et la monarchie française au XVIIe siècle," *Provinces et Etats dans la France de l'Est* (Bésançon, 1978).

53. AN K 2044/3, letter of duc de Choiseul to baron de Thun, including a "Réponse aux observations du conseil de Montbéliard," 2 November 1766.

54. Ibid., letter of the regency council to the duc de Württemberg, 28 October 1768.

55. Ibid., letter of baron de Thun to the regency council, 27 August 1777.

56. Ibid., letter of Vergennes to the baron de Thun, 28 November 1777; and letter of baron de Thun to the regency council, 27 March 1778. In fact, a similar clause on "transmigration" was replaced with the formal declaration that "the respective subjects will be held to the laws, formalities, and rights in the states and countries where the said successions were opened," even though more formal control of "transmigration" can be found in the treaties negotiated with the principalities of Hesse-Cassel (1767) and Hesse-d'Armstadt (1767). See the final text of the Württemberg accord in BN MS 4254(13) and the commentary by Gaschon in *Code diplomatique*, 202–7.

57. AAE ADP France 1, fols. 35–38, "Droit d'émigration." His commentary on the patent letters was this: "It is clear that the king wishes to confirm these proximate seigneurs in their exercise of the Abzug, but only on the inhabitants of their lands who go to settle outside the kingdom. Nothing has been expressed, in any fashion, about inheritances exported abroad, which proves invincibly that His Majesty has reserved for himself the exercise of the droit de détraction, which like the aubaine itself cannot be transferred." Meanwhile, the courts litigated the question: see, for example, *Gazette des Tribuneaux* 17, no. 27 (1783): 350 et seq., and 19 (1785): 125–26, concerning the duc de Valentois, hereditary prince of Monaco's collection of the "droit de détraction ou d'émigration" in Alsace contested by the royal tax-farmers.

58. AAE ADP France 1, no. 92, letter of Antoine in Nancy to M. de Boislecomte, 16 November 1783.

59. AN H1 158850, fols. 16–17.

60. *The Spirit of the Laws*, trans. A. M. Cohler, B. C. Miller, and H. S. Stone (Cambridge, 1989 [1748]), 386.

61. A. Hirschman, *The Passions and the Interests: Arguments for Capitalism before Its Triumph* (Princeton, 1977), 71–74.

62. C. Larrère, *L'Invention de l'économie au XVIIIe siècle* (Paris, 1992); on François Quesnay's early work representing the "transition from mercantilism to mature physiocracy," see E. Fox-Genovese, *The Origins of Physiocracy: Economic Revolution and Social Order in Eighteenth-Century France* (Ithaca, 1976), 109 et. seq.

63. R. L. Meek, *The Economics of Physiocracy: Essays and Translations* (London, 1962), 30; Conventionally, scholars have identified the beginnings of Physiocracy in 1756 and 1757, but important works were composed by the abbé André Morellet and Pierre-Samuel Dupont de Nemours in the early 1750s: see A. Murphy, "Le Développement des idées économiques en France

(1750–1756)," *Revue d'histoire moderne et contemporaine* 33 (1986): 521–41. Moreover, the older scholarship tends to credit Quesnay more than to emphasize his collaboration with Mirabeau: cf. Fox-Genovese, *Origins of Physiocracy*, esp. 134–66. On Physiocracy as a "kind of catechism, precisely laid out, and done such that each lesson can be broken down and subdivided by the teachers," see Mirabeau's remarks quoted in H. Ripert, *Le Marquis de Mirabeau (L'Ami des Hommes): Ses Théories politiques et économiques* (Paris, 1901), 416–17.

64. The renamed *Nouvelles Ephémérides économiques* were published again in 1774–76 and in 1788, at moments when Turgot and later Necker were engaged in the projects of conceiving a new citizenship of provincial assemblies. On Mirabeau and his "school," see Ripert, *Le Marquis de Mirabeau*, esp. 404–26; and on the participation of the Rhineland princes, 416–17. The margrave wrote to Mirabeau in July 1770 of how "it seems like the portico of Athens, except that I believe economic philosophy to be more useful to humanities that that which was taught by Greek philosophers." Mirabeau, in a later letter in reference to the prince of Saxe-Weimar, commented how "I will nonetheless try to give my class in the morning, and to give them economic works that they can study afterwards in a more leisurely fashion" (407–8). For the complete correspondence, see C. Knies, *Correspondance inédite de Dupont de Nemours et du marquis de Mirabeau avec le margrave et le prince héréditaire de Bade*, 2 vols. (Paris, 1892).

65. M. Marion, *Machault d'Arnouville: Etude sur l'histoire du contrôle général des finances de 1749 à 1754* (Paris, 1892), 422–42. Physiocratic thought never considered the international grain trade at the center of its program, although this element was consistently present and formed part of the critique of mercantilism: see G. Weulersse, *La Physiocratie à la fin du règne de Louis XV (1770–74)* (Paris, 1959), 180–81 et seq.; and A. I. Bloomfield, "The Foreign-Trade Doctrines of the Physiocrates," *American Economic Review* 28 (1938): 716–35.

66. M. Einaudi, *The Physiocratic Doctrine of Judicial Control* (Cambridge, Mass., 1938), 12. Classical studies of the economic liberalism of the Physiocrats include R. L. Meek, *The Economics of Physiocracy: Essays and Translations* (London, 1962); and the works of G. Weulersse, esp. *Le Mouvement physiocratique en France de 1756 à 1770*. 2 vols. (Paris, 1910).

67. Quesnay thus denounced the merchant as a "foreigner in his fatherland," quoted in Roche, *La France des lumières*, 131; on the physiocratic conception of "sterile" classes (including merchants), see A. Lorion, *Les Théories politiques des premiers physiocrates* (Paris, 1918), 116–27.

68. Quoted in Ripert, *Le Marquis de Mirabeau*, 222; on Physiocracy and the "new diplomacy," see Gilbert, "The 'New Diplomacy,' " 11–14. On Quesnay's different ideas about the free circulation within and outside the kingdom that did not depend on reciprocity, see Dockès, *L'Espace*, 260–94. Positions on "free trade" thus varied, including attitudes toward the removal of internal customs barriers: J. Bosher, *The Single Duty Project: A Study of the Movement for a French Customs Union in the Eighteenth Century* (London, 1964), argues that the Physiocrats did not support the single duty project: 69–72, 170–71, passim.

69. Bouchaud, *Théories des traités de commerce entre les nations* (Paris, 1777), 8.

70. Mirabeau, *L'Ami des Hommes* (Avignon, 1756), 93, 290.

71. Le Trosne, *De l'administration provinciale et de la réforme de l'impot*, 3 vols. (Basel, 1788), 1:364–68; more generally, on the Physiocratic condemnation of the droit d'aubaine, see G. Weulersse, *La Physiocratie sous les ministères de Turgot et de Necker (1774–1781)* (Paris, 1950), 308–9.

72. AAE ADP France 2, fol. 21, marquis de Boynes to duc d'Aiguillon, 30 November 1771.

73. Grieder, *Anglomania in France, 1740–1789*, passim.

74. J.-C. Perrot, "Les Économistes, les philosophes, et la population," in *Histoire de la population française*, vol. 2: *De la Renaissance à 1789*, ed. J. Dupâquier (Paris, 1988), 515–18.

75. *Recherches et considerations sur la population en France* (Paris, 1778), 246–48; see J. J. Spengler, "Moheau: Prophet of Depopulation," in *Journal of Political Economy* 47, no. 5 (1939): 648–77.

76. Vattel, *Law of Nations*, 147–48 (bk. 2, chap. 8, par. 112); on eighteenth-century international law, see F. Ruddy, *International Law in the Enlightenment: The Background of Emmerich de Vattel's Droit des Gens* (Dobbs Ferry, N.Y., 1975).

77. Cited in S. Aragon, "Les Belles étrangères vues par les femmes auteurs des lumières," in *Visions de l'étranger au siècle des Lumières*, ed. M.-O. Bernez (Dijon, 2002), 161.

78. *Journals et mémoires du marquis d'Argenson*, ed. E. J. B. Rathery, 9 vols. (Paris, 1859–67), 9:128.

79. *Oeuvres de Turgot*, 2 vols. (Paris, 1844), 1:399. Already in 1755, Turgot had translated and annotated a pamphlet of Josiah Tucker supporting the bill naturalizing foreign Protestants before the English Parliament: "Questions importantes sur le Commerce, à l'occasion des oppositions au dernier Bill de Naturalisation. Pamphlet économique de Josiah Tucker, traduit et annoté par Turgot," quoted in Rapport, " 'A Languishing Branch,' " 20. On Turgot, see the still classic study by D. Dakin, *Turgot and the Ancien Régime in France* (New York, 1965).

80. In a parenthetical "little history of French nationality," the Protestant-born and unnaturalized minister consulted with the jurisconsult François Tronchet in April 1786 on the extent of his ability to will his property to his wife. The question required assessing the legal capacities of Madame Necker, born in a Swiss Catholic canton whose inhabitants were exempted from the droit d'aubaine, and Jacques himself. Tronchet denied the controller-general's capacity to make a valid will in France as a "citizen of Geneva." Because inheritance was ineffably part of civil law ["it only belongs to those who are members of a corps and state that has established specific laws"], Tronchet argued that the conventions of exemption, both before and during the eighteenth century, could not confer privileges on foreigners that were not shared by French natives. Genevans had no rights to inherit from Frenchmen or women; foreigners, as *peregrini*, could not hold property or privileges that set them apart from "the authority of the territorial law [in this case, the customary law of Paris] in the jurisdiction where the goods are located." AP ACA Fonds Tronchet, vol. 16, n. 1616, 15 April 1786. Tronchet makes the same argument as Emmerich de Vattel in *The Law of Nations*, 146 (bk. 2, chap. 8)

81. On the fate of physiocratic thought in the later eighteenth century, see Weulersse, *La Physiocratie sous les ministères de Turgot et de Necker*, passim.

82. *De l'Administration des finances de la France* (Paris, 1784), 3:270–6 [bk. 3, chap. 25]: "Sur le droit d'aubaine." The standard biography is R. Harris, *Necker, Reform Statesman of the Ancien Régime* (Berkeley, 1979).

83. AAE ADP France 2, letter of Calonne to the comte de Vergennes, 25 January 1786.

84. Ibid., fol. 151, Calonne to Vergennes, 9 April 1787.

85. *Oeuvres de Turgot*, 1:399. On the opposition and rivalry, personal and political, of Turgot and Vergennes, especially over French participation in the American War of Independence, see Price, *Preserving the Monarchy*, 49–50; on that of Vergennes and Necker, see ibid., 55–56.

86. AAE ADP France 1, no. 142, "Réponses aux observations de M. le Garde des Sceaux," n.d. [but ca. September 1785].

87. AAE CP England, 554, fol. 324, Calonne to Vergennes, 16 November 1785. See M. Donaghay, "Calonne and the Anglo-French Commercial Treaty of 1786," *Journal of Modern History* 50, no. 3, supp. (1978): D1157–D1184, and W. O. Henderson, "The Anglo-French Commercial Treaty of 1789," *Economic History Review*, n.s., 10 (1957): 104–12. See also Murphy, *Charles Gravier*, 432–46; and Bosher, *Single Duty Project*, 72–75, on physiocratic views of England, considered incapable of competing with France because of its stifling of agriculture.

88. For an overview of Anglo-French relations from the French perspective, see Black, *From Louis XIV to Napoleon*, chap. 5. Bell's *Cult of the Nation* explores the pamphlet literature, especially in his essay on "Jumontville's Death: Nation and Race in Eighteenth-Century France." More generally, Bell follows Linda Colley's model of how England itself had constructed its own national identity in the eighteenth century against the "Catholic Other" that was France: L. Colley, *Britons: Forging the Nation, 1707–1837* (New Haven, 1992), a model adapted from my book on the French-Spanish borderland: *Boundaries*. For an older view, see F. Acomb, *Anglophobia in France: An Essay in the History of Constitutionalism and Nationalism* (Durham, 1950).

89. On the rhetoric of Anglophobia during the Revolution, see especially Wahnich, *L'Impossible citoyen*.

90. On Vergennes's relation to the Physiocratic program, see G. Weulersse, *La Physiocratie à l'aube de la Révolution, 1781–1792*, ed. C. Beutler (Paris, 1985), 32–33, 186–89; Murphy, *Charles Gravier*, 432–46; and J.-F. Labourdette, *Vergennes: Ministre principal de Louis XVI* (Paris, 1990), 257 et seq.

91. Mayer, *Vie publique et privée de Charles Gravier, comte de Vergennes, ministre d'état; Discours couronné par l'Académie d'Amiens le 25 août 1788* (Paris, 1789), 130.

92. Quoted in P.-A. Fenet, *Recueil complet des travaux préparatoires du Code civil*, 15 vols. (Paris, 1827), 7:229–30, by Boissy d'Anglade (see below, chapter 8).

93. BN MS JF 268, fols. 146–47, "Droit d'aubaine." The text represents the commentary of Gullaume François Joly de Fleury, solicitor-general at the Paris parlement, on a no longer extant project that de Fleury strongly opposed, the project of enforcing a "universal" droit d'aubaine.

94. Lefebvre de la Planche, *Mémoires*, 2:8, n. (a).

95. Price, *Preserving the Monarchy*, perhaps overemphasizes Vergennes's conservatism, 19 et seq.; for a more balanced view, see Murphy, *The Comte de Vergennes*, passim.

96. AAE ADP France 1, fols. 98–99, anon. report to the council of state, 11 December 1785, relating the report of the comte de Vergennes to Louis XVI.

97. D'Holbach's definition of the citizen was put forth in the *Encyclopédie*, s. v. "Représentants," cited in Rosanvallon, *Le Sacre du Citoyen*, 46; G.-F. Le Trosne, *De l'administration provinciale et de la réforme de l'impot*, 3 vols. (Basel, 1788[1779]). Le Trosne, a magistrate, emphasized judicial control of sovereign authority: see Einaudi, *Physiocratic Doctrine*, 34–40.

98. Cited in Lorion, *Les Théories politiques*, 122; obversely, merchants and manufacturers should not be considered citizens (ibid., 125–26); see also Rosanvallon, *Le Sacre du citoyen*, 48–50 et seq., who distinguishes the prerevolutionary projects of "proprietor citizen" (*citoyen proprietaire*) from the "taxed citizen" (*citoyenneté contributaire*) that took shape, in tandem with ideas of equality, individuality, and the universality of political rights, during the Revolution itself. The former, informed by physiocratic thinking, relied on an ideological framework of "dependence," which continued during the Revolution but was abandoned in the late 1790s in favor of strict and highly limited property requirements, whose variation set the conditions of political participation in the nineteenth century (see below, chap. 8).

99. The classical works on provincial assemblies under Louis XVI include P. Renouvin, *Les Assemblées provinciales de 1787* (Paris, 1921), and L. de Lavergne, *Les Assemblées provinciales sous Louis XVI* (Paris, 1879); a more recent and balanced assessment can be found in Kwass, *Privilege and Politics*, 255–73; on the opposition of republican reformers generally to the principles of Physiocracy, see Baker, "Transformations," 38, citing the *Doutes proposés au philosophes économiques* by Mably, published in 1768, which, according to Baker, appealed to the "ancient" republicanism that insisted on the "sustained assertion of a political will" and not a "modern" republicanism created by "the purportedly self-necessitating rule of reason." Specifically, on Mably's opposition to Physiocracy, see Weulersse, *La Physiocratie*, 24–25.

100. Bell, *Lawyers and Citizens*, passim; citation, 9. For a synthetic discussion of the "classical" French Bar Association, the professional culture, and the "political liberalism" of lawyers in the eighteenth century, see L. Karpick, *French Lawyers: A Study in Collective Action, 1274 to 1994*, trans. N. Scott (Oxford, 1999), 36–86; see also Fumaroli, *L'Age de l'éloquence*, pt. 3, on the rhetorical movement, mediated by Jansenism, from "men of law" to "men of letters" in the eighteenth century.

101. Denisart, *Collection* (1783), 4:561.

102. The traditional conservatism of French lawyers in the late eighteenth century is emphasized by Watson (who writes that "though the concerns of the citizens had become politicized, lawyers were still trained to think of law as private law": *Making of Civil Law*, 156) and Halperin, *L'Impossible Code civil*, 74.

103. Halperin, *L'Impossible Code civil*, 63–64; cf., Watson, *Making of Civil Law*, 88–89, who argues that the growth of natural law in the seventeenth and eighteenth centuries, following the influence of Grotius, was matched by the decline in the authority of the *Corpus juris*.

104. Justinian is quoted in Bosquet, *Dictionnaire raisonné*, 1:170–84: Questions of succession, he wrote, "depend absolutely on civil law, in which all citizens participate, and from which foreigners are entirely excluded" (70).

105. Chêne, *L'Enseignement du droit français*, 230–35; Martinage, *Bourjon*, 113–22; B. Beignier, "Portalis et le droit naturel dans le Code civil," *Revue d'histoire des facultés de droit et de la science juridique*, no. 6 (1988): 77–101.

106. Watson, *Making of Civil Law*, chap. 7, on the indebtedness of French civil law before and after the Civil Code to Justinian's *Institutes*; for contemporary opinions, see the remarks by the

minor barrister Loeuilliet, *Principes des lois romaines comparés aux principes des lois français* (Douai, 1787), 9; and the anonymously published epistolary treatise by André-Jean Boucher d'Argis, *Lettres d'un magistrat de Paris à un magistrat de province sur le droit romain et la manière dont on l'enseigne en France* (1782).

107. *Mémoires*, 2:68; see also Denisart, *Collection* (1783), 1:580–85.

108. Bosquet, *Dictionnaire*, 1:171.

109. Lefebvre de la Planche, *Mémoires*, 2:68, n.(a). Other eighteenth-century commentators, not as sophisticated juridically, also insisted that the treaties of exemption contained a variety of greater or lesser derogations to the "common and general law," ranging from simple exemptions from the droit d'aubaine to full-scale privileges permitting foreigners to gather successions from native-born kinsmen: see, for example, J.-L. Moreau de Beaumont, *Mémoires concernant les impositions et droits en Europe*, 4 vols. (Paris, 1787 [1768]), 4:629. Beaumont is the source of much of the factual evidence used by the Physiocrat Le Trosne (e.g., *De l'Administration provinciale*, 1:338).

110. Overviews of the early modern efforts to codify and unify private law include J. Vanderlinden, *Le Concept de code en Europe occidentale du XIIIe au XIXe siecle: Essai de définition* (Brussels, 1967); J. Krynen, "The Absolute Monarchy and the French Unification of Private Rights," in *Privileges and Rights of Citizenship: Law and the Juridical Construction of Society*, ed. J. Kirshner and L. Mayali (Berkeley, 2002), 27–56; J. Van Kan, *Les Efforts de codification en France: Etude historique et psychologique* (Paris, 1929); and J. Gaudemet, "Les Tendances à l'unification du droit en France dans les derniers siècles de l'Ancien Régime (XVIe–XVIIIe)," in *La Formazione storica del diritto moderno in Europa*, Atti del terzo congresso internazionale della societa italiana di storia del diritto (Florence, 1972), 157–94.

111. H. Regnault, *Les Ordonnances civiles du chancelier Daguesseau: Les Testaments et l'ordonnance de 1735* (Paris, 1938); Regnault, *Les Ordonnances civiles du chancelier Daguesseau: Les Donations et l'ordonnance de 1731* (Paris, 1929), esp. 31–48. On the efforts of Laverdy and Langlois, two Parisian magistrates, to continue Chancellor d'Aguesseau's unification of civil law in 1759, see the document reproduced by V. Azimi, "Une Tentative d'unification du droit civil: Le Projet inédit de Laverdy et Langlois," *Mémoires de la Société pour l'histoire du droit et des institutions des anciens pays Bourguignons, Comtois, et Romands*, no. 42 (1985): 123–56.

112. AN K 873, nos. 41–46, contains the responses of the parlements, inventoried and studied in detail by M. Folain-Le Bras, *Un projet d'ordonnance du Chancelier Daguesseau: Etude de quelques incapacités de donner et de recevoir sous l'Ancien Régime* (Paris, 1941), 10–17. Some of the responses were printed: [H.-F. d'Aguesseau], *Recueil des questions de jurisprudence proposés par M. d'Aguesseau . . . à tous les parlements du royaume concernant les donations, les testaments, les substitutions, les incapacités de donner et de recevoir, et les matières bénéficiales. Avec les réponses du parlement de Toulouse sur ces mêmes questions. . . .* (n.p., 1749).

113. The early nineteenth-century lawyer J. B. Gaschon astutely observed that the "ancient jurisconsultes" had not used the idea of civil disability (*incapacité*) as a foundation of the droit d'aubaine, but had used the droit d'aubaine as a foundation of this disability: *Code diplomatique*, 133.

114. AN K 873, no. 43 (3) and (4) [Grenoble]; ibid., no. 46 (8) [Toulouse].

115. Ibid., no. 41 (1).

116. Folain-Le Bras, *Un Projet d'ordonnance*, 82.

117. AN K 873, nos. 38, 39.

118. AN AD XV 1, no. 128, "Arrest de la cour de parlement en faveur des hollandois, qui les juge capables de Succeder en France, meme a leurs parens François," 1715. In a frequently cited case from 1761, François Antoine Jabach (born of a father from Köln but naturalized by the Estates of the Netherlands, thus considered a Dutch citizen) was upheld in his claim to inherit against the receiver general of the domain, in the name of the king: ABP Recueil Gaultier de Breuil, vol. 12, no. 27. "Les Hollandais sont-ils affranchis en France du droit d'aubaine? . . . ," signed Damours (1761).

119. AP BACA Recueil Gaultier de Breil, vol. 77, no. 35 (1786).

120. Ibid., 15. On the Enlightened language of "human rights," see Hunt, "The Paradoxical Origins of Human Rights," 8–11.

121. AP BACA Receuil Gaultier de Breuil, vol. 77, no. 35, 50–53. The Doria case is reported by Merlin, *Répertoire*, 7: 416–25.

122. Details of this "cause célèbre" were reported by Merlin, *Répertoire*, 7:416–25.

123. AP BACA Receuil Gaultier de Breuil, vol. 77, no. 35 (1786).

124. AP BACA Recueil Martineau, vol. 11, no. 12, "Mémoire pour M. Rouxeau des Fontenelles . . . contre le sieur Abbé Lemmens . . . ," 1783.

125. Ibid.

126. Gaschon, *Code diplomatique*, 39, 52.

127. AP BACA Recueil Gaultier de Breuil, vol. 77, no. 35, 48. Although the Paris parlement was willing to make decisions, other courts jumped directly to the judgment that only the royal council could decide the question. Such was the lesson of the lawsuit brought by Charles Howard, baron of Greystock, in 1763. Howard and his English wife claimed the execution of Article 13 of the Utrecht Treaty and the declaration of 1739, in which subjects of the king of Great Britain were allowed to inherit movables from their kin who died in France, just as French subjects could inherit similar properties from their kinsmen who died in England. But reciprocity was not the rule because in English common law all foreigners (including Frenchmen and women) could inherit, while French "common law" required naturalization or a particular treaty to that effect. The Châtelet turned the case down, and the plaintiffs were instructed to seek naturalization, and pointed in the direction of the royal council, where they might have more success: AP BACA Recueil Gaultier de Breuil, vol. 8, nos. 27, 11–13.

128. For brief biographical sketches of the comte de Mercy-Argenteau, see F.-C. Mercy-Argenteau, *Correspondance secrète du comte de Mercy-Argenteau avec l'empereur Joseph II et le prince de Kaunitz*, ed. A. d'Arneth and M. J. Flammermont, 3 vols. (Paris, 1891), introduction to vol. 1; and T. Juste, *Le Comte de Mercy-Argenteau* (Brussels, 1863). Florimond de Mercy was himself a beneficiary of a letter of naturalization, or more precisely its fictional juridical equivalent: to inherit an estate from his father the comte de Mercy, in Lorraine near Longwy, he acquired through the offices of the duc de Choiseul in 1761 a permission to inherit and not be subjected to the droit d'aubaine, itself only abolished between France and the subjects of Austria in 1766: ibid., xxiii.

129. AAE MD America 16, fols. 150–150v, Mercy-Argenteau to duc d'Aiguillon, 3 May 1773.

130. AP BACA Recueil Martineau, no. 12, 54 ff.

131. Ghachem, "Sovereignty and Slavery," 175 ff.

132. Ibid., chap. 4.

133. AAE ADP France 2, no. 21, "Observations . . . sur les differents traités par lesquels le droit d'aubaine a été aboli," marquis de Boynes to the duc d'Aiguillon, 30 November 1779. The marquis de Boynes thus opposed the extension of the droit d'aubaine's exemption to the colonies, although he did realize that the conventions and treaties produced a central confusion. The treaties, he argued, failed to distinguish between the right of the king and that of his subjects: the king's right was that of collecting the droit d'aubaine only if there was no subject of the king, of whatever degree of relatedness. If there were a French kinsman, however distant, he would supersede the king's right to the droit d'aubaine. But the conventions, studiously examined by de Boynes, made no mention of this distinction. According to de Boynes, this had unintentionally deprived the king's subjects of their rights to collect or gather inheritances, since the treaties explicitly stipulated that foreigners and regnicoles were co-equal. This argument figured among his reasons for opposing the extension of the droit d'aubaine's abolition to the colonies, a step that "would leave the boundaries of sound policies."

134. AAE Fonds Divers Amerique 16, fol. 144v, marquis de Boynes to duc d'Aiguillon, 27 September 1772.

135. Or on boats that had left Saint-Domingue, as was the case of François Rizial, from Turin, who died in 1771 having left the island, and in whose will a French native had been named the universal heir: ibid.; see also AP BACA Chanclaire, vol. 105, no. 8, n.d., ca. 1778: the suit was brought by the *receveur du droit d'aubaine* on 29 November 1777.

136. AP BACA Martineau, vol. 11, no. 12, 65. See the two letters by the ministry, dated 4 January 1777 and 25 July 1779, regarding the continued application of the droit d'aubaine in the colonies, because it was not explicitly mentioned in the treaties; in Gaschon, *Code diplomatique*, 158–60.

137. AAE ADP France 1, fol. 163; Chancellor de Maupeou to duc d'Aiguillon, 19 May 1773.

138. AAE ADP France 2, no. 21, marquis de Boynes to duc d'Aiguillon, 30 November 1771.

139. Weiss, *Traité théorique et pratique*, 2:71, n. 1. Of course, many eighteenth-century jurists had already made these claimes: see Merlin, *Répertoire*, 7:416–30.

140. Quoted in Hirschman, *Passions and the Interests*, 80.

141. Quoted in Sorel, *L'Europe et la Révolution française*, 1:313.

142. On eighteenth century notions of police, see A. Williams, *The Police of Paris* (Baton Rouge, La., 1979), esp. 5–16; and P. Napoli, " 'Police': La Conceptualisation d'un modèle juridico-politique sous l'Ancien Régime," *Droits* (1994): 151–60, (1995): 183–96. On the Paris police in the late eighteenth century, see also the older work by H. de Montbas, *La Police parisienne sous Louis XVI* (Paris, 1949); and the more recent studies by E.-M. Bénabou, *La Prostitution et la police des mœurs* (Paris, 1987); and F. El Ghoul, "La Police parisienne dans la seconde moitié du XVIIIe siècle (1760–1785)," Thèse de lettres, Université de Rennes, 1993.

143. The declaration of 1777 and its justification by Sartine are reproduced in M. Blesson, "La Police des Noirs sous Louis XVI en France," *Revue de l'histoire des colonies françaises* (1928): 443–46. On the declaration within a more general racialization of slavery during the Enlightenment, see Peabody, "*There are no Slaves in France*," chap. 7; and P. Pluchon, *Nègres et Juifs au XVIIe siècle: Le Racisme au siècle des Lumières* (Paris, 1984), esp. 116–57. The following account of administrative changes involved in the police of foreigners is largely drawn from Dubost, "Les Étrangers à Paris"; see also R. Rey, "La Police des étrangers en France," Thèse de Droit (Paris, 1937); M. Louit, "Essai sur l'histoire de la police des étrangers de la fin de l'Ancien Régime à la IIIème République," Thèse de Droit (Paris, 1949); and G. Carrot, *Histoire de la police française* (Paris, 1992), 71–90.

144. Roche, "Les Migrants parisiens," 3–20; Henry and Courgeau, "Deux analyses," passim.

145. Bibliothèque de l'Arsenal, Archives de la Bastille 10283–10293, *Surveillance des étrangers*, 1725, 1729–48, 1750, 1753–54, 1761, 1767, and other undated pieces.

146. BN MS 21714, fols. 1–2 (ordinances of 1707); Lefebvre de la Planche, *Mémoires*, 2:140, whose editor wrote how the requirements had "fallen into abandon," and Millot, "La Surveillance," 24–32.

147. Dubost, "Les Etrangers à Paris," 227–29; see also J.-B. Lemaire, "La Police de Paris en 1770: Mémoire inédit composé par ordre de Sartine, sur la demande de Marie Thérèse d'Autriche," *Mémoires de la Société d'histoire de Paris et de l'Isle de France* 5 (1879): 2–131.

Chapter 8: Naturalization and the Droit d'Aubaine from the French Revolution to the Bourbon Restoration

1. K. M. Baker, "The Idea of a Declaration of Rights," in Van Kley, ed., *French Idea of Freedom*, 154–98. On the distinct discursive and political trajectory of the "nation" in revolutionary political culture, see P. Nora, "Nation," in *Dictionnaire critique de la Révolution française*, ed. F. Furet and M. Ozouf (Paris, 1988), 801–11; and Bell, *Cult of the Nation*, esp. chaps. 4–5.

2. Quoted in Brubaker, *Citizenship and Nationhood*, 47; on Tallien, see A. Kuscinkski, *Dictionnaire des Conventionnnels* (Paris, 1917), 178–79. For biographical data on the revolutionaries and figures of the Napoleonic Empire, I have also relied on J. Tulard, J.-F. Fayard, and A. Fierro, eds., *Histoire et dictionnaire de la Révolution française, 1789–1799* (Paris, 1998); A. Fierro, A. Palleul-Guillard, and J. Tullard, *Histoire et dictionnaire du Consulat et de l'Empire* (Paris, 1995); J. Tulard, ed., *Dictionnaire Napoléon* (Paris, 1987); and the older but still useful A. Robert, E. Bouleton, and G. Cougny, eds., *Dictionnaire des parlementaires français . . . depuis le 1e mai 1789 jusqu'au 1 mai 1889*, 5 vols. (Paris, 1889–91).

3. Recent overviews include Waldinger et al., eds., *The French Revolution and the Meaning of Citizenship*; Le Cour Grandmaison, *Les Citoyennetés en révolution*; and Heuer, "Foreigners, Families, and Citizens." Rapport's recent study, *Nationality and Citizenship in Revolutionary France*, is a timely revision of Albert Mathiez's dated work, *La Révolution et les étrangers: Cosmopolitisme et défense nationale* (Paris, 1918), but, despite its title, it underconceptualizes and insufficiently documents the question of French nationality law during the revolutionary decade. Weil, *Qu'est-ce qu'un Français?* chap. 1, fills this gap in our knowledge of nationality law, but does not link it to the fate of the droit d'aubaine.

4. The Third Estate of Versailles, in Article 47 of its grievances, declared that "the droit d'aubaine will be suppressed with regard to all peoples of the world. All foreigners, after three years of residence in the kingdom, will exercise all rights of citizens": *Archives parlementaires de 1787 à 1860: Recueil complet des débats législatifs et politiques des chambres françaises*, 1st ser., 96 vols. (Paris, 1877–1990) (hereafter cited as *AP* I), 5:183. Meanwhile, the grievances of Clichy-la-Garnenne did not mention the droit d'aubaine, but made aliens and citizens equal in their conditional exercise of civil rights, framed by the fiction of a Catholic France: "The inhabitants of France, natives or foreigners, who contribute to state finances and usefully serve the king and the nation shall be reputed to be citizens and possess full civil rights, whatever religion they may profess, provided that they respect the Catholic, Apostolic, and Roman faith, which must always be the dominant religion in France": *AP* I, 4:477.

5. AN o/1/238, fol. 246, draft declaration, 5 February 1789. The text noted that the archbishop of Paris (the ambassador's brother), with the consent of the bishop of Orléans, had already officially "incorporated" Desforge in the diocese.

6. Ibid., fol. 268, draft declaration, 27 May 1789.

7. On the discussion surrounding the terms "for reasons of religion," which were eventually kept as "reparation of a persecution that we all deplore," see *AP* I, 29:302, 9 August 1791; see also R. Birn, "Religious Toleration and Freedom of Expression," in *French Idea of Freedom*, ed. Van Kley, 265–99. The issue was not entirely resolved, as a court case about the bequests of *religionnaires fugitifs* suggests. *Gazette des Tribuneaux, et mémorial des corps administratifs et municipaux* 7 (1 March–1 July 1793): 121.

8. AN o/1/238, fol. 286; 237, fol. 119, draft naturalization, May 1782; Parin's dossier can be found in AAE MD France 1454, fol. 234. Parin, or his lawyer, pulled out all the stops in his claims to already be French: his momentary residence and "accidental birth" outside the kingdom, the "spirit of return" maintained by his family, the relations of neighborliness and the administrative confusion in the border area between Bésançon and the bishopric of Basel, where he was born . . .

9. AN o/1/238, fol. 296, draft declaration of Jean-Baptiste Chevalier, 30 December 1789.

10. AN BB 30/52, draft naturalization, 21 July 1790.

11. Weil, *Qu'est-ce qu'un Français?* 23–25.

12. *AP* I, 15:340; AD II(34) (b); see also J. Imbert, "La Capacité de l'étranger à succéder en France: Concession humanitaire ou intéressée," in *Humanité et droit international, Mélanges R. Dupuy* (Paris, 1991), 180–82.

13. See W. H. Sewell, "Le Citoyen/la citoyenne: Activity, Passivity, and the Revolutionary Concept of Citizenship," in *The French Revolution and the Creation of Modern Political Culture*, ed. C. Lucas (New York, 1988), 105–23; and also his recent revision of Sieyès, *The Rhetoric of Bourgeois Revolution:* The Abbé Sièyes and What Is the Third Estate? (Durham, 1994), esp. chap. 5. Sieyès wrote that because the "civiciat" or civic order was composed "of all stories of the social building, it follows that the weaker classes, the men the most barren, are even more foreign, by their mental capacities and their sentiments, to the interests of association," and that as a result "the greatest majority of our fellow citizens have neither the education nor the leisure to want to be occupied directly with the laws that must govern France": quoted in Larrère, *L'Invention de l'économie*, 297–98.

14. All citations from the constitutions of 1791, 1793, 1795, and 1799 are taken from *Les Constitutions de la France*, ed. C. Debbasch and J.-M. Pontier (Paris, 1983). On the continuities with Old Regime jurisprudence, see Vanel, *Evolution historique*, 69, and Weil, *Qu'est-ce qu'un Français?* 20.

15. On the exclusions of revolutionary citizenship more generally, see Le Cour Grandmaison, *Les Citoyennetés en Révolution*, passim; and S. M. Singham, "Betwixt Cattle and Men: Jews, Blacks, and Women, and the Declaration of the Rights of Man," in *French Idea of Freedom*, ed. Van Kley, 114–53; and F. Hincker, "La Citoyenneté révolutionaire saisie à travers ses exclus," in *Le Citoyen Fou*, ed. N. Robatel (Paris, 1991), 7–28.

16. Rosanvallon, *Le Sacre du citoyen*, 45–54. The most well-treated of these exclusions is that of women: see, for example, M. Gutwirth, "*Citoyens, Citoyennes:* Cultural Regression and the Subversion of Female Citizenship in the French Revolution," in Waldinger et al., eds., *French Revolution*,

17–28; and the recent work on gender and revolution discussed in S. Desan, "What's after Political Culture? Recent Revolutionary Historiography," *French Historical Studies* 23 (2000): 187–93.

17. G. Kates, "Jews into Frenchmen: Nationality and Representation in Revolutionary France," in *The French Revolution and the Birth of Modernity*, ed. F. Feher (Berkeley, 1990), 103–16; cf. J. Portemer, "Les Étrangers dans le droit de la révolution francaise," in *RSJB* 10 (Paris, 1958), 538; and Hertzberg, *French Enlightenment*, passim. On the Bordeaux Jews, see also F. Malino, *Les Juifs sépharades de Bordeaux: Assimilation et émancipation dans la France révolutionnaire et impériale* (Bordeaux, 1984). Contemporary pamphleteers made the same point that Jews had already acquired "passive" citizenship: see Scaramuzza, *Les Juifs d'Alsace doivent-ils être admis au droit des citoyens actifs* (Paris, 1790).

18. Weil, *Qu'est-ce qu'un Français?* 24–25.

19. Wahnich, *L'Impossible citoyen*, 67–78, explores the unexpectedly local and communal "origins" of national citizenship in what represented historically a far more "Spanish" model of communal self-definition than a French absolutist denial of the role of local communities (and the "integration" of foreigners into "daily social practices" as a condition of citizenship).

20. Heuer, "Foreigners, Families, and Citizens," 240–41 and passim; Heuer, " 'Afin d'obtenir le droit de citoyen . . . en tout ce qui peut concerner une personne de son sexe': Devenir ou cesser d'etre femme française à l'époque napoléonienne," *Clio* 12 (2000): 17.

21. AN BB11/2, letter of 25 May 1792; G. Gorani, *Recherches sur la science du gouvernement*, 2 vols. (Paris, 1792), 1:97–101, where, arguing against the droit d'aubaine, he claimed that "the right to bequeath property by last will and testament is a safeguard of civil liberty, for without this right, taxation would become piracy. Public revenue founded on inheritance can only impoverish a state and diminish its population" (98–99).

22. *AP* I, 44:113, 160–61, Hobe's speech to the Assembly, followed by Koch's recommendation, 27 May 1792; AN BB 11/2, dossier including the letters of Hobes, his father, Luckner, and his baptismal abstract.

23. *AP* I, 44:692–94; *Proceedings in the National Assembly of France on the Admission of Mr. William Priestley and the motion for his naturalization* (London, 1792), with a preface signed by the editor and translator, C. L., attributed to Capel Lofft.

24. AN BB 11/2, rapport de M. Navier sur diverses demandes en naturalisation, n.d. [but before 10 August 1792].

25. Ibid. After the proclamation of the Republic on 21 September, the projected grant was rewritten, this time in more radical language, noting the need to naturalize those foreigners who "flee the lands of slavery and request an asylum in the French republic," and adding another foreigner, Jean-Baptiste Dasory, a Genoese merchant who lived in Port-Vendres (Roussillon) but only since 1788—less than the stated five years in the 1791 Constitution, hence the need for a discretionary legislative naturalization.

26. *AP* I, 48:689–91. Historians have never been able to figure out why certain individuals proposed by Chénier, including the Englishmen Horne Tooch and William Bolts and the Irish citizen Naper-Tandi, were dropped from the final list, while Jeremy Bentham, George Washington, John Hamilton, Tadeusz Kościusko, and others were added to it. See the complete lists and speculation in Rapport, *Nationality and Citizenship*, 138; Weil, *Qu'est-ce qu'un Français?* 21; Mathiez, *La Révolution française*, 15–16; and R. R. Palmer, *The Age of Democratic Revolution*, 2 vols. (Princeton, 1959), 1:55.

27. *AP* I, 48:690–91.

28. AN D III 368–70/2; Rapport, *Nationality and Citizenship*, 138–40. It is perhaps significant that at this moment, a deputy of the Convention proposed a decree that would abolish all legal fictions, recognizing only those past ones "expressly authorized by laws and customs." The Old Regime practice of naturalization as legal fiction had no meaning within radical revolutionary discourse: see AN D III 361, no. 5, piece 237, 1 floréal an II.

29. On the latter, see Weil, *Que c'est qu'un Français?* 20–22, 280 n. 38.

30. Buonarotti appears to be the only one whose naturalization was published: *Recueil des lois publiées du 5 juillet 1788 jusqu'à nivôse an II*, no. 1027, 27 May 1793. On the first two, see K. Dietrich-Chénel and M.-H. Varnier, "Intégration d'étrangers en France par naturalisation ou admission à domicile de 1790/1814 au 10 mai 1871," 9 vols (Thesis, Department of German Studies,

University of Aix-Marseille I, 1994), 6:215–33. On Barlow, see Rapport, *Nationality and Citizenship*, 127–28, et seq.; and R. F. Durden, "Joel Barlow in the French Revolution," *William and Mary Quarterly*, 3d ser., 8 (1951): 328–31. A draft of Barlow's letter can be found in AN D II 34, no. 3.

31. *AP* I, 15:349, 1 May 1790.

32. Barère de Vieuzac (1755–41) was to become a radical Republican in the Convention who rallied, however, on the side of the Robespierre's enemies: he was convicted during the Terror, but escaped and came to hold legislative office in his native department of the Hautes-Pyrénées under Napoleon. Nonetheless, his earlier radicalism (he voted for the regecide in January 1793) led to his banishment during the Restoration.

33. *AP* I, 17:629, 6 August 1790.

34. *AP* I, 23:329.

35. Moreau de Saint-Méry, *Loix et constitutions*, 597 et seq.

36. *AP* I, 22:147–48, report of Barère, 12 January 1791; *AP* I, 15:11, adoption of the decree.

37. *AP* I, 17:629, 1 August 1790.

38. This new classification based on degrees of successability was the schema elaborated by Roederer in 1802 and Gaschon in 1817. My own classification of the treaties and conventions thus returns to the principles of 1781 and the concerns of the eighteenth-century French foreign office. The debate over whether the 1790 abolition included the possibility of "active" succession continued in the courts: Lainé cites a decision of the appellate court of 2 prairial an IX (22 May 1800) concerning a foreigner who died before the passage of the 1791 law, in which the court ruled that the foreigner in question had no right to inherit from a Frenchman: *Etude*, 29, n. 1.

39. *AP* I, 17:629, 1 August 1790.

40. *AP* I, 24:496, 1 April 1791.

41. Roederer's account appears in his report on the droit d'aubaine presented to the council of state during the debates over the first proposal of the first title of the Civil Code ("Des personnes"), and appears in P.-A. Fenet, *Recueil complet des travaux préparatoires du Code civil*, 15 vols. (Paris, 1827), 7:74–75.

42. M. Troper, "La Notion de citoyen sous la Révolution française," in *Etudes en l'honneur de Georges Dupuis. Droit Public* (Paris, 1997), 320. After the adjournment of the first project to write a civil code, the Convention passed a provisional law on inheritance on 17 nivôse II (3 January 1794). Article 59 stated that "any time that the dispositions of the present law are found to profit foreigners who are subjects of powers with which the French Republic is at war, they will cease to have their effect, and contrary dispositions done in favor of *républicoles* or allies or neutral [states] remain, in this case, maintained": *AP* I, 80:627–31.

43. In abolishing the droit d'aubaine, the Constituent Assembly nonetheless left two minor legal distinctions in place: the *cautio judicatum solvi*, and the *contrainte par corps* for foreign debtors. These were dismantled by the Convention between 9 and 12 March 1793, when Danton argued that no one—foreigner or French—could be forced to give their person as collateral (Rapport, *Nationality and Citizenship*, 89), but both were reintroduced in legislation of years V and VI (1796–97): V. Azimi, "L'Etat révolutionnaire et les intérêts privés étrangers," in *Révolutions et droit international*. [Actes du 23e] Colloque [organisé par la] Société française pour le droit international, Dijon [1–3 June 1989] (Paris, 1990), 222–23. The *cautio* was reintroduced by Article 16 of the Civil Code: G. Lepointe, "Le Statut des étrangers dans la France du XIXe siècle," *RSJB* 10 (1958): 569.

44. Wahnich, *L'Impossible citoyen*, passim.

45. V. Guiraudon, "Cosmopolitanism and National Priority: Attitudes towards Foreigners in France between 1789 and 1794," *History of European Ideas* 13 (1991), 594–98; Rapport, *Nationality and Citizenship*, chap. 3. The Paris court of appeals ruled on 3 vendémiaire an X (25 September 1801) that the laws abolishing the droit d'aubaine, having made no distinction between "foreigners" and "enemies" in times of peace and war, remained in place: Weiss, *Traité théorique et pratique de droit international privé*, 2:83–84.

46. *AP* I, 88:613–22. More generally, on these and other interdictions of foreigners in the republic at war, see Rapport, *Nationality and Citizenship*, chap. 3; and, on exemptions in these laws for foreign workers, see Azimi, "L'Etat révolutionnaire," 228–29. On the responses of "foreigners"

subjected to the decree of 26 germinal year II, see below, 288–89. In the mature republican model of citizenship, put in place during the 1870s, the distinction between the civil (or private) rights of foreigners as allies or enemies was definitively dropped: see Lainé, *Etude sur la capacité successorale*, 2.

47. Mathiez, *La Révolution et les étrangers*; the model persists in Vanel, *Evolution historique*; and can be found in the more recent work of Brubaker, *Citizenship and Nationhood*, 43–48, and Guiraudon, "Cosmopolitanism and National Priority," 591–604.

48. Quoted in Brubaker, *Nationality and Citizenship*, 47.

49. Traditional interpretations of the constitutional failure to define nationality include Vanel, *Evolution historique*, 95–97; Troper, "La Notion de citoyen," 320 et seq.; and M. Borgetto, "Etre français sous la Révolution," *Crises* 2 (1994): 80 et seq. More sophisticated revisionist readings include V. Azimi, "Le Suffrage 'universaliste,' les étrangers et le droit electoral de 1793," in *La Constitution du 24 juin 1793, l'utopie dans le droit public français*, Actes du Colloque de Dijon, 16–17 September 1993, ed. J.-J. Clère and M. Verpeaux (Dijon, 1997), 204–39; and Weil, *Qu'est-ce qu'un Français?* 26–27, who usefully points out that the question of whether the 1793 Constitution defined citizenship as nationality depended on whether legal cases were decided before or after the application of the Civil Code of 1803.

50. Wahnich *L'Impossible citoyen*; Heuer, "Foreigners, Families, and Citizens," passim.

51. Halpérin, *L'Impossible Code civil*, 3–18. Cambacères had been a royal solicitor at the Chambre des comptes of Montpellier before the Revolution, and he was later to play an essential role in the elaboration of the Civil Code. His three projects were failures, often leading legal historians to dismiss the insignificance of what is disparagingly called the "intermediary" law of revolutionary France: and passim; J.-J. Régis de Cambacères, *Projet de code civil: Presenté au Conseil des cinq-cents au nom de la Commission de la classification des lois* (Paris, year IV [1796]). The classic work on the civil legislation of the Revolution remains P. Sagnac, *La Législation civile de la Révolution française (1789–1804): Essai d'histoire sociale* (Geneva, 1979 [1898]). The "intermediate law" of the revolutionary regimes has recently been revalorized, both in relation to the absolutist efforts at codification and to the eventual success of Napoleon: see, for example, J. Goy, "Code civil," in *Dictionnaire critique*, ed. Furet and Ozouf, 508–19.

52. *AP* I, 52:576–77.

53. Lanjuinais might have mentioned a third sense of the word citizen: that of being "irreprochable," virtuous, and a supporter of the Revolution itself, the final expression of the "good citizen" who appeared in the eighteenth-century citizenship revolution. *AP* I, 63:561–67, 29 April 1793; see also the printed version in BN Le38, no. 2342, and the final project ibid., no. 2344.

54. Vanel, *Evolution historique*, 97–99.

55. "Lettre à la Convention nationale sur les vices de la Constitution de 1791," annexed to the summary of the session of 7 November 1792, in *AP* I, 3:266. Only a few speakers, including Thomas Paine, were to query the Assembly about what the "others" who were not politically capable citizens might be called. *Ancien Moniteur* 25, 171, 5 messidor III (32 June 1795). The question was unanswered.

56. *AP* I, 60:615, 27 March 1792.

57. *AP* I, 62:388–90, 17 April 1793.

58. *AP* I, 63:205, 24 April 1793.

59. *AP* I, 62:291, 17 April 1793.

60. Azimi, "Le Suffrage 'universaliste,' " 210–15.

61. *AP* I, 62:594, 7 April 1793; see also ibid., 63:583 et seq., 29 April 1793.

62. As Patrick Weil has pointed out, there was little discussion over the article, only Thuriot's amendment to substitute "domiciled" for "resident." the former was less subject to abuse on the part of a "rich man who could take care that a large number of workers or servants would vote in his favor." Weil, *Qu'est-ce qu'un Français?* 281, n. 49.

63. A small number of petitions for naturalization in 1794 and 1795 survive in AN BB 11/2. That of Antoine Guiny, a Greek sea captain who served as a provisioner and courier for the French republican ambassador to Constantinople, reflected the tension between naturalization conferred and "automatically" acquired by the foreigner. Guiny wrote that "since the dangers

he has risked have attached him even more to the French Nation, from which he has experienced loyalty and justice, he requests to be placed among its children by obtaining the permission to naturalize himself as French citizen [*la permission de se naturaliser citoyen français*]," petitions of 18 frimaire year III (8 December 1794) and 13 frimaire year III (3 December 1794) to the legislation committee. See also the petitions of Nicolas Lynch, an Irish native already naturalized in France in 1784 (draft naturalization in O/1/237, fol. 265, 291 [October 1784]); and of François Drago, a captain of a Piedmontese regiment (petition of 25 frimaire year III [14 January 1795]).

64. *AP* I 88:613–22, report by Saint-Just on the general police of the republic. Project and decree, Article 6.

65. AN D III 373, nos. 429 (Belz), 436 (Vermeulan), 233 (Lallemand), 234 (Campbell), 597 (Bernard), 471 (Deschamps).

66. For Daunou's views on citizenship more generally, including the importance of property rights and the obligations of the citizen, see A. Dauteribes, "L'Idée de république dans la pensée politique de Daunou," in *Nation et république*, 77–97.

67. Weil, *Qu'est-ce qu'un Francais?* 25.

68. Quoted ibid., 282, n. 58.

69. Cf. Weil, *Que c'est qu'un Français?* 26.

70. Heuer, "Foreigners, Families, and Citizens," 137, citing the pamphlet of Bonnier, *Recherches sur l'ordre de Malte et examen d'une question relative aux Français par ci-devant membres de cet ordre* (Paris, year VI [1798–79]).

71. Merlin, *Répertoire*, 7:13–21, esp. 14. "The title of citizen is exclusively reserved by the constitution of those French who have political rights [*droit de cité*], that is, the right to vote in the political assemblies of their districts, and to be elected there. As for the French who do not have this right, they are not properly speaking citizens, and cannot become so except by constitutional means. Until then, they must be considered by the simple qualification of French, which assures them civil liberty and all its advantages."

72. For a nuanced understanding of the continuities and ruptures more generally in the politics, law, and institutions of the New Regime, see I. Woloch, *The New Regime: Transformations of the French Civic Order, 1789–1820s* (New York, 1994).

73. On the parliamentary system established by Bonaparte after Brumaire, see I. Collins, *Napoleon and His Parliaments, 1800–1815* (New York, 1979), 8–17.

74. AP ACA Fonds Tronchet. The Tronchet papers contain some thirty volumes, uselessly indexed, but extraordinarily rich. On his career, which desperately seeks its historian, see M. de Royer, "Discours sur la vie et les travaux de M. Tronchet," *Cour de Cassation: Audience de rentrée du 3 novembre 1753* (Paris, 1853), 1–70. Already aged sixty-three when the French Revolution broke out, he was one of the twenty deputies of the Third Estate elected from Paris, and immediately established his identity within the Constituent Assembly as a constitutional royalist. His politics, reputation, and legal expertise were attractive to Louis XVI, and Tronchet was to defend him—obviously unsuccessfully—in his trial in December 1792 and January 1793. Hidden during the Terror, he returned to public service in 1795, and in 1799, having just been named a judge on the appellate court in Paris, Napoleon tapped him to serve as president of the commission of lawyers who designed the Civil Code.

75. Fenet, *Recueil*, 7:6.

76. Weil, *Qu'est-ce qu'un Français?* 27–35, quote 35. On the "purge" of 1802, see Collins, *Napoleon and His Parliaments*, 56–67.

77. Tronchet was not alone: fellow jurists and jurisconsults Bigot-Préameneu, Portalis, Maleville, Cretet, all in the commission and in the council of state, helped build the legal bridge across the rupture of the revolutionary divide, even if they did not all share Tronchet's predeliction for descent as the principal criterion defining French nationality. See the remarks in Halpérin, *L'Impossible Code civil*, passim; and J. Charbonnier, "The French Civil Code," in *Rethinking France: Les Lieux de mémoire*; vol. 1: *The State*, ed. P. Nora (Chicago, 2001), 336–37; and especially D. R. Kelley, "Men of Law and the French Revolution," *Politics, Ideology, and the Law in Early Modern Europe: Essays in Honor of J. H. M. Salmon*, ed. A. E. Bakos (Rochester, 1994), 127–46.

78. Professor of Roman Law at the Legislative Academy, Henri-Jean-Baptiste Dard, author of the *Code civil des Français, avec des notes indicatives des lois romaines, coutumes, ordonnances, edits et déclarations, qui ont rapport à chaque article, ou Conférence du Code Civil avec les lois anciennes* (Paris, 1827), offered no commentary on this article, whereas his search for precedents for the other articles yielded frequent if often misleading references to both Roman law and that of the Old Regime jurists.

79. Fenet, *Recueil complet*, 7:138–39; on the "sociological continuity" of the Civil Code as a "realm of memory," see Charbonnier, "French Civil Code," 352 and passim.

80. Instituted in 1803, this statute became obsolete in 1889, and disappeared entirely in 1927: see Weil, *Qu'est-ce qu'un Français?* 397 and passim; and below, conclusion.

81. Dard noted with respect to Article 13 that "the authorization of the government has the same effect of letters of naturalization that the king accorded to foreigners in the past," *Code civil des français*, n. 2 to Article 13. The same perspective was adopted by Jacques de Maleville, who himself had worked on the Civil Code, and was later a member of the Senate under Napoleon: see his *Analyse raisonnée de la discussion du Code Civil au Conseil d'Etat*, 3d ed. (Paris, 1822), art. 13; a further confirmation can be found in Dufour, *Le Code Civil des Français avec les sources où toutes ses dispositions ont été prises* (Paris, 1806).

82. Fenet, *Recueil complet*, 7:10–11.

83. Fenet, *Recueil complet*, 7:69–76; another copy can be found in ADP France 1, fols. 166–91.

84. When the English king had claimed Gascony as the crown of his maternal grandfather, he momentarily banished the French living in his kingdom (despite his reputation as "the champion of the foreign trader"): see E. F. Churchill, "The Crown and the Alien: A Review of the Crown's Protection of the Alien from the Norman Conquest Down to 1689," *Law Quarterly Review* 36 [1920]: 404). According to Roederer and others, drawing on Enlightenment accounts, Philip VI of France retaliated by imposing the droit d'aubaine—as inheritance restriction and royal right of escheat—in the kingdom.

85. Fenet, *Recueil*, 7:69–76; Roederer's table appears to be an adaptation of another one, produced by the director of the archives of the foreign ministry, who claimed to have sent Roederer all the information necessary: see the surviving pages of the "Tableau par ordre classique des rapports que les traités ou autres actes politiques ont établis . . . relativement à l'abolition ou à la modification reciproque des droits d'aubaine ou de détraction . . . ," n.a., n.d., but ca. thermidor year IX (July 1801), in AAE ADP France 1, fols. 153–55. An unsigned manuscript approximating Roederer's table—is ibid., fol. 161 et seq.

86. The adoption occurred shortly after the Paris court of appeals overruled, on 25 September 1801, Article 59 of the law of 17 nivôse year II (6 January 1794) that had distinguished between foreigners from states at war or at peace with France, and upheld the regime of the droit d'aubaine as an inheritance restriction.

87. Fenet, *Recueil*, 7:138–47.

88. The Provençal lawyer Siméon, originally associated with the Girondins, sat among the moderates in the Council of Five Hundred, was named a councillor of state and prefect under Napoleon, and eventually became a deputy under the Restoration and later a French peer in 1821. He participated vigorously in the movement to finally abolish the droit d'aubaine as a deputy to the lower chamber in 1819, when he looked back on the decision to uphold reciprocity, explaining how it was a moment when "jurisconsults, leaving their domain, entered that of politics. They gave with all their talent their favorable counsel to a potentate [Napoleon] who wished for reciprocity": *Archives parlementaires: Recueil compet des débats législatifs et politiques des chambres françaises de 1800 à 1860*, 2d ser., 127 vols. (Paris, 1862–1913) (hereafter cited as *AP* II), 23:239, 16 March 1819.

89. Tulard et al., *Histoire et dictionnaire*, 587–88. Boissy d'Anglas's *Opinion sur le projet de loi relatif à la jouissance et à la privation des droits civils*, along with those of the twenty or so deputies of the Tribunate who intervened specifically in the debate for or against the principle of reciprocity and the reestablishment of the droit d'aubaine, were published as pamphlets in December 1801, and can be found in AN AD II 34 (B). These, along with the other "opinions" and interventions concerning the remaining articles of the law, are reproduced in Frenet, *Recueil*, 7:195–590.

90. AN AD II 34 (B), 18, 3.

91. Fenet, *Recueil*, 7:231

92. AN AD II 34 (B), 15, 27.

93. *Opinion de Mathieu*, ibid., no. 29, 2. Mathieu's consultation quoted extensively from the Roman law tradition, citing the seventeenth-century Toulouse jurist Caseneuve (who had identified "this right as an enemy of public hospitality and public liberty"), the Estates General of Tours in 1483, and the ordinances of Louis XII as evidence that neither Roman law nor the province of Languedoc ever fully admitted the droit d'aubaine: ibid., no. 22, 12–14.

94. AN AD 34 II (B), no. 26, *Opinion de Saint-Aubin*, 34–35.

95. Ibid., no. 23, *Opinion de Curée*, 3.

96. Article 726 of the Civil Code read: "A foreigner is not permitted to inherit goods that his foreign or French kin possess on the territory of the Republic except in the case and the manner in which a Frenchman inherits from his kin goods in the country of this foreigner, as per the dispositions relative to the possession of civil rights." In addition, two other articles of the Civil Code touched on the status of foreigners: Article 912 stated "One can bequeath [property] to a foreigner only in the instance when this foreigner can bequeath to a Frenchman," and Article 912 stated that "the foreigner can be called before French courts for obligations he has contracted towards Frenchmen in foreign countries": see Lainé, *Etude*, 37–41 et seq., who notes that the additional articles amounted to a "double reciprocity," between nations on the one hand and co-heirs on the other, even if, in decisions in 1808 and 1813, the appellate court upheld individual reciprocity when a deceased foreigner left goods in a foreign country.

97. AAE ADP France 1, fols. 193–95.

98. The classic study of revolutionary expansion before 1799 remains J. Godechot, *La Grande Nation*, 2 vols. (Paris, 1956); an excellent synthesis of the Napoleonic period is S. Woolf, *Napoleon's Integration of Europe* (London, 1991), which unfortunately fails to examine in detail the legal assimilation of the annexed territories, especially in relation to Old Regime law. The practice of the droit d'aubaine remained ambiguous at times: for example, when the Hanseatic ports were annexed to the French Empire by decree of 9 October 1811, the "droit d'aubaine" was originally retained, despite the formal abolition of feudalism, only to be suppressed by a further decree of 9 December: see AAE ADP France 2, fols. 104–111, and Rapport, " 'A Languishing Branch,' " 34.

99. Imbert, "La Capacité de l'étranger," 184–85, lists some of the subsequent imperial decrees of 1806 that reestablished the droit d'aubaine in the "Great Empire," the same year that decrees exempted the subjects of the kingdom of Italy; see also Gaschon, *Code diplomatique*, 84 et seq.; Cotelle, *Dissertation*, pt. 4. The administrator-general of Parma, which had been ceded to France in March 1801, was none other than the ex-colonial administrator Moreau de Saint-Méry, who had favored the abolition of the droit d'aubaine in France's Caribbean colonies in the 1780s, and spoke in favor of its abolition in 1791: see Woolf, *Napoleon's Integration of Europe*, 50–51.

100. AN F2(1) 437.

101. AN F2(1) 43, 1. On 24 brumaire year V (14 November 1796), the minister of foreign relations, Delacroix, inquired of the minister of justice whether Article 10 of the Constitution of 1795 required a prior declaration, to which the answer two weeks later was unequivocal, as was the jurisprudence on this question reaching 1829.

102. B. Schnapper, "La Naturalisation française au XIXe siècle: Les Variations d'une politique," in *La Condition juridique de l'étranger*, 213.

103. Duvergier, 8:312; on the preparation, Repertoire Dalloz 1850, vol. 18, s.v. "Droits civils," no. 97. Biographies of the successive chancellars and ministers under the empire can be found in T. Lentz, *Dictionnaire des ministres de Napoléon: Dictionnaire analytique statistique et comparé des trente-deux ministres de Napoléon* (Paris, 1999).

104. BN Le 49–16, printed *Motifs du projet de Sénatus-Consulte organique sur la naturalisation des étrangers, présenté au Sénat dans la séance du 16 vendémiaire an XI, par les conseillers d'état Regnault de Saint-Jean-d'Angely et Bigot-Préameneu, orateurs du Gouvernement*, 1.

105. The *senatus consulte* of 26 vendemiaire year XI (18 October 1802) [BN Le 49–16] was ignored in a later, unsigned draft report to the council of state on 12 thermidor an XII (12 August 1804) that did not mention the legislation, but complained about the large number of foreigners

already resident in France from before the Revolution who had been given "either by their acquisition of lands, or by their services rendered, a guarantee of their attachment to France and of their trust of its laws." Other foreigners "have made useful discoveries in the arts, bring to France successful procedures, or are disposed to invest considerable sums in our industry, but hesitate to establish themselves in the Republic." Heavily edited, the document's last interlocutor reiterated that "the government could still reserve for itself, like the last government, the faculty of granting letters of naturalization based on the report of the interior minister": AN F2(1) 436, no. 11.

106. AN F2(1) 436, nos. 8–15, including a report of the council of state to the interior minister, 14 fructidor an 12 (1 September 1804). The Neapolitan Ciolly actually received his naturalization on 5 brumaire an XIII [27 October 1804] once he produced a certificate that attested to his residence in France since 24 prairial an XI [13 June 1803]: see F 2 I 437. The council did give an exception to another foreigner, a certain M. Douglas from England, because "it believed that this mechanic, having brought to France instruments that are infinitely useful in commerce for which he received a fifteen-year patent, and having formed a wealthy establishment, could be seen as holding to his new fatherland through property and as having the intention to establish himself here."

107. *AP* II, vols. 10, 11; other copies are in AAE ADP France 1, and in Duvergier, *Collection des lois*, 16:220–21. A subsequent decree of 1 March 1808 (Article 11) regulated the attributions of the Conseil du sceau des titres, which was further specified in three subsequent decrees of 1811–12: Duvergier, *Collection des lois*, 18:33–34, passim.

108. Wahnich, *L'Impossible citoyen*, 56–81, discusses only the discourses of the early revolutionary years; Heuer, "Foreigners, Families, and Citizens," is a model case study of Strasbourg and other Alsatian towns whose Old Regime practices of conferring citizenship had been unusually strong.

109. AN F2(1) 436, no. 14, "Mode de déclaration de l'acquisition faite, conformément aux constiutions de l'empire, du titre de citoyen français. Rapport à l'empereur, 1808." See the text of the 1809 decree in *Code de la nationalité francais, suivi de documents annexes*, vol. 1: *Partie officielle*, Melun, Imprimerie administrative, 1946, 131, "1. When a foreigner, in conformity with the dispositions of the constitutional act of 22 frimaire year VIII, fulfills the required conditions to become a French citizen, his naturalization will be pronounced by Us. 2. The demand for naturalization and the supporting documents shall be transmitted by the mayor of the petitioner's domicile to the prefect who will send them, with his opinion, to Our Great Judge, the minister of justice, who is charged with the execution of the said decree" (49); see also Weil, *Qu'est-ce qu'un Français?* 38–39.

110. AN BB 11/3; AN F(2) 1 437.

111. The case of the English cloth merchant Arthur Spear was to decide administrative practice. On 27 July 1808, he made his declaration to the mayoralty of the second Paris district requesting permission to reside; more than two years later, on 22 September 1810, the minister of interior deferred to the justice minister in producing the report that recommended his admission, following the favorable recommendations of the departmental prefect, the minister of police, and the minister of war (AD BB [11] 4).

112. AN BB 11/3.

113. Ibid. Most requests for naturalization apparently took less time, especially if they involved men of standing and reputation. Thus the case of Georges Axel Adelsward, born in Sweden in 1781, who had requested in an 1808 declaration to the mayoralty of Longwy (Moselle) to "enjoy the rights of French citizenship" (*jouir des droits de citoyen français*). He explained how he had come to France as a Swedish officer made prisoner of war in 1804, had obtained permission to marry (the daughter of a notary of Longwy), and how in his own kingdom he was a "wealthy proprietor" of iron and copper works: "Son intention est de former un établissement de fabrication qui serait utile pour sa nouvelle patrie et d'entretenir des relations de commerce avec la Suède." Four years later—on 20 June 1812—he was naturalized (ibid.).

114. AN F(2) 1 437. More generally, see Heuer, " 'Afin d'obtenir le droit de citoyen,' " 15–32.

115. AN BB 11/3.

116. Ibid., the case of Frederik Eck, born in Bavaria, established in Nancy, who had musical talents—or lack thereof, according to the director of the municipal conservatory at Nancy. The council of state's decision on 4 frimaire year XII (26 November 1803) was that "the establishment

of M. Eck in Nancy was not of the kind designated by the senatus-consulte of 26 vendémiaire year XI and the other claims . . . are not sufficient to merit an exception."

117. Ibid.

118. Ibid.

119. L. B. Cotèle, *Notice sur la justice et l'intérêt de la France, comme des autres Etats de l'Europe, d'abolir le droit d'aubaine* (Orléans, 1814), 23–24.

120. AN D III. The list includes Andre Masséna, Prince d'Essling; comte Pierre-Marie-Barthelemy Ferino (b. Craveggia, named senator in Florence in 1807); and the comte Charles-Leopold de Belderblusch (b. near Koln, senator since 1810), who was one of the first to rally to Talleyrand and sign the decree stripping the emperor of his authority. Others include Charles Joseph Mathieu, comte de Lambrechts, Corvetto, Amiral, Verhuel; for brief biographies of these "foreigners," see the relevant entries in Tulard, ed., *Dictionnaire Napoléon*.

121. *AP* II, 12:35–36, 4 June 1814.

122. AN D III, no. 46. *Chambre des Pairs, séance du 13 décembre 1814. Rapport à la Chambre.*

123. *AP* II, 12:277–78.

124. Ibid., 345–47; see also AN CC 258, *Procès-verbaux des séances*, sessions of 13 August 1814, fols. 63–65.

125. Ibid., 638–39.

126. AD II (4) B, n. 42, 28 September 1814.

127. Ibid., n. 39, 27 September 1814.

128. Weiss, *Traité théorique et pratique de droit international privé*, 1:614–18.

Conclusion: Ending the Old Regime in 1819

1. Noiriel, *French Melting Pot*, 101 (figure showing that the increase in "foreigners" began in the 1870s); for an overview of migratory patterns, see also Y. Lequin, ed., *La Mosaïque France: Histoire des étrangers et de l'immigration* (Paris, 1988), 335–72; and A. Perotti, "L'immigration en France: Son histoire, ses nouvelles réalités et ses nouveaux enjeux," in *La Citoyenneté et les changements de structures sociales et nationales de la population française*, ed. C. Wihtol de Wendon (Paris, 1988), 59–72, who argues for the shift from "proximate immigration" to migration as a "mechanism of social reproduction" in the same period. On asylum laws and political practices, see G. Noiriel, *La Tyrannie du national: Le Droit d'asile en Europe, 1793–1993* (Paris, 1991).

2. Rosanvallon, *Le Sacre du citoyen*, 209–98; G. Noiriel and M. Offerlé, "Citizenship and Nationality in Nineteenth-Century France," in *European Integration in Social and Historical Perspective*, ed. J. Klausen and L. A. Tilly (Boston, 1997), 71–84.

3. The establishment of military conscription is conventionally seen as the reason behind the development of modern nationality law: see C. Parry, *Nationality and Citizenship Laws of the Commonwealth and the Republic of Ireland*, 2 vols. (London, 1957), 1:3 et seq.; and for France, Brubaker, *Citizenship and Nationhood*, esp. chap. 5. But cf. the more convincing arguments of Weil, *Qu'est-ce qu'un Français?* 37–62, pointing to republican notions of equality, and not the demands of universal conscription, as the source of political reform in the 1889 law. More generally, recent work on French citizenship during the Second Empire (1851–70) underscores the importance of the decades prior to the proclamation of the Third Republic in establishing both the institutional development of national unity (conscription and primary schools) and in the language of citizenship itself: see S. Hazareesingh, *From Subject to Citizen: The Second Empire and the Emergence of Modern French Democracy* (Princeton, 1998); and P. Nord, *The Republican Moment: Struggles for Democracy in Nineteenth-Century France* (Cambridge, Mass., 1995).

4. As we shall see, an average of some thirty "naturalizations" a year were accorded between the 1820s and 1880s, but between two thousand and twenty-five hundred naturalizations were accorded in 1848 and 1849, respectively, following the provisional decree of 28 March 1848 allowing the justice minister to naturalize foreigners resident in France for at least five years. Most of these cases emanated from prefectures in the Bas-Rhin and the Isère and involved foreigners who were denied grants in previous years: see Weil, *Qu'est-ce qu'un Français?* 44–45; and Schnapper, "La Naturalisation française au XIXe siècle, 211–12.

5. Maza, *Private Lives and Public Affairs*, passim.

6. Dietrich-Chénel and Varnier, "Intégration d'étrangers en France," passim. The study is based on the published legal record of the *Bulletin des Lois*, and unfortunately too often collapses the varieties of naturalization and permissions to establish domicile in practice.

7. On the parallel history of the French *état civil*, see G. Noiriel, "L'identification des citoyens, Naissance de l'état civil républicain," in *Etat, nation et immigration*, 233–37.

8. AAE ADP France 2, fol. 259–61.

9. Dietrich-Chanel and Varnier, "Intégration d'étrangers," vol. 1, 36–37 and annexes.

10. Weil, *Qu'est-ce qu'un Français?* 43.

11. Ibid., 42–43.

12. The 1799 Constitution had declared that naturalization in a foreign country resulted in the loss of the *qualité de français*, a law that was reiterated in the Civil Code Articles 17 and 21, and later in the imperial decrees of 6 April 1809 and 26 August 1811 that forbade French men and women to naturalize abroad—an image of the emperor's discretionary monopoly of the authority to naturalize foreigners in France that resulted in the increasingly "exclusionary" quality of naturalization in the New Regime: *Code de la nationalité*, 48, 50–52.

13. On the administrative reconstitution under Napoleon of an Old Regime "keeper of the seals" (*garde des sceau*), see Dainville-Barbiche, "Les Archives du sceau," 127–52; and Weil, *Qu'est-ce qu'un Français?* 64–66. The arch-chancellor and then the chancellor of France presided over the commission, which was not incorporated into the ministry of justice until the royal ordinance of Louis-Philippe of 31 October 1830.

14. AN F2 (1) 436, no. 63, letter of 21 September 1822 from the minister of justice to the minister of interior, marginal notation.

15. AN BB 11/97 2 2381 B2, no. 4. Presumably, he could be naturalized after ten years' residence, although no such record survives. Dietrich-Chénel and Varnier ("Intégration d'étrangers") count some 550 requests for permission to reside that eventually became naturalizations for the period 1815–71.

16. AN BB 11/97 2 2381 B2, no. 1. The administrative acts of local officials in Dunkerque refer to "naturalization," while the royal ordinance of the chancellery confirms that these concerned "declarations of naturalization."

17. On the unattractive status of being a naturalized citizen, see Weil, *Qu'est ce qu'un Français?* 42–43.

18. AN F2 (1) 436, no. 66: "Tableau nominatif des individus naturalisés français qui n'ont point retiré leurs lettres patentes," listing a total of seventy-one between 1815 and 1821. Note the confusion over the vocabulary: *lettres de naturalité* was sometimes used, and once crossed out and replaced with the term *lettres de naturalisation*.

19. Lainé, *Etude*, 46–47 and passim.

20. *AP* II, 21:637, 4 April 1818.

21. Ibid., 751 et seq. Other proponents were more expansive in their citations: the marquis de Pastoureau cited, in addition, Grotious, Wolf, Vattel, Gorani, Rayneval, and Necker: Ibid., 638.

22. Ibid., 749.

23. Ibid., 593.

24. Ibid., 631, 26 January 1819.

25. Had they done so, they would have noted how Gaschon was clear that "national" inheritance restrictions were distinct from the "droit d'aubaine" of absolutism: see above, chap. 7. In the debate, no one cited the law school dissertation of August Cramer, written at the same moment, which put forth a far more expansive list than Gaschon's of treaties that permitted foreigners active succession rights to French estates : see his *Dissertation sur le droit d'aubaine, soutenue à la faculté de Droit de Strasbourg . . .* (Strasbourg, 1818) [BN 4-F-5695].

26. Ibid., 626–27, 26 January 1819.

27. Ibid., 686–87, 26 January 1819.

28. Ibid., 23:200–205, 11 March 1819.

29. Ibid., 233.

30. Ibid., 22:627–31, 26 January 1819.

31. Ibid., 24:553, marquis de Marbois, 25 May 1819.

32. Ibid., 22:628–29.

33. Ibid., 636–37; above, chap. 8.

34. Ibid., 553, 25 May 1819

35. Ibid., 596, 18 January 1819.

36. The Chamber of Peers passed the proposition on 30 January 1819 by a vote of 79 to 36 (*AP* II, 22:694); and the proposal that the king draft a law was approved by the Chamber of Deputies by a margin of 121 to 68 votes on 16 March 1819 (ibid., 23:239).

37. *Bulletin des Lois*, no. 294 (7th ser., vol. 9, 17–18): "Loi relative à l'abolition du droit d'aubaine et de détraction," 14 July 1819.

38. *AP* II, 24:176, 4 May 1819.

39. Ibid., 568, 22 May 1819.

40. Ibid., 24:614; Lainé, *Etude*, 57–59; M. Coin-Delisle, *Commentaire analytique du Code civil. Livre III, Titre II. Donations et Testaments*, 3d ed. (Paris, 1851), esp. 117–19.

41. In fact, it is unclear whether the law was applied to the colonies: Martens and Cussy, eds., *Recueil manuel et pratique de traités*, 1:viii, cite a further royal act to ensure that these applied to France's colonial possessions on 20 November 1821, but I have found no further evidence in the *AP* or Duvergnier.

42. AAE ADP France 2, fol. 245, 19 July 1820.

43. Weiss, *Traité théorique*, 2:71.

44. AAE ADP France 2, no. 27, minister of finances to foreign minister, 14 April 1829.

45. See Lainé, *Etude*, 61–97 and passim on the late-nineteenth-century jurisprudence engendered by the law of 14 July 1819 in relation to foreign legislation concerning succession. In general, the question of residual inheritance taxes among European states in the nineteenth and early twentieth centuries often revolved around their continued levies in the colonies: see, for example, the case of Sweden and Great Britain, "Nielsen v. Johnson [Supreme Court of the United States]," *American Journal of International Law* 23, no. 2 (1929): 422–28. The question was also raised continuously in lawsuits involving U.S. citizens, because many state constitutions prohibited foreigners from inheriting without establishing residence (New Hampshire, Kentucky, Iowa, Nevada, Virginia, Connecticut), or declaring their intention to become citizens (Arkansas, Delaware, Maryland, South Carolina), although the federal law of the United States usually prevailed: Lainé, *Etude*, 94–96. Before the unification of Germany, the United States signed a number of treaties with the German principalities mutually abolishing "the *droit d'aubaine* and taxes on emigration" (e.g., convention with the Duke of Nassau, 27 May 1846). By the 1930s, it would seem, international treaties and "universal reason" had succeeded in eliminating all the "feudal" remnants concerning the succession of properties, although a legal scholar in 1933, commenting on the International Conference on the Treatment of Foreigners of 1929, argued that "the droit d'aubaine is not out of date, even now": J. W. Cutler, "The Treatment of Foreigners: In Relation to the Draft Convention and Conference of 1929," *American Journal of International Law* 27, no. 2. (1933): 225–46. Following the Second World War, the "droit d'aubaine" was once again reinvented and invoked in lawsuits involving German businesses in the United States: see Q. Wright, "International Law and Guilt by Association," *American Journal of International Law* 43, no. 4 (1949): 746–55.

Appendix 1: Sources of the Statistical Study of Naturalizations, 1660–1790

1. *Les Etrangers en France*, 25–54.

2. In 1693, the Bureau des finances and the Chambre du trésor et du domaine were reorganized into the Chambre du domaine: see Bély, ed., *Dictionnaire*, s.v. "Chambre du domaine." Neither the archives of the Chambre du trésor nor those of the Chambre du domaine have survived intact. Partial traces of registrations of patent letters at the Bureau des finances are scattered in AN Z/IF/555–638 (1588–1790): see below, note 9.

3. AN O/1/218–238. Although bound in the nineteenth century, the collection may date from Colbert's efforts in the royal ordinance of 1674 to establish registries of expeditions from the royal household. See the index of names and persons prepared by G. de Bauffremont, J. de la Trollière, and F. de La Houssaye, 334 pages, which includes the series V/1/542 and 612 (AN, inv. 1088).

The Savoyards in this series AN O/1/218–238 have been inventoried by M. Pointet, "Les Savoyards de Nation ayant demandé et obtenu leur nationalité française (1633–1792)," Centre généalogique de Savoie, 1988, copy in the bibliothèque du Service d'Onomastique des Archives Nationales (S.TOP.1298 [17]).

4. J. Félix, *Economie et finances sous l'Ancien Régime: Guide du chercheur, 1523–1789* (Paris, 1994), 85–87. See the index of personal names by Ch. De Lapeyrouse, G. Saige, F. Gerbaux, H. de Curzon, Ch. Samaran, E. Guillemot, G. Vilar, E. Thomas, M. Langlois, and D. Dallet-Guerne, 1868–1968, twenty-eight volumes (AN, inv. 264).

5. AN V/1/542, patent letters involving name changes, marriage dispensations, legitimations, naturalizations, and ennoblements, 1673–1718. AN K 174–75, copies of letters from the registers of the Paris Chambre des comptes, 1685–1714. The surviving registers of the chancellery (series JJ) contains numerous naturalizations but only covering the period to 1568, and were thus not systematically collected for the database that begins with the advent of Louis XIV's reign.

6. Dubost and Sahlins, *Et si on faisait payer.* The tax rolls are found within AN E 370611–12. Dubost has used these extensively for his study of Italians in the kingdom during the sixteenth and seventeenth centuries (*La France italienne*), while other researchers have produced useful inventories of specific populations: thus, for example, the Jacobite population of Catholic refugees from England who settled in Saint-Germain-en-Laye after 1688 have been inventoried by the Cercle généalogique de Versailles et des Yvelines (78220 Viroflay), including the Jacobites mentioned in AN K 174–75. The inventory is deposited in the Archives Nationales.

7. See the bibliography of archival sources cited, including AN M 612 (Maltese); AN M 1031 dossier VI (Colonials); AAE MD 1454 (Austrian clerics); and the contentious cases found in BN MS JF.

8. For a general description of the Chambres and their archives, see Félix, *Economie et finances,* 235–43. I have not, however, searched for registrations in the remnants of the archives of the Chambre du trésor (above, note 2) classed in AN/Z/1F (most of which involve traces from the provincial bureaux des finances, and end in 1693). In this same series, however, can be found the procedure and protocol of confiscation by the Chambre du domaine, occasionally revealing of the local social relations into which the "foreigner" was assimilated: see, for example, the dossier on Jean Georges Nasezold, "Bourgeois de Paris allemand de nation," a banker who died in Paris in 1752, and whose properties were adjudicated to the king by the droit d'aubaine: AN Z/1F/863, "Sentences et pièces provenant de confiscations, désherences et bastardise." Nor have I systematically exploited any of the local registers of registrations (and insinuations after 1704) at the provincial financial bureaux: see, for example, the series for Paris in the Archives départementales de la Seine, C 6 1–33; or for those of Bordeaux in Archives départementales de la Gironde, C 3837–39, 38–41, 3846–47, 3857, 3865–69, 4848. Françoise Bayard has exploited the registers of the bureau des finances of Lyon and the seneschal records of Lyon in her valuable study "Naturalization in Lyon," on which I have occasionally drawn for additional information on specific naturalized foreigners.

9. AN K 174–75. For the broader period 1441–1737 (AN K 168–75), there is an alphabetical inventory of ennoblements, naturalizations, and legitimations prepared by G. Demay in 1872 (AN, inv. 240).

10. AN P 2590–2601. See the analytical inventory in alphabetical order, "Lettres de naturalité enregistrées dans les registres des chartes de la Chambre des comptes (1737–1787)," in AN, inv. 303; and also the index of J. P. Babelon, "Lettres de naturalité et de légitimation relevées dans les plumitifs de la Chambre des comptes (1635–1742)." Copies and extracts of the *plumitifs* can also be found (for the period 1574–1759) in BN MS 10991–11082.

11. Archives départementales de Loire-Atlantique (ADLA) B. As research instruments, I used the *Inventaire sommaire des Archives départementales antérieures à 1790. Tome premier, archives civils, série B: Chambre des comptes de Bretagne. Art. B1–1952,* L. Maître (Nantes, 1952); and the contemporaneous inventory of the B series register in ADLA B 111–15.

12. Archives départementales des Bouches-du-Rhône (ADBR), *Les Fonds des archives départementales des Bouches-du-Rhône,* Raoul Busquet, vol. 2, pt. 1, série B (Marseille, 1939).

13. Archives départementales de la Seine-Maritime (ADSM) 2B 361, patent letters of naturalization registered at the Chambre des comptes de Rouen. The archives of the intendancy (ADSM C 641, 1266, 1268, 2373) contain mentions of naturalizations as well.

14. Archives départementales de l'Hérault (ADH), *Inventaire analytique—série B; Cour des comptes, aides, finances de Languedoc*, M. de Dainville and D. Neirincl, vol. 7 (Montpellier, 1976). See the excellent study by Santucci of these registrations and inquiries at the Montpellier Chambre, "Devenir regnicole."

15. Archives départemales de l'Isère (ADI) B II 2–4 (inventory and index). Many of the archives of the Chambre de Grenoble, covering the Dauphiné (and now surviving in the departmental archives of the Isère), were burned in 1793: those in the database come from the expeditionary clauses of the letters.

16. The few naturalizations from Pau and the southwest were taken from the expeditionary addresses of drafts found in the O/1 series of the National Archives: according to local archivists and inventories of the Archives départementales des Pyrénees-Atlantique no surviving naturalizations or verifications exist. Thanks to the many directors of archives who took the time to reply in detail to my inquiries.

17. Archives départementales de la Côte-d'Or (ADCO) B 49, 68–70, 93 (registration of patent letters including naturalizations at the Chambre des comptes, Dijon); and ADCO C 2713 (ennoblement and naturalizations, 1697–1769). See the *Inventaire sommaire de la série B*, vol. 1., ed. C. Rossignol (Paris, 1869); vol. 4, ed. J. Garnier (Dijon, 1876).

18. The Chambre de Besançon (transferred from Dôle in 1676 and then suppressed in 1771) contains a number of mentions of naturalizations, most, however, from before the reign of Louis XIV: Archives départementales du Doubs (ADD) B 582–83, 604, 611, etc. (see manuscript inventory in ADD in Bésançon).

19. Data for the Chambres at Nancy and Metz were taken from expeditionary addresses of draft letters from other series, notably AN O/1. No archives of the Chambre des comptes at Bar-le-Duc survive; the Chambre des comptes at Blois was suppressed in 1775, although it is believed that few documents from the Chambre survive within the the existing Archives départementales de Loir-et-Cher, and many fragments can be found disbursed in the AN K, KK, and P series, although excavations yielded no naturalizations for the period 1660–1790.

20. I have not, however, considered the royal acts registered in the Paris parlement, or the registration of letters from (mostly seventeenth-century) clerics seeking benefices transcribed in the registers of the Grand Conseil: on these and other possible sources for the study of naturalizations, see Dubost, *Les Etrangers en France*, 35–39.

21. For the purposes of offering a general if limited view of the geographic distribution of naturalizations in the kingdom (above, chap. 6), I have constructed two categories that are historically illegitimate for the early modern period: "Flanders" (including the jurisdictions of the parlements and sovereign councils of Tournai and Douai) and "Alsace-Lorraine," relying principally on expeditionary addresses to these sovereign courts and to the Chambres des comptes at Nancy and Metz. The limitations of this approach are evident, but an effort nonetheless was made to determine the approximate geographic distribution of settled foreigners seeking to be naturalized.

22. See the determined if somewhat misguided efforts of Dietrich-Chénel and Varnier, "Intégration d'étrangers en France," esp. vol. 1, and the discussion of sources in chap. 8.

23. I have consulted the mentions of naturalizations in AN BB 11/2 (1789–92), 11/3–4 (1808–11), 29/175–76 (requests to establish domicile, 1803–09); 30/50–3; and 30/512 (naturalizations, 1789–91). I have also read several hundred dossiers of naturalization, requests to establish domicile, and associated correspondence dispersed in AN BB (see bibliography).

BIBLIOGRAPHY

I. Archival Sources

Note: Archival sources and abbreviations used in the construction of the database of naturalized foreigners (1660–1790) are listed in appendix 1.

AAE Archives des Affaires Etrangères, Paris

ADP Affaires diverses politiques, France: 1–2, 7–8, 10, 12, 14, 302
MD Mémoires et documents: America (11, 16, 18) Austria (7), England (8, 59), Geneva (1–2), Genoa (21), Germany (94), Low Countries [Holland] (5, 60), Portugal (1–2), Spain (51, 132–33), Fonds France et Fonds divers (10, 36, 934, 1347, 1434, 1454–57, 1463–64, 1747, 2020, 2032–34), Petit Fonds Alsace (58)

AN Archives Nationales, Paris

AD Archives Imprimés, Législation civil. II 34 (B) (opinions on the abolition of the droit d'aubaine, 1801); XV 1 ("Etrangers")
BB Justice. 11 (2–4, dossiers on naturalizations, 1789–92); 29 (175–76, requests to establish domicile, 1803–9); 30 (50–53, 512, naturalizations, 1789–91); 76–90, 91, 94–95, 97, 132, 147, 157, 200, 246 (several hundred incomplete dossiers of individual naturalizations, consulted by extract with permission).
D Révolution
  III: 46, 321, 361, 373
  XXXIX, 3–7: Civil Code, 1790–an VII
E Conseil du roi. 3706[11-12], "Minutes des rôles de legitimations et de naturalités arrêtés au Conseil des finances et Conseil royal des finances, 1646–1716"
G7 Contrôle Générale des Finances. 5–22, 559, 1542 (affaires extraordinaires: naturalités, 1702–15)
H1 Pays d'Etats, Pays d'Elections, Intendances. 1588: mémoires sur les généralités (1697–99)
K Monuments Historiques
  118: no. 1, "Discours sur l'employ des étrangers aux charges et dignités de ce royaume"
  173–75: copies de lettres de naturalité tirées des registres des chartes de la Chambre des Comptes de Paris (1685–1714)
  873: responses of the parlements from regions of "written law" to the questionnaire by d'Aguesseau in 1728 on civil incapacities
  2043/2–3, 2044: concerning the droit d'aubaine dans le comté de Montbéliard (seventeenth to eighteenth centuries)
  KK 627: "Formules de lettres de chancellerie, lettres de naturalité, etc., XVIIIe": naturalizations, declarations, dispensations, permissions to hold benefices, etc.

M Mélanges

  612: naturalizations of members of the Order of Malta

  1031 dossier VI: naturalizations of foreigners in the colonies of Saint-Domingue, Martinique, Guadeloupe, and Ile-Bourbon, 1711–85

O/1 Maison du Roi

  218–38: "Minutes et copies de lettres et déclarations de naturalité et légitimation, 1506–1789"

P Chambre des comptes de Paris

  2592–601: Registers of the Chambre des Comptes, 1737–90

PP 151 Table of naturalizations and declarations registered at the Paris Chambre des comptes

Q/3 88–92 "Taxes perçues à l'occasion des naturalités," 1718

V/1/542 lettres patentes (including naturalizations and legitimations), 1673–1718

AP *Archives du Palais (Ile Saint-Louis, Paris)*

ACA Archives de la Cour de Cassation, Fonds Tronchet

BACA Bibliothèque des Avocats à la Cour d'Appel Recueils Chanclaire, Martineau, and Breuil (factums, eighteenth century)

BN *Bibliothèque Nationale, Paris*

MS Manuscrits Français: 1848, 3497, 4254, 4429, 17957, 18271, 21082, 21714, 21754, 21805, 21308, 23612, 23622, 338501,

  JF: Fonds Joly de Fleury: 42, 124, 268, 306, 443, 540, 543, 554, 559, 563, 604, 1733, 2393, 2401, 2417, 2494, 2527, 2547–55 (Tables)

NAF Nouvelles Acquisitions Françaises: 9801

Collection Dupuy: 603, 854, 857

II. Published Primary Sources

Académie française. *Dictionnaire de l'Académie française.* Paris, 1694. 2d ed. 2 vols. Paris, 1718.

Actes Royaux. Catalogue général des livres imprimés de la Bibliothèque nationale. Ed. S. Honoré. 7 vols. N.d. (AN X/50–51).

Aguesseau, H.-F. d'. *Oeuvres complètes.* 16 vols. Paris, 1819.

——. *Recueil des questions de jurisprudence proposes par M. d'Aguesseau . . . à tous les parlements du royaume concernant les donations, les testaments, les substitutions, les incapacités de donner et de recevoir, et les matières bénéficiales. Avec les réponses du parlement de Toulouse sur ces mêmes questions.* N.p., 1749.

Albert, J. *Arrests de la Cour du Parlement de Toulouse.* Toulouse, 1686.

Ancien Moniteur, réimpression depuis la réunion des Etats Généraux jusqu'au Consulat, mai 1789–novembre 1799. Paris, 1932.

Archives départementales des Bouches-du-Rhône. *Les Fonds des archives départementales des Bouches-du-Rhône.* Raoul Busquet. Vol. 2, pt. 1, série B. Marseille, 1939.

Archives départementales de la Côte d'Or. *Inventaire sommaire de la série B.* Vol. 1. C. Rossignol. Paris, 1869. Vol. 4. J. Garnier. Dijon, 1876.

Archives départementales de l'Hérault. *Inventaire analytique—série B; Cour des comptes, aides, finances de Languedoc.* M. de Dainville and D. Neirincl. Vol. 7. Montpellier, 1976.

Archives départementales de la Loire-Atlantique. *Inventaire sommaire des Archives départementales antérieures à 1790. Tome premier, archives civils, série B: Chambre des comptes de Bretagne. Art. B1–1952.* L. Maître. Nantes, 1952.

Archives parlementaires de 1787 à 1860: Recueil complet des débats législatifs et politiques des chambres françaises. 1st ser. 96 vols. Paris, 1877–1990.

Archives parlementaires: Recueil compet des débats législatifs et politiques des chambres françaises de 1800 à 1860. 2d ser. 127 vols. Paris, 1862–1913.

Argenson, marquis d'. *Journal et mémoires du marquis d'Argenson.* Ed. E. J. B. Rathery. 9 vols. Paris, 1859–67.

Argou, G. *Institutions du droit françois.* 11th ed. 2 vols. Paris, 1787 [1692].

Augéard, M. *Arrests notables des différents tribunaux du Royaume.* 2 vols. Paris, 1756.

Automne, B. *La Conférence du Droict François avec le Droict Romain.* Paris, 1610.

Bacquet, J. *Les Oeuvres de maistre Jean Bacquet, Advocat du Roy en la Chambre du Trésor . . . augmentées de plusieurs questions . . . par M. Claude de Ferrière, avocat au parlement . . . et augmentées considerablement par M. Claude-Josephe de Ferrière, avocat au parlement et doyen des professeurs de la faculté des droits de Paris.* 2 vols. Lyon, 1744 [1576]. Vol. 2, *Traité du droit d'aubaine,* 1–144.

Barbier, E.-J.-F. *Chronique de la Régence.* Vol. 8. Paris, 1857 [1763].

Bardet, P. *Recueil d'arrests du Parlement de Paris pris des Memoires de feu M. Pierre Bardet, ancien avocat en la Cour avec les notes et Dissertations de M. Claude Berroyer, Avocat au même Parlement. Nouvelle edition . . . par M. C. N. Lalaure.* 2 vols. Avignon, 1773 [1690].

Basnage, H. *Oeuvres.* 2 vols. Rouen, 1778.

Basset, J. G. *Notables arrêts de la Cour de Parlement, Aydes et Finances de Dauphiné.* Grenoble, 1730 [1676].

Bergeal, C., ed. *Protestantisme et tolérance au XVIIIe siècle, de la Révocation à la Révolution (1689–1789).* Textes d'histoire protestantes. Carrières-sous-Poissy, 1988.

Blondeau, C., and G. Gueret. *Journal du Palais, ou Recueil des Principales Décisions de tous les Parlements et Cours Souveraines de France sur les questions les plus important de droit civil.* 4th ed. 2 vols. Paris, 1755.

Bodin, J. *Les Six livres de la République.* 4th ed. Paris, 1583 [1576].

Boislisle, A.-R. de. *Correspondance des contrôleurs-généraux des finances avec les intendants des provinces.* 3 vols. Paris, 1874–97.

Boniface, H. *Arrests notables de la Cour du Parlement de Provence, Cour des Comptes, Aydes, et Finances du Même Pais.* 5 vols. Lyon, 1708.

Bosquet, J. B. *Dictionnaire raisonné des domaines et droits domaniaux.* 2 vols. Paris, 1763.

Bouchaud, M.-A. *Théories des traités de commerce entre les nations.* Paris, 1777.

Bouchel, L. *Bibliothèque du Trésor du Droit français, où sont traitées les matières civiles, criminelles, et bénéficiales.* 3d (?) ed. 3 vols. Paris, 1671 [1615].

Boucher d'Argis, A.-J. *Lettres d'un magistrat de Paris à un magistrat de province sur le droit romain et la manière dont on l'enseigne en France.* 1782. Reprinted with an introduction by W. Wolodkiewicz, Naples, 1984.

Boug, F.-H d'Orschwiller de. *Recueil des édits, déclarations, lettres patentes, arrêts du Conseil d'état et du Conseil souverain d'Alsace.* 2 vols. Colmar, 1775.

Bourjon, F. *Le Droit commun de la France et la Coutume de Paris réduits en principes.* 2 vols. Paris, 1770 [1747].

Bretonnier, B.-J. *Recueil par ordre alphabétique des principales questions de droit qui se jugent diversement dans les différens tribunaux du Royaume.* 5th ed. Paris, 1783 [1718].

Brillon, P.-J. *Dictionnaire des arrêts ou jurisprudence universelle des Parlements de France et autre tribunaux.* 2d ed. 6 vols. Paris, 1727 [1711].

———. *Dictionnaire civil et canonique contenant les étymologies, définitions, divisions et principes du droit françois, conféré avec le Droit Romain et de la Pratique, accomodée aux nouvelle ordonnances.* Paris, 1707.

Brizard, G. *Du Massacre de la Saint Barthélémy et de l'influence des étrangers en France durant la Ligue. Discours historique.* 2 vols. Paris, 1790.

Cambacères, J.-J. Régis de. *Projet de code civil: Presenté au Conseil des cinq-cents au nom de la Commission de la classification des lois.* Paris, an IV [1796].

Cambolas, J. de. *Décisions notables sur diverses questions du Droit jugées par plusieurs arêts de la Cour du Parlement de Tolouse.* 6th ed. Toulouse, 1744 [1659].

Catellan, J. *Arrêts remarquables du Parlement de Toulouse,* 2d (?) ed. Toulouse, 1733 [1723].

Choppin, R. *Oeuvres.* 5 vols. Paris, 1662.

Collection complète des lois, decrets, ordonnances, reglemens et avis du Conseil d'Etat. . . . 71 vols. Paris, 1824–71.

Clercq, A., and J. de. Clercq, eds. *Recueil des traités de la France depuis 1713 jusqu'à nos jours.* 23 vols. Paris, 1864–1917.

Les Constitutions de la France. Ed. C. Debbasch and J.-M. Pontier. Paris, 1983.

Cotèle, L. B. *Notice sur la justice et l'intérêt de la France, comme des autres Etats de l'Europe, d'abolir le droit d'aubaine.* Orléans, 1814.

Cramer, A. *Dissertation sur le droit d'aubaine, soutenue à la faculté de Droit de Strasbourg. . . .* Strasbourg, 1818. [BN 4–F–5695]

Dangeau, Ph. de Courcillon, marquis de. *Journal du marquis Dangeau [1684–1686].* Paris, 1854–60.

Dard, H.-J.-B. *Code civil des français avec les notes indicatives des lois romaines, coutumes, ordonnances, édits et déclarations qui ont rapport à chaque article, ou Conférence du Code Civil avec les lois anciennes.* Paris, 1827.

Denisart, J.-B. *Collection de décisions nouvelles et de notions relatives à la jurisprudence actuelle.* 8th ed. 4 vols. Paris, 1773.

——. *Collection de décisions nouvelles et de notions relatives à la jurisprudence, mise dans un nouvel ordre, corrigée et augmentée par MM. Camus et Bayard, Avocats au Parlement.* 9th ed. 4 vols. Paris, 1783.

Depping, G. B., ed. *Correspondance administrative sous le règne de Louis XIV.* 4 vols. Paris, 1855.

Diderot, D., and J. d'Alembert. *Encyclopédie, ou Dictionnaire raisonné des sciences, des arts, et des métiers, par une société des gens de lettres.* 23 vols. and 4 suppls. Neufchatel, 1751–77.

Dionis du Séjour. *Mémoires pour servir à l'histoire du droit public de la France en matière d'impots ou Recueil de ce qui s'est passé de plus interessant à la cour des aides de Paris depuis 1756 jusqu'au mois de juin 1775.* Brussels, 1779.

Domat, J. *The Civil Law in Its Natural Order.* Trans. W. Strahan. 2 vols. Boston, 1853 [1696].

——. *Les Quatre livres du droit public.* Caen, 1989 [1697].

Droz. *Essai sur l'histoire des bourgeois du roi, des seigneurs, et des villes.* Besancon, 1760.

Dufour. *Le Code Civil des Français avec les sources où toutes ses dispositions ont été prises.* Paris, 1806.

Du Fresne. *Journal des principales audiences du Parlement.* 6 vols. Paris, 1757.

Du Massacre de la Saint Barthélémy et de l'influence des étrangers en France durant la Ligue. Discours historique. 2 vols. Paris, 1790.

Du Rousseau de la Combe, G. *Arrests et reglements notables du Parlement de Paris.* Paris, 1743.

——. *Recueil de jurisprudence canonique et bénéficiale.* Paris, 1755.

——. *Recueil de jurisprudence civile du pays de droit écrit et coutumier par ordre alphabétique.* 5th (?) ed. Paris, 1785.

Dupuy, P. *Traité touchant les droits du Roy.* Rouen, 1670.

Edits, déclarations et Arrests concernans la Réligion P[rétendue] Réformée, 1662–1751. Paris, 1885.

Fénelon, F. Salignac de la Mothe de. *Les Aventures de Télémaque.* Paris, 1987 [1699].

Fenet, P.-A. *Recueil complet des travaux préparatoires du Code civil.* 15 vols. Paris, 1827.

Ferrière, C. de. *Corps et compilation de tous les commentateurs anciens et modernes sur la Coutume de Paris.* 4 vols. Paris, 1714.

——. *Les Instituts du droit français.* Paris, 1687.

Ferrière, C.-J. de. *Dictionnaire de Droit et de Pratique contenant l'explication des termes de droit, d'ordonnances, de coutumes et de pratique: Avec les jurisdictions de France.* 2 vols. Toulouse, 1779 [first published as *Nouvelle introduction à la pratique.* Paris, 1718].

Flammermont, J., ed. *Les Correspondances des agents diplomatiques étrangers en France avant la Révolution conservées dans les archives de Berlin, Dresde, Genève, Turin, Gênes, Florences, Naples, Simancas, Lisbonne, Londres, La Haye et Vienne.* Paris, 1896.

——. *Rémonstrances du parlement de Paris au XVIIIe siècle.* 3 vols. Paris, 1888–98.

Flassan, G. *Histoire générale et raisonnée de la diplomatiè française; ou de la politique de la France; depuis la fondation de la monarchie jusqu'à la fin du règne de Louis XVI.* Paris, 1811.

Frain, S. *Arrests du Parlement de Bretagne . . . Troisieme édition, revue . . . par Pierre Hévin.* 3d ed. 2 vols. Rennes, 1684 [1659].

Furetière, A. *Dictionaire universel, contenant généralement tous les mots françois tant vieux que modernes, et les termes de toutes les sciences et des arts. . . .* Paris, 1727 [1685]; new ed. in 3 vols. Paris, 1978.

Gabriel, C.-J. *Observations détachées sur les coutumes et les usages anciens et modernes du ressort du Parlement de Metz.* 2 vols. Bouillon, 1787.

Gama, E. de. *Dissertation sur le droit d'aubaine.* Paris, 1706.

Gaschon, J. B. *Code Diplomatique des aubains.* Paris, 1818.

Gazette des Tribuneaux, et Mémorial des corps administratifs et municipaux. 7 vols. Paris, 1791–93.

Gazette des Tribunaux, ouvrage periodique, contenant les nouvelles des tribuneaux . . . par M. Mars, avocat au parlement. . . . 26 vols. Paris, 1775–89.

Goldoni, C. *Memorie.* Ed. Guido Davico Bonino. Trans. Eugenio Levi. Turin, 1993 [orig. French ed., 1787].

Gorani, G. *Recherches sur la science du gouvernement.* 2 vols. Paris, 1792.

Grotius, H. *De Jure Belli ac Pacis.* Reproduction of 1646 ed., trans. Francis W. Kelsey et al. 2 vols. Oxford, 1925.

Guyot, J.-N. *Répertoire universel et raisonné de jurisprudence en matière civile, criminelle, canonique et bénéficiale.* 27 vols. Paris, 1784–85.

Héricourt du Vautier, L. de. *Les Loix ecclésiastiques de France dans leur ordre naturel, et une analyse des livres du droit canonique conferés avec les usages de l'Église gallicane.* Paris, 1771.

Hévin, P. *Arrêts du Parlement de Bretagne.* Rennes, 1684.

Isambert, F.-A., A. J. L. Jourdan, and Decrusy, eds. *Recueil général des anciennes lois de la France, de l'an 420 jusqu'à la Révolution de 1789 . . . avec les notes de concordance, table chronologique et table générale alphabétique des matières. . . .* 29 vols. Paris, 1821–33.

Journal des principales audiences du Parlement. 7 vols. Paris, 1733–54.

Knies, C. *Correspondance inédite de Dupont de Nemours et du marquis de Mirabeau avec le margrave et le prince héréditaire de Bade.* 2 vols. Paris, 1892.

Koch, C. *Table des traités entre la France et les puissances étrangères depuis la paix de Westphalie jusqu'à nos jours.* 2 vols. Basel, 1802.

Laffemas, B. de. *Recueil présenté au roi de ce qui se passe en l'assemblée du commerce au Palais à Paris, fait par Laffemas, contrôleur-général dudit commerce* [1604]. In *Archives curieuses de l'histoire de France.* 1st ser., vol. 14. Paris, 1837.

Lapeyrère, A. *Décisions sommaires du Palais.* 7th ed. Bordeaux, 1808 [1749].

La Roche-Flavin, B. de. *Arrests notables du Parlement de Toulouse.* Toulouse, 1745 [1682].

Le Bret, C. *Les Oeuvres de Messire Cardin Le Bret, conseiller ordinaire du Roy en ses conseils d'état et privé, cy-devant Avocat General en la Cour des Aydes, et depuis au Parlement de Paris.* Paris, 1689.

———. *Recueil d'aucuns plaidoyez faict en la cour des aides.* Paris, 1604.

Le Brun, D. *Traité des successions.* 2 vols. Paris, 1775.

Le Chanteur. *Dissertation historique et critique sur la Chambre des comptes.* Paris, 1765.

Lefebvre de la Planche, J.-J. A. *Mémoires sur les matières domaniales, ou Traité du domaine.* 3 vols. Paris, 1764–65.

Le Trosne, G.-F. *De l'administration provinciale et de la réforme de l'impôt.* 3 vols. Basel, 1788 [1779].

"Lettres d'un magistrat de Paris à un magistrat de province" [1782]. In "Les Études de droit en France à la veille de la Révolution." *Revue internationale de l'enseignement* 5 (1883): 291–300.

Loeuilliet. *Principes des lois romaines comparés aux principes des lois français.* Douai, 1787.

Loüet, G. *Recueil de plusieurs arrests notables du Parlement de Paris contenant un grand nombre de décisions recueillies par Maître Julien Brodeau.* 2 vols. Paris, 1742.

Loyseau, C. *Cinq livres du droit des offices.* Paris, 1613 [1610].

Loysel, A. de. *Divers opuscules tirez des mémoires de M. Antoine Loisel.* Ed. Claude Joly. Paris, 1652 [1578].

Mably, G. Bonnot de. *Des Droits et des devoirs du citoyen.* Paris, 1879.

Maisons, F. de. *Nouveau traité des aydes, tailles et gabelles.* 4th (?) ed. Paris, 1666 [1622].

Maleville, J. de. *Analyse raisonnée de la discussion du Code Civil au Conseil d'Etat.* 3d ed. Paris, 1822.

Malesherbes, C.-G. de Lamoignon de. *Très-humbles et très respectueuses remonstrances, que présentent au roi notre très honoré souverain et seigneur, les gens tenants sa Cour des Aides à Paris.* Paris, 1778. Published in Dionis du Séjour, *Mémoires pour servir à l'histoire du droit public de la France en matieres d'impots,* 628–93. Brussels, 1779. Reprinted with a translation by G. Robinson in *Translations and Reprints from the Original Sources of European History* 5, no. 2. Philadelphia, 1912.

Martens, C. de, and F. de Cussy, eds. *Recueil manuel et pratique de traités, conventions, et autres actes diplomatiques . . . de l'année 1760 jusqu'à l'époque actuelle.* 4 vols. Leipzig, 1846.

Mayer, C.-J. de. *Vie publique et privée de Charles Gravier, comte de Vergennes, ministre d'état; Discours couronné par l'Académie d'Amiens le 25 août 1788.* Paris, 1789.

Maynard, G. de. *Notables et singulières questions de droit escrit et jugées par arrests mémorables de la cour souveraine du Parlement de Tholose.* Toulouse, 1638.

Mémoire pour répondre aux plaintes faites par MM. Les Ambassadeurs plénipotentiares d'Espagne, d'Angleterre et d'Hollande contre la déclaration du 22 juillet 1697. [BNF Lg(6) 338].

Mémoires du clergé. 14 vols. Paris, 1716.

Mercy-Argenteau, F.-C., comte de, *Correspondence secrète du comte de Mercy-Argenteau avec l'empereur Joseph II et le prince de Kaunitz.* Ed. A. d'Arneth and M. J. Flammermont. 3 vols. Paris, 1891.

Merlin, P.-A. *Répertoire universel et raisonné de jurisprudence.* . . . 5th ed. 18 vols. Paris, 1827–28 [1812–15].

Mirabeau, V., marquis de. *L'Ami des hommes, ou Traité de la population.* 2 vols. Darmstadt, 1970 [Avignon, 1756].

Moheau, J.-B. *Recherches et considérations sur la population de la France.* Paris, 1912 [1778].

Montchrétien, A. de. *Traicté de l'Economie politique.* Ed. T. Funck-Brentano. Paris, 1889 [1615].

Montesquieu, Ch.-L. de Secondat, baron de. *The Spirit of the Laws.* Trans. A. M. Cohler, B. C. Miller, and H. S. Stone. Cambridge, 1989 [1748].

Moreau de Beaumont, J.-L. *Mémoires concernant les impositions et droits en Europe.* 4 vols. Paris, 1787 [1768].

Moreau de Saint-Méry, M. L.-E. *Loix et constitutions des colonies françaises de l'Amérique sous le vent.* Paris, 1785.

Nahon, G. *Les "nations" juives portugaises du sud-ouest de la France (1684–1791). Documents.* Fontes Documentais Portugesas XV. Paris, 1981.

Necker, J. *De l'Administration des finances de la France.* Paris, 1784.

———. *Oeuvres complètes.* 15 vols. Paris, 1820–21.

"Nielsen v. Johnson" [Supreme Court of the United States], *American Journal of International Law* 23, no. 2. (1929): 422–28.

Pape, G. *La Jurisprudence du célèbre conseiller et jurisconsulte Guy Pape dans ses décisions, avec plusieurs remarques importantes, dans lesquelles sont entr'autres employés plus de mille arrêts du Parlement de Grenoble.* 2d ed. Grenoble, 1769 [1692].

Papon, J. *Secrets du troisième et dernier notaire.* Lyon, 1578.

———, ed. *Recueil d'arrêts notables des Cours souveraines de France.* 6th (?) ed. Paris, 1607 [1565].

Picardet, H. *Plaidoyer de Hugues Picardet, procureur général de Sa Majesté au parlement de Dijon en Bourgogne, sur une veille erreur populaire, que le droit d'aubaine était aboli en la ville de Dijon, avec les arrêts et ordonnances.* Dijon, 1609.

Pithou, P. *Traitez des droits et libertez de l'Eglise Gallicane.* 2 vols. Paris, 1651.

Pothier, R. J. *Oeuvres de Pothier, contenant les traités du droit français. Nouvelle edition de M. Dupin.* 11 vols. Paris, 1825.

Poullain du Parc, A. M. *Principes du Droit français suivant les maximes de Bretagne.* 12 vols. Rennes, 1767–71.

Prévost, Abbé. *Manuel lexique ou Dictionnaire portatif de mots françois dont la signification n'est pas familière à tout le monde.* Paris, 1750.

Proceedings in the National Assembly of France on the Admission of Mr. William Priestly and the Motion for His Naturalization. 1792, London.

Ragueau, F. *Glossaire du droit francais, contenant l'explication des mots difficiles qui se trouvent dans les ordonnances roys de France, dans les coustumes du royaume, dans les anciens arrests et les anciens titres.* Ed. E. de Laurière. Paris, 1882 [1583].

Ricard. *Traité des donations entre vifs et testamentaires.* 2 vols. Paris, 1783 [1713].

Richelet, P. *Dictionnaire françois augmenté par Pierre Richelet.* Amsterdam, 1706.

Rochefort, César de. *Dictionnaire généralé et curieux.* Lyon, 1684.

Rondonneau, L. *Table générale, alphabétique et raisonnée des matières contenues dans le répertoire de jurisprudence et dans le recueil des questions de droit de M. Merlin.* Paris, 1828.

Rousseau, J.-J. *The Social Contract.* Trans. M. Cranston. London, 1968 [1762].

Royer, M. de. "Discours sur la vie et les travaux de M. Tronchet." In *Cour de Cassation. Audience de rentrée du 3 novembre 1753,* 1–70. Paris, 1853.

Sault, du. *Nouveau stile des lettres des chancelleries de France.* Paris, 1666.

Scaramuzza. *Les Juifs d'Alsace doivent-ils être admis au droit des citoyens actifs?* Paris, 1790.

Serres, C. de. *Les Institutions du droit français suivant l'ordre de celles de Justinien.* Paris, 1753.

Soëfve, L. *Nouveau recueil de plusieurs questions notables tant de droit que de coutumes jugées par arrests d'audiences du Parlement de Paris depuis 1640 jusques à présent.* 2 vols. Paris, 1682.

Tessereau, A. *Histoire chronologique de la grande chancellerie de France.* 2 vols. Paris, 1710.

Turgot, A.-R. J. *Oeuvres de Turgot, classée par ordre de matières, avec les notes de Dupont de Nemours, augm. de lettres inédites, des Questions sur le commerce, et d'observations et de notes nouvelles.* 2 vols. Paris, 1844.

Valabrègue, B. de. *Odes prononcées par les Juifs d'Avignon et de Bordeaux résidants à Paris dans leur Assemblée à l'occasion du sacre de Louis XVI.* [n.d., 1774]

Vattel, E. de. *The Law of Nations or the Principles of Natural Law Applied to the Conduct and to the Affairs of Nations and Sovereigns.* Vol. 3. Buffalo, 1995 [1758, trans. C. G. Fenwick].

Zur-Lauben, A. de. *Histoire militaire des Suisses au service de la France.* Paris, 1751.

III. Secondary Sources

Acomb, F. *Anglophobia in France: An Essay in the History of Constitutionalism and Nationalism.* Durham, 1950.

Alteroche, B. d'. *De l'Etranger à la seigneurie à l'étranger au royaume, XIe–XVe siècle.* Paris, 2002.

Alvarez-Valdès y Valdès, M. *La Extrangería en la historia del derecho español.* Oviedo, 1992.

Anderson, B. *Imagined Communities: Reflections on the Origin and Spread of Nationalism.* London, 1983.

André, L. *Louis XIV et l'Europe.* Paris, 1950.

André, L., and E. Bourgeois. *Les Sources de l'histoire de la France. XVIIe siècle (1610–1715).* Vol. 5, *Histoire politique et militaire.* Paris, 1926.

Antoine, M. *Le Conseil du roi sous le regne de Louis XV.* Geneva, 1970.

——. *Louis XV.* Paris, 1989.

——. "La Monarchie absolue." In *The Political Culture of the Old Regime*, ed. K. Baker, 3–24. Oxford, 1987.

Antonetti, G. "Traditionalistes et novateurs à la faculté des droits de Paris au XVIIIe siècle." *Annales d'histoire des facultés de droit*, no. 3 (1986): 37–50.

Aragon, S. "Les Belles étrangères vues par les femmes auteurs des lumières." In *Visions de l'étranger au siècle des Lumières*, ed. M.-O. Bernez, 161–71. Dijon, 2002.

Asséo, H. "Marginalité et exclusion, le traitement administratif des Bohémiens dans la société française du XVIIe siècle." In *Problèmes socio-culturels en France au XVIIIe siècle*, 11–87. Paris, 1974.

——. "Le Roi, la marginalité, et les marginaux." In *L'Etat Classique, 1652–1715*, ed. H. Méchoulan and J. Cornette, 355–71. Paris, 1996.

Augustin, J. "Trois familles hollandaises et protestantes à la Rochelle au XVIIe siècle." In *La Condition juridique de l'étranger, hier et aujourd'hui.* Actes du Colloque organisé à Nimègue les 9–11 May 1988, 247–62. Nijmegen, 1988.

L'Autre exil: Les Jacobites en France au début du XVIIIe siècle. Actes du Colloque "La Cour des Stuarts à Saint-Germain-en-Laye au temps de Louis XIV," Saint-Germain-en-Laye, February 1992. Aubenas, 1993.

Azimi, V. "L'Etat révolutionnaire et les intérets privés étrangers." In *Révolutions et droit international.* [Actes du 23e] Colloque [organisé par la] Société française pour le droit international, Dijon, 1–3 June 1989, 207–50. Paris, 1990.

——. "Le Suffrage 'universaliste,' les étrangers et le droit electoral de 1793." In *La Constitution du 24 juin 1793, l'utopie dans le droit public français*, ed. J.-J. Clère and M. Verpeaux, 204–39. Actes du Colloque de Dijon, 16–17 September 1993. Dijon, 1997.

——. "Une Tentative d'unification du droit civil: Le Projet inédit de Laverdy et Langlois." *Mémoires de la Société pour l'histoire du droit et des institutions des anciens pays Bourguignons, Comtois et Romands*, no. 42 (1985): 123–56.

Babelon, E. "Les Bourgeois du Roi au Moyen Age." Thèse de l'Ecole de Chartes, 1878 [AN AB XXVIII 197].

Baker, K. M. "The Idea of a Declaration of Rights." In *The French Idea of Freedom*, ed. D. Van Kley, 154–98. Stanford, 1994.

——. *Inventing the French Revolution: Essays on French Political Culture in the Eighteenth Century.* Cambridge, 1990.

——. "Transformations of Classical Republicanism in Eighteenth-Century France." *Journal of Modern History* 3, no. 1 (2001): 32–53.

Balibar, E. *Les Frontières de la démocratie.* Paris, 1992.

——. "Is a European Citizenship Possible?" *Public Culture* 8 (1996): 355–76.

Balteau, J., M. Barroux, M. Prévost, and R. d'Amat, eds. *Dictionnaire de biographie française.* Paris, 1933–42.

Baratier, E., G. Duby, and E. Hidesheimer. *Atlas historique: Provence, Comtat, Orange, Nice, Monaco.* Paris, 1989.

Barret-Kriegel, B. "La Politique juridique de la monarchie française." In *L'Etat moderne: Le Droit, l'espace, et les formes de l'etat,* ed. N. Coulet and J.-P. Genet, 91–108. Paris, 1990.

Baschet, A. *Histoire du Dépôt des Archives des Affaires étrangères.* Paris, 1875.

Baulant, M. "Les Salaires des ouvriers du batiment de Paris de 1400 à 1726." *Annales ESC* (March–April 1971), no. 2: 463–97.

Bayard, F. "Naturalization in Lyon during the Ancien Régime." *French History* 4, no. 3 (1990): 277–316.

——. *Le Monde des financiers au XVIIe siècle.* Paris, 1988.

Beaune, C. *The Birth of an Ideology: Myths and Symbols of Nation in Late Medieval France.* Ed. F. L. Cheyette. Trans. S. R. Huston. Berkeley, 1991.

Beaurepaire, P.-Y. *L'Autre et le frère étranger, la franc-maçonnerie au XVIIIe siècle.* Paris, 1999.

Beignier, B. "Portalis et le droit naturel dans le Code civil." *Revue d'histoire des facultés de droit et de la science juridique,* no. 6 (1988): 77–101.

Bell, D. A. "Les Avocats parisiens d'ancien régime: Guide de recherches." *Revue de la Société internationale d'histoire de la profession d'avocat,* no. 5 (1993): 213–54.

——. *The Cult of the Nation in France: Inventing Nationalism, 1680–1800.* Cambridge, Mass., 2001.

——. "Forgotten Frenchmen." *Times Literary Supplement.* 24 January 1997.

——. *Lawyers and Citizens: The Making of a Political Elite in Old Regime France.* New York, 1994.

Bell, D. A., L. Pimenova, and S. Pujol, eds. *La Recherche dix-huitièmiste: Raison universelle et culture nationale au siècle des Lumières / Eighteenth-Century Research: Universal Reason and National Culture during the Enlightenment.* Paris, 1999.

Bély, L., ed. *Dictionnaire de l'Ancien Régime: Royaume de France, XVIe–XVIIIe siècle.* Paris, 1996.

——. *Espions et ambassadeurs au temps de Louis XIV.* Paris, 1990.

——. *Les Relations internationales en Europe, XVIIe–XVIIIe siècles.* Paris, 1992.

Bénabou, E.-M. *La Prostitution et la police des moeurs.* Paris, 1987.

Benoit, M. *Versailles et les musiciens du Roi (1661–1733): Etude institutionelle et sociale.* Paris, 1971.

Berlanstein, L.-R. *The Barristers of Toulouse in the Eighteenth Century (1740–1793).* Baltimore, 1975.

Bernard, B. "Les XVIIe et XVIIIe siècles: Une hospitalité parcimonieuse." In *Histoire des étrangers et de l'immigration en Belgique de la préhistoire à nos jours,* ed. A. Morelli, 75–90. Brussels, 1992.

Bertrand, L. *Histoire des séminaires de Bordeaux et de Bazas.* 2 vols. Paris, 1894.

Bickart, R. *Les Parlements et la notion de souveraineté nationale au XVIIIe siècle.* Paris, 1932.

Bien, D. "Manufacturing Nobles: The Chancelleries in France to 1789." *Journal of Modern History* 61 (1989): 445–86.

——. "Offices, Corps, and a System of State Credit: The Uses of Privilege under the Ancien Régime." In *The Political Culture of the Old Regime,* ed. K. Baker, 89–114. Oxford, 1987.

——. "Old Regime Origins of Democratic Liberty." In *The French Idea of Freedom: The Old Regime and the Declaration of Rights of 1789,* ed. D. Van Kley, 23–71. Stanford, 1994.

——. "The *Secrétaires du Roi:* Absolutism, Corps, and Privileges under the Ancien Régime." In *Vom Ancien Regime zur Französischen Revolution: Forschungen und Perspektiven,* ed E. Hinrichs, E. Schmitt, and R. Vierhaus, 153–68. Göttingen, 1978.

Billot, C. "L'Assimilation des étrangers dans le royaume de France au XIVe et XVe siècles." *Revue historique* 270, no. 2 (1983): 273–96.

——. "Les Italiens naturalisés sous le regne de François I." In *Struttura familiari, epidemie, migrazioni nell'Italia medievale,* ed. R. Comba, G. Piccini, and G. Pinto, 477–91. Siena, 1984.

Birn, R. "Religious Toleration and Freedom of Expression." In *The French Idea of Freedom: The Declaration of the Rights of Man,* ed. D. Van Kley, 265–99. Stanford, 1994.

Black, J. *From Louis XIV to Napoleon: The Fate of a Great Power.* London, 1999.

Blesson, M. "La Police des Noirs sous Louis XVI en France." *Revue de l'histoire des colonies françaises* (1928): 443–46.

Bloch, J. R. *L'Annoblissement en France au temps de François I: Essai d'une définition de la condition juridique et sociale de la noblesse au début du XVIe siècle.* Paris, 1934.

Bloomfield, A. I. "The Foreign-Trade Doctrines of the Physiocrates." *American Economic Review* 28 (1938): 716–35.

Blumenkranz, B. ed. *Juifs en France au XVIIIè siècle*. Paris, 1994.

———. *Juifs en France: Ecrits dispersés*. Paris, 1980.

Bodin, J. *Les Suisses au service de la France de Louis XI à la Légion étrangère*. Paris, 1988.

Bois, J. P. *Les Anciens soldats dans la société française au XVIIIe siècle*. Paris, 1990.

Boizet, J. *Les Lettres de naturalité sous l'Ancien Régime*. Paris, 1943.

Bonner, E. "French Naturalization of the Scots in the Fifteenth and Sixteenth Centuries." *Historical Journal* 40, no. 4 (1997): 1085–1115.

Bonolas, Ph. "La Question des étrangers à la fin du XVIe siècle et au début du XVIIe siècle." *Revue d'histoire moderne et contemporaine* 36 (1989): 304–17.

Borgetto, M. "Métaphore de la famille et idéologies." In *Le Droit non-civil de la famille*. Publication de la Faculté de Droit et des Sciences Sociales de Poitiers, vol. 10, 1–21. Paris, 1983.

Bornecque-Winandye, E. *Histoire de la Police: Police de l'antiquité Gallo-Romaine, Police de Paris, Police intérieure et extérieure de la France*. Paris, 1950.

Bosher, J. *French Finances, 1770–1795: From Business to Bureaucracy*. Cambridge, 1970.

———. *The Single Duty Project: A Study of the Movement for a French Customs Union in the Eighteenth Century*. London, 1964.

Bossenga, G. "City and State: An Urban Perspective on the Origins of the French Revolution." In *The Political Culture of the Old Regime*, ed. K. Baker, 115–40. Oxford, 1987.

———. "From *Corps* to Citizenship: The Bureaux des Finances before the French Revolution." *Journal of Modern History* 58, no. 3 (1986): 610–42.

———. "Rights and Citizens in the Old Regime." *French Historical Studies* 20, no. 2 (1997): 217–43.

Bottin, J., and D. Calabi, eds. *Les Etrangers dans la ville*. Paris, 1999.

Bouamama, S. "Nationalité et citoyen: Le Divorce inévitable." In *La Citoyenneté dans tous ses états: De l'immigration à la nouvelle citoyenneté*, ed. S. Bouamama, A. Cordeiro, and M. Roux, 145–70. Paris, 1992.

Boulet-Sautel, M. "L'Aubain dans la France coutumière au Moyen Age." *RSJB* 10 (1958): 65–100.

Bourilly, V.-L. "Les Protestants à Marseille au XVIIIe siècle." *BSHPF* 59 (1910): 518–53.

Bouwsma, W. *A Usable Past: Essays in European Cultural History*. Berkeley, 1990.

Bowsky, W. M. "Medieval Citizenship: The Individual and the State in the Commune of Siena, 1287–1355." *Studies in Medieval and Renaissance History* 4 (1967): 195–243.

Branca-Rosoff, S. "Les Mots de parti pris: *Citoyen, Aristocrate* et *Insurrection* dans quelques dictionnaires (1762–1798)." In *Dictionnaire des usages socio-politiques (1770–1815)*. Vol. 3, *Dictionnaires, Normes, Usages*, 2. Société française d'étude du 18e siècle, 47–73. Paris, 1988.

Braudel, F. *Civilization and Capitalism, Fifteenth–Eighteenth Century*. 3 vols. Trans. S. Reynolds. New York, 1986.

———. *The Identity of France*. Trans. S. Reynolds. 2 vols. New York, 1988–90.

Braudel, F., and E. Labrousse, eds. *Histoire économique et sociale de la France*. Vol. 1, *1450–1660*; vol. 2, *Des derniers temps de l'âge seigneurial aux préludes de l'âge industriel (1660–1789)*. Paris, 1970–77.

Brockliss, B. *French Higher Education in the Seventeenth and Eighteenth Centuries: A Cultural History*. Oxford, 1987.

Broglie, duc de. *Le Secret du Roi. Correspondance secrète de Louis XV avec ses agents diplomatiques*. Paris, 1878.

Brubaker, R. *Citizenship and Nationhood in France and Germany*. Cambridge, Mass., 1992.

Brunelle, G. "Immigration, Assimilation, and Success: Three Families of Spanish Origin in Sixteenth-Century Rouen." *Sixteenth Century Journal* 20 (1989): 203–19.

Bruschi, C. "Note sur l'étranger et la nation au XVIII siècle." In *Nation et République: Les Éléments d'un débat*. Actes du colloque de Dijon, 6–7 April 1994, Association française des idées politiques, 41–50. Aix, 1995.

Burg, A. M. *Les Suisses et le repeuplement de Haguenau dans la seconde moitié du XVIIe siècle*. Paris, 1952.

Burguière, A. "Groupe d'immigrant ou minorité réligieuse? Les Juifs à Paris au XVIIIe siècle." In *Le Migrant: "France, terre de migrations internes; France, terre d'immigration."* Actes du colloque d'Aurillac, 5–7 June 1985, 183–200. Aurillac, 1986.

Butel, P. *Les Dynasties bordelaises de Colbert à Chaban*. Paris, 1991.

———. *Les Négotiants bordelais, l'Europe et les Iles au XVIIe siècle*. Paris, 1974.

Cahen, A. "Les Juifs dans les colonies françaises au XVIIIe siècle." *Revue des études juives* 4 (1881): 127–45, 236–48; 5 (1882): 68–92, 258–72.

Campbell, P. *Power and Politics in Old Regime France, 1720–1745*. London, 1996.

Camon, G. *Maurice de Saxe, Maréchal de France*. Paris, 1934.

Canning, J. "A Fourteenth-Century Contribution to the Theory of Citizenship: Political Man and the Problem of Created Citizenship in the Thought of Baldus de Ubaldis." In *Authority and Power: Studies in Medieval Law and Government Presented to Walter Ullmann on His Seventieth Birthday*, ed. B. Tierney and P. A. Linehan, 197–212. Cambridge, 1980.

——. *The Political Thought of Baldus of Ubaldis*. Cambridge, 1987.

Canny, N., ed. *Europeans on the Move: Studies on European Migration, 1500–1800*. Oxford, 1994.

Cans, A. "Les Registres d'expéditions du Secrétariat d'Etat de la Maison du Roi." *Revue d'histoire moderne et contemporaine* 4 (1902–3): 257–61.

Carey, J. A. *Judicial Reform in France before the Revolution of 1789*. Cambridge, Mass., 1981.

Carpenter, A. H. "Naturalization in England and the American Colonies." *American Historical Review* 9 (1904): 288–303.

Carrière, Ch. *Négociants marseillais au XVIIIe siècle: Contribution à l'étude des économies maritimes*. Marseilles, 1973.

Carrot, G. *Histoire de la police française*. Paris, 1992.

Cavignac, J. "A Bordeaux et Bayonne: Des 'marchands portugais' aux citoyens français." In *Juifs en France au XVIIIe siècle*, ed. B. Blumenkranz, 53–72. Paris, 1994.

——. "L'Immigration des Juifs portugais a Bordeaux au XVIIIe siècles." In *Les Relations entre le Sud-Ouest et la péninsule ibérique*. Actes du XXXVIIIe Congrès de la Fédération historique du Sud-Ouest, Pau, 5–6 October 1985, 125–38. Pau, 1987.

Chabrun, C. *Les Bourgeois du roi*. Paris, 1908.

Charbonnier, J. "The French Civil Code." In *Rethinking France. Les Lieux de mémoire*. Vol. 1, *The State*, ed. P. Nora, 335–60. Chicago, 2001.

Charmeil, J.-P. *Les Trésoriers de France à l'époque de la Fronde: Contribution à l'histoire de l'administration financière sous l'Ancien Régime*. Paris, 1964.

Chartier, R. *The Cultural Origins of the French Revolution*. Trans. L. G. Cochrane. Durham, 1991.

——. "La Formation de la population lyonnaise: Apports savoyards au XVIIIe siecle." *Revue de géographie de Lyon* 25 (1951): 345–49.

Chaussinard-Nogaret, G. *Le Citoyen des Lumières*. Paris, 1994.

——. "La Diaspora jacobite et l'Europe moderne." *Revue de la Bibliothèque Nationale*, no. 46 (1992): 2–3.

——. "Une Elite insulaire au service de l'Europe: Les Jacobites au XVIIIe siècle." *Annales ESC* (September–October 1973), no. 5: 1097–1122.

——. *Gens de finance au XVIIIe siècle*. Paris, 1993.

Chaussinard-Nogaret, G., J.-M. Constant, C. Durandin, and A. Jouanna. *Histoire des élites en France du XVIe au XXe siècle. L'Honneur—Le Mérite—L'Argent*. Paris, 1991.

Chêne, C. "L'Arrestographie, science fort douteuse." *Recueil des mémoires de la Société d'histoire du droit et des institutions des pays de droit écrit* (1985): 179–87.

——. *L'Enseignement du droit français en pays de droit écrit (1679–1793)*. Geneva, 1982.

——. "Les Facultés de droit françaises du XVIIe siècle à la Révolution, éléments de bibliographie." *Annales d'histoire des facultés de droit*, no. 3 (1986): 199–242.

——. "La Politique royale de l'enseignement du droit en France au XVIIIe siècle: Les Survivances dans le régime moderne." *Revue d'histoire des facultés de droit et de la science juridique*, no. 7 (1988): 21 et seq.

Chevrier, G. "Remarques sur l'introduction de la distinction et les vicissitudes du 'jus privatum' et du 'jus publicum' dans les oeuvres des anciens juristes francais." *Archives de philosophie du droit*, n.s., 1 (1952): 5–77.

Christian, M. "Du citadinage à la naturalité: L'Intégration des étrangers à Marseille (XIIIe–XVIe siècles)." *Provence historique* 49 (1999): 333–52.

Church, W. F. "The Decline of the French Jurists as Political Theorists, 1660–1789." *French Historical Studies* 5 (1967): 1–16.

Çinar, D. "From Aliens to Citizens: A Comparative Analysis of the Rules of Transition." In *From Aliens to Citizens: Redefining the Status of Immigrants in Europe*, ed. R. Baubock, 49–72. Aldershot, 1994.

Clarke de Dromantin, P. "Condition juridiques et sociales de l'assimilation d'une famille jacobite réfugiée en France." In *L'Autre exil: Les Jacobites en France au début du XVIIIe siècle*. Actes du Colloque "La Cour des Stuarts à Saint-Germain-en-Laye au temps de Louis XIV." Saint-Germain-en-Laye, February 1992, 157–70. Aubenas, 1993.

Coin-Delisle. *Commentaire analytique du Code civil.Livre III, Titre II. Donations et Testaments.* 3d ed. Paris, 1851.

Cole, C. *Colbert and a Century of French Mercantilism.* 2 vols. New York, 1939.

Colley, L. *Britons: Forging the Nation, 1707–1837.* New Haven, 1992.

Collins, I. *Napoleon and His Parliaments, 1800–1815.* New York, 1979.

Collins, J. B. "Geographic and Social Mobility in Early-Modern France." *Journal of Social History* 24 (1991): 563–77.

Corcia, J. di. "*Bourg, Bourgeois, Bourgeoisie de Paris* from the Eleventh to the Eighteenth Centuries." *Journal of Modern History* 50 (1978): 207–33.

Cornette, J. *Chronique du règne de Louis XIV.* Paris, 1997.

Cornevin, R., and M. Cornevin. *La France et les Français outre-mer.* Paris, 1990.

Corvisier, A. *L'Armée française de la fin du XVIIe siècle au ministère de Choiseul.* 2 vols. Paris, 1964.

——. *Les Contrôles de troupes de l'Ancien Régime.* 4 vols. Paris, 1968.

Cosandey, F., and R. Descimon. *L'Absolutisme en France: Histoire et historiographie.* Paris, 2002.

Costa, P. "The Discourse of Citizenship in Europe." In *Privileges and Rights of Citizenship: Law and the Juridical Construction of Society,* ed. J. Kirshner and L. Mayali, 199–225. Berkeley, 2002.

Costamagna, H. "Notes sur les migrations dans le comté de Nice au XVIIIe siècle." In *Les Migrations dans les pays méditerranéens au XVIIIe et au début du XIXe siècle,* 80–89. Nice, 1974.

Cotteret, B. *The Huguenots in England: Immigration and Settlement, 1550–1700.* Cambridge, 1991.

Le Cour des Comptes. Pref. M. André Chandernagor. Paris, 1984.

Coustant d'Yanville, comte H. *La Chambre des comptes de Paris.* Paris, 1866–75.

Crook, M., ed. *Revolutionary France, 1788–1880.* Oxford, 2002.

Cullen, L. M. "The Irish Disapora of the Seventeenth and Eighteenth Centuries." In *Europeans on the Move: Studies on European Migration, 1500–1800,* ed. N. Canny, 113–49. Oxford, 1994.

——. "The Irish Merchant Communities at Bordeaux, La Rochelle, and Cognac in the Eighteenth Century." In *Négoce et industrie en France et en Irlande aux XVIIIe et XIXe siècles,* ed. L. M. Cullen and P. Butel, 51–64. Paris, 1980.

Curzon, A. de. "L'Enseignement du droit français dans les universités de France aux XVIIe et XVIIIe siècles." *Revue historique de droit Français et étranger* 42 (1919): 209–69, 305–64.

Cutler, J. W. "The Treatment of Foreigners: In Relation to the Draft Convention and Conference of 1929." *American Journal of International Law* 27, no. 2. (1933): 225–46.

Dainville-Barbiche, S. de. "Les Archives du sceau." *La Gazette des archives,* nos. 160–61 (1993): 127–51.

Dakin, D. *Turgot and the Ancien Régime in France.* New York, 1965.

Darnton, R. *The Literary Underground of the Old Regime.* Cambridge, Mass., 1982.

Dauteribes, A. "L'Idée de république dans la pensée politique de Daunou." In *Nation et République: Les Éléments d'un débat.* Actes du colloque de Dijon, 6–7 April 1994, Association française des idées politiques, 77–97. Aix, 1995.

Davis, N. Z. *Fiction in the Archives: Pardon Tales and Their Tellers in Sixteenth-Century France.* Stanford, 1987.

Dekkers, R. *La Fiction juridique: Etude de droit romain et droit comparé.* Paris, 1935.

Debard, J. M. "La Principauté de Montbéliard et la monarchie française au XVIIe siècle." In *Provinces et Etats dans la France de l'Est.* Besançon, 1978.

Delbez, L. *De la légitimation par lettres royaux.* Montpellier, 1923.

Demangeat, J. C. *Histoire de la condition civile des étrangers en France.* Paris, 1844.

Demotz, R. "La Géographie administrative médiévale: L'Exemple du comté de Savoie, début XIIIe siècle–début Xve siècle." *Moyen Age* 1 (1974): 261–300.

Desan, S. "What's after Political Culture? Recent Revolutionary Historiography." *French Historical Studies* 23 (2000): 163–96.

Descimon, R. " 'Bourgeois de Paris': Les Migrations sociales d'un privilège, XIV–XVIIIe siècle." In *Histoire social, histoire globale? Actes du colloque des 27–9 janvier 1989,* ed. C. Charles, 173–82. Paris, 1993.

——. "Les Fonctions de la métaphore du mariage politique du Roi et de la République France, XVe–XVIe siècle." *Annales HSS* (November–December 1992), no. 6: 1127–47.

Dessert, D. *Argent, pouvoir et société au Grand Siècle*. Paris, 1984.

Devos, R., and B. Grosperrin. *La Savoie de la Réforme à la Révolution française*. Rennes, 1985.

Devyer, A. *Le Sang épuré: Les Préjuges de race chez les gentilshommes français de l'Ancien Régime, 1560–1620*. Brussels, 1973.

Dietrich-Chénel, K., and M.-H. Varnier. "Intégration d'étrangers en France par naturalisation ou admission à domicile de 1790/1814 au 10 mai 1871." 9 vols. Doctoral thesis, Department of German Studies, University of Aix-Marseille I, 1994.

Dockès, P. *L'Espace dans la pensée économique du XVIe au XVIIIe siècle*. Paris, 1969.

Dolan, C. "Famille et intégration des etrangers à Aix-en-Provence au XVIe siècle." *Provence historique* 35, no. 142 (1989): 401–13.

Dominguez Ortiz, A. "La Concesión de 'naturalezas par comerciar en Indias' durante el siglo XVII." *Revista de Indias* 19 (1959): 227–39.

Donaghay, M. "Calonne and the Anglo-French Commercial Treaty of 1786." *Journal of Modern History* 50, no. 3, supplt. (1978): D1157–D1184.

Driancourt-Giroud, J. *La Chapelle de l'ambassade de Suède à Paris, 1626–1806*. Paris, 1976.

———. *L'Insolite histoire de luthériens de Paris, de Louis XIII à Napoleon*. Paris, 1992.

Dubois, S. *Les Bornes immuables de l'Etat: La Rationalisation du tracé des frontières au siècle des Lumières (France, Pays-Bas autrichiens et principauté de Liège)*. Courtrai-Heule, 1999.

Dubost, J.-F. "Les Etrangers à Paris au siècle des lumières." In *La Ville promise: Mobilité et accueil à Paris (fin XVIIe–début XIXe siècle)*, ed. D. Roche, 221–90. Paris, 2000.

———. *Les Etrangers en France, XVIe siecle–1789: Guide des recherches aux Archives Nationales*. Paris, 1993.

———. *La France italienne, XVIe–XVIIe siècle*. Paris, 1997.

———. "Les Italiens dans les villes françaises aux XVIe et XVIIe siècles." In *Les Immigrants à la ville: Insertion, intégration, discrimination (XIIe–XXe siècles)*, ed. D. Menjot and J.-L. Pinol, 91–105. Paris, 1996.

———. "Refuge religieux et politique en France." In *Dictionnaire de l'Ancien Régime. Royaume de France, XVIe–XVIIIe siècle*, ed. L. Bély, 518–22; 1061–63. Paris, 1996.

———. "Significations de la lettre de naturalité dans la France des XVIe et XVIIe siecles." Institut Universitaire Européen Working Papers in History, no. 90/3. Florence, 1990.

Dubost, J.-F., and P. Sahlins. *Et si on faisait payer les étrangers? Louis XIV, les immigrés et quelques autres*. Paris, 1999.

Dubouchet, P. *La Pensée juridique avant et apres le Code Civil*. Paris, 1991.

Duccini, H. "L'Entourage des Concini: Les Étrangers et leur image entre 1610 et 1617." In *Le Sentiment national dans l'Europe moderne: Actes du colloque de 1990*. Association des historiens modernes, actes du colloque de 1990, bulletin no. 15, 25–52. Paris, 1991.

Duclos, P. "L'Accession des Naturalisés aux fonctions publiques." *Revue du droit public*, no. 1 (1938): 5–86.

Ducos, M. *Rome et le droit*. Paris, 1996.

Dummett, A., and A. Nicol. *Subjects, Citizens, Aliens, and Others: Nationality and Immigration Law*. London, 1990.

Dupâquier, J., ed. *Histoire de la population française*. Vol. 2, *De la Renaissance à 1789*. Paris, 1988.

———. *La Population rurale du Bassin parisien à l'époque de Louis XIV*. Paris, 1972.

Durden, R. F. "Joel Barlow in the French Revolution." *William and Mary Quarterly*, 3d ser., 8 (1951): 328–31.

Dussieux, L. *Les Artistes français à l'étranger: Recherche sur leurs travaux et leur influence en Europe*. Paris, 1956.

Dziembowski, E. *Un Nouveau patriotisme français, 1750–1770: La France face à la puissance anglaise à l'époque de la guerre de Sept Ans*. Studies on Voltaire and the Eighteenth Century, vol. 365. Oxford: Voltaire Foundation, 1998.

Echinard, P., and E. Temime. *Migrance: Histoire des migrations à Marseille*. Vol. 1, *La Préhistoire de la migration (1482–1830)*. Aix en Provence, 1989.

Egret, J. *Louis XV et l'opposition parlementaire, 1715–1774*. Paris, 1970.

Einaudi, M. *The Physiocratic Doctrine of Judicial Control*. Cambridge, Mass., 1938.

Eiseman, C. "La Cité de Jean-Jacques Rousseau." In *Etudes sur le contrat social de Jean-Jacques Rousseau*, 191–201. Paris, 1964.

El Ghoul, F. "La Police parisienne dans la seconde moitié du XVIIIe siècle (1760–1785)." Thèse de lettres, Université de Rennes, 1993.

Ellis, H. A. *Boulainvilliers and the French Monarchy: Aristocratic Politics in Early Eighteenth-Century France.* Ithaca, 1988.

Emmanuelli, F.-X. *L'Intendance de Provence à la fin du XVIIe siècle.* Paris, 1980.

Engel, C.-E. *L'Ordre de Malte en Méditerranée (1530–1798).* Monaco, 1957.

Englund, S. "The Ghost of Nation Past" [Review of Nora, ed., *Les Lieux de mémoire*]. *Journal of Modern History* 44, no. 2 (1992): 299–320.

Fagniez, G. *La Condition des commerçants étrangers en France au début du XVIIe siècle.* Paris, 1908.

Favre-Lejeune, C. *Les Secrétaires du Roi de la Grande Chancellerie de France: Dictionnaire biographique et généalogique.* 2 vols. Paris, 1986.

Feenstra, R., and H. Klompmaker. "Le Statut des étrangers aux Pays-Bas." *RSJB* 10 (1958): 333–73.

Félix, J. *Economie et finances sous l'Ancien Régime: Guide du chercheur, 1523–1789.* Paris, 1994.

Fenske, H. "International Migration: Germany in the Eighteenth Century." *Central European History* 3 (1980): 332–47.

Ferenc, T. "Identité nationale en exile: Le Rôle du sentiment national hongrois dans la constitution des régiments de Hussards en France au XVIIIe siècle." In *La Recherche dix-huitièmiste: Raison universelle et culture nationale au siècle des Lumières / Eighteenth-century Research: Universal Reason and National Culture during the Enlightenment*, ed. D. A. Bell, L. Pimenova, and S. Pujol, 91–107. Paris, 1999.

Ferrone, V., and D. Roche, eds. *Le Monde des lumières.* Paris, 1999.

Fieffé, E. *Histoire des troupes étrangères au service de la France.* 2 vols. Paris, 1854.

Fierro, A., A. Palleul-Guillard, and J. Tulard. *Histoire et dictionnaire du Consulat et de l'Empire.* Paris, 1995.

Fitzsimmons, M. P. "The National Assembly and the Invention of Citizenship." In *The French Revolution and the Meaning of Citizenship*, ed. R. Waldinger, P. Dawson, and I. Woloch, 29–42. Westport, Conn., 1993.

Folain-Le Bras, M. *Un Projet d'ordonnance du Chancelier Daguesseau: Etude sur quelques incapacités de donner et de recevoir sous l'Ancien Régime.* Paris, 1941.

Fontaine, L. *History of Peddlers in Europe.* Trans. V. Whittaker. Durham, 1996.

Foucault, M. *The Order of Things: An Archaeology of the Human Sciences.* New York, 1971.

Fournier, G. M. "L'Immigration savoyarde en Franche-Comté avant 1789." *Mémoires de la Société d'émulation du Doubs*, n.s. (1959): 1–99.

Fox, E. W. *History in Geographic Perspective: The Other France.* New York, 1971.

Fox-Genovese, E. *The Origins of Physiocracy: Economic Revolution and Social Order in Eighteenth-Century France.* Ithaca, 1976.

Les Français en Espagne à l'époque moderne (XVIe–XVIIIe siècles). Paris, 1990.

François, E. "L'Acceuil des refugiés huguenots en Allemagne." In *La Révocation de l'Edit de Nantes et les Provinces Unies, 1685.* International Congress of the Tricentennial, Leyden, 1–3 April 1685, 207–16. Amsterdam, 1986.

François, E., ed. *Immigration et société urbaine en Europe occidentale (XVIe siècle–XXe siècle).* Paris, 1985.

Franklin, J. H. *Jean Bodin and the Rise of Absolutist Theory.* Cambridge, 1973.

Frijhoff, W. "Cosmopolitisme." In *Le Monde des lumières*, ed. V. Ferrone and D. Roche, 31–40. Paris, 1999.

Fumaroli, M. *L'Age de l'éloquence.* Paris, 1980.

Furet, F. *Revolutionary France, 1770–1880.* Trans. A. Neville. Oxford, 1995.

Gager, K. *Blood Ties and Fictive Ties: Adoption and Family Life in Early Modern France.* Princeton, 1996.

Garden, M. *Lyon et les Lyonnais au XVIIIe siècle.* Paris, 1975.

[Les] Gardes Suisses et leurs familles aux XVIIe et XVIIIe siecles en région parisienne. Colloque du 30 Septembre et 1er Octobre 1988. Reuil-Malmaison, 1989.

Garreta, J.-C. "Les Sources de la législation de l'Ancien Régime." *Mémoires de la Société pour l'histoire du droit et des institutions des anciens pays Bourguignons, Comtois, et Romands* 29 (1968–69): 275–364.

Garrisson, J. *L'Edit de Nantes et sa révocation: Histoire d'une intolérance.* Paris, 1985.

Gascon, R. *Grand commerce et vie urbaine au XVIe siècle: Lyon et ses marchands.* 2 vols. Paris, 1971.

Gaudemet, J. "Les Tendances à l'unification du droit en France dans les derniers siècles de l'Ancien Régime (XVIe–XVIIIe)." *La Formazione storica del diritto moderno in Europa.* Atti del terzo congresso internazionale della societa italiana di storia del diritto, 157–94. Florence, 1972.

Gazzaniga, J.-L. "Quand les avocats formaient les juristes et la doctrine." *Droits*, no. 20 (1994): 31–41.

Geffroy, A. "Citoyen/citoyenne (1753–1829)." In *Dictionnaire des usages socio-politiques (1770–1815).* Vol. 3, *Designants socio-politiques*, part 2. Société française d'étude du 18e siècle, 63–86. Paris, 1989.

Genet-Rouffiac, N. "Les Jacobites à Paris et à Saint-Germain-en-Laye." *Revue de la bibliothèque nationale*, no. 46 (1992): 44–49.

Gérardin, J. *Etude sur les bénéfices ecclésiastiques aux XVIe et XVIIe siecles.* Geneva: Slatkine, 1971 [1897].

Gerber, M. "The End of Bastardy: Illegitimacy in France from the Reformation to the Revolution." Ph.D. diss, University of California, Berkeley, 2003.

Ghachem, M. W. "Sovereignty and Slavery in the Age of Revolution: Haitian Variations on a Metropolitan Theme." Ph.D. diss., Stanford University, 2001.

Gibbs, C. B. "The Reception of Huguenots in England and the Dutch Republic, 1680–1690." In *From Persecution to Moderation: The Glorious Revolution and Religion in England*, ed. O. P. Grell, J. I. Israel, and N. Tyake Grell, 275–306. Oxford, 1991.

Gibert, R. "La Condición de los extranjeros en el antiguo derecho español." *RSJB* 10 (1958): 151–200.

Gilbert, F. "The 'New Diplomacy' of the Eighteenth Century." *World Politics* 4, no. 1 (1951): 1–38.

Gilissen, J. "Le Statut des étrangers, à la lumière de l'histoire comparative." *RSJB* 9 (1958): 1–57.

——. "Le Statut des étrangers en Belgique du XIIIe au XXe siècle." *RSJB* 9 (1958): 231–332.

Gilli, P. "Comment cesser d'être étranger: Citoyens et non-citoyens dans la pensée juridique italienne de la fin du Moyen Age." In *L'Etranger au Moyen Age*, XXXe Congrès de la S.H.M.E.S. Gottingen, June 1999, 59–78. Paris, 2000.

Girard, A. *Le Commerce français à Séville et Cadix au temps des Hapsbourgs: Contribution à l'étude du commerce étranger au XVI et XVIIe siècles.* Paris, 1932.

Girard d'Albissin, N. *Genèse de la frontière franco-belge: Les Variations des limites septentrionales de la France de 1659 à 1789.* Paris, 1970.

Glasson, E. *Histoire du droit et des institutions de la France.* 8 vols. Paris, 1896–1903.

Godechot, J. *La Grande Nation.* 2 vols. Paris, 1956.

Gonnet, P. *L'Adoption Lyonnaise des orphelins legitimes (1536–1793).* 2 vols. Paris, 1935.

Gordon, D. "Citizenship." In *The Oxford Encyclopedia of the Enlightenment*, ed. A. Kors et al. Oxford, 2002.

——. *Citizens without Sovereignty: Equality and Sociability in French Thought, 1670–1789.* Princeton. 1994.

——. "The Origins of a Polarity: Cosmopolitanism versus Citizenship in Early Modern Europe." Unpublished manuscript.

Goubert, P. *Beauvais et le beauvaisie au XVIIe siècle.* Paris, 1960.

——. *The French Peasantry in the Seventeenth Century.* Cambridge, 1989.

Gouhier, P. "Mercenaires irlandais en France, 1635–1664." *Revue d'histoire moderne et contemporaine* (1964): 612–90.

Goy, J. "Code civil." In *Dictionnaire critique de la Révolution française*, ed. F. Furet and M. Ozouf, 508–19. Paris, 1988.

Goyard-Fabre, S. *Jean Bodin (1529–1596) et sa politique philosophique.* Paris, 1999.

Green, N. L. "The Comparative Method and Poststructural Structuralism: New Perspectives for Migration Studies." In *Migration, Migration History, History: Old Paradigms and New Perspectives*, ed. J. Lucassen and L. Lucassen, 41–56. Bern, 1997.

Greenfeld, L. *Nationalism: Five Roads to Modernity.* Cambridge, Mass., 1992.

Greenleaf, W. H. "Bodin and the Idea of Order." In *Jean Bodin: Proceedings of the International Conference on Bodin in Munich*, ed. H. Denzer, 23–38. Munich, 1973.

Gres-Gayer, J. "Le Culte de l'ambassade de Grande-Bretagne à Paris au début de la Régence, 1715–1720." *BSHPF* 130, no. 2 (1984): 29–46.

Grewe, W. G. *The Epochs of International Law.* Trans. and revised by M. Byers. Berlin, 2000.

Grieder, J. *Anglomania in France, 1740–1789: Fact, Fiction, and Political Discourse.* Geneva, 1985.

Grimmer, C. "Juifs et Italiens dans l'Auvergne du XVIIIe siècle." In *Le Migrant: "France, terre de migrations internes; France, terre d'immigration."* Actes du colloque d'Aurillac, 5–7 June 1985, 201–8. Aurillac, 1986.

Groebner, V. "Describing the Person, Reading the Signs in Late Medieval and Renaissance Europe: Identity Papers, Vested Figures, and the Limits of Identification, 1400–1600." In *Documenting Individual Identity: The Development of State Practices in the Modern World*, ed. J. Caplan and J. Torpey, 15–27. Princeton, 2001.

Guichonnet, P., ed. *Histoire et civilisations des Alpes.* 2 vols. Toulouse, 1980.

Guiffrey, J. "Lettres de naturalité accordées à des artistes étrangers pour les permettre de s'établir en France (1612–1699)." In *Nouvelles Archives de l'Art français.* 34 vols., 2:222–61. Paris, 1873.

Guiraudon, V. "Cosmopolitanism and National Priority: Attitudes Towards Foreigners in France Between 1789 and 1794." *History of European Ideas* 13 (1991): 591–604.

Gutton, J.-P. *Histoire de l'adoption en France.* Paris, 1993.

Gutwirth, M. "*Citoyens, Citoyennes:* Cultural Regression and the Subversion of Female Citizenship in the French Revolution." In *The French Revolution and the Meaning of Citizenship,* ed. R. Waldinger, P. Dawson, and I. Woloch, 17–28. Westport, Conn., 1993.

Habermas, J. *The Structural Transformations of the Public Sphere: An Inquiry into a Category of Bourgeois Society.* Trans. T. Burger. Cambridge, Mass., 1989.

Halpérin, J.-L. *L'Impossible code civil.* Paris, 1992.

Hampton, T. *Literature and the Nation in the Sixteenth Century: Inventing Renaissance France.* Ithaca, 2001.

Hanley, S. "Engendering the State: Family Formation and State-building in Early Modern France." *French Historical Studies* 16 (1989): 4–27.

——. *The "Lit de Justice" of the Kings of France: Constitutional Ideology in Legend, Ritual, and Discourse.* Princeton, 1983.

——. "The Monarchic State in Early Modern France: Marital Regime Government and Male Right." In *Politics, Ideology, and the Law in Early Modern Europe,* ed. A. E. Bakos, 107–26. Rochester, 1994.

Harris, R. *Necker, Reform Statesman of the Ancien Régime.* Berkeley, 1979.

Harsin, P. *Les Doctrines monétaires et financières en France du XVIe au XVIIe siècles.* Paris, 1928.

Hayes, R., Chr. Preston, and J. Weygand, eds. *Les Irlandais en Aquitaine.* Bordeaux, 1971.

Hazard, P. "Cosmopolite." In *Mélanges d'histoire littéraire générale et comparée offerts à Fernand Baldensperger.* 2 vols., 1:354–64. Paris, 1930.

Hazareesingh, S. *From Subject to Citizen: The Second Empire and the Emergence of Modern French Democracy.* Princeton, 1998.

Henderson, W. O. "The Anglo-French Commercial Treaty of 1786." *Economic History Review,* n.s., 10 (1957): 104–12.

Henry, L., and D. Courgeau. "Deux analyses de l'immigration à Paris au XVIIIe siècle." *Population* 6 (1971): 1073–92.

Herman, Jr., A. L. "The Language of Fidelity in Early Modern France." *The Journal of Modern History* 67 (1995): 1–24.

Herry, S. *Une Ville en mutation: Strasbourg au tournant du Grand Siècle.* Strasbourg, 1996.

Hertzberg, A. *The French Enlightenment and the Jews.* New York, 1968.

Herzog, T. *Defining Nations: Immigrants and Citizens in Early Modern Spain and Spanish America.* New Haven, 2003.

——. "Municipal Citizenship and Empire: Communal Definition in Eighteenth-Century Spain and Spanish America." In *Privileges and Rights of Citizenship: Law and the Juridical Construction of Society,* ed. J. Kirshner and L. Mayali, 147–68. Berkeley, 2002.

——. " 'A Stranger in a Strange Land': The Conversion of Foreigners into Members in Colonial Latin America (Seventeenth–Eighteenth Centuries)." *Social Identities* 3 (1997): 247–63.

Heuer, J. " 'Afin d'obtenir le droit de citoyen . . . en tout ce qui peut concerner une personne de son sexe': Devenir ou cesser d'etre femme française à l'époque napoléonienne." *Clio* 12 (2000): 15–32.

——. "Foreigners, Families, and Citizens: Contradictions of National Citizenship in France, 1789–1830." Ph.D. diss., University of Chicago, 1998.

Hildenfinger, P. ed. *Documents sur les Juifs à Paris au XVIIIe siècle.* Paris, 1913.

Hildesheimer, F. "Aubains ou regnicoles: La Capacité à succeder des Niçois en Provence." *Nice historique* 83, no. 3 (1980): 122–26.

——. "La Présence juive en Provence à la fin de l'Ancien Régime: Sources et bilan." In *Juifs en France au XVIIIè siècle,* ed. B. Blumenkranz, 111–23. Paris, 1994.

Hincker, F. "La Citoyenneté révolutionaire saisie à travers ses exclus." In *Le Citoyen Fou,* ed. N. Robatel, 7–28. Paris, 1991.

Hirschman, A. O. *The Passions and the Interests: Political Arguments for Capitalism before Its Triumph.* Princeton, 1977.

Honig, B. *Democracy and the Foreigner.* Princeton, 2001.

Hunt, L. "The Paradoxical Origins of Human Rights." In *Human Rights and Revolutions,* ed. J. N. Wasserstrom, L. Hunt, and M. B. Young, 3–17. Lanham, Md., 2000.

Imbert, J. "La Capacité de l'étranger à succéder en France: Concession humanitaire ou intéressée." In *Humanité et droit international, Mélanges R. Dupuy*, 179–86. Paris, 1991.

——. "L'Exercise du droit d'aubaine à l'égard des habitants du Hainault à la fin de l'Ancien Régime." *Revue d'histoire du droit français et étranger,* 1950: 548–59.

——. *Postliminium.* Paris, 1944.

——. "Les Rapports entre l'aubaine et la bourgeoisie en Lorraine." *Annales de l'Est,* 5th ser., no. 4 (1952): 349–64.

Ingold, D. "Note sur l'immigration marchande savoyarde à Thann [Haut Rhin] sous l'Ancien Regime." *Amis Thann,* no. 3 (1988): 2–6.

Jackson, R. *Vive le roi!: A History of the French Coronation from Charles V.* Chapel Hill, 1984.

Jandot-Danjou, C. "La Condition civile de l'étranger dans les trois derniers siècles de la monarchie." Thèse de Droit, Université de Paris, 1939.

Jaume, L. "Citoyenneté et souveraineté: Les Poids de l'absolutisme." In *The Political Culture of the Old Regime,* ed. K. Baker, 515–34. Oxford, 1987.

Job, F. *Les Juifs de Nancy.* Nancy, 1991.

Jordan, W. C. "Home Again: The Jews in the Kingdom of France, 1315–1322." In *The Stranger in Medieval Society.* Medieval Cultures, vol. 12, ed. F. R. P. Akehurst and S. C. Vand'Elden, 27–45. Minneapolis, 1997.

Jouanna, A. *L'Idee de race en France au XVIe siècle et au debut du XVIIe siècle (1498–1614).* Montpellier, 1981.

Juste, T. *Le Comte de Mercy-Argenteau.* Brussels, 1863.

Kagan, R. "Law Students and Legal Careers in Eighteenth-Century France." *Past and Present* 68 (1975): 38–72.

Kahn, L. *Les Juifs de Paris au XVIIIe siècle d'après les archives de la lieutenance générale de police à la Bastille: Histoire de la communauté israélite de Paris.* Paris, 1894.

——. "Les Juifs de Paris de 1755 à 1759." *Revue d'Etudes Juives* 39 (1904): 121–24.

Kahn, S. "Les Juifs à Nimes au XVIIe et XVIIIe siècle." *Revue des études juives* 47 (1914): 225–61.

Kantorowicz, E. H. *The King's Two Bodies: A Study in Medieval Political Theology.* Princeton, 1957.

——. "Pro Patria Mori in Medieval Political Thought." *American Historical Review* 56 (1951): 472–92.

Karpick, L. *French Lawyers: A Study in Collective Action, 1274 to 1994.* Trans. N. Scott. Oxford, 1999.

Kates, G. "Jews into Frenchmen: Nationality and Representation in Revolutionary France." In *The French Revolution and the Birth of Modernity,* ed. F. Feher, 103–16. Berkeley, 1990.

Katz, D. S. *Philo-Semitism and the Readminission of the Jews to England, 1603–1655.* Oxford, 1982.

Kelley, D. R. *Foundations of Modern Historical Scholarship: Language, Law, and History in the French Renaissance.* New York, 1970.

——. "Men of Law and the French Revolution." In *Politics, Ideology, and the Law in Early Modern Europe: Essays in Honor of J. H. M. Salmon,* ed. A. E. Bakos, 127–46. Rochester, 1994.

Keohane, N. O. *Philosophy and the State in France: The Renaissance to the Enlightenment.* Princeton, 1980.

Kettner, J. *The Development of American Citizenship, 1608–1870.* Chapel Hill, 1978.

Khatibi, A. *Figures de l'étranger dans la littérature française.* Paris, 1987.

Kiefé, R. "L'Allégeance." In *La Nationalité dans la science sociale et dans le droit contemporain,* 47–68. Paris, 1933.

Kim, K. "L'Etranger chez Bodin, l'étranger chez nous." *Revue de l'histoire de droit* 76 (1998): 75–92.

Kirshner, J. " 'Ars imitatur naturam': A *Consilium* of Baldus of Perugia on Naturalization in Florence." *Viator* 5 (1974): 289–331.

——. "Between Nature and Culture: An Opinion of Baldus of Perugia on Venetian Citizenship as Second Nature." *Journal of Medieval and Renaissance Studies* 9 (1979): 179–208.

——. " 'Civitas sibi faciat civem': Bartolus of Sassoferrato's Doctrine of the Making of a Citizen." *Speculum* 48 (1973): 694–713.

Kirtz, J.-P. "La Mobilité humaine en Alsace, XVIe–XVIIIe siecle." *Annales de démographie historique* (1970): 157–83.

Klintz, J. P. "Savoyards et Grand Commerce à l'aube du XVIIIe siècle: L'Exemple de la Compagnie des Trois Frères." In *L'Europe, l'Alsace et la France: Hommage à Georges Livet,* 32–39. Strasbourg, 1986.

Kohn, R. S. "Le Statut forain: Marchands étrangers, Lombards, et Juifs en France et en Bourgogne (deuxième moitié du XV siècle)." *Revue historique de droit français et étranger* 61 (1983): 7–24.

Konetzke, R. "La Legislación sobre inmigración de extranjeros en América durante el reinado de Carlos V." In *Charles Quint et son temps*, 93–111. Paris, 1959.

Kosselleck, R. *Futures Past: On the Semantics of Historical Time*. Trans. K. Tribe. Cambridge, Mass., 1985.

Kozakai, T. *L'Etranger, l'identité: Essai sur l'intégration culturelle*. Paris, 2000.

Krafft, O. "Les Classes sociales à Genève et la notion de citoyen." In *Jean-Jacques Rousseau et son oeuvre: Problèmes et Recherches*. Commémoration et Colloque de Paris (16–20 October 1962), 219–27. Paris, 1964.

Krynen, J. "The Absolute Monarchy and the French Unification of Private Rights." In *Privileges and Rights of Citizenship: Law and the Juridical Construction of Society*, ed. J. Kirshner and L. Mayali, 27–56. Berkeley, 2002.

———. " 'Naturel': Essai sur l'argument de la nature dans la pensée politique française à la fin du Moyen Age." *Journal des Savants* (1982): 169–90.

Kuscinkski, A. *Dictionnaire des Conventionnels*. Paris, 1917.

Kwass, M. "A Kingdom of Taxpayers: State Formation, Privilege, and Political Culture in Eighteenth-Century France. *Journal of Modern History* 52, no. 2 (1998): 295–339.

———. *Privilege and the Politics of Taxation in Eighteenth-Century France*. Cambridge, 2000.

Kymlicka, W., and W. Norman. "Return of the Citizen: A Survey of Recent Work on Citizenship Theory." In *Theorizing Citizenship*, ed. R. Beiner, 283–322. Albany, 1995.

Lach, D. F., and E. J. Van Kley. *Asia in the Making of Europe*. Vol. 3, pt. 4: *Southeast Asia*. Chicago, 1993.

Labourdette, J.-F. *Vergennes: Ministre principal de Louis XVI*. Paris, 1990.

Labrousse, C. E. *Esquisse du mouvement des prix et des revenus en France au XVIIIe siècle*. 2 vols. Paris, 1933.

Lagarde, P. *La Nationalité française*. Paris, 1997.

Lainé, P. *Etude sur la capacité successorale des étrangers en France*. Paris, 1900.

Lalinde Abadia, J. "De la nacionalidad aragonesa a la regionalidad." *Revista juridica de Cataluña* 72 (1973): 536–80.

Lalou, E. "La Chambre des comptes de Paris: Sa mise en place et son fonctionement (fin XIIIe–XIVe siecle)." In *La France des principautés: Les Chambres des comptes, XIV et XVe siècles*. Paris, 1996.

Landré, C. "Les Protestants hollandais à Bordeaux, avant et après la révocation de l'édit de Nantes." *Bulletin de la Commission pour l'histoire des Eglises wallones* 2 (1887): 269–75.

Laprat, R. "Les Aubains en droit canonique." In *Dictionnaire de droit canonique*, ed. R. Naz. 7 vols. Vol. 1, 1332–46. Paris, 1935–66.

Larrère, C. *L'Invention de l'économie au XVIIIe siècle*. Paris, 1992.

Lavergne, L. de. *Les Assemblées provinciales sous Louis XVI*. Paris, 1879.

Le Cour Grandmaison, O. *Les Citoyennetés en révolution (1789–1794)*. Paris, 1992.

Lefebvre-Teillard, A. "Citoyen." *Droits* 17 (1993): 33–42.

———. *Introduction historique au droit des personnes et de la famille*. Paris, 1996.

———. "Ius sanguinis: L'Emergence d'un principe (Eléments d'histoire de la nationalité française)." *Revue critique de droit international privé* 82, no. 2 (1993): 223–50.

Lefèvre, J. "La Compénétration Hispano-Belge aux Pays Bas Catholiques pendant le XVIIe siècle." *Revue belge de philologie et d'histoire* 16 (1937): 599–621.

Leith, W. F. *The Scots men of arms and life-guards in France*. Edinburgh, 1882.

Lemalet, M. "Juifs et Intendants au XVIIe siecle." *XVIIe siècle*, no. 183 (1994): 287–302.

Lentz, T. *Dictionnaire des ministres de Napoléon: Dictionnaire analytique statistique et comparé des trente-deux ministres de Napoléon*. Paris, 1999.

Lepointe, G. *Petit précis des sources de l'histoire du droit Francais*. Paris: 1937.

———. "Le Statut des étrangers dans la France du XIXe siècle." *RSJB* 10 (1958): 553–74.

Lequin, Y., ed. *La Mosaïque France: Histoire des étrangers et de l'immigration*. Paris, 1988.

Leroux, A. *La Colonie germanique de Bordeaux: Etude historique, juridique, statistique, économique d'après les sources allemandes et françaises*. 2 vols. Bordeaux, 1917–18.

Le Roy Ladurie, E. *Les Paysans de Languedoc*. 2 vols. Paris, 1966.

———, ed. *La Ville classique de la Renaissance aux révolutions*. Vol. 3 of *Histoire de la France urbaine*, ed. G. Duby. Paris, 1981.

Limousin, A. "L'Histoire de l'immigration en France: Une histoire impossible." *Pouvoirs: Revue française d'etudes constitutionnelles et politiques* 47 (1988): 5–22.

Livet, G. "Croissance économique et privileges commerciaux des Suisses sous l'Ancien Régime: Note sur les commercants suisses établis en France au XVIIIe siècle." In *Lyon et L'Europe: Hommes et Sociétés. Melanges d'histoire offerts à Richard Gascon*. 2 vols., 2:43–63. Lyon, 1980.

——. "Louis XIV et les provinces conquises." *XVIIe siècle* 22 (1952): 481–507.

——. "Une Page d'histoire sociale: Les Savoyards à Strasbourg au début du XVIIIe siècle." *Cahiers d'histoire* 4, no. 2 (1959): 131–45.

Lloyd, H. A. *The State, France, and the Sixteenth Century*. London, 1983.

Lochak, D. "La Citoyenneté: Un concept juridique flou." In *Citoyenneté et nationalité*, ed. D. Colas, C. Emeri, and J. Zulberg. Paris, 1991.

Loeb, I. "Un Baron juif français au XVIII siècle: Liefman Calmer." *Annuare des archives israélites de France* 46 (1885): 188–90, 196–98.

Lombard-Jourdan, A. "Des Malgaches à Paris sous Louis XIV: Exotisme et mentalités en France au XVIIe siècle." *Archipel: Etudes interdisicplinaires sur le monde insulindien* 9 (1975): 79–90.

Lopez, R. "Les Suisses à Marseille: Une immigration de longue durée." *Recherches Regionales* 28, no. 1 (1987): 49–74.

Lorion, A. *Les Théories politiques des premiers physiocrates*. Paris, 1918.

Louit, M. "Essai sur l'histoire de la police des étrangers de la fin de l'Ancien Régime à la IIIème République." Thèse de Droit, Paris, 1949.

Loupès, Ph. "Les Ecclésiastiques irlandais dans le diocèse de Bordeaux au XVIIe et XVIIIe siècles." In *Bordeaux et les Iles Britanniques du XIIIe au XXe siècle*. Actes du colloque, York, 1973. Fédération Historique du Sud-Ouest, 80–98. Bordeaux, 1975.

Loupès, Ph., and L. Lucassen, eds. *Migration, Migration History, History: Old Paradigms and New Perspectives*. Bern, 1997.

Lucassen, L. "Eternal Vagrants? State Formation, Migration, and Travelling Groups in Western-Europe, 1350–1914." In *Migration, Migration History, History: Old Paradigms and New Perspectives*, ed. J. Lucassen and L. Lucassen, 225–51. Bern, 1997.

Lüthy, H. *La Banque protestante en France, de la révocation de l'édit de Nantes à la Révolution*. 2 vols. Paris, 1961.

MacClean, I. *Interpretation and Meaning in the Renaissance: The Case of Law*. Cambridge, 1992.

Maine, Sir H. *Ancient Law*. London, 1878.

Malino, F. *Les Juifs sépharades de Bordeaux: Assimilation et émancipation dans la France révolutionnaire et impériale*. Bordeaux, 1984.

Mandy, G. A. *La Cautio judicatum solvi: Les Étrangers devant la justice en droit international privé: Étude de législation comparée*. Paris, 1897.

Marion, M. *Histoire financière de la France depuis 1715*. 5 vols. Paris, 1919.

——. *Machault d'Arnouville: Etude sur l'histoire du contrôle-général des finances de 1749 à 1754*. Paris, 1892.

Marquand, D. "Civic Republics and Liberal Individualists: The Case of Britain." In *Citizenship: Critical Concepts*, ed. B. S. Turner and P. Hamilton, 238–50. London, 1994.

Marshall, T. H. *Citizenship and Social Class and Other Essays*. Cambridge, 1950.

Martin, G. *La Grande industrie sous le règne de Louis XIV*. Geneva, 1979 [Paris, 1899].

Martinage, R. *Bourjon et le code Civil*. Paris, 1971.

Massaloux, J.-P. *La Régie de l'enregistrement et des domaines au XVIIIe–XIXe siècles*. Geneva, 1988.

Mathiez, A. *La Révolution et les étrangers: Cosmopolitisme et défense nationale*. Paris, 1918.

Mathorez, J. *Les Etrangers en France sous l'Ancien Régime*. 2 vols. Paris, 1919.

——. "Notes sur la colonie irlandaise de Nantes du XVIe au XVIIIe siècles." *Bulletin de la Société archéologique de Nantes et du département de la Loire Inférieure* 53 (1912): 169–95.

——. "Notes sur les Espagnols en France depuis le XVIe siècle jusqu'au regne de Louis XIII." *Bulletin Hispanique* 16 (1914): 335–71.

——. "Notes sur les rapports de Nantes avec l'Espagne." *Bulletin Hispanique* 14 (1912): 119–26; 15 (1913): 383–407.

——. "Petits métiers exercés en France par les Italiens au XVIIe et XVIIIe siècle." *Ethnographie* (1922–25): 65–71.

Maza, S. *Private Lives and Public Affairs: The Causes Célèbres of Prerevolutionary France*. Berkeley, 1993.

——. "Stories in History: Cultural Narratives in Recent Works in European History." *American Historical Review* 101 (1996): 1493–1515.

McGurk, J. "Wild Geese: The Irish in European Armies (Sixteenth to Eighteenth Centuries)." In *The Irish World Wide: History, Heritage, Identity.* Vol. 1., *Patterns of Migration*, ed. P. O'Sullivan, 36–62. Leicester, 1992.

McLoughlin, T. O. "A Crisis for the Irish in Bordeaux, 1756." In *Nations and Nationalisms: France, Britain, Ireland, and the Eighteenth-Century Context*, ed. M. O'Dea and K. Whelan. Studies on Voltaire and the Eighteenth Century 335, 129–45. Oxford, 1995.

Meek, R. L. *The Economics of Physiocracy: Essays and Translations.* London, 1962.

Merrick, J. "Conscience and Citizenship in Eighteenth-Century France." *Eighteenth Century Studies* 21 (1987): 48–71.

———. *The Desacralization of the French Monarchy in the Eighteenth Century.* Baton Rouge, 1990.

———. "Fathers and Kings: Patriarchalism and Absolutism in Eighteenth-Century French Politics." *Studies on Voltaire and the Eighteenth Century* 308 (1993): 281–303.

———. "Subjects and Citizens in the Remonstrances of the Parlement of Paris in the Eighteenth Century." *Journal of the History of Ideas* 51 (1990): 453–60.

Metz, R. *La Monarchie française et la provision de bénéfices ecclesiastiques en Alsace de la paix de Westphalie à la fin de l'Ancien Regime.* Strasbourg, 1947.

Meyer, J. "Noblesse française au XVIIIe siècle." *Acta poloniae historica* 26 (1977): 15–21.

Michaud, H. *La Grande Chancellerie et les écritures royales au XVI siècle.* Paris, 1967.

Michaud, J. "L'Immigration savoyarde à Poligny [Jura] au XVIIe siecles." *Généalogie et Histoire*, no. 62 (1990): 31–37; no. 63 (1991): 23–27.

Michaud, L. G. *Biographie universelle ancienne et moderne.* 45 vols. Paris, 1854–65.

Mijhardt, W. "The Batavian Citizen: Dutch Ideas on Moral Citizenship in the Batavian Period." In *Civisme et citoyenneté: Une longue histoire.* Journées scientifiques du Pôle Universitaire Européen de Montpellier et du Languedoc-Roussillon, 143–66. Montpellier, 1999.

Milliot, V. "La Surveillance des migrants et des lieux d'acceuil à Paris du XVIe siècle aux années 1830." In *La Ville promise: Mobilité et accueil à Paris (fin XVIIe–début XIXe siècle)*, ed. D. Roche, 21–76. Paris, 2000.

Minard, Ph. *La Fortune du colbertisme.* Paris, 1998.

Mitard, S. *La Crise financière en France à la fin du XVIIe siècle: La Première capitation (1695–1698).* Rennes, 1934.

Moch, L. *Moving Europeans: Migration in Western Europe since 1650.* Bloomington, 1992.

Montbas, H. de. *La Police parisienne sous Louis XVI.* Paris, 1949.

Morel, O. *Les Lombards dans la Flandre français et le Hainault.* Dijon, 1908.

Morineau, M. "Lyon l'Italienne, Lyon la Grande." *Annales ESC* (July–August 1977), no. 6: 1537–50.

Morini-Comby, J. *Mercantilisme et protectionisme.* Paris, 1980.

Moulinas, R. *Les Juifs du Pape en France: Les Communautés d'Avignon et du Comtat Vénaissin aux XVIIe et XVIIIe siècles.* Toulouse, 1972.

Mousnier, R. E. *The Institutions of France under the Absolute Monarchy, 1598–1789.* Trans. B. Pearce. 2 vols. Chicago, 1979–84.

Murphy, A. "Le Développement des idées économiques en France, 1750–1756." *Revue d'histoire moderne et contemporaine* 33 (1986): 521–41.

Murphy, O. T. *Charles Gravier, Comte de Vergennes: French Diplomacy in the Age of Revolution, 1719–1787.* Albany, 1982.

Nahon, G. *Les Nations juives du sud-ouest de la France (1684–1791): Documents.* Paris, 1981.

Napoli, P. " 'Police': La Conceptualisation d'un modèle juridico-politique sous l'Ancien Régime. *Droits* (1994) 151–60; (1995): 183–96.

Nève, P. L. "La Statut juridique des réfugiés huguenots: Quelques remarques comparatives." In *La Condition juridique de l'étranger, hier et aujourd'hui.* Actes du Colloque organisé à Nimegue, 9–11 May 1988, 223–46. Nijmegen, 1988.

———. *The World of the Citizen in Republican Rome.* Trans. P. S. Falla. Berkeley, 1988.

Noël, J. F. "Le Concept de nation allemande dans l'Empire au XVIIe siecle." *XVIIe siècle* 44, no. 176 (1992): 325–344.

———. "Les Problèmes des frontières entre la France et L'Empire dans la second moité du XVIIIe siècle." *Revue historique* 235 (1966): 333–46.

Noiriel, G. *Etat, nation et immigration: Vers une histoire du pouvoir.* Belin, 2001.

——. "French and Foreigners." In *Realms of Memory: Rethinking the French Past*. Vol. 1, *Conflicts and Divisions*, ed. P. Nora, trans. A. Goldhammer, 145–78. New York, 1996.

——. *The French Melting Pot: Immigration, Citizenship, and National Identity*. Trans. G. de Laforcade. Minneapolis, 1996.

——. "Socio-histoire d'un concept: Les Usages du mot 'nationalité' au XIXe siècle." *Genèses* 20 (1995): 4–23.

——. *La Tyrannie du national: Le Droit d'asile en Europe, 1793–1993*. Paris, 1991.

Noiriel, G., and M. Offerlé. "Citizenship and Nationality in Nineteenth-Century France." In *European Integration in Social and Historical Perspective*, ed. J. Klausen and L. A. Tilly, 71–84. Boston, 1997.

Nora, P. "Nation." In *Dictionnaire critique de la Révolution française*, ed. F. Furet and M. Ozouf, 801–11. Paris, 1988.

Nora, P., ed. *Les Lieux de mémoire*. 7 vols. Paris, 1984–92. Trans. selections in *Realms of Memory: Rethinking the French Past*. 3 vols. Trans. A. Goldhammer. New York, 1996; and *Rethinking France: Les Lieux de mémoire*. Trans. M. Trouille. Chicago, 2001.

Nord, P. *The Republican Moment: Struggles for Democracy in Nineteenth-Century France*. Cambridge, Mass., 1995.

Nordman, D. *Frontières de France: De l'espace au territoire, XVIe–XVIIe siècle*. Paris, 1998.

——. "Sauf-conduits et passeports, en France, la Renaissance." In *Voyages et voyageurs à la Renaissance*, ed. J. Céard and J.-C. Margolin, 145–58. Paris, 1987.

Oldfield, A. *Citizenship and Community: Civic Republicanism and the Modern World*. London, 1990.

Olivier-Martin, F. "Les Professeurs royaux de droit français et l'unification du droit civil français." In *Mélanges juridiques dédiés à M. le Professeur Sugiyama*, 263–81. Paris, 1970.

Onclin, W. "Le Statut des étrangers dans la doctrine canonique médiévale." *RSJB* 10 (1958): 37–64.

Ourliac, P. "La Condition civile des étrangers dans la region Toulousaine au Moyen-Age." *RSJB* 10 (1958): 101–8.

Ourliac, P., and J.-L. Gazzaniga. *Histoire du droit privé français de l'an mil au Code civil*. Paris, 1985.

Pagès, G. *La Monarchie française de Henri IV à Louis XIV*. Paris, 1928.

Palmer, R. R. *The Age of the Democratic Revolution*. 2 vols. Princeton, 1959.

——. "The National Idea in France before the Revolution." *Journal of the History of Ideas* 1 (1940): 95–111.

Paquot, M. *Les Etrangers dans les divertissements de la cour, de Beaujoyeulz à Molière, 1581–1673*. Brussels, 1933.

Parisse, M., ed. *Histoire de la Lorraine*. Toulouse, 1977.

Parker, D. "Absolutism." In *Encyclopedia of European Social History*. 6 vols., 4:439–448. New York, 2001.

Parry, C. *Nationality and Citizenship Laws of the Commonwealth and the Republic of Ireland*. 2 vols. London, 1957.

Peabody, S. *"There Are No Slaves in France": The Political Culture of Race and Slavery in the Ancien Régime*. New York, 1996.

Perrot, J.-Cl., "Les Economistes, les philosophes, et la population." In *Histoire de la population française*, ed. J. Dupâquier. Vol. 2, *De la Renaissance à 1789*, 499–52. Paris, 1988.

Perotti, A. "L'Immigration en France: Son histoire, ses nouvelles réalités et ses nouveaux enjeux." In *La Citoyenneté et les changements de structures sociales et nationales de la population française*, ed. C. Wihtol de Wendon, 59–72. Paris, 1988.

Perry, E. I. *From Theory to History: French Religious Controversy and the Revocation of the Edict of Nantes*. The Hague, 1973.

Perry, T. W. *Public Opinion, Propaganda, and Politics in Eighteenth-Century England: A Study of the Jew Bill of 1753*. Cambridge, Mass., 1962.

Peytavin, M. "Españoles e italianos en Sicilia, Nápoles y Milán durante los siglos XVII y XVII: Sobre la oportunidad de ser nacional o natural." *Relaciones* 19, no. 73 (1998): 85–114.

Piccioni, C. *Les Premiers commis des Affaires étrangeres au XVII et XVIIIe siècle*. Paris, 1928.

Picot, G. *Histoire des Etats Généraux considérés au point de vue de leur influence sur le gouvernement de la France de 1355 à 1614*. 5 vols. Geneva, 1979 [Paris, 1872].

Pluchon, P. *Nègres et Juifs au XVIIIe siècle: Le Racisme au siècle des Lumières*. Paris, 1984.

Pocock, J. G. A. "The Ideal of Citizenship since Classical Times." In *The Citizenship Debates*, ed. G. Schafir, 31–42. Minneapolis, 1998.

——. *The Machiavellian Moment*. Princeton, 1975.

Poitrineau, A. *Ils travaillaient la France: Métiers et mentalités du XVIe au XXe siècle*. Paris, 1992.

——. *Remues d'hommes: Les Migrations montagnardes en France, XVIIe–XVIIIe siècles*. Paris, 1983.

Poland, B. C. *French Protestantism and the French Revolution: A Study in Church and State, Thought and Religion, 1685–1815*. Princeton, 1957.

Portemer, J. "L'Enseignement du droit public au XVIIIe siècle." *Revue historique de droit français et étranger*, 4th ser., 37 (1959): 341–97.

——. "L'Etranger dans le droit de la revolution francaise." *RSJB* 10 (1958): 533–52.

Poussou, J.-P. "Migrations et mobilité en France à l'epoque moderne." In *Les Mouvements migratoires dans l'Occident moderne*, Civilisations 19 (Paris, 1994), 39–62.

——. "Mobilité et migrations." In *Histoire de la population française*. Vol. 2, *De la renaissance à 1789*, ed. J. Dupâquier, 98–137. Paris, 1988.

——. "Les Mouvement migratoires en France et à partir de la France du XVe au début du XIXe siècles: Approches pour une synthèse." *Annales de démographie historique* 1970: 11–78.

——. "Recherches sur l'immigration anglo-irlandaise à Bordeaux au XVIIIe siècle." In *Bordeaux et les Iles Britanniques du XIIIe au XXe siècle*. Actes du colloque, York, 1973. Fédération Historique du Sud-Ouest. Bordeaux, 1975.

Price, M. *Preserving the Monarchy: The Comte de Vergennes, 1774–1787*. Cambridge, 1995.

Quaglioni, D. "Les Citoyens envers l'Etat: L'Individu en tant que citoyen de la *République* de Bodin au *Contrat social* de Rousseau." In *L'Individu dans la théorie et dans la pratique*, ed. J. Coleman, 311–21. Paris, 1996.

Rampelberg, R.-M. *Aux Origines du Ministère de l'Intérieur: Le Ministre de la Maison du Roi, 1783–1788. Baron de Breteuil*. Paris, 1975.

Rapport, M. " 'A Languishing Branch of the Old Tree of Feudalism': The Death, Resurrection, and Final Burial of the *Droit d'Aubaine* in France." *French History* 14, no. 1 (2000): 13–40.

——. *Nationality and Citizenship in Revolutionary France: The Treatment of Foreigners, 1789–1799*. Oxford, 2000.

Read, Ch. "Cimetières et inhumations des Huguenots, principalement à Paris, aux XVIe, XVIIe, et XVIIIe siècles, 1563–1792." *BSHPF* 11 (1862), 132–50; 351–59; 12 (1863): 33, 141, 143, 247, 367; 13 (1864): 224; 14 (1866): passim.

Reeves, J. S. "The First Edition of Grotius' *De Jure Belli Ac Pacis*, 1625." *American Journal of International Law* 19, no. 1 (1925): 12–22.

Regnault, H. *Les Ordonnances civiles du chancelier Daguesseau: Les Testaments et l'ordonnance de 1735*. Paris, 1938.

——. *Les Ordonnances civiles du chancelier Daguesseau: Les Donations et l'ordonnance de 1731*. Paris, 1929.

Le Règne de Louis XIV (1661–1715). Paris, 1998.

Reisenberg, P. *Citizenship in the Western Tradition: Plato to Rousseau*. Chapel Hill, 1992.

——. "Civism and Roman Law in Fourteenth-Century Italian Society." In *Economy, Society, and Government in Medieval Italy: Essays in Honor of Robert L. Reynolds*, ed. D. Herliy, R. Lopez, and V. Slessarev, 237–54. Kent, Ohio, 1969.

Rémy-Limousin, M. ed, *Traités internationaux de l'Ancien Régime*. Paris, 1997.

Renouvin, P. *Les Assemblées provinciales de 1787*. Paris, 1921.

Rétat, P. "Citoyen-Sujet, Civisme." In *Handbüch politisch-sozialer Grundbegriffe in Frankreich 1680–1829*, ed. R. Reichardt and E. Schmitt. 10 vols, 9:75–105. Munich, 1985–.

——. "The Evolution of the Citizen from the Ancien Regime to the Revolution." In *The French Revolution and the Meaning of Citizenship*, ed. R. Waldinger, P. Dawson, and I. Woloch, 3–15. Westport, Conn., 1993.

Reulos, M. "Les Sources juridiques de Bodin: Textes, auteurs, pratique." In *Jean Bodin: Proceedings of the International Conference on Bodin in Munich*, ed. H. Denzer, 187–94. Munich, 1973.

Reuss, R. *L'Alsace au XVIIe siècle*. Paris, 1904.

Rey, R. "La Police des étrangers en France." Thèse de Droit, Paris, 1937.

Richet, D. *La France moderne: L'Esprit des institutions*. Paris, 1973.

——. "La Monarchie au travail sur elle-même?" In *The Political Culture of the Old Regime*, ed. K. Baker, 25–39. Oxford, 1987.

Rigault, J. "La Population de Metz au XVIIe siècle: Quelques problèmes de démographie." *Annales de l'Est* 3 (1951): 307–15.

Riley, J. C. *The Seven Years War and the Old Regime in France: The Economic and Financial Toll.* Princeton, 1986.

Ripert, H. "Le Marquis de Mirabeau (*L'Ami des Hommes*): Ses théories politiques et économiques." Thèse de Droit, Paris, 1901.

Robert, A., E. Bouleton, and G. Cougny, eds. *Dictionnaire des parlementaires français . . . depuis le 1e mai 1789 jusqu'au 1 mai 1889.* 5 vols. Paris, 1889–91.

Robin, P. *La Compagnie des secrétaires du Roi (1351–1791).* Paris, 1933.

Roche, D., ed. *La France des lumières.* Paris, 1993.

——. "Nouveaux Parisiens au XVIIIe siècle." *Cahiers d'histoire*, no. 3 (1979): 3–20.

——. *Le Peuple de Paris.* Paris, 1981.

——. *La Ville promise: Mobilité et accueil à Paris (fin XVIIe–début XIXe siècle).* Paris, 2000.

Rodière, A. *Les Grands jurisconsultes.* Toulouse, 1874.

Roos, G. *Relations entre le gouvernement royal et les juifs du nord-est de la France au XVIIe siècle.* Paris, 2000.

Rosanvallon, P. *Le Sacre du citoyen: Histoire du suffrage universel en France.* Paris, 1992.

Rosenberg, H. *A Negotiated World: Three Centuries of Change in a French Alpine Community.* Toronto, 1988.

Rosenblatt, H. *Rousseau and Geneva: From the First Discourse to the Social Contract, 1749–1762.* Cambridge, 1997.

Rothkrug, L. *Opposition to Louis XIV: The Political and Social Origins of the French Enlightenment.* Princeton, 1965.

Roumy, F. *L'Adoption dans le droit savant du XII au XVIe siècle.* Paris, 1998.

Roux, Marquis de. *Louis XIV et les provinces conquises: Artois, Alsace, Flandres, Roussillon, Franche-Comté.* Paris, 1938.

Ruddy, F. *International Law in the Enlightenment: The Background of Emmerich de Vattel's Droit des Gens.* Dobbs Ferry, N.Y., 1975.

Sagnac, Ph. *La Législation civile de la Révolution française (1789–1804): Essai d'histoire sociale.* Geneva, 1979 [1898].

Sahlins, P. *Boundaries: The Making of France and Spain in the Pyrenees.* Berkeley, 1989.

——. "Fictions of a Catholic France: The Naturalization of Foreigners, 1685–1787." *Representations*, no. 47 (1994): 85–110.

——. "La Nationalité avant la lettre: Les Pratiques de naturalisation en France sous l'Ancien Régime." *Annales HSS* (September–October 2000), no. 5: 1081–1108.

——. "Natural Frontiers Revisited: France's Boundaries since the Seventeenth Century." *American Historical Review* 95, no. 5 (1990): 1423–51.

Sala-Molins, L. *Le Code Noir, ou le calvaire de Canaan.* Paris, 1987.

Sales, N. *De Tuïr a Catarroja: Estudis sobre institucions catalanes i de la Corona d'Aragó (segles XV–XVIII).* Valencia, 2002.

Salmon, J. H. M. *Society in Crisis: France in the Sixteenth Century.* Toronto, 1975.

Salomon, A. "Les Alsaciens employés au ministère des affaires étrangères au XVIIe et XVIIIe siècle." *Revue d'histoire diplomatique* 54 (1931): 449–72.

Samoyault, J.-P. *Les Bureaux du Secretariat d'Etat des Affaires étrangeres sous Louis XV.* Paris, 1971.

Santucci, M. R. "Devenir régnicole: Les Enquêtes de la Chambre de comptes." *Recueil de mémoires et travaux publiées par la Société d'histoire du droit et des institutions des anciens pays de droit écrit*, no. 13 (1985): 129–51.

Schalk, L. *From Valor to Pedigree: Ideas of Nobility in France in the Sixteenth and Seventeenth Centuries.* Princeton, 1986.

Schnapper, B. "La Naturalisation française au XIXe siècle: Les Variations d'une politique." In *La Condition juridique de l'étranger, hier et aujourd'hui.* Actes du Colloque organisé à Nimègue, 9–11 May 1988, 209–21. Nijmegen, 1988.

Schwob, E. *Un Formulaire de Chancellerie au XVIIIe siècle.* Paris, 1936.

Sée, H. *Les Idées politiques en France au XVIIe siècle.* Paris, 1923.

Sélosse, R. *Traité de l'annexion au territoire français et de son démembrement.* Paris, 1880.

Sewell, W. H. "Le Citoyen/la citoyenne: Activity, Passivity, and the Revolutionary Concept of Citizenship." In *The French Revolution and the Creation of Modern Political Culture*, ed. C. Lucas, 105–23. Oxford, 1988.

——. *A Rhetoric of Bourgeois Revolution: The Abbé Sieyès and "What Is the Third Estate?"* Durham, 1994.

Shennan, J. H. "The Political Vocabulary of the Parlement of Paris in the Eighteenth Century." In *Diritto e potere nella storia europea: Atti in onore di Bruno Paradesi*, 951–64. Florence, 1982.

Sherwin-White, A. N. *The Roman Citizenship*. Oxford, 1973.

Siat, J. *Histoire du rattachement de l'Alsace à la France*. Saint-Etienne, 1997.

Simon-Sandras, R. *Les Curés à la fin de l'Ancien Régime*. Paris, 1988.

Singham, S. M. "Betwixt Cattle and Men: Jews, Blacks, and Women, and the Declaration of the Rights of Man." In *The French Idea of Freedom: The Declaration of the Rights of Man*, ed. D. Van Kley, 114–53. Stanford, 1994.

———. "A Conspiracy of Twenty Million Frenchmen: Public Opinion, Patriotism, and the Assault on Absolutism, 1770–1775." Ph.D. diss., Princeton, 1991.

Small, C. M. "The Royal Bourgeoisies in the Duchy of Burgundy." *Proceedings of the Annual Meeting for the Western Society for French History* 13 (1986): 1–9.

Somers, M. "Citizenship and the Place of the Public Sphere: Law, Community, and Political Culture in the Transition to Democracy." *American Sociological Review* 1993 (58): 587–620.

Sopheau, P. "Les Variations de la frontière française des Alpes depuis le XVIe siècle." *Annales de géographie* 3 (1893–94): 183–200.

Sorel, A. *L'Europe et la Révolution française*. 4 vols. Paris, 1906.

Spengler, J. J. "Moheau: Profit of Depopulation." *Journal of Political Economy* 47, no. 5 (1939): 648–77.

Spitz, J.-F., *Bodin et la souveraineté*. Paris, 1988.

Statt, D. 1984. "The Birthright of an Englishman: The Practice of Naturalization and Denization of Immigrants under the Later Stuarts and Early Hanoverians." *Proceedings of the Huguenot Society of London/Great Britain and Ireland* 25 (1989): 61–74.

———. *Foreigners and Englishmen: The Controversy over Immigration and Population, 1660–1760*. Newark, Del., 1995.

Stein, P. *Roman Law in European History*. Cambridge, 1999.

Storez, I. *Le Chancelier Henri François d'Aguesseau (1688–1751): Monarchiste et libéral*. Paris, 1996.

Storti-Storchi, C. "The Legal Status of Foreigners in Italy (XVth–XVIth Centuries): General Rules and Their Enforcement in Some Cases concerning the *Executio Parata*." In *Of Strangers and Foreigners (Late Antiquity–Middle Ages)*, ed. L. Mayali and M. M. Mart, 97–135. Berkeley, 1993.

Sueur, P. *Histoire du droit public français, XVe–XVIIIe siècle*. 2 vols. Paris, 1989.

Swann, J. *Politics and the Parlement of Paris under Louis XV, 1754–1774*. Cambridge, 1995.

Szajkowski, Z. *The Economic Status of the Jews in Alsace, Metz, and Lorraine (1648–1789)*. New York, 1954.

———. *Franco-Judaica: An Analytical Bibliography of Books, Pamphlets, Decrees, Briefs, and Other Printed Documents Pertaining to the Jews in France, 1500–1788*. New York, 1962.

———. "Jewish Emigration from Bordeaux during the Eighteenth and Nineteenth Centuries." *Jewish Social Studies* 18 (1956): 118–24.

———. "The Jewish Problem in Alsace, Metz, and Lorraine on the Eve of the Revolution of 1789." *Jewish Quarterly Review* 44 (1954): 205–43.

———. "The Jewish Status in Eighteenth-Century France and the 'Droit d'Aubaine.'" *Historia Judaica* 19 (1957): 147–63.

Taisand, P. *Vie des plus celebres jurisconsultes*. Paris, 1837.

Terré, F. "Réflections sur la notion de nationalité." *Revue de droit internationale privé* 99 (1975): 197–214.

Tessier, G. "L'Audience du sceau." *Bibliothèque de l'Ecole des chartes*, no. 109 (1951): 51–95.

———. *Diplomatique royale française*. Paris, 1962.

Thieme, H. "Die Rechtsstellung der Fremden in Eutschland von 11. bis zum 18. Jahrhundert." *RSJB* 10 (1958): 217–30.

Thillay, A. "Les Artisans étrangers au faubourg Saint-Antoine à Paris (1650–1793)." In *Les Etrangers à la ville*, ed. J. Bottin and D. Calabi, 261–69. Paris, 1999.

Thomas, Y. "Citoyens et résidents dans les cités de l'Empire romain: Essai sur le droit d'origine." In *Identité et droit de l'Autre*, ed. L. Mayali, 1–56. Berkeley, 1994.

———. "*Origine*" et "*Commune Patrie*": Etude de droit public romain (89 av. J.-C. —212 ap. J.-C.). Collection de l'Ecole Française de Rome 221. Rome, 1996.

Tilly, C. "The Emergence of Citizenship in France and Elsewhere." In *Citizenship, Identity, and Social History*, ed. C. Tilly. *International Review of Social History* 40, supplement 3 (1995): 223–36.

Tison, R. H. *La Prise de l'autonomie de la volonté dans l'ancien droit français.* Paris, 1931.

Tocqueville, A. de. *The Old Regime and the Revolution,* ed. F. Furet and M. Melonio, trans. A. S. Kahn. 2 vols. Chicago, 1998–2001.

Torpey, J. *The Invention of the Passport: Surveillance, Citizenship, and the State.* Cambridge, 2000.

Trénard, L. "La Notion de 'naturalité' à Lille au XVIIIe siècle." *Cahiers Plisnier* (Brussels) (1959): 87–93.

Troper, M. "La Notion de citoyen sous la Révolution française." In *Etudes en l'honneur de Georges Dupuis: Droit Public,* 301–22. Paris, 1997.

Tulard, J., ed. *Dictionnaire Napoléon.* Paris, 1987.

Tulard, J., J.-F. Fayard, and A. Fierro, eds. *Histoire et dictionnaire de la Révolution française, 1789–1799.* Paris, 1988.

Turner, B. S., and P. Hamilton, eds. *Citizenship: Critical Concepts.* London, 1994.

Ullman, W. "The Rebirth of the Citizen on the Eve of the Renaissance Period." In *Aspects of the Renaissance,* ed. A. R. Lewis, 5–25. Austin, 1967.

Van Caenegeam, R. C. *An Historical Introduction to Private Law.* Cambridge, 1992.

Van Horn Melton, J. *The Rise of the Public in Enlightenment Europe.* Cambridge, 2001.

Van Kan, J. *Les Efforts de codification en France: Etude historique et psychologique.* Paris, 1929.

Van Kley, D. *The Damiens Affair and the Unraveling of the Ancien Régime.* Princeton, 1983.

———. *The Religious Origins of the French Revolution, 1560–1791.* New Haven, 1996.

Vandenbossche, A. "Contribution à l'étude des privilèges: Quelques problèmes posé par l'exemption du droit d'aubaine en Flandre Maritime au XVIIIe siècle." *Annales de la faculté de droit de l'université de Bordeaux, Série juridique* (1955): 117–48.

Vanderlinden, J. *Le Concept de code en Europe occidentale du XIIIe au XIXe siecle: Essai de définition.* Brussels, 1967.

Vanel, M. *Evolution historique de la notion de français d'origine du XVIe siècle au Code civil: Contribution à l'étude de la nationalité française d'origine.* Paris, 1945.

Vaux le Foletier, F. "Les Portugais à Rouen au XVIIe–XVIIIe siècle." *Revue des Sociétés savantes de Haute Normandie* 7 (1957): 33–42.

Vernon, R. A. *Citizenship and Order: Studies in French Political Thought.* Toronto, 1986.

Vial, H., A. Marcel, and A. Girodie. *Les Artistes décorateurs du bois: Répertoires alphabétiques des ébénistes, menuisiers, sculpteurs, doreurs sur bois, etc., ayant travaillé en France aux XVIIe et XVIIIe siècles.* Paris, 1912.

Villers, R. "La Condition des étrangers en France dans les trois derniers siècles de la monarchie." *RSJB* 10 (1958): 139–50.

Viroli, M. *For Love of Country: An Essay on Patriotism and Nationalism.* Oxford, 1995.

Visscher, F. de. "La Condition des pérégrins à Rome, jusqu'à la Constitution Antonine de l'an 212." *RSJB* 9 (1958): 195–208.

Voigt, K. "Huguenots et Vaudois en Allemagne à partir de 1685." In *Emigrés français en Allemagne, Emigrés allemands en France, 1685–1945,* 10–42. Paris, 1983.

Voss, J. "La Lorraine et sa situation politique entre la France et l'Empire vues par le duc de Saint-Simon." In *Les Habsbourg et la Lorraine,* ed. J.-P. Bled et al., 91–99. Nancy, 1988.

Vovelle, M. "Gavots et Italiens: Les Alpes et leur bordure dans la population marseillaise au XVIIIe siècle." *Provence historique* 108 (1977): 137–69.

———. "Piémontais en Provence occidentale au XVIIIe siècle." In *Migrazioni attraverso le Alpi occidentali: Relazioni tra Piemonte, Provenza e Delfinato dal Medioevo ai nostri giorni.* Atti del Convegno Internazionale, Cuneo, 1–3 Giugno 1984, 73–92. Turin, 1988.

Waddington, F. "Cimetières et inhumation des huguenots, principalement à Paris, aux XVIe, XVIIe, et XVIIIe siècles." *BSHPF* 11 (1862): 132–50.

Waddington, R. *Louis XV et le renversement des alliances.* Paris, 1896.

Wahnich, S. *L'Impossible citoyen: L'Etranger dans le discours de la Révolution française.* Paris, 1997.

Waldinger, R., P. Dawson, and I. Woloch, eds., *The French Revolution and the Meaning of Citizenship.* Westport, Conn., 1993.

Walker, M. *German Home Towns: Community, State, and General Estate, 1648–1871.* Ithaca, 1971.

Wallerstein, I. *The Modern World System.* 2 vols. New York, 1974–80.

Watson, A. *The Making of Civil Law.* Cambridge, Mass., 1981.

———. *Sources of Law, Legal Change, and Ambiguity.* Philadelphia, 1984.

——. *The Spirit of Roman Law*. Athens, Ga., 1995.

Waxin, M. "Statut de l'étudiant étranger dans son développement historique." Thèse de Droit, Paris, 1939.

Weil, P. "Access to Citizenship: A Comparison of Twenty-Five Nationality Laws." In *Citizenship Today: Global Perspectives and Practices*, ed. T. A. Aleinikoff and D. Klusmeyer, 17–35. Washington, D.C., 2001.

——. *Mission d'étude des législations de la nationalité et de l'immigration*. Paris, 1997.

——. *Qu'est-ce qu'un Français? Histoire de la nationalité française de la Révolution à nos jours*. Paris, 2002.

Weiss, A. *Traité théorique et pratique de droit international privé*. 6 vols. Paris, 1908–1913.

Weiss, G. L. "Back from Barbary: Captivity, Redemption, and French Identity in the Seventeenth and Eighteenth Century Mediterranean World." Ph.D. diss., Stanford University, 2002.

Wells, C. "The Language of Citizenship in the French Religious Wars." *Sixteenth Century Journal* 30, no. 2 (1999): 441–56.

——. *Law and Citizenship in Early Modern France*. Baltimore, 1995.

——. "Leeches on the Body Politic: Xenophobia and Witchcraft in Early Modern French Political Thought," *French Historical Studies* 22 (1999): 351–77.

Weulersse, G. *Le Mouvement physiocratique en France de 1756 à 1770*. 2 vols. Paris, 1910.

——. *La Physiocratie à l'aube de la Révolution, 1781–1792*. Ed. C. Beutler. Paris, 1985.

——. *La Physiocratie sous les ministères de Turgot et de Necker (1774–1781)*. Paris, 1950.

Wihtol de Wenden, C. "Citizenship and Nationality in France." In *From Aliens to Citizens: Redefining the Status of Immigrants in Europe*, ed. R. Baubock, 85–94. Aldershot, 1994.

——. *Citoyenneté, Nationalité, et Immigration*. Paris, 1987.

——. "Les Pays européens face à l'immigration." *Pouvoirs* 47 (1988): 133–44.

Williams, A. *The Police of Paris, 1718–1789*. Baton Rouge, La., 1979.

Woloch, I. *The New Regime: Transformations of the French Civic Order, 1789–1820s*. New York, 1994.

Wolodkiewicz, W. "Bodin et le droit privé romain." In *Jean Bodin*. Actes du Colloque Interdisciplinaire d'Angers, 24–27 May 1984, 303–10. Angers, 1985.

Woolf, S. *Napoleon's Integration of Europe*. London, 1991.

Wright, Q. "International Law and Guilt By Association." *American Journal of International Law* 43, no. 4 (1949): 746–55.

Yardeni, M. *La Conscience nationale en France pendant les Guerres de Religion (1559–1598)*. Louvain, 1971.

——. *Le Refuge protestant*. Paris, 1985.

Zeller, G. *Les Temps Modernes: II. de Louis XIV à 1789*. Vol. 3 of *Histoire des Relations internationales*, ed. P. Renouvin. Paris, 1955.

Zeller, O. "L'Implantation savoyarde à Lyon à la fin du XVIe siecle." In *Habiter la Ville, XVe–XXe siècles*, ed. M. Garden and Y. Lequin, 25–35. Lyon, 1984.

——. *Les Recensements lyonnais de 1597 et 1636: Démographie historique et géographie sociale*. Lyon, 1983.

Zernatto, G. "Nation: The History of a Word." *Review of Politics* 6 (1944): 351–66.

Zink, A. "Communautés et corps social: Les Juifs à Saint-Esprit-lès-Bayonne du XVIIe au début du XIXe siècle." In *Les Etrangers dans la ville*, ed. J. Bottin and D. Calabi, 313–28. Paris, 1999.

——. "Une Niche juridique: L'Installation des juifs à Saint Esprit." *Annales HSS* (May–June 1993), no. 4: 639–70.

INDEX

Note: Italicized page numbers indicate illustrations; those with a *t* indicate tables.

Habsburg Empire, 70–71, 165, 175
Haiti. *See* Saint-Domingue
Hamburg, 49, 179, 227, 337t
Henry II, 25–26, 38, 47, 52, 273
Henry III, 38, 61, 103, 181
Henry IV, 25, 45, 97, 118
Hesse, principality of, 103–4
Hesse-Cassel, landgrave of, 231, 336t
Hesse-Darmstadt, principality of, 231, 234, 336t
Hesse-Homburg, landgrave of, 339t
Holland. *See* Low Countries
Holy Roman Empire, 47, 111–12, 119, 159t, 162,
197, 230–35
citizenship in, 20, 33
droit d'aubaine and, 168, 179
See also Austria; Low Countries; Rhineland-
principalities
Huguenots, 84, 150–51
descendants of, 60–61, 95, 173, 197–98, 269–70
diaspora of, 7, 56, 59–60, 94, 192, 356 n. 104
See also Protestants
Hungary, 32, 119–20, 159t, 180, 181t, 231

India, 159t, 162, 181t, 182–84
Ireland, 158, 172, 191, *203*, 206
droit d'aubaine and, 171–72
taxation of naturalized Irish, 159t, 172–73, 202
See also Jacobites
Islam. *See* Muslims
Italy, 8, 31–32, 39, 49, 96, 114–16, 175–77, 201, 241
city-states of, 3, 20, 67, 216, 337t
under Napoleon, 300–301
taxation of immigrants from, 157, 159t, 175
treaties with, 231, 233, 337t–338t

Jacobites, 146–47, 158, 171–72
See also England; Ireland
Jansenism, 206, 222–23, 249, 398 n. 22
Jews
citizenship of, 7, 115, 222, 271–73
converted, 126–27
droit d'aubaine and, 51–52, 178
naturalization of, 88, 96–99, 162–63
"Portuguese merchants," 52, 162–64, 178, 272
See also Alsace; Avignon; Lorraine
Joly de Fleury, 83, 119, 257, 331–32, 370 n. 88
Justinian. *See* Law: Roman

Languedoc
droit d'aubaine in, 37–38, 46–47, 58, 356 n. 104
foreigners in, 152, 158–59, 159t, 183
Roman law in, 69–70
Lanjuinais, Jean, 285, 289
Law
civil law, 14, 26, 28, 39, 283, 360 n. 134
droit d'aubaine and, 46, 55–56, 237, 240,
249–62, 295

fictions of, 37, 52, 66–75, 80, 85, 88, 96, 98–
99, 107, 109, 111–20, 126, 164, 173, 222
inheritance and, 43, 62, 262
law of nations versus, 250–51
vice in, 31, 34, 63, 252, 257
customary, 27, 91
"French," 27–28, 33, 40, 62, 249
international, 7, 43, 55, 237, 250–51
natural, 237–38, 240, 250
Roman, 1–2, 20–23, 26–28, 33, 51, 61–64, 66–67,
69–70, 250–53
training in, 26–27
Law, John, 97, 105, 150
Laws
Blois ordinances, 38, 40
Caracalla edict, 23, 63
cautio judicatum solvi, 36–38
Civil Code, 15, 27, 31, 251, 291–300
citizenship and, 58, 64, 71, 268–69, 291–94
droit d'aubaine and, 282, 291, 294–95
nationality and, 85, 268–69, 313–14
Code Noir (1685), 182–83
Corpus juris civilis, 3, 26, 347 n. 4
droit de bourgeoisie, 21, 41, 47–48, 51, 99
droit de chevage, 32, 41, 99
droit de cité, 248, 290, 314–15, 324, 411 n. 71
droit de détraction, 33, 231–36, 295–96, 301t, 307
droit de formariage, 34, 41, 99
droit d'épave, 237, 280
droit de sceau, 99–100
Institutes, 3, 26, 403 n. 106
iuris postliminum, 61–62
ius albiganii, 32
ius domicilium, 62
ius gentium, 43
ius sanguinis, 57–59, 62–63, 91, 256, 272, 293–
94, 314
ius soli, 57–59, 63–64, 272, 292–93, 314
Judicatum solvi, 258
Lex faldicia, 33
Nationality Law of 1889, 314, 327
Omnes peregrini, 33
Le Brun, Denis, 73
Lefebvre de la Planche, Jean-Jacques Auguste,
27–28, 30
anti-Semitism of, 97
on droit d'aubaine, 35, 46–47, 251–52
on emigrants, 94–95
on letters of naturalization, 72, 74, 92, 103–4,
106, 107
See also Lorry, Paul Charles
Leiden, county of, 228, 339t
Le Trosne, Guillaume-François, 238, 240, 247–
48, 298
Letters of naturalization. *See* Naturalization
L'Hôpital, Michel de, 97
L'Huillier, Jérôme, 40, 44, 99

Vergennes, Charles Gravier, comte de, 93, 122–23, 225, 234–35, 242–47, 259
Versailles, Treaty of, 204, 227–28
    See also Seven Years War
Vienna, Treaty of, 307

Waldeck, principality of, 301t
Wied-Neuwied, county of, 338t

Women
    and citizenship, 21–22, 60–61, 120–21, 218–20, 224, 289
    civil rights and, 272, 305–6
    naturalization of, 128–30
    Naturalization Tax and, 136
    See also Citizenship; Family; Naturalization
Württemberg, duchy of, 233, 339t
Würzburg, principality of, 337t